THE COMPLETE WORKS OF
SAINT JOHN OF THE CROSS
IN THREE VOLUMES:
VOLUME I

THE 'MOUNT OF PERFECTION'

(See pp. xxxii–xxxiii)

THE COMPLETE WORKS OF SAINT JOHN OF THE CROSS

DOCTOR OF THE CHURCH

Translated and edited by

E. ALLISON PEERS

from the critical edition of

P. SILVERIO DE SANTA TERESA, C.D.

I

GENERAL INTRODUCTION
ASCENT OF MOUNT CARMEL
DARK NIGHT OF THE SOUL

LONDON
BURNS OATES & WASHBOURNE LTD.
PUBLISHERS TO THE HOLY SEE

NIHIL OBSTAT: GEORGIVS SMITH, S.T.D., PH.D.
CENSOR DEPVTATVS
IMPRIMATVR: E. MORROGH BERNARD
VICARIVS GENERALIS
WESTMONASTERII: DIE XXIV SEPTEMBRIS MCMLII

First published 1935
Second impression 1943
Third impression 1947
New Edition, revised 1953

Made and printed in Great Britain by
William Clowes and Sons, Limited, London and Beccles
for Burns Oates and Washbourne Limited
*28 Ashley Place, London, S.W.*1

CONTENTS

BOOK III

DARK NIGHT OF THE SOUL

BOOK I

BOOK II

TRANSLATOR'S PREFACE
TO THE FIRST EDITION

I

FOR at least twenty years, a new translation of the works of St. John of the Cross has been an urgent necessity. The translations of the individual prose works now in general use go back in their original form to the eighteen-sixties, and, though the later editions of some of them have been submitted to a certain degree of revision, nothing but a complete retranslation of the works from their original Spanish could be satisfactory. For this there are two reasons.

First, the existing translations were never very exact renderings of the original Spanish text even in the form which held the field when they were first published. Their great merit was extreme readableness: many a disciple of the Spanish mystics, who is unacquainted with the language in which they wrote, owes to these translations the comparative ease with which he has mastered the main lines of St. John of the Cross's teaching. Thus for the general reader they were of great utility; for the student, on the other hand, they have never been entirely adequate. They paraphrase difficult expressions, omit or add to parts of individual sentences in order (as it seems) to facilitate comprehension of the general drift of the passages in which these occur, and frequently retranslate from the Vulgate the Saint's Spanish quotations from Holy Scripture instead of turning into English the quotations themselves, using the text actually before them.

A second and more important reason for a new translation, however, is the discovery of fresh manuscripts and the consequent improvements which have been made in the Spanish text of the works of St. John of the Cross during the present century. Seventy years ago, the text chiefly used was that of the collection known as the *Biblioteca de Autores Españoles* (1853), which itself was based, as we shall later see, upon an edition going back as far as 1703, published before modern methods of editing were so much as imagined. Both the text of the *B.A.E.* edition and the unimportant commentary which accompanied it were highly unsatisfactory, yet until the beginning of the present century nothing appreciably better was attempted.

In the last twenty years, however, we have had two new editions, each based upon a close study of the extant manuscripts and each representing a great advance upon the editions preceding it. The three-volume Toledo edition of P. Gerardo de San Juan de la Cruz, C.D. (1912–14), was the first attempt made to produce an accurate text by modern critical methods. Its execution was perhaps less laudable than its conception, and faults were pointed out in it from the time of its appearance, but it served as a new starting-point for Spanish scholars and stimulated them to a new interest in St. John of the Cross's writings. Then, seventeen years later, came the magnificent five-volume edition of P. Silverio de Santa Teresa, C.D. (Burgos, 1929–31), which forms the basis of this present translation. So superior is it, even on the most casual examination, to all its predecessors that to eulogize it in detail is superfluous. It is founded upon a larger number of texts than has previously been known and it collates them with greater skill than that of any earlier editor. It can hardly fail to be the standard edition of the works of St. John of the Cross for generations.

Thanks to the labours of these Carmelite scholars and of others whose findings they have incorporated in their editions, Spanish students can now approach the work of the great Doctor with the reasonable belief that they are reading, as nearly as may be, what he actually wrote. English-reading students, however, who are unable to master sixteenth-century Spanish, have hitherto had no grounds for such a belief. They cannot tell whether, in any particular passage, they are face to face with the Saint's own words, with a translator's free paraphrase of them or with a gloss made by some later copyist or early editor in the supposed interests of orthodoxy. Indeed, they cannot be sure that some whole paragraph is not one of the numerous interpolations which has its rise in an early printed edition—i.e., the timorous qualifications of statements which have seemed to the interpolator over-bold. Even some of the most distinguished writers in English on St. John of the Cross have been misled in this way and it has been impossible for any but those who read Spanish with ease to make a systematic and reliable study of such an important question as the alleged dependence of Spanish quietists upon the Saint, while his teaching on the mystical life has quite unwittingly been distorted by persons who would least wish to misrepresent it in any particular.

It was when writing the chapter on St. John of the Cross in the first volume of my *Studies of the Spanish Mystics* (in which, as it was published in 1927, I had not the advantage of using P. Silverio's edition) that I first realized the extent of the harm caused by the lack of an accurate and modern translation. Making my own versions of all the passages quoted, I had sometimes occasion to compare them with those of other translators, which at their worst were almost unrecognizable as versions of the same originals. Then and there I resolved that, when time allowed, I would make a fresh translation of the works of a saint to whom I have long had great devotion—to whom, indeed, I owe more than to any other writer outside the Scriptures. Just at that time I happened to visit the Discalced Carmelites at Burgos, where I first met P. Silverio, and found, to my gratification, that his edition of St. John of the Cross was much nearer publication than I had imagined. Arrangements for sole permission to translate the new edition were quickly made and work on the early volumes was begun even before the last volume was published.

II

These preliminary notes will explain why my chief preoccupation throughout the performance of this task has been to present as accurate and reliable a version of St. John of the Cross's works as it is possible to obtain. To keep the translation, line by line, *au pied de la lettre*, is, of course, impracticable: and such constantly occurring Spanish habits as the use of abstract nouns in the plural and the verbal construction '*ir* + present participle' introduce shades of meaning which cannot always be reproduced. Yet wherever, for stylistic or other reasons, I have departed from the Spanish in any way that could conceivably cause a misunderstanding, I have scrupulously indicated this in a footnote. Further, I have translated, not only the text, but the variant readings as given by P. Silverio,[1] except where they are due merely to slips of the copyist's pen or where they differ so slightly from the readings of the text that it is impossible to render the differences in English. I beg students not to think that some of the smaller changes noted are of no importance; closer examination will often show that, however slight they may seem, they are, in relation to their context, or to some particular aspect of the Saint's teaching, of real interest; in other places they help to give the reader an idea, which may be useful to him in some crucial passage, of the general characteristics of the manuscript

[1] The footnotes are P. Silverio's except where they are enclosed in square brackets.

or edition in question. The editor's notes on the manuscripts and early editions which he has collated will also be found, for the same reason, to be summarized in the introduction to each work; in consulting the variants, the English-reading student has the maximum aid to a judgment of the reliability of his authorities.

Concentration upon the aim of obtaining the most precise possible rendering of the text has led me to sacrifice stylistic elegance to exactness where the two have been in conflict; it has sometimes been difficult to bring oneself to reproduce the Saint's often ungainly, though often forceful, repetitions of words or his long, cumbrous parentheses, but the temptation to take refuge in graceful paraphrases has been steadily resisted. In the same interest, and also in that of space, I have made certain omissions from, and abbreviations of, other parts of the edition than the text. Two of P. Silverio's five volumes are entirely filled with commentaries and documents. I have selected from the documents those of outstanding interest to readers with no detailed knowledge of Spanish religious history and have been content to summarize the editor's introductions to the individual works, as well as his longer footnotes to the text, and to omit such parts as would interest only specialists, who are able, or at least should be obliged, to study them in the original Spanish.

The decision to summarize in these places has been made the less reluctantly because of the frequent unsuitability of P. Silverio's style to English readers. Like that of many Spaniards, it is so discursive, and at times so baroque in its wealth of epithet and its profusion of imagery, that a literal translation, for many pages together, would seldom have been acceptable. The same criticism would have been applicable to any literal translation of P. Silverio's biography of St. John of the Cross which stands at the head of his edition (Vol. I, pp. 7–130). There was a further reason for omitting these biographical chapters. The long and fully documented biography by the French Carmelite, P. Bruno de Jésus-Marie, C.D., written from the same standpoint as P. Silverio's, has recently been translated into English, and any attempt to rival this in so short a space would be foredoomed to failure. I have thought, however, that a brief outline of the principal events in St. John of the Cross's life would be a useful preliminary to this edition; this has therefore been substituted for the biographical sketch referred to.

In language, I have tried to reproduce the atmosphere of a sixteenth-century text as far as is consistent with clarity. Though following the paragraph divisions of my original, I have not scrupled, where this has seemed to facilitate understanding, to divide into shorter sentences the long and sometimes straggling periods in which the Saint so frequently indulged. Some attempt has been made to show the contrast between the highly adorned, poetical language of much of the commentary on the 'Spiritual Canticle' and the more closely shorn and eminently practical, though always somewhat discursive style of the *Ascent* and *Dark Night*. That the *Living Flame* occupies an intermediate position in this respect should also be clear from the style of the translation.

Quotations, whether from the Scriptures or from other sources, have been left strictly as St. John of the Cross made them. Where he quotes in Latin, the Latin has been reproduced; only his quotations in Spanish have been turned into English. The footnote references are to the Vulgate, of which the Douai Version is a direct translation; if the Authorized Version differs, as in the Psalms, the variation has been shown in square brackets for the convenience of those who use it.

A word may not be out of place regarding the translations of the poems as they appear in the prose commentaries. Obviously, it would have been impossible to use the comparatively free verse renderings which appear in Volume II of this translation, since the commentaries discuss each line and often each word of the poems. A literal version of the poems in their original verse-lines, however, struck me as being inartistic, if not repellent, and as inviting continual comparison with the more polished verse renderings which, in spirit, come far nearer to the poet's aim. My first intention was to translate the poems, for the purpose of the commentaries, into prose. But later I hit upon the long and metrically unfettered verse-line, suggestive of Biblical poetry in its English dress, which I have employed throughout. I believe that, although the renderings often suffer artistically from their necessary literalness, they are from the artistic standpoint at least tolerable.

III

The debts I have to acknowledge, though few, are very large ones. My gratitude to P. Silverio de Santa Teresa for telling me so much about his edition before its publication, granting my publishers the sole translation rights and discussing with me a number of crucial passages cannot be disjoined from the many kindnesses I have received during my work on the Spanish mystics, which is still proceeding, from himself and from his fellow-Carmelites in the province of Castile.

In dedicating this translation to them, I think particularly of P. Silverio in Burgos, of P. Florencio del Niño Jesús in Madrid, and of P. Crisógono de Jesús Sacramentado, together with the Fathers of the 'Convento de la Santa' in Ávila.

The long and weary process of revising the manuscript and proofs of this translation has been greatly lightened by the co-operation and companionship of P. Edmund Gurdon, Prior of the Cartuja de Miraflores, near Burgos, with whom I have freely discussed all kinds of difficulties, both of substance and style, and who has been good enough to read part of my proofs. From the quiet library of his monastery, as well as from his gracious companionship, I have drawn not only knowledge, but strength, patience and perseverance. And when at length, after each of my visits, we have had to part, we have continued our labours by correspondence, shaking hands, as it were, 'over a vast' and embracing 'from the ends of opposèd winds.'

Finally, I owe a real debt to my publishers for allowing me to do this work without imposing any such limitations of time as often accompany literary undertakings. This and other considerations which I have received from them have made that part of the work which has been done outside the study unusually pleasant and I am correspondingly grateful.

E. Allison Peers.

University of Liverpool.
    Feast of St. John of the Cross,
    November 24, 1933.

Note.—Wherever a commentary by St. John of the Cross is referred to, its title is given in italics (e.g. *Spiritual Canticle*); where the corresponding poem is meant, it is placed between quotation marks (e.g. 'Spiritual Canticle'). The abbreviation 'e.p.' stands for *editio princeps* throughout.

TRANSLATOR'S PREFACE
TO THE SECOND EDITION

D URING the sixteen years which have elapsed since the publication of the first edition, several reprints have been issued, and the demand is now such as to justify a complete resetting. I have taken advantage of this opportunity to revise the text throughout, and hope that in some of the more difficult passages I may have come nearer than before to the Saint's mind. Recent researches have necessitated a considerable amplification of introductions and footnotes and greatly increased the length of the bibliography.

The only modification which has been made consistently throughout the three volumes relates to St. John of the Cross's quotations from Scripture. In translating these I still follow him exactly, even where he himself is inexact, but I have used the Douai Version (instead of the Authorized, as in the first edition) as a basis for all Scriptural quotations, as well as in the footnote references and the Scriptural index in Vol. III.

Far more is now known of the life and times of St. John of the Cross than when this translation of the *Complete Works* was first published, thanks principally to the *Historia del Carmen Descalzo* of P. Silverio de Santa Teresa, C.D., now General of his Order, and to the admirably documented Life of the Saint written by P. Crisógono de Jesús Sacramentado, C.D., and published (in *Vida y Obras de San Juan de la Cruz*) in the year after his untimely death. This increased knowledge is reflected in many additional notes, and also in the 'Outline of the Life of St. John of the Cross' (Vol. I, pp. xxv–xxviii), which, for this edition, has been entirely recast. References are given to my *Handbook to the Life and Times of St. Teresa and St. John of the Cross*, which provides much background too full to be reproduced in footnotes and too complicated to be compressed. The *Handbook* also contains numerous references to contemporary events, omitted from the 'Outline' as being too remote from the main theme to justify inclusion in a summary necessarily so condensed.

My thanks for help in revision are due to kindly correspondents, too numerous to name, from many parts of the world, who have made suggestions for the improvement of the first edition; to the Rev. Professor David Knowles, of Cambridge University, for whose continuous practical interest in this translation I cannot be too grateful; to Miss I. L. McClelland, of Glasgow University, who has read a large part of this edition in proof; to Dom Philippe Chevallier, for material which I have been able to incorporate in it; to P. José Antonio de Sobrino, S.J., for allowing me to quote freely from his recently published *Estudios*; and, most of all, to M. R. P. Silverio de Santa Teresa, C.D., and the Fathers of the International Carmelite College at Rome, whose learning and experience, are, I hope, faintly reflected in this new edition.

E. A. P.

June 30, 1951.

PRINCIPAL ABBREVIATIONS

A.V.—Authorized Version of the Bible (1611).

D.V.—Douai Version of the Bible (1609).

C.W.S.T.J.—*The Complete Works of Saint Teresa of Jesus*, translated and edited by E. Allison Peers from the critical edition of P. Silverio de Santa Teresa, C.D. London, Sheed and Ward, 1946. 3 vols.

H.—E. Allison Peers: *Handbook to the Life and Times of St. Teresa and St. John of the Cross*. London, Burns Oates and Washbourne, 1953.

LL.—*The Letters of Saint Teresa of Jesus*, translated and edited by E. Allison Peers from the critical edition of P. Silverio de Santa Teresa, C.D. London, Burns Oates and Washbourne, 1951. 2 vols.

N.L.M.—National Library of Spain (Biblioteca Nacional), Madrid.

Obras (*P. Silv.*)—*Obras de San Juan de la Cruz*, Doctor de la Iglesia, editadas y anotadas por el P. Silverio de Santa Teresa, C.D. Burgos, 1929–31. 5 vols.

S.S.M.—E. Allison Peers: *Studies of the Spanish Mystics*. Vol. I, London, Sheldon Press, 1927; 2nd ed., London, S.P.C.K., 1951. Vol. II, London, Sheldon Press, 1930.

Sobrino.—José Antonio de Sobrino, S.J.: *Estudios sobre San Juan de la Cruz y nuevos textos de su obra*. Madrid, 1950.

AN OUTLINE OF THE LIFE OF ST. JOHN OF THE CROSS[1]

1542. Birth of Juan de Yepes at Fontiveros (Hontiveros), near Ávila.

> The day generally ascribed to this event is June 24 (St. John Baptist's Day). No documentary evidence for it, however, exists, the parish registers having been destroyed by a fire in 1544. The chief evidence is an inscription, dated 1689, on the font of the parish church at Fontiveros.

? c. 1543. Death of Juan's father. 'After some years' the mother removes, with her family, to Arévalo, and later to Medina del Campo.

? c. 1552–6. Juan goes to school at the Colegio de los Niños de la Doctrina, Medina.

c. 1556–7. Don Antonio Álvarez de Toledo takes him into a Hospital to which he has retired, with the idea of his (Juan's) training for Holy Orders under his patronage.

? c. 1559–63. Juan attends the College of the Society of Jesus at Medina.

c. 1562. Leaves the Hospital and the patronage of Álvarez de Toledo.

1563. Takes the Carmelite habit at St. Anne's, Medina del Campo, as Juan de San Matías (Santo Matía).

> The day is frequently assumed (without any foundation) to have been the feast of St. Matthias (February 24), but P. Silverio postulates a day in August or September and P. Crisógono thinks February definitely improbable.

1564. Makes his profession in the same priory—probably in August or September and certainly not earlier than May 21 and not later than October.

1564 (November). Enters the University of Salamanca as an *artista*. Takes a three-year course in Arts (1564–7).

[1] Cf. p. xviii.

xxv

1565 (January 6). Matriculates at the University of Salamanca.

1567. Receives priest's orders (probably in the summer).

1567 (? September). Meets St. Teresa at Medina del Campo. Juan is thinking of transferring to the Carthusian Order. St. Teresa asks him to join her Discalced Reform and the projected first foundation for friars. He agrees to do so, provided the foundation is soon made.

1567 (November). Returns to the University of Salamanca, where he takes a year's course in theology.

1568. Spends part of the Long Vacation at Medina del Campo. On August 10, accompanies St. Teresa to Valladolid. In September, returns to Medina and later goes to Ávila and Duruelo.

1568 (November 28). Takes the vows of the Reform at Duruelo as St. John of the Cross, together with Antonio de Heredia (Antonio de Jesús), Prior of the Calced Carmelites at Medina, and José de Cristo, another Carmelite from Medina.

1570 (June 11). Moves, with the Duruelo community, to Mancera de Abajo.

1570 (October, or possibly February 1571). Stays for about a month at Pastrana, returning thence to Mancera.

1571 (? January 25). Visits Alba de Tormes for the inauguration of a new convent there.

1571 (? April). Goes to Alcalá de Henares as Rector of the College of the Reform and directs the Carmelite nuns.

1572 (shortly after April 23). Recalled to Pastrana to correct the rigours of the new novice-master, Ángel de San Gabriel.

1572 (between May and September). Goes to Ávila as confessor to the Convent of the Incarnation. Remains there till 1577.

1574 (March). Accompanies St. Teresa from Ávila to Segovia, arriving on March 18. Returns to Ávila about the end of the month.

1575–6 (Winter of: before February 1576). Kidnapped by the Calced and imprisoned at Medina del Campo. Freed by the intervention of the Papal Nuncio, Ormaneto.

1577 (December 2 or 3). Kidnapped by the Calced and carried off to the Calced Carmelite priory at Toledo as a prisoner.

1577–8. Composes in prison 17 (or perhaps 30) stanzas of the 'Spiritual Canticle' (i.e., as far as the stanza: 'Daughters of Jewry'); the poem with the refrain 'Although 'tis night'; and the stanzas beginning 'In principio erat verbum.' He may also have composed the paraphrase of the psalm *Super flumina* and the poem 'Dark Night.' (*Note*: All these poems, in verse form, will be found in Vol. II of this edition.)

1578 (August 16 or shortly afterwards). Escapes to the Convent of the Carmelite nuns in Toledo, and is thence taken to his house by D. Pedro González de Mendoza, Canon of Toledo.

1578 (October 9). Attends a meeting of the Discalced superiors at Almodóvar. Is sent to El Calvario as Vicar, in the absence in Rome of the Prior.

1578 (end of October). Stays for 'a few days' at Beas de Segura, near El Calvario. Confesses the nuns at the Carmelite Convent of Beas.

1578 (November). Arrives at El Calvario.

1578–9 (November–June). Remains at El Calvario as Vicar. For a part of this time (probably from the beginning of 1579), goes weekly to the convent of Beas to hear confessions. During this period, begins his commentaries entitled *The Ascent of Mount Carmel* (cf. pp. 9–314, below) and *Spiritual Canticle* (translated in Vol. II).

1579 (June 14). Founds a college of the Reform at Baeza.

1579–82. Resides at Baeza as Rector of the Carmelite college. Visits the Beas convent occasionally. Writes more of the prose works begun at El Calvario and the rest of the stanzas of the 'Spiritual Canticle' except the last five, possibly with the commentaries to the stanzas.

1580. Death of his mother.

1581 (March 3). Attends the Alcalá Chapter of the Reform. Appointed Third Definitor and Prior of the Granada house of Los Mártires. Takes up the latter office only on or about the time of his election by the community in March 1582.

1581 (November 28). Last meeting with St. Teresa, at Ávila. On the next day, sets out with two nuns for Beas (December 8– January 15) and Granada.

1582 (January 20). Arrives at Los Mártires.

1582–8. Mainly at Granada. Re-elected (or confirmed) as Prior of Los Mártires by the Chapter of Almodóvar, 1583. Resides at Los Mártires more or less continuously till 1584 and intermittently afterwards. Visits the Beas convent occasionally. Writes the last five stanzas of the 'Spiritual Canticle' during one of these visits. At Los Mártires, finishes the *Ascent of Mount Carmel* and composes his remaining prose treatises. Writes *Living Flame of Love* about 1585, in fifteen days, at the request of Doña Ana de Peñalosa.

1585 (May). Lisbon Chapter appoints him Second Definitor and (till 1587) Vicar-Provincial of Andalusia. Makes the following foundations: Málaga, February 17, 1585; Córdoba, May 18, 1586; La Manchuela (de Jaén), October 12, 1586; Caravaca, December 18, 1586; Bujalance, June 24, 1587.

1587 (April). Chapter of Valladolid re-appoints him Prior of Los Mártires. He ceases to be Definitor and Vicar-Provincial.

1588 (June 19). Attends the first Chapter-General of the Reform in Madrid. Is elected First Definitor and a *consiliario*.

1588 (August 10). Becomes Prior of Segovia, the central house of the Reform and the headquarters of the Consulta. Acts as deputy for the Vicar-General, P. Doria, during the latter's absences.

1590 (June 10). Re-elected First Definitor and a *consiliario* at the Chapter-General Extraordinary, Madrid.

1591 (June 1). The Madrid Chapter-General deprives him of his offices and resolves to send him to Mexico. (This latter decision was later revoked.)

1591 (August 10). Arrives at La Peñuela.

1591 (September 12). Attacked by fever. (September 22) Leaves La Peñuela for Úbeda. (December 14) Dies at Úbeda.

· · · · ·

January 25, 1675. Beatified by Clement X.

December 26, 1726. Canonized by Benedict XIII.

August 24, 1926. Declared Doctor of the Church Universal by Pius XI.

GENERAL INTRODUCTION TO THE WORKS OF ST. JOHN OF THE CROSS

I

DATES AND METHODS OF COMPOSITION. GENERAL CHARACTERISTICS

WITH regard to the times and places at which the works of St. John of the Cross were written, and also with regard to the number of these works, there have existed, from a very early date, considerable differences of opinion. Of internal evidence from the Saint's own writings there is practically none, and such external testimony as can be found in contemporary documents needs very careful examination.

There was no period in the life of St. John of the Cross in which he devoted himself entirely to writing. He does not, in fact, appear to have felt any inclination to do so: his books were written in response to the insistent and repeated demands of his spiritual children. He was very much addicted, on the other hand, to the composition of apothegms or maxims for the use of his penitents and this custom he probably began as early as the days in which he was confessor to the Convent of the Incarnation at Ávila, though his biographers have no record of any maxims but those written at Beas. One of his best beloved daughters, however, Ana María de Jesús, of the Convent of the Incarnation, declared in her deposition, during the process of the Saint's canonization, that he was accustomed to 'comfort those with whom he had to do, both by his words and by his letters, of which this witness received a number, and also by certain papers concerning holy things which this witness would greatly value if she still had them.' Considering the number of nuns to whom the Saint was director at Ávila, it is to be presumed that M. Ana María was not the only person whom he favoured. We may safely conclude, indeed, that there were many others who shared the same privileges, and that, had we all these 'papers,' they would comprise a large volume, instead of the few pages reproduced elsewhere in this translation.

There is a well-known story, preserved in the documents of the

canonization process, of how, on a December night of 1577, St. John
of the Cross was kidnapped by the Calced Carmelites of Ávila and
carried off from the Incarnation to their priory.[1] Realizing that he had
left behind him some important papers, he contrived, on the next
morning, to escape, and returned to the Incarnation to destroy them
while there was time to do so. He was missed almost immediately and
he had hardly gained his cell when his pursuers were on his heels. In
the few moments that remained to him he had time to tear up these
papers and swallow some of the most compromising. As the original
assault had not been unexpected, though the time of it was uncertain,
they would not have been very numerous. It is generally supposed
that they concerned the business of the infant Reform, of which the
survival was at that time in grave doubt. But it seems at least equally
likely that some of them might have been these spiritual maxims, or
some more extensive instructions which might be misinterpreted by
any who found them. It is remarkable, at any rate, that we have none
of the Saint's writings belonging to this period whatever.

All his biographers tell us that he wrote some of the stanzas of the
'Spiritual Canticle,' together with a few other poems, while he was
imprisoned at Toledo. 'When he left the prison,' says M. Magdalena
del Espíritu Santo, 'he took with him a little book in which he had
written, while there, some verses based upon the Gospel *In principio
erat Verbum*, together with some couplets which begin: "How well I
know the fount that freely flows, Although 'tis night," and the stanzas
or *liras* that begin "Whither hast vanishèd?" as far as the stanzas
beginning "Daughters of Jewry." The remainder of them the Saint
composed later when he was Rector of the College at Baeza. Some of
the expositions were written at Beas, as answers to questions put to
him by the nuns; others at Granada. This little book, in which the
Saint wrote while in prison, he left in the Convent of Beas and on
various occasions I was commanded to copy it. Then someone took
it from my cell—who, I never knew. The freshness of the words in
this book, together with their beauty and subtlety, caused me great
wonder, and one day I asked the Saint if God gave him those words
which were so comprehensive and so lovely. And he answered:
"Daughter, sometimes God gave them to me and at other times I
sought them."[2]

[1] [H., III, ii.]
[2] M. Magdalena is a very reliable witness, for she was not only a most discreet and
able woman, but was also one of those who were very near to the Saint and gained most
from his spiritual direction. The quotation is from MS. 12,944.

M. Isabel de Jesús María, who was a novice at Toledo when the Saint escaped from his imprisonment there, wrote thus from Cuerva on November 2, 1614. 'I remember, too, that, at the time we had him hidden in the church, he recited to us some lines which he had composed and kept in his mind, and that one of the nuns wrote them down as he repeated them. There were three poems—all of them upon the Most Holy Trinity, and so sublime and devout that they seem to enkindle the reader. In this house at Cuerva we have some which begin:

"Far away in the beginning,
Dwelt the Word in God Most High." [1]

The frequent references to keeping his verses in his head and the popular exaggeration of the hardships (great though these were) which the Saint had to endure in Toledo have led some writers to affirm that he did not in fact write these poems in prison but committed them to memory and transferred them to paper at some later date. The evidence of M. Magdalena, however, would appear to be decisive. We know, too, that the second of St. John of the Cross's gaolers, Fray Juan de Santa María, was a kindly man who did all he could to lighten his captive's sufferings; and his superiors would probably not have forbidden him writing materials provided he wrote no letters.[2]

It seems, then, that the Saint wrote in Toledo the first seventeen (or perhaps thirty) stanzas of the 'Spiritual Canticle,' the nine parts of the poem 'Far away in the beginning . . . ,' the paraphrase of the psalm *Super flumina Babylonis* and the poem 'How well I know the fount. . . .' This was really a considerable output of work, for, except perhaps when his gaoler allowed him to go into another room, he had no light but that of a small oil-lamp or occasionally the infiltration of daylight that penetrated a small interior window.

Apart from the statement of M. Magdalena already quoted, little more is known of what the Saint wrote in El Calvario than of what he wrote in Toledo. From an amplification made by herself of the sentences to which we have referred it appears that almost the whole of

---

[1] MS. 12,738, fol. 835. Fr. Jerónimo de S. José, too, says that the nuns of Toledo also copied certain poems from the Saint's dictation. M. Ana de S. Alberto heard him say of his imprisonment: 'God sought to try me, but His mercy forsook me not. I made some stanzas there which begin: "Whither hast vanishèd, Beloved"; and also those other verses, beginning "Far above the many rivers That in Babylon abound." All these verses I sent to Fray José de Jesús María, who told me that he was interested in them and was keeping them in his memory in order to write them out.'
[2] [H., III, ii.]

what she had copied was taken from her; as the short extracts transcribed by her are very similar to passages from the Saint's writings we may perhaps conclude that much of the other material was also incorporated in them. In that case he may well have completed a fair proportion of the *Ascent of Mount Carmel* before leaving Beas.

It was in El Calvario, too, and for the nuns of Beas, that the Saint drew the plan called the 'Mount of Perfection' (referred to by M. Magdalena[1] and in the *Ascent of Mount Carmel* and reproduced as the frontispiece to this volume) of which copies were afterwards multiplied and distributed among Discalced houses. Its author wished it to figure at the head of all his treatises, for it is a graphical representation of the entire mystic way, from the starting-point of the beginner to the very summit of perfection. His first sketch, which still survives, is a rudimentary and imperfect one; before long, however, as M. Magdalena tells us, he evolved another that was fuller and more comprehensive.

Just as we owe to PP. Gracián and Salazar many precious relics of St. Teresa, so we owe others of St. John of the Cross to M. Magdalena. Among the most valuable of these is her own copy of the 'Mount,' which, after her death, went to the 'Desert'[2] of Our Lady of the Snows established by the Discalced province of Upper Andalusia in the diocese of Granada. It was found there by P. Andrés de la Encarnación, of whom we shall presently speak, and who immediately made a copy of it, legally certified as an exact one and now in the National Library of Spain (MS. 6,296).

The superiority of the second plan over the first is very evident. The first consists simply of three parallel lines corresponding to three different paths—one on either side of the Mount, marked 'Road of the spirit of imperfection' and one in the centre marked 'Path of Mount Carmel. Spirit of perfection.' In the spaces between the paths are written the celebrated maxims which appear in Book I, Chapter xiii, of the *Ascent of Mount Carmel*, in a somewhat different form, together with certain others. At the top of the drawing are the words 'Mount Carmel,' which are not found in the second plan, and below them is the legend: 'There is no road here, for there is no law for the righteous man,' together with other texts from Scripture.

The second plan represents a number of graded heights, the loftiest

---

[1] MS. 12,944. 'He also occasionally wrote spiritual things that were of great benefit. There, too, he composed the *Mount* and drew a copy with his own hand for each of our breviaries; later, he added to these copies and made some changes.'

[2] [See, on this term, *S.S.M.*, II, 282, and *Catholic Encyclopædia*, sub. 'Carmelites.']

of which is planted with trees. Three paths, as in the first sketch, lead from the base of the mount, but they are traced more artistically and have a more detailed ascetic and mystical application. Those on either side, which denote the roads of imperfection, are broad and somewhat tortuous and come to an end before the higher stages of the mount are reached. The centre road, that of perfection, is at first very narrow but gradually broadens and leads right up to the summit of the mountain, which only the perfect attain and where they enjoy the *iuge convivium*—the heavenly feast. The different zones of religious perfection, from which spring various virtues, are portrayed with much greater detail than in the first plan. As we have reproduced the second plan in this volume, it need not be described more fully.

We know that St. John of the Cross used the 'Mount' very frequently for all kinds of religious instruction. 'By means of this drawing,' testified one of his disciples, 'he used to teach us that, in order to attain to perfection, we must not desire the good things of earth, nor those of Heaven; but that we must desire naught save to seek and strive after the glory and honour of God our Lord in all things . . . and this "Mount of Perfection" the said holy father himself expounded to this witness when he was his superior in the said priory of Granada.'[1]

It seems not improbable that the Saint continued writing chapters of the *Ascent* and the *Spiritual Canticle* while he was Rector at Baeza,[2] whether in the College itself, or in El Castellar, where he was accustomed often to go into retreat. It was certainly here that he wrote the remaining stanzas of the *Canticle* (as M. Magdalena explicitly tells us in words already quoted), except the last five, which he composed rather later, at Granada. One likes to think that these loveliest of his verses were penned by the banks of the Guadalimar, in the woods of the Granja de Santa Ana, where he was in the habit of passing long hours in communion with God. At all events the stanzas seem more in harmony with such an atmosphere than with that of the College.

With regard to the last five stanzas, we have definite evidence from a Beas nun, M. Francisca de la Madre de Dios, who testifies in the Beatification process (April 2, 1618) as follows:

And so, when the said holy friar John of the Cross was in this convent one Lent (for his great love for it brought him here from the said city of Granada, where he was prior, to confess the nuns and preach to them) he was preaching to them one day in the parlour, and this witness observed that on two separate occasions he was rapt and lifted up from the ground; and when he

---

[1] Fray Martín de San José in MS. 12,738, fol. 125.   [2] [H., IV, i.]

came to himself he dissembled and said : 'You saw how sleep overcame me!'
And one day he asked this witness in what her prayer consisted, and she
replied : 'In considering the beauty of God and in rejoicing that He has such
beauty.' And the Saint was so pleased with this that for some days he said
the most sublime things concerning the beauty of God, at which all marvelled.
And thus, under the influence of this love, he composed five stanzas, beginning 'Beloved, let us sing, And in thy beauty see ourselves portray'd.' And
in all this he showed that there was in his breast a great love of God.

From a letter which this nun wrote from Beas in 1629 to P. Jerónimo de San José, we gather that the stanzas were actually written at
Granada and brought to Beas, where

. . . with every word that we spoke to him we seemed to be opening a door
to the fruition of the great treasures and riches which God had stored up in
his soul.

If there is a discrepancy here, however, it is of small importance ; there
is no doubt as to the approximate date of the composition of these
stanzas and of their close connection with Beas.

The most fruitful literary years for St. John of the Cross were those
which he spent at Granada. Here he completed the *Ascent* and wrote
all his remaining treatises. Both M. Magdalena and the Saint's closest
disciple, P. Juan Evangelista, bear witness to this. The latter writes
from Granada to P. Jerónimo de San José, the historian of the Reform :

With regard to having seen our venerable father write the books, I saw
him write them all ; for, as I have said, I was ever at his side. The *Ascent of
Mount Carmel* and the *Dark Night* he wrote here at Granada, little by little,
continuing them only with many breaks. The *Living Flame of Love* he also
wrote in this house, when he was Vicar-Provincial, at the request of Doña
Ana de Peñalosa, and he wrote it in fifteen days when he was very busy here
with an abundance of occupations. The first thing that he wrote was *Whither
hast vanishèd?* and that too he wrote here ; the stanzas he had written in the
prison at Toledo.[1]

In another letter (February 18, 1630), he wrote to the same corres-
pondent :

With regard to our holy father's having written his books in this house,
I will say what is undoubtedly true—namely, that he wrote here the commentary on the stanzas *Whither hast vanishèd?* and the *Living Flame of Love*,
for he began and ended them in my time. The *Ascent of Mount Carmel* I
found had been begun when I came here to take the habit, which was a year

[1] MS. 12,738, fol. 1,431. The letter is undated as to the year.

and a half after the foundation of this house; he may have brought it from yonder already begun. But the *Dark Night* he certainly wrote here, for I saw him writing a part of it, and this is certain, because I saw it.[1]

These and other testimonies might with advantage be fuller and more concrete, but at least they place beyond doubt the facts that we have already set down. Summarizing our total findings, we may assert that part of the 'Spiritual Canticle,' with perhaps the 'Dark Night,' and the other poems enumerated, were written in the Toledo prison; that at the request of some nuns he wrote at El Calvario (1578–79) a few chapters of the *Ascent* and commentaries on some of the stanzas of the 'Canticle'; that he composed further stanzas at Baeza (1579–81), perhaps with their respective commentaries; and that, finally, he completed the *Canticle* and the *Ascent* at Granada and wrote the whole of the *Dark Night* and of the *Living Flame*—the latter in a fortnight. All these last works he wrote before the end of 1585, the first year in which he was Vicar-Provincial.

Other writings, most of them brief, are attributed to St. John of the Cross; they will be discussed in the third volume of this edition, in which we shall publish the minor works which we accept as genuine. The authorship of his four major prose works—the *Ascent, Dark Night, Spiritual Canticle* and *Living Flame*—no one has ever attempted to question, even though the lack of extant autographs and the large number of copies have made it difficult to establish correct texts. To this question we shall return later.

The characteristics of the writings of St. John of the Cross are so striking that it would be difficult to confuse them with those of any other writer. His literary personality stands out clearly from that of his Spanish contemporaries who wrote on similar subjects. Both his style and his methods of exposition bear the marks of a strong individuality.

If some of these derive from his native genius and temperament, others are undoubtedly reflections of his education and experience. The Aristotelian-Thomistic philosophy, then at the height of its splendour, which he learned so thoroughly in the classrooms of Salamanca University, characterizes the whole of his writings, giving them a granite-like solidity even when their theme is such as to defy human speculation. Though the precise extent of his debt to this Salamancan training in philosophy has not yet been definitely assessed, the fact of its influence is evident to every reader. It gives massiveness,

[1] MS. 12,738, fol. 1,435.

harmony and unity to both the ascetic and the mystical work of St. John of the Cross—that is to say, to all his scientific writing.

Deeply, however, as St. John of the Cross drew from the School-men, he was also profoundly indebted to many other writers. He was distinctly eclectic in his reading and quotes freely (though less than some of his Spanish contemporaries) from the Fathers and from the mediæval mystics, especially from St. Thomas, St. Bonaventura, Hugh of St. Victor and the pseudo-Areopagite. All that he quotes, however, he makes his own, with the result that his chapters are never a mass of citations loosely strung together, as are those of many other Spanish mystics of his time.

When we study his treatises—principally that great composite work known as the *Ascent of Mount Carmel* and the *Dark Night*—we have the impression of a master-mind that has scaled the heights of mystical science and from their summit looks down upon and domin-ates the plain below and the paths leading upward. We may well wonder what a vast contribution to the subject he would have made had he been able to expound all the eight stanzas of his poem since he covered so much ground in expounding no more than two. Observe with what assurance and what mastery of subject and method he defines his themes and divides his arguments, even when treating the most abstruse and controversial questions. The most obscure pheno-mena he appears to illumine, as it were, with one lightning flash of understanding, as though the explanation of them were perfectly natural and easy. His solutions of difficult problems are not timid, questioning and loaded with exceptions, but clear, definite and virile like the man who proposes them. No scientific field, perhaps, has so many zones which are apt to become vague and obscure as has that of mystical theology; and there are those among the Saint's predecessors who seem to have made their permanent abode in them. They give the impression of attempting to cloak vagueness in verbosity, in order to avoid being forced into giving solutions of problems which they find insoluble. Not so St. John of the Cross. A scientific dictator, if such a person were conceivable, could hardly express himself with greater clarity. His phrases have a decisive, almost a chiselled quality; where he errs on the side of redundance, it is not with the intention of cloaking uncertainty, but in order that he may drive home with double force the truths which he desires to impress.

No less admirable are, on the one hand, his synthetic skill and the logic of his arguments, and, on the other, his subtle and discriminating analyses, which weigh the finest shades of thought and dissect each subject with all the accuracy of science. To his analytical genius we owe those finely balanced statements, orthodox yet bold and fearless, which have caused clumsier intellects to misunderstand him. It is not remarkable that this should have occurred. The ease with which the un-skilled can misinterpret genius is shown in the history of many a heresy.

How much of all this St. John of the Cross owed to his studies of scholastic philosophy in the University of Salamanca, it is difficult to say. If we examine the history of that University and read of its severe discipline we shall be in no danger of under-estimating the effect which it must have produced upon so agile and alert an intellect. Further, we note the constant parallelisms and the comparatively infrequent (though occasionally important) divergences between the doctrines of St. John of the Cross and St. Thomas, to say nothing of the close agreement between the views of St. John of the Cross and those of the Schoolmen on such subjects as the passions and appetites, the nature of the soul, the relations between soul and body. Yet we must not forget the student tag: *Quod natura non dat, Salmantica non præstat.* Nothing but natural genius could impart the vigour and the clarity which enhance all St. John of the Cross's arguments and nothing but his own deep and varied experience could have made him what he may well be termed—the greatest psychologist in the history of mysticism.

Eminent, too, was St. John of the Cross in sacred theology. The close natural connection that exists between dogmatic and mystical theology and their continual interdependence in practice make it impossible for a Christian teacher to excel in the latter alone. Indeed, more than one of the heresies that have had their beginnings in mysti-cism would never have developed had those who fell into them been well grounded in dogmatic theology. The one is, as it were, the lantern that lights the path of the other, as St. Teresa realized when she began to feel the continual necessity of consulting theological teachers. If St. John of the Cross is able to climb the greatest heights of mysticism and remain upon them without stumbling or dizziness it is because his feet are invariably well shod with the truths of dogmatic theology. The great mysteries—those of the Trinity, the Creation, the Incarna-tion and the Redemption—and such dogmas as those concerning grace, the gifts of the Spirit, the theological virtues, etc., were to him guide-posts for those who attempted to scale, and to lead others to scale, the symbolic mount of sanctity.

It will be remembered that the Saint spent but one year upon his theological course at the University of Salamanca, for which reason many have been surprised at the evident solidity of his attainments. But, apart from the fact that a mind so keen and retentive as that of Fray Juan de San Matías could absorb in a year what others would have failed to imbibe in the more usual two or three, we must of necessity assume a far longer time spent in private study. For in one year he could not have studied all the treatises of which he clearly demonstrates his knowledge—to say nothing of many others which he must have known. His own works, apart from any external evidence, prove him to have been a theologian of distinction.

In both fields, the dogmatic and the mystical, he was greatly aided by his knowledge of Holy Scripture, which he studied continually, in the last years of his life, to the exclusion, as it would seem, of all else. Much of it he knew by heart; the simple devotional talks that he was accustomed to give were invariably studded with texts, and he made use of passages from the Bible both to justify and to illustrate his teaching. In the mystical interpretation of Holy Scripture, as every student of mysticism knows, he has had few equals even among his fellow Doctors of the Church Universal.

Testimonies to his mastery of the Scriptures can be found in abundance. P. Alonso de la Madre de Dios, *el Asturicense*, for example, who was personally acquainted with him, stated in 1603 that 'he had a great gift and facility for the exposition of the Sacred Scripture, principally of the Song of Songs, Ecclesiasticus, Ecclesiastes, the Proverbs and the Psalms of David.'[1] His spiritual daughter, that same Magdalena del Espíritu Santo to whom we have several times referred, affirms that St. John of the Cross would frequently read the Gospels to the nuns of Beas and expound the letter and the spirit to them.[2] Fray Juan Evangelista says in a well-known passage:

He was very fond of reading in the Scriptures, and I never once saw him read any other books than the Bible,[3] almost all of which he knew by heart, St. Augustine *Contra Hæreses* and the *Flos Sanctorum*. When occasionally he preached (which was seldom) or gave informal addresses [*pláticas*], as he more commonly did, he never read from any book save the Bible. His conversation, whether at recreation or at other times, was continually of

---

[1] MS. 12,738, fol. 3. Cf. a letter of April 28, 1614, by the same friar (*ibid.*, fol. 865), which describes the Saint's knowledge of the Holy Scriptures, and skill in expounding them, as 'inspired' and 'Divine.'   [2] *Ibid.*, fol. 18.

[3] Jerónimo de la Cruz (*ibid.*, fol. 639) describes the Saint on his journeys as 'frequently reading the Bible' as he went along on his 'beast.'

God, and he spoke so delightfully that, when he discoursed upon sacred things at recreation, he would make us all laugh and we used greatly to enjoy going out. On occasions when we held chapters, he would usually give devotional addresses (*pláticas divinas*) after supper, and he never failed to give an address every night.[1]

Fray Pablo de Santa María, who had also heard the Saint's addresses, wrote thus:

He was a man of the most enkindled spirituality and of great insight into all that concerns mystical theology and matters of prayer; I consider it impossible that he could have spoken so well about all the virtues if he had not been most proficient in the spiritual life, and I really think he knew the whole Bible by heart, so far as one could judge from the various Biblical passages which he would quote at chapters and in the refectory, without any great effort, but as one who goes where the Spirit leads him.[2]

Nor was this admiration for the expository ability of St. John of the Cross confined to his fellow-friars, who might easily enough have been led into hero-worship. We know that he was thought highly of in this respect by the University of Alcalá de Henares, where he was consulted as an authority. A Dr. Villegas, Canon of Segovia Cathedral, has left on record his respect for him. And Fray Jerónimo de San José relates the esteem in which he was held at the University of Baeza, which in his day enjoyed a considerable reputation for Biblical studies:

There were at that time at the University of Baeza many learned and spiritually minded persons, disciples of that great father and apostle Juan de Ávila.[3] . . . All these doctors . . . would repair to our venerable father as to an oracle from heaven and would discuss with him both their own spiritual progress and that of souls committed to their charge, with the result that they were both edified and astonished at his skill. They would also bring him difficulties and delicate points connected with Divine letters, and on these, too, he spoke with extraordinary energy and illumination. One of these doctors, who had consulted him and listened to him on various occasions, said that, although he had read deeply in St. Augustine and St. John Chrysostom and other saints, and had found in them greater heights and depths, he had found in none of them that particular kind of spirituality in exposition which this great father applied to Scriptural passages.[4]

[1] MS. 12,738, fol. 559. P. Alonso writes similarly in a letter to Fray Jerónimo de San José: 'And in this matter of speaking of God and expounding passages from Scripture he made everyone marvel, for they never asked him about a passage which he could not explain in great detail, and sometimes at recreation the whole hour and much more went by in the explanation of passages about which they asked him' (fol. 1,431).
[2] *Ibid.*, fol. 847.   [3] [Cf. *S.S.M.*, II, 123–48.]
[4] *Vida*, Bk. IV, Chap. xiv, § 1.

The Scriptural knowledge of St. John of the Cross was, as this passage makes clear, in no way merely academic. Both in his literal and his mystical interpretations of the Bible, he has what we may call a 'Biblical sense,' which saves him from such exaggerations as we find in other expositors, both earlier and contemporary. One would not claim, of course, that among the many hundreds of applications of Holy Scripture made by the Carmelite Doctor there are none that can be objected to in this respect; but the same can be said of St. Augustine, St. Ambrose, St. Gregory or St. Bernard, and no one would assert that, either with them or with him, such instances are other than most exceptional.

To the three sources already mentioned in which St. John of the Cross found inspiration we must add a fourth—the works of ascetic and mystical writers. It is not yet possible to assert with any exactness how far the Saint made use of these; for, though partial studies of this question have been attempted, a complete and unbiased treatment of it has still to be undertaken. Here we can do no more than give a few indications of what remains to be done and summarize the present content of our knowledge.[1]

We may suppose that, during his novitiate in Medina, the Saint read a number of devotional books, one of which would almost certainly have been the *Imitation of Christ*, and others would have included works which were translated into Spanish by order of Cardinal Cisneros. The demands of a University course would not keep him from pursuing such studies at Salamanca; the friar who chose a cell from the window of which he could see the Blessed Sacrament, so that he might spend hours in its company, would hardly be likely to neglect his devotional reading. But we have not a syllable of direct external evidence as to the titles of any of the books known to him.

Nor, for that matter, have we much more evidence of this kind for any other part of his life. Both his early Carmelite biographers and the numerous witnesses who gave evidence during the canonization process describe at great length his extraordinary penances, his love for places of retreat beautified by Nature, the long hours that he spent in prayer and the tongue of angels with which he spoke on things spiritual. But of his reading they say nothing except to describe his attachment to the Bible, nor have we any record of the books contained in the libraries

[1] [On this subject cf. P. Crisógono de Jesús Sacramentado: *San Juan de la Cruz*, Madrid, 1929, Vol. II, pp. 17–34 *et passim*.]

of the religious houses that he visited. Yet if, as we gather from the process, he spent little more than three hours nightly in sleep, he must have read deeply of spiritual things by night as well as by day.

Some clues to the nature of his reading may be gained from his own writings. It is true that the clues are slender. He cites few works apart from the Bible and these are generally liturgical books, such as the Breviary. Some of his quotations from St. Augustine, St. Gregory and other of the Fathers are traceable to these sources. Nevertheless, we have not read St. John of the Cross for long before we find ourselves in the full current of mystical tradition. It is not by means of more or less literal quotations that the Saint produces this impression; he has studied his precursors so thoroughly that he absorbs the substance of their doctrine and incorporates it so intimately in his own that it becomes flesh of his flesh. Everything in his writings is fully matured: he has no *juvenilia*. The mediæval mystics whom he uses are too often vague and undisciplined; they need someone to select from them and unify them, to give them clarity and order, so that their treatment of mystical theology may have the solidity and substance of scholastic theology. To have done this is one of the achievements of St. John of the Cross.

We are convinced, then, by an internal evidence which is chiefly of a kind in which no chapter and verse can be given, that St. John of the Cross read widely in mediæval mystical theology and assimilated a great part of what he read. The influence of foreign writers upon Spanish mysticism, though it was once denied, is to-day generally recognized. It was inevitable that it should have been considerable in a country which in the sixteenth century had such a high degree of culture as Spain. Plotinus, in a diluted form, made his way into Spanish mysticism as naturally as did Seneca into Spanish asceticism. Plato and Aristotle entered it through the two greatest minds that Christianity has known—St. Augustine and St. Thomas. The influence of the Platonic theories of love and beauty and of such basic Aristotelian theories as the origin of knowledge is to be found in most of the Spanish mystics, St. John of the Cross among them.

The pseudo-Dionysius was another writer who was considered a great authority by the Spanish mystics. The importance attributed to his works arose partly from the fact that he was supposed to have been one of the first disciples of the Apostles; many chapters from mystical works of those days all over Europe are no more than glosses of the pseudo-Areopagite. He is followed less, however, by St. John of the Cross than by many of the latter's contemporaries.

Other influences upon the Carmelite Saint were St. Gregory, St. Bernard and Hugh and Richard of St. Victor, many of whose maxims were in the mouths of the mystics in the sixteenth century. More important, probably, than any of these was the Fleming, Ruysbroeck, between whom and St. John of the Cross there were certainly many points of contact. The Saint would have read him, not in the original, but in Surius' Latin translation of 1552, copies of which are known to have been current in Spain.[1] Together with Ruysbroeck may be classed Suso, Denis the Carthusian, Herp, Kempis and various other writers.

Many of the ideas and phrases which we find in St. John of the Cross, as in other writers, are, of course, traceable to the common mystical tradition rather than to any definite individual influence. The striking metaphor of the ray of light penetrating the room, for example, which occurs in the first chapter of the pseudo-Areopagite's *De Mystica Theologia*, has been used continually by mystical writers ever since his time. The figures of the wood consumed by fire, of the ladder, the mirror, the flame of love and the nights of sense and spirit had long since become naturalized in mystical literature. There are many more such examples.

The originality of St. John of the Cross is in no way impaired by his employment of this current mystical language: such an idea might once have been commonly held, but has long ceased to be put forward seriously. His originality, indeed, lies precisely in the use which he made of language that he found near to hand. It is not going too far to liken the place taken by St. John of the Cross in mystical theology to that of St. Thomas in dogmatic; St. Thomas laid hold upon the immense store of material which had accumulated in the domain of dogmatic theology and subjected it to the iron discipline of reason. That St. John of the Cross did the same for mystical theology is his great claim upon our admiration. Through St. Thomas speaks the ecclesiastical tradition of many ages on questions of religious belief; through St. John speaks an equally venerable tradition on questions of Divine love. Both writers combined sainthood with genius. Both opened broad channels to be followed of necessity by Catholic writers through the ages to come till theology shall lose itself in that vast

[1] On Flemish influences on Spanish mysticism, see P. Groult: *Les Mystiques des Pays-Bas et la littérature espagnole du seizième siècle*, Louvain, 1927 [, and Joaquín Sanchis Alventosa, O.F.M.: *La Escuela mística alemana y sus relaciones con nuestros místicos del Siglo de Oro*, Madrid, 1946].

ocean of truth and love which is God. Both created instruments adequate to the greatness of their task: St. Thomas' clear, decisive reasoning processes give us the formula appropriate to each and every need of the understanding; St. John clothes his teaching in mellower and more appealing language, as befits the exponent of the science of love. We may describe the treatises of St. John of the Cross as the true *Summa Angelica* of mystical theology.

II

OUTSTANDING QUALITIES AND DEFECTS OF THE SAINT'S STYLE

THE profound and original thought which St. John of the Cross bestowed upon so abstruse a subject, and upon one on which there was so little classical literature in Spanish when he wrote, led him to clothe his ideas in a language at once energetic, precise and of a high degree of individuality. His style reflects his thought, but it reflects the style of no school and of no other writer whatsoever.

This is natural enough, for thought and feeling were always uppermost in the Saint; style and language take a place entirely subordinate to them. Never did he sacrifice any idea to artistic combinations of words; never blur over any delicate shade of thought to enhance some rhythmic cadence of musical prose. Literary form (to use a figure which he himself might have coined) is only present at all in his works in the sense in which the industrious and deferential servant is present in the ducal apartment, for the purpose of rendering faithful service to his lord and master. This subordination of style to content in the Saint's work is one of its most eminent qualities. He is a great writer, but not a great stylist. The strength and robustness of his intellect everywhere predominate.

This to a large extent explains the negligences which we find in his style, the frequency with which it is marred by repetitions and its occasional degeneration into diffuseness. The long, unwieldy sentences, one of which will sometimes run to the length of a reasonably sized paragraph, are certainly a trial to many a reader. So intent is the Saint upon explaining, underlining and developing his points so that they shall be apprehended as perfectly as may be, that he continually recurs to what he has already said, and repeats words, phrases and even passages of considerable length without scruple. It is only fair to remind the reader that such things were far commoner in the Golden Age than they are to-day; most didactic Spanish prose of that period would be notably improved, from a modern standpoint, if its volume were cut down by about one-third.

Be that as it may, these defects in the prose of St. John of the Cross are amply compensated by the fullness of his phraseology, the wealth and profusion of his imagery, the force and the energy of his argument. He has only to be compared with the didactic writers who were his contemporaries for this to become apparent. Together with Luis de Granada, Luis de León, Juan de los Ángeles and Luis de la Puente,[1] he created a genuinely native language, purged of Latinisms, precise and eloquent, which Spanish writers have used ever since in writing of mystical theology.

The most sublime of all the Spanish mystics, he soars aloft on the wings of Divine love to heights known to hardly any of them. Though no words can express the loftiest of the experiences which he describes, we are never left with the impression that word, phrase or image has failed him. If it does not exist, he appears to invent it, rather than pause in his description in order to search for an expression of the idea that is in his mind or be satisfied with a prolix paraphrase. True to the character of his thought, his style is always forceful and energetic, even to a fault.

We have said nothing of his poems, for indeed they call for no purely literary commentary. How full of life the greatest of them are, how rich in meaning, how unforgettable and how inimitable, the individual reader may see at a glance or may learn from his own experience. Many of their exquisite figures their author owes, directly or indirectly, to his reading and assimilation of the Bible. Some of them, however, have acquired a new life in the form which he has given them. A line here, a phrase there, has taken root in the mind of some later poet or essayist and has given rise to a new work of art, to many lovers of which the Saint who lies behind it is unknown.

It is perhaps not an exaggeration to say that the verse and prose works combined of St. John of the Cross form at once the most grandiose and the most melodious spiritual canticle to which any one man has ever given utterance. It is impossible, in the space at our disposal, to quote at any length from the Spanish critics who have paid tribute to its comprehensiveness and profundity. We must content ourselves with a short quotation characterizing the Saint's poems, taken from the greatest of these critics, Marcelino Menéndez Pelayo,

[1] [Cf. *S.S.M.*, I (1927), 33–76, 291–405; (1951), 25–61, 235–328; II (1930), 309–43.]

who, besides referring frequently to St. John of the Cross in such of his mature works as the *Heterodoxos*, *Ideas Estéticas* and *Ciencia Española*, devoted to him a great part of the address which he delivered as a young man at his official reception into the Spanish Academy under the title of 'Mystical Poetry.'

'So sublime,' wrote Menéndez Pelayo, 'is this poetry [of St. John of the Cross] that it scarcely seems to belong to this world at all; it is hardly capable of being assessed by literary criteria. More ardent in its passion than any profane poetry, its form is as elegant and exquisite, as plastic and as highly figured as any of the finest works of the Renaissance. The spirit of God has passed through these poems every one, beautifying and sanctifying them on its way.'

III

DIFFUSION OF THE WRITINGS OF ST. JOHN OF THE CROSS—LOSS OF THE AUTOGRAPHS—GENERAL CHARACTERISTICS OF THE MANUSCRIPTS

THE outstanding qualities of St. John of the Cross's writings were soon recognized by the earliest of their few and privileged readers. All such persons, of course, belonged to a small circle composed of the Saint's intimate friends and disciples. As time went on, the circle widened repeatedly; now it embraces the entire Church, and countless individual souls who are filled with the spirit of Christianity.

First of all, the works were read and discussed in those foci of evangelical zeal which the Saint had himself enkindled, by his word and example, at Beas, El Calvario, Baeza and Granada. They could not have come more opportunely. St. Teresa's Reform had engendered a spiritual alertness and energy reminiscent of the earliest days of Christianity. Before this could in any way diminish, her first friar presented the followers of them both with spiritual food to nourish and re-create their souls and so to sustain the high degree of zeal for Our Lord which He had bestowed upon them.

In one sense, St. John of the Cross took up his pen in order to supplement the writings of St. Teresa; on several subjects, for example, he abstained from writing at length because she had already treated of them.[1] Much of the work of the two Saints, however, of necessity

---

[1] One well-known example will be found in the commentary on the 'Spiritual Canticle,' Chap. xii (cf. p. lvi, below).

covers the same ground, and thus the great mystical school of the
Spanish Carmelites is reinforced at its very beginnings in a way which
must be unique in the history of mysticism. The writings of St. Teresa
and St. John of the Cross, though of equal value and identical aim, are
in many respects very different in their nature; together they cover
almost the entire ground of orthodox mysticism, both speculative and
experimental. The Carmelite mystics who came after them were able
to build upon a broad and sure foundation.

The writings of St. John of the Cross soon became known outside
the narrow circle of his sons and daughters in religion. In a few years
they had gone all over Spain and reached Portugal, France and Italy.
They were read by persons of every social class, from the Empress
Maria of Austria, sister of Philip II, to the most unlettered nuns of St.
Teresa's most remote foundations. One of the witnesses at the process
for the beatification declared that he knew of no works of which there
existed so many copies, with the exception of the Bible.

We may fairly suppose (and the supposition is confirmed by the
nature of the extant manuscripts) that the majority of the early copies
were made by friars and nuns of the Discalced Reform. Most Discalced
houses must have had copies and others were probably in the possession
of members of other Orders. We gather, too, from various sources,
that even lay persons managed to make or obtain copies of the
manuscripts.

How many of these copies, it will be asked, were made directly from
the autographs? So vague is the available evidence on this question
that it is difficult to attempt any calculation of even approximate
reliability. All we can say is that the copies made by, or for, the Discalced friars and nuns themselves are the earliest and most trustworthy,
while those intended for the laity were frequently made at third or
fourth hand. The Saint himself seems to have written out only one
manuscript of each treatise and none of these has come down to us.
Some think that he destroyed the manuscripts copied with his own
hand, fearing that they might come to be venerated for other reasons
than that of the value of their teaching. He was, of course, perfectly
capable of such an act of abnegation; once, as we know, in accordance
with his own principles, he burned some letters of St. Teresa, which
he had carried with him for years, for no other reason than that he
realized that he was becoming attached to them.[1]

The only manuscript of his that we possess consists of a few pages

[1] MS. 12,738, fol. 639.

of maxims, some letters and one or two documents which he wrote when he was Vicar-Provincial of Andalusia.[1] So numerous and so thorough have been the searches made for further autographs during the last three centuries that further discoveries of any importance seem most unlikely. We have, therefore, to console ourselves with manuscripts, such as the Sanlúcar de Barrameda Codex of the *Spiritual Canticle*, which bear the Saint's autograph corrections as warrants of their integrity.

The vagueness of much of the evidence concerning the manuscripts to which we have referred extends to the farthest possible limit—that of using the word 'original' to indicate 'autograph' and 'copy' indifferently. Even in the earliest documents we can never be sure which sense is intended. Furthermore, there was a passion in the seventeenth and eighteenth centuries for describing all kinds of old manuscripts as autographs, and thus we find copies so described in which the hand bears not the slightest resemblance to that of the Saint, as the most superficial collation with a genuine specimen of his hand would have made evident. We shall give instances of this in describing the extant copies of individual treatises. One example of a general kind, however, may be quoted here to show the extent to which the practice spread. In a statement made, with reference to one of the processes, at the convent of Discalced Carmelite nuns of Valladolid, a certain M. María de la Trinidad deposed 'that a servant of God, a Franciscan tertiary named Ana María, possesses the originals of the books of our holy father, and has heard that he sent them to the Order.' Great importance was attached to this deposition and every possible measure was taken to find the autographs—needless to say, without result.[2]

With the multiplication of the number of copies of St. John of the Cross's writings, the number of variants naturally multiplied also. The early copies having all been made for devotional purposes, by persons with little or no palæographical knowledge, many of whom did not even exercise common care, it is not surprising that there is not

[1] To these we shall refer in the third volume of this edition.

[2] If any single person could have spoken from knowledge of this matter it would be P. Alonso de la Madre de Dios, as all papers connected with St. John of the Cross passed through his hands and he took hundreds of depositions in connection with the Beatification process. His statements, however (MS. 19,404, fol. 176 [P. Silverio, I, 179]), are as vague as any others. Rather more reliable are the Saint's two early biographers, P. José de Jesús María (Quiroga) and P. Jerónimo de San José. The former states in one place that he is using an autograph of the *Ascent of Mount Carmel*, but again it seems likely that he was mistaken, since the archives of the Reform were still intact in the next century and no genuine autograph of any length was found in them.

a single one which can compare in punctiliousness with certain extant eighteenth-century copies of documents connected with St. John of the Cross and St. Teresa. These were made by a painstaking friar called Manuel de Santa María, whose scrupulousness went so far that he reproduced imperfectly formed letters exactly as they were written, adding the parts that were lacking (e.g., the *tilde* over the letter *ñ*) with ink of another colour.

We may lament that this good father had no predecessor like himself to copy the Saint's treatises, but it is only right to say that the copies we possess are sufficiently faithful and numerous to give us reasonably accurate versions of their originals. The important point about them is that they bear no signs of bad faith, nor even of the desire (understandable enough in those unscientific days) to clarify the sense of their original, or even to improve upon its teaching. Their errors are often gross ones, but the large majority of them are quite easy to detect and put right. The impression to this effect which one obtains from a casual perusal of almost any of these copies is quite definitely confirmed by a comparison of them with copies corrected by the Saint or written by the closest and most trusted of his disciples. It may be added that some of the variants may, for aught we know to the contrary, be the Saint's own work, since it is not improbable that he may have corrected more than one copy of some of his writings, and not been entirely consistent.

There are, broadly speaking, two classes into which the copies (more particularly those of the *Ascent* and the *Dark Night*) may be divided. One class aims at a more or less exact transcription; the other definitely sets out to abbreviate. Even if the latter class be credited with a number of copies which hardly merit the name, the former is by far the larger, and, of course, the more important, though it must not be supposed that the latter is unworthy of notice. The abbreviators generally omit whole chapters, or passages, at a time, and, where they are not for the moment doing this, or writing the connecting phrases necessary to repair their mischief, they are often quite faithful to their originals. Since they do not, in general, attribute anything to their author that is not his, no objection can be taken, on moral grounds, to their proceeding, though, in actual fact, the results are not always happy. Their ends were purely practical and devotional and they made no attempt to pass their compendia as full-length transcriptions.

With regard to the *Spiritual Canticle* and the *Living Flame of Love*, of each of which there are two redactions bearing indisputable marks of the author's own hand, the classification of the copies will naturally depend upon which redaction each copy the more nearly follows. This question will be discussed in the necessary detail in the introduction to each of these works, and to the individual introductions to the four major treatises we must refer the reader for other details of the manuscripts. In the present pages we have attempted only a general account of these matters. It remains to add that our divisions of each chapter into paragraphs follow the manuscripts throughout except where indicated. The printed editions, as we shall see, suppressed these divisions, but, apart from their value to the modern reader, they are sufficiently nearly identical in the various copies to form one further testimony to their general high standard of reliability.

IV

INTEGRITY OF THE SAINT'S WORK—INCOMPLETE CONDITION OF THE 'ASCENT' AND THE 'NIGHT'—DISPUTED QUESTIONS

THE principal lacuna in St. John of the Cross's writings, and, from the literary standpoint, the most interesting, is the lack of any commentary to the last five stanzas[1] of the poem 'Dark Night.' Such a commentary is essential to the completion of the plan which the Saint had already traced for himself in what was to be, and, in spite of its unfinished condition, is in fact, his most rigorously scientific treatise. 'All the doctrine,' he wrote in the Argument of the *Ascent*, 'whereof I intend to treat in this *Ascent of Mount Carmel* is included in the following stanzas, and in them is also described the manner of ascending to the summit of the Mount, which is the high estate of perfection which we here call union of the soul with God.' This leaves no doubt but that the Saint intended to treat the mystical life as one whole, and to deal in turn with each stage of the road to perfection, from the beginnings of the Purgative Way to the crown and summit of the life of Union. After showing the need for such a treatise as he proposes to write, he divides the chapters on Purgation into four parts corresponding to the Active and Passive nights of Sense and of Spirit. These, however, correspond only to the first two stanzas of his poem; they are not, as we shall shortly see, complete, but their incompleteness is slight compared with that of the work as a whole.

---

[1] [The commentary on the third stanza is begun in II, xxv (p. 456, below). If this be not counted, the number of stanzas left uncommented is six.]

Did St. John of the Cross, we may ask, ever write a commentary on those last five stanzas, which begin with a description of the state of Illumination:

> 'Twas that light guided me,
> More surely than the noonday's brightest glare—

and end with that of the life of Union:

> All things for me that day
> Ceas'd, as I slumber'd there,
> Amid the lilies drowning all my care?

If we suppose that he did, we are faced with the question of its fate and with the strange fact that none of his contemporaries makes any mention of such a commentary, though they are all prolific in details of far less importance.

Conjectures have been ventured on this question ever since critical methods first began to be applied to St. John of the Cross's writings. A great deal was written about it by P. Andrés de la Encarnación, to whom his superiors entrusted the task of collecting and editing the Saint's writings, and whose findings, though they suffer from the defects of an age which from a modern standpoint must be called un-scientific, and need therefore to be read with the greatest caution, are often surprisingly just and accurate. P. Andrés begins by referring to various places where St. John of the Cross states that he has treated certain subjects and proposes to treat others, about which nothing can be found in his writings. This, he says, may often be due to an over-sight on the writer's part or to changes which new experiences might have brought to his mode of thinking. On the other hand, there are sometimes signs that these promises have been fulfilled: the sharp truncation of the argument, for example, at the end of Book III of the *Ascent* suggests that at least a few pages are missing, in which case the original manuscript must have been mutilated,[1] for almost all the extant copies break off at the same word. It is unthinkable, as P. Andrés says, that the Saint 'should have gone on to write the *Night* without completing the *Ascent*, for all these five books[2] are integral parts of one whole, since they all treat of different stages of one spiritual path.'[3]

---

[1] This is not so unlikely as it may seem, for the early manuscripts were all either un-bound, or very roughly stitched together, and several of the extant copies have leaves missing.   It was not till the time of the Beatification Process that greater care began to be taken of the Saint's writings, and they were bound strongly and even luxuriously.

[2] i.e., the three books of the *Ascent* and the two of the *Night*.

[3] MS. 3,180, Adición B.

It may be argued in the same way that St. John of the Cross would not have gone on to write the commentaries on the 'Spiritual Canticle' and the 'Living Flame of Love' without first completing the *Dark Night*. P. Andrés goes so far as to say that the very unwillingness which the Saint displayed towards writing commentaries on the two latter poems indicates that he had already completed the others; otherwise, he could easily have excused himself from the later task on the plea that he had still to finish the earlier.

Again, St. John of the Cross declares very definitely, in the prologue to the *Dark Night*, that, after describing in the commentary on the first two stanzas the effects of the two passive purgations of the sensual and the spiritual part of man, he will devote the six remaining stanzas to expounding 'various and wondrous effects of the spiritual illumination and union of love with God.'[1] Nothing could be clearer than this. Now, in the commentary on the 'Living Flame,' argues P. Andrés, he treats at considerable length of simple contemplation and adds that he has written fully of it in several chapters of the *Ascent* and the *Night*, which he names; but not only do we not find the references in two of the chapters enumerated by him, but he makes no mention of several other chapters in which the references are of considerable fullness. The proper deductions from these facts would seem to be, first, that we do not possess the *Ascent* and the *Night* in the form in which the Saint wrote them, and, second, that in the missing chapters he referred to the subject under discussion at much greater length than in the chapters we have.

Further, the practice of St. John of the Cross was not to omit any part of his commentaries when for any reason he was unable or unwilling to write them at length, but rather to abbreviate them. Thus, he runs rapidly through the third stanza of the *Night* and through the fourth stanza of the *Living Flame*: we should expect him in the same way to treat the last three stanzas of the *Night* with similar brevity and rapidity, but not to omit them altogether.

Such are the principal arguments used by P. Andrés which have inclined many critics to the belief that St. John of the Cross completed these treatises. Other of his arguments, which to himself were even more convincing, have now lost much weight. The chief of these are the contention that, because a certain Fray Agustín Antolínez (b. 1554), in expounding these same poems, makes no mention of the Saint's having failed to expound five stanzas of the *Night*, he did therefore

[1] Cf. p. 325, below.

write an exposition of them ;[1] and the supposition that the *Living Flame* was written before the *Spiritual Canticle*, and that therefore, when the prologue to the *Living Flame* says that the author has already described the highest state of perfection attainable in this life, it cannot be referring to the *Canticle* and must necessarily allude to passages, now lost, from the *Dark Night*.[2]

Our own judgment upon this much debated question is not easily delivered. On the one hand, the reasons why St. John of the Cross should have completed his work are perfectly sound ones and his own words in the *Ascent* and the *Dark Night* are a clear statement of his intentions. Furthermore, he had ample time to complete it, for he wrote other treatises at a later date and he certainly considered the latter part of the *Dark Night* to be more important than the former. On the other hand, it is disconcerting to find not even the briefest clear reference to this latter part in any of his subsequent writings, when both the *Living Flame* and the *Spiritual Canticle* offered so many occasions for such a reference to an author accustomed to refer his readers to his other treatises. Again, his contemporaries, who were keenly interested in his work, and mention such insignificant things as the *Cautions*, the *Maxims* and the 'Mount of Perfection,' say nothing whatever of the missing chapters. None of his biographers speaks of them, nor does P. Alonso de la Madre de Dios, who examined the Saint's writings in detail immediately after his death and was in touch with his closest friends and companions. We are inclined, therefore, to think that the chapters in question were never written.[3] Is not the following sequence of probable facts the most tenable? We know from P. Juan Evangelista that the *Ascent* and the *Dark Night* were written at different times, with many intervals of short or long duration. The Saint may well have entered upon the *Spiritual Canticle*, which was a concession to the affectionate importunity of M. Ana de Jesús, with

---

[1] It would be natural enough, of course, for Fray Agustín Antolínez to have noted this fact, but, as he makes no mention of St. John of the Cross at all, nothing can be safely inferred from his silence. It may be added that Fray Agustín's commentary is to be published by the Spanish Augustinians [and that P. Silverio (I, 190–3) gives a specimen of it which shows how well it deserves publication. Cf. also Vol. II, pp. 20–1, below.]

[2] As we shall later see, the *Living Flame* was written after the first redaction of the *Spiritual Canticle*, but before the second redaction, which mentions the *Living Flame* in the exposition of Stanza XXXI, thus misleading P. Andrés as to its date. There is no doubt, in our mind, that the reference in the preface to the *Living Flame* is to the *Canticle*: the description fits it exactly.

[3] [P. Silverio's words are: 'For my own part, I think it very probable that he never composed them.' I myself give a little less weight to the negative evidence brought forward, and, though I too am inclined to the negative solution, I should hold the scales between the two rather more evenly.]

every intention of returning later to finish his earlier treatise. But, having completed the *Canticle*, he may equally well have been struck with the similarity between a part of it and the unwritten commentary on the earlier stanzas, and this may have decided him that the *Dark Night* needed no completion, especially as the *Living Flame* also described the life of Union. This hypothesis will explain all the facts, and seems completely in harmony with all we know of St. John of the Cross, who was in no sense, as we have already said, a writer by profession. If we accept it, we need not necessarily share the views which we here assume to have been his. Not only would the completion of the *Dark Night* have given us new ways of approach to so sublime and intricate a theme, but this would have been treated in a way more closely connected with the earlier stages of the mystical life than was possible in either the *Living Flame* or the *Canticle*.

We ought perhaps to notice one further supposition of P. Andrés, which has been taken up by a number of later critics: that St. John of the Cross completed the commentary which we know as the *Dark Night*, but that on account of the distinctive nature of the contents of the part now lost he gave it a separate title.[1] The only advantage of this theory seems to be that it makes the hypothesis of the loss of the commentary less improbable. In other respects it is as unsatisfactory as the theory of P. Andrés,[2] of which we find a variant in M. Baruzi,[3] that the Saint thought the commentary too bold, and too sublime, to be perpetuated, and therefore destroyed it, or, at least, forbade its being copied. It is surely unlikely that the sublimity of these missing chapters would exceed that of the *Canticle* or the *Living Flame*.

This seems the most suitable place to discuss a feature of the works of St. John of the Cross to which allusion is often made—the little interest which he took in their division into books and chapters and his lack of consistency in observing such divisions when he had once made them. A number of examples may be cited. In the first chapter of the *Ascent of Mount Carmel*, using the words 'part' and 'book' as synonyms, he makes it clear that the *Ascent* and the *Dark Night* are to him one single treatise. 'The first night or purgation,' he writes, 'is of the sensual part of the soul, which is treated in the present stanza, and

---

[1] If this were so, we might even hazard a guess that the title was that given in the *Living Flame* (I, 21) and not exactly applicable to any of the existing treatises, viz. *The Dark Night of the Ascent of Mount Carmel*.

[2] *Memorias Historiales*, C. 13.

[3] *Saint Jean de la Croix*, pp. 13–15.

will be treated in the first part of this book. And the second is of the spiritual part; of this speaks the second stanza, which follows; and of this we shall treat likewise, in the second and the third part, with respect to the activity of the soul; and in the fourth part, with respect to its passivity.'[1] The author's intention here is evident. Purgation may be sensual or spiritual, and each of these kinds may be either active or passive. The most logical proceeding would be to divide the whole of the material into four parts or books: two to be devoted to active purgation and two to passive.[2] St. John of the Cross, however, devotes two parts to active spiritual purgation—one to that of the understanding and the other to that of the memory and the will. In the *Night*, on the other hand, where it would seem essential to devote one book to the passive purgation of sense and another to that of spirit, he includes both in one part, the fourth. In the *Ascent*, he divides the content of each of his books into various chapters; in the *Night*, where the argument is developed like that of the *Ascent*, he makes a division into paragraphs only, and a very irregular division at that, if we may judge by the copies that have reached us. In the *Spiritual Canticle* and the *Living Flame* he dispenses with both chapters and paragraphs. The commentary on each stanza here corresponds to a chapter.

Another example is to be found in the arrangement of his expositions. As a rule, he first writes down the stanzas as a whole, then repeats each in turn before expounding it, and repeats each line also in its proper place in the same way. At the beginning of each treatise he makes some general observations—in the form either of an argument and prologue, as in the *Ascent*; of a prologue and general exposition, as in the *Night*; of a prologue alone, as in the first redaction of the *Canticle* and in the *Living Flame*; or of a prologue and argument, as in the second redaction of the *Canticle*. In the *Ascent* and the *Night*, the first chapter of each book contains the 'exposition of the stanzas,' though some copies describe this, in Book III of the *Ascent*, as an 'argument.' In the *Night*, the book dealing with the Night of Sense begins with the usual 'exposition'; that of the Night of the Spirit, however, has nothing to correspond with it.

---

[1] Cf. p. 18, below.

[2] Some manuscripts do in fact divide the treatise in this way; but apart from the fact that we have the authority of St. John of the Cross himself, in the passage just quoted (confirmed in *Ascent*, I, xiii), for a different division, the Alcaudete MS., which we believe to be the most reliable, follows the division laid down by the Saint. We may add that St. John of the Cross is not always a safe guide in these matters, no doubt because he trusted too much to his memory; in *Ascent*, II, xi (p. 100), for example, he calls the fourth book the third.

In the first redaction of the *Spiritual Canticle*, St. John of the Cross first sets down the poem, then a few lines of 'exposition' giving the argument of the stanza, and finally the commentary upon each line. Sometimes he comments upon two or three lines at once. In the second redaction, he prefaces almost every stanza with an 'annotation,' of which there is none in the first redaction except before the commentary on the thirteenth and fourteenth stanzas. The chief purpose of the 'annotation' is to link the argument of each stanza with that of the stanza preceding it; occasionally the annotation and the exposition are combined.

It is clear from all this that, in spite of his orderly mind, St. John of the Cross was no believer in strict uniformity in matters of arrangement which would seem to demand such uniformity once they had been decided upon. They are, of course, of secondary importance, but the fact that the inconsistencies are the work of St. John of the Cross himself, and not merely of careless copyists, who have enough else to account for, is of real moment in the discussion of critical questions which turn on the Saint's accuracy.

Another characteristic of these commentaries is the inequality of length as between the exposition of certain lines and stanzas. While some of these are dealt with fully, the exposition of others is brought to a close with surprising rapidity, even though it sometimes seems that much more needs to be said: we get the impression that the author was anxious to push his work forward or was pressed for time. He devotes fourteen long chapters of the *Ascent* to glossing the first two lines of the first stanza and dismisses the three remaining lines in a few sentences. In both the *Ascent* and the *Night*, indeed, the stanzas appear to serve only as a pretext for introducing the great wealth of ascetic and mystical teaching which the Saint has gathered together. In the *Canticle* and the *Living Flame*, on the other hand, he keeps much closer to his stanzas, though here, too, there is a considerable inequality. One result of the difference in nature between these two pairs of treatises is that the *Ascent* and the *Night* are more solidly built and more rigidly doctrinal, whereas in the *Canticle* and the *Flame* there is more movement and more poetry.

V

HISTORY OF THE PUBLICATION OF ST. JOHN OF THE CROSS'S WRITINGS—THE FIRST EDITION

IT seems strange that mystical works of such surpassing value should not have been published till twenty-seven years after their author's death, for not only were the manuscript copies insufficient to propagate them as widely as those who made them would have desired, but the multiplication of these copies led to an ever greater number of variants in the text. Had it but been possible for the first edition of them to have been published while their author still lived, we might to-day have a perfect text. But the probability is that, if such an idea had occurred to St. John of the Cross, he would have set it aside as presumptuous. In allowing copies to be made he doubtless never envisaged their going beyond the limited circle of his Order.

We have found no documentary trace of any project for an edition of these works during their author's lifetime. The most natural time for a discussion of the matter would have been in September 1586, when the Definitors of the Order, among whom was St. John of the Cross, met in Madrid and decided to publish the works of St. Teresa.[1] Two years earlier, when he was writing the *Spiritual Canticle*, St. John of the Cross had expressed a desire for the publication of St. Teresa's writings and assumed that this would not be long delayed.[2] As we have seen, he considered his own works as complementary to those of St. Teresa,[3] and one would have thought that the simultaneous publication of the writings of the two Reformers would have seemed to the Definitors an excellent idea.

After his death, it is probable that there was no one at first who was both able and willing to undertake the work of editor; for, as is well known, towards the end of his life the Saint had powerful enemies within his Order who might well have opposed the project, though, to do the Discalced Reform justice, it was brought up as early as ten years after his death. A resolution was passed at the Chapter-General of the Reform held in September 1601, to the effect 'that the works of Fr. Juan de la Cruz be printed and that the Definitors, Fr. Juan de Jesús María and Fr. Tomás [de Jesús], be instructed to examine and

---

[1] [H., V, iii.]
[2] *Spiritual Canticle*, Stanza XII, § 6 [Second Redaction, XIII, § 7].
[3] In the same passage as that referred to in the last note he declares his intention of not repeating what she has said (cf. p. xlv, above).

approve them.'[1] Two years later (July 4, 1603), the same Chapter, also meeting in Madrid, 'gave leave to the Definitor, Fr. Tomás [de Jesús], for the printing of the works of Fr. Juan de la Cruz, first friar of the Discalced Reform.'[2]

It is not known (since the Chapter Book is no longer extant) why the matter lapsed for two years, but Fr. Tomás de Jesús, the Definitor to whom alone it was entrusted on the second occasion, was a most able man, well qualified to edit the works of his predecessor.[3] Why, then, we may wonder, did he not do so? The story of his life in the years following the commission may partly answer this question. His definitorship came to an end in 1604, when he was elected Prior of the 'desert' of San José de las Batuecas. After completing the customary three years in this office, during which time he could have done no work at all upon the edition, he was elected Prior of the Discalced house at Zaragoza. But at this point Paul V sent for him to Rome and from that time onward his life followed other channels.

The next attempt to accomplish the project was successful. The story begins with a meeting between the Definitors of the Order and Fr. José de Jesús María, the General, at Vélez-Málaga, where a new decision to publish the works of St. John of the Cross was taken and put into effect (as a later resolution has it) 'without any delay or condition whatsoever.'[4] The enterprise suffered a setback, only a week after it had been planned, in the death of the learned Jesuit P. Suárez, who was on terms of close friendship with the Discalced and had been appointed one of the censors. But P. Diego de Jesús (Salablanca), Prior of the Discalced house at Toledo, to whom its execution was entrusted, lost no time in accomplishing his task; indeed, one would suppose that he had begun it long before, since early in the next year it was completed and published in Alcalá. The volume, entitled *Spiritual Works which lead a soul to perfect union with God*, has 720 pages and bears the date 1618. The works are preceded by a preface addressed to the reader and a brief summary of the author's 'life and virtues.' An engraving of the 'Mount of Perfection' is included.[5]

There are several peculiarities about this *editio princeps*. In the first place, although the pagination is continuous, it was the work of two different printers; the reason for this is quite unknown, though various

---

[1] Our authority for this statement is P. Andrés de la Encarnación (*Memorias Historiales*, B. 32), who found the Chapter Book in the General Archives of the Reform at Madrid.
[2] Op. cit. (B. 33).
[3] [For a study of Tomás de Jesús, see *S.S.M.*, II, 281–306.]
[4] *Memorias Historiales*, B. 35.   [5] Cf. p. xxxii, above.

reasons might be suggested. The greatest care was evidently taken so
that the work should be well and truly approved : it is recommended,
in terms of the highest praise, by the authorities of the University of
Alcalá, who, at the request of the General of the Discalced Carmelites,
had submitted it for examination to four of the professors of that
University. No doubt for reasons of safety, the *Spiritual Canticle* was
not included in that edition : it was too much like a commentary on the
Song of Songs for such a proceeding to be just then advisable.

We have now to enquire into the merits of the edition of P. Salablanca, which met with such warm approval on its publication, yet
very soon afterwards began to be recognized as defective and is little
esteemed for its intrinsic qualities to-day.

It must, of course, be realized that critical standards in the early
seventeenth century were low and that the first editor of St. John of
the Cross had neither the method nor the available material of the
twentieth century. Nor were the times favourable for the publication
of the works of a great mystic who attempted fearlessly and fully
to describe the highest stages of perfection on the road to God.
These two facts are responsible for most of the defects of the
edition.

For nearly a century, the great peril associated with the mystical life
had been that of Illuminism, a gross form of pseudo-mysticism which
had claimed many victims among the holiest and most learned, and of
which there was such fear that excessive, almost unbelievable, precautions had been taken against it. These precautions, together with the
frequency and audacity with which Illuminists invoked the authority
and protection of well-known contemporary ascetic and mystical
writers, give reality to P. Salablanca's fear lest the leaders of the sect
might shelter themselves behind the doctrines of St. John of the Cross
and so call forth the censure of the Inquisition upon passages which
seemed to him to bear close relation to their erroneous teaching. It was
for this definite reason, and not because of an arbitrary meticulousness,
that P. Salablanca omitted or adapted such passages as those noted in
Book I, Chapter xiii of the *Ascent of Mount Carmel* and in a number of
chapters in Book II. A study of these, all of which are indicated in the
footnotes to our text, is of great interest.

Less important are a large number of minor corrections made with
the intention of giving greater precision to some theological concept;
the omission of lines and even paragraphs which the editor considered

redundant, as in fact they frequently are; and corrections made with the aim of lending greater clearness to the argument or improving the style. A few changes were made out of prudery: such are the use of *sensitivo* for *sensual*, the suppression of phrases dealing with carnal vice and the omission of several paragraphs from that chapter of the *Dark Night* which speaks of the third deadly sin of beginners. There was little enough reason for these changes: St. John of the Cross is particularly inoffensive in his diction and may, from that point of view, be read by a child.

The sum total of P. Salablanca's mutilations is very considerable. There are more in the *Ascent* and the *Living Flame* than in the Dark *Night*; but hardly a page of the *editio princeps* is free from them and on most pages they abound. It need not be said that they are regrettable. They belong to an age when the garments of dead saints were cut up into small fragments and distributed among the devout and when their cells were decked out with indifferent taste and converted into oratories. It would not have been considered sufficient had the editor printed the text of St. John of the Cross as he found it and glossed it to his liking in footnotes; another editor would have put opposite interpretations upon it, thus cancelling out the work of his predecessor. Even the radical mutilations of P. Salablanca did not suffice, as will now be seen, to protect the works of the Saint from the Inquisition.

VI

DENUNCIATION OF THE 'WORKS' TO THE INQUISITION—DEFENCE
OF THEM MADE BY FR. BASILIO PONCE DE LEÓN—EDITIONS
OF THE SEVENTEENTH AND EIGHTEENTH CENTURIES

NEITHER the commendations of University professors nor the scissors of a meticulous editor could save the treatises of St. John of the Cross from that particular form of attack which, more than all others, was feared in the seventeenth century. We shall say nothing here of the history, nature and procedure of the Spanish Inquisition, which has had its outspoken antagonists and its unreasoning defenders but has not yet been studied with impartiality. It must suffice to set down the facts as they here affect our subject.

Forty propositions, then, were extracted from the edition of 1618 and presented to the Holy Office for condemnation with the object of causing the withdrawal of the edition from circulation. The attempt would probably have succeeded but for the warm, vigorous and learned defence put up by the Augustinian Fray Basilio Ponce de León, a theological professor in the University of Salamanca and a nephew of the Luis de León who wrote the *Names of Christ* and took so great an interest in the works of St. Teresa.[1]

It was in the very convent of San Felipe in Madrid where thirty-five years earlier Fray Luis had written his immortal eulogy of St. Teresa[2] that Fray Basilio, on July 11, 1622, signed a most interesting 'Reply' to the objections which had been raised to the Alcalá edition of St. John of the Cross. Although we propose, in our third volume, to reproduce Fray Basilio's defence, it is necessary to our narrative to say something of it here, for it is the most important of all extant documents which reveal the vicissitudes in the history of the Saint's teaching.

Before entering upon an examination of the censured propositions, the learned Augustinian makes some general observations, which must have carried great weight as coming from so high a theological authority. He recalls the commendations of the edition by the professors of the University of Alcalá 'where the faculty of theology is so famous,' and by many others, including several ministers of the Holy Office and two Dominicans who 'without dispute are among the most learned of their Order.' Secondly, he refers to the eminently saintly character of the first friar of the Discalced Reform: 'it is not to be presumed that God would set a man whose teaching is so evil . . . as is alleged, to be the corner-stone of so great a building.' Thirdly, he notes how close a follower was St. John of the Cross of St. Teresa, a person who was singularly free from any taint of unorthodoxy. And finally he recalls a number of similar attacks on works of this kind, notably that on Laredo's *Ascent of Mount Sion*,[3] which have proved to be devoid of foundation, and points out that isolated 'propositions' need to be set in their context before they can be fairly judged.

Fray Basilio next refutes the charges brought against the works of St. John of the Cross, nearly all of which relate to his teaching on the passivity of the faculties in certain degrees of contemplation. Each proposition he copies and afterwards defends, both by argument and by quotations from the Fathers, from the mediæval mystics and from

---

[1] [Cf. *S.S.M.*, I (1927), 291–344; (1951), 235–79. An abridged English edition of the *Names of Christ*, translated by a Benedictine of Stanbrook, was published by Messrs. Burns Oates and Washbourne in 1926.]

[2] [Cf. *S.S.M.*, I (1927), 295–6; (1951), 240.]

[3] [Cf. *S.S.M.*, II, 41–76.]

his own contemporaries. It is noteworthy that among these authorities he invariably includes St. Teresa, who had been beatified in 1614, and enjoyed an undisputed reputation. This inclusion, as well as being an enhancement of his defence, affords a striking demonstration of the unity of thought existing between the two great Carmelites.

Having expounded the orthodox Catholic teaching in regard to these matters, and shown that the teaching of St. John of the Cross is in agreement with it, Fray Basilio goes on to make clear the true attitude of the Illuminists and thus to reinforce his contentions by showing how far removed from this is the Saint's doctrine.

Fray Basilio's magnificent defence of St. John of the Cross appears to have had the unusual effect of quashing the attack entirely: the excellence of his arguments, backed by his great authority, was evidently unanswerable. So far as we know, the Inquisition took no proceedings against the Alcalá edition whatsoever. Had this at any time been prohibited, we may be sure that Llorente would have revealed the fact, and, though he refers to the persecution of St. John of the Cross during his lifetime,[1] he is quite silent about any posthumous condemnation of his writings.

The *editio princeps* was reprinted in 1619, with a different pagination and a few corrections, in Barcelona.[2] Before these two editions were out of print, the General of the Discalced Carmelites had entrusted an able historian of the Reform, Fray Jerónimo de San José, with the preparation of a new one. This was published at Madrid, in 1630. It has a short introduction describing its scope and general nature, a number of new and influential commendations and an admirable fifty-page 'sketch' of St. John of the Cross by the editor which has been reproduced in most subsequent editions and has probably done more than any other single work to make known the facts of the Saint's biography. The great feature of this edition, however, is the inclusion of the *Spiritual Canticle*, placed (by an error, as a printer's note explains) at the end of the volume, instead of before the *Living Flame*, which is, of course, its proper position.

The inclusion of the *Canticle* is one of the two merits that the editor claims for his new edition. The other is that he 'prints both the *Canticle* and the other works according to their original manuscripts,

---

[1] *Historia crítica de la Inquisición de España*, Vol. V, Chap. xxx, and elsewhere. [The original of this work is in French: *Histoire critique de l'Inquisition d'Espagñe*, 1817–18.]

[2] Here we have a curious parallelism with the works of St. Teresa, first published at Salamanca in 1588 and also reprinted in Barcelona in the year following.

written in the hand of the same venerable author.' This claim is, of course, greatly exaggerated, as what has been said above with regard to the manuscripts will indicate. Not only does Fray Jerónimo appear to have had no genuine original manuscript at all, but of the omissions of the *editio princeps* it is doubtful if he makes good many more than one in a hundred. In fact, with very occasional exceptions, he merely reproduces the *princeps*—omissions, interpolations, well-meant improvements and all.[1]

In Fray Jerónimo's defence it must be said that the reasons which moved his predecessor to mutilate his edition were still potent, and the times had not changed. It is more surprising that for nearly three centuries the edition of 1630 should have been followed by later editors. The numerous versions of the works which saw the light in the later seventeenth and the eighteenth century added a few poems, letters and maxims to the corpus of work which he presented and which assumed great importance as the Saint became better known and more deeply venerated. But they did no more. It suffices, therefore, to enumerate the chief of them.

The Barcelona publisher of the 1619 edition produced a new edition in 1635, which is a mere reproduction of that of 1630. A Madrid edition of 1649, which adds nine letters, a hundred maxims and a small collection of poems, was reproduced in 1672 (Madrid), 1679 (Madrid), 1693 (Barcelona) and 1694 (Madrid), the last reproduction being in two volumes. An edition was also published in Barcelona in 1700.

If we disregard a 'compendium' of the Saint's writings published in Seville in 1701, the first eighteenth-century edition was published in Seville in 1703—the most interesting of those that had seen the light since 1630. It is well printed on good paper in a folio volume and its editor, Fr. Andrés de Jesús María, claims it, on several grounds, as an advance on preceding editions. First, he says, 'innumerable errors of great importance' have been corrected in it; then, the *Spiritual Canticle* has been amended according to its original manuscript 'in the hand of the same holy doctor, our father, kept and venerated in our convent of Discalced Carmelite nuns at Jaén'; next, he adds two new poems and increases the number of maxims from 100 to 365; and lastly, the letters are increased from nine to seventeen, all of which are found in P.

---

[1] He also supplies the Latin text of Scriptural quotations which St. John of the Cross gives in the vernacular, corrects the punctuation and spelling of the *princeps* and substitutes his 'Sketch' of the Saint's life for the biographical notes of that edition. The treatise in which he corrects most of the defects of the *princeps* is the *Ascent of Mount Carmel*.

Jerónimo de San José's history. The first of these claims is as great an exaggeration as was P. Jerónimo's; to the second we shall refer in our introduction to the *Spiritual Canticle*. The third and fourth, however, are justified, and for these, as for a few minor improvements, the editor deserves every commendation.

The remaining years of the eighteenth century produced few editions; apart from a reprint (1724) of the compendium of 1701, the only one known to us is that published at Pamplona in 1774, after which nearly eighty years were to pass before any earlier edition was so much as reprinted. Before we resume this bibliographical narrative, however, we must go back over some earlier history.

VII

NEW DENUNCIATIONS AND DEFENCES—FRAY NICOLÁS DE JESÚS MARÍA—THE CARMELITE SCHOOL AND THE INQUISITION

WE remarked, apropos of the edition of 1630, that the reasons which led Fray Diego de Jesús to mutilate his texts were still in existence when Fray Jerónimo de San José prepared his edition some twelve years later. If any independent proof of this statement is needed, it may be found in the numerous apologias that were published during the seventeenth century, not only in Spain, but in Italy, France, Germany and other countries of Europe. If doctrines are not attacked, there is no occasion to write vigorous defences of them.

Following the example of Fray Basilio Ponce de León, a professor of theology in the College of the Reform at Salamanca, Fray Nicolás de Jesús María, wrote a learned Latin defence of St. John of the Cross in 1631, often referred to briefly as the *Elucidatio*.[1] It is divided into two parts, the first defending the Saint against charges of a general kind that were brought against his writings, and the second upholding censured propositions taken from them. On the general ground, P. Nicolás reminds his readers that many writers who now enjoy the highest possible reputation were in their time denounced and unjustly persecuted. St. Jerome was attacked for his translation of the Bible from Hebrew into Latin; St. Augustine, for his teaching about grace and freewill. The works of St. Gregory the Great were burned at Rome; those of St. Thomas Aquinas at Paris. Most mediæval and

---

[1] *Phrasium mysticæ Theologiæ V.P. Fr. Joannis a Cruce, Carmelitarum excalceatorum Parentis primi elucidatio.* Compluti, 1631.

modern mystics have been the victims of persecution—Ruysbroeck, Tauler and even St. Teresa. Such happenings, he maintains, have done nothing to lessen the eventual prestige of these authors, but rather have added to it.

Nor, he continues, can the works of any author fairly be censured, because misguided teachers make use of them to propagate their false teaching. No book has been more misused by heretics than Holy Scripture and few books of value would escape if we were to condemn all that had been so treated. Equally worthless is the objection that mystical literature is full of difficulties which may cause the ignorant and pusillanimous to stumble. Apart from the fact that St. John of the Cross is clearer and more lucid than most of his contemporaries, and that therefore the works of many of them would have to follow his own into oblivion, the same argument might again be applied to the Scriptures. Who can estimate the good imparted by the sacred books to those who read them in a spirit of uprightness and simplicity? Yet what books are more pregnant with mystery and with truths that are difficult and, humanly speaking, even inaccessible?

But (continues P. Nicolás), even if we allow that parts of the work of St. John of the Cross, for all the clarity of his exposition, are obscure to the general reader, it must be remembered that much more is of the greatest attraction and profit to all. On the one hand, the writings of the Saint represent the purest sublimation of Divine love in the pilgrim soul, and are therefore food for the most advanced upon the mystic way. On the other, every reader, however slight his spiritual progress, can understand the Saint's ascetic teaching: his chapters on the purga-tion of the senses, mortification, detachment from all that belongs to the earth, purity of conscience, the practice of the virtues, and so on. The Saint's greatest enemy is not the obscurity of his teaching but the inflexible logic with which he deduces, from the fundamental principles of evangelical perfection, the consequences which must be observed by those who would scale the Mount. So straight and so hard is the road which he maps out for the climber that the majority of those who see it are at once dismayed.

These are the main lines of P. Nicolás' argument, which he develops at great length. We must refer briefly to the chapter in which he makes a careful synthesis of the teaching of the Illuminists, to show how far it is removed from that of St. John of the Cross. He divides these false contemplatives into four classes. In the first class he places those who suppress all their acts, both interior and exterior, in prayer. In the second, those who give themselves up to a state of pure quiet, with no loving attention to God. In the third, those who allow their bodies to indulge every craving and maintain that, in the state of spiritual intoxication which they have reached, they are unable to commit sin. In the fourth, those who consider themselves to be instruments of God and adopt an attitude of complete passivity, maintaining also that they are unable to sin, because God alone is working in them. The division is more subtle than practical, for the devotees of this sect, with few exceptions, professed the same erroneous beliefs and tended to the same degree of licence in their conduct. But, by isolating these tenets, P. Nicolás is the better able to show the antithesis between them and those of St. John of the Cross.

In the second part of the *Elucidatio*, he analyses the propositions already treated by Fray Basilio Ponce de León, reducing them to twenty and dealing faithfully with them in the same number of chapters. His defence is clear, methodical and convincing and follows similar lines to those adopted by Fray Basilio, to whom its author acknowledges his indebtedness.

Another of St. John of the Cross's apologists is Fray José de Jesús María (Quiroga), who, in a number of his works,[1] both defends and eulogizes him, without going into any detailed examination of the propositions. Fray José is an outstanding example of a very large class of writers, for, as Illuminism gave place to Quietism, the teaching of St. John of the Cross became more and more violently impugned and almost all mystical writers of the time referred to him. Perhaps we should single out, from among his defenders outside the Carmelite Order, that Augustinian father, P. Antolínez, to whose commentary on three of the Saint's works we have already made reference.

As the school of mystical writers within the Discalced Carmelite Reform gradually grew—a school which took St. John of the Cross as its leader and is one of the most illustrious in the history of mystical theology—it began to share in the same persecution as had befallen its founder. It is impossible, in a few words, to describe this epoch of purgation, and indeed it can only be properly studied in its proper context—the religious history of the period as a whole. For our purpose, it suffices to say that the works of St. John of the Cross were once more denounced to the Inquisition, though, once more, no

---

[1] *Subida del Alma a Dios; Apología mística en defensa de la contemplación divina; Don que tuvo San Juan de la Cruz para guiar las almas*, etc.

notice appears to have been taken of the denunciations, for there exists no record ordering the expurgation or prohibition of the books referred to. The *Elucidatio* was also denounced, together with several of the works of P. José de Jesús María, at various times in the seventeenth century, and these attacks were of course equivalent to direct attacks on St. John of the Cross. One of the most vehement onslaughts made was levelled against P. José's *Subida del Alma a Dios* ('Ascent of the Soul to God'), which is in effect an elaborate commentary on St. John of the Cross's teaching. The Spanish Inquisition refusing to censure the book, an appeal against it was made to the Inquisition at Rome. When no satisfaction was obtained in this quarter, P. José's opponents went to the Pope, who referred the matter to the Sacred Congregation of the Index; but this body issued a warm eulogy of the book and the matter thereupon dropped.

In spite of such defeats, the opponents of the Carmelite school continued their work into the eighteenth century. In 1740, a new appeal was made to the Spanish Inquisition to censure P. José's *Subida*. A document of seventy-three folios denounced no less than one hundred and sixty-five propositions which it claimed to have taken direct from the work referred to, and this time, after a conflict extending over ten years, the book (described as 'falsely attributed' to P. José[1]) was condemned (July 4, 1750), as 'containing doctrine most perilous in practice, and propositions similar and equivalent to those condemned in Miguel de Molinos.'

We set down the salient facts of this controversy, without commenting upon them, as an instance of the attitude of the eighteenth century towards the mystics in general, and, in particular, towards the school of the Discalced Carmelites. In view of the state and tendencies of thought in these times, the fact of the persecution, and the degree of success that it attained, is not surprising. The important point to bear in mind is that it must be taken into account continually by students of the editions of the Saint's writings and of the history of his teaching throughout the eighteenth and nineteenth centuries.

---

[1] This phrase, no doubt, was inserted in order to save the reputation of P. José's earlier supporters, and out of respect to his uncle, who had been a Cardinal and Inquisitor-General.

VIII

FURTHER HISTORY OF THE EDITIONS—P. ANDRÉS DE LA ENCAR-
NACIÓN—EDITIONS OF THE NINETEENTH AND TWENTIETH
CENTURIES

WHAT has just been said will fully explain the paucity of the editions
of St. John of the Cross which we find in the eighteenth century. This
century, however, was, scientifically speaking, one of great progress.
Critical methods of study developed and became widespread; and
there was a great desire to obtain purer and more nearly perfect texts
and to discover the original sources of the ideas of great thinkers.
These tendencies made themselves felt within the Discalced Carmelite
Order, and there also arose a great ambition to republish in their
original forms the works both of St. Teresa and of St. John of the Cross.
The need was greater in the latter case than in the former; so urgent
was it felt to be as to admit of no delay. 'There have been discovered
in the works [of St. John of the Cross],'says a document of about 1753,
'many errors, mutilations and other defects the existence of which
cannot be denied.'¹ The religious who wrote thus to the Chapter-
General of the Reform set out definite and practical schemes for a
thorough revision of these works, which were at once accepted. There
thus comes into our history that noteworthy friar, P. Andrés de la
Encarnación, to whom we owe so much of what we know about the
Saint to-day. P. Andrés was no great stylist, nor had he the usual
Spanish fluency of diction. But he was patient, modest and industrious,
and above all he was endowed with a double portion of the critical
spirit of the eighteenth century. He was selected for the work of in-
vestigation as being by far the fittest person who could be found for
it. A decree dated October 6, 1754 ordered him to set to work. As a
necessary preliminary to the task of preparing a corrected text of the
Saint's writings, he was to spare no effort in searching for every extant
manuscript; accordingly he began long journeys through La Mancha
and Andalusia, going over all the ground covered by St. John of the
Cross in his travels and paying special attention to the places where he
had lived for any considerable period. In those days, before the religious
persecutions of the nineteenth century had destroyed and scattered
books and manuscripts, the archives of the various religious houses
were intact. P. Andrés and his amanuensis were therefore able to copy
and collate valuable manuscripts now lost to us and they at once began

¹ Quoted by P. Andrés de la Encarnación (MS. 3,653, Previo 1).

to restore the phrases and passages omitted from the editions. Unhappily, their work has disappeared and we can judge of it only at
second hand; but it appears to have been in every way meritorious.
So far as we can gather from the documents which have come down to
us, it failed to pass the rigorous censorship of the Order. In other
words, the censors, who were professional theologians, insisted upon
making so many corrections that the Superiors, who shared the enlightened critical opinions of P. Andrés, thought it better to postpone
the publication of the edition indefinitely.

The failure of the project, however, to which P. Andrés devoted so
much patient labour, did not wholly destroy the fruits of his skill and
perseverance. He was ordered to retire to his priory, where he spent
the rest of his long life under the burden of a trial the magnitude of
which any scholar or studiously minded reader can estimate. He did
what he could in his seclusion to collect, arrange and recopy such notes
of his work as he could recover from those to whom they had been
submitted. His defence of this action to the Chapter-General is at
once admirable in the tranquillity of its temper and pathetic in the
eagerness and affection which it displays for the task that he has been
forbidden to continue:

Inasmuch as I was ordered, some years ago . . . to prepare an exact edition
of the works of our holy father, and afterwards was commanded to suspend
my labours for just reasons which presented themselves to these our fathers
and prevented its accomplishment at the time, I obeyed forthwith with the
greatest submissiveness, but, as I found that I had a rich store of information which at some future time might contribute to the publication of a truly
illustrious and perfect edition, it seemed to me that I should not be running
counter to the spirit of the Order if I gave it some serviceable form, so that I
should not be embarrassed by seeing it in a disorderly condition if at some
future date it should be proposed to carry into effect the original decisions of
the Order.

With humility and submissiveness, therefore, I send to your Reverences
these results of my private labours, not because it is in my mind that the
work should be recommenced, or that, if this is to be done, it should be at
any particular time, for that I leave to the disposition of your Reverences and
of God, but to the end that I may return to the Order that which belongs to
it; for, since I was excused from religious observances for nearly nine years
so that I might labour in this its own field, the Order cannot but have a
right to the fruits of my labours, nor can I escape the obligation of deliver-
ing what I have discovered into its hand. . . .[1]

[1] MS. 3,653, Previo 1.

We cannot examine the full text of the interesting memorandum to the Censors which follows this humble exordium. One of their allegations had been that the credit of the Order would suffer if it became known that passages of the Saint's works had been suppressed by Carmelite editors. P. Andrés makes the sage reply: 'There is certainly the risk that this will become known if the edition is made; but there is also a risk that it will become known in any case. We must weigh the risks against each other and decide which proceeding will bring the Order into the greater discredit if one of them materializes.' He fortifies this argument with the declaration that the defects of the existing editions were common knowledge outside the Order as well as within it, and that, as manuscript copies of the Saint's works were also in the possession of many others than Carmelites, there was nothing to prevent a correct edition being made at any time. This must suffice as a proof that P. Andrés could be as acute as he was submissive.

Besides collecting this material, and leaving on record his opposition to the short-sighted decision of the Censors, P. Andrés prepared 'some *Disquisitions* on the writings of the Saint, which, if a more skilful hand should correct and improve their style, cannot but be well received.' Closely connected with the *Disquisitions* are the *Preludes* in which he glosses the Saint's writings. These studies, like the notes already described, have all been lost—no doubt, together with many other documents from the archives of the Reform in Madrid, they disappeared during the pillaging of the religious houses in the early nineteenth century.

The little of P. Andrés' work that remains to us gives a clear picture of the efforts made by the Reform to bring out a worthy edition of St. John of the Cross's writings in the eighteenth century; it is manifestly insufficient, however, to take a modern editor far along the way. Nor, as we have seen, are his judgments by any means to be followed otherwise than with the greatest caution; he greatly exaggerates, too, the effect of the mutilations of earlier editors, no doubt in order to convince his superiors of the necessity for a new edition. The materials for a modern editor are to be found, not in the documents left by P. Andrés, but in such Carmelite archives as still exist, and in the National Library of Spain, to which many Carmelite treasures found their way at the beginning of the last century.

The work sent by P. Andrés to his superiors was kept in the archives of the Discalced Carmelites, but no new edition was prepared till a hundred and fifty years later. In the nineteenth century such a task was made considerably more difficult by religious persecution, which resulted in the loss of many valuable manuscripts, some of which P. Andrés must certainly have examined. For a time, too, the Orders were expelled from Spain, and, on their return, had neither the necessary freedom, nor the time or material means, for such undertakings. In the twenty-seventh volume of the well-known series of classics entitled *Biblioteca de Autores Españoles* (1853) the works of St. John of the Cross were reprinted according to the 1703 edition, without its engravings, indices and commendations, and with a 'critical estimate' of the Saint by Pi y Margall, which has some literary value but in other respects fails entirely to do justice to its subject.

Neither the Madrid edition of 1872 nor the Barcelona edition of 1883 adds anything to our knowledge and it was not till the Toledo edition of 1912–14 that a new advance was made. This edition was the work of a young Carmelite friar, P. Gerardo de San Juan de la Cruz, who died soon after its completion. It aims, according to its title, which is certainly justified, at being 'the most correct and complete edition of all that have been published down to the present date.' If it was not as successful as might have been wished, this could perhaps hardly have been expected of a comparatively inexperienced editor confronted with so gigantic a task—a man, too, who worked almost alone and was by temperament and predilection an investigator rather than a critic. Nevertheless, its introductions, footnotes, appended documents, and collection of apocryphal works of the Saint, as well as its text, were all considered worthy of extended study and the edition was rightly received with enthusiasm. Its principal merit will always lie in its having restored to their proper places, for the first time in a printed edition, many passages which had heretofore remained in manuscript.

We have been anxious that this new edition [Burgos, 1929–31] should represent a fresh advance in the task of establishing a definitive text of St. John of the Cross's writings. For this reason we have examined, together with two devoted assistants, every discoverable manuscript, with the result, as it seems to us, that both the form and the content of our author's works are as nearly as possible as he left them.

In no case have we followed any one manuscript exclusively, preferring to assess the value of each by a careful preliminary study and to consider each on its merits, which are described in the introduction to each of the individual works. Since our primary aim has been to present an accurate text, our footnotes will be found to be almost exclusively textual. The only edition which we cite, with the occasional exception of that of 1630, is the *princeps*, from which alone there is much to be learned. The Latin quotations from the Vulgate are not, of course, given except where they appear in the manuscripts, and, save for the occasional correction of a copyist's error, they are reproduced in exactly the form in which we have found them. Orthography and punctuation have had perforce to be modernized, since the manuscripts differ widely and we have so few autographs that nothing conclusive can be learned of the Saint's own practice.[1]

[1] [The last two paragraphs form P. Silverio's description of his own edition. The lines followed in the present translation have been described in the Translator's Preface.]

THE COMPLETE WORKS OF SAINT JOHN OF THE CROSS

ASCENT OF MOUNT CARMEL

INTRODUCTION

As will be seen from the biographical outline which we have given of the life of St. John of the Cross, this was the first of the Saint's treatises to be written; it was begun at El Calvario, and, after various intervals, due to the author's preoccupation with the business of government and the direction and care of souls, was completed at Granada.

The treatise presents a remarkable outline of Christian perfection from the point at which the soul first seeks to rise from the earth and soar upward towards union with God. It is a work which shows every sign of careful planning and great attention to detail; as an ascetic treatise it is noteworthy for its detailed psychological analysis; as a contribution to mystical theology, for the skill with which it treats the most complicated and delicate questions concerning the Mystic Way.

Both the great Carmelite reformers pay close attention to the early stages of the mystical life, beyond which many never pass, and both give the primacy to prayer as a means of attaining perfection. To St. Teresa prayer is the greatest of all blessings of this life, the channel through which all the favours of God pass to the soul, the beginning of every virtue and the plainly marked highroad which leads to the summit of Mount Carmel. She can hardly conceive of a person in full spiritual health whose life is not one of prayer. Her coadjutor in the Carmelite Reform writes in the same spirit. Prayer, for St. John of the Cross as for St. Teresa, is no mere exercise made up of petition and meditation, but a complete spiritual life which brings in its train all the virtues, increases all the soul's potentialities and may ultimately lead to 'deification' or transformation in God through love. It may be said that the exposition of the life of prayer, from its lowest stages to its

I

highest, is the common aim of these two Saints, which each pursues and accomplishes in a peculiarly individual manner.

St. John of the Cross assumes his reader to be familiar with the rudiments of the spiritual life and therefore omits detailed description of the most elementary of the exercises incumbent upon all Christians. The plan of the *Ascent of Mount Carmel* (which, properly speaking, embraces its sequel, the *Dark Night*) follows the lines of the poem with the latter title (p. 10). Into two stanzas of five lines each, St. John of the Cross has condensed all the instruction which he develops in this treatise. In order to reach the Union of Light, the soul must pass through the Dark Night—that is to say, through a series of purifications, during which it is walking, as it were, through a tunnel of impenetrable obscurity and from which it emerges to bask in the sunshine of grace and to enjoy the Divine intimacy.

Through this obscurity the thread which guides the soul is that of 'emptiness' or 'negation.' Only by voiding ourselves of all that is not God can we attain to the possession of God, for two contraries cannot co-exist in one individual, and creature-love is darkness, while God is light, so that from any human heart one of the two cannot fail to drive out the other.[1]

Now the soul, according to the Saint's psychology, is made up of interior and exterior senses and of the faculties. All these must be free from creature impurities in order to be prepared for Divine union. The necessary self-emptying may be accomplished in two ways: by our own efforts, with the habitual aid of grace, and by the action of God exclusively, in which the individual has no part whatsoever. Following this order, the Ascent is divided into two parts, which deal respectively with the 'Active' night and the 'Passive.' Each of these parts consists of several books. Since the soul must be purified in its entirety, the Active Night is logically divided into the Night of Sense and the Night of the Spirit; a similar division is observed in treating of the Passive Night. One book is devoted to the Active Night of Sense; two are needed for the Active Night of the Spirit. Unhappily, however, the treatise was never finished; not only was its author unable to take us out of the night into the day, as he certainly intended to do, but he has not even space to describe the Passive Night in all the fullness of its symbolism.

A brief glance at the outstanding parts of the *Ascent of Mount Carmel* will give some idea of its nature. The first obstacle which the pilgrim

[1] *Ascent*, Bk. III, Chap. ii.

soul encounters is the senses, upon which St. John of the Cross expends his analytical skill in Book I. Like any academic professor (and it will be recalled that he had undergone a complete university course at Salamanca), he outlines and defines his subject, goes over the necessary preliminary ground before expounding it, and treats it, in turn, under each of its natural divisions. He tells us, that is to say, what he understands by the 'dark night'; describes its causes and its stages; explains how necessary it is to union with God; enumerates the perils which beset the soul that enters it; and shows how all desires must be expelled, 'however small they be,' if the soul is to travel through it safely. Finally he gives a complete synthesis of the procedure that must be adopted by the pilgrim in relation to this part of his journey: the force of this is intensified by those striking maxims and distichs which make Chapter xiii of Book I so memorable.

The first thirteen chapters of the *Ascent* are perhaps the easiest to understand (though they are anything but easy to put into practice) in the entire works of St. John of the Cross. They are all a commentary on the very first line of the poem. The last two chapters of the first book glance at the remaining lines, rather than expound them, and the Saint takes us on at once to Book II, which expounds the second stanza and enters upon the Night of the Spirit.

Here the Saint treats of the proximate means to union with God— namely, faith. He uses the same careful method of exposition, showing clearly how faith is to the soul as a dark night, and how, nevertheless, it is the safest of guides. A parenthetical chapter (v) attempts to give some idea of the nature of union, so that the reader may recognize from afar the goal to which he is proceeding. The author then goes on to describe how the three theological virtues—faith, hope and charity —must 'void and dispose for union' the three faculties of the soul— understanding, memory and will.

He shows how narrow is the way that leads to life and how nothing that belongs to the understanding can guide the soul to union. His illustrations and arguments are far more complicated and subtle than are those of the first book, and give the reader some idea of his knowledge, not only of philosophy and theology, but also of individual souls. Without this last qualification he could never have written those penetrating chapters on the impediments to union—above all, the passages on visions, locutions and revelations—nor must we overlook his description (Chapter xiii) of the three signs that the soul is ready to pass from meditation to contemplation. It may be doubted if in its own field this second book has ever been surpassed. There is no mystic who gives a more powerful impression than St. John of the Cross of an absolute mastery of his subject. No mistiness, vagueness or indecision clouds his writing: he is as clear-cut and definite as can be.

In his third book St. John of the Cross goes on to describe the obstacles to union which come from the memory and the will. Unlike St. Thomas, he considered the memory as a distinct and separate faculty of the soul. Having written, however, at such length of the understanding, he found it possible to treat more briefly of that other faculty, which is so closely related to it.[1] Fourteen chapters (ii–xv) describe the dark night to be traversed by the memory; thirty (xvi–xlv) the passage of the will, impelled by love.[2] The latter part is the more strikingly developed. Four passions—joy, hope, sorrow and fear—invade the will, and may either encompass the soul's perdition, or, if rightly directed, lead it to virtue and union. Once more St. John of the Cross employs his profound familiarity with the human soul to turn it away from peril and guide it into the path of safety. Much that he says, in dealing with passions so familiar to us all, is not only purely ascetic, but is even commonplace to the instructed Christian. Yet these are but parts of a greater whole.

Of particular interest, both intrinsically and as giving a picture of the Saint's own times, are the chapters on ceremonies and aids to devotion —the use of rosaries, medals, pilgrimages, etc. It must be remembered, of course, that he spent most of his active life in the south of Spain, where exaggerations of all kinds, even to-day, are more frequent than in the more sober north. In any case there is less need, in this lukewarm age, to warn Christians against the abuse of these means of grace, and more need, perhaps, to urge them to employ aids that will stimulate and quicken their devotion.

In the seventeenth chapter of this third book, St. John of the Cross enumerates the 'six kinds of good' which can give rise to rejoicing and sets down his intention of treating each of them in its turn. He carries out his purpose, but, on entering his last division, subdivides it at considerable length and subsequently breaks off with some brusqueness while dealing with one of these sub-heads, just as he is introducing another subject of particular interest historically—namely, pulpit methods considered from the standpoint of the preacher. In all probability we shall never know what he had to say about the hearers of sermons, or what were his considered judgments on confessors and

---

[1] *Ascent*, Bk. III, Chap. iii, § 1.   [2] Cf. *Ascent*, Bk. III, Chap. xvi, §§ 1–2.

penitents—though of these judgments he has left us examples else-where in this treatise, as well as in others.

We cannot estimate of how much the sudden curtailment of the *Ascent of Mount Carmel* has robbed us.[1] Orderly as was the mind of St. John of the Cross, he was easily carried away in his expositions, which are apt to be unequal. No one would have suspected, for example, that, after going into such length in treating the first line of his first stanza, he would make such short work of the remaining four. Nor can we disregard the significance of his warning that much of what he had written on the understanding was applicable also to the memory and the will. He may, therefore, have been nearer the end of his theme than is generally supposed. Yet it is equally possible that much more of his subtle analysis was in store for his readers. Any truncation, when the author is a St. John of the Cross, must be considered irreparable.

THE MANUSCRIPTS[2]

Unfortunately there is no autograph of this treatise extant, though there are a number of early copies, some of which have been made with great care. Others, for various reasons, abbreviate the original con-siderably. The MSS. belonging to both classes will be enumerated.

Alba de Tormes. The Discalced Carmelite priory of Alba de Tormes has a codex which contains the four principal treatises of St. John of the Cross (*Ascent, Dark Night, Spiritual Canticle* and *Living Flame*). This codex belonged from a very early date (perhaps from a date not much later than that of the Saint's death) to the family of the Duke of Alba, which was greatly devoted to the Discalced Carmelite Reform and to St. Teresa, its foundress. It remained in the family until the beginning of the eighteenth century, when it came into the hands of a learned Carmelite, Fray Alonso de la Madre de Dios, who presented it to the Alba monastery on April 15, 1705. The details of this history are given by Fray Alonso himself in a note bearing this date.

For over half a century the MS. was believed to be an autograph, partly, no doubt, on account of its luxurious binding and the respect paid to the noble house whence it came. In February 1761, however, it was examined carefully by P. Manuel de Santa María, who, by his Superiors' orders, was assisting P. Andrés de la Encarnación in his

---

1 [On the question of the curtailment of the *Ascent*, see Sobrino, pp. 159–66.]

2 [On MSS. not described by P. Silverio, see *Ephemerides Carmeliticae*, Florence, 1950, IV, 95–148, and in particular p. 103, n. 9. As the variants and annotations in these MSS. will be of interest only to specialists, and few of them can be reproduced in a translation, those who wish to study them are referred to that article.]

search for, and study of, manuscripts of the Saint's writings. P. Manuel soon discovered that the opinion commonly held was erroneous—greatly, it would seem, to the disillusionment of his contemporaries. Among the various reasons which he gives in a statement supporting his conclusions is that in two places the author is described as 'santo'—a proof not only that the MS. is not an autograph but also that the copyist had no intention of representing it as such.

Although this copy is carefully made and richly bound—which suggests that it was a gift from the Reform to the house of Alba—it contains many errors, of a kind which indicate that the copyist, well educated though he was, knew little of ascetic or mystical theology. A number of omissions, especially towards the end of the book, give the impression that the copy was finished with haste and not compared with the original on its completion. There is no reason, however, to suppose that the errors and omissions are ever intentional; indeed, they are of such a kind as to suggest that the copyist had not the skill necessary for successful adulteration.

MS. 6,624. This copy, like the next four, is in N.L.M. [National Library of Spain, Madrid], and contains the same works as that of Alba de Tormes. It was made in 1755, under the direction of P. Andrés de la Encarnación, from a manuscript, now lost, which was venerated by the Benedictines of Burgos: this information is found at the end of the volume. P. Andrés had evidently a good opinion of the Burgos MS., as he placed this copy in the archives of the Discalced Reform, whence it passed to the National Library early in the nineteenth century.

As far as the *Ascent* is concerned, this MS. is very similar to that of Alba. With a few notable exceptions, such as the omission of the second half of Book I, Chapter iv, the errors and omissions are so similar as to suggest a definite relationship, if not a common source.

MS. 13,498. This MS., which gives us the *Ascent* and the *Dark Night*, also came from the Archives of the Reform and is now in the National Library. The handwriting might be as early as the end of the sixteenth century. The author did not attempt to make a literal transcription of the *Ascent*, but summarized where he thought advisable, reducing the number of chapters and abbreviating many of them—this last not so much by the method of paraphrase as by the free omission of phrases and sentences.

MS. 2,201. This, as far as the *Ascent* is concerned, is an almost literal transcription of the last MS., in a seventeenth-century hand; it was bound in the eighteenth century, when a number of other treatises were added to it, together with some poems by St. John of the Cross and others. The variants as between this MS. and 13,498 are numerous, but of small importance, and seem mainly to have been due to carelessness.

MS. 18,160. This dates from the end of the sixteenth century and contains the four treatises named above, copied in different hands and evidently intended to form one volume. Only the first four chapters of the *Ascent* are given, together with the title and the first three lines of the fifth chapter. The transcription is poorly done.

MS. 13,507. An unimportant copy, containing only a few odd chapters of the *Ascent* and others from the remaining works of St. John of the Cross and other writers.

Pamplona. A codex in an excellent state of preservation is venerated by the Discalced Carmelite nuns of Pamplona. It was copied, at the end of the sixteenth century, by a Barcelona Carmelite, M. Magdalena de la Asunción, and contains a short summary of the four treatises enumerated above, various poems by St. John of the Cross and some miscellaneous writings. The *Ascent* is abbreviated to the same extent as in 13,498 and 2,201 and by the same methods; many chapters, too, are omitted in their entirety.

Alcaudete. This MS., which contains the *Ascent* only, was copied by St. John of the Cross's close friend and companion, P. Juan Evangelista, as a comparison with manuscripts (N.L.M., 12,738) written in his well-known and very distinctive hand, puts beyond all doubt. P. Juan, who took the habit of the Reform at Christmas 1582, knew the Saint before this date; was professed by him at Granada in 1583; accompanied him on many of his journeys; saw him write most of his books; and, as his close friend and confessor, was consulted repeatedly by his biographers.[1] It is natural that he should also have acted as the Saint's copyist, and, in the absence of autographs, we should expect no manuscripts to be more trustworthy than copies made by him. Examination of this MS. shows that it is in fact highly reliable. It corrects none of those unwieldy periods in which the Saint's work abounds, and which the *editio princeps* often thought well to emend, nor, like the early editions and even some manuscripts, does it omit whole paragraphs and substitute others for them. Further, as this copy was being made solely for the use of the Order, no passages are omitted or altered in it because they might be erroneously interpreted as illuministic. It is true that P. Juan Evangelista is not, from the technical standpoint, a

[1] [H., *sub* Juan Evangelista (2)]

perfect copyist, but, frequent as are his slips, they are always easy to recognize.

The Alcaudete MS. was found in the Carmelite priory in that town by P. Andrés de la Encarnación, who first made use of it for his edition. When the priory was abandoned during the religious persecutions of the early nineteenth century, the MS. was lost. Nearly a hundred years passed before it was re-discovered by P. Silverio de Santa Teresa in a second-hand bookshop [and forms a most important contribution to that scholar's edition, which normally follows it]. It bears many signs of frequent use; eleven folios are missing from the body of the MS. (corresponding approximately to Book III, Chapters xxii to xxvi) and several more from its conclusion.

In the footnotes to the *Ascent*, the following abbreviations are used:

A =MS. of the Discalced Carmelite Friars of Alba.
Alc. =Alcaudete MS.
B =MS. of the Benedictines of Burgos.
C =N.L.M., MS. 13,498.
D =N.L.M., MS. 2,201.
P =MS. of the Discalced Carmelite Nuns of Pamplona.
E.p. = *Editio princeps* (Alcalá, 1618).

Other editions or manuscripts cited are referred to without abbreviation.

ASCENT OF MOUNT CARMEL

Treats of how the soul may prepare itself in order to attain in a short time to Divine union. Gives very profitable counsels and instruction, both to beginners and to proficients, that they may know how to disencumber themselves of all that is temporal and not to encumber themselves with the spiritual,[1] and to remain in complete detachment and liberty of spirit, as is necessary for Divine union.[2]

ARGUMENT

ALL the doctrine whereof I intend to treat[3] in this *Ascent of Mount Carmel* is included in the following stanzas, and in them is also described the manner of ascending to the summit of the Mount, which is the high estate of perfection which we here call union of the soul with God. And because I must continually base upon them that which I shall say, I have desired to set them down here together, to the end that all the substance of that which is to be written may be seen and comprehended together; although it will be fitting to set down each stanza separately before expounding it, and likewise the lines of each stanza, according as the matter and the exposition require. The poem, then, runs as follows:[4]

[1] A omits: 'and not . . . spiritual.'
[2] So Alc. On his own account P. Juan Evangelista adds: 'composed by P. Fray Juan de la Cruz, Discalced Carmelite.' Other Codices, like Alc., give the name of the author. E.p. alone reads: '*Ascent of Mount Carmel*, composed by the Venerable Father Fr. Juan de la Cruz, first Discalced friar of the Reform of Our Lady of Carmel founded by the virgin Saint Teresa.'
[3] So Alc., e.p.—A, B read: 'All the doctrine which is to be treated.'
[4] [*Lit.*: 'It says, then, thus.'] Only Alc. has these words.

STANZAS[1]

Wherein the soul sings of the happy chance which it had in passing through the dark night of faith, in detachment and purgation of itself, to union with the Beloved.[2]

1. On a dark night,   Kindled[3] in love with yearnings—oh, happy chance!—
I went forth without being observed,   My house being now at rest.[4]

2. In darkness and secure,   By the secret ladder, disguised— oh, happy chance!—
In darkness and in concealment,   My house being now at rest.

3. In the happy night,   In secret, when none saw me,
Nor I beheld aught,   Without light or guide, save that which burned in my heart.

4. This light guided me   More surely than the light of noonday,
To the place where he (well I knew who!) was awaiting me— A place where none appeared.

5. Oh, night that guided me,   Oh, night more lovely than the dawn,
Oh, night that joined Beloved with lover,   Lover transformed in the Beloved!

6. Upon my flowery breast,   Kept wholly for himself alone,
There he stayed sleeping, and I caressed him,   And the fanning of the cedars made a breeze.

7. The breeze blew from the turret   As I parted his locks ;
With his gentle hand he wounded my neck   And caused all my senses to be suspended.

8. I remained, lost in oblivion ;[5]   My face I reclined on the Beloved.
All ceased and I abandoned myself,   Leaving my cares forgotten among the lilies.

[1] For a verse translation in the metre of the original, see Vol. II, pp. 417–18.
[2] Several editions read: 'to union of love.' E.p., Alc., A, B all have the reading of the text above.
[3] [The adjectives are feminine throughout.]
[4] [The word translated 'at rest' is a past participle: more literally, 'stilled.']
[5] [*Lit.*: 'I remained and forgot.']

PROLOGUE

IN order to expound and describe this dark night, through which the soul passes in order to attain to the Divine light of the perfect union of the love of God, as far as is possible in this life, it would be necessary to have illumination of knowledge and experience other and far greater than mine; for this darkness and these trials, both spiritual and temporal,[1] through which happy souls are wont to pass in order to be able to attain to this high estate of perfection, are so numerous and so profound that neither does human knowledge suffice for the understanding of them, nor experience for the description of them; for only he that passes this way can understand it, and even he cannot describe it.

2. Therefore, in order to say a little about this dark night, I shall trust neither to experience nor to knowledge, since both may fail and deceive; but, while not omitting to make such use as I can of these two things, I shall avail myself, in all that, with the Divine favour, I have to say, or at the least, in that which is most important and dark to the understanding, of Divine Scripture; for, if we guide ourselves by this, we shall be unable to stray, since He Who speaks therein is the Holy Spirit. And if in aught I stray, whether through my imperfect understanding of that which is said in it or of matters unconnected with it, it is not my intention[2] to depart from the sound sense and doctrine of our Holy Mother the Catholic Church; for in such a case I submit and resign myself wholly, not only to her command,[3] but to whatever better judgment she may pronounce concerning it.

3. To this end I have been moved,[4] not by any possibility that I see in myself of accomplishing so arduous a task, but by the confidence

---

[1] E.p.: 'both spiritual and corporeal.' The correction was no doubt made because 'corporeal' is the usual antithesis of 'spiritual'; all the MSS., however, have 'temporal.'

[2] E.p. modifies: '. . . since both may fail and deceive; but to Divine Scripture, for, if we guide ourselves by this, we cannot stray, since He Who speaks therein is the Holy Spirit. Nevertheless I shall make use of these two things—knowledge and experience— whereof I speak. And if in aught I stray, through my imperfect understanding thereof, it is not my intention, etc.'

[3] E.p.: 'to her light and command.' A, B: 'to her opinion.' There are slight variations in these last few lines in different MSS. We follow Alc., with which A and B agree very closely.

[4] A, B: 'To write this I have been moved.'

which I have in the Lord that He will help me to say something to relieve the great necessity which is experienced by many souls, who, when they set out upon the road of virtue, and Our Lord desires to bring them into this dark night that they may pass through it to Divine union, make no progress. At times this is because they have no desire to enter it or to allow themselves to be led into it; at other times, because they understand not themselves and lack competent and alert directors[1] who will guide them to the summit. And so it is sad to see many souls to whom God gives both aptitude and favour with which to make progress (and who, if they would take courage, could attain to this high estate), remaining in an elementary stage[2] of communion with God, for want of will, or knowledge, or because there is none who will lead them in the right path or teach them how to get away from[3] these beginnings. And at length, although Our Lord grants them such favour as to make them to go onward without this hindrance or that, they arrive at their goal very much later, and with greater labour, yet with less merit, because they have not conformed themselves to God, and allowed themselves to be brought freely[4] into the pure and sure road of union. For, although it is true that God is leading them, and that He can lead them without their own help, they will not allow themselves to be led; and thus they make less progress, because they resist Him Who is leading them, and they have less merit, because they apply not their will, and on this account they suffer more. For there are souls who, instead of committing themselves to God and making use of His help, rather hinder God by the indiscretion of their actions or by their resistance; like children who, when their mothers desire to carry them in their arms, start stamping and crying, and insist upon being allowed to walk, with the result that they can make no progress; and, if they advance at all, it is only at the pace of a child.

4. Wherefore, to the end that all, whether beginners or proficients, may know how to commit themselves to God's guidance, when His Majesty desires to lead them onward, we shall give instruction and counsel, by His help, so that they may be able to understand His will, or, at the least, allow Him to lead them. For some confessors and spiritual fathers,[5] having no light and experience concerning these roads, are wont to hinder and harm such souls rather than to help them

---

1 [*Lit.* 'and wideawake guides.'] E.p. reads 'skilled,' and B 'prepared,' for 'alert.'
2 [*Lit.*, 'a low manner.']
3 So e.p. [P. Silverio's text, following Alc., reads: 'disengage themselves from.']
4 E.p. omits 'freely.'
5 Thus A, B, e.p. Alc. omits: 'confessors and.'

on the road;[1] they are like the builders of Babel, who, when told to
furnish suitable material, gave and applied other very different material,
because they understood not the language, and thus nothing was done.
Wherefore, it is a difficult and troublesome thing at such seasons[2] for a
soul not to understand itself or to find none who understands it. For it
will come to pass that God will lead the soul[3] by a most lofty path of
dark contemplation and aridity, wherein it seems to be lost, and, being
thus full of darkness and trials, constraints and temptations, will meet
one who will speak to it like Job's comforters, and say that[4] it is suffering from melancholy, or low spirits, or a morbid disposition, or that
it may have some hidden sin, and that it is for this reason that God has
forsaken it. Such comforters are wont to declare immediately that that
soul must have been very evil, since such things as these are befalling it.

5. And there will likewise be those who tell the soul to retrace its
steps, since it is finding no pleasure or consolation in the things of God
as it did aforetime. And in this way they double the poor soul's trials;
for it may well be that the greatest affliction which it is feeling is that
of the knowledge of its own miseries, thinking that it sees itself, more
clearly than daylight, to be full of evils and sins, for God gives it that
light of knowledge[5] in that night of contemplation, as we shall presently show. And, when the soul finds someone whose opinion agrees
with its own, and who says that these things must be due to its own
fault, its affliction and trouble increase infinitely and are wont to
become more grievous than death. And, not content with this, such
confessors, thinking that these things proceed from sin, make these
souls go over their lives and cause them to make many general confessions, and crucify them afresh; not understanding that this may quite
well not be the time for any of such things, and that their penitents
should be left in the state of purgation which God gives them, and be
comforted and encouraged to desire it until God be pleased to dispose
otherwise; for until that time, no matter what the souls themselves may
do and their confessors may say, there is no remedy for them.

6. This, with the Divine favour, we shall consider hereafter, and
also how the soul should conduct itself at such a time, and how the
confessor must treat it, and what signs there will be whereby it may be
known if this is the purgation of the soul; and, in such case, whether

---

[1] E.p. omits: 'on the road.'
[2] 'Reasons,' found in many editions, is a copyist's or printer's error. E.p. has 'occasions.'
[3] E.p.: 'For it will happen that God will lead it.'
[4] E.p.: 'who will say to it what Job's comforters said to Job, that it, etc.'
[5] E.p.: 'for God gives it to understand this.'

it be of sense or of spirit (which is the dark night whereof we speak), and how it may be known if it be melancholy or some other imperfection with respect to sense or to spirit. For there may be some souls who will think, or whose confessors will think, that God is leading them along this road of the dark night of spiritual purgation, whereas they may possibly be suffering only from some of the imperfections aforementioned. And, again, there are many souls who think that they have no aptitude for prayer, when they have very much; and there are others who think[1] that they have much when they have hardly any.

7. There are other souls who labour and weary themselves to a piteous extent, and yet go backward, seeking profit in that which is not profitable, but is rather a hindrance; and there are still others who, by remaining at rest and in quietness, continue to make great progress. There are others who are hindered and disturbed and make no progress, because of the very consolations and favours that God is granting them in order that they may make progress. And there are many other things on this road that befall those who follow it, both joys and afflictions and hopes and griefs:[2] some proceeding from the spirit of perfection and others from imperfection. Of all these, with the Divine favour, we shall endeavour to say something, so that each soul[3] who reads this may be able to see something of the road that he ought to follow, if he aspire to attain to the summit of this Mount.

8. And, since this introduction relates to the dark night through which the soul must go to God, let not the reader marvel if it seem to him somewhat dark also. This, I believe, will be so at the beginning when he begins to read; but, as he passes on, he will find himself understanding the first part better, since one part will explain another. And then, if he read it a second time, I believe it will seem clearer to him and the instruction will appear sounder.[4] And if any persons find themselves disagreeing with this instruction,[5] it will be due to my ignorance and poor style; for in itself the matter is good and of the first importance. But I think that, even were it written in a more excellent and perfect manner than it is, only the minority would profit by it,[6] for we shall not here set down things that are very moral and delect-

---

[1] E.p.: 'and others, on the contrary, think.'
[2] E.p.: 'and disturbed on this road, wherein to those who follow it there befall many things—joys and afflictions and hopes and griefs.'
[3] E.p.: 'each one.'
[4] E.p.: 'will appear more certain.'
[5] So Alc. [and P. Silverio]. The other codices and editions have 'reading' [i.e., 'that which they read'].
[6] E.p.: 'than it is, it would not be appreciated by many.'

able[1] for all spiritual persons who desire to travel toward God by pleasant and delectable ways,[2] but solid and substantial instruction, as well suited to one kind of person as to another, if they desire to pass to the detachment of spirit which is here treated.

9. Nor is my principal intent to address all, but rather certain persons of our sacred Order of Mount Carmel of the primitive observance, both friars and nuns—since they have desired me to do so—to whom God is granting the favour of setting them on the road to this Mount; who, as they are already detached from the temporal things of this world, will better understand the instruction concerning detachment of spirit.

[1] Needless to say, the Saint does not here mean that he will not write in conformity with moral standards—no writer is more particular in this respect—nor that he will deal with no delectable matters at all, but rather that he will go to the very roots of spiritual teaching and expound the 'solid and substantial instruction,' which not only forms its basis but also leads the soul toward the most intimate union with God in love.

[2] E.p.: 'for spiritual persons who desire to travel, by [ways] that are pleasant, to God.' There are various other readings in these lines—all of them, however, differing from the text extremely slightly.

BOOK THE FIRST

Wherein is described the nature of dark night and how necessary it is to pass through it to Divine union; and in particular this book describes the dark night of sense, and desire, and the evils which these work in the soul.[1]

CHAPTER I

Sets down the first stanza. Describes two different nights through which spiritual persons pass, according to the two parts of man, the lower and the higher. Expounds the stanza which follows.

STANZA THE FIRST[2]

**On a dark night,   Kindled in love with yearnings—oh, happy chance!—
I went forth without being observed,   My house being now at rest.**

IN this first stanza[3] the soul sings of the happy fortune and chance which it experienced in going forth from all things that are without,[4] and from the desires[5] and imperfections[6] that are in the sensual[7] part of man because of the disordered state of his reason. For the understanding of this it must be known that, for a soul to attain to the state of perfection, it has ordinarily first[8] to pass through two principal kinds of night, which spiritual persons call purgations or purifications of the soul; and here we call them nights, for in both of them the soul journeys, as it were, by night, in darkness.

---

[1] The Codices give neither title nor sub-title: both were inserted in e.p. ['Desire' is to be taken as the direct object of 'describes'; 'these' refers to 'sense' and 'desire,' not to the dark night.]

[2] So A, D, e.p.   Omitted from Alc., B, C.

[3] Alc.: 'In this happy stanza.'   [4] E.p. omits: 'that are without.'

[5] [*Lit.*, 'appetites,' but this word is uniformly translated 'desires,' as the Spanish context frequently will not admit the use of the stronger word in English.]

[6] A, B: 'and affections.'

[7] [The word translated 'sensual' is sometimes *sensual*, and sometimes, as here, *sensitivo*. The meaning in either case is simply 'of sense.']

[8] E.p. omits 'first.'

2. The first night or[1] purgation is of the sensual part of the soul, which is treated in the present stanza, and will be treated in the first part of this book. And the second is of the spiritual part; of this speaks the second stanza, which follows; and of this we shall treat likewise, in the second and the third part,[2] with respect to the activity of the soul; and in the fourth part, with respect to its passivity.

3.[3] And this first night pertains to beginners, occurring at the time when God begins to bring them into the state of contemplation; in this night the spirit likewise has a part, as we shall say in due course. And the second night, or purification, pertains to those who are already proficient, occurring at the time when God desires to bring them to the state of union with God. And this latter night is a more obscure and dark and terrible purgation, as we shall say afterwards.

EXPOSITION OF THE STANZA

4. Briefly, then, the soul means by this stanza that it went forth (being led by God) for love of Him alone, enkindled in love of Him, upon a dark night, which is the privation and purgation of all its sensual desires, with respect to all outward things of the world and to those which were delectable to its flesh, and likewise with respect to the desires of its will. This all comes to pass in this purgation of sense; for which cause the soul says that it went forth while its house was still at rest[4]; which house is its sensual part, the desires being at rest and asleep in it, as it is to them.[5] For there is no going forth from the pains and afflictions of the secret places of the desires until these be mortified and put to sleep. And this, the soul says, was a happy chance for it— namely, its going forth without being observed: that is, without any desire of its flesh or any other thing being able to hinder it. And likewise, because it went out by night—which signifies the privation of all these things wrought in it by God, which privation was night for it.

---

[1] So Alc. The other authorities read 'and' for 'or.'
[2] So Alc. The other authorities read: 'and of this we shall treat likewise, in the second part with respect to the activity [of the soul] [*these last three words are not contained in the Spanish of any authority*], and in the third and the fourth part with respect to its passivity.' E.p. follows this division. Alc., however, seems to correspond more closely with the Saint's intentions; for he did not divide each of his 'books' into 'parts' and appears therefore to indicate by 'part' what we know as 'book.' Now Book I is in fact devoted to the active purgation of sense, as are Books II and III to the active purgation of the spirit. For the 'fourth book,' see Introduction, pp. liii–liv above.
[3] This paragraph is omitted from e.p.
[4] [On the phrase 'at rest,' cf. p. 10, n. 4, above.]
[5] [*Lit.*, 'and it in them.' This 'it' means the soul; the preceding 'it,' the house.]

5. And it was a happy chance that God should lead it into this night, from which there came to it so much good;[1] for of itself the soul would not have succeeded in entering therein, because no man of himself can succeed in voiding himself of all his desires in order to come to God.[2]

6. This is, in brief, the exposition of the stanza; and we shall now have to go through it, line by line, setting down one line after another, and expounding that which pertains to our purpose.[3] And the same method is followed in the other stanzas, as I said in the Prologue[4]— namely, that each stanza will be set down and expounded, and afterwards each line.[5]

CHAPTER II

Explains the nature of this dark night through which the soul says that it has passed on the road to union.[6]

On a dark night

WE may say that there are three reasons[7] for which this journey[8] made by the soul to union with God is called night. The first has to do with the point from which the soul goes forth, for it has gradually to deprive itself of desire for all the worldly things which it possessed, by denying them to itself;[9] the which denial and deprivation are, as it were, night to all the senses[10] of man. The second reason has to do with the mean,[11] or the road along which the soul must travel to this union—that is, faith, which is likewise[12] as dark as night to the understanding. The third has to do with the point to which it travels—namely, God, Who, equally, is dark night to the

---

[1] A, e.p.: 'from which there comes so much good.'
[2] E.p.: 'to go to God.'
[3] The rest of the paragraph is omitted from e.p., possibly because it was already in the 'Argument' above (p. 9).
[4] I.e., in the 'Argument.'
[5] A: 'each line separately.'
[6] So A, Alc., C, D.   B, e.p. read: 'to union with God.' A, B, C, D, e.p. add further: 'Sets down the causes thereof.'
[7] Alc., D: 'three things.'
[8] [More exactly, this 'passage' or 'transition' (*tránsito*).]
[9] [*Lit.*, 'in negation of them.']
[10] E.p.: 'to all the desires and senses.'
[11] E.p.: 'the manner.' [By 'the mean' is meant the middle, or main part, of the journey.]
[12] E.p. omits 'likewise.'

soul in this life.[1] These three nights must pass through the soul—or, rather, the soul must pass through them—in order that it may come to Divine union with God.[2]

2. In the book of the holy Tobias these three kinds of night were shadowed forth by the three nights which, as the angel commanded, were to pass ere the youth Tobias should be united with his bride. In the first he commanded him to burn the heart of the fish in the fire, which signifies the heart that is affectioned to, and set upon, the things of the world; which, in order that one may begin to journey toward God, must be burned and purified from all that is creature, in the fire of the love of God. And in this purgation the devil flees away, for he has power over the soul only when it is attached to things[3] corporeal and temporal.

3. On the second night the angel told him that he would be admitted into the company of the holy patriarchs, who are the fathers of the faith. For, passing through the first night, which is self-privation of all objects of sense, the soul at once enters into the second night, and abides alone in faith to the exclusion, not of charity, but of other knowledge acquired by the understanding, as we shall say hereafter,[4] which is a thing that pertains not to sense.

4. On the third night the angel told him that he would obtain a blessing, which is God; Who, by means of the second night, which is faith, continually communicates Himself to the soul in such a secret and intimate manner that He becomes another night to the soul, inasmuch as this said communication is far darker than those others, as we shall say presently. And, when this third night is past, which is the complete accomplishment of the communication of God in the spirit, which is ordinarily wrought in great darkness of the soul, there then follows its union with the Bride, which is the Wisdom of God. Even so the angel said likewise to Tobias that, when the third night was past, he should be united with his bride in the fear of the Lord; for, when this fear of God is perfect, love is perfect, and this comes to pass when the transformation of the soul is wrought through its love.[5]

5. These three parts of the night are all one night; but, after the

---

[1] E.p. glosses the text by substituting: 'Who, since He is incomprehensible and infinitely transcendent, may also be called dark night.'

[2] E.p. shortens this sentence: 'Through these three nights the soul must pass in order to come to Divine union with God.'

[3] E.p.: 'to the pleasures of things.'

[4] The words 'to the exclusion . . . hereafter' are found only in Alc.

[5] E.p. reads: 'for, when this is perfect, the love of God is so likewise, and this comes to pass when the transformation of the soul is wrought through its love for God.'

manner of night, it has three parts.[1] For the first part, which is that of sense, is comparable to the beginning of night, the point at which things begin to fade from sight. And the second part, which is faith, is comparable to midnight, which is total darkness. And the third part is like the close of night, which is God, the which part is now near to the light of day. And, that we may understand this the better, we shall treat of each of these reasons separately as we proceed.[2]

CHAPTER III

Speaks of the first cause of this night, which is that of the privation of the desire in all things, and gives the reason for which it is called night.[3]

WE here describe as night the privation of every kind of pleasure which belongs to the desire; for, even as night is naught but the privation of light, and, consequently, of all objects that can be seen by means of light, whereby the visual faculty[4] remains unoccupied[5] and in darkness, even so likewise the mortification of desire may be called night to the soul. For, when the soul is deprived of the pleasure of its desire in all things, it remains, as it were, unoccupied and in darkness. For even as the visual faculty, by means of light, is nourished and fed by objects which can be seen, and which, when the light is quenched, are not seen,[6] even so, by means of the desire, the soul is nourished and fed by all things wherein it can take pleasure according to its faculties; and, when this also is quenched, or rather, mortified,[7] the soul ceases to feed upon the pleasure of all things, and thus, with respect to its desire, it remains unoccupied and in darkness.

2. Let us take an example from each of the faculties. When the soul deprives its desire of the pleasure of all that can delight the sense of hearing, the soul remains unoccupied and in darkness with respect to this faculty. And, when it deprives itself of the pleasure of all that can

---

[1] E.p. reads: 'And, that we may the better understand it, we shall treat of each one of these reasons separately as we proceed. And it will be noted that these three nights are all one night, which has three parts.'

[2] E.p. omits this sentence, which it has prefixed to the beginning of the paragraph. Alc. alone reads 'reasons'; the other authorities have 'things.'

[3] Alc. alone has the words 'and . . . night.'

[4] A adds: 'as to all things.'   [5] [*Lit.*, 'without anything (*sc.* to do).']

[6] E.p. has: 'and, when the light is quenched, this ceases.'

[7] E.p.: 'and when this is mortified.'

please the sense of sight, it remains unoccupied and in darkness with respect to this faculty also.[1] And, when it deprives itself of the pleasure of all the sweetness of perfumes which can give it pleasure through the sense of smell, it remains equally unoccupied and in darkness according to this faculty. And, if it also denies itself the pleasure of all food that can satisfy the palate, the soul likewise remains unoccupied and in darkness. And finally, when the soul mortifies itself with respect to all the delights and pleasures that it can receive from the sense of touch, it remains, in the same way, unoccupied and in darkness with respect to this faculty. So that the soul that has denied and thrust away from itself the pleasures which come from all these things, and has mortified its desire with respect to them, may be said to be, as it were, in the darkness of night, which is naught else than an emptiness within itself of all things.

3. The reason for this is that, as the philosophers say, the soul, as soon as God infuses it into the body, is like a smooth, blank board[2] upon which nothing is painted; and, save for that which it experiences through the senses, nothing is communicated to it, in the course of nature, from any other source. And thus, for as long as it is in the body, it is like one who is in a dark prison and who knows nothing, save what he is able to see through the windows of the said prison; and, if he saw nothing through them, he would see nothing in any other way. And thus the soul, save for that which is communicated to it through the senses, which are the windows of its prison, could acquire nothing, in the course of nature, in any other way.

4. Wherefore, if the soul rejects and denies that which it can receive through the senses, we can quite well say that it remains, as it were, in darkness and empty; since, as appears from what has been said, no light can enter it, in the course of nature, by any other means of illumination than those aforementioned.[3] For, although it is true that the soul cannot help hearing and seeing and smelling and tasting and touching, this is of no greater import, nor, if the soul denies and rejects the object, is it hindered more than if it saw it not, heard it not, etc. Just so a man who desires to shut his eyes will remain in darkness, like[4] the blind man who has not the faculty of sight. And to this purpose David says these words: *Pauper sum ego, et in laboribus a juventute*

---

[1] E.p. omits the next three sentences, continuing: 'And the same may be said of the other senses. So that the soul that has denied, etc.'

[2] ['Blank board': Sp., *tabla rasa*; Lat., *tabula rasa*.]

[3] E.p. omits: 'than those aforementioned'

[4] E.p. has 'as much as' for 'like.'

mea.[1] Which signifies: I am poor and in labours from my youth. He calls himself poor, although it is clear that he was rich, because his will was not set upon riches, and thus it was as though he were really poor. But if he had been really poor and had not been so in his will, he would not have been truly poor, for his soul, as far as its desire was concerned, would have been rich and replete. For that reason we call this detachment night to the soul, for we are not treating here of the lack of things, since this implies no detachment on the part of the soul if it has a desire for them; but we are treating of the detachment from them of the taste and desire, for it is this that leaves the soul free and void of them, although it may have them; for it is not the things of this world that either occupy the soul or cause it harm, since they enter it not, but rather the will and desire for them, for it is these that dwell within it.

5. This first kind of night, as we shall say hereafter, belongs to the soul according to its sensual part,[2] which is one of the two parts, whereof we spoke above, through which the soul must pass in order to attain to union.[3]

6. Let us now say how meet it is for the soul to go forth from its house into this dark night of sense, in order to travel to union with God.

CHAPTER IV

Wherein is declared how necessary it is for the soul truly to pass through this dark night of sense, which is mortification of desire, in order that it may journey to union with God.[4]

THE reason for which it is necessary for the soul, in order to attain to Divine union with God, to pass through this dark night of mortification of the desires and denial of pleasures in all things, is because all the affections which it has for creatures are pure darkness in the eyes of God, and, when the soul is clothed in these affections, it has no capacity for being enlightened and possessed by the pure and simple light of God,[5] if it first cast them not from it; for

---

[1] Psalm lxxxvii, 16 [A.V. lxxxviii, 15]. E.p. omits the Latin text and the words 'Which signifies.'

[2] E.p. omits the rest of this paragraph, and also: 'as we shall say hereafter.' It had been said already.

[3] Only Alc. gives: 'in order to attain to union.'

[4] A adds: 'This is proved by comparisons of passages and figures from Sacred Scripture, etc.'

[5] E.p.: 'for being possessed in the pure and simple light of God.'

light cannot agree with darkness; since, as Saint John says: *Tenebræ eam non comprehenderunt*.[1] That is: The darkness could not receive the light.

2. The reason is that two contraries (even as philosophy teaches us) cannot coexist in one person; and that darkness, which is affection set upon the creatures, and light, which is God, are contrary to each other, and have no likeness or accord between one another, even as Saint Paul taught the Corinthians, saying: *Quæ conventio luci ad tenebras?*[2] That is to say: What communion can there be between light and darkness? Hence it is that the light of Divine union cannot dwell in the soul if these affections first flee not away from it.

3. In order that we may the better prove what has been said, it must be known that the affection and attachment which the soul has for creatures renders the soul like to these creatures; and, the greater is its affection, the closer is the equality and likeness between them; for love creates a likeness between that which loves and that which is loved. For which reason David, speaking of those who set their affections upon idols, said thus: *Similes illis fiant qui faciunt ea: et omnes qui confidunt in eis*.[3] Which signifies: Let them that set their heart upon them be like to them. And thus, he that loves a creature becomes as low as that creature, and, in some ways, lower; for love not only makes the lover equal to the object of his love, but even subjects him to it. Hence in the same way it comes to pass that the soul that loves any-thing else[4] becomes incapable of pure union with God and transforma-tion in Him. For the low estate of the creature is much less capable of union with the high estate of the Creator than is darkness with light. For all things of earth and heaven, compared with God, are nothing, as Jeremias says in these words: *Aspexi terram, et ecce vacua erat, et nihil; et cœlos, et non erat lux in eis*.[5] 'I beheld the earth,' he says, 'and it was void, and it was nothing; and the heavens, and saw that they had no light.' In saying that he beheld the earth void, he means that all its creatures were nothing, and that the earth was nothing likewise. And, in saying that he beheld the heavens and saw no light in them, he says that all the luminaries of heaven, compared with God, are pure dark-ness. So that in this way all the creatures are nothing; and their affec-tions, we may say, are less than nothing, since they are an impediment to transformation in God and the privation thereof, even as darkness is

---

1 St. John i, 5. Neither this nor any of the other Latin texts in this chapter is found in e.p.
2 2 Corinthians vi, 14.   3 Psalm cxiv, 8 [A.V. cxv, 8].
4 The editions add, for a better understanding of the phrase, 'apart from God.'
5 Jeremias iv, 23.

not only nothing, but less than nothing, since it is privation of light. And even as he that is in darkness comprehends not the light, so the soul that sets its affection upon[1] creatures will be unable to comprehend God; and, until it be purged, it will neither be able to possess Him here below, through pure transformation of love, nor yonder in clear vision. And, for greater clarity, we will now speak in greater detail.

4. All the being of creation, then, compared with the infinite Being of God, is nothing. And therefore the soul that sets its affection upon the being of creation is likewise nothing in the eyes of God, and less than nothing; for, as we have said, love makes equality and similitude, and even sets the lover below the object of his love. And therefore such a soul will in no wise be able to attain to union with the infinite Being of God; for that which is not can have no communion with that which is. And, coming down in detail to some examples,[2] all the beauty of the creatures, compared with the infinite beauty of God, is the height of deformity,[3] even as Solomon says in the Proverbs: *Fallax gratia, et vana est pulchritudo*.[4] 'Favour is deceitful and beauty is vain.' And thus the soul that is affectioned to the beauty of any creature is the height of deformity[5] in the eyes of God. And therefore this soul that is deformed will be unable to become transformed in beauty, which is God, since deformity cannot attain to beauty; and all the grace and beauty of the creatures, compared with the grace of God, is the height of misery[6] and of uncomeliness. Wherefore the soul that is ravished by the graces and beauties of the creatures has only supreme[7] misery and unattractiveness in the eyes of God; and thus it cannot be capable of the infinite grace and loveliness of God; for that which has no grace is far removed from that which is infinitely gracious; and all the goodness of the creatures of the world, in comparison with the infinite goodness of God, may be described as wickedness. 'For there is naught good, save only God.'[8] And therefore the soul that sets its heart upon the good things of the world is supremely[9] evil in the eyes of God. And, even

---

[1] A, B, e.p.: 'that has affection for.'
[2] The words 'And . . . examples' are found in Alc. only.
[3] [The words often translated 'deformity,' 'deformed,' or 'vileness,' 'vile,' are the ordinary contraries of 'beauty,' 'beautiful,' and might be rendered, more literally but less elegantly, 'ugliness,' 'ugly.']
[4] Proverbs xxxi, 30.   [5] E.p. softens this phrase to: 'has its share of deformity.'
[6] [For 'grace . . . misery' the Spanish has *gracia . . . desgracia*. The latter word, however, does not, as might be supposed, correspond to English 'disgrace.']
[7] E.p. omits 'supreme'; the Spanish word [having a more literally superlative force than the English] can hardly be applied, save in a restricted sense, to what is finite.
[8] St. Luke xviii, 19.   [9] This word, too, is omitted from e.p.

S.J.C. I—4

as wickedness comprehends not goodness, even so such a soul cannot be united with God,[1] Who is supreme goodness.

5. All the wisdom of the world and all human ability, compared with the infinite wisdom of God, are pure and supreme ignorance,[2] even as Saint Paul writes *ad Corinthios*, saying: *Sapientia hujus mundi stultitia est apud Deum.*[3] 'The wisdom of this world is foolishness with God.'[4] Wherefore any soul that makes account of all its knowledge and ability in order to come to union with the wisdom of God is supremely ignorant in the eyes of God and will remain far removed from that wisdom; for ignorance knows not what wisdom is, even as Saint Paul says that this wisdom seems foolishness to God; since, in the eyes of God,[5] those who consider themselves to be persons with a certain amount of knowledge are very ignorant, so that the Apostle, writing to the Romans, says of them: *Dicentes enim se esse sapientes, stulti facti sunt.* That is: Professing themselves to be wise, they became foolish.[6] And those alone acquire wisdom of God who are like ignorant children, and, laying aside their knowledge, walk in His service with love. This manner of wisdom Saint Paul taught likewise *ad Corinthios: Si quis videtur inter vos sapiens esse in hoc sæculo, stultus fiat ut sit sapiens. Sapientia enim hujus mundi stultitia est apud Deum.*[7] That is: If any man among you seem to be wise, let him become ignorant that he may be wise; for the wisdom of this world is foolishness with God. So that, in order to come to union with the wisdom of God, the soul has to proceed rather by unknowing than by knowing; and all the dominion and liberty of the world, compared with the liberty and dominion of the Spirit of God, is the most abject[8] slavery, affliction and captivity.

6. Wherefore the soul that is enamoured of prelacy,[9] or of any other such office, and longs for liberty of desire, is considered and treated, in the sight of God, not as a son, but as a base slave and captive,[10] since it has not been willing to accept His holy doctrine, wherein He teaches us that whoso would be greater must be less, and whoso would be less must be greater.[11] And therefore such a soul will be unable to attain to

---

[1] E.p. adds: 'in perfect union.'
[2] B abbreviates greatly here and then omits the remainder of the chapter.
[3] 1 Corinthians iii, 19.
[4] [In P. Silverio's edition § 4 ends here, but the sense of the passage seems to demand a break where it has been made above.]
[5] E.p. abbreviates: 'knows not what wisdom is, and, in the eyes of God. . . .'
[6] Romans i, 22.   [7] 1 Corinthians iii, 18–19.   [8] [*Lit.*, 'is supreme.']
[9] [The word is applicable to any kind of preferential position.]
[10] E.p. reads: 'not as a dear son, but as a base person, a captive of its passions,' etc.
[11] E.p.: '. . . doctrine, which teaches us that whoso would be greater must be less.

that true liberty of spirit which is attained in His Divine union. For slavery can have no part with liberty; and liberty cannot dwell in a heart that is subject to desires, for this is the heart of a slave; but it dwells in the free man, because he has the heart of a son. It was for this cause that Sara bade her husband Abraham cast out the bondwoman and her son, saying that the son of the bondwoman should not be heir with the son of the free woman.[1]

7. And all the delights and pleasures of the will in all the things of the world, in comparison with all those delights which are God, are supreme affliction, torment and bitterness. And thus he that sets his heart upon them is considered, in the sight of God, as worthy of supreme affliction, torment and bitterness; and thus he will be unable to attain to the delights of the embrace of union with God, since he is worthy of affliction and bitterness.[2] All the wealth and glory of all creation, in comparison with the wealth which is God, is supreme poverty and wretchedness. Thus the soul that loves and possesses creature wealth is supremely poor and wretched in the sight of God, and for that reason will be unable to attain to that wealth and glory which is the state of transformation in God;[3] for that which is miserable and poor is supremely far removed from that which is supremely rich and glorious.

8. And therefore Divine Wisdom, grieving for such as these, who make themselves vile, low, miserable and poor, because they love the things in this world which seem to them so rich and beautiful, addresses an exclamation to them in the Proverbs, saying: *O viri, ad vos clamito, et vox mea ad filios hominum. Intelligite, parvuli, astutiam, et insipientes, animadvertite. Audite quia de rebus magnis locutura sum.* And farther on he continues: *Mecum sunt divitæ, et gloria, opes superbæ et justitia. Melior est fructus meus auro, et lapide pretioso, et genimina mea argento electo. In viis justitiæ ambulo, in medio semitarum judicii, ut ditem diligentes me, et thesauros eorum repleam.*[4] Which signifies: O ye men, to you I call, and my voice is to the sons of men. Attend,[5] little ones, to subtlety and sagacity; ye that are foolish, take notice. Hear, for I have to speak of great things. With me are riches and glory, high riches and justice. Better is the fruit that ye will find in me than gold and precious stones; and my generation—namely, that which ye will engender of me in your souls—is better than choice silver. I walk in the ways of

---

[1] Genesis xxi, 10.   [2] E.p. omits: 'since . . . bitterness.'
[3] The remainder of the paragraph is found only in A and e.p.
[4] Proverbs viii, 4–6, 18–21.
[5] So A, Alc.   E.p.: 'Understand.' The other authorities omit this passage.

justice, in the midst of the paths of judgment, that I may enrich those that love me and fill[1] their treasures perfectly.—Herein Divine Wisdom speaks to all those that set their hearts and affections upon anything of the world, according as we have already said. And she calls them 'little ones,' because they make themselves like to that which they love, which is little. And therefore she tells them to be subtle and to take note that she is treating of great things and not of things that are little like themselves. That the great riches and the glory that they love are with her and in her, and not where they think. And that high riches and justice dwell in her; for, although they think the things of this world to be all this, she tells them to take note that her things are better, saying that the fruit that they will find in them will be better for them than gold and precious stones; and that that which she engenders in souls is better than the choice silver which they love; by which is understood any kind of affection that can be possessed in this life.

CHAPTER V

Wherein the aforementioned subject is treated and continued, and it is shown by passages and figures from Holy Scripture how necessary it is for the soul to journey to God through this dark night of the mortification of desire in all things.

FROM what has been said it may be seen in some measure how great a distance there is between all that the creatures are in themselves and that which God is in Himself, and how souls[2] that set their affections upon any of these creatures are at as great a distance as they from God; for, as we have said, love produces equality and likeness. This distance was clearly realized by Saint Augustine, who said in the *Soliloquies*, speaking with God:[3] 'Miserable man that I am, when will my littleness and imperfection be able to have fellowship with Thy uprightness? Thou indeed art good, and I am evil; Thou art merciful, and I am impious; Thou art holy, I am miserable; Thou

---

[1] A, Alc. both have 'fulfil' [*cumplir*] but in the archaic Spanish sense of 'swell,' which is the reading of e.p. and later editions. [For the rendering of the text cf. A.V. and D.V.: 'I . . . . . fill their treasures.']

[2] E.p.: 'We have already spoken of the distance that there is between the creatures and God, and how souls,' etc.

[3] A, B omit: 'speaking with God.'

art just, I am unjust; Thou art light, I am blind; Thou, life, I, death; Thou, medicine, I, sick; Thou, supreme truth, I, utter vanity.'[1] All this is said by this Saint.[2]

2. Wherefore, it is supreme ignorance for the soul to think that it will be able to pass to this high estate of union with God if first it void not the desire of all things, natural and supernatural, which may hinder it, according as we shall explain hereafter;[3] for there is the greatest possible distance between these things and that which comes to pass in this estate, which is naught else than transformation in God. For this reason Our Lord, when showing us this path, said through Saint Luke: *Qui non renuntiat omnibus quæ possidet, non potest meus esse discipulus.*[4] This signifies: He that renounces not all things that he possesses with his will cannot be My disciple. And this is evident; for the doctrine that the Son of God came to teach[5] was contempt for all things, whereby a man might receive as a reward the Spirit of God in himself. For, as long as the soul rejects not all things, it has no capacity to receive the Spirit of God in pure transformation.

3. Of this we have a figure in Exodus, wherein we read that God[6] gave not the children of Israel the food from Heaven, which was manna, until the flour which they had brought from Egypt failed them. By this is signified that first of all it is meet to renounce all things, for this angels' food is not fitting for the palate that would find delight in the food of men. And not only does the soul become incapable of receiving the Divine Spirit when it stays and pastures on other strange pleasures, but those souls greatly offend the Divine Majesty who desire spiritual food and are not content with God alone, but desire rather to intermingle desire and affection for other things. This can likewise be seen in the same book of Holy Scripture,[7] wherein it is said that, not content with that simplest of food, they desired and craved fleshly

---

[1] A, B, C: 'universal vanity.' D: 'supreme vanity.'

[2] *Soliloq.*, chap. ii (Migne: *Patr. lat.*, Vol. XL, p. 866). E.p. has: 'The which this Saint says concerning the inclination of man toward the creatures.'

[3] So Alc. The other authorities have merely: 'which may pertain to it,' and e.p. adds to this: 'through self-love.' Even when softened by Diego de Jesús this phrase of the Saint did not escape denunciation, and it was the first of the 'propositions' condemned in his writings (cf. p. lix, above). It was defended by P. Basilio Ponce de León in his *Reply* (p. lx), and more extensively by P. Nicolás de Jesús María (*Elucidatio*, Pt. II, Chap. i, pp. 125–40). In reality, little defence is needed other than that contained in the last chapters of the *Ascent of Mount Carmel*, which clearly show the harm caused by supernatural favours, when these are abused, to the memory, the understanding and the will. Who, after all, can doubt that we may abuse 'things supernatural' and by such abuse hinder the soul from attaining union with God?

[4] St. Luke xiv, 33.   [5] A, e.p.: 'to teach the world.'

[6] E.p.: 'that God's Majesty.'

[7] E.p. alters this to: 'in the same Scripture.' [It does not, in fact, occur in the same book.]

food.[1] And that Our Lord was greatly wroth that they should desire to intermingle a food that was so base and so coarse with one that was so noble[2] and so simple; which, though it was so, had within itself the sweetness and substance[3] of all foods.[4] Wherefore, while they yet had the morsels in their mouths, as David says likewise: *Ira Dei descendit super eos.*[5] The wrath of God came down upon them, sending fire from Heaven and consuming many thousands of them; for God held it an unworthy thing that they should have a desire for other food when He had given them food from Heaven.

4. Oh, did spiritual persons but know how much good and what great abundance of spirit they lose through not seeking to raise up their desires above childish things, and how in this simple spiritual food they would find the sweetness of all things, if they desired not to taste those things! But such food gives them no pleasure, for the reason why the children of Israel received not the sweetness of all foods that was contained in the manna was that they would not reserve their desire for it alone. So that they failed to find in the manna all the sweetness and strength that they could wish, not because it was not contained in the manna, but because they desired some other thing. Thus he that will love some other thing together[6] with God of a certainty makes little account of God, for he weighs in the balance against God that which, as we have said, is at the greatest possible distance from God.

5. It is well known by experience that, when the will of a man is affectioned to one thing, he prizes it more than any other; although some other thing may be much better, he takes less pleasure in it. And if he wishes to enjoy both, he is bound to wrong the more important, because he makes an equality between them.[7] Wherefore, since there is naught that equals God, the soul that loves some other thing together with Him, or clings to it, does Him a grievous wrong. And if this is so, what would it be doing if it loved anything more than God?

6. It is this, too, that was denoted by the command of God to Moses[8] that he should ascend the Mount to speak with Him: He commanded him not only to ascend it alone, leaving the children of Israel

---

[1] Numbers xi, 4.   [2] [*Lit.*, 'so high.']
[3] E.p. omits: 'and substance.' [4] [Wisdom xvi, 20.]
[5] Psalm lxxvii, 31 [A.V. lxxviii, 31]. [6] E.p. omits: 'together.'
[7] E.p. substitutes for the last clause: 'because of the unjust equality that he makes between them.'
[8] A, B: 'This likewise is that which God intended to teach when He commanded Moses,' etc.

below, but not even to allow the beasts to feed over against the Mount.[1] By this He signified that the soul that is to ascend this mount of perfection, to commune with God, must not only renounce all things and leave them below,[2] but must not even allow the desires, which are the beasts, to pasture over against this mount—that is, upon other things which are not purely God, in Whom—that is, in the state of perfection—every desire ceases. So he that journeys on the road and makes the ascent to God must needs be habitually careful to quell and mortify the desires; and the greater the speed wherewith a soul does this, the sooner will it reach the end of its journey. Until these be quelled, it cannot reach the end, however much it practise the virtues, since it is unable to attain to perfection in them; for this perfection consists in voiding and stripping and purifying the soul of every desire. Of this we have another very[3] striking figure in Genesis, where we read that, when the patriarch Jacob desired to ascend Mount Bethel, in order to build an altar there to God whereon he should offer Him[4] sacrifice, he first commanded all his people to do three things: one was that they should cast away from them all strange gods; the second, that they should purify themselves; the third, that they should change their garments.[5]

7. By these three things it is signified that any soul that will ascend this mount in order to make of itself an altar whereon it may offer to God the sacrifice of pure love and praise and pure reverence, must, before ascending to the summit of the mount, have done these three things aforementioned perfectly. First, it must cast away all strange gods—namely, all strange affections and attachments; secondly, it must purify itself of the remnants which the desires aforementioned have left in the soul, by means of the dark night of sense whereof we are speaking, habitually[6] denying them and repenting itself of them; and thirdly, in order to reach the summit of this high mount, it must have changed its garments, which, through its observance of the first two things, God will change for it, from old to new, by giving it a new understanding of God in God, the old[7] human understanding being cast aside; and a new love of God in God, the will being now stripped of all its old desires and human pleasures, and the soul being brought

---

1 [Exodus xxxiv, 2–3.] E.p.: 'within sight of the Mount.' A, B: 'near the Mount.'
2 E.p. omits: 'and leave them below.'
3 E.p. omits 'very.'
4 The Codices have: 'whereon he offered Him.' The editions change this to: 'whereon to offer Him.'
5 Genesis xxxv, 2.   6 A, B have 'duly' for 'habitually.'
7 A reads: 'the new.'

into a new state of knowledge and profound delight,[1] all other old images and forms of knowledge having been cast away, and all that belongs to the old man, which is the aptitude of the natural self, quelled, and the soul clothed with a new supernatural aptitude with respect to all its faculties. So that its operation, which before was human, has become Divine, which is that that is attained in the state of union, wherein the soul becomes naught else than an altar whereon God is adored in praise and love, and God alone is upon it. For this cause God commanded that the altar whereon the Ark of the Covenant was to be laid[2] should be hollow within;[3] so that the soul may understand how completely empty of all things God desires it to be, that it may be an altar worthy of the presence of His Majesty. On this altar it was likewise forbidden that there should be any strange fire, or that its own fire should ever fail; and so essential was this that, because Nadab and Abiu, who were the sons of the High Priest Aaron, offered strange fire upon His altar, Our Lord was wroth and slew them there before the altar.[4] By this we are to understand that the love of God must never fail in the soul, so that the soul may be a worthy altar, and also that no other love must be mingled with it.

8. God permits not that any other thing should dwell together with Him. Wherefore we read in the First Book of the Kings that, when the Philistines put the Ark of the Covenant into the temple where their idol was, the idol was cast down upon the ground at the dawn of each day,[5] and broken to pieces[6]. And He permits and wills that there should be only one desire where He is, which is to keep the law of God perfectly, and to bear upon oneself the Cross of Christ. And thus naught else is said in the Divine Scripture to have been commanded by God to be put in the Ark, where the manna was, save the book of the Law,[7] and the rod of Moses,[8] which signifies the Cross. For the soul that aspires to naught else than the keeping of the law of the Lord perfectly and the bearing of the Cross of Christ will be a true Ark, containing within itself the true manna, which is God,[9] when that soul

---

[1] [More literally: 'and abysmal delight.'] Alc. omits these words by a copyist's oversight. A, B, C give them; D has: 'and habitual delight.' The Saint certainly wrote *abisal*, a word which had passed out of use when the *editio princeps* was published, in 1618.

[2] E.p.: 'whereon sacrifices were to be offered.' The reading is nearer to Scripture than that of the Codices.

[3] Exodus xxvii, 8.

[4] Leviticus x, 1–2. E.p. reads: 'before the same altar.'

[5] A, B: 'of each morning.'   [6] 1 Kings [A.V., 1 Samuel] v, 3–5.

[7] Deuteronomy xxxi, 26.

[8] Numbers xvii, 10. [More properly, 'the rod of Aaron.']

[9] E.p. ends the chapter here.

attains to a perfect possession within itself of this law and this rod, without any other thing soever.

CHAPTER VI

Wherein are treated two serious evils caused in the soul by the desires, the one evil being privative and the other positive.[1]

IN order that what we have said may be the more clearly and fully understood, it will be well to set down here and state how[2] these desires are the cause of two serious evils in the soul: the one is that they deprive it of the Spirit of God, and the other is that the soul wherein they dwell is wearied, tormented, darkened, defiled and weakened, according to that which is said in Jeremias, Chapter II: *Duo mala fecit Populus meus: dereliquerunt fontem aquæ vivæ, et foderunt sibi cisternas, dissipatas, quæ continere non valent aquas.* Which signifies: They have forsaken Me, Who am the fountain of living water, and they have hewed them out broken cisterns, that can hold no water.[3] Those two evils—namely, the privative and the positive—may be caused by any disordered act of the desire. And, speaking first of all of the privative, it is clear[4] from the very fact that the soul becomes affectioned to a thing which comes under the head of creature, that the more the desire for that thing fills the soul,[5] the less capacity has the soul for God; inasmuch as two contraries, according to the philosophers, cannot coexist in one person;[6] and further, since, as we said in the fourth chapter, affection for God and affection for creatures are contraries, there cannot be contained within one will affection for creatures and affection for God.[7] For what has the creature to do with the Creator? What has sensual to do with spiritual? Visible with invisible? Temporal with eternal? Food that is heavenly, spiritual and pure with food that is of sense alone and is purely sensual? Christlike poverty of spirit with attachment to aught soever?

2. Wherefore, as in natural generation no form can be introduced

---

[1] E.p. adds: 'This is proved by passages from Scripture.'
[2] E.p.: 'it will be well to state here how.'   [3] Jeremias ii, 13.
[4] So Alc.—A, B, e.p. read: 'These two evils are caused by one act of the desire. For it is clear,' etc.
[5] [*Lit.,* 'the greater the bulk that that desire has in the soul.']
[6] E.p. modifies: '. . . it has for God; for, as we said in Chapter iv, two contraries cannot coexist in one person; and affection for God and affection for creatures are contraries and so cannot coexist in one person.' A, B omit 'according to the philosophers' and 'as we said in the fourth chapter.'   [7] Cf. p. 25, above.

unless the preceding, contrary form is first expelled from the subject, which form, while present, is an impediment to the other by reason of the contrariety which the two have between each other; even so, for as long as the soul is subjected to the sensual spirit,[1] the spirit which is pure and spiritual cannot enter it. Wherefore our Saviour said through Saint Matthew: *Non est bonum sumere panem filiorum, et mittere canibus*.[2] That is: It is not meet to take the children's bread and to cast it to the dogs. And elsewhere, too, he says through the same Evangelist[3]: *Nolite sanctum dare canibus*.[4] Which signifies: Give not that which is holy to the dogs. In these passages Our Lord compares those who renounce their creature-desires, and prepare themselves to receive the Spirit of God in purity, to the children of God; and those who would have their desire feed upon the creatures, to dogs. For it is given to children to eat with their father at table and from his dish, which is to feed upon His Spirit, and to dogs are given the crumbs which fall from the table.

3. From this we are to learn that all created things are crumbs that have fallen from the table of God. Wherefore he that feeds ever upon[5] the creatures is rightly called a dog, and therefore the bread is taken from the children, because they desire not to rise above feeding upon the crumbs, which are created things, to the table of the Uncreated Spirit of their Father. Therefore, like dogs, they are ever hungering, and justly so, because the crumbs serve to whet their appetite rather than to satisfy their hunger. And thus David says of them: *Famem patientur ut canes, et circuibunt civitatem. Si vero non fuerint saturati, et murmurabunt.*[6] Which signifies: They shall suffer hunger like dogs and shall go round about the city, and, if they find not enough to fill them, they shall murmur. For this is the nature of one that has desires, that he is ever discontented and dissatisfied, like one that suffers hunger; for what has the hunger which all the creatures suffer to do with the fullness which is caused by the Spirit of God? Wherefore this fullness that is uncreated[7] cannot enter the soul, if there be not first cast out that other created hunger which belongs to the desire of the soul; for, as we have said,[8] two contraries cannot dwell in one person, the which contraries in this case[9] are hunger and fullness.

---

[1] E.p.: 'sensual and animal spirit.'   [2] St. Matthew xv, 26.
[3] So Alc.   A, B: *Et alibi.*   E.p.: 'And elsewhere.'
[4] St. Matthew vii, 6.   [5] [*Lit.*, 'he that goes feeding upon.']
[6] Psalm lviii, 15–16 [A.V., lix, 14–15].   [7] E.p.: 'this fullness of God.'
[8] E.p.: '. . . cast out from it this hunger of the desire; for, as has been said,' etc.
[9] E.p. omits: 'in this case.'

4. From what has been said it will be seen how much greater is the work of God[1] in the cleansing and the purging of a soul from these contrarieties than in the creating of that soul from nothing. For these contrarieties, these contrary desires and affections, are more completely opposed to God and offer Him greater resistance than does nothingness;[2] for nothingness resists not at all.[3] And let this suffice with respect to the first of the important evils which are inflicted upon the soul by the desires—namely, resistance to the Spirit of God—since much has been said of this above.

5. Let us now speak of the second effect which they cause in the soul. This is of many kinds, because the desires weary the soul and torment and darken it, and defile it and weaken it. Of these five things we shall speak separately, in their turn.

6. With regard to the first, it is clear that the desires weary and fatigue the soul; for they are like restless and discontented children, who are ever demanding this or that from their mother, and are never contented. And even as one that digs because he covets a treasure is wearied and fatigued, even so is the soul wearied and fatigued in order to attain that which its desires demand of it; and although in the end it may attain it, it is still weary, because it is never satisfied; for, after all, the cisterns which it is digging are broken, and cannot hold water to satisfy thirst. And thus, as Isaias says: *Lassus adhuc sitit, et anima ejus vacua est.*[4] Which signifies: His desire is empty. And the soul that has desires is wearied and fatigued; for it is like a man that is sick of a fever, who finds himself no better until the fever leaves him, and whose thirst increases with every moment. For, as is said in the Book of Job: *Cum satiatus fuerit, arctabitur, æstuabit, et omnis dolor irruet super eum.*[5] Which signifies: When he has satisfied his desire, he will be the more oppressed and straitened; the heat of desire hath increased in his soul and thus every sorrow will fall upon him. The soul is wearied and fatigued by its desires, because it is wounded and moved and disturbed by them as is water by the winds; in just the same way they disturb it, allowing it not to rest in any place or in any thing soever. And of such a soul says Isaias: *Cor impii quasi mare fervens.*[6] 'The heart of the wicked man is like the sea when it rages.' And he is a wicked

---

[1] [*Lit.*, 'how much more God does.'] E.p. adds: 'in a certain way.'

[2] E.p.: '. . . affections seem to hinder (*estorbar*) God more than does nothingness.'

[3] E.p.: 'for nothingness resists not His Majesty at all, and creature desire does resist Him.'

[4] Isaias xxix, 8. The editions supply the translation of the first part of the Latin text, which the Saint and the Codices omitted: 'After being wearied and fatigued, he yet thirsteth,' etc.   [5] Job xx, 22.   [6] Isaias lvii, 20.

man that conquers not his desires. The soul that would fain satisfy its desires grows wearied and fatigued; for it is like one that, being an hungered, opens his mouth that he may sate himself with wind, whereupon, instead of being satisfied, his craving becomes greater, for the wind is no food for him. To this purpose said Jeremias :[1] *In desiderio animæ suæ attraxit ventum amoris sui*.[2] As though he were to say: In the desire of his will he snuffed up the wind of his affection. And he then tries to describe the aridity wherein such a soul remains, and warns it, saying: *Prohibe pedem tuum a nuditate, et guttur tuum a siti*.[3] Which signifies: Keep thy foot (that is, thy thought) from being bare and thy throat from thirst (that is to say, thy will from the indulgence of the desire which causes greater dryness) ;[4] and, even as the lover is wearied and fatigued upon the day of his hopes, when his attempt has proved to be vain, so the soul is wearied and fatigued by all its desires and by indulgence in them, since they all cause it greater emptiness and hunger; for, as is often said, desire is like the fire, which increases as wood is thrown upon it, and which, when it has consumed the wood, must needs die.

7. And in this regard it is still worse with desire; for the fire goes down when the wood is consumed, but desire, though it increases when fuel is added to it, decreases not correspondingly when the fuel is consumed; on the contrary, instead of going down, as does the fire when its fuel is consumed, it grows weak through weariness, for its hunger is increased and its food diminished. And of this Isaias speaks, saying: *Declinabit ad dexteram, et esuriet: et comedet ad sinistram, et non saturabitur*.[5] This signifies: He shall turn to the right hand, and shall be hungry; and he shall eat on the left hand, and shall not be filled. For they that mortify not their desires, when they 'turn,' justly see the fullness of the sweetness of spirit of those who are at the right hand of God, which fullness is not granted to themselves; and justly, too, when they eat on the left hand,[6] by which is meant the satisfaction of their desire with some creature comfort, they are not filled, for, leaving aside that which alone can satisfy, they feed on that which causes them greater hunger. It is clear, then, that the desires weary and fatigue the soul.

---

[1] E.p.: 'And thus Jeremias says of such a soul.'
[2] Jeremias ii, 24.   [3] Jeremias ii, 25.
[4] E.p. here omits several lines, continuing: 'Desire is like the fire,' etc.
[5] Isaias ix, 20.
[6] Thus Alc. [with 'run' for 'eat']. A, B, e.p. read: '. . . when they turn from the way of God (which is the right hand) are justly hungered, for they merit not the fullness of the sweetness of spirit. And justly, too, when they eat on the left hand,' etc. [While agreeing with P. Silverio that Alc. gives the better reading, I prefer 'eat' to 'run': it is nearer the

CHAPTER VII

Wherein is shown how the desires torment the soul. This is proved likewise by comparisons and quotations.[1]

THE second kind of positive evil which the desires cause the soul is in their tormenting and afflicting of it, after the manner of one who is in torment through being bound with cords from which he has no relief until he be freed. And of these David says: *Funes peccatorum circumplexi sunt me.*[2] The cords of my sins, which are my desires, have constrained me round about. And, even as one that lies naked upon thorns and briars is tormented and afflicted, even so is the soul tormented and afflicted when it rests upon its desires. For they take hold upon it and wound it and distress it and cause it pain, even as do thorns. Of these David says likewise: *Circumdederunt me sicut apes: et exarserunt sicut ignis in spinis.*[3] Which signifies: They compassed me about like bees,[4] wounding me with their stings, and they were enkindled against me, like fire among thorns; for in the desires, which are the thorns, increases the fire of anguish and torment. And even as the husbandman, coveting the harvest for which he hopes, afflicts and torments the ox in the plough, even so does concupiscence afflict a soul that is subject to its desire to attain that for which it longs. This can be clearly seen in that desire which Dalila had to know whence Samson derived his strength that was so great, for the Scripture says that it fatigued and tormented her so much that it caused her to swoon, almost to the point of death, and she said: *Defecit anima ejus, et ad mortem usque lassata est.*[5]

2. The more intense is the desire, the greater is the torment which it causes the soul. So that the torment increases with the desire; and the greater are the desires which possess the soul, the greater are its torments; for in such a soul is fulfilled, even in this life, that which is said in the Apocalypse concerning Babylon,[6] in these words: *Quantum glorificavit se, et in deliciis fuit, tantum date illi tormentum, et luctum.*[7]

Scriptural passage and the two Spanish words, *comen* and *corren*, could easily be confused in MS.]

[1] Thus Alc. and e.p. A, B read: 'This is proved by comparisons and quotations from the Sacred Scripture.'   [2] Psalm cxviii, 61 [A.V., cxix, 61].

[3] Psalm cxvii, 12 [A.V., cxviii, 12].   [4] A, B: 'like stinging bees.'

[5] Judges xvi, 16. [Actually it was Samson, not Dalila, who was 'wearied even until death.']   [6] E.p. omits: 'concerning Babylon.'

[7] Apocalypse xviii, 7.

That is: As much as she has wished to exalt and fulfil her desires, so much give ye to her torment and anguish. And even as one that falls into the hands of his enemies is tormented and afflicted, even so is the soul tormented and afflicted that is led away by its desires. Of this there is a figure in the Book of the Judges, wherein it may be read that that strong man, Samson, who at one time was strong[1] and free and a judge of Israel, fell into the power of his enemies, and they took his strength from him, and put out his eyes, and bound him in a mill, to grind corn,[2] wherein they tormented and afflicted him greatly;[3] and thus it happens to the soul in which these its enemies, the desires, live and rule; for the first thing that they do is to weaken the soul and blind it, as we shall say below; and then they afflict and torment it, binding it to the mill of concupiscence; and the bonds with which it is bound are its own desires.

3. Wherefore God, having compassion on these that with such great labour, and at such cost to themselves, go about endeavouring to satisfy the hunger and thirst of their desire in the creatures, says to them through Isaias: *Omnes sitientes, venite ad aquas; et qui non habetis argentum, properate, emite, et comedite: venite, emite absque argento vinum et lac. Quare appenditis argentum non in panibus, et laborem vestrum non in saturitate?*[4] As though He were to say: All ye that have thirst of desire, come to the waters, and all ye that have no silver of your own will and desires, make haste; buy from Me and eat; come and buy from Me wine and milk (that is, spiritual sweetness and peace) without the silver of your own will, and without giving Me any labour in exchange for it, as ye give for your desires.[5] Wherefore do ye give the silver of your will[6] for that which is not bread—namely, that of the Divine Spirit—and set the labour of your desires upon that which cannot satisfy you? Come, hearkening to Me, and ye shall eat the good that ye desire and your soul shall delight itself in fatness.

4. This attaining to fatness is a going forth from all pleasures of the creatures; for the creatures torment, but the Spirit of God refreshes. And thus He calls us through Saint Matthew, saying: *Venite ad me omnes, qui laboratis et onerati estis, et ego reficiam vos, et invenietis requiem animabus vestris.*[7] As though He were to say: All ye that go

---

[1] E.p.: '. . . figure in that strong man, Samson, who at one time was so strong,' etc.
[2] [*Lit.*, 'bound him to grind in a mill.']   [3] Judges xvi, 21.
[4] Isaias lv, 1–2.
[5] A, B repeat: 'wine and milk—that is, peace and sweetness.'
[6] E.p.: 'of your own will.'   [7] St. Matthew xi, 28–9.

about tormented, afflicted and burdened with the burden of your cares and desires, go forth from them, come to Me, and I will refresh you and ye shall find for your souls the rest which your desires take from you, wherefore they are a heavy burden, for David says of them: *Sicut onus grave gravatæ sunt super me.*[1]

CHAPTER VIII

Wherein is shown how the desires darken and blind the soul.[2]

THE third evil that the desires cause in the soul is that they blind and darken it. Even as vapours darken the air and allow not the bright sun to shine; or as a mirror that is clouded over cannot receive within itself a clear image; or as water defiled by mud reflects not the visage of one that looks therein; even so the soul that is clouded by the desires is darkened in the understanding and allows neither[3] the sun of natural reason nor that of the supernatural Wisdom of God to shine upon it and illumine it clearly. And thus David, speaking to this purpose, says: *Comprehenderunt me iniquitates meæ, et non potui, ut viderem.*[4] Which signifies: Mine iniquities[5] have taken hold upon me, and I could have no power to see.

2. And, at this same time, when the soul is darkened in the understanding, it is benumbed also in the will, and the memory becomes dull and disordered in its due operation. For, as these faculties in their operations depend upon the understanding, it is clear that, when the understanding is impeded, they will become disordered and troubled. And thus David says: *Anima mea turbata est valde.*[6] That is: My soul is sorely troubled. Which is as much as to say, 'disordered in its faculties.' For, as we say, the understanding has no more capacity for receiving enlightenment from the wisdom of God than has the air, when it is dark, for receiving enlightenment from the sun; neither has the will any power to embrace God within itself in pure love, even as the mirror that is clouded with vapour has no power to reflect clearly within itself

---

1 Psalm xxxvii, 5 [A.V., xxxviii, 4].
2 A, B, e.p. add: 'This is proved by quotations from the Sacred Scripture.'
3 [*Lit.*, 'gives no occasion either for,' etc.] Only Alc. reads thus. All the other authorities have: 'gives no light.'
4 Psalm xxxix, 13 [A.V., xl, 12].
5 So e.p. The other authorities have: 'My wickednesses.'
6 Psalm vi, 4 [A.V., vi, 3].

any visage,[1] and even less power has the memory which is clouded by the darkness of desire to take clearly upon itself the form of the image of God, just as the muddied water cannot show forth clearly the visage of one that looks at himself therein.[2]

3. Desire blinds and darkens the soul; for desire, as such, is blind, since of itself it has no understanding in itself, the reason being to it always, as it were, a child leading a blind man.[3] And hence it comes to pass that, whensoever the soul is guided by its desire, it becomes blind; for this is as if one that sees were guided by one that sees not, which is, as it were, for both to be blind. And that which follows from this is that[4] which Our Lord says through Saint Matthew: *Si cæcus cæco ducatum præstet, ambo in foveam cadunt.*[5] 'If the blind lead the blind, both fall into the pit.' Of little use are its eyes to a moth, since desire for the beauty of the light dazzles it and leads it into the flame.[6] And even so we may say that one who feeds upon desire is like a fish that is dazzled, upon which the light acts rather as darkness, preventing it from seeing the snares which the fishermen are preparing for it. This is very well expressed by David himself, where he says of such persons: *Supercecidit ignis, et non viderunt solem.*[7] Which signifies: There came upon them the fire, which burns with its heat and dazzles with its light.[8] And it is this that desire does to the soul, enkindling its concupiscence and dazzling its understanding so that it cannot see its light. For the cause of its being thus dazzled is that, when another light of a different kind is set before the eye, the visual faculty is attracted by[9] that which is interposed so that it sees not the other; and, as the desire is set so near to the soul as to be within the soul itself, the soul meets this first light and is attracted by[10] it; and thus it is unable to see the light of clear understanding, neither will see it until the dazzling power of desire is taken away from it.

4. For this reason one must greatly lament the ignorance of certain men, who burden themselves with extraordinary penances and with

---

[1] [*Lit.*, 'the present visage.'] A, B, e.p. have 'object' for 'visage.'
[2] 'Therein' is in e.p. only.
[3] E.p. has: '. . . is blind, since of itself it is unreasonable; and it is reason that always guides and directs the soul rightly in its operations.'
[4] E.p.: 'is exactly that.'
[5] St. Matthew xv, 14.
[6] [*hoguera.* More exactly: 'fire,' 'bonfire,' 'blaze.']
[7] Psalm lvii, 9 [cf. A.V., lviii, 8].
[8] So Alc. The other MSS. have: 'The light fell upon them and struck their eyes and dazzled them.' E.p. reads: 'The fire came upon them and they saw not the sun.'
[9] Alc. has: 'is blinded by,' probably a copyist's error [*ciégase* for *cébase*].
[10] Here A and B have *ciégase*, whereas Alc. and e.p. read *cébase*.

many other voluntary practices, and think that this practice or that will suffice to bring them to the union of Divine Wisdom[1]; but such will not be the case if they endeavour not diligently to mortify their desires. If they were careful to bestow half of that labour on this, they would profit more in a month than they profit by all the other practices in many years. For, just as it is necessary to till the earth if it is to bear fruit, and unless it be tilled it bears naught but weeds, just so is mortification of the desires necessary if the soul is to profit. Without this mortification, I make bold to say, the soul no more achieves progress on the road to perfection and to the knowledge of God and of itself, however many efforts it may make, than the seed grows when it is cast upon[2] untilled ground. Wherefore the darkness and rudeness of the soul will not be taken from it until the desires be quenched. For these desires are like cataracts, or like motes in the eye, which obstruct the sight until they be taken away.

5. And thus David, realizing how blind are these souls, and how completely impeded from beholding the light of truth, and how wroth is God with them, speaks to them, saying: *Priusquam intelligerent spinæ vestræ rhamnum: sicut viventes, sic in ira absorbet eos.*[3] And this is as though He had said: Before your thorns (that is, your desires) harden and grow, changing from tender thorns into a thick hedge and shutting out the sight of God even as oft-times the living find their thread of life broken in the midst of its course, even so will God swallow them up in His wrath.[4] For the desires that are living in the soul, so that it cannot understand Him,[5] will be swallowed up by God by means of chastisement and correction, either in this life or in the next, and this will come to pass through purgation. And He says that He will swallow them up in wrath, because that which is suffered in the mortification of the desires is punishment for the ruin which they have wrought in the soul.[6]

---

1 E.p. has: 'who burden themselves with unrestrained [*lit.*, *desordenadas*, 'disordered', 'unruly'] penances and with many other unrestrained practices—I mean voluntary ones—and place their confidence in these, and think that these alone, without any mortification of their desires in other respects, will be sufficient to bring them to the union of Divine Wisdom.'

2 E.p.: 'being scattered over.'

3 Psalm lvii, 10 [A.V., lviii, 9].

4 [P. Silverio following] Alc. reads: 'Before your thorns (that is, your desires) understood, even as the living, after this manner He will swallow them up in His wrath.' All the other MSS., however, and also e.p., read as in the text.

5 [*Lit.*, 'before it can understand God.']

6 E.p. reads: 'For God in His wrath will swallow up those whose desires live in the soul and shut out the knowledge of God, either in the next life in the affliction and purgation of purgatory, or in this life with afflictions and trials which He sends to detach them

6. Oh, if men but knew how great is the blessing of Divine light whereof they are deprived by this blindness which proceeds from their affections and desires, and into what great hurts and evils these make them to fall day after day, for so long as they mortify them not! For a man must not rely upon a clear understanding, or upon gifts that he has received from God, and think that he may indulge his affection or desire, and will not be blinded and darkened, and fall gradually into a worse estate. For who would have said that a man so perfect in wisdom and the gifts of God as was Solomon would have been reduced to such blindness and torpor of the will as to make altars to so many idols and to worship them himself, when he was old?[1] Yet no more was needed to bring him to this than the affection which he had for women and his neglect to deny the desires and delights of his heart. For he himself says concerning himself, in Ecclesiastes, that he denied not his heart that which it demanded of him.[2] And this man was capable of being so completely led away by his desires that, although it is true that at the beginning he was cautious, nevertheless, because he denied them not, they gradually blinded and darkened his understanding, so that in the end they succeeded in quenching that great light of wisdom which God had given him, and therefore in his old age he forsook God.

7. And if unmortified desires could do so much in this man who knew so well the distance that lies between good and evil, what will they not be capable of accomplishing by working upon our ignorance? For we, as God[3] said to the prophet Jonas concerning the Ninivites, cannot discern between[4] our right hand and our left.[5] At every step we hold evil to be good, and good, evil, and this arises from our own nature. What, then, will come to pass if to our natural darkness is added the hindrance of desire[6]? Naught but that which Isaias describes thus: *Palpavimus, sicut cœci parietem, et quasi absque oculis attrectavimus: impegimus meridie, quasi in tenebris.*[7] The prophet is speaking with those who love to follow these their desires. It is as if he had said: We have groped for the wall as though we were blind, and we have been groping as though we had no eyes, and our blindness has attained to

---

from their desires, or through the mortification of their own desires. This God does that He may remove thereby the false light of desire which is between Himself and us, and which was dazzling us and hindering us from knowing Him; so that, the sight of the understanding being enlightened, the ruin wrought by the desires may be repaired.'

[1] 3 Kings [A.V., 1 Kings] xi, 4.
[2] Ecclesiastes ii, 10.   [3] E.p.: 'as the Lord.'
[4] [*Lit.*, 'we . . . know not what there is between.']
[5] Jonas iv, 11.   [6] [*Lit.*, 'is added desire.']
[7] Isaias lix, 10.

such a point that we have stumbled at midday as though it were in the darkness.[1] For he that is blinded by desire has this property, that, when he is set in the midst of truth and of that which is good for him, he can no more see them than if he were in darkness.

CHAPTER IX

Wherein is described how the desires defile the soul. This is proved by comparisons and quotations from Holy Scripture.

THE fourth evil which the desires cause in the soul is that they stain and defile it, as is taught in Ecclesiasticus, in these words: *Qui tetigerit picem, inquinabitur ab ea.*[2] This signifies: He that toucheth pitch shall be defiled with it. And a man touches pitch when he allows the desire of his will to be satisfied by any creature. Here it is to be noted that the Wise Man compares the creatures to pitch; for there is more difference between excellence of soul[3] and the best of the creatures[4] than there is between pure diamond,[5] or fine gold, and pitch. And just as gold or diamond, if it were heated and placed upon pitch, would become foul and be stained by it, inasmuch as the heat would have cajoled and allured the pitch, even so the soul that is hot with desire for any creature draws forth[6] foulness from it through the heat of its desire and is stained by it. And there is more difference between the soul and other corporeal creatures than between a liquid that is highly clarified and mud that is most foul. Wherefore, even as such a liquid would be defiled if it were mingled with mud, so is the soul defiled that clings to creatures, since by doing this it becomes like to the said creatures. And in the same way that traces of soot would defile a face that is very lovely and perfect, even in this way do disordered desires befoul and defile the soul that has them, the which soul is in itself a most lovely and perfect image of God.

2. Wherefore Jeremias, lamenting the ravages of foulness which

---

[1] E.p. has slight verbal variations here, the chief being 'as in darkness' for 'as though we had no eyes,' and 'in obscurity' for 'in the darkness.'

[2] Ecclesiasticus xiii, 1.

[3] E.p.: 'between the excellence which the soul may have.'

[4] [More literally: 'and all the best that is of the creatures.' 'Best' is neuter and refers to qualities, appurtenances, etc.]

[5] [*Lit.*, 'bright diamond.']

[6] E.p.: 'even so the soul, in the heat of its desire which it has for any creature, derives,' etc.

these disordered affections cause in the soul, speaks first of its beauty, and then of its foulness, saying: *Candidiores sunt Nazaræi ejus nive, nitidiores lacte, rubicundiores ebore antiquo, sapphiro pulchriores. Deni-grata est super carbones facies eorum, et non sunt cogniti in plateis.*[1] Which signifies: Its hair—that is to say, that of the soul—is more excellent in whiteness[2] than the snow, clearer[3] than milk, and ruddier than old ivory, and lovelier than the sapphire stone. Their face has now become blacker than coal and they are not known in the streets.[4] By the hair we here understand the affections and thoughts of the soul, which, ordered as God orders them—that is, in God Himself[5]—are whiter than snow, and clearer[6] than milk, and ruddier than ivory,[7] and lovelier than the sapphire. By these four things is understood every kind of beauty and excellence of corporeal creatures, higher than which, says the writer, are the soul and its operations, which are the Nazarites or the hair aforementioned; the which Nazarites, being unruly,[8] with their lives ordered in a way that God ordered not—that is, being set upon the creatures—have their face (says Jeremias) made and turned blacker than coal.

3. All this harm, and more, is done to the beauty of the soul by its unruly desires for the things of this world;[9] so much so that, if we set out to speak of the foul and vile appearance that the desires can give the soul, we should find nothing, however full of cobwebs and worms it might be, not even the corruption of a dead body, nor aught else that is impure and vile, nor aught that can exist and be imagined in this life, to which we could compare it. For, although it is true that the unruly soul, in its natural being,[10] is as perfect as when God created it, yet, in its reasonable being, it is vile, abominable,[11] foul, black and full of all the evils that are here being described, and many more. For, as we shall afterwards say, a single unruly desire, although there be in it no matter of mortal sin, suffices to bring a soul into such bondage, foulness and

1 Lamentations iv, 7–8.
2 A: 'is whiter than whiteness, than the snow.' B: 'is lovelier than whiteness, than the snow.'
3 [*Lit., más resplandecientes,* 'more brilliant,' 'more luminous.']
4 [*Lit., plazas* (derived from the Latin *plateas*), which now, however, has the meaning of 'squares,' '(market) places.']
5 Alc. omits, perhaps by an oversight: 'that . . . Himself.'
6 [' Clearer' here is *más claros;* the adjective is rendered ' bright ' on p. 43, n. 5.]
7 E.p.: 'than old ivory.'
8 [The words translated 'unruly,' 'disordered,' here and elsewhere, and occasionally 'unrestrained,' are the same in the original: *desordenado.* Cf. p. 41, n. 1.]
9 E.p. omits: 'for the things of this world.'
10 E.p.: 'natural substance.'
11 E.p. omits 'abominable.'

vileness that it can in no wise come to accord with God in union[1] until the desire be purified. What, then, will be the vileness of the soul that is completely unrestrained with respect to its own passions and given up to its desires, and how far removed will it be from God and from His purity?

4. It is impossible to explain in words, or to cause to be understood by the understanding, what variety of impurity is caused in the soul by a variety of desires. For, if it could be expressed and understood, it would be a wondrous thing, and one also which would fill us with pity, to see how each desire, in accordance with its quality and degree, be it greater or smaller, leaves in the soul its mark and deposit[2] of impurity and vileness, and how one single disorder of the reason can be the source of innumerable different impurities, some greater, some less, each one after its kind.[3] For, even as the soul of the righteous man has in one single perfection, which is uprightness of soul, innumerable gifts of the greatest richness, and many virtues of the greatest loveliness, each one different and full of grace after its kind according to the multitude and the diversity of the affections of love which it has had in God, even so the unruly soul, according to the variety of the desires which it has for the creatures, has in itself a miserable variety of impurities and meannesses, wherewith it is endowed[4] by the said desires.

5. The variety of these desires[5] is well illustrated in the Book of Ezechiel, where it is written that God showed this Prophet, in the interior of the Temple, painted around its walls, all likenesses of creeping things which crawl on the ground, and all the abomination of unclean beasts.[6] And then God said to Ezechiel: 'Son of man, hast thou not indeed seen the abominations that these do, each one in the secrecy of his chamber?'[7] And God commanded the Prophet to go in farther and he would see greater abominations; and he says that he there saw women seated, weeping for Adonis, the god of love.[8] And God commanded him to go in farther still, and he would see yet greater abominations, and he says that he saw there five-and-twenty old men whose backs were turned toward the Temple.[9]

---

[1] E.p.: '. . . of mortal sin, befouls and stains the soul and renders it unfit to come to accord with God in perfect union.' A, B: 'in any union.' [The Spanish of the text reads literally: 'in a union.']

[2] E.p.: '. . . how each desire, in agreement with its quality and intention, leaves its mark and deposit,' etc.

[3] E.p. omits: 'and how . . . its kind.'

[4] [The verb is *pintar*, 'paint': perhaps 'corrupt' is intended. The same verb occurs in the following sentence.]

[5] A, B, e.p. have: 'of impurities.'

[6] Ezechiel viii, 10.

[7] [Ezechiel viii, 12.]   [8] Ezechiel viii, 14.   [9] Ezechiel viii, 16

6. The diversity of creeping things and unclean beasts that were painted in the first chamber of the Temple are the thoughts and conceptions which the understanding fashions from the lowly things of earth, and from all the creatures, which are painted, just as they are, in the temple of the soul, when the soul[1] embarrasses its understanding with them, which is the soul's first habitation. The women that were farther within, in the second habitation, weeping for the god Adonis, are the desires that are in the second faculty of the soul, which is the will; the which are, as it were, weeping, inasmuch as they covet that to which the will is affectioned, which are the creeping things painted in the understanding. And the men that were in the third habitation[2] are the images and representations of the creatures, which the third part[3] of the soul—namely memory—keeps and reflects upon[4] within itself. Of these it is said that their backs are turned toward the Temple because when the soul, according to these three faculties, completely and perfectly embraces anything that is of the earth, it can be said to have its back turned toward the Temple of God, which is the right reason of the soul, which admits within itself nothing that is of creatures.[5]

7. And let this now suffice for the understanding of this foul disorder of the soul with respect to its desires. For if we had to treat in detail of the lesser foulness[6] which these imperfections and their variety make and cause in the soul, and that which is caused by venial sins, which is still greater than that of the imperfections, and their great variety, and likewise that which is caused by the desires for mortal sin, which is complete foulness of the soul, and its great variety, according to the variety and multitude of all these three things, we should never end, nor would the understanding of angels suffice to understand it.[7] That which I say, and that which is to the point for my purpose, is that any desire, although it be for but the smallest imperfection, stains and defiles the soul.[8]

---

[1] E.p.: 'which, being so contrary to things eternal, defile the temple of the soul, and the soul,' etc.
[2] So Alc., e.p.   A, B and some editions have: 'third chamber.'
[3] E.p.: 'third faculty.'
[4] [*Lit.*, 'revolves'—'turns over in its mind' in our common idiom.]
[5] E.p.: 'admits within itself no created thing that is opposed to God.'
[6] E.p.: 'of the impediment to this union.'
[7] E.p. shortens: 'and its great diversity, we should never end.'
[8] E.p. omits: 'stains . . . soul,' leaving the sentence incomplete.

CHAPTER X

Wherein is described how the desires weaken the soul in virtue and make it lukewarm.[1]

THE fifth way in which the desires harm the soul is by making it lukewarm and weak, so that it has no strength to follow after virtue and to persevere therein. For as the strength of the desire, when it is set upon various aims, is less than if it were set wholly on one thing alone, and as, the more are the aims whereon it is set, the less of it there is for each one of them, for this cause philosophers say that virtue in union is stronger than if it be dispersed. Wherefore it is clear that, if the desire of the will be dispersed among other things than virtue, it must be weaker as regards virtue. And thus the soul whose will is set upon various trifles is like water, which, having a place below wherein to empty itself, never rises; and such a soul has no profit. For this cause the patriarch Jacob compared his son Ruben to water poured out, because in a certain sin he had given rein to his desires. And he said: 'Thou art poured out like water; grow thou not.'[2] As though he had said: Since thou art poured out like water as to the desires, thou shalt not grow in virtue. And thus, as hot water, when uncovered, readily loses heat, and as aromatic spices, when they are unwrapped,[3] gradually lose the fragrance and strength of their perfume, even so the soul that is not recollected in one single desire for God loses heat and vigour in its virtue. This was well understood by David, when he said, speaking with God: I will keep my strength for Thee.[4] That is, concentrating the strength of my desires[5] upon Thee alone.

2. And the desires weaken the virtue of the soul, because they are to it like the shoots[6] that grow about a tree, and take away its virtue so that it cannot bring forth so much fruit. And of such souls as these says the Lord: *Væ prægnantibus, et nutrientibus in illis diebus.*[7] That is: Woe to them that in those days are with child and to them that give suck. This being with child and giving suck is understood with respect to the desires; which, if they be not pruned, will ever be taking more virtue from the soul, and will grow to the harm of the soul, like the shoots upon the tree. Wherefore Our Lord counsels us, saying: Have

[1] E.p. adds: 'This is proved by comparisons and quotations from the Sacred Scripture.'
[2] Genesis xlix, 4.   [3] A, B: '. . . spices, not being covered.'
[4] Psalm lviii, 10 [A.V., lix, 9].   [5] E.p.: 'my affections.'
[6] A, B, e.p.: 'like the twigs and shoots.'   [7] St. Matthew xxiv, 19.

your loins girt about[1]—the loins signifying here the desires. And indeed, they are also like leeches, which are ever sucking the blood from the veins, for thus the Preacher terms them when he says: The leeches are the daughters—that is, the desires—saying ever: *Daca, daca*.[2]

3. From this it is clear that the desires bring no good to the soul but rather take from it that which it has; and, if it mortify them not, they will not cease till they have wrought in it that which the children of the viper are said to work in their mother; who, as they are growing within her womb, consume her and kill her, and they themselves remain alive at her cost. Just so the desires that are not mortified grow to such a point that they kill the soul with respect to God because it has not first killed them. And they alone live in it. Wherefore the Preacher says: *Aufer a me Domine ventris concupiscentias*.[3]

4. And, even though they reach not this point, it is very piteous to consider how the desires that live in this poor soul treat it, how unhappy it is with regard to itself, how dry with respect to its neighbours, and how weary and slothful with respect to the things of God. For there is no evil humour that makes it as wearisome and difficult for a sick man to walk, or gives him a distaste for eating comparable to the weariness and distaste for following virtue which is given to a soul by desire for creatures. And thus the reason why many souls have no diligence and eagerness to gain[4] virtue is, as a rule, that they have desires and affections which are not pure and are not fixed upon God.[5]

CHAPTER XI

Wherein it is proved necessary that the soul that would attain to Divine union should be free from desires, however slight they be.[6]

I EXPECT that for a long time the reader has been wishing to ask whether it be necessary, in order to attain to this high estate of perfection, to undergo first of all total mortification in all the desires, great and small, or if it will suffice to mortify some of them and to leave

---

[1] St. Luke xii, 35.

[2] Proverbs xxx, 15. All the codices have this reading. E.p. reads: 'saying ever: "Give me, give me."'

[3] Ecclesiasticus xxiii, 6. [In the original the last two sentences are transposed.]

[4] A, B: 'to work virtue.' E.p.: 'to work virtues.'

[5] [*Lit.*, 'not pure on (or 'in') God.'] E.p. adds: 'our Lord.'

[6] So e.p. Alc. differs slightly here, chiefly by using a stronger word [*mínimos*] for 'slight.' We might read: 'how very slight soever.'

others, those at least which seem of little moment. For it appears to be a severe and most difficult thing for the soul to be able to attain to such purity and detachment that it has no will and affection for anything.

2. To this I reply: first, that it is true that all the desires are not equally hurtful, nor do they all equally embarrass the soul.[1] I am speaking of those that are voluntary, for the natural desires hinder the soul little, if at all, from attaining to union, when they are not consented to nor pass beyond the first movements (I mean,[2] all those wherein the rational will has had no part, whether at first or afterward); and to take away these—that is, to mortify them wholly in this life—is impossible. And these hinder not the soul in such a way as to prevent its attainment to Divine union, even though they be not, as I say, wholly mortified; for the natural man may well have them, and yet the soul may be quite free from them according to the rational spirit. For it will sometimes come to pass that the soul will be in the full[3] union of the prayer of quiet in the will at the very time when these desires are dwelling in the sensual part of the soul,[4] and yet the higher part, which is in prayer, will have nothing to do with them. But all the other voluntary desires, whether they be of mortal sin, which are the gravest, or of venial sin, which are less grave, or whether they be only of imperfections, which are the least grave of all, must be driven away every one, and the soul must be free from them all, howsoever slight they be, if it is to come to this complete union; and the reason is that the state of this Divine union consists in the soul's total transformation, according to the will, in the will of God, so that there may be naught in the soul that is contrary to the will of God, but that,[5] in all and through all, its movement may be that of the will of God alone.

3. It is for this reason that we say of this state that it is the making of two wills into one—namely, into the will of God, which will[6] of God is likewise the will of the soul. For if this soul desired any imperfection that God wills not, there would not be made one will of God, since the soul would have a will for that which God has not. It is clear, then, that for the soul to come to unite itself perfectly with God through love and will, it must first be free from all desire of the will, howsoever

[1] Alc. omits several lines here, but apparently only through the copyist's negligence.
[2] [The original has no such explanatory phrase.] E.p. [however] reads: 'And I mean by "natural" and "first movements" all those. . . . etc.'
[3] [That is, will be enjoying all the union that the prayer of quiet gives.] B, e.p. have: 'in high union.'
[4] Thus A, B. The other authorities [and P. Silverio] read: 'of man.'
[5] E.p.: '[and] so that.'
[6] E.p.: 'the making into one will of God—that is, of my will and the will of God, so that the will,' etc.

slight. That is, that it must not intentionally and knowingly consent with the will to imperfections, and it must have power and liberty to be able not so to consent intentionally. I say knowingly, because, unintentionally and unknowingly, or without having[1] the power to do otherwise, it may well fall into imperfections and venial sins, and into the natural desires whereof we have spoken; for of such sins as these which are not voluntary and surreptitious[2] it is written that the just man shall fall seven times in the day and shall rise up again.[3] But of the voluntary desires, which, though they be for very small things, are, as I have said, intentional venial sins, any one that is not conquered suffices to impede union.[4] I mean, if this habit be not mortified; for sometimes certain acts of different desires have not as much power when the habits are mortified.[5] Still, the soul will attain to the stage of not having even these, for they likewise proceed from a habit of imperfection. But some habits of voluntary imperfections, which are never completely conquered, prevent not only the attainment of Divine union, but also progress in perfection.

4. These habitual imperfections are, for example, a common custom of much speaking, or some slight attachment which we never quite wish to conquer—such as that to a person, a garment, a book, a cell, a particular kind of food, tittle-tattle, fancies for tasting, knowing or hearing certain things, and suchlike. Any one of these imperfections, if the soul has become attached and habituated to it, is of as great harm to its growth and progress in virtue as though it were to fall daily into many other imperfections and casual venial sins[6] which proceed not from a habitual indulgence in any habitual[7] and harmful attachment, and will not hinder it so much as when it has attachment to anything. For as long as it has this there is no possibility that it will make progress in perfection, even though the imperfection[8] be extremely slight. For it comes to the same thing whether a bird be held by a slender cord or by a stout one; since, even if it be slender, the bird will be as well held as though it were stout, for so long as it breaks it not and flies not

---

[1] E.p.: 'without wholly having.'
[2] These last two words occur in Alc. alone.
[3] Proverbs xxiv, 16.
[4] [The original omits 'union.'] Only Alc. reads: 'which are intentional venial sins.' E.p. reads: 'But of desires which are voluntary and quite intentional, though they be for very small things, as has been said, any one that is not conquered suffices to impede.'
[5] Alc. only has: 'when . . . mortified.' E.p. substitutes: 'since they have not become a definite habit.' A, B read similarly, but omit 'not.'
[6] E.p.: 'many other and even greater imperfections.'
[7] E.p. omits this second 'habitual.'
[8] E.p.: 'that the soul will reach perfection, though the thing,' etc.

away. It is true that the slender one is the easier to break; still, easy though it be, the bird will not fly away if it be not broken. And thus the soul that has attachment to anything, however much virtue it possess, will not attain to the liberty of Divine union. For the desire and the attachment of the soul have that power which the sucking-fish[1] is said to have when it clings to a ship; for, though but a very small fish, if it succeed in clinging to the ship, it makes it incapable of reaching the port, or of sailing on at all. It is sad to see certain souls in this plight; like rich vessels, they are laden with wealth and good works and spiritual exercises, and with the virtues and the favours that God grants them; and yet, because they have not the resolution to break with some whim or attachment or affection (which all come to the same thing), they never make progress or reach the port of perfection,[2] though they would need to do no more than make one good flight and thus to snap that cord of desire right off, or to rid themselves of that sucking-fish of desire which clings to them.[3]

5. It is greatly to be lamented that, when God has granted them strength to break other and stouter cords[4]—namely, affections for sins and vanities—they should fail to attain[5] to such blessing because they have not shaken off some childish thing which God had bidden them conquer[6] for love of Him, and which is nothing more than a thread or a hair.[7] And, what is worse, not only do they make no progress, but because of this attachment they fall back,[8] lose that[9] which they have gained, and retrace that part of the road along which they have travelled[10] at the cost of so much time and labour; for it is well known that, on this road, not to go forward is to turn back, and not to be gaining is to be losing. This Our Lord desired to teach us when He said: 'He that is not with Me is against Me; and he that gathereth not with Me scattereth.'[11] He that takes not the trouble to repair the vessel, however slight be the crack in it, is likely to spill all the liquid that is within it. The Preacher taught us this clearly when he said: He

---

[1] [Or 'remora.']   [2] E.p.: 'neither can reach the port of perfect union.'
[3] E.p. omits: 'which clings to them.'
[4] [*cordeles:* a stronger word than that used above (*hilo*), which, if the context would permit, might better be translated 'string'—its equivalent in modern speech. Below, *hilo* is translated 'thread.']
[5] E.p.: 'fail to progress and to attain.'   [6] A, B, e.p.: 'God left them to conquer.'
[7] E.p. omits: 'or a hair.' [*Hilo*, rendered 'thread,' as explained in n. 4 above, can also be taken in the stronger sense of 'cord.']
[8] E.p. adds: 'in the matter of perfection.'   [9] E.p.: 'losing something of that.'
[10] E.p. omits: 'and retrace . . . travelled.'
[11] St. Matthew xii, 30. E.p. reads: 'For we know that, on this spiritual road, not to go forward conquering is to turn back; and not to be gaining is to be losing. This Our Lord desired to teach us when He said: He that gathereth not with Me, scattereth.'

that contemneth small things shall fall by little and little.[1] For, as he himself says, a great fire cometh from a single spark.[2] And thus one imperfection is sufficient to lead to another; and these lead to yet more; wherefore you will hardly ever see a soul that is negligent in conquering one desire, and that has not many more arising from the same weakness and imperfection that this desire causes. In this way they are continually falling; we have seen many persons to whom God has been granting the favour of leading them a long way, into a state of great detachment and liberty, yet who, merely through beginning to indulge some slight attachment, under the pretext of doing good, or in the guise of conversation and friendship, often lose their spirituality and desire for God and holy solitude, fall from the joy and wholehearted devotion which they had in their spiritual exercises, and cease not until they have lost everything; and this because they broke not with that beginning of sensual desire and pleasure and kept not themselves in solitude for God.

6. Upon this road we must ever journey in order to attain our goal; which means that we must ever be mortifying our desires and not indulging them; and if they are not all completely mortified we shall not completely attain. For even as a log of wood may fail to be transformed in the fire because a single degree of heat is wanting to it, even so the soul will not be transformed in God if it have but one imperfection, although it be something less than voluntary desire;[3] for, as we shall say hereafter concerning the night of faith, the soul has only one will, and that will, if it be embarrassed by aught and set upon aught, is not free,[4] solitary and pure, as is necessary for Divine transformation.

7. Of this that has been said we have a figure in the Book of the Judges, where it is related that the angel came to the children of Israel and said to them that, because they had not destroyed that froward people, but had made a league with some of them, they would therefore be left among them as enemies, that they might be to them an occasion of stumbling and perdition.[5] And just so does God deal with certain souls: though He has taken them out of the world,[6] and slain the giants, their sins, and destroyed the multitude of their enemies, which are the occasions of sin that they encountered in the world, solely that they

---

[1] Ecclesiasticus xix, 1. E.p. adds: 'in great things.'
[2] [Lit., 'the fire is increased by a single spark.'] Ecclesiasticus xi, 34 [A.V., xi, 32].
[3] E.p. omits: 'although . . . desire.'
[4] A, B, e.p.: 'is not completely free.'   [5] Judges ii, 3.
[6] A, B: 'of the perils of the world.' E.p.: 'of the Egypt of the world.'

may enter this Promised Land of Divine union with greater liberty, yet they harbour friendship and make alliance with the insignificant peoples[1]—that is, with imperfections—and mortify them not completely; therefore Our Lord is angry, and allows them[2] to fall into their desires and go from bad to worse.

8. In the Book of Josue, again, we have a figure of what has just been said—where we read that God commanded Josue, at the time that he had to enter into possession of the Promised Land, to destroy all things that were in the city of Jericho, in such wise as to leave therein nothing alive, man or woman, young or old, and to slay all the beasts, and to take naught, neither to covet aught, of all the spoils.[3] This He said that we may understand how, if a man is to enter this Divine union, all that lives in his soul must die, both little and much, small and great, and that the soul must be without desire for all this, and detached from it, even as though it existed not for the soul, neither the soul for it. This Saint Paul teaches us clearly in his epistle *ad Corinthios*, saying: 'This I say to you, brethren, that the time is short; it remains, and it behoves you, that they that have wives should be as if they had none; and they that weep for the things of this world, as though they wept not; and they that rejoice, as if they rejoiced not;[4] and they that buy, as though they possessed not; and they that use this world, as if they used it not.'[5] This the Apostle says to us in order to teach us how complete must be the detachment of our soul from all things if it is to journey to God.

CHAPTER XII

Which treats of the answer to another question,[6] explaining what the desires are that suffice to cause the evils aforementioned in the soul.

WE might write at greater length upon this matter of the night of sense, saying all that there is to say concerning the harm which is caused by the desires, not only in the ways aforementioned, but in many others. But for our purpose that which has

---

[1] [The original phrase (*gente menuda*) means 'little folk.' It is used of children and sometimes also of insects and other small creatures. There is a marked antithesis between the 'giants,' or sins, and the 'little folk,' or imperfections.]

[2] E.p.: 'therefore, since they live negligently and slothfully, His Majesty is wroth and allows them,' etc. [3] Josue vi, 21.

[4] E.p. omits this clause. [5] 1 Corinthians vii, 29–31.

[6] E.p.: 'Answers another question.'

been said suffices; for we believe we have made it clear in what way the mortification of these desires is called night, and how it behoves us to enter this night in order to journey to God. The only thing that remains, before we treat of the manner of entrance therein, in order to bring this part to a close, is a question concerning what has been said which might occur to the reader.

2. It may first be asked if any desire can be sufficient to work and produce in the soul the two evils aforementioned—namely, the privative, which consists in depriving the soul of the grace of God, and the positive, which consists in producing within it the five serious evils whereof we have spoken.[1] Secondly, it may be asked if any desire, however slight it be and of whatever kind, suffices to produce all these together,[2] or if some desires produce some and others produce others. If, for example, some produce torment; others, weariness; others, darkness, etc.

3. Answering this question, I say, first of all, that with respect to the privative evil—which consists in the soul's being deprived of God —this is wrought wholly,[3] and can only be wrought, by the voluntary desires, which are of the matter of mortal sin; for they deprive the soul of grace in this life, and of glory, which is the possession of God, in the next. In the second place, I say that both those desires which are of the matter of mortal sin, and the voluntary desires, which are of the matter of venial sin, and those that are of the matter of imperfection, are each sufficient to produce in the soul all these positive evils together; the which evils, although in a certain way they are privative, we here call positive, since they correspond to a turning towards the creature, even as the privative evils correspond to a turning away from God.[4] But there is this difference, that the desires which are of mortal sin produce total blindness, torment, impurity, weakness, etc. Those others, however, which are of the matter of venial sin or imperfection,[5] produce not these evils in a complete and supreme degree, since they deprive not the soul of grace, upon the loss of which depends the possession of them,[6] since the death of the soul is their life; but they produce them in the soul remissly, proportionately to the remission of grace which these

---

[1] E.p. abbreviates: '. . . produce in the soul the two evils, positive and privative, already described.'

[2] So Alc.   A, e.p. have: 'all these five evils together.' B: 'all these evils together.'

[3] E.p. omits 'wholly.'

[4] E.p. omits: 'the which . . . from God.'

[5] E.p.: 'or known imperfection.'

[6] E.p.: '. . . of grace, with the which privation goes together the possession of them.'

desires produce in the soul.[1] So that that desire which most weakens grace will produce the most abundant torment, blindness and defilement.[2]

4. It should be noted, however, that, although each desire produces all these evils, which we here term positive, there are some which, principally and directly, produce some of them, and others which produce others, and the remainder are produced consequently upon these. For, although it is true that one sensual desire produces all these evils, yet its principal and proper effect is the defilement of soul and body. And, although one avaricious desire likewise produces them all, its principal and direct result is to produce misery. And, although similarly one vainglorious desire produces them all, its principal and direct result is to produce darkness and blindness.[3] And, although one gluttonous desire produces them all, its principal result is to produce lukewarmness in virtue. And even so is it with the rest.

5. And the reason why any act of voluntary desire produces in the soul all these effects together lies in the direct contrariety which exists between them and all the acts of virtue which produce the contrary effects in the soul. For, even as an act of virtue produces and begets in the soul sweetness, peace, consolation, light, cleanness and fortitude all together, even so an unruly desire causes torment, fatigue, weariness, blindness and weakness. All the virtues grow through the practice of any one of them, and all the vices grow through the practice of any one of them likewise, and the remnants[4] of each grow in the soul. And although all these evils are not evident at the moment when the desire is indulged, since the resulting pleasure gives no occasion for them, yet the evil remnants which they leave are clearly perceived, whether before or afterwards. This is very well illustrated by that book which the angel commanded Saint John to eat, in the Apocalypse, the which book was sweetness to his mouth, and in his belly bitterness.[5] For the desire, when it is carried into effect, is sweet and appears to be good, but its bitter taste is felt afterwards; the truth of this can be clearly proved by anyone who allows himself to be led away by it. Yet I am not ignorant that there are some men so blind and insensible as not to

---

[1] E.p.: 'But they produce something of these evils, although remissly, proportionately to the lukewarmness and remissness which they produce in the soul.' [The word here translated 'remissness' is rendered 'remission' in the text, where it seems to have a slightly different meaning.]

[2] E.p.: 'will more abundantly produce torment, blindness and non-purity.'

[3] Alc. unintentionally omits this sentence.

[4] E.p.: 'the effects.' [The word translated 'remnants' also means 'after-taste.']

[5] Apocalypse x, 9. This sentence is omitted by e.p.

feel this, for, as they do not walk in God, they are unable to perceive that which hinders them from approaching Him.

6. I am not writing here of the other natural desires which are not voluntary, and of thoughts that go not beyond the first movements, and other temptations to which the soul is not consenting; for these produce in the soul none of the evils aforementioned. For, although a person who suffers from them may think that the passion and disturbance which they then produce in him are defiling and blinding him, this is not the case; rather they are bringing him the opposite advantages.[1] For, in so far as he resists them, he gains fortitude, purity, light and consolation, and many blessings, even as Our Lord said to Saint Paul: That virtue was made perfect in weakness.[2] But the voluntary desires work all the evils aforementioned, and more. Wherefore the principal care of spiritual masters is to mortify their disciples immediately with respect to any desire soever, by causing them to remain without the objects of their desires, in order to free them from such great misery.

CHAPTER XIII

Wherein is described the manner and way which the soul must follow in order to enter this night of sense.[3]

IT now remains for me to give certain counsels whereby the soul may know how to enter this night of sense and may be able so to do. To this end it must be known that the soul habitually enters this night of sense in two ways: the one is active; the other passive. The active way consists in that which the soul can do, and does,[4] of itself, in order to enter therein, whereof we shall now treat in the counsels which follow. The passive way is that wherein the soul does nothing,[5] and God works in it, and it remains, as it were, patient.[6] Of this we shall treat in the fourth book,[7] where we shall be treating of

---

[1] E.p. inserts the important modifying adverb 'occasionally.'

[2] 2 Corinthians xii, 9. ['Virtue' had often, in the author's day, much of the meaning of the modern word 'strength.']

[3] The title in e.p. is: 'Of the manner and way which the soul must follow in order to enter this night of sense through faith.'

[4] The earlier editions add: 'aided by grace.'

[5] The earlier editions add: 'as of itself or by its own effort.'

[6] The earlier editions have: 'but God works it in the soul with more special aids, and the soul is, as it were, patient, consenting thereto freely.'

[7] The earlier editions have: 'in the *Dark Night*': it is, of course, that treatise that is referred to.

beginners. And because there, with the Divine favour, we shall give many counsels to beginners, according to the many imperfections which they are apt to have while on this road, I shall not spend time in giving many here. And this, too, because it belongs not to this place to give them, as at present we are treating only of the reasons for which this journey is called a night, and of what kind it is, and how many parts it has. But, as it seems that it would be incomplete, and less profitable than it should be, if we gave no help or counsel here for walking in this night of desires, I have thought well to set down briefly here the way which is to be followed: and I shall do the same at the end of each of the next two parts, or causes, of this night, whereof, with the help of the Lord, I have to treat.

2. These counsels for the conquering of the desires, which now follow, albeit brief and few, I believe to be as profitable and efficacious as they are concise; so that one who sincerely desires to practise them will need no others, but will find them all included in these.

3. First, let him have an habitual desire[1] to imitate Christ in everything that he does, conforming himself to His life; upon which life he must meditate so that he may know how to imitate it, and to behave in all things as Christ would behave.

4. Secondly, in order that he may be able to do this well, every pleasure that presents itself to the senses, if it be not purely for the honour and glory of God, must be renounced and completely rejected for the love of Jesus Christ, Who in this life had no other pleasure, neither desired any, than to do the will of His Father, which He called His meat and food.[2] I take this example. If there present itself to a man the pleasure of listening to things that tend not to the service and honour of God, let him not desire that pleasure, nor desire to listen to them; and if there present itself the pleasure of looking at things that help him not Godward,[3] let him not desire the pleasure or look at these things; and if in conversation or in aught else soever such pleasure present itself, let him act likewise. And similarly with respect to all the senses, in so far as he can fairly avoid the pleasure in question; if he cannot, it suffices that, although these things may be present to his senses, he desire not to have this pleasure. And in this wise he will be able to mortify and void his senses of such pleasure, as though they were in darkness. If he takes care to do this, he will soon reap great profit.

---

[1] E.p. has 'care and affection' for 'desire.' [The word used for desire is *apetito*, which has been used in the past chapters for desires of sense (cf. p. 17, n. 5, above).]

[2] [St. John iv, 34.]

[3] E.p.: 'that lead him not Godward.'

5. For the mortifying and calming of the four natural passions, which are joy, hope, fear and grief, from the concord and pacification whereof come these and other blessings, the counsels here following are of the greatest help, and of great merit, and the source of great virtues.

6. Strive always to prefer, not that which is easiest, but that which is most difficult;

Not that which is most delectable, but that which is most unpleasing;

Not that which gives most pleasure, but rather that which gives least;[1]

Not that which is restful, but that which is wearisome;

Not that which is consolation, but rather that which is disconsolateness;

Not that which is greatest, but that which is least;

Not that which is loftiest and most precious, but that which is lowest and most despised;

Not that which is[2] a desire for anything, but that which is a desire for nothing;

Strive to go about seeking not the best of temporal things, but the worst.

Strive thus to desire to enter into complete detachment and emptiness and poverty, with respect to everything that is in the world, for Christ's sake.

7. And it is meet that the soul embrace these acts with all its heart and strive to subdue its will thereto. For, if it perform them with its heart, it will very quickly come to find in them great delight and consolation, and to act with order and discretion.

8. These things that have been said, if they be faithfully put into practice, are quite sufficient for entrance into the night of sense; but, for greater completeness, we shall describe another kind of exercise which teaches us to mortify the concupiscence of the flesh and the concupiscence of the eyes, and the pride of life, which, says Saint John,[3] are the things that reign in the world, from which all the other desires proceed.[4]

9. First, let the soul strive to work in its own despite, and desire all

---

[1] B, e.p.: 'that which gives none.' E.p. omits 'rather.'
[2] [Lit., 'Not that which is to desire anything, etc.']
[3] [1 St. John ii, 16.]
[4] E.p. abbreviates: 'which teaches us to mortify truly the desire for honour, whence originate many other [desires].'

to do so.[1] Secondly, let it strive to speak in its own despite and desire all to do so.[2] Third, let it strive to think humbly of itself, in its own despite, and desire all to do so.[3]

10. To conclude these counsels and rules, it will be fitting to set down here those lines which are written in the Ascent of the Mount,[4] which is the figure that is at the beginning of this book; the which lines are instructions for ascending to it, and thus reaching the summit of union. For, although it is true that that which is there spoken of is spiritual and interior, there is reference likewise to the spirit of imperfection according to sensual and exterior things, as may be seen by the two roads which are on either side of the path of perfection. It is in this way and according to this sense that we shall understand them here; that is to say, according to that which is sensual. Afterwards, in the second part of this night, they will be understood according to that which is spiritual.[5]

11. The lines are these:

In order to arrive at having[6] pleasure in everything,
Desire to have pleasure in nothing.
In order to arrive at possessing everything,
Desire to possess nothing.[7]
In order to arrive at being everything,
Desire to be nothing.
In order to arrive at knowing everything,
Desire to know nothing.
In order to arrive at that wherein thou hast no pleasure,
Thou must go by a way wherein thou hast no pleasure.
In order to arrive at that which thou knowest not,
Thou must go by a way that thou knowest not.
In order to arrive at that which thou possessest not,
Thou must go by a way that thou possessest not.
In order to arrive at that which thou art not,
Thou must go through that which thou art not.

[1] A, B, e.p.: 'others to do so.' A, B add: 'and this is against the concupiscence of the flesh.'

[2] A, B add: 'and this is against the concupiscence of the eyes.'

[3] A, B add: 'likewise against it; and this is against the pride of life.'

[4] A, B, C, D, e.p. have 'figure' for 'ascent.' The reference is to the diagram which is reproduced as the frontispiece to this volume. Cf. also p. xxxii, above.

[5] The Saint does not, however, allude to these lines again. The order followed below is that of Alc., which differs somewhat from that followed in the diagram.

[6] E.p.: 'to have.'

[7] [This line, like ll. 6, 8 of the paragraph, reads more literally: 'Desire not to possess (be, know) anything in anything.' It is more emphatic than l. 2.]

THE WAY NOT TO IMPEDE THE ALL

12.   When thy mind dwells upon anything,
Thou art ceasing to cast thyself upon the All.
For, in order to pass from the all to the All,
Thou hast to deny thyself[1] wholly[2] in all.
And, when thou comest to possess it wholly,
Thou must possess it without desiring anything.
For, if thou wilt have anything in having all,[3]
Thou hast not thy treasure purely in God.

13. In this detachment the spiritual soul finds its quiet and repose; for, since it covets nothing, nothing wearies it when it is lifted up, and nothing oppresses it when it is cast down, because it is in the centre of its humility; but, when it covets anything, at that very moment it becomes wearied.[4]

CHAPTER XIV

Wherein is expounded the second line of the stanza.[5]

Kindled in love with yearnings.

Now that we have expounded the first line of this stanza, which treats of the night of sense, explaining what this night of sense is, and why it is called night; and now that we have likewise described the order and manner which are to be followed for a soul to enter therein actively, the next thing to be treated in due sequence is its properties and effects, which are wonderful, and are described in the next lines of the stanza aforementioned, upon which I will briefly touch for the sake of expounding the said lines,[6] as I promised in the Prologue;[7] and I will then pass on at once to the second book, treating of the other part of this night, which is the spiritual.

2. The soul, then, says that, 'kindled in love with yearnings,' it passed through this dark night of sense and came out thence to the

---

[1] Thus Alc., A, B, C, D.   E.p. repeats: 'cast thyself.'
[2] [There is a repetition here which could only be indicated by translating 'all-ly.' So, too, in the next couplet.]
[3] [*Lit.*, 'anything in all.']   [4] A, B add: 'and tormented.'
[5] E.p.: 'of the above-mentioned stanza.'   [6] E.p. omits: 'for . . . lines.'
[7] This confirms our point (p. 19, n. 4, above) that the Saint considers the Argument as part of the Prologue. A and B omit the rest of this paragraph.

union of the Beloved. For, in order to conquer all the desires and to
deny itself the pleasures which it has in everything, and for which its
love and affection are wont to enkindle the will that it may enjoy them,
it would need to experience another and a greater enkindling by another
and a better love, which is that of its Spouse; to the end that, having
its pleasure set upon Him and deriving from Him its strength, it should
have courage and constancy to deny itself all other things with ease.
And, in order to conquer the strength of the desires of sense, it would
need, not only to have love for its Spouse, but also to be enkindled by
love and to have yearnings. For it comes to pass, and so it is, that with
such yearnings of desire the sensual nature is moved and attracted toward sensual things, so that, if the spiritual part be not enkindled with
other and greater yearnings for that which is spiritual, it will be
unable to throw off the yoke of nature[1] or to enter this night of sense,
neither will it have courage to remain in darkness as to all things,
depriving itself of desire for them all.

3. And the nature and all the varieties of these yearnings of love
which souls experience in the early stages of this road to union; and
the diligent means and contrivances which they employ in order to
leave their house, which is self-will, during the night of the mortification of their senses; and how easy, and even sweet and delectable,[2]
these yearnings for the Spouse make all the trials and perils of this
night to appear to them, this is not the place to describe, neither is such
description possible; for it is better to know and meditate upon these
things than to write of them. And so we shall pass on to expound the
remaining lines in the next chapter.

[1] [*Lit.*, 'to conquer the natural yoke.'] E.p. has: 'the sensual and material yoke.'
[2] E.p. omits: 'and delectable.'

CHAPTER XV

Wherein are expounded the remaining lines of the aforementioned stanza.[1]

. . . oh, happy chance!—
I went forth without being observed, My house being now at rest.

THESE lines take as a metaphor the miserable estate of captivity, a man's deliverance from which, when none of the gaolers[2] hinder his release, he considers a 'happy chance.' For the soul, on account of[3] original sin, is truly as it were a captive in this mortal body, subject to the passions and desires of nature, from bondage and subjection to which it considers its having gone forth without being observed as a 'happy chance'—having gone forth, that is, without being impeded or engulfed[4] by any of them.

2. For to this end the soul profited by going forth upon a 'dark night'—that is, in the privation of all pleasures and mortification of all desires, after the manner whereof we have spoken. And by its 'house being now at rest' is meant the sensual part, which is the house of all the desires, and is now at rest because they have all been overcome and lulled to sleep. For until the desires are lulled to sleep through the mortification of the sensual nature, and until at last the sensual nature itself is at rest from them, so that they make not war upon the spirit, the soul goes not forth to true liberty and to the fruition of union with its Beloved.

END OF THE FIRST BOOK[5]

---

[1] A has no chapter-heading, considering this chapter as the termination of the last.
[2] A, B have 'gaolers'; Alc., C, D, 'prisoners.' The first reading is the more apt, though we should not say that the second is inadmissible.
[3] [*Lit.*, 'after.']   [4] [*Lit.*, 'comprehended.']
[5] So end both the codices and e.p.

BOOK THE SECOND

OF THE 'ASCENT OF MOUNT CARMEL'[1]

Wherein is treated the proximate means of ascending to union with God, which is faith; and wherein therefore is described the second part of this night, which, as we said, belongs to the spirit, and is contained in the second stanza, which is as follows.[2]

STANZA THE SECOND

CHAPTER I[3]

In darkness and secure, By the secret ladder, disguised—oh, happy chance!—
In darkness and in concealment, My house being now at rest.

IN this second stanza the soul sings of the happy chance which it experienced in stripping the spirit of all spiritual imperfections and desires for the possession of spiritual things. This was a much greater happiness to it, by reason of the greater difficulty that there is in putting to rest this house of the spiritual part, and of being able to enter this interior darkness, which is spiritual detachment from all things, whether sensual or spiritual, and a leaning on pure faith[4] alone[5] and an ascent thereby to God. The soul here calls this a 'ladder,' and 'secret,' because all the rungs and parts of it[6] are secret and hidden from all sense and understanding. And thus the soul has remained in darkness as to all light[7] of sense and understanding, going forth beyond all

---

[1] So both Codices and e.p.

[2] E.p. abbreviates: 'Treats of the proximate means of attaining to union with God, which is faith, and of the second night of the spirit, contained in the second stanza.' It should be observed that the Saint calls this Second Book 'the second (spiritual) night' (e.g., on p. 74, below, and elsewhere).

[3] The chapter-headings vary considerably in the Codices and editions. B treats this chapter as an exposition and numbers from the next onward.

[4] E.p.: 'on living faith.'

[5] In parenthesis e.p. adds: 'and of this I am ordinarily speaking because I am dealing with persons who journey to perfection.'

[6] [*Lit.*, 'all the steps and articles that it has.']   [7] E.p.: 'all natural light.'

63

limits of nature and reason in order to ascend by this Divine ladder of faith, which attains[1] and penetrates even to the heights[2] of God. The soul says that it was travelling 'disguised,' because the garments and vesture[3] which it wears and its natural condition are changed into the Divine, as it ascends by faith. And it was because of this disguise that it was not recognized or impeded, either by time or by reason or by the devil; for none of these things can harm one that journeys in faith. And not only so, but the soul travels in such wise concealed and hidden and is so far from all the deceits of the devil that in truth it journeys (as it also says here) 'in darkness and in concealment'—that is to say, hidden from the devil, to whom the light of faith is more than darkness.

2. And thus the soul that journeys through this night, we may say, journeys in concealment and in hiding from the devil, as will be more clearly seen hereafter. Wherefore the soul says that it went forth 'in darkness and secure'; for one that has such happiness as to be able to journey through the darkness of faith, taking faith for his guide, like to one that is blind,[4] and leaving behind all natural imaginings and spiritual reasonings, journeys very securely, as we have said. And so the soul says furthermore that it went forth through this spiritual night, its 'house being now at rest'—that is to say, its spiritual and rational parts. When, therefore, the soul attains to union which is of God, its natural faculties are at rest, as are likewise its impulses and yearnings of the senses,[5] in its spiritual part. For this cause the soul says not here that it went forth with yearnings, as in the first night of sense. For, in order to journey in the night of sense, and to strip itself of that which is of sense, it needed yearnings of sense-love so that it might go forth perfectly; but, in order to put to rest the house of its spirit, it needs no more than denial[6] of all faculties and pleasures and desires of the spirit in pure faith. This attained, the soul is united with the Beloved in a union of simplicity and purity and love and similitude.

3. And it must be remembered that the first stanza, speaking of the sensual part, says that the soul went forth upon 'a dark night,' and

---

[1] [*Lit.*, 'climbs': the verb (*escala*) is identical with the noun 'ladder' (*escala*).]
[2] [*Lit.*, 'to the depths.']　　　[3] Only Alc. has: 'vesture.'
[4] [The literal translation is shorter, viz. 'taking faith for a blind man's guide.']
[5] Alc. omits: 'of the senses.'
[6] [*Lit.*, 'negation.'] This is the reading of Alc. 'Affirmation' is found in A, B, C, D, e.p. Though the two words are antithetical, they express the same underlying concept. [The affirmation, or establishment, of all the powers and desires of the spirit upon pure faith, so that they may be ruled by pure faith alone, is equivalent to the denial, or negation, of those powers and desires in so far as they are not ruled by pure faith.]

here, speaking of the spiritual part, it says that it went forth 'in darkness.' For the darkness of the spiritual part is by far the greater, even
as darkness is a greater obscurity than that of night. For, however dark
a night may be, something can always be seen, but in true darkness
nothing can be seen; and thus in the night of sense there still remains
some light, for the understanding and reason remain, and are not
blinded. But this spiritual night, which is faith, deprives the soul of
everything, both as to understanding and as to sense. And for this
cause the soul in this night says that it was journeying 'in darkness and
secure,' which it said not in the other. For, the less the soul works
with its own ability, the more securely it journeys, because it journeys
more in faith. And this will be expounded at length in the course of
this second book, wherein it will be necessary for the devout reader to
proceed attentively,[1] because there will be said herein things of great
importance to the person that is truly spiritual.[2] And, although they
are somewhat obscure, some of them will pave the way to others, so
that I believe they will all be quite clearly understood.

CHAPTER II

Which begins to treat of the second part or cause of this night, which is
faith. Proves by two arguments how it is darker than the first and than the
third.

WE now go on to treat of the second part of this night, which
is faith; this is the wondrous means[3] which, as we said, leads
to the goal, which is God, Who, as we said,[4] is also to the
soul, naturally, the third cause or part of this night. For faith, which is
the mean,[5] is compared with midnight. And thus we may say that it is
darker for the soul either than the first part or, in a way, than the third;
for the first part, which is that of sense, is compared to the beginning
of night, or the time when sensible objects can no longer be seen, and
thus it is not so far removed from light as is midnight. The third part,
which is the period preceding the dawn, is quite close to the light of
day, and it, too, therefore, is not so dark as midnight; for it is now close

---

[1] So e.p. The clause 'wherein . . . attentively' is omitted in A, B, C, D. Alc. reads:
'wherein I request the benevolent attention of the devout reader.'
[2] [*Lit.*, 'to true spirit.'] A, B end the chapter here.
[3] E.p. has 'manner' for 'means.'   [4] [I, ii: p. 19, above.]
[5] [Cf. p. 19, n. 11, above.]

to the enlightenment and illumination of the light[1] of day, which is compared with God. For, although it is true, if we speak after a natural manner, that God is as dark a night to the soul as is faith, still, when these three parts of the night are over, which are naturally night to the soul, God begins to illumine the soul by supernatural means with the ray of His Divine light;[2] which is the beginning of the perfect union that follows, when the third night is past, and it can thus be said to be less dark.[3]

2. It is likewise darker than the first night, for this belongs to the lower part of man, which is the sensual part, and, consequently, the more exterior; and this second part, which is of faith, belongs to the higher part of man, which is the rational part, and, in consequence, more interior and more obscure, since it deprives it of the light of reason, or, to speak more clearly, blinds it;[4] and thus it is aptly compared to midnight, which is the depth of night and the darkest part thereof.

3. We have now to prove how this second part, which is faith, is night to the spirit, even as the first part is night to sense. And we shall then also describe the things that are contrary to it, and how the soul must prepare itself actively to enter it. For, concerning the passive part, which is that which God works in it, when He brings it into that night, we shall speak in its place, which I intend shall be the third book.[5]

[1] So Alc.   A, B, e.p.: 'of the brightness.'
[2] E.p. adds these words, which occur in none of the codices: 'and in a loftier, higher and more experimental manner.'
[3] A, B: 'to be dark.'
[4] This was another of the propositions which were cited by those who denounced the writings of St. John of the Cross to the Holy Office. It is interpretable, nevertheless, in a sense that is perfectly true and completely in conformity with Catholic doctrine. The Saint does not, in these words, affirm that faith destroys nature or quenches the light of human reason (St. Thomas, *Summa*, Pt. I, q. 1, a. 8, *et alibi*); what he endeavours to show is that the coming of knowledge through faith excludes a simultaneous coming of natural knowledge through reason. It is only in this way that, in the act of faith, the soul is deprived of the light of reason, and left, as it were, in blindness, so that it may be raised to another nobler and sublimer kind of knowledge, which, far from destroying reason, gives it dignity and perfection. Philosophy teaches that the proper and connatural object of the understanding, in this life, is things visible, material and corporeal. By his nature, man inclines to knowledge of this kind, but cannot lay claim to such knowledge as regards the things which belong to faith. For, to quote a famous verse of Scripture: *Fides est sperandarum substantia rerum, argumentum non apparientium* (Hebrews xi, 1). This line of thought is not confined to St. John of the Cross, but is followed by all the mystics and is completely in agreement with theological doctrine. Cf. *Respuesta* [Reply] of P. Basilio Ponce de León and *Dilucidatio*, Pt. II, Chap. ii, and also the following chapter in this present book.
[5] Here end Alc. and e.p.   A, B add: 'as we have already spoken and promised to speak of the passive [part] of the first [night] in the second [book].' The subject in question is actually treated in the *Dark Night of the Soul*.

CHAPTER III

How faith is dark night to the soul. This is proved with arguments and quotations and figures from Scripture.[1]

FAITH, say the theologians, is a habit of the soul, certain and obscure. And the reason for its being an obscure habit is that it makes us believe truths revealed by God Himself, which transcend all natural light, and exceed all human understanding, beyond all proportion.[2] Hence it follows that, for the soul, this excessive light of faith which is given to it is thick darkness, for it overwhelms greater things and does away with smaller things, even as the light of the sun overwhelms all other lights whatsoever, so that when it shines and disables our visual faculty they appear not to be lights at all. So that it blinds it and deprives it of the sight that has been given to it, inasmuch as its light is great beyond all proportion and transcends the faculty of vision. Even so the light of faith, by its excessive greatness, oppresses and disables that of the understanding;[3] for the latter, of its own power, extends only to natural knowledge, although it has a faculty[4] for the supernatural, whenever Our Lord is pleased to give it supernatural activity.

2. Wherefore a man can know nothing by himself, save after a natural manner,[5] which is only that which he attains by means of the senses. For this cause he must have the phantasms and the forms[6] of objects present in themselves and in their likenesses;[7] otherwise it

---

[1] A, B omit this sentence.   [2] E.p. omits: 'beyond all proportion.'
[3] E.p.: 'by its excessive greatness and by the way wherein God communicates it, transcends that of our understanding.'
[4] E.p.: 'an obediential faculty' [*potencia obediencial*] : this phrase is borrowed from the Schoolmen. Among the various divisions of the faculty are two, natural and obediential. The first is that which is directed towards an act within the sphere of nature, such as the cooling action of water and the heating action of fire; the second is directed towards an act which exceeds these powers, brought about by God, Who is outside the laws of nature and can therefore work outside the natural domain. This obediential faculty (called also 'receptive' or 'passive') frequently figures in mystical theology, since it is this that disposes the faculties of the soul for the supernatural reception of the gifts of grace, all of which exceed natural capacity.
[5] E.p.: 'a natural manner which has its beginning in the senses.' Here the Saint expounds a principle of scholastic philosophy summarized in the axiom: *Nihil est in intellectu quin prius non fuerit in sensu*. This principle, like many other great philosophical questions, has continually been debated. St. John of the Cross will be found as a rule to follow the philosophy most favoured by the Church and is always rigidly orthodox.
[6] E.p.: 'the phantasms and senses.'
[7] E.p. uses *semejanzas*, the abstract noun; the Codices have *semejantes* [a word which can be either abstract or concrete, in the latter case with the sense of 'fellow-creatures'].

cannot be, for, as philosophers say: *Ab objecto et potentia paritur notitia.*
That is: From the object that is present and from the faculty, knowledge is born in the soul. Wherefore, if one should speak to a man of
things which he has never been able to understand, and whose likeness
he has never seen, he would have no more illumination from them
whatever than if naught had been said of them to him. I take an
example. If one should say to a man that on a certain island there is an
animal which he has never seen, and give him no idea of the likeness
of that animal, that he may compare it with others that he has seen, he
will have no more knowledge of it, or idea of its form, than he had
before, however much is being said to him about it. And this will be
better understood by another and a more apt example. If one should
describe to a man that was born blind, and has never seen any colour,
what is meant by a white colour or by a yellow, he would understand
it but indifferently, however fully one might describe it to him; for, as
he has never seen such colours or anything like them by which he may
judge them, only their names would remain with him; for these he
would be able to comprehend through the ear, but not their forms or
figures, since he has never seen them.

3. Even so[1] is faith with respect to the soul; it tells us of things
which we have never seen or understood, nor have we seen or understood aught that resembles them, since there is naught that resembles
them at all.[2] And thus we have no light of natural knowledge concerning them, since that which we are told of them bears no relation to any
sense of ours; we know it by the ear alone, believing that which we are
taught, bringing our natural light into subjection and treating it as if it
were not.[3] For, as Saint Paul says, *Fides ex auditu.*[4] As though he were
to say: Faith is not knowledge which enters by any of the senses, but is
only the consent given by the soul to that which enters[5] through the ear.

4. And faith far transcends even that which is indicated by the
examples given above. For not only does it give no information and
knowledge,[6] but, as we have said, it deprives us of all other information and knowledge, and blinds us to them, so that they cannot judge
it well.[7] For other knowledge can be acquired by the light of the

---

[1] E.p. adds in parenthesis: 'though the equivalence is not exact.'
[2] E.p.: 'aught that resembles them, which might bring us to a knowledge of them
without revelation.'
[3] [*Lit.,* 'subjecting and blinding our natural light.']
[4] Romans x, 17.   [5] E.p.: 'but is superior light which enters.'
[6] E.p.: 'no evidence or knowledge.'
[7] E.p.: 'but, as we have said, it surpasses and transcends any other knowledge and
science, so that we may only judge of it in perfect contemplation.'

understanding; but the knowledge that is of faith is acquired without the illumination of the understanding, which is rejected for faith; and in its own light, if that light be not darkened, it is lost. Wherefore Isaias said: *Si non credideritis, non intelligetis.*[1] That is: If ye believe not, ye shall not understand. It is clear, then, that faith is dark night for the soul, and it is in this way that it gives it light; and the more the soul is darkened, the greater is the light that comes to it. For it is by blinding that it gives light, according to this saying of Isaias. For if ye believe not, ye shall not (he says) have light.[2] And thus faith was foreshadowed by that cloud which divided the children of Israel and the Egyptians when the former were about to enter the Red Sea, whereof Scripture says: *Erat nubes tenebrosa, et illuminans noctem.*[3] This is to say that that cloud was full of darkness and gave light to the night.

5. A wondrous thing it is that, though it was dark, it should give light to the night. This was said to show that faith, which is a black and dark cloud to the soul (and likewise is night, since in the presence of faith the soul is deprived of its natural light and is blinded), can with its darkness give light and illumination to the darkness of the soul, for it was fitting that the disciple should thus be like the master. For man, who is in darkness, could not fittingly be enlightened save by other darkness, even as David teaches us, saying: *Dies diei eructat verbum et nox nocti indicat scientiam.*[4] Which signifies: Day unto day uttereth and aboundeth in speech, and night unto night showeth knowledge. Which, to speak more clearly, signifies: The day, which is God in bliss, where it is day to the blessed angels and souls who are now day, communicates and reveals[5] to them the Word, which is His Son, that they may know Him and enjoy Him. And the night, which is faith in the Church Militant, where it is still night, shows knowledge to the Church, and consequently to every soul, which knowledge is night to it, since it is without[6] clear beatific wisdom; and, in the presence of faith, it is blind as to its natural light.

6. So that which is to be inferred from this is that faith, because it is dark night, gives light to the soul, which is in darkness, that there

[1] Isaías vii, 9. So Alc. The passage seems to be taken from the Septuagint. [The Vulgate has *non permanebitis*.]
[2] [*Lit.,* 'If ye believe not, that is, ye shall not have light.'] E.p. evidently found this not clear, for it expands the sentence thus: For if ye believe not—that is, if ye blind not yourselves—ye shall not understand—that is, ye shall not have light and knowledge both lofty and supernatural.
[3] Exodus xiv, 20.   [4] Psalm xviii, 3 [A.V., xix, 2].
[5] Thus e.p. modifies the reading of the codices [followed by P. Silverio]: 'and pronounces.'
[6] E.p.: 'since it does not yet enjoy.'

may come to be fulfilled[1] that which David likewise says to this purpose, in these words: *Et nox illuminatio mea in deliciis meis*.[2] Which signifies: The night will be my illumination in my delights. Which is as much as to say: In the delights of my pure contemplation and union with God, the night of faith shall be my guide. Wherein he gives it clearly to be understood[3] that the soul must be in darkness in order to have light for this road.[4]

CHAPTER IV

Treats in general of how the soul likewise must be in darkness, in so far as this rests with itself, to the end that it may be effectively guided by faith to the highest contemplation.

IT is now, I think, becoming clear how faith is dark night to the soul, and how the soul likewise must be dark, or in darkness as to its own light,[5] so that it may allow itself to be guided by faith to this high goal of union. But, in order that the soul may be able to do this, it will now be well to continue describing, in somewhat greater detail, this darkness which it must have, in order that it may enter into this abyss of faith. And thus in this chapter I shall speak of it in a general way; and hereafter, with the Divine favour, I shall continue to describe more minutely the way in which the soul is to conduct itself that it may neither stray therein nor impede this guide.

2. I say, then, that the soul, in order to be effectively guided to this state by faith, must not only be in darkness with respect to that part that concerns the creatures and temporal things, which is the sensual and the lower part (whereof we have already treated), but that likewise it must be blinded and darkened according to the part which has respect to God and to spiritual things, which is the rational and higher part,[6] whereof we are now treating. For, in order that one may attain supernatural transformation, it is clear that he must be plunged into darkness and carried far away from all contained in his nature[7] that is sensual and rational. For the word supernatural means that which soars

---

[1] E.p.: 'that there may come and may be fulfilled.'
[2] Psalm cxxxviii, 11 [A.V., cxxxix, 11].
[3] E.p. abbreviates: 'Giving it to be understood.'
[4] E.p.: 'in order to have light and to be able to walk on this road.'
[5] A, e.p.: 'its own natural light.'
[6] Alc. alone reads: 'the reason and the higher part.'
[7] E.p.: 'all belonging to his nature.'

above the natural; the natural self, therefore, remains beneath it. For, although this transformation and union is something that cannot be comprehended by human ability and sense, the soul must completely and voluntarily void itself of all that can enter into it,[1] whether from above or from below—I mean according to the affection and will—so far as this rests with itself. For who shall prevent God from doing that which He will in the soul that is resigned, annihilated and detached? But the soul must be voided of all such things as can enter[2] its capacity, so that,[3] however many supernatural experiences it may have, it will ever remain as it were detached from them and in darkness. It must be like to a blind man, leaning upon dark faith, taking it for guide and light, and leaning upon none of the things that he understands, experiences, feels and imagines. For all these are darkness, which will cause him to stray; and faith is above all that he understands and experiences and feels and imagines. And, if he be not blinded as to this, and remain not in total darkness,[4] he attains not to that which is greater —namely, that which is taught by faith.

3. A blind man, if he be not quite blind, refuses to be led by a guide; and, since he sees a little, he thinks it better to go in whatever happens to be the direction which he can distinguish, because he sees none better; and thus he can lead astray a guide who sees more than he, for after all it is for him to say where he shall go rather than for the guide.[5] In the same way a soul may lean upon any knowledge of its own, or any feeling or experience of God, yet, however great this may be, it is very little and far different from what God is; and, in going along this road, a soul is easily led astray, or brought to a standstill, because it will not remain in faith like one that is blind, and faith is its true guide.

4. It is this that was meant by Saint Paul when he said: *Accedentem ad Deum oportet credere quod est.*[6] Which signifies: He that would journey towards union with God must needs believe in His Being. As though he had said: He that would attain to being joined in a union with God must not walk by understanding, neither lean upon experience or feeling or imagination, but he must believe in His Being,[7]

---

[1] So Alc. The other authorities have: 'that can be contained in it.' [The difference is slight: *caer* for *caber*.]

[2] The variant of the preceding note is repeated here.

[3] E.p. abbreviates: 'But the soul must be voided of all things, so that.'

[4] A, B, e.p. add: 'with respect to it.'

[5] E.p.: '. . . lead astray his guide, because he acts as if he saw and it is for him to say where he shall go rather than for the guide.'

[6] Hebrews xi, 6.

[7] E.p.: 'but he must believe in the perfection of the Divine Being.'

which is not perceptible to the understanding, neither to the desire nor to the imagination nor to any other sense, neither can it be known[1] in this life at all. Yea, in this life, the highest thing that can be felt and experienced concerning God is infinitely remote from God and from the pure possession of Him. Isaias and Saint Paul say: *Nec oculus vidit, nec auris audivit, nec in cor hominis ascendit, quæ præparavit Deus iis, qui diligunt illum.*[2] Which signifies: That which God hath prepared for them that love Him neither eye hath seen, nor ear heard, neither hath it entered into the heart or thought of man. So, however much the soul aspires to be perfectly united through grace in this life with that to which it will be united through glory in the next (which, as Saint Paul here says, eye hath not seen, nor ear heard, neither hath it entered into the heart of man in the flesh[3]), it is clear that, in order perfectly to attain to union in this life through grace and through love, a soul must be in darkness with respect to all that can enter through the eye, and to all that can be received through the ear, and can be imagined with the fancy, and understood with the heart, which here signifies the soul. And thus a soul is greatly impeded from reaching this high estate of union with God when it clings to any understanding or feeling or imagination or appearance or will or manner of its own, or to any other act or to anything of its own, and cannot detach and strip itself of all these. For, as we say, the goal which it seeks lies beyond all this, yea, beyond even the highest thing that can be known or experienced; and thus a soul must pass beyond everything to unknowing.

5. Wherefore, upon this road, to enter upon the road is to leave the road; or, to express it better, it is to pass on to the goal and to leave one's own way,[4] and to enter upon that which[5] has no way, which is God. For the soul that attains to this state has no longer any ways or methods, still less is it attached to ways and methods, or is capable of being attached to them. I mean ways of understanding, or of perception, or of feeling. Nevertheless it has within itself all ways, after the way of one that possesses nothing, yet possesses all things.[6] For, if it have courage to pass beyond its natural limitations, both interiorly and exteriorly, it enters within the limits of the supernatural,[7] which has no way, yet in substance[8] has all ways. Hence for the soul to arrive at these

---

[1] E.p.: 'known as it is.'   [2] Isaias lxiv, 4; 1 Corinthians ii, 9.
[3] A, B: 'heart of the flesh.'
[4] [The word translated 'way' is *modo*, which, in the language of scholastic philosophy, would rather be translated 'mode.']
[5] A, B: 'to enter upon the goal which . . .'   [6] [2 Corinthians vi, 10.]
[7] E.p.: 'it enters, without any limit, into the supernatural.'
[8] E.p. has 'eminently' for 'in substance.'

limits is for it to leave these limits, in each case going forth out of itself a great way, from this lowly state to that which is high above all others.

6. Wherefore, passing beyond all that can be known and understood, both spiritually and naturally,[1] the soul will desire with all desire to come to that which in this life cannot be known, neither can enter into its heart. And, leaving behind all that it experiences and feels, both temporally and spiritually,[2] and all that it is able to experience and feel in this life, it will desire with all desire to come to that which surpasses all feeling and experience. And, in order to be free and void to that end, it must in no wise lay hold upon that which it receives, either spiritually or sensually, within itself[3] (as we shall explain presently, when we treat this in detail), considering it all to be of much less account. For the more emphasis the soul lays upon what it understands, experiences and imagines, and the more it esteems this, whether it be spiritual or no, the more it loses of the supreme good, and the more it is hindered from attaining thereto. And the less it thinks of what it may have, however much this be, in comparison with the highest good, the more it dwells upon that good and esteems it, and, consequently, the more nearly it approaches it. And in this wise the soul approaches a great way towards union, in darkness, by means of faith, which is likewise dark, and in this wise faith wondrously illumines it. It is certain that, if the soul should desire to see, it would be in darkness much more quickly,[4] with respect to God, than would one who opens his eyes to look upon the great brightness of the sun.

7. Wherefore, by blinding itself in its faculties upon this road, the soul will see the light, even as the Saviour says in the Gospel, in this wise: *In judicium veni in hunc mundum: ut qui non vident, videant, et qui vident, cæci fiant.*[5] That is: I am come into this world for judgment; that they which see not may see, and that they which see may become blind. This, as it will be supposed, is to be understood of this spiritual road, where the soul that is in darkness,[6] and is blinded as regards all its natural and proper lights, will see supernaturally; and the soul that would depend upon any light of its own will become the blinder and will halt upon the road to union.

8. And, that we may proceed with less confusion, I think it will be

---

[1] E.p.: 'and temporally.'
[2] Thus Alc.   A, B have 'spiritually' only; e.p.: 'both spiritually and senusally.'
[3] [*Lit.*, 'either spiritually or sensually, in its soul.']
[4] A, B: 'it would be in much greater darkness.'
[5] St. John ix, 39.
[6] E.p. omits the quotation and its exposition, abbreviating thus: 'the soul will see the light, so that the soul that is in darkness . . .'

necessary to describe, in the following chapter, the nature of this that we call union of the soul with God; for, when this is understood, that which we shall say hereafter will become much clearer. And so I think the treatment of this union comes well at this point, as in its proper place. For, although the thread of that which we are expounding is interrupted thereby, this is not done without a reason, since it serves to illustrate in this place the very thing that is being described.[1] The chapter which follows, then, will be a parenthetical one, placed, as it were, between the two terms of an enthymeme,[2] since we shall afterwards have to treat in detail of the three faculties of the soul, with respect to the three theological virtues, in relation to this second night.

CHAPTER V

Wherein is described what is meant by union of the soul with God. A comparison is given.[3]

FROM what has been said above it becomes clear to some extent what we mean by union of the soul with God; what we now say about it, therefore, will be the better understood. It is not my intention here to treat of the divisions of this union, nor of its

---

[1] A, B end the chapter here.   [2] E.p. omits this phrase.

[3] As the Saint has explained above, this is a parenthetical chapter necessary to an understanding of the following chapters on the active purification of the three faculties of the soul; for, in order to make an intelligent use of the means to an end, it is important to know what that end is. St. John of the Cross begins by setting aside the numerous divisions under which the mystics speak of union with God and deals only with that which most usually concerns the soul, namely union which is active, and acquired by our own efforts, together with the habitual aid of grace. This is the kind of union which is most suitably described in this treatise, which deals with the intense activity of the soul as regards the purgation of the senses and faculties as a necessary means for the loving transformation of the soul in God—the end and goal of all the Saint's writings. In order to forestall any grossly erroneous pantheistic interpretations, we point out, with the author of the *Médula Mística* (Trat. V, Chap. i, No. 2), that by union the Saint understands 'a linking and conjoining of two things which, though united, are still different, each, as St. Thomas teaches (Pt. III, q. 2, a. 1), keeping its own nature, for otherwise there would not be union but identity. Union of the soul with God, therefore, will be a linking and conjoining of the soul with God and of God with the soul, for the one cannot be united with the other if the other be not united with the one, so that the soul is still the soul and God is still God. But just as, when two things are united, the one which has the most power, virtue and activity communicates its properties to the other, just so, since God has greater strength, virtue and activity than the soul, He communicates His properties to it and makes it, as it were, deific, and leaves it, as it were, divinized, to a greater or a lesser degree, corresponding to the greater or the lesser degree of union between the two.' This conception, which is a basic one in Christian mysticism, is that of St. John of the Cross. Had all his commentators understood that fact, some of them would have been saved from making ridiculous comparisons of him with Gnostics,

parts,[1] for I should never end if I were to begin now to explain what is the nature of union of the understanding, and what is that of union according to the will, and likewise according to the memory; and likewise what is transitory and what permanent in the union of the said faculties; and then what is meant by total union, transitory and permanent, with regard to the said faculties all together. All this we shall treat gradually in our discourse—speaking first of one and then of another. But here this is not to the point in order to describe what we have to say concerning them; it will be explained[2] much more fittingly in its place, when we shall again be treating the same matter, and shall have a striking illustration to add to the present explanation, so that everything will then be considered and explained and we shall judge of it better.

2. Here I treat only of this permanent and total union according to the substance of the soul and its faculties with respect to the obscure habit of union: for with respect to the act, we shall explain later, with the Divine favour, how there can be no permanent union in the faculties, in this life, but a transitory union only.

3. In order, then, to understand what is meant by this union whereof we are treating, it must be known that God dwells and is present substantially in every soul, even in that of the greatest sinner in the world. And this kind of union[3] is ever wrought between God and all the creatures, for in it He is preserving their being: if union of this kind were to fail them, they would at once become annihilated and would cease to be. And so, when we speak of union of the soul with God, we speak not of this substantial union which is continually being wrought,[4] but of the union and transformation of the soul with God,[5] which is

Illuminists or even the Eastern seekers after Nirvana. Actually, this Saint and Doctor of the Church applies the tenets of Catholic theology to the union of the soul with God, presenting them in a condensed and vigorous form and keeping also to strict psychological truth, as in general do the other Spanish mystics. This is one of his greatest merits. In this chapter he is speaking, not of essential union, which has nothing to do with his subject, but (presupposing the union worked through sanctifying grace received in the substance of the soul, which is the source of the infused virtues, such as faith, hope and charity, and the gifts of the Holy Spirit) of active actual union, after which we can and should strive, so that we may will what God wills and abhor what He abhors. Though not the only kind of union, it is this which chiefly concerns the soul; and, when once this is attained, God readily grants all other mystical gifts. Cf. St. Teresa's *Interior Castle*, V, iii [*C.W.S.T.J.*, II, 259–60].

1 Only Alc., A, B have: 'nor of its parts.'

2 E.p. abbreviates: 'And it is not now our intention to explain in detail what is the union of the understanding, what is that of the will, and what likewise is that of the memory; and what is transitory and what permanent in the said faculties, for this we shall treat hereafter and it will be explained . . .'

3 E.p. adds: 'or presence (which we may describe as being in the order of nature).'

4 E.p.: 'we speak not of this presence of God which ever exists in all the creatures.'

5 E.p. adds: 'through love.'

not being wrought continually, but only when there is produced that likeness that comes from love; we shall therefore term this the union of likeness, even as that other union is called substantial or essential. The former is natural; the latter supernatural. And the latter comes to pass when the two wills—namely that of the soul and that of God—are conformed together in one, and there is naught in the one that is repugnant to the other. And thus, when the soul rids itself totally of that which is repugnant to the Divine will and conforms not with it, it is transformed in God through love.

4. This is to be understood of that which is repugnant, not only in action, but likewise in habit, so that not only must the voluntary acts of imperfection cease, but the habits of any such imperfections must be annihilated.[1] And since no creature whatsoever, and none of its actions or abilities, can conform or can attain to that which is God, therefore must the soul be stripped of all things created, and of its own actions and abilities—namely, of its understanding, perception and feeling—so that, when all that is unlike God and unconformed to Him is cast out, the soul may receive the likeness of God; and nothing will then remain in it that is not the will of God and it will thus be transformed in God. Wherefore, although it is true that, as we have said, God is ever in the soul, giving it, and through His presence conserving within it, its natural being, yet He does not always communicate supernatural being to it. For this is communicated only by love and grace, which not all souls possess; and all those that possess it have it not in the same degree; for some have attained more degrees of love and others fewer. Wherefore God communicates Himself most to that soul that has progressed farthest in love; namely, that has its will in closest conformity with the will of God. And the soul that has attained complete conformity and likeness of will is totally united and transformed in God supernaturally. Wherefore, as has already been explained, the more completely a soul is wrapped up in[2] the creatures and in its own abilities, by habit and affection, the less preparation it has for such union; for it gives not God a complete opportunity to transform it supernaturally. The soul, then, needs only to strip itself of these natural dissimilarities and contrarieties, so that God, Who is communicating Himself naturally to it, according to the course of nature, may communicate Himself to it supernaturally, by means of grace.[3]

---

[1] E.p. abbreviates: 'but also the habits.'   [2] [*Lit.*, 'is clothed with.']
[3] E.p. reads: 'The soul, then, needs to strip itself of these natural dissimilarities and contrarieties, so that God, Who is naturally present in it by means of essence, may communicate Himself supernaturally to it by means of grace, in the transformation of union.'

5. And it is this that Saint John desired to explain when he said: *Qui non ex sanguinibus, neque ex voluntate carnis, neque ex voluntate viri, sed ex Deo nati sunt.*[1] As though he had said: He gave power to be sons of God—that is, to be transformed in God—only to those who are born, not of blood—that is, not of natural constitution and temperament— neither of the will of the flesh—that is, of the free will of natural capacity and ability—still less of the will of man—wherein is included every way and manner of judging and comprehending with the under- standing. He gave power to none of these to become sons of God, but only to those that are born of God—that is, to those who, being born again through grace, and dying first of all to everything that is of the old man, are raised above themselves to the supernatural, and receive from God this rebirth and adoption, which transcends all that can be imagined. For, as Saint John himself says elsewhere: *Nisi quis renatus fuerit ex aqua, et Spiritu Sancto, non potest videre regnum Dei.*[2] This signifies: He that is not born again in the Holy Spirit will not be able to see this kingdom of God, which is the state of perfection; and to be born again in the Holy Spirit[3] in this life[4] is to have a soul most like to God in purity, having in itself no admixture of imperfection, so that pure transformation can be wrought in it through participation of union, albeit not essentially.

6. In order that both these things may be the better understood, let us make a comparison. A ray of sunlight is striking a window. If the window is in any way stained or misty, the sun's ray will be unable to illumine it and transform it into its own light, totally, as it would if it were clean of all these things, and pure; but it will illumine it to a lesser degree, in proportion as it is less free from those mists and stains; and will do so to a greater degree, in proportion as it is cleaner from them,[5] and this will not be because of the sun's ray, but because of itself; so much so that, if it be wholly pure and clean, the ray of sun- light will transform it and illumine it in such wise that it will itself seem to be a ray and will give the same light as the ray. Although in reality the window has a nature distinct from that of the ray itself, however much it may resemble it, yet we may say that that window is a ray of the sun or is light by participation. And the soul is like this window, whereupon is ever beating (or, to express it better, wherein is ever

---

[1] St. John i, 13.   [2] St. John iii, 5.
[3] E.p. omits the whole of the first part of this paragraph, beginning thus: 'For the estate of perfection and re-birth in the Holy Spirit . . .'
[4] A, B: 'in this life perfectly.'
[5] E.p. omits: 'and will . . . from them.'

dwelling) this Divine light of the Being of God according to nature, which we have described.

7. In thus allowing God to work in it, the soul (having rid itself of every mist and stain of the creatures, which consists in having its will perfectly united with that of God, for to love is to labour to detach and strip itself for God's sake of all that is not God) is at once illumined and transformed in God, and God communicates to it His supernatural Being, in such wise that it appears to be God Himself, and has all that God Himself has. And this union comes to pass when God grants the soul this supernatural favour,[1] that all the things of God and the soul are one in participant transformation; and the soul seems to be God rather than a soul, and is indeed God by participation; although it is true that its natural being, though thus transformed, is as distinct from the Being of God as it was before, even as the window has likewise a nature distinct from that of the ray, though the ray gives it brightness.

8. This makes it clearer that the preparation of the soul for this union, as we said, is not that it should understand or perceive or feel or imagine anything, concerning either God or aught else, but that it should have purity and love—that is, perfect resignation and detachment from everything for God's sake alone;[2] and, as there can be no perfect transformation if there be not perfect purity, and as the enlightenment, illumination and union of the soul with God will be according to the proportion of its purity, in greater or in less degree; yet the soul will not be perfect, as I say, if it be not wholly and perfectly[3] bright and clean.

9. This will likewise be understood by the following comparison. A picture is truly perfect, with many and most sublime beauties and delicate and subtle illuminations, and some of its beauties are so fine and subtle[4] that they cannot be completely realized, because of their delicacy and excellence. Fewer beauties and less delicacy will be seen in this picture by one whose vision is less clear and refined; and he whose vision is somewhat more refined will be able to see in it more beauties and perfections; and, if another person has a vision still more refined, he will see still more perfection;[5] and, finally, he who has the clearest and purest faculties will see[6] the most beauties and perfections

---

[1] A, B, C, e.p. have: 'this sovereign favour.'
[2] E.p. modifies: 'that the preparation for this union is purity and love—that is, perfect resignation and total detachment, for God's sake alone.'
[3] [Lit., 'wholly perfect and . . .']   [4] E.p. omits 'and subtle.'
[5] E.p.: 'and he whose vision is more refined will be able to see greater beauties; and, if another person has a vision still more refined, he will be able to see still greater perfection.'   [6] E.p.: 'will be able to see.'

of all; for there is so much to see in the picture that, however far one may attain, there will ever remain higher degrees of attainment.

10. After the same manner we may describe the condition of the soul with relation to God in this enlightenment or transformation. For, although it is true that a soul, according to its greater or lesser capacity, may have attained to union, yet not all do so in an equal degree, for this depends upon what the Lord is pleased to grant to each one. It is in this way that souls see God in Heaven; some more, some less[1]; but all see Him, and all are content,[2] for their capacity is satisfied.

11. Wherefore, although in this life here below we find certain souls enjoying equal peace and tranquillity in the state of perfection, and each one of them satisfied, yet some of them may be many degrees higher than others. All, however, will be equally satisfied, because the capacity of each one is satisfied.[3] But the soul that attains not to such a measure of purity as is in conformity with its capacity[4] never attains true peace and satisfaction, since it has not attained to the possession of that detachment and emptiness in its faculties which is required for simple union.[5]

CHAPTER VI

Wherein is described how it is the three theological virtues that perfect the three faculties of the soul, and how the said virtues produce emptiness and darkness within them.[6]

HAVING now to endeavour to show how[7] the three faculties of the soul—understanding, memory and will—are brought into this spiritual night, which is the means to Divine union, it is necessary first of all to explain in this chapter how the three theological virtues—faith, hope and charity—which have respect to the three faculties aforesaid as their proper supernatural objects, and[8] by means

---

[1] E.p.: 'some more perfectly, some less so.'
[2] E.p.: 'content and satisfied.'
[3] E.p.: 'equally satisfied, each one according to his preparation and the knowledge that he has of God.'
[4] E.p.: 'to such a measure of purity as seems to be demanded by the enlightenment and vocation [that have been granted it] from God.'
[5] A, B: 'union with God.'
[6] E.p. adds: 'To this purpose are quoted two passages, one from Saint Luke and the other from Isaias.'
[7] [*Lit.*, 'to lead . . . into,' as at the beginning of § 6, below.]
[8] E.p. omits: 'which have . . . objects, and.'

whereof the soul is united with God according to its faculties, produce the same emptiness and darkness, each one in its own faculty. Faith, in the understanding; hope, in the memory; and charity, in the will. And afterwards we shall go on to describe how the understanding is perfected in the darkness of faith; and the memory in the emptiness of hope; and likewise how the will must be buried by[1] withdrawing and detaching every affection so that the soul may journey to God. This done, it will be clearly seen how necessary it is for the soul, if it is to walk securely on this spiritual road, to travel through this dark night, leaning upon these three virtues, which empty it of all things and make it dark with respect to them. For, as we have said, the soul is not united with God in this life through understanding, nor through enjoyment, nor through the imagination, nor through any sense whatsoever; but only through faith, according to the understanding; and through hope, according to the memory; and through love, according to the will.[2]

2. These three virtues, as we have said, all cause emptiness in the faculties: faith, in the understanding, causes an emptiness and darkness with respect to understanding; hope, in the memory, causes emptiness of all possessions; and charity causes emptiness in the will and detachment from all affection and from rejoicing in all that is not God. For, as we see, faith tells us what cannot be understood with the understanding.[3] Wherefore Saint Paul spoke of it *ad Hebræos* after this manner: *Fides est sperandarum substantia rerum, argumentum non apparentium.*[4] This we interpret as meaning that faith is the substance of things hoped for; and, although the understanding may be firmly and certainly consenting to them, they are not things that are revealed to the understanding, since, if they were revealed to it, there would be no faith. So faith, although it brings certainty to the understanding, brings it not clearness, but obscurity.

3. Then, as to hope, there is no doubt but that it renders the memory empty and dark with respect both to things below and to things above. For hope always relates to that which is not possessed; for, if it were possessed, there would be no more hope. Wherefore Saint Paul says

---

[1] So Alc., B [*enterrar*]. A, e.p. have [*entrar*, which changes the reading to] 'must enter into the withdrawal and detachment of.'

[2] E.p.: 'and through hope, which may be attributed to the memory (although it be in the will) with respect to the emptiness and forgetfulness of every other temporal and fleeting thing which it causes, the soul keeping itself entirely for the supreme good for which it hopes; and through love, according to the will.'

[3] E.p. adds: 'according to its natural light and reason.'

[4] Hebrews xi, 1.

ad Romanos: Spes, quæ videtur, non est spes: nam quod videt quis, quid sperat?[1] That is to say: Hope that is seen is not hope; for what a man seeth—that is, what a man possesseth—how doth he hope for it?[2] This virtue, then, also produces emptiness, for it has to do with that which is not possessed and not with that which is possessed.

4. Similarity, charity causes emptiness in the will with respect to all things, since it obliges us to love God above them all; which cannot be unless we withdraw our affection from them all in order to set it wholly upon God. Wherefore Christ[3] says, through Saint Luke : *Qui non renuntiat omnibus quæ possidet, non potest meus esse discipulus.*[4] Which signifies: He that renounces not all that he possesses with the will cannot be My disciple. And thus all these three virtues set the soul in obscurity and emptiness with respect to all things.

5. And here we must consider that parable which our Redeemer related in the eleventh chapter of Saint Luke, wherein He said that a friend had to go out at midnight in order to ask his friend for three loaves;[5] the which loaves signify these three virtues. And he said that he asked for them at midnight in order to signify that the soul that is in darkness as to all things must acquire these three virtues[6] according to its faculties and must perfect itself in them in this night. In the sixth chapter of Isaias we read that the two seraphim whom this Prophet saw on either side of God had each six wings; with two they covered their feet, which signified the blinding and quenching of the affections of the will with respect to all things for the sake of God; and with two they covered their face, which signified the darkness of the understanding in the presence of God; and with the other two they flew.[7] This is to signify the flight of hope to the things that are not possessed, when it is raised above all that it can possess, whether below or above, apart from God.

6. To these three virtues, then, we have to lead the three faculties of the soul, informing each faculty by each one of them, and stripping it and setting it in darkness[8] concerning all things save only these three virtues. And this is the spiritual night which just now we called active; for the soul does that which in it lies in order to enter therein. And

---

[1] Romans viii, 24.
[2] A, B: 'for if a man possesseth what he seeth, how doth he hope for it?'
[3] A, B: 'Christ our Lord,' as in several other places below.
[4] St. Luke xiv, 33.   [5] St. Luke xi, 5.   E.p. omits: 'his friend.'
[6] E.p.: 'must prepare itself for the perfection of these three virtues.'
[7] Isaias vi, 2.
[8] E.p.: 'informing the understanding by faith, stripping the memory of every possession and informing the will by charity, stripping them and setting them in darkness . . .'

even as, in the night of sense, we described a method of voiding the faculties of sense of their sensible objects, with regard to the desire, so that the soul might go forth from the beginning of its course to the mean,[1] which is faith; even so, in this spiritual night, with the favour of God, we shall describe a method whereby the spiritual faculties are voided and purified of all that is not God, and are set in darkness concerning these three virtues, which, as we have said, are the means and preparation for the union of the soul with God.

7. In this method is found all security against the crafts of the devil and against the efficacy[2] of self-love and its ramifications, which is wont most subtly to deceive and hinder spiritual persons on their road, when they know not how to become detached and to govern themselves according to these three virtues; and thus they are never able to reach the substance and purity of spiritual good, nor do they journey by so straight and short a road as they might.

8. And it must be noted that I am now speaking particularly to those who have begun to enter the state of contemplation, because as far as this concerns beginners it must be described somewhat more amply,[3] as we shall note in the second book, God willing, when we treat of the properties of these beginners.

CHAPTER VII

Wherein is described how strait is the way that leads to eternal[4] life and how completely detached and disencumbered must be those that will walk in it. We begin to speak of the detachment of the understanding.

WE have now to describe the detachment and purity of the three faculties of the soul and for this are necessary a far greater knowledge and spirituality than mine, in order to make clear to spiritual persons how strait is this road which, said Our Saviour, leads to life; so that, persuaded of this, they may not marvel at the emptiness and detachment to which, in this night, we have to abandon the faculties of the soul.

2. To this end must be carefully noted the words which Our

---

[1] [Or 'middle.' Cf. p. 19, n. 11, above.]   [2] E.p. reads 'craft' for 'efficacy.'
[3] So Alc.   A, B end the chapter here. E.p. omits the reference to the 'second book' as being inexact, and adds simply: '[more amply] when we treat of the properties of these beginners.'
[4] E.p. omits 'eternal.'

Saviour used, in the seventh chapter of Saint Matthew, concerning this road,[1] as follows: *Quam angusta porta, et arcta via est, quæ ducit ad vitam, et pauci sunt, qui inveniunt eam.*[2] This signifies: How strait is the gate and how narrow the way that leadeth unto life, and few there are that find it! In this passage we must carefully note the emphasis and insistence which are contained in that word *Quam*. For it is as if He had said: In truth the way is very strait, more so than you think. And likewise it is to be noted that He says first that the gate is strait, to make it clear that, in order for the soul to enter by this gate, which is Christ, and which comes at the beginning of the road, the will must first be straitened and detached in all things sensual and temporal, and God must be loved above them all; which belongs to the night of sense, as we have said.

3. He then says that the way is narrow—that is to say, the way of perfection—in order to make it clear that, to travel upon the way of perfection, the soul has not only to enter by the strait gate,[3] emptying itself of things of sense, but has also to straiten[4] itself, freeing and disencumbering itself completely in that which pertains to the spirit. And thus we can apply what He says of the strait gate to the sensual part of man; and what He says of the narrow road we can understand of the spiritual or the rational part; and, when He says 'Few there are that find it,' the reason of this must be noted, which is that there are few who can enter, and desire to enter, into this complete detachment and emptiness of spirit. For this path ascending the high mountain of perfection leads upward, and is narrow, and therefore requires travellers that have no burden weighing upon them with respect to lower things, neither aught that embarrasses them with respect to higher things; and, as this is a matter wherein we must seek after and attain to God alone, God alone must be the object of our search and attainment.

4. Hence it is clearly seen that the soul must not only be disencumbered from that which belongs to the creatures, but likewise, as it travels, must be annihilated and detached from all that belongs to its spirit. Wherefore Our Lord, instructing us and leading us into this road, gave, in the eighth chapter of Saint Mark, that wonderful teaching of which I think it may almost be said that, the more necessary it is

---

[1] E.p. adds: 'which [words] we shall now apply to this dark night and lofty road of perfection.'

[2] St. Matthew vii, 14.

[3] A alone reads: 'by the way of perfection, that is, by the strait gate.'

[4] [The Spanish verb, used also at the end of the preceding paragraph, is derived from the adjective.]

for spiritual persons, the less it is practised by them.[1] As this teaching is so important and so much to our purpose, I shall reproduce it here in full, and expound it according to its genuine, spiritual sense. He says, then, thus: *Si quis vult me sequi, deneget semetipsum: et tollat crucem suam, et sequatur me. Qui enim voluerit animam suam salvam facere, perdet eam: qui autem perdiderit animam suam propter me . . . salvam faciet eam.*[2] This signifies: If any man will follow My road, let him deny himself and take up his cross and follow Me. For he that will save his soul shall lose it; but he that loses it for My sake, shall gain it.

5. Oh, that one could show us how to understand, practise and experience what this counsel is which[3] our Saviour here gives us concerning self-denial,[4] so that spiritual persons might see in how different a way they should[5] conduct themselves upon this road from that which many of them think proper! For they believe that any kind of retirement and reformation of life suffices; and others are content with practising the virtues and continuing in prayer and pursuing mortification; but they attain not to detachment and poverty or selflessness[6] or spiritual purity (which are all one), which the Lord here commends to us; for they prefer feeding and clothing their natural selves with spiritual feelings and consolations,[7] to stripping themselves of all things, and denying themselves all things, for God's sake. For they think that it suffices to deny themselves worldly things without annihilating and purifying themselves of spiritual attachment. Wherefore it comes to pass that, when there presents itself to them any of this solid and perfect[8] spirituality, consisting in the annihilation of all sweetness in God, in aridity, distaste and trial, which is the true spiritual cross, and the detachment of the spiritual poverty of Christ, they flee from it as from death, and seek only sweetness and delectable communion with God. This is not self-denial and detachment of spirit, but spiritual gluttony. Herein, spiritually, they become enemies of the Cross of Christ; for true spirituality seeks for God's sake that which is distasteful rather than that which is delectable; and inclines itself rather to suffering than to consolation; and desires to go without all blessings

---

[1] The lines from this point to the Latin text are omitted by A and B.
[2] St. Mark viii, 34-5.
[3] E.p.: 'what is contained in this so lofty instruction which . . .'
[4] [*Lit.*, 'the denial of ourselves to our very selves.']
[5] A, B, e.p. have 'it behoves them to' for 'they should.'
[6] [*enagenación*, a word which to-day means 'alienation,' 'rapture,' 'derangement (of mind),' but in Covarrubias' dictionary (1611) is also defined as 'giving to another what is one's own.']
[7] E.p.: 'with consolations.'
[8] E.p. omits: 'and perfect.'

for God's sake rather than to possess them; and to endure aridities and afflictions rather than to enjoy sweet communications, knowing that this is to follow Christ and to deny oneself, and that the other is perchance to seek oneself in God, which is clean contrary to love.[1] For to seek oneself in God is to seek the favours and refreshments of God; but to seek God in oneself is not only to desire to be without both of these for God's sake, but to be disposed to choose, for Christ's sake, all that is most distasteful, whether in relation to God or to the world; and this is love of God.

6. Oh, that one could tell us how far Our Lord desires this self-denial to be carried! It must certainly be like to death and annihilation, temporal, natural and spiritual, in all things that the will esteems, wherein consists all self-denial.[2] And it is this that Our Lord meant when He said: 'He that will save his life, the same shall lose it.' That is to say: He that will possess anything or seek anything for himself, the same shall lose it; and he that loses his soul for My sake, the same shall gain it. That is to say: He who for Christ's sake renounces all that his will can desire and enjoy, and chooses that which is most like to the Cross (which the Lord Himself, through Saint John, describes as hating his soul[3]), the same shall gain it. And this His Majesty taught to those two disciples who went and begged Him for a place on His right hand and on His left; when, giving no countenance to their request for such glory, He offered them the chalice which He had to drink, as a thing more precious and more secure upon this earth than is fruition.[4]

7. This chalice is death to the natural self, a death attained through the detachment and annihilation of that self, in order that the soul may travel by this narrow path, with respect to all its connections with sense, as we have said, and according to the spirit,[5] as we shall now say; that is, in its understanding and in its enjoyment and in its feeling. And, as a result, not only has the soul made its renunciation as regards both sense and spirit, but it is not hindered, even by that which is spiritual, in taking the narrow way, on which there is room only for self-denial (as the Saviour explains), and the Cross, which is the staff wherewith one may reach one's goal,[6] and whereby the road is greatly

---

[1] A, B omit this last clause.
[2] So Alc., A, B, C, D.   E.p. has: 'all gain.' The gain, however [says P. Silverio], is rather a result of the complete self-denial of which the Saint is here speaking.
[3] St. John xii, 25.   [4] St. Matthew xx, 22.
[5] Thus e.p.   Alc., A, B [and P. Silverio] read 'soul' for 'spirit.'
[6] E.p.: 'the staff whereon to lean.'

lightened and made easy. Wherefore Our Lord said through Saint Matthew: 'My yoke is easy and My burden is light';[1] which burden is the cross. For if a man resolve to submit himself to carrying this cross —that is to say, if he resolve to desire in truth to meet trials and to bear them in all things for God's sake, he will find in them all great relief and sweetness wherewith he may travel upon this road, detached from all things and desiring nothing. Yet, if he desire to possess anything— whether it come from God or from any other source—with any feeling of attachment, he has not stripped and denied himself in all things; and thus he will be unable to walk along this narrow path or to climb upward by it.[2]

8. I would, then, that I could convince spiritual persons that this road to God consists not in a multiplicity of meditations nor in ways or methods of such, nor in consolations, although these things may in their own way be necessary to beginners; but that it consists only in the one thing that is needful, which is the ability to deny oneself truly, according to that which is without and to that which is within, giving oneself up to suffering for Christ's sake, and to total annihilation. For the soul that practises this suffering and annihilation will achieve all that those other exercises can achieve, and that can be found in them, and even more. And if a soul be found wanting in this exercise, which is the sum and root of the virtues, all its other methods are so much beating about the bush, and profiting not at all, although its meditations and communications may be as lofty as those of the angels.[3] For progress comes not save through the imitation of Christ, Who is the Way, the Truth and the Life, and no man comes to the Father but by Him, even as He Himself says through Saint John.[4] And elsewhere He says: 'I am the door; by Me if any man enter in he shall be saved.'[5] Wherefore, as it seems to me, any spirituality that would fain walk in sweetness and with ease, and flees from the imitation of Christ, is worthless.

9. And, as I have said that Christ is the Way, and that this Way is death to our natural selves, in things both of sense and of spirit, I will now explain how we are to die, following the example of Christ, for He is our example and light.

10. In the first place, it is certain that He died as to sense, spiritually, in His life, besides dying naturally, at His death. For, as He said, He

---

[1] St. Matthew xi, 30.   [2] E.p. omits 'upward.'
[3] E.p. has 'very lofty' and omits 'as those of the angels,' which is found, however, in all the Codices.
[4] St. John xiv, 6.   [5] St. John x, 9.

had not in His life where to lay His head, and at His death this was even truer.

11. In the second place, it is certain that, at the moment of His death, He was likewise annihilated[1] in His soul, and was deprived of any relief and consolation, since His Father left Him in[2] the most intense aridity, according to the lower part of His nature.[3] Wherefore He had perforce to cry out, saying: 'My God! My God! Why hast Thou forsaken Me?'[4] This was the greatest desolation, with respect to sense, that He had suffered in His life.[5] And thus He wrought herein[6] the greatest work that He had ever wrought, whether in miracles or in mighty works, during the whole of His life, either upon earth or in Heaven,[7] which was the reconciliation and union of mankind, through grace, with God. And this, as I say, was at the moment and the time when this Lord was most completely annihilated in everything. Annihilated, that is to say, with respect to human reputation; since, when men saw Him die,[8] they mocked Him rather than esteemed Him; and also with respect to nature, since His nature was annihilated when He died; and further with respect to the spiritual[9] consolation and protection of the Father, since at that time He forsook Him, that He might pay the whole of man's debt and unite him with God, being thus annihilated and reduced as it were[10] to nothing. Wherefore David says concerning Him: *Ad nihilum redactus sum, et nescivi.*[11] This he said that the truly spiritual man may understand the mystery of the gate and of the way of Christ, and so become united with God, and may know that, the more completely he is annihilated for God's sake, according to these two parts, the sensual and the spiritual, the more completely is he united to God and the greater is the work which he accomplishes. And when at last he is reduced to nothing, which will be the greatest extreme of humility, spiritual[12] union will be wrought between the soul and God, which in this life is the greatest and the highest state attainable. This consists not, then, in refreshment and in consolations and spiritual feelings, but in a living death of the Cross, both as to sense and as to spirit—that is, both inwardly and outwardly.

---

1 E.p.: 'He was likewise forsaken and, as it were, annihilated.'
2 E.p.: 'left Him without consolation and in.'
3 E.p. omits: 'according to . . . His nature.'
4 St. Matthew xxvii, 46.   5 E.p. omits this sentence.
6 E.p. has 'then' for 'herein.'
7 E.p. omits: 'either upon earth or in Heaven.'
8 E.p. adds: 'on a tree.'   9 E.p. omits 'spiritual.'
10 E.p.: 'and as though reduced, as it were.'
11 Psalm lxxii, 22 [A.V., lxxiii, 22].   12 E.p. omits 'spiritual.'

12. I will not pursue this subject farther, although I have no desire to finish speaking of it, for I see that Christ[1] is known very little by those who consider themselves His friends : we see them seeking in Him their own pleasures and consolations because of their great love for themselves, but not loving His bitter trials and His death because of their great love for Him. I am speaking now of those who consider themselves His friends; for such as live far away, withdrawn from Him, men of great learning and influence, and all others who live yonder, with the world, and are eager about their ambitions and their prelacies, may be said not to know Christ; and their end, however good, will be very bitter. Of such I make no mention in these lines; but mention will be made of them on the Day of Judgment, for to them it was fitting to speak first this word of God,[2] as to those whom God set up as a target for it,[3] by reason of their learning and their high position.

13. But let us now address the understanding of the spiritual man, and particularly that of the man to whom God has granted the favour of leading him into the state of contemplation (for, as I have said, I am now speaking to these in particular),[4] and let us say how such a man must direct himself toward God in faith, and purify himself from contrary things, constraining himself[5] that he may enter upon this narrow path of obscure contemplation.

CHAPTER VIII

Which describes in a general way how no creature and no knowledge that can be comprehended by the understanding can serve as a proximate means of Divine union with God.

BEFORE we treat of the proper and fitting means of union with God, which is faith, it behoves us to prove how no thing, created or imagined, can serve the understanding as a proper means of union with God; and how all that the understanding can attain serves

---

[1] E.p.: 'that Jesus Christ.'
[2] [The reference seems to be to Acts xiii, 46, the point of it being in the second part of that verse. The Spanish will also bear the interpretation: 'for them it behoved first (i.e., before others) to speak this word of God, as (being) those whom God set up as guides, etc.']
[3] [By this vivid phrase the author seems to mean: 'whom God held to be suitable recipients of it.']
[4] A, B omit the parenthesis.
[5] E.p. has 'girding' for 'constraining.'

it rather as an impediment than as such a means, if it should desire to cling to it. And now, in this chapter, we shall prove this in a general way, and afterwards we shall begin to speak in detail, treating in turn of all kinds of knowledge that the understanding may receive from any sense, whether inward or outward, and of the inconveniences and evils that may result from all these kinds of inward and outward knowledge,[1] when it clings not, as it progresses, to the proper means, which is faith.

2. It must be understood, then, that, according to a rule of philosophy, all means must be proportioned to the end; that is to say, they must have some connection and resemblance with the end, such as is enough and sufficient for the desired end to be attained through them. I take an example. A man desires to reach a city; he has of necessity to travel by the road, which is the means that brings him to this same city and connects[2] him with it. Another example.[3] Fire is to be combined and united with wood; it is necessary that heat, which is the means, shall first prepare the wood, by conveying to it so many degrees of warmth that it will have great resemblance and proportion to fire. Now if one would prepare the wood by any other than the proper means—namely, with heat—as, for example, with air or water or earth, it would be impossible for the wood to be united with the fire, just as it would be to reach the city without going by the road that leads to it.[4] Wherefore, in order that the understanding may be united with God in this life, so far as is possible,[5] it must of necessity employ that means that unites it with Him and that bears the greatest resemblance to Him.

3. Here it must be pointed out that, among all the creatures, the highest or the lowest, there is none that comes near to God or bears any resemblance to His Being. For, although it is true that all creatures have, as theologians say, a certain relation to God, and bear a Divine impress (some more and others less, according to the greater or lesser excellence of their nature), yet there is no essential resemblance or connection between them and God—on the contrary, the distance between their being and His Divine Being is infinite. Wherefore it is impossible for the understanding to attain to God[6] by means of the creatures, whether these be celestial or earthly, inasmuch as there is no proportion or resemblance between them. Wherefore, when David speaks of the heavenly creatures, he says: 'There is none among the

---

1 E.p.: 'kinds of knowledge.'
3 E.p. adds 'likewise.'
5 E.p. adds: 'in it' [i.e., in this life].

2 [*Lit.*, 'unites.']
4 E.p. omits: 'just as . . . leads to it.'
6 E.p. adds 'perfectly.'

gods like unto Thee, O Lord';[1] meaning by the gods the angels[2] and holy souls. And elsewhere: 'O God, Thy way is in the holy place. What God is there so great as our God?'[3] As though he were to say: The way of approach to Thee, O God, is a holy way—that is, the purity of faith. For what God can there be so great? That is to say: What angel will there be so exalted in his being, and what saint so exalted in glory, as to be a proportionate and sufficient road by which a man may come to Thee? And the same David, speaking likewise of earthly and heavenly things both together, says: 'The Lord is high and looketh on lowly things, and the high things He knoweth afar off.'[4] As though he had said: Lofty in His own Being, He sees that the being of things here below[5] is very low in comparison with His lofty Being;[6] and the lofty things, which are the celestial creatures, He sees and knows to be very far from His Being. All the creatures, then, cannot serve as a proportionate means to the understanding whereby it may reach God.[7]

4. Just so all that the imagination can imagine and the understanding can receive and understand in this life is not, nor can it be, a proximate means of union with God. For, if we speak of natural things, since understanding can understand naught save that which is contained within, and comes under the category of, forms and imaginings of things that are received through the bodily senses, the which things, we have said, cannot serve as means, it can make no use of natural intelligence. And, if we speak of the supernatural (in so far as is possible in this life of our ordinary faculties[8]), the understanding in its bodily prison has no preparation or capacity for receiving the clear knowledge of God; for such knowledge belongs not to this state, and we must either die or remain without receiving it. Wherefore Moses, when he entreated God for this clear knowledge, was told by God that he would be unable to see Him, in these words[9]: 'No man shall see Me and remain alive.'[10] Wherefore Saint John says: 'No man hath seen God at any time,[11] neither aught that is like to Him.' And Saint Paul says, with Isaias: 'Eye hath not seen Him, nor hath ear heard Him,

---

[1] Psalm lxxxv, 8 [A.V., lxxxvi, 8].   [2] E.p.: 'the holy angels.'
[3] Psalm lxxvi, 14 [A.V., lxxvii, 13] [*lit.*, 'in that which is holy'].
[4] Psalm cxxxvii, 6 [A.V., cxxxviii, 6].
[5] E.p.: 'of the things of the earth.'   [6] B omits this sentence.
[7] E.p.: '. . . means for perfectly reaching God.'
[8] These last four words are found only in Alc.
[9] E.p. abbreviates: '. . . receiving it. Wherefore God said to Moses: No man . . .'
[10] Exodus xxxiii, 20.
[11] St. John i, 18. E.p. omits 'neither . . . Him,' which is found in all the Codices.

neither hath it entered into the heart of man.'[1] And it is for this reason that, as is said in the Acts of the Apostles,[2] Moses, in the bush, durst not consider for as long as God was present; for he knew that his understanding could make no consideration that was fitting concerning God, corresponding to the sense which he had of God's presence.[3] And of Elias, our father,[4] it is said that he covered his face on the Mount in the presence of God[5]— an action signifying the blinding of his understanding, which he wrought there, daring not to lay so base a hand upon that which was so high, and seeing clearly that whatsoever he might consider or understand with any precision would be very far from God and completely unlike Him.

5. Wherefore no supernatural apprehension or knowledge in this mortal state can serve as a proximate means to the high union of love with God. For all that can be understood by the understanding, that can be tasted by the will, and that can be invented by the imagination is most unlike to God and bears no proportion to Him, as we have said. All this Isaias admirably explained in that most noteworthy passage,[6] where he says: 'To what thing have ye been able to liken God? Or what image will ye make that is like to Him? Will the workman in iron perchance be able to make a graven image? Or will he that works gold be able to imitate Him[7] with gold, or the silversmith with plates of silver?'[8] By the workman in iron is signified the understanding, the office of which is to form intelligences and strip them of the iron of species and images. By the workman in gold is understood the will, which is able to receive the figure and the form of pleasure, caused by the gold of love.[9] By the silversmith, who is spoken of as being unable to form[10] Him with plates of silver, is understood the memory, with the imagination, whereof it may be said with great propriety that its knowledge and the imaginings that it can invent[11] and make are like plates of silver. And thus it is as though he had said: Neither the understanding with its intelligence will be able to understand aught that is like Him, nor can the will taste pleasure and sweetness that bears any resemblance

---

[1] 1 Corinthians ii, 9; Isaias lxiv, 4.   [2] Acts vii, 32.

[3] E.p.: '. . . concerning God, though this sprang from the profound sense which he had of God['s presence].'

[4] Only Alc., C read: 'our father.'

[5] 3 Kings [A.V., 1 Kings] xix, 13.

[6] Alc. alone has: 'in that most noteworthy passage.'

[7] [Lit., 'feign Him.'] E.p.: 'figure Him' [or 'form Him']. A, B: 'make Him.'

[8] Isaias xl, 18-19.

[9] A, B, e.p.: '. . . gold of the love wherewith it loves.'

[10] [All authorities read 'form' (or 'figure') here. Cf. n. 7, above.]

[11] [This is the word (fingir, 'feign'), translated above as 'imitate.' Cf. n. 7, above.]

to that which is God, neither can the memory set in the imagination ideas and images that represent Him. It is clear, then, that none of these kinds of knowledge can lead the understanding direct to God; and that, in order to reach Him, a soul must rather proceed by not understanding than by desiring to understand; and by blinding itself and setting itself in darkness, rather than by opening its eyes, in order the more nearly to approach the ray Divine.

6. And thus it is that contemplation, whereby the understanding has the loftiest knowledge of God,[1] is called mystical theology, which signifies secret wisdom of God; for it is secret even to the understanding that receives it. For that reason Saint Dionysius calls it a ray of darkness. Of this the prophet Baruch says: 'There is none that knoweth its way, nor any that can think of its paths.[2]' It is clear, then, that the understanding must be blind to all the paths that are open to it in order that it may be united with God. Aristotle says that, even as are the eyes of the bat with regard to the sun, which is total darkness to it, even so is our understanding to that which is greater light in God, which is total darkness to us. And he says further that, the loftier and clearer are the things of God in themselves, the more completely unknown and obscure are they to us. This likewise the Apostle affirms, saying: 'The lofty things of God are the least known unto men.'[3]

7. But we should never end if we continued at this rate to quote authorities and arguments to prove and make clear that among all created things, and things that can be apprehended by the understanding, there is no ladder whereby the understanding can attain to this high Lord. Rather it is necessary to know that, if the understanding should seek to make use of all these things, or of any of them, as a proximate means to such union, they would be not only a hindrance, but even an occasion of numerous errors and delusions in the ascent of this mount.

[1] So Alc. All other authorities read: '. . . the understanding is enlightened by God.'
[2] Baruch iii, 23.
[3] [Possibly a further reference to I Corinthians ii, 9–10, quoted above.]

CHAPTER IX

How faith is the proximate and proportionate means to the understanding
whereby the soul may attain to the Divine union of love. This is proved
by passages and figures from Divine Scripture.[1]

FROM what has been said it is to be inferred that, in order for the
understanding to be prepared for this Divine union, it must be
pure and void of all that pertains to sense, and detached[2] and
freed from all that can clearly be apprehended by the understanding,
profoundly hushed and put to silence, and leaning upon faith, which
alone is the proximate and proportionate means whereby the soul is
united with God; for such is the likeness between itself and God that[3]
there is no other difference, save that which exists between seeing God
and believing in Him. For, even as God is infinite, so faith sets Him
before us as infinite; and, as He is Three and One, it sets Him before us
as Three and One; and, as God is darkness to our understanding, even
so does faith likewise blind and dazzle our understanding.[4] And thus,
by this means alone, God manifests Himself to the soul in Divine light,
which passes all understanding. And therefore, the greater is the faith
of the soul, the more closely is it united with God. It is this that Saint
Paul meant in the passage which we quoted above, where he says: 'He
that will be united with God must believe.'[5] That is, he must walk by
faith as he journeys to Him, the understanding being blind and in darkness, walking in faith alone;[6] for beneath this darkness the understanding is united with God, and beneath it God is hidden, even as David
said in these words: 'He set darkness under His feet. And He rose
upon the cherubim, and flew upon the wings of the wind. And He
made darkness, and the dark water, His hiding-place.'[7]

2. By his saying that He set darkness beneath His feet, and that He
took the darkness for a hiding-place, and that His tabernacle round
about Him was in the dark water, is denoted the obscurity of the faith
wherein He is concealed. And by his saying that He rose upon the
cherubim and flew upon the wings of the winds, is understood His

[1] This last sentence is found only in Alc. and in e.p.
[2] E.p. omits: 'and detached.'
[3] E.p. omits: 'such is . . . God that,' which is found in all the Codices.
[4] This clause ('and as God . . . our understanding') is omitted from e.p.
[5] Hebrews xi, 6.   [6] E.p. omits: 'It is this that St. Paul . . . in faith alone.'
[7] Psalm xvii, 10–12 [A.V., xviii, 9–11]. E.p. modifies thus: 'And He made darkness
His hiding-place; round about Him He set His tabernacle, which is dark water, among
the clouds of the air.'

soaring above all understanding. For the cherubim denote those who understand or contemplate. And the wings of the winds signify the subtle and lofty ideas and conceptions of spirits, above all of which is His Being, and to which none, by his own power, can attain.

3. This we learn from an illustration in the Scriptures. When Solomon had completed the building of the Temple, God came down in darkness and filled the Temple so that the children of Israel could not see; whereupon Solomon spake and said: 'The Lord hath promised that He will dwell in darkness.'[1] Likewise He appeared in darkness to Moses on the Mount, where God was concealed. And whensoever God communicated Himself intimately, He appeared in darkness, as may be seen in Job, where the Scripture says that God spoke with him from the darkness of the air.[2] All these mentions of darkness signify the obscurity of the faith wherein the Divinity is concealed, when It communicates Itself to the soul; which will be ended when, as Saint Paul says, that which is in part shall be ended,[3] which is this darkness of faith, and that which is perfect shall come, which is the Divine light. Of this we have a good illustration in the army of Gedeon, whereof it is said that all the soldiers had lamps in their hands, which they saw not, because they had them concealed in the darkness of the pitchers; but, when these pitchers were broken, the light was seen.[4] Just so does faith, which is foreshadowed by those pitchers, contain within itself Divine light;[5] which, when it is ended and broken, at the ending and breaking of this mortal life, will allow the glory and light of the Divinity, which was contained in it,[6] to appear.

4. It is clear, then, that, if the soul in this life is to attain to union with God, and commune directly with Him, it must unite itself with the darkness whereof Solomon spake, wherein God had promised to dwell, and must draw near to the darkness of the air wherein God was pleased to reveal His secrets to Job, and must take in its hands, in darkness, the jars of Gedeon, that it may have in its hands (that is, in the works of its will) the light, which is the union of love, though it be in the darkness of faith, so that, when the pitchers of this life are broken, which alone have kept from it the light of faith, it may see God[7] face to face in glory.

---

[1] 3 Kings [A.V., 1 Kings] viii, 12.   [2] Job xxxviii, 1; xl, 1.
[3] 1 Corinthians xiii, 10.   [4] Judges vii, 16.
[5] A, e.p. add: 'that is, the truth of that which God is in Himself.'
[6] E.p. omits: 'which was contained in it.'
[7] E.p. omits 'which . . . of faith' and inserts 'God,' which word is not found in the Codices.

5. It now remains to describe in detail all the types of knowledge and the apprehensions which the understanding can receive; the hindrance and the harm which it can receive upon this road of faith; and the way wherein the soul must conduct itself so that, whether they proceed from the senses or from the spirit, they may cause it, not harm, but profit.

CHAPTER X

Wherein distinction is made between all apprehensions and types of knowledge which can be comprehended by the understanding.

IN order to treat in detail of the profit and the harm which may come to the soul, with respect to this means to Divine union which we have described—namely, faith—through the ideas and apprehensions of the understanding, it is necessary here to make a distinction between all the apprehensions, whether natural or supernatural, that the soul may receive, so that then, with regard to each of them in order, we may direct the understanding with greater clearness into the night and obscurity of faith. This will be done with all possible brevity.

2. It must be known, then, that the understanding can receive knowledge and intelligence by two channels: the one natural and the other supernatural. By the natural channel is meant all that the understanding can understand, whether by means of the bodily senses or by its own power.[1] The supernatural channel is all that is given to the understanding over and above its natural ability and capacity.

3. Of these kinds of supernatural knowledge, some are corporeal and some are spiritual. The corporeal are two in number: some are received by means of the outward bodily senses; others, by means of the inward bodily senses, wherein is comprehended all that the imagination can comprehend,[2] form and conceive.

4. The spiritual supernatural knowledge is likewise of two kinds: that which is distinct and special in its nature, and that which is confused, general and dark. Of the distinct and special kind there are four manners of apprehension which are communicated to the spirit without the aid of any bodily sense: these are visions, revelations, locutions

---

[1] [*Lit.*, 'by itself.'] E.p. adds: 'after these [senses].' A, B read: 'or by the channel of itself.'
[2] E.p.: 'can apprehend.'

and spiritual feelings. The obscure and general type of knowledge is of one kind alone, which is contemplation that is given in faith. To this we have to lead the soul by bringing it thereto[1] through all these other means, beginning with the first and detaching it from them.

CHAPTER XI

Of the hindrance and harm that may be caused by apprehensions of the understanding which proceed from that which is supernaturally represented to the outward bodily senses; and how the soul is to conduct itself therein.

THE first kinds of knowledge whereof we have spoken in the preceding chapter are those that belong to the understanding and come through natural channels. Of these, since we have treated them already in the first book, where we led the soul into the night of sense, we shall here say not a word, for in that place we gave suitable instruction to the soul concerning them. What we have to treat, therefore, in the present chapter, will be solely those kinds of knowledge and those apprehensions which belong to the understanding and come supernaturally, by way of the outward bodily senses—namely, by seeing, hearing, smelling, tasting and touching. With respect to all these there may come, and there are wont to come,[2] to spiritual persons representations and objects of a supernatural kind.[3] With respect to sight, they are apt to picture figures and forms of persons belonging to the life to come—the forms of certain saints, and representations of angels, good and evil, and certain lights and brightnesses of an extraordinary kind. And with the ears they hear certain extraordinary words, sometimes spoken by those figures[4] that they see, sometimes without seeing the person who speaks them. As to the sense of smell, they sometimes perceive the sweetest perfumes with the senses, without knowing whence they proceed. Likewise, as to taste, it comes to pass that they are conscious of the sweetest savours, and, as to touch, they experience great delight[5]—sometimes to such a degree that it is as though all the bones and the marrow rejoice and sing[6] and are bathed in delight;[7]

---

[1] Alc. breaks off the chapter here.
[2] A, B, e.p. have 'happen [*acaecer*]' for 'come' [which in the Spanish is *nacer*, 'be born'],' both here and in the preceding clause.
[3] E.p.: 'and objects represented and set before them in a supernatural way.'
[4] E.p.: 'those persons.'
[5] E.p.: 'and, as to touch, of its own kind of enjoyment and sweetness.'
[6] [*Lit.*, 'and blossom.']   [7] E.p.: 'are bathed therein.'

this is like that which we call spiritual unction, which in pure souls[1] proceeds from the spirit and flows into the very members. And this sensible sweetness is a very ordinary thing with[2] spiritual persons, for it comes to them from their sensible affection and devotion,[3] to a greater or a lesser degree, to each one after his own manner.

2. And it must be known that, although all these things may happen to the bodily senses in the way of God, we must never rely upon them or accept them, but must always fly from them, without trying to ascertain whether they be good or evil; for, the more completely exterior and corporeal they are, the less certainly are they of God.[4] For it is more proper and habitual[5] to God to communicate Himself to the spirit, wherein there is more security and profit for the soul, than to sense, wherein there is ordinarily much danger and deception; for bodily sense judges and makes its estimate of spiritual things by thinking that they are as it feels them to be, whereas they are as different as is the body from the soul and sensuality[6] from reason. For the bodily sense is as ignorant of spiritual things as is a beast of rational things, and even more so.

3. So he that esteems such things errs greatly and exposes himself to great peril of being deceived; in any case he will have within himself a complete[7] impediment to the attainment of spirituality. For, as we have said, between spiritual things and all these bodily things there exists no kind of proportion whatever. And thus it may always be supposed that such things as these are more likely to be of the devil than of God; for the devil has more influence in that which is exterior and corporeal, and can deceive a soul more easily thereby than by that which is more interior and spiritual.

4. And the more exterior are these corporeal forms and objects in themselves, the less do they profit the interior and spiritual nature, because of the great distance and the lack of proportion existing between the corporeal and the spiritual. For, although there is communicated by their means a certain degree of spirituality, as is always the case with things that come from God, much less is communicated than would be the case if the same things were more interior and spiritual. And thus they very easily become the means whereby error

---

[1] E.p.: 'in simple souls.'   [2] E.p.: 'is wont to happen to.'
[3] [Lit., 'from the affection and devotion of the sensible spirit.']
[4] E.p.: 'the less certainty is there of their being of God.'
[5] E.p. omits: 'and habitual.'
[6] [P. Silverio remarks here that] we must understand [as frequently elsewhere] 'sensibility' and not sensuality in the grosser sense.
[7] E.p.: 'a great.'

and presumption and vanity grow in the soul; since, as they are so palpable and material, they stir the senses greatly, and it appears to the judgment of the soul that they are of greater importance because they are more readily felt. Thus the soul goes after them, abandoning faith and[1] thinking that the light which it receives from them is the guide and means to its desired goal, which is union with God. But the more attention it pays to such things, the farther it strays from the true way and means, which are faith.

5. And, besides all this, when the soul sees that such extraordinary things happen to it, it is often visited, insidiously and secretly by a certain complacency, so that it thinks itself to be of some importance in the eyes of God; which is contrary to humility. The devil, too, knows how to insinuate into the soul a secret satisfaction with itself, which at times becomes very evident; wherefore he frequently represents these objects to the senses, setting before the eyes figures of saints and most beauteous lights; and before the ears words very much dissembled; and representing also sweetest perfumes, delicious tastes[2] and things delectable to the touch; to the end that, by producing desires for such things, he may lead the soul into much evil. These representations and feelings, therefore, must always be rejected; for, even though some of them be of God, He is not offended by their rejection, nor is the effect and fruit which He desires to produce in the soul by means of them any the less surely received because the soul rejects them and desires them not.

6. The reason for this is that corporeal vision, or feeling in respect to any of the other senses, or any other communication of the most interior kind, if it be of God, produces its effect[3] upon the spirit at the very moment when it appears or is felt, without giving the soul time or opportunity to deliberate whether it will accept or reject it. For, even as God gives these things supernaturally, without effort[4] on the part of the soul, and independently of its capacity, even so likewise, without respect to its effort or capacity, God produces in it the effect that He desires by means of such things; for this is a thing that is wrought and brought to pass in the spirit passively;[5] and thus its acceptance or non-acceptance consists not in the acceptance or the rejection of it by the will. It is as though fire were applied to a person's

---

[1] E.p. omits: 'abandoning faith and.'

[2] [*Lit.*, 'and sweetnesses in the mouth.']   [3] E.p.: 'its first effect.'

[4] E.p.: 'For, even as God [i.e., His work] begins in these things supernaturally without active effort . . .'

[5] The 1630 edition adds: 'without its free consent.'

naked body: it would matter little whether or no he wished to be burned; the fire would of necessity accomplish its work. Just so is it with visions and representations that are good: even though the soul desire it not,[1] they work their effect upon it, chiefly and especially in the soul, rather than in the body. And likewise those that come from the devil (without the consent of the soul) cause it disturbance or aridity or vanity or presumption in the spirit. Yet these are not so effective to work evil as are those of God to work good; for those of the devil can only set in action the first movements of the will,[2] and move it no farther, unless the soul be consenting thereto; and such trouble continues not long unless the soul's lack of courage and prudence be the occasion of its continuance. But the visions that are of God penetrate the soul and move the will to love, and produce their effect,[3] which the soul cannot resist even though it would, any more than the window can resist the sun's rays when they strike it.

7. The soul, then, must never presume to desire to receive them, even though, as I say, they be of God; for, if it desire to receive them, there follow six inconveniences.

The first is that faith[4] grows gradually less; for things that are experienced by the senses derogate from faith; since faith, as we have said, transcends every sense. And thus the soul withdraws itself from the means of union with God when it closes not its eyes to all these things of sense.

Secondly, if they be not rejected, they are a hindrance to the spirit, for the soul rests in them and its spirit soars not to the invisible. This was one of the reasons why the Lord said to His disciples that it was needful for Him to go away that the Holy Spirit might come; so, too, He forbade Mary Magdalene to touch His feet, after His resurrection, that she might be grounded in faith.

Thirdly, the soul becomes attached to these things and advances not to true resignation and detachment of spirit.

Fourthly, it begins to lose the effect of them and the inward

---

[1] E.p. omits: 'even . . . not.'

[2] E.p.: 'for those of the devil stop at the first movements and cannot move the will.' This, no doubt, was the Saint's meaning, for the Church teaches that the devil cannot influence the will directly, though he may do so indirectly, principally through the senses and the imagination.

[3] E.p.: '. . . effect of excitement and overpowering delight, which makes ready and prepares [the soul] to give its free and loving consent to good.' It omits the rest of the paragraph as in the text and continues: 'But although these outward visions and feelings be of God, if the soul make much account of them and endeavour to desire to accept them, there follow six inconveniences. The first . . .'

[4] E.p.: 'that the perfection of guidance through faith.'

spirituality which they cause it, because it sets its eyes upon their sensual aspect, which is the least important. And thus it receives not so fully the spirituality which they cause,[1] which is impressed and preserved more securely when all things of sense are rejected, since these are very different from pure spirit.

Fifthly, the soul begins to lose the favours of God, because it accepts them as though they belonged to it and profits not by them as it should. And to accept them in this way and not to profit by them is to seek after them; but God gives them not that the soul may seek after them;[2] nor should the soul take upon itself to believe that they are of God.[3]

Sixthly, a readiness to accept them opens the door to the devil that he may deceive the soul by other things like to them, which he very well knows how to dissimulate and disguise, so that they may appear to be good; for, as the Apostle says, he can transform himself into an angel of light.[4] Of this we shall treat hereafter, by the Divine favour, in our third book, in the chapter upon spiritual gluttony.[5]

8. It is always[6] well, then, that the soul should reject these things, and close its eyes to them, whencesoever they come. For, unless it does so, it will prepare the way for those things that come from the devil, and will give him such influence that, not only will his visions come in place of God's, but his visions will begin to increase, and those of God to cease, in such manner that the devil will have all the power and God will have none. So it has happened[7] to many incautious and ignorant souls, who rely on these things to such an extent that many of them have found it hard to return to God in purity of faith; and many have been unable to return,[8] so securely has the devil rooted himself in them; for which reason it is well to resist and reject them all.[9] For, by the rejection of evil visions, the errors of the devil are avoided, and by the rejection of good visions no hindrance is offered to faith and the spirit harvests the fruit of them. And just as, when the soul allows them

---

[1] A here repeats the phrase above: 'because it sets . . . least important.'

[2] E.p. endeavours to bring out the sense more clearly here: 'is to seek after them and to rest in them, and God gives them not for this.'

[3] St. John of the Cross means that the soul should not rely upon its own judgment in such matters but upon some discreet and learned director.

[4] 2 Corinthians xi, 14.

[5] Only Alc. and e.p. have this sentence. The 'third book' must be the *Dark Night* (I, vi).

[6] Alc. alone has 'always.'

[7] E.p. abbreviates: 'that his visions will come in place of the others, as has happened . . .'

[8] E.p.: 'have not returned.' This is more exact, since the backslider has always the *power* to return, if he so wills.

[9] E.p.: 'and fear them all.'

entrance, God begins to withhold them because the soul is becoming attached to them and is not profiting by them as it should, while the devil insinuates and increases his own visions, where he finds occasion and cause for them;[1] just so, when the soul is resigned, or even averse to them,[2] the devil begins to desist, since he sees that he is working it no harm; and contrariwise God begins to increase and magnify[3] His favours in a soul that is so humble and detached, making it ruler over[4] many things, even as He made the servant who was faithful in small things.[5]

9. In these favours, if the soul be faithful and humble,[6] the Lord will not cease until He has raised it from one step to another, even to Divine union and transformation. For Our Lord continues to prove the soul and to raise it ever higher, so that He first gives it things that are very unpretentious and exterior and in the order of sense,[7] in conformity with the smallness of its capacity; to the end that, when it behaves as it should, and receives these first morsels with moderation for its strength and sustenance, He may grant it further and better food. If, then, the soul conquer the devil upon the first step, it will pass to the second; and if upon the second likewise, it will pass to the third; and so onward, through all seven mansions,[8] which are the seven steps of love, until the Spouse shall bring it to the cellar of wine of His perfect charity.

10. Happy the soul that can fight against that beast of the Apocalypse,[9] which has seven heads, set over against these seven steps of love, and which makes war therewith against each one, and strives therewith against the soul in each of these mansions, wherein the soul is being exercised and is mounting step by step in the love of God. And undoubtedly if it strive faithfully against each of these heads, and gain the victory, it will deserve to pass from one step to another, and from one mansion to another, even unto the last, leaving the beast vanquished after destroying its seven heads, wherewith it made so furious a war upon it. So furious is this war that Saint John says in that place[10] that it was given unto the beast to make war against the saints and to be able to overcome them upon each one of these steps of love,

---

[1] A, B, e.p.: 'because the soul gives occasion for them and makes room for them.'
[2] E.p.: 'resigned, and has no attachment to them.'
[3] E.p. omits: 'and magnify.'
[4] [*Lit.*, 'making it over.'] E.p. has: 'setting it and placing it over.']
[5] [St. Matthew xxv, 21.]   [6] [*Lit.*, 'and retired.']
[7] E.p.: 'so that He rather visits it first according to sense.'
[8] [The phrase is suggestive of St. Teresa, though the Spanish word is not *moradas*, but *mansiones*.]
[9] [Apocalypse xiii, 1.]   [10] [Apocalypse xiii, 7.]

arraying against each one many weapons and munitions of war. And it is therefore greatly to be lamented that many who engage in this spiritual battle against the beast do not even destroy its first head by denying themselves the sensual things of the world. And, though some destroy and cut off this head, they destroy not the second head, which is that of the visions of sense whereof we are speaking. But what is most to be lamented is that some, having destroyed not only the first and the second but even the third, which is that of the interior senses,[1] pass out of the state of meditation, and travel still farther onward, and are overcome by this spiritual[2] beast at the moment of their entering into purity of spirit, for he rises up against them once more, and even his first head comes to life again, and the last state of those souls is worse than the first, since, when they fall back, the beast brings with him seven other spirits worse then himself.[3]

11. The spiritual person, then, has to deny himself all the apprehensions, and the temporal delights,[4] that belong to the outward senses, if he will destroy the first and the second head of this beast, and enter into the first chamber of love, and the second, which is of living faith,[5] desiring neither to lay hold upon, nor to be embarrassed by, that which is given to the senses, since it is this that derogates most from faith.[6]

12. It is clear, then, that these sensual apprehensions and visions cannot be a means to union, since they bear no proportion to God; and this was one of the reasons why Christ desired that the Magdalene and Saint Thomas[7] should not touch Him. And so the devil rejoices greatly when a soul desires to receive revelations, and when he sees it inclined to them, for he has then a great occasion and opportunity to insinuate errors and, in so far as he is able, to derogate from faith; for, as I have said, he renders the soul that desires them very gross, and at times even leads it into many temptations and unseemly ways.

13.[8] I have written at some length of these outward apprehensions in order to throw and shed rather more light on the others, whereof we have to treat shortly. There is so much to say on this part of my subject that I could go on and never end. I believe, however, that I

---

[1] So e.p. The other authorities [and P. Silverio] read: 'the interior sensual senses.'
[2] Only Alc. has 'spiritual.'
[3] [St. Luke xi, 26.]   [4] E.p.: 'and the bodily delights.'
[5] E.p.: 'into the first and the second chamber of love in living faith.'
[6] E.p.: '. . . this that is the greatest hindrance to this spiritual night of faith.'
[7] E.p.: 'that Mary Magdalene and the apostle Saint Thomas.'
[8] This paragraph is not in A or B. It is given as found in Alc.; C, D, e.p. give it with slight variants.

am summarizing it sufficiently by merely saying that the soul must take care never to receive these apprehensions, save occasionally on another person's advice, which should very rarely be given, and even then it must have no desire for them. I think that on this part of my subject what I have said is sufficient.[1]

CHAPTER XII

Which treats of natural imaginary apprehensions. Describes their nature and proves that they cannot be a proportionate means of attainment to union with God. Shows the harm which results from inability to detach oneself from them.[2]

BEFORE we treat of the imaginary visions which are wont to occur supernaturally to the interior sense, which is the imagination and the fancy, it is fitting here, so that we may proceed in order, to treat of the natural apprehensions of this same interior bodily sense, in order that we may proceed from the lesser to the greater, and from the more exterior to the more interior, until we reach the most interior[3] recollection wherein the soul is united with God;[4] this same order we have followed up to this point. For we treated first of all the detachment of the exterior senses[5] from the natural apprehensions of objects,[6] and, in consequence, from the natural power of the desires—this was contained in the first book, wherein we spoke of the night of sense. We then began to detach these same senses from[7] supernatural exterior apprehensions (which, as we have just shown in the last chapter, affect the exterior senses), in order to lead the soul into the night of the spirit.

2. In this second book, the first thing that has now to be treated is the interior bodily sense—namely, the imagination and the fancy; this we must likewise void of all the imaginary apprehensions and forms

---

1 E.p. has: '. . . never to receive them, save in some rare case and after close examination by a learned, spiritual and experienced person, and even then [the soul must receive them] without any desire to do so.' This is clearly an editorial attempt to clarify [and improve upon] the Saint's directions.

2 E.p. adds: 'in time.'

3 [*Lit.*, 'the intimate'; but the superlative idea is clearly present.] Alc. has: 'the last' —probably a copyist's error [*último* for *íntimo*].

4 A, B omit the rest of this paragraph and the whole of the next.

5 E.p.: 'the detachment of the soul.'

6 E.p.: 'of exterior objects.'

7 E.p.: '. . . began the detachment in particular from . . .'

that may belong to it by nature, and we must prove how impossible it is that the soul should attain to union with God until its operation cease in them, since they cannot be the proper and proximate means of this union.

3. It is to be known, then, that the senses whereof we are here particularly speaking are two interior bodily senses which are called imagination and fancy, which subserve each other in due order. For the one sense reasons, as it were, by imagining, and the other forms the imagination, or that which is imagined, by making use of the fancy.[1] For our purpose the discussion of the one is equivalent to that of the other, and, for this reason, when we name them not both, it must be understood that we are speaking of either, as we have here explained.[2] All the things, then, that these senses can receive and fashion are known as imaginations and fancies, which are forms that are represented to these senses by bodily figures and images. This can happen in two ways. The one way is supernatural, wherein representation can be made, and is made, to these senses passively, without any effort of their own; these we call imaginary visions, produced after a supernatural manner, and of these we shall speak hereafter. The other way is natural, wherein, through the ability of the soul, these things can be actively fashioned in it through its operation,[3] beneath forms, figures and images. And thus to these two faculties belongs meditation, which is a discursive action wrought by means of images, forms and figures that are fashioned and imagined by the said senses, as when we imagine Christ crucified, or bound to the column, or at another of the stations; or when we imagine God seated upon a throne with great majesty; or when we consider and imagine glory to be like a most beauteous light, etc.; or when we imagine all kinds of other things, whether Divine or human, that can belong to the imagination. All these imaginings[4] must be cast out from the soul, which will remain in darkness as far as this sense is concerned, that it may attain to Divine union; for they can bear no proportion to proximate means of union with God, any more than can the bodily imaginings, which serve as objects to the five exterior senses.

[1] [Lit., 'by fancying.'] E.p.: 'For in the one there is something of reasoning, though it is imperfect and is [produced] imperfectly, and the other forms the image, which is the imagination.'

[2] [The Codices omit 'that we are speaking of either,' leaving the sense uncompleted.] E.p. adds: 'that what we say of the one is applicable likewise to the other and that we are speaking of both indifferently.'

[3] E.p.: 'The other way is natural, when through its operation these things can be actively produced.'   [4] A, B: 'All these apprehensions.'

4. The reason of this is that the imagination cannot fashion or imagine anything whatsoever beyond that which it has experienced through its exterior senses—namely, that which it has seen with the eyes, or heard with the ears, etc. At most it can only compose likenesses of those things that it has seen or heard or felt, which are of no more consequence than[1] those which have been received by the senses afore-mentioned, nor are they even of as much consequence. For, although a man imagines palaces of pearls and mountains of gold, because he has seen gold and pearls, all this is in truth less[2] than the essence of a little gold or of a single pearl, although in the imagination it be greater in quantity and in beauty.[3] And since, as has already been said, no created things can bear any proportion to the Being of God, it follows that nothing that is imagined in their likeness can serve as proximate means to union with Him, but, as we say, quite the contrary.[4]

5. Wherefore those that imagine God beneath any of these figures, or as a great fire or brightness, or in any other such form, and think that anything like this will be like to Him, are very far from approaching Him. For, although these considerations and forms and manners of meditation are necessary to beginners, in order that they may gradually feed and enkindle their souls with love by means of sense, as we shall say hereafter, and although they thus serve them as remote means to union with God, through which a soul has commonly to pass in order to reach the goal and abode of spiritual repose, yet they must merely pass through them, and not remain ever in them, for in such a manner they would never reach their goal, which does not resemble these remote means, neither has aught to do with them. The stairs of a staircase have naught to do with the top of it and the abode to which it leads, yet are means to the reaching of both; and if the climber left not behind the stairs below him until there were no more to climb, but desired to remain upon any one of them, he would never reach the top of them nor would he mount to the pleasant[5] and peaceful room which is the goal. And just so the soul that is to attain in this life to the union of that supreme repose and blessing, by means of all these stairs of meditations, forms and ideas, must pass through them and have done with them,[6] since they have no resemblance and bear no proportion to

---

[1] E.p.: 'which are of no greater excellence than . . .'
[2] E.p. has 'no more' for 'less.'
[3] E.p.: 'although in the imagination it may have the order and trace of beauty.'
[4] E.p. omits: 'but . . . contrary.'
[5] [*Lit.*, 'the level'—i.e., by contrast with the steep stairs.]
[6] E.p. omits: 'and have done with them.'

the goal to which they lead, which is God. Wherefore Saint Paul says in the Acts of the Apostles: *Non debemus æstimare, auro, vel argento, aut lapidi sculpturæ artis, et cogitationis hominis, Divinum esse similem.*[1] Which signifies: We ought not to think of the Godhead by likening Him to gold or to silver, neither to stone that is formed by art, nor to aught that a man can fashion with his imagination.

6. Great, therefore, is the error of many[2] spiritual persons who have practised approaching God by means of images and forms and meditations, as befits beginners. God would now lead them on to[3] further spiritual blessings, which are interior and invisible, by taking from them the pleasure and sweetness of discursive meditation; but they cannot, or dare not, or know not how to detach themselves from those palpable methods to which they have grown accustomed. They continually labour to retain them, desiring to proceed, as before, by the way of consideration and meditation upon forms, for they think that it must be so with them always. They labour greatly to this end and find little sweetness or none; rather the aridity and weariness and disquiet of their souls are increased and grow, in proportion as they labour for that earlier sweetness. They cannot find this in that earlier manner, for the soul no longer enjoys that food of sense, as we have said; it needs not this but another food, which is more delicate, more interior and partaking less of the nature of sense; it consists not in labouring with the imagination, but in setting the soul at rest, and allowing it to remain in its quiet and repose, which is more spiritual. For, the farther the soul progresses in spirituality, the more it ceases from the operation of the faculties in particular acts, since it becomes more and more occupied in one act that is general and pure; and thus the faculties that were journeying to a place whither the soul has arrived cease to work, even as the feet stop and cease to move when their journey is over. For if all were motion, one would never arrive, and if all were means, where or when would come the fruition of the end and goal?

7. It is piteous, then, to see many a one who,[4] though his soul would fain tarry in this peace and rest of interior quiet, where it is filled with the peace and refreshment of God, takes from it its tranquillity, and leads it away to the most exterior things, and would make it return and

---

[1] Acts xvii, 29.   [2] E.p.: 'of certain.'

[3] [The verb, *recoger*, of which the derived noun is translated 'recollection,' has more accurately the meaning of 'gather,' 'take inwards.']

[4] [*Lit.*, 'to see that there are many who.'] E.p. omits 'many who,' making the subject of the sentence an unspecified 'they.'

retrace the ground it has already traversed, to no purpose,[1] and abandon the end and goal wherein it is already reposing for the means which led it to that repose,[2] which are meditations. This comes not to pass without great reluctance and repugnance of the soul, which would fain be in that peace that it understands not,[3] as in its proper place; even as one who has arrived, with great labour, and is now resting, suffers pain if he is made to return to his labour. And, as such souls know not the mystery of this new experience, the idea comes to them that they are being idle and doing nothing; and thus they allow not themselves to be quiet, but endeavour to meditate and reason. Hence they are filled[4] with aridity and affliction, because they seek to find sweetness where it is no longer to be found; we may even say of them that the more they strive the less they profit,[5] for, the more they persist after this manner, the worse is the state wherein they find themselves, because their soul is drawn farther away from spiritual peace; and this is to leave the greater for the less, and to retrace the ground already traversed, and to seek to do that which has been done.[6]

8. To such as these the advice must be given to learn to abide attentively and wait lovingly upon God in that state of quiet, and to pay no heed either to imagination or to its working; for here, as we say, the faculties are at rest, and are working, not actively, but passively, by receiving that which God works in them; and, if they work at times, it is not with violence[7] or with carefully elaborated meditation, but with sweetness of love, moved less by the ability of the soul itself than by God, as will be explained hereafter. But let this now suffice to show how fitting and necessary it is for those who aim at making further progress to be able to detach themselves from all these methods and manners and works of the imagination at the time and season when the profit of the state which they have reached demands and requires it.

9. And, that it may be understood how this is to be, and at what season, we shall give in the chapter following[8] certain signs which the

---

[1] E.p. omits: 'to no purpose.'

[2] [P. Silverio prints *a Él*—'to Him'; but he now agrees with me that *a él*—'to it,' i.e., the repose just mentioned—is the correct reading.]

[3] E.p. omits: 'that it understands not.'

[4] A, B: 'Hence comes it that they are filled' [using a stronger word for 'filled', with the sense of 'stuffed,' 'swollen'].

[5] E.p.: 'the more they freeze, the more they bind' [a popular saying].

[6] Alc. omits: 'and to . . . been done,' probably only by an oversight.

[7] E.p.: '. . . and work not, save in that simple and sweet loving attentiveness; and if at times they work more [than this] it is not with violence . . .' The reading in the text is that of Alc.

[8] Only Alc. and e.p. have: 'in the chapter following.'

spiritual person will see in himself and whereby he may know at what time and season he may freely avail himself of the goal mentioned above, and may cease from journeying by means of meditation and the work of the imagination.

CHAPTER XIII

Wherein are set down the signs which the spiritual person will find in himself whereby he may know at what season it behoves him to leave meditation and reasoning and pass to the state of contemplation.[1]

IN order that there may be no confusion in this instruction it will be meet in this chapter to explain at what time and season it behoves the spiritual person to lay aside the task of discursive meditation as carried on through the imaginations and forms and figures above mentioned, in order that he may lay them aside neither sooner nor later than when the Spirit[2] bids him; for, although it is meet for him to lay them aside at the proper time in order that he may journey to God and not be hindered by them, it is no less needful for him not to lay aside the said imaginative meditation before the proper time lest he should turn backward. For, although the apprehensions of these faculties serve not as proximate means of union to the proficient, they serve nevertheless as remote means to beginners in order to dispose and habituate[3] the spirit to spirituality by means of sense, and in order to void the sense, in the meantime, of all the other low forms and images, temporal, worldly and natural. We shall therefore speak here of certain signs and examples which the spiritual person will find in himself, whereby he may know whether or not it will be meet for him to lay them aside at this season.[4]

2. The first sign is his realization that he can no longer meditate or reason[5] with his imagination, neither can take pleasure therein as he was wont to do aforetime; he rather finds aridity in that which aforetime

---

[1] E.p.: 'Sets down the signs which the spiritual person may recognize in himself, in order that he may begin to detach the understanding from the imaginary forms and reasonings of meditation.'

[2] [The MSS. and editions, including P. Silverio, have 'spirit,' but P. Silverio agrees with me that the correct reading is 'Spirit.']

[3] A, B: 'and habilitate.'

[4] A, B add here: 'The signs which the spiritual person will observe in himself for laying aside discursive meditation are three.' Alc., C, D add none of these words. E.p. adds only: 'which [signs] are three.'

[5] A, e.p.: 'or work.'

was wont to captivate his senses and to bring him sweetness. But, for as long as he finds sweetness in meditation,[1] and is able to reason, he should not abandon this, save when his soul is led into the peace and quietness[2] which is described under the third head.

3. The second sign is a realization that he has no desire to fix his meditation or his sense upon other particular objects, exterior or interior. I do not mean that the imagination neither comes nor goes (for even at times of deep[3] recollection it is apt to move freely), but that the soul has no pleasure in fixing it of set purpose upon other objects.

4. The third and surest sign is that the soul takes pleasure in being alone, and waits with loving attentiveness upon God, without making any particular meditation, in inward peace and quietness and rest, and without acts and exercises of the faculties—memory, understanding and will—at least, without discursive acts, that is, without passing from one thing to another; the soul is alone, with an attentiveness and a knowledge, general and loving, as we said, but without any particular understanding, and adverting not to that which it is contemplating.[4]

5. These three signs, at least, the spiritual person must observe in himself, all together, before he can venture safely to abandon the state of meditation and sense,[5] and to enter that of contemplation and spirit.

---

[1] Alc. [and P. Silverio]: 'as he extracts sweetness from meditation.' A, B, C, D, e.p. have 'finds.'

[2] E.p. omits: 'and quietness.' The Saint's description of this first sign at which a soul should pass from meditation to contemplation was denounced as disagreeing with Catholic doctrine, particularly the phrase: 'that he can no longer meditate or reason with his imagination, neither can take pleasure therein as he was wont to do aforetime.' This language, however, is common to mystics and theologians, not excluding St. Thomas (2a 2æ, q. 180, a. 6) and Suárez (*De Oratione*, Bk. II, Chap. x), as is proved, with eloquence and erudition, by P. Basilio Ponce de León and the *Elucidatio*, in their refutations of the Saint's critics. All agree that, in the act of contemplation of which St. John of the Cross here speaks, the understanding must be stripped of forms and species of the imagination and that the reasonings and reflections of meditation must be set aside. This is to be understood, both of the contemplation that transcends all human methods, and also of that which is practised according to these human methods with the ordinary aid of grace. But there is this important difference, that those who enjoy the first kind of contemplation set aside all intellectual reasoning as well as processes of the fancy and the imagination, whereas, for the second kind, reasoning *prior* to the act of contemplation is normally necessary, though it ceases *at* the act of contemplation, and there is then substituted for it simple and loving intuition of eternal truth. It should be clearly understood that this is not of habitual occurrence in the contemplative soul, but occurs only *during the act* of contemplation, which is commonly of short duration. St. Teresa makes this clear in Chap. xxvii of her *Life*, and treats this same doctrinal question in many other parts of her works—e.g., *Life*, Chaps. x, xii; *Way of Perfection*, Chap. xxvi; *Interior Castle*, IV, Chap. iii, etc.

[3] [*Lit.*, 'much.']

[4] Only Alc., B, C, D have: 'and adverting . . . it is contemplating.'

[5] E.p. omits: 'and sense.' Since sense plays so great a part in meditation, St. John of the Cross places it in contradistinction to contemplation, which, the more nearly it attains perfection, becomes the more sublime and spiritual and the more completely freed from the bonds of nature. Cf. *Elucidatio*, Pt. II, Chap. iii, p. 180.

6. And it suffices not for a man to have the first alone without the second, for it might be that the reason for his being unable to imagine and meditate upon the things of God, as he did aforetime, was distraction on his part and lack of diligence;[1] for the which cause he must observe in himself the second likewise, which is the absence of inclination or desire to think upon other things; for, when the inability to fix the imagination and sense upon the things of God proceeds from distraction or lukewarmness, the soul then has the desire and inclination to fix it upon other and different things, which lead it thence altogether. Neither does it suffice that he should observe in himself the first and second signs, if he observe not likewise, together with these, the third; for, although he observe his inability to reason and think upon the things of God, and likewise his distaste for thinking upon other and different things, this might proceed from melancholy or from some other kind of humour in the brain or the heart, which habitually produces a certain absorption and suspension of the senses, causing the soul to think not at all, nor to desire or be inclined to think, but rather to remain in that pleasant state of reverie.[2] Against this must be set the third sign, which is loving attentiveness and knowledge, in peace, etc., as we have said.

7. It is true, however, that, when this condition first begins, the soul is hardly aware of this loving knowledge, and that for two reasons. First, this loving knowledge is apt at the beginning to be very subtle and delicate, and almost imperceptible to the senses. Secondly, when the soul has been accustomed to that other exercise of meditation, which is wholly[3] perceptible, it is unaware, and hardly conscious, of this other new and imperceptible condition, which is purely spiritual; especially when, not understanding it, the soul allows not itself to rest in it, but strives after the former, which is more readily perceptible; so that abundant though the loving interior peace may be, the soul has no opportunity of experiencing and enjoying it. But the more accustomed the soul grows to this,[4] by allowing itself to rest, the more it will grow therein and the more conscious it will become of that loving general knowledge of God, in which it has greater enjoyment than in aught else, since this knowledge causes it peace, rest, pleasure and delight without labour.

8. And, to the end that what has been said may be the clearer, we

---

[1] A, B, C: 'and lack of recollectedness.'

[2] [*embelesamiento*, a word denoting a pleasurable condition somewhere between a reverie and a swoon.]

[3] E.p.: 'which is more.'   [4] A, e.p.: 'becomes habilitated for this.'

shall give, in this chapter following, the causes and reasons why the three signs aforementioned appear to be necessary for the soul that is journeying to pure spirit.[1]

CHAPTER XIV

Wherein is proved the fitness of these signs, and the reason is given why that which has been said in speaking of them is necessary to progress.

WITH respect to the first sign whereof we are speaking—that is to say, that the spiritual person who would enter upon the spiritual road[2] (which is that of contemplation) must leave the way of imagination and of meditation through sense when he takes no more pleasure therein and is unable to reason—there are two reasons why this should be done, which may almost be comprised in one. The first is, that in one way the soul has received all the spiritual good which it would be able to derive from the things of God by the path of meditation and reasoning, the sign whereof is that it can no longer meditate or reason as before,[3] and finds no new sweetness or pleasure therein as it found before, because up to that time it had not progressed[4] as far as the spirituality which was in store for it; for, as a rule, whensoever the soul receives some spiritual blessing, it receives it with pleasure, at least in spirit, in that means whereby it receives it and profits by it; otherwise it is astonishing if it profits by it, or finds in the cause of it that help and that sweetness which it finds when it receives it.[5] For this is in agreement with a saying of the philosophers, *Quod sapit, nutrit.* That is: That which is palatable nourishes and fattens. Wherefore holy Job said: *Numquid poterit comedi insulsum, quod non est sale conditum?*[6] Can that which is unsavoury perchance be eaten when it is not seasoned with salt? It is for this cause that the soul is unable to meditate or reason as before: the little pleasure which the spirit finds therein and the little profit which it gains.

2. The second reason is that the soul at this season has now both the substance and the habit of the spirit of meditation. For it must be known that the end of reasoning and meditation on the things of God

---

[1] [*Lit.*, 'appear to be necessary in order to journey to spirit.'] E.p.: 'in order to guide the spirit.'
[2] E.p.: 'spiritual life.'   [3] E.p.: 'as it was wont to do before.'
[4] E.p.: '. . . pleasure therein as before, because before this it had not progressed . . .'
[5] E.p. omits: 'or finds . . . receives it.'
[6] Job vi, 6.

is the gaining of some knowledge and love of God, and each time that the soul gains this through meditation,[1] it is an act; and just as many acts, of whatever kind, end by forming a habit in the soul, just so, many of these acts of loving knowledge which the soul has been making one after another from time to time come through repetition to be so continuous in it that they become habitual. This end God is wont also to effect in many souls without the intervention of these acts[2] (or at least without many such acts having preceded it), by setting them at once in contemplation.[3] And thus that which aforetime the soul was gaining gradually through its labour of meditation upon particular facts has now through practice, as we have been saying, become converted and changed into a habit and substance of loving knowledge, of a general kind, and not distinct or particular as before. Wherefore, when it gives itself to prayer, the soul is now like one to whom water has been brought, so that he drinks peacefully, without labour, and is no longer forced to draw the water through the aqueducts of past meditations and forms and figures.[4] So that, as soon as the soul comes before God, it makes an act of knowledge, confused, loving, passive and tranquil, wherein it drinks of wisdom and love and delight.

3. And it is for this cause that the soul feels great weariness and distaste, when, although it is in this condition of tranquillity, men try to make it meditate and labour in particular acts of knowledge. For it is like a child, which, while receiving the milk that has been collected and brought together for it in the breast, is taken from the breast and then forced to try to gain and collect food by its own diligent squeezing and handling. Or it is like one who has removed the rind from a fruit, and is tasting the substance of the fruit, when he is forced to cease doing this and to try to begin removing the said[5] rind, which has been removed already. He finds no rind to remove, and yet he is unable to enjoy the substance of the fruit which he already had in his hand; herein he is like to one who leaves a prize[6] which he holds for another which he holds not.

4. And many act thus when they begin to enter this state; they think that the whole business consists in a continual reasoning and learning to understand particular things by means of images and forms,

---

[1] E.p. omits: 'through meditation.'
[2] E.p.: 'This God is wont to do likewise without the intervention of these acts of meditation.'
[3] A adds: 'and love.'
[4] [Cf. the simile of the Waters in St. Teresa, *Life*, Chap. xi, and *Interior Castle*, IV, ii, iii.]
[5] E.p.: 'the same.'   [6] [*Lit.*, 'booty,' 'prey.']

which are to the spirit as rind. When they find not these in that substantial and loving quiet wherein their soul desires to remain, and wherein it understands nothing clearly, they think that they are going astray and wasting time, and they begin once more to seek the rind of their imaginings and reasonings,[1] but find it not, because it has already been removed. And thus they neither enjoy the substance nor make progress in meditation, and they become troubled by the thought that they are turning backward and are losing themselves. They are indeed losing themselves,[2] though not in the way they think, for they are becoming lost to their own senses and to their first manner of perception;[3] and this means gain in that spirituality which is being given them. The less they understand, however, the farther they penetrate into the night of the spirit, whereof we are treating in this book, through the which night they must pass in order to be united with God, in a union that transcends all knowledge.

5. With respect to the second sign, there is little to say, for it is clear that at this season the soul cannot possibly take pleasure in other and different objects of the imagination, which are of the world, since, as we have said, and for the reasons already mentioned, it has no pleasure in those which are in closest conformity with it—namely, those of God. Only, as has been noted above, the imaginative faculty in this state of recollection is in the habit of coming and going and varying of its own accord; but neither according to the pleasure nor at the will of the soul, which is troubled thereby, because its peace and joy are disturbed.

6. Nor do I think it necessary to say anything here concerning the fitness and necessity of the third sign whereby the soul may know if it is to leave the meditation aforementioned, which is a knowledge of God or a general and loving attentiveness to Him. For something has been said of this in treating of the first sign, and we shall treat of it again hereafter, when we speak in its proper place of this confused and general knowledge, which will come after our description of all the particular apprehensions of the understanding. But we will speak[4] of one reason alone by which it may clearly be seen how, when the contemplative has to turn aside from the way of meditation and reasoning, he needs this general and loving attentiveness or knowledge of God. The reason is that, if the soul at that time had not this knowledge of God or this realization of His presence, the result would be that it

---

[1] A: 'the rind of reasoning.'
[3] A, B, e.p. add: 'and understanding.'
[2] E.p.: 'And they are indeed doing so.'
[4] E.p.: 'will now speak.'

would do nothing and have nothing; for, having turned aside from meditation (by means whereof the soul has been reasoning with its faculties of sense), and being still without contemplation, which is the general knowledge whereof we are speaking,[1] wherein the soul makes use of its spiritual faculties[2]—namely, memory, understanding and will—these being united in this knowledge which is then wrought and received in them, the soul[3] would of necessity be without any exercise in the things of God, since the soul can neither work, nor can it receive[4] that which has been worked in it, save only by way of these two kinds of faculty,[5] that of sense and that of spirit. For, as we have said, by means of the faculties of sense it can reason and search out and gain knowledge of things and by means of the spiritual faculties it can have fruition of the knowledge[6] which it has already received in these faculties aforementioned, though the faculties themselves take no part herein.[7]

7. And thus the difference between the operation of these two kinds of faculty in the soul is like the difference between working and enjoying the fruit of work which has been done; or like that between the labour of journeying and the rest and quiet which comes from arrival at the goal; or, again, like that between preparing a meal and partaking and tasting of it, when it has been both prepared and masticated, without having any of the labour of cooking it, or it is like the difference between receiving something and profiting by that which has been received.[8] Now if the soul be occupied neither with respect to the operation[9] of the faculties of sense, which is meditation and reasoning, nor with respect to that which has already been received and effected in the spiritual faculties, which is[10] the contemplation and knowledge whereof we have spoken, it will have no occupation, but will be wholly idle, and there would be no way in which it could be said to be

[1] B: 'whereof we were speaking.'

[2] [*Lit.*, 'the soul keeps in act its spiritual faculties.'] B reads: 'the soul has present spiritual faculties.' [The difference in the Spanish between this reading and that of the text is very slight and might be due to a careless copyist.]

[3] E.p. omits: 'the soul'; [as a result, the clause may be interpreted impersonally, but the general sense is the same].

[4] E.p.: 'nor can it continue in.'   [5] A, B: 'of these two faculties.'

[6] E.p.: 'the object of the knowledge.'

[7] E.p. adds: 'with labour, search or reasoning.'

[8] So Alc., but the other Codices and e.p. place this last clause after 'has been done' above.

[9] E.p. omits 'and masticated' and the following clauses, continuing thus: '. . . [been prepared]. And if it be not occupied in any kind of exercise, whether it have respect to the operation . . . or . . .'

[10] E.p. omits: 'in the spiritual faculties, which is.'

employed. This knowledge, then, is needful for the abandonment of the way of meditation and reasoning.

8. But here it must be made clear that this general knowledge whereof we are speaking is at times so subtle and delicate, particularly when it is most pure and simple and perfect, most spiritual and most interior, that, although the soul be occupied therein, it can neither realize it nor perceive it. This is most frequently the case when we can say that it is in itself most clear, perfect and simple; and this comes to pass when it penetrates a soul that is unusually pure and far withdrawn from other particular kinds of knowledge and intelligence, which the understanding or the senses might fasten upon. Such a soul, since it no longer has those things wherein the understanding and the senses have the habit and custom of occupying themselves, is not conscious of them, inasmuch as it has not its accustomed powers of sense. And it is for this reason that, when this knowledge is purest and simplest and most perfect, the understanding is least conscious of it and thinks of it as most obscure. And similarly, in contrary wise, when it[1] is in itself least pure and simple in the understanding, it seems to the understanding to be clearest and of the greatest importance, since it is clothed in, mingled with or involved in certain intelligible forms which understanding or sense[2] may seize upon.[3]

9. This will be clearly understood by the following comparison. If we consider a ray of sunlight entering through a window, we see that, the more the said ray is charged with atoms and particles of matter, the more palpable, visible and bright it appears to the eye of sense;[4] yet it is clear that the ray is in itself least pure, clear, simple and perfect at that time, since it is full of so many particles and atoms. And we see likewise that, when it is purest and freest from those particles and atoms, the least palpable and the darkest[5] does it appear to the material eye; and the purer it is, the darker and less apprehensible it appears to it. And if the ray were completely pure and free from all these atoms and particles, even from the minutest specks of dust, it would appear completely dark and invisible[6] to the eye, since everything that could be seen would be absent from it—namely, the objects

---

[1] E.p.: 'when this knowledge.'   [2] E.p. omits: 'or sense.'

[3] [The verb is *tropeçar en*, which may mean either 'stumble upon'—i.e., 'come across (and make use of),' or 'stumble over'—i.e., the forms may be a stumbling-block, or a snare. I think there is at least a suggestion of the latter meaning.]

[4] [*Lit.*, 'to the sight of sense.'] E.p. has: 'to the sense of sight.'

[5] E.p.: 'and the least pure.'

[6] All the MSS. have 'incomprehensible.' E.p. reads 'imperceptible' and [says P. Silverio] rightly so.

of sight. For the eye would find no objects whereon to rest, since light
is no proper[1] object of vision, but the means whereby that which is
visible is seen; so that, if there be no visible objects wherein the sun's
ray or any light can be reflected, nothing will be seen. Wherefore, if
the ray of light entered by one window and went out by another, without meeting anything that has material form, it would not[2] be seen at
all; yet, notwithstanding, that ray of light would be purer and clearer
in itself than when it was more clearly seen and perceived through
being full of visible objects.

10. The same thing happens in the realm of spiritual light with
respect to the sight of the soul, which is the understanding, and which
this general[3] and supernatural knowledge and light whereof we are
speaking strikes so purely and simply. So completely is it detached and
removed from all intelligible forms, which are objects[4] of the understanding, that it is neither perceived nor observed. Rather, at times
(that is, when it is purest), it becomes darkness, because it withdraws
the understanding from its accustomed lights, from forms and from
fancies, and then the darkness is more clearly felt and realized. But,
when this Divine light strikes the soul with less force, it neither
perceives darkness nor observes light, nor apprehends aught that it
knows,[5] from whatever source; hence at times the soul remains as it
were in a great forgetfulness, so that it knows not where it has been[6]
or what it has done, nor is it aware of the passage of time. Wherefore
it may happen, and does happen, that many hours are spent in this
forgetfulness, and, when the soul returns to itself, it believes that less
than a moment has passed, or no time at all.[7]

11. The cause of this forgetfulness is the purity and simplicity of
this knowledge which occupies the soul[8] and simplifies, purifies and
cleanses it from all apprehensions and forms of the senses and of the
memory, through which it acted when it was conscious of time,[9] and
thus leaves it in forgetfulness and without consciousness of time.[10]
This prayer, therefore, seems to the soul extremely brief, although, as

---

[1] A, B: 'no visible.' E.p.: 'since simple and pure light is not as properly an object
of vision as a means whereby,' etc.   [2] E.p.: 'it seems that it would not.'
[3] E.p. omits: 'general and.'   [4] E.p.: 'which are proportionate objects.'
[5] E.p. begins this sentence thus: 'At other times, too, this Divine light strikes the
soul with such force that it neither perceives darkness, nor observes light, neither does it
seem to apprehend aught that it knows.'
[6] A, B: 'has entered.'   [7] E.p. omits: 'or no time at all.'
[8] E.p. adds: 'being itself clear and pure.'
[9] [Or: 'when it was dependent on time.' Lit., 'acted in time.']
[10] [Or: 'and independent of time.' Lit., 'without time.'] E.p.: 'without noticing differences of time.'

we say,[1] it may last for a long period; for the soul has been united[2] in pure intelligence, which belongs not to time; and this is the brief prayer which is said to pierce the heavens, because it is brief and because it belongs not to time.[3] And it pierces the heavens, because the soul is united in heavenly intelligence; and when the soul awakens, this knowledge leaves in it the effects which it created in it without its being conscious of them, which effects are the lifting up of the spirit to the heavenly intelligence, and its withdrawal and abstraction from all things and forms and figures and memories thereof. It is this that David describes as having happened to him when he returned to himself out of this same forgetfulness, saying: *Vigilavi, et factus sum sicut passer solitarius in tecto.*[4] Which signifies: I have watched and I have become like the lonely bird[5] on the house-top. He uses the word 'lonely' to indicate that he was withdrawn and abstracted from all things. And by the house-top he means the elevation of the spirit on high; so that the soul remains as though ignorant of all things, for it knows God only, without knowing how. Wherefore the Bride declares in the Songs that among the effects which that sleep and forgetfulness of hers produced was this unknowing. She says that she came down to the garden, saying: *Nescivi.*[6] That is: I knew not whence. Although, as we have said, the soul in this state of knowledge believes itself to be doing nothing, and to be entirely unoccupied, because it is working neither with the senses nor with the faculties, it should realize that it is not wasting time.[7] For, although the harmony of the faculties of the soul may cease, its intelligence is as we have said. For this cause the Bride, who

---

[1] E.p.: 'as I have said.'   [2] E.p. omits 'united.'

[3] E.p. modifies these lines thus: '. . . it has been in pure intelligence, which is the brief prayer that is said to pierce the heavens. Because it is brief and because the soul is not conscious or observant of time.' P. José de Jesús María comments thus upon this passage: 'In contemplation the soul withdraws itself from the seashore, and entirely loses sight of land, in order to whelm itself in that vast sea and impenetrable abyss of the Divine Essence; hiding itself in the region of time, it enters within the most extensive limits of eternity. For the pure and simple intelligence whereinto the soul is brought in this contemplation, as was pointed out by the ancient Dionysius (*Myst. Theol.*, Chap. ii), and by our own Father, is not subject to time. For, as St. Thomas says (Pt. I, q. 118, a. 3, *et alibi*), the soul is a spiritual substance, which is above time and superior to the movements of the heavens, to which it is subject only because of the body. And therefore it seems that, when the soul withdraws from the body, and from all created things, and by means of pure intelligence whelms itself in eternal things, it recovers its natural dominion and rises above time, if not according to substance, at least according to its most perfect being; for the noblest and most perfect being of the soul resides rather in its acts than in its faculties. Wherefore St. Gregory said (*Morals*, Bk. VIII): "The Saints enter eternity even in this life, beholding the eternity of God."'

[4] Psalm ci, 8 [A.V. cii, 7].

[5] [The Spanish *pájaro*, 'bird,' is derived from *passer*, 'sparrow.']

[6] Canticles vi, 11.   [7] E.p. adds: 'nor acting uselessly.'

was wise, answered this question herself in the Songs, saying: *Ego dormio et cor meum vigilat.*[1] As though she were to say: Although I sleep with respect to my natural self, ceasing to labour, my heart waketh, being supernaturally lifted up in supernatural knowledge.[2]

12. But, it must be realized, we are not to suppose that this knowledge necessarily causes this forgetfulness when the soul is in the state that we are here describing: this occurs only when[3] God suspends in the soul the exercise of all its faculties, both natural and spiritual, which happens very seldom,[4] for this knowledge does not always fill the soul entirely. It is sufficient for the purpose, in the case which we are treating, that the understanding should be withdrawn from all particular knowledge, whether temporal or spiritual, and that the will should not desire to think with respect to either, as we have said, for this is a sign that the soul is occupied.[5] And it must be taken as an indication that this is so[6] when this knowledge is applied and communicated to the understanding only, which sometimes happens when the soul is unable to observe it. For, when it is communicated to the will also, which happens almost invariably, the soul does not cease to understand in the very least degree, if it will reflect hereon, that it is employed and occupied in this knowledge, inasmuch as it is conscious of a sweetness of love therein, without particular knowledge or understanding of that which it loves. It is for this reason that this knowledge

---

[1] Canticles v, 2.

[2] The words which conclude this paragraph in the edition of 1630 ('The sign by which we may know if the soul is occupied in this secret intelligence is if it is seen to have no pleasure in thinking of aught, whether high or low') are not found either in the Codices or in e.p. When St. John of the Cross uses the words 'cessation,' 'idleness' [*ocio*, Lat. *otium*], 'quiet,' 'annihilation,' 'sleep' (of the faculties), etc., he does not mean, as the Illuminists did, that the understanding and will in the act of contemplation are so passive as to have lost all their force and vitality, and that the contemplative is therefore impeccable, although he commit the grossest sins. The soul's vital powers, according to St. John of the Cross, are involved even in the highest contemplation; the understanding is attentive to God and the will is loving Him. They are not working, it is true, in the way which is usual and natural with them—that is, by reason and imagination—but supernaturally, through the unction of the Holy Spirit, which they receive passively, without any effort of their own. It is in this sense that such words as those quoted above ('cessation,' 'idleness,' etc.) are both expressively and appropriately used by the Saint, for what is done without labour and effort may better be described by images of passivity than by those of activity. Further, the soul is unaware that its faculties are working in this sublime contemplation, though they undoubtedly do work.

St. John of the Cross, philosopher as well as mystic, would not deny the vital and intrinsic activity of the understanding and the will in contemplation. His reasoning is supported by P. José de Jesús María (*Apología Mística de la Contemplación Divina*, Chap. ix) [quoted at length by P. Silverio, *Obras*, etc., Vol. II, p. 130, note].

[3] E.p.: 'when in a particular way.'

[4] E.p. abbreviates: '. . . suspends the soul, and this happens very seldom.'

[5] E.p. omits: 'for this . . . occupied.'

[6] E.p.: 'it must be taken to show that the soul is in this forgetfulness.'

is described as general and loving; for, just as it is so in the understanding, being communicated to it obscurely, even so is it in the will, sweetness and love being communicated to it confusedly, so that it cannot have a distinct knowledge of the object of its love.

13. Let this suffice now to explain how meet it is that the soul should be occupied in this knowledge, so that it may turn aside from the way of spiritual[1] meditation, and be sure that, although it seem to be doing nothing, it is well occupied, if it discern within itself these signs. It will also be realized, from the comparison which we have made, that if this light presents itself to the understanding in a more comprehensible and palpable manner, as the sun's ray presents itself to the eye when it is full of particles, the soul must not for that reason consider it purer, brighter and more sublime. It is clear that, as Aristotle and the theologians say,[2] the higher and more sublime is the Divine light, the darker is it to our understanding.

14. Of this Divine knowledge there is much to say, concerning both itself and the effects which it produces upon contemplatives. All this we reserve for its proper place,[3] for, although we have spoken of it here, there would be no reason for having done so at such length, save our desire not[4] to leave this doctrine rather more confused than it is already, for I confess it is certainly very much so. Not only is it a matter which is seldom treated in this way, either verbally or in writing, being in itself so extraordinary and obscure, but my rude style and lack of knowledge make it more so. Further, since I have misgivings as to my ability to explain it, I believe I often write at too great length and go beyond the limits which are necessary for that part of the doctrine which I am treating.[5] Herein I confess that I sometimes err purposely; for that which is not explicable by one kind of reasoning will perhaps be better understood by another, or by others yet; and I believe, too, that in this way I am shedding more light upon that which is to be said hereafter.

15. Wherefore it seems well to me also, before completing this part of my treatise, to set down a reply[6] to one question which may arise with respect to the continuance of this knowledge, and this shall be briefly treated[7] in the chapter following.

---

[1] E.p. omits 'spiritual.' [2] A, B omit: 'as ... say.'
[3] In spite of this promise, the Saint does not return to this subject at such length as his language here would suggest.
[4] Alc., B omit 'not,' which, however, is required by the context.
[5] A, B omit the rest of this paragraph.
[6] E.p.: 'not to fail to reply.' [7] E.p.: 'and this I will do.'

CHAPTER XV

Wherein is explained how it is sometimes well for progressives who are beginning to enter upon this general knowledge of contemplation to make use of natural[1] reasoning and the work of the natural faculties.

WITH regard to that which has been said, there might be raised one question—if progressives (that is, those whom God is beginning to bring into this supernatural knowledge of contemplation whereof we have spoken) must never again, because of this that they are beginning to experience, return to the way of meditation and reasoning and natural forms. To this the answer is that it is not to be understood that such as are beginning to experience this loving knowledge must, as a general rule, never again try to return to meditation;[2] for, when they are first making progress in proficiency, the habit of contemplation is not yet so perfect that they can give themselves to the act thereof whensoever they wish, nor, in the same way, have they reached a point so far beyond meditation that they cannot occasionally meditate and reason in a natural way,[3] as they were wont, using the figures and the steps that they were wont to use,[4] and finding something new in them. Rather, in these early stages, when, by means of the indications already given, they are able to see that the soul is not occupied in that repose and knowledge, they will need to make use of meditation until by means of it they come to acquire in some degree of perfection the habit which we have described. This will happen when, as soon as they seek to meditate, they experience this knowledge and peace, and find themselves unable to meditate and no longer desirous of doing so, as we have said. For until they reach this stage, which is that of the proficient in this exercise, they use sometimes the one and sometimes the other, at different times.[5]

2. The soul, then, will frequently find itself in this loving or peaceful state of waiting upon God[6] without in any way exercising its faculties—that is, with respect to particular acts—and without working actively at all, but only receiving.[7] In order to reach this state, it will

---

[1] E.p. omits 'natural.'

[2] E.p. : 'this loving and simple knowledge must never meditate again or strive to do so.'

[3] Alc. alone has: 'in a natural way.'   [4] E.p. omits: 'using . . . to use.'

[5] E.p. omits: 'at different times.'

[6] [*Lit.*, 'in this loving or peaceful presence,' the original of 'presence' having also the sense of 'attendance.']

[7] The words: 'that is . . . only receiving' occur only in Alc. E.p. substitutes: 'as has been explained.'

frequently need to make use of meditation, quietly and in moderation; but, when once the soul is brought into this other state,[1] it acts not at all with its faculties,[2] as we have already said. It would be truer to say that understanding and sweetness work in it and are wrought within it, than that the soul itself works at all, save only by waiting upon God and by loving Him without desiring to feel or to see anything.[3] Then God communicates Himself to it passively, even as to one who has his eyes open, so that light is communicated to him passively, without his doing more than keep them open.[4] And this reception of light which is infused supernaturally is passive understanding. We say that the soul works not at all, not because it understands not, but because it understands things without taxing its own industry and receives only that which is given to it, as comes to pass in the illuminations and enlightenments or inspirations of God.[5]

3. Although in this condition the will freely receives this general and confused knowledge of God, it is needful, in order that it may receive this Divine light more simply and abundantly, only that it should not try to interpose other lights which are more palpable, whether forms or ideas or figures having to do with any kind of meditation; for none of these things is similar to that pure and serene light. So that if at this time the will desires to understand and consider particular things, however spiritual they be, this would obstruct the pure and simple general light[6] of the spirit, by setting those clouds in the way; even as a man might set something before his eyes which impeded his vision and kept from him both the light and the sight of things in front of him.

4. Hence it clearly follows that, when the soul has completely purified and voided itself of all forms and images that can be apprehended, it will remain in this pure and simple light, being transformed therein into a state of perfection. For, though this light never fails in the soul,[7] it is not infused into it because of the creature forms and veils wherewith the soul is veiled and embarrassed; but, if these impediments and these veils were wholly removed (as will be said hereafter),

---

[1] E.p.: 'when once this [other state] is attained.'
[2] E.p.: 'the soul neither reflects nor labours with its faculties.'
[3] E.p. adds: 'save only to let itself be carried away by God.'
[4] E.p. abbreviates: '. . . his eyes open, light is communicated.'
[5] This passage ('And this reception . . . inspirations of God') together with the first clause of the next paragraph ('Although . . . knowledge of God') is found only in Alc.
[6] E.p.: 'this would obstruct the subtle and simple light.'
[7] E.p. reads: 'For, though this light is always made ready to be communicated to the soul.'

the soul would then find itself in a condition of pure detachment and poverty of spirit, and, being simple and pure, would be transformed into simple and pure Wisdom, which is the Son of God. For the enamoured soul finds that that which is natural has failed it, and it is then imbued with that which is Divine, both naturally and supernaturally, so that there may be no vacuum in its nature.[1]

5. When the spiritual person cannot meditate, let him learn to be still in God, fixing his loving attention upon Him, in the calm of his understanding, although he may think himself to be doing nothing. For thus, little by little and very quickly, Divine calm and peace will be infused into his soul, together with a wondrous and sublime knowledge of God, enfolded in Divine love. And let him not meddle with forms, meditations and imaginings, or with any kind of reasoning, lest his soul be disturbed, and brought out of its contentment and peace, which can only result in its experiencing distaste and repugnance. And if, as we have said, such a person has scruples that he is doing nothing, let him note that he is doing no small thing by pacifying the soul and bringing it into calm and peace, unaccompanied by any act or desire, for it is this that Our Lord asks of us, through David, saying: *Vacate, et videte quoniam ego sum Deus*.[2] As though he had said: Learn to be empty of all things (that is to say, inwardly and outwardly[3]) and you will see[4] that I am God.

CHAPTER XVI

Which treats of the imaginary apprehensions that are supernaturally represented in the fancy. Describes how they cannot serve the soul as a proximate means to union with God.

Now that we have treated of the apprehensions which the soul can receive within itself by natural means, and whereon the fancy and the imagination can work by means of reflection,[5] it will be suitable to treat here of the supernatural apprehensions, which are called imaginary visions, which likewise belong to these senses,

---

[1] C, D: 'for no vacuum occurs in nature.' E.p.: 'it is imbued with that which is Divine, supernaturally, for God leaves no vacuum without filling it.'
[2] Psalm xlv, 11 [A.V., xlvi, 10].
[3] E.p. omits: 'and outwardly.'
[4] E.p. adds: 'with delight.'
[5] E.p.: 'and whereon it can work by means of the fancy and the imagination.'

since they come within the category of images, forms and figures, exactly[1] as do the natural apprehensions.

2. It must be understood that beneath this term 'imaginary vision' we purpose to include all things which can be represented to the imagination supernaturally by means of any image, form, figure and species.[2] For all the apprehensions and species which, through all the five bodily senses, are represented to the soul, and dwell within it, after a natural manner, may likewise occur in the soul after a supernatural manner, and be represented to it without any assistance of the outward senses. For this sense of fancy, together with memory, is, as it were, an archive and storehouse of the understanding, wherein are received all forms and images that can be understood; and thus the soul has them within itself as it were in a mirror, having received them by means of the five senses, or, as we say, supernaturally; and thus it presents them to the understanding, whereupon the understanding considers them and judges them. And not only so, but the soul can also prepare and imagine others like to those with which it is acquainted.[3]

3. It must be understood, then, that, even as the five outward senses represent[4] the images and species of their objects to these inward senses, even so, supernaturally, as we say, without using the outward senses, both God and the devil can represent[5] the same images and species, and much more beautiful[6] and perfect ones. Wherefore, beneath these images, God often represents many things to the soul, and teaches it much wisdom; this is continually seen in the Scriptures, as when Isaias saw God in His glory[7] beneath the smoke which covered the Temple, and beneath the seraphim who covered their faces and their feet with their wings;[8] and as Jeremias saw the rod watching,[9] and Daniel a multitude of visions,[10] etc. And the devil, too, strives to deceive the soul with his visions, which in appearance are good, as may be seen in the Book of the Kings, when he deceived all the prophets of

---

[1] E.p. omits 'exactly.'

[2] E.p. here adds a passage which is found in none of the Codices: 'and this with species that are very perfect and that [have power to] make representations and cause influences more vivid and more perfect than [any brought about] through the connatural order of the senses.'

[3] E.p. abbreviates: '. . . and images which it has to make intelligible, and thus the understanding beholds and judges them.'

[4] E.p.: 'propose and represent.'

[5] E.p. has (for 'both . . . represent'): 'may be represented.'

[6] E.p.: 'more vivid.'

[7] E.p.: 'as when God showed His glory.'

[8] Isaias vi, 4.   [9] Jeremias i, 11.   [10] Daniel vii, 10.

Achab, presenting to their imaginations the horns wherewith he said the King was to destroy the Assyrians, which was a lie.[1] Even such were the visions of Pilate's wife, warning him not to condemn Christ;[2] and there are many other places where it is seen how, in this mirror of the fancy and the imagination,[3] these imaginary visions come more frequently to proficients than do outward and bodily visions. These, as we say, differ not in their nature (that is, as being images and species) from those which enter by the outward senses; but, with respect to the effect which they produce, and in the degree of their perfection, there is a great difference; for imaginary visions are subtler and produce a deeper impression upon the soul, inasmuch as they are supernatural, and are also more interior than the exterior supernatural visions. Nevertheless, it is true that some of these exterior bodily visions may produce a deeper impression; the communication, after all, is as God wills. We are speaking, however, merely as concerns their nature, and in this respect they are more spiritual.[4]

4. It is to these senses of imagination and fancy that the devil habitually betakes himself with his wiles—now natural, now supernatural;[5] for they are the door and entrance to the soul, and here, as we have said,[6] the understanding comes to take up or set down its goods, as it were in a harbour or in a store-house where it keeps its provisions. And for this reason it is hither that both God and the devil always come with their jewels of supernatural forms and images,[7] to offer them to the understanding; although God does not make use of this means alone to instruct the soul, but dwells within it in substance, and is able to do this by Himself and by other methods.

5. There is no need for me to stop here in order to give instruction concerning the signs by which it may be known which visions are of God and which not, and which are of one kind and which of another; for this is not my intention, which is only to instruct the understanding herein, that it may not be hindered or impeded as to union with Divine Wisdom by the good visions, neither may be deceived by those which are false.

6. I say, then, that with regard to all these imaginary visions and apprehensions and to all other forms and species whatsoever, which

---

[1] 3 Kings xxii, 11 [A.V., 1 Kings xxii, 11].   [2] [St. Matthew xxvii, 19.]
[3] E.p. has only: 'and [in] many other places.'   [4] E.p.: 'more interior.'
[5] E.p. omits: 'now natural, now supernatural.' The Saint employs this last word, in this passage, with the sense of 'preternatural.' Only God can transcend the bounds of nature, but the devil can act in such a way that he appears to be doing so, counterfeiting miracles, and so forth.
[6] E.p. omits: 'as we have said.'   [7] E.p.: 'come hither with images and forms.'

present themselves beneath some particular kind of knowledge or image or form, whether they be false and come from the devil or are recognized as true and coming from God, the understanding must not be embarrassed by them or feed upon them, neither must the soul desire to receive them or to have them,[1] lest it should no longer be detached, free, pure and simple, without any mode or manner, as is required for union.[2]

7. The reason of this is that all these forms which we have already mentioned are always represented, in the apprehension of the soul, as we have said, beneath certain modes and manners which have limitations; and that the Wisdom of God, wherewith the understanding is to be united, has no mode or manner, neither is it contained within any particular or distinct kind of intelligence or limit, because it is wholly pure and simple. And as, in order that these two extremes may be united—namely, the soul and Divine Wisdom—it will be necessary for them to attain to agreement, by means of a certain mutual resemblance,[3] hence it follows that the soul must be pure and simple, neither bounded by, nor attached to, any particular kind of intelligence, nor modified by any limitation of form, species and image. As God comes not within[4] any image or form, neither is contained within any particular kind of intelligence, so the soul, in order to reach God,[5] must likewise come within no distinct form or kind of intelligence.

8. And that there is no form or likeness in God is clearly declared by the Holy Spirit in Deuteronomy, where He says: *Vocem verborum ejus audistis, et formam penitus non vidistis.*[6] Which signifies: Ye heard the voice of His words, and ye saw in God no form whatsoever. But He says that there was darkness there, and clouds and thick darkness, which are the confused and dark knowledge whereof we have spoken, wherein the soul is united with God. And afterwards He says further: *Non vidistis aliquam similitudinem in die, qua locutus est vobis Dominus in Horeb de medio ignis.* That is: Ye saw no likeness in God upon the day when He spoke to you on Mount Horeb, out of the midst of the fire.[7]

9. And that the soul cannot reach the height of God,[8] even as far as is possible in this life, by means of any form and figure, is declared likewise by the same Holy Spirit in the Book of Numbers, where God

[1] E.p.: 'or to set its foot upon them.'   [2] E.p.: 'for Divine union.'
[3] E.p.: 'by a certain manner of resemblance.'
[4] E.p.: 'As God is not contained within.'
[5] [*Lit.*, 'to come within God.'] E.p.: 'to be united with God.'
[6] Deuteronomy iv, 12.   [7] Deuteronomy iv, 15.
[8] E.p.: 'cannot reach the summit of union with God.'

reproves Aaron and Miriam, the brother and sister of Moses, because they murmured against him, and, desiring to convey to them the loftiness of the state of union and friendship with Him wherein He had placed him, said: *Si quis inter vos fuerit Propheta Domini, in visione apparebo ei, vel per somnium loquar ad illum. At non talis servus meus Moyses, qui in omni domo mea fidelissimus est: ore enim ad os loquor ei, et palem, et non per ænigmata, et figuras Dominum videt.*[1] Which signifies: If there be any prophet of the Lord among you, I will appear to him in some vision or form, or I will speak with him in his dreams; but there is none like My servant Moses, who is the most faithful in all My house, and I speak with him mouth to mouth, and he sees not God by comparisons, similitudes and figures. Herein He says clearly that, in this lofty state of union whereof we are speaking, God is not communicated to the soul by means of any disguise of imaginary vision or similitude or form, neither can He be so communicated; but mouth to mouth—that is, in the naked and pure essence of God, which is the mouth of God in love, with the naked and pure essence of the soul,[2] which is the mouth of the soul in love of God.

10. Wherefore, in order to come to this essential union of love in God,[3] the soul must have a care not to lean upon[4] imaginary visions, nor upon forms or figures or particular objects of the understanding; for these cannot serve it as a proportionate and proximate means to such an end; rather they would disturb it, and for this reason the soul must renounce them and strive not to have them. For if in any circumstances they were to be received and prized, it would be for the sake of the profit which true visions bring to the soul and the good effect which they produce upon it. But, for this to happen, it is not necessary to receive them;[5] indeed, for the soul's profit, it is well always to reject them. For these imaginary visions, like the outward bodily visions whereof we have spoken, do the soul good by communicating to it intelligence or love or sweetness; but for this effect to be produced by them in the soul it is not necessary that it should desire to receive them; for, as has also been said above, at this very time[6] when they are present to the imagination, they produce in the soul and infuse into it

---

[1] Numbers xii, 6–8. [D.V. has 'Mary' for 'Miriam'.]

[2] The editions of 1630 and later dates add here: 'by means of the will.' But these words are found neither in e.p. nor in the Codices.

[3] E.p.: 'to this so perfect union of God.'

[4] [The progressive form is used in the Spanish: 'not to go (or 'be') leaning upon.']

[5] A, B: 'but it is necessary, for this to happen, not to admit them.' The second part of this sentence shows that the reading of the text, which is that of both Alc. and e.p., is the correct one.   [6] E.p. omits : 'at this very time.'

intelligence and love, or sweetness, or whatever effect God wills them to produce. And not only do they produce this joint effect, but principally, although not simultaneously, they produce their effect in the soul passively,[1] without its being able to hinder this effect, even if it so desired,[2] just as it was also powerless to acquire it, although it had been able previously to prepare itself.[3] For, even as the window is powerless[4] to impede the ray of sunlight which strikes it, but, when it is prepared by being cleansed, receives its light passively without any diligence or labour on its own part, even so the soul, although against its will,[5] cannot fail to receive in itself the influences and communications of those figures, however much it might desire to resist them.[6] For the will that is negatively inclined cannot, if coupled with loving and humble resignation, resist supernatural infusions; only the impurity and imperfections of the soul can resist them[7] even as the stains upon a window impede the brightness of the sunlight.[8]

11. From this it is evident that, when the soul completely detaches itself, in its will and affection, from the apprehensions of the stains of those forms, images and figures wherein are clothed[9] the spiritual communications which we have described, not only is it not deprived of these communications and the blessings which they cause within it, but it is much better prepared to receive them with greater abundance, clearness, liberty of spirit and simplicity, when all these apprehensions are set on one side, for they are, as it were, curtains and veils covering the spiritual thing[10] that is behind them. And thus, if the soul desire to feed upon them, they occupy spirit and sense in such a way that the spirit cannot communicate itself simply and freely; for, while they are still occupied with the outer rind, it is clear that the understanding is not free to receive the substance.[11] Wherefore, if the soul at that time desires to receive these forms and to set store by them, it

---

1 E.p.: 'And thus the soul receives their quickening effect passively.'

2 E.p. omits: 'even if it so desired.'

3 E.p. substitutes for this last clause: 'notwithstanding its having laboured previously to prepare itself.'

4 E.p.: 'To some extent it resembles a window, which is powerless . . .'

5 E.p. omits: 'although against its will.'   6 E.p. omits: 'however . . . resist them.'

7 E.p.: 'For the will cannot resist supernatural infusions, although without doubt the impurity and imperfections of the soul are an obstruction.'

8 [Lit., 'impede the brightness.']

9 E.p.: 'from the stains of the apprehensions, images and figures wherein are clothed.' A: 'from the apprehensions and the stains of them and the affections wherein are clothed.' B: 'from the apprehensions of the stains of those forms and figures wherein are clothed.'

10 E.p.: 'the more spiritual thing.'

11 This is the reading of e.p. A, B [followed by P. Silverio] read: 'to receive those forms.' Alc. reads merely: 'to receive.'

would be embarrassing itself, and contenting itself with the least important part of them—namely, all that it can apprehend and know of them, which is the form and image and particular object of the understanding in question. The most important part of them, which is the spiritual part that is infused into the soul, it can neither apprehend nor understand, nor can it even know what it is, or be able to express it, since it is purely spiritual. All that it can know of them, as we say, according to its manner of understanding, is but the least part of what is in them—namely, the forms perceptible by sense. For this reason I say that what it cannot understand or imagine is communicated to it by these visions, passively, without any effort of its own to understand and without its even knowing how to make such an effort.

12. Wherefore the eyes of the soul must ever be withdrawn from all these apprehensions which it can see and understand distinctly, which are communicated through sense, and do not make for a foundation of faith, or for reliance on faith, and must be set upon that which it sees not, and which belongs not to sense, but to spirit, which can be expressed by no figure of sense; and it is this which leads the soul to union in faith, which is the true medium, as has been said. And thus these visions will profit the soul substantially, in respect of faith, when it is able completely to renounce the sensible and intelligible part[1] of them, and to make good use of the purpose for which God gives them to the soul, by casting them aside; for, as we said of corporeal visions, God gives them not so that the soul may desire to have them and to set its affection upon them.

13. But there arises here this question: If it be true that God gives the soul supernatural visions, but not so that it may desire to have them or be attached to them or set store by them, why does He give them at all, since by their means the soul may fall into many errors and perils, or at the least may find in them such hindrances to further progress as are here described, especially since God can come to the soul, and communicate to it, spiritually and substantially, that which He communicates to it through sense, by means of the sensible forms and visions aforementioned?

14. We shall answer this question in the following chapter:[2] it involves important teaching, most necessary, as I see it, both to spiritual persons and to those who instruct them. For herein is taught the way and purpose of God with respect to these visions, which many know

---

[1] E.p.: 'the particular intelligible part.'
[2] The words 'in the following chapter' occur in Alc. and e.p. only.

not, so that they cannot rule themselves or guide themselves to union, neither can they guide others to union, through these visions. For they think that, just because they know them to be true and to come from God, it is well to receive them and to trust them,[1] not realizing that the soul will become attached to them, cling to them and be hindered by them, as it will by things of the world, if it know not how to renounce these as well as those. And thus they think it well to receive one kind of vision and to reject another, causing themselves, and the souls under their care, great labour and peril in discerning between the truth and the falsehood of these visions. But God does not command them to undertake this labour, nor does He desire that sincere and simple souls should be led into this conflict and danger; for they have safe and sound teaching, which is that of the faith, wherein they can go forward.

15. This, however, cannot be unless they close their eyes to all that is of particular and clear intelligence and sense. For, although Saint Peter was quite certain of that vision of glory which he saw in Christ at the Transfiguration, yet, after having described it in his second canonical Epistle, he desired not that it should be taken for an important and sure testimony, but rather directed his hearers to faith, saying: *Et habemus firmiorem propheticum sermonem: cui benefacitis attendentes, quasi lucernæ lucenti in caliginoso loco, donec dies elucescat.*[2] Which signifies: And we have a surer testimony than this vision of Tabor— namely, the sayings and words of the prophets who bear testimony to Christ, whereunto ye must indeed cling, as to a candle which gives light in a dark place. If we will think upon this comparison, we shall find therein the teaching which we are now expounding. For, in telling us to look to the faith whereof the prophets spake, as to a candle that shines in a dark place, he is bidding us remain in the darkness, with our eyes closed to all these other lights; and telling us that in this darkness, faith alone, which likewise is dark, will be the light to which we shall cling; for if we desire to cling to these other bright lights—namely, to distinct objects of the understanding—we cease to cling to that dark light, which is faith, and we no longer have that light in the dark place whereof Saint Peter speaks. This place, which here signifies the under-standing, which is the candlestick wherein this candle of faith is set, must be dark until the day when the clear vision of God dawns upon it in the life to come, or, in this life, until the day of transformation and union with God to which the soul is journeying.[3]

---

[1] E.p.: 'it is well to lean on them and cleave to them.'   [2] 2 St. Peter i, 19.
[3] Alc. ends the chapter with the words: 'transformation and union.' E.p. has 'with Him' for 'with God.'

CHAPTER XVII

Wherein is described the purpose and manner of God in His communication of spiritual blessings to the soul by means of the senses. Herein is answered the question which has been referred to.

THERE is much to be said concerning the purpose of God, and concerning the manner wherein He gives these visions in order to raise up the soul from its lowly estate to His Divine union. All spiritual books deal with this and in this treatise of ours the method which we pursue is to explain it;[1] therefore I shall only say in this chapter as much as is necessary to answer our question, which was as follows: Since in these supernatural visions there is so much hindrance and peril to progress, as we have said, why does God, Who is most wise and desires to remove stumbling-blocks and snares from the soul, offer and communicate them to it?

2. In order to answer this, it is well first of all to set down three fundamental points.[2] The first is from Saint Paul *ad Romanos*, where he says: *Quæ autem sunt, a Deo ordinatæ sunt.*[3] Which signifies: The works that are done are ordained of God. The second is from the Holy Spirit in the Book of Wisdom, where He says: *Disponit omnia suaviter.*[4] And this is as though He had said: The wisdom of God, although it extends from one end to another—that is to say, from one extreme to another—orders all things with sweetness. The third is from the theologians, who say that *Omnia movet secundum modum eorum.* That is, God moves all things according to their nature.

3. It is clear, then, from these fundamental points, that if God is to move the soul and to raise it up from the extreme depth of its lowliness to the extreme height of His loftiness, in Divine union with Him, He must do it with order and sweetness and according to the nature of the soul itself. Then, since the order[5] whereby the soul acquires knowledge is through forms and images of created things, and the natural way wherein it acquires this knowledge and wisdom is through the senses, it follows that, if God is to raise up the soul to supreme knowledge, and to do so with sweetness, He must begin to work from the lowest and extreme end of the senses of the soul, in order that He may gradually

---

[1] E.p. omits: 'and in this treatise . . . to explain it.'
[2] E.p.: 'to take for granted three principles.'
[3] Romans xiii, 1.   [4] Wisdom viii, 1.
[5] B: 'since the method and order.' ['Method' is the *modo* translated above as 'nature.']

lead it,[1] according to its own nature, to the other extreme of His
spiritual wisdom, which belongs not to sense. Wherefore He first leads
it onward by instructing it through forms, images and ways of sense,
according to its own method of understanding, now naturally, now
supernaturally, and by means of reasoning, to this supreme Spirit of
God.

4. It is for this reason that God gives the soul visions and forms,
images and other kinds of sensible and intelligible knowledge of a
spiritual nature;[2] not that God would not give it spiritual wisdom[3]
immediately, and all at once, if the two extremes—which are human
and Divine, sense and spirit—could in the ordinary way concur and
unite in one single act, without the previous intervention of many other
preparatory acts which concur among themselves in order and sweetness, and are a basis and a preparation one for another, like natural
agents; so that the first acts serve the second, the second the third, and
so onward, in exactly the same way.[4] And thus God brings man to
perfection according to the way of man's own nature, working from
what is lowest and most exterior up to what is most interior and
highest. First, then, He perfects his bodily senses, impelling him to
make use of good things which are natural, perfect and exterior, such as
hearing sermons and masses, looking on holy things, mortifying the
palate at meals and chastening the sense of touch by penance and holy
rigour. And, when these senses are in some degree prepared, He is
wont to perfect them still further, by bestowing on them certain
supernatural favours and gifts, in order to confirm them the more
completely in that which is good, offering them certain supernatural
communications, such as visions of saints or holy things, in corporeal
shape, the sweetest perfumes, locutions, and exceeding great delights of
touch, wherewith[5] sense is greatly confirmed in virtue and is withdrawn from a desire for evil things. And besides this He continues at
the same time to perfect the interior bodily senses, whereof we are
here treating, such as imagination and fancy, and to habituate[6] them to
that which is good, by means of considerations, meditations, and
reflections of a sacred kind, in all of which He is instructing the spirit.
And, when these are prepared by this natural exercise, God is wont to

---

[1] E.p.: 'may gradually raise it.'   [2] E.p. omits: 'of a spiritual nature.'
[3] E.p.: 'spiritual substance.'
[4] E.p. modifies: '. . . preparation one for another; even as with natural agents the first
serve the second, the second the third, and so onward.'
[5] E.p.: locutions, together with pure and singular sweetness, wherewith . . .'
[6] A, B: 'and to habilitate.'

enlighten and spiritualize them still more by means of certain supernatural visions, which are those that we are here calling imaginary;
wherein, as we have said, the spirit, at the same time, profits greatly, for
both kinds of vision help to take away its grossness and gradually to
reform it. And after this manner God continues to lead the soul step
by step till it reaches that which is the most interior of all; not that it is
always[1] necessary for Him to observe this order, and to cause the soul to
advance exactly in this way, from the first step to the last; sometimes
He allows the soul to attain one stage and not another, or leads it from
the more interior to the less, or effects two stages of progress together.
This happens when God sees it to be meet for the soul, or when He
desires to grant it His favours in this way;[2] nevertheless His ordinary
method is as has been said.

5. It is in this way, then, that God instructs[3] the soul and makes it
more spiritual, communicating spirituality to it first of all by means of
outward and palpable things, adapted to sense, on account of the soul's
feebleness and incapacity, so that, by means of the outer husk of those
things of sense which in themselves are good, the spirit may make[4]
particular acts and receive so many spiritual communications[5] that it
may form a habit as to things spiritual, and may acquire actual and
substantial spirituality,[6] which is completely removed from every
sense. To this, as we have said, the soul cannot attain except very
gradually, and in its own way—that is, by means of sense—to which
it has ever been attached.[7] And thus, in proportion as the spirit attains
more nearly to converse with God, it becomes ever more detached and
emptied of the ways of sense, which are those of imaginary meditation
and reflection. Wherefore, when the soul attains perfectly to spiritual
converse with God, it must of necessity have been voided of all that
relates to God and yet might come under the head of sense. Even so,
the more closely a thing grows attracted to one extreme, the farther
removed and withdrawn[8] it becomes from the other; and, when it
comes to rest perfectly in the one, it will also have withdrawn itself

---

[1] E.p. omits 'always.'

[2] E.p.: '. . . and not another, when He sees that it so befits the soul and desires to grant
it favours in this way.'

[3] [The verb is progressive ('goes (on) instructing').] A, B, e.p. add: 'ordinarily.'

[4] [This verb also is progressive: 'may go (on) making.']

[5] [Lit., 'mouthfuls of spiritual communication.' Cf. p. 135, n. 2, below.]

[6] E.p.: 'may acquire the most substantial of the spirit' [i.e., the most substantial
spirituality].

[7] A, B add: 'and has come near.'

[8] E.p.: 'and rejected.' [All the verbs in these last two clauses are in the progressive
form.]

perfectly from the other. Wherefore there is a commonly quoted spiritual adage which says: *Gustato spiritu, desipit omnis caro.* Which signifies: After the taste and sweetness of the spirit have been experienced, everything carnal is insipid.[1] That is: No profit or enjoyment is afforded by all the ways of the flesh,[2] wherein is included all communication of sense with the spiritual. And this is clear: for, if it is spirit, it has no more to do with sense; and, if sense can comprehend it, it is no longer pure spirit. For, the more can be known of it by natural apprehension and sense, the less it has of spirit and of the supernatural, as has been explained above.

6. The spirit[3] that has become perfect, therefore, pays no heed to sense, nor does it receive anything through sense, nor make any great use of it, neither does it need to do so, in its relations with God, as it did aforetime when it had not grown spiritually. It is this that is signified by that passage from Saint Paul's Epistle to the Corinthians which says: *Cum essem parvulus, loquebar ut parvulus, sapiebam ut parvulus, cogitabam ut parvulus. Quando autem factus sum vir, evacuavi quæ erant parvuli.*[4] This signifies: When I was a child, I spake as a child, I knew as a child, I thought as a child; but, when I became a man, I put away[5] childish things. We have already explained how the things of sense, and the knowledge that spirit can derive[6] from them, are the business of a child. Thus, if the soul should desire to cling to them for ever, and not to throw them aside, it would never be aught but a little child; it would speak ever of God as a child, and would know of God as a child, and would think of God as a child;[7] for, clinging to the outer husk of sense, which pertains to the child, it would never attain to the substance of the spirit, which pertains to the perfect man. And thus the soul must not desire to receive the said revelations in order to continue in growth, even though God offer them to it, just as the child must leave the breast in order to accustom its palate to strong meat, which is more substantial.

7. You will ask, then, if, when the soul is immature, it must take these things, and, when it is grown, must abandon them; even as an infant must take the breast, in order to nourish itself, until it be older and can leave it. I answer that, with respect to meditation and natural reflection by means of which the soul begins to seek God, it is true that

---

[1] E.p.: 'is tasteless.'   [2] E.p.: 'all the tastes or roads of sense.'
[3] E.p.: 'the spiritual man.'   [4] 1 Corinthians xiii, 11.
[5] [*Lit.,* 'I emptied.'] A, B, e.p.: 'I voided.'   [6] E.p.: 'that can be derived.'
[7] A, B: 'it would never be aught but a little child; it would ever speak of, know and think of God as a child.'

it must not leave the breast of sense in order to continue taking in nourishment until the time and season to leave it have arrived, and this comes when God brings the soul into a more spiritual communion, which is contemplation, concerning which we gave instruction in the eleventh chapter of this book.[1] But, when it is a question of imaginary visions, or other supernatural apprehensions, which can enter the senses without the co-operation of man's free will, I say that at no time and season must it receive them,[2] whether the soul be in the state of perfection, or whether in a state less perfect—not even though they come from God. And this for two reasons. The first is that, as we have said, He produces His effect in the soul,[3] without its being able to hinder it, although, as often happens, it can and may hinder visions;[4] and consequently that effect[5] which was to be produced in the soul is communicated to it much more substantially, although not after that manner. For, as we said likewise, the soul cannot hinder the blessings that God desires to communicate to it, since it is not in the soul's power to do so, save when it has some imperfection and attachment; and there is neither imperfection nor attachment in renouncing these things with humility and misgiving.[6] The second reason is that the soul may free itself from the peril and effort inherent in discerning between evil visions and good, and in deciding whether an angel be of light or of darkness. This effort brings the soul no advantage; it merely wastes its time, and hinders it, and becomes to it an occasion of many imperfections and of failure to make progress. The soul concerns not itself, in such a case, with what is important, nor frees itself of trifles in the shape of apprehensions and perceptions of some particular kind. This has already been said in the discussion of corporeal visions; and more will be said on the subject hereafter.

8. Let it be believed, too, that, if Our Lord were not about to lead the soul in a way befitting its own nature, as we say here, He would never communicate to it the abundance of His Spirit through these

---

[1] In reality, this instruction is given in Chap. xiii.

[2] E.p.: 'must it seek them, or remain for long in them.'

[3] So Alc. The other MSS. and e.p. read: '. . . that, as we have said, they produce their effect passively in the soul.'

[4] E.p. has: 'although it do something to hinder the manner of the vision,' and omits: 'as often happens.'

[5] E.p.: 'that second effect.'

[6] E.p. omits the passage: 'For, as we said likewise . . . and attachment,' and substitutes for 'and there . . . misgiving': 'For, in renouncing these things with humility and misgiving, there is neither imperfection nor attachment.' The Codices end the sentence at the word 'misgiving,' but e.p. continues: 'but rather disinterestedness and emptiness, which is the best preparation for union with God.'

aqueducts, which are so narrow—these forms and figures and particular perceptions—by means whereof He gives the soul enlightenment by crumbs. For this cause David says: *Mittit crystallum suam sicut buccellas.*[1] Which is as much as to say: He sent His wisdom to the souls as in morsels.[2] It is greatly to be lamented that, though the soul has infinite capacity,[3] it should be given its food by morsels conveyed through the senses, by reason of the small degree of its spirituality and its incapacitation by sense. Saint Paul was also grieved by this lack of preparation and this incapability of men for receiving the Spirit, when he wrote to the Corinthians, saying: 'I, brethren, when I came to you, could not speak to you as to spiritual persons, but as to carnal; for ye could not receive it, neither can ye now.' *Tamquam parvulis in Christo lac potum vobis dedi, non escam.*[4] That is: I have given you milk to drink, as to infants in Christ, and not solid food to eat.[5]

9. It now remains, then, to be pointed out that the soul must not allow its eyes to rest upon that outer husk—namely, figures and objects set before it supernaturally. These may be presented to the exterior senses, as are locutions and words audible to the ear; or, to the eyes, visions of saints, and of beauteous radiance; or perfumes to the sense of smell; or tastes and sweetnesses to the palate; or other delights to the touch, which are wont to proceed from the spirit, a thing that very commonly happens to spiritual persons.[6] Or the soul may have to avert its eyes from visions of interior sense, such as imaginary[7] visions, all of which it must renounce entirely. It must set its eyes only upon the spiritual good which they produce, striving to preserve it in its works and to practise that which is for the due[8] service of God, paying no heed to those representations nor desiring any pleasure of sense. And in this way the soul takes from these things only that which God intends and wills—namely, the spirit of devotion—for there is no other important purpose for which He gives them; and it casts aside that which He would not give if these gifts could be received in the spirit without it,[9] as we have said—namely, the exercise and apprehension of the senses.

---

[1] Psalm cxlvii, 17.
[2] C, D: 'as morsels.' [*Lit.*, 'mouthfuls.']
[3] E.p.: 'has as it were infinite capacity.' All the MSS. have the reading of the text.
[4] 1 Corinthians iii, 1–2.
[5] E.p. omits: 'in Christ' and 'to eat.'
[6] E.p. omits: 'a thing . . . persons.'
[7] E.p.: 'interior imaginary.'
[8] So Alc., C, D.   A, B, e.p. read 'naked' [i.e., 'pure'] for 'due.'
[9] The remainder of the sentence is omitted in Alc.

CHAPTER XVIII

Which treats of the harm that certain spiritual masters may do to souls when they direct them not by a good method with respect to the visions aforementioned. Describes also how these visions may cause deception even though they be of God.

IN this matter of visions we cannot be as brief as we should desire, since there is so much to say about them. Although in substance we have said what is relevant in order to explain to the spiritual person how he is to behave with regard to the visions aforementioned, and to the master who directs him, the way in which he is to deal with his disciple,[1] yet it will not be superfluous to go into somewhat greater detail about this doctrine, and to give more enlightenment as to the harm which can ensue, either to spiritual souls or to the masters who direct them, if they are over-credulous about them, although they be of God.

2. The reason which has now moved me to write at length about this is the lack of discretion, as I understand it, which I have observed in certain spiritual masters. Trusting to these supernatural apprehensions, and believing that they are good and come from God, both masters and disciples have fallen into great error and found themselves in dire straits, wherein is fulfilled the saying of Our Saviour: *Si cæcus cæco ducatum præstet, ambo in foveam cadunt.*[2] Which signifies: If a blind man lead another blind man, both fall into the pit. And He says not 'shall fall,' but 'fall.' For they may fall without falling into error, since the very venturing of the one to guide the other is a going astray, and thus they fall in this respect alone,[3] at the very least. And, first of all, there are some whose way and method with souls that experience these visions cause them to stray, or embarrass them with respect to their visions, or guide them not along the road of humility, but encourage them to fix their eyes upon them in some way (for which reason they remain without the true spirit of faith[4]) and edify them not in faith, but lead them to speak highly of those things.[5] By doing

---

1 A, B, e.p. add: 'concerning them.'
2 St. Matthew xv, 14.
3 E.p. omits 'alone.'
4 E.p.: 'for which reason they journey not by way of the pure and perfect spirit of faith.'
5 E.p.: 'and edify them not, neither fortify them in it [i.e., in faith], making these things of great account.'

this they make them realize that they themselves set some value upon them, or[1] make great account of them, and, consequently, their disciples do the same. Thus their souls have been set upon these apprehensions, instead of being edified in faith, so that they may be empty and detached, and freed from those things and can soar to the heights of dark faith. All this arises from the terms and language which the soul observes its master to employ with respect to these apprehensions; somehow it very easily develops a satisfaction and an esteem for them, which is not in its own control, and which averts its eyes from the abyss of faith.

3. And the reason why this is so easy must be that the soul is so greatly occupied with these things of sense that, as it is inclined to them by nature, and is likewise disposed to enjoy the apprehension of distinct and sensible things, it has only to observe in its confessor, or in some other person, a certain esteem and appreciation for them, and not merely will it at once conceive the same itself, but also, without its realizing the fact, its desire will become lured away by them, so that it will feed upon them and will be ever more inclined toward them and will set a certain value[2] upon them. And hence arise many imperfections, at the very least; for the soul is no longer as humble as before, but thinks that all this is of some importance and productive of good, and that it is itself esteemed by God, and that He is pleased and somewhat satisfied with it, which is contrary to humility. And thereupon the devil secretly sets about increasing this, without the soul's realizing it, and begins to suggest ideas to it about others, as to whether they have these things or have them not, or are this or are that; which is contrary to holy simplicity and spiritual solitude.

4. There is much more to be said about these evils, and of how such souls, unless they withdraw themselves, grow not in faith, and also of how there are other evils of the same kind which, although they be not so palpable and recognizable[3] as these, are subtler and more hateful in the Divine eyes, and which result from not living in complete detachment. Let us, however, leave this subject now,[4] until we come to treat of the vice of spiritual gluttony[5] and of the other six vices, whereof, with the help of God,[6] many things will be said, concerning these subtle

---

[1] E.p. omits: 'set some value upon them, or.'
[2] So all the MSS.   E.p. alters to 'much value' [bringing out the general sense of the passage by the change].
[3] E.p. omits: 'and recognizable.'
[4] E.p. omits 'complete' and reads: 'We shall leave' for 'Let us leave.'
[5] A, B omit the remainder of the paragraph.
[6] E.p. has: 'God willing.'

and delicate stains which adhere to the spirit when its director cannot guide it in detachment.

5. Let us now say something of this manner wherein certain confessors deal with souls, and instruct them ill. And of a truth I could wish that I knew how to describe it, for I realize that it is a difficult thing to explain how the spirit of the disciple grows in conformity with that of his spiritual father, in a hidden and secret way; and this matter is so tedious that it wearies me,[1] for it seems impossible to speak of the one thing without describing the other also, as they are spiritual things, and the one corresponds with the other.

6. But it is sufficient to say here that[2] I believe, if the spiritual father has an inclination toward revelations of such a kind that they mean something to him,[3] or satisfy or delight his soul, it is impossible but that he will impress that delight and that aim[4] upon the spirit of his disciple, even without realizing it, unless the disciple be more advanced than he; and, even in this latter case, he may well do him grievous harm if he continue with him. For, from that inclination of the spiritual father toward such visions, and the pleasure which he takes in them, there arises a certain kind of esteem for them, of which, unless he watch it carefully, he cannot fail to communicate some indication or impression to other persons; and if any other such person is like-minded and has a similar inclination, it is impossible, as I understand, but that there will be communicated from the one to the other a readiness to apprehend these things and a great esteem for them.

7. But we need not now go into detail about this. Let us speak of the confessor who, whether or no he be inclined toward these things, has not the prudence that he ought to have in disencumbering the soul of his disciple and detaching his desire from them, but begins to speak to him about these visions and devotes the greater part of his spiritual conversation to them, as we have said, giving him signs by which he may distinguish good visions from evil. Now, although it is well to know this, there is no reason for him to involve the soul in such labour, anxiety and peril.[5] By paying no heed[6] to visions, and refusing to receive them, all this is prevented, and the soul acts as it should. Nor is this all, for such confessors, when they see that their penitents

1 E.p. omits: 'and this . . . wearies me.'
2 E.p. omits this phrase. A, B have: 'And, treating of that which I promised.'
3 E.p. : 'that they have much weight with him.'
4 E.p. : 'that same pleasure and esteem.'
5 E.p. adds: 'save in a case of stringent necessity, as has been said.'
6 E.p. : 'By paying little heed.'

are receiving visions from God, beg them to entreat God to reveal them to themselves also, or to say such and such things to them, with respect to themselves or to others, and the foolish souls[1] do so, thinking that it is lawful to desire knowledge by this means. For they suppose that, because God is pleased to reveal or say something by supernatural means, in His own way or for His own purpose, it is lawful for them to desire Him to reveal it to them, and even to entreat Him to do so.

8. And, if it come to pass that God answers their petition and reveals it, they become more confident, thinking that, because God answers them, it is His will and pleasure to do so; whereas, in reality, it is neither God's will nor His pleasure. And they frequently act or believe according to that which He has revealed to them, or according to the way wherein He has answered them; for, as they are attached to that manner of communion with God, the revelation makes a great impression upon them and their will acquiesces in it. They take a natural pleasure in their own way of thinking and therefore naturally acquiesce in it; and frequently they go astray.[2] Then they see that something happens in a way they had not expected; and they marvel, and then begin to doubt if the thing were of God,[3] since it happens not, and they see it not, according to their expectations. At the beginning they thought two things: first, that the vision was of God, since at the beginning it agreed so well with their disposition, and their natural inclination to that kind of thing may well have been the cause of this agreement, as we have said; and secondly that, being of God, it would turn out as they thought or expected.

9. And herein lies a great delusion, for revelations or locutions which are of God do not always turn out as men expect or as they imagine inwardly. And thus they must never be believed or trusted blindly, even though they are known to be revelations or answers or sayings of God. For, although they may in themselves be certain and true, they are not always so[4] in their causes, and according to our

---

[1] All the MSS. have this reading, but the editor of e.p. evidently disliked the exact and expressive phrase, for he substituted 'good souls' for it.

[2] E.p. abbreviates: '. . . they become more confident about other occasions and think that this manner of communion with God is His pleasure, whereas, in truth, it is neither His pleasure nor His will. And, as they are attached to that manner of communion with God, the revelation makes a great impression upon them, and their will acquiesces naturally in it. For, as they take a natural pleasure in their own way of thinking, they naturally acquiesce in it, and they frequently go astray in what they say.'

[3] [*Lit.*, 'if it were of God.'] E.p.: 'if they were of God or no.' A: 'if it were of God or were not God [*sic*].' B: 'if it were of God or were not of God.'

[4] E.p. adds: 'of necessity' and omits 'in their causes.'

manner of understanding,[1] as we shall prove in the chapter following. And afterwards we shall further say and prove that, although God sometimes gives a supernatural answer to that which is asked of Him, it is not His pleasure to do so, and sometimes, although He answers, He is angered.

CHAPTER XIX

Wherein is expounded and proved how, although visions and locutions which come from God are true,[2] we may be deceived about them. This is proved by quotations from Divine Scripture.[3]

FOR two reasons we have said that, although visions and locutions which come from God are true, and in themselves are always certain, they are not always so with respect to ourselves. One reason is the defective way in which we understand them; and the other, the variety of their causes.[4] In the first place, it is clear that they are not always as they seem, nor do they turn out as they appear to our manner of thinking. The reason for this is that, since God is vast and boundless, He is wont, in His prophecies, locutions and revelations, to employ ways, concepts and methods of seeing things which differ greatly from such purpose and method as can normally be understood by ourselves; and these are the truer and the more certain the less they seem so to us. This we constantly see in the Scriptures. To many of the ancients many prophecies and locutions of God came not to pass as they expected, because they understood them after their own manner, in the wrong way, and quite literally. This will be clearly seen in these passages.

2. In Genesis, God said to Abraham, when He had brought him to the land of the Chanaanites: *Tibi dabo terram hanc.*[5] Which signifies, I will give thee this land. And when He had said it to him many times, and Abraham was by now very old, and He had never given it to him, though He had said this to him, Abraham answered God once again

---

[1] A, B end the chapter here.   [2] A, B, e.p. add: 'in themselves.'
[3] This sentence is omitted in A, B.
[4] E.p. amplifies thus: '. . . always certain, they are not always so in our understanding. One reason is the defective way in which we understand them; and the other is the causes and foundations of them, which are minatory, and, as it were, conditional, depending on the amendment of this or the accomplishment of that, although the locution itself may seem to be of an absolute character. These two things we shall prove with a few quotations from Scripture' [*lit.*, 'with some Divine authorities'].
[5] Genesis xv, 7.

and said: *Domine, unde scire possum, quod possessurus sim eam?* That is: Lord, whereby or by what sign am I to know that I am to possess it? Then God revealed to him that he was not to possess it in person, but that his sons would do so after four hundred years; and Abraham then understood the promise, which in itself was most true; for, in giving it to his sons for love of him, God was giving it to himself. And thus Abraham was deceived by the way in which he himself had understood the prophecy. If he had then acted according to his own understanding of it, those that saw him die without its having been given to him might have erred greatly; for they were not to see the time of its fulfilment. And, as they had heard him say that God would give it to him,[1] they would have been confounded and would have believed it to have been false.

3. Likewise to his grandson Jacob, when Joseph his son brought him to Egypt because of the famine in Chanaan, and when he was on the road, God appeared and said: *Jacob, Jacob, noli timere, descende in Aegiptum, quia in gentem magnam faciam te ibi. Ego descendam tecum illuc. . . . Et inde adducam te revertentem.*[2] Which signifies: Jacob, fear not; go down into Egypt, and I will go down there with thee; and, when thou goest forth thence again, I will bring thee out and guide thee. This promise, as it would seem according to our own manner of understanding, was not fulfilled, for, as we know, the good old man Jacob died in Egypt and never left it alive. The word of God was to be fulfilled in his children, whom He brought out thence after many years, being Himself their guide upon the way. It is clear that anyone who had known of this promise made by God to Jacob would have considered it certain that Jacob, even as he had gone to Egypt alive, in his own person,[3] by the command and favour of God, would of a certainty leave it, alive and in his own person,[4] in the same form and manner as he went there, since God had promised him a favourable return; and such a one would have been deceived, and would have marvelled greatly, when he saw him die in Egypt, and the promise, in the sense in which he understood it, remain unfulfilled. And thus, while the words of God are in themselves most true, it is possible to be greatly mistaken with regard to them.

4. In the Judges, again, we read that, when all the tribes of Israel had come together to make war against the tribe of Benjamin, in order to punish a certain evil to which that tribe had been consenting, they

---

[1] E.p.: 'that God had promised it to him.'   [2] Genesis xlvi, 3–4.
[3] E.p. omits: 'in his own person.'   [4] E.p. omits: 'and in his own person.'

were so certain of victory because God had appointed them a captain
for the war, that, when twenty-two thousand of their men were conquered and slain, they marvelled very greatly; and, going into the
presence of God, they wept all that day, knowing not the cause of the
fall, since they had understood[1] that the victory was to be theirs. And,
when they enquired of God if they should give battle again or no, He
answered that they should go and fight against them. This time they
considered victory to be theirs already, and went out with great boldness,[2] and were conquered again the second time, with the loss of
eighteen thousand of their men. Thereat they were greatly confused,
and knew not what to do, seeing that God had commanded them to
fight and yet each time they were vanquished, though they were
superior[3] to their enemies in number and strength, for the men of
Benjamin were no more than twenty-five thousand and seven hundred
and they were four hundred thousand. And in this way they were mistaken in their manner of understanding the words of God. His words
were not deceptive, for He had not told them that they would conquer,
but that they should fight; for by these defeats God wished to chastise
a certain neglect and presumption of theirs, and thus to humble them.
But, when in the end He answered that they would conquer, it was so,
although they conquered only after the greatest stratagem and toil.[4]

5. In this way, and in many other ways, souls are oftentimes
deceived with respect to locutions and revelations that come from God,
because they interpret them according to their apparent sense[5] and
literally; whereas, as has already been explained, the principal intention
of God in giving these things is to express and convey the spirit that is
contained in them, which is difficult to understand. And the spirit is
much more pregnant in meaning than the letter, and is very extraordinary, and goes far beyond its limits. And thus, he that clings to the
letter, or to a locution or to the form or figure of a vision,[6] which can be
apprehended, will not fail to go far astray, and will forthwith fall into
great confusion and error, because he has guided himself by sense
according to these visions, and not allowed the spirit to work in detachment from sense. *Littera enim occidit, spiritus autem vivificat,*[7] as Saint
Paul says. That is: The letter killeth and the spirit giveth life.[8] Wherefore in this matter of sense the letter must be set aside, and the soul

---

[1] E.p.: 'understood and considered.'
[2] So Alc.   A, B: 'with great courage.' E.p.: 'with great daring.'
[3] A, B, e.p.: 'were so greatly superior.'   [4] Judges xx, 12 ff.
[5] [*Lit.*, 'according to the rind.' Cf. p. 113, above.]
[6] Alc., clearly in error, reads 'of a union.'
[7] 2 Corinthians iii, 6.   [8] A, B: 'The letter surely killeth, but the spirit giveth life.'

must remain in darkness, in faith, which is the spirit, and this cannot be comprehended by sense.

6. For which cause, many of the children of Israel, because they took the sayings and prophecies of the prophets according to the strict letter, and these were not fulfilled as they expected, came to make little account of them and believed them not; so much so, that there grew up a common saying among them—almost a proverb, indeed—which turned prophets into ridicule.[1] Of this Isaias complains, speaking and exclaiming in the manner following: *Quem docebit Dominus scientiam? et quem intelligere faciet auditum? ablactatos a lacte, avulsos ab uberibus. Quia manda remanda, manda remanda, expecta reexpecta, expecta reexpecta, modicum ibi, modicum ibi. In loquela enim labii, et lingua altera loquetur ad populum istum.*[2] This signifies: To whom shall God teach knowledge? And whom shall He make to understand His word and prophecy? Only them that are already weaned from the milk and drawn away from the breasts. For all say (that is, concerning the prophecies[3]): Promise and promise again; wait and wait again; wait and wait again;[4] a little there, a little there; for in the words of His lips and in another tongue will He speak to this people. Here Isaias shows quite clearly that these people were turning prophecies into ridicule, and that it was in mockery that they repeated this proverb: 'Wait and then wait again.' They meant that the prophecies were never fulfilled for them, for they were wedded to the letter, which is the milk of infants, and to their own sense, which is the breasts,[5] both of which contradict the greatness of spiritual knowledge. Wherefore he says: To whom shall He teach the wisdom of His prophecies? And whom shall He make to understand His doctrine, save them that are already weaned from the milk of the letter and from the breasts of their own senses? For this reason these people understand it not, save according to this milk[6] of the husk and letter, and these breasts of their own sense, since they say: Promise and promise again;[7] wait and wait again, etc. For it is in the doctrine of the mouth of God, and not in their own doctrine, and it is in another tongue than their own, that God shall speak to them.

7. And thus, in interpreting prophecy, we have not to consider our

---

[1] Alc. alone has this last clause.   [2] Isaias xxviii, 9–11.
[3] Only Alc., e.p. have the parenthesis.
[4] [For 'wait,' we may also read 'hope,' the Spanish word (*esperar*) here used expressing both these ideas.]
[5] A, B omit: 'which is the breasts.'
[6] E.p.: 'but follow this milk.' [This involves only the slight variant of *siguen* for *según*.   [7] This phrase is repeated in Alc. only.

own sense and language, knowing that the language of God is very different from ours, and that it is spiritual language, very far removed from our understanding and exceedingly difficult. So much so is it that even Jeremias, though a prophet of God, when he sees that the significance of the words of God is so different from the sense commonly attributed to them by men, is himself deceived by them and defends the people, saying: *Heu, heu, heu, Domine Deus, ergone decepisti populum istum et Jerusalem, dicens: Pax erit vobis; et ecce pervenit gladius usque ad animam?*[1] Which signifies: Ah, ah, ah, Lord God, hast Thou perchance deceived this people and Jerusalem, saying, 'Peace will come upon you,' and seest Thou here that the sword reacheth unto their soul? For the peace that God promised them was that which was to be made between God and man by means of the Messiah Whom He was to send them, whereas they understood it of temporal peace; and therefore, when they suffered wars and trials, they thought that God was deceiving them, because there befell them the contrary of that which they expected. And thus they said, as Jeremias says likewise: *Exspectavimus pacem, et non erat bonum.*[2] That is: We have looked for peace and there is no boon of peace. And thus it was impossible for them not to be deceived, since they took the prophecy merely in its literal sense.[3] For who would fail to fall into confusion and to go astray if he confined himself to a literal interpretation of that prophecy which David spake concerning Christ, in the seventy-first Psalm, and[4] of all that he says therein, where he says: *Et dominabitur a mari usque ad mare; et a flumine usque ad terminos orbis terrarum.*[5] That is: He shall have dominion from one sea even to the other sea, and from the river even unto the ends of the earth. And likewise in that which he says in the same place: *Liberabit pauperem a potente, et pauperem, cui non erat adjutor.*[6] Which signifies: He shall deliver the poor man from the power of the mighty, and the poor man that had no helper. But later it became known that Christ was born[7] in a low estate and lived in poverty and died in misery; not only had He no dominion over the earth, in a temporal sense, while He lived, but He was subject to lowly people, until He died under the power of Pontius Pilate. And not only did He not deliver poor men—namely, His disciples—from the hands of the mighty, in a temporal sense, but He allowed them to be slain and persecuted for His name's sake.

---

[1] Jeremias iv, 10.   [2] Jeremias viii, 15.
[3] The 1630 edition has: 'literal and grammatical sense.'
[4] E.p.: 'and in particular.'   [5] Psalm lxxi, 8 [A.V., lxxii, 8].
[6] Psalm lxxi, 12 [A.V., lxxii, 12].   [7] [*Lit.,* 'seeing Him later to be born.']

8. The fact is that these prophecies concerning Christ had to be understood spiritually, in which sense they were entirely true. For Christ was not only Lord of earth alone,[1] but likewise of Heaven, since He was God; and the poor who were to follow Him He was not only to redeem and free from the power of the devil,[2] that mighty one against whom they had no helper,[3] but also to make heirs of the Kingdom of Heaven. And thus God was speaking, in the most important sense, of Christ, and of the reward of His followers,[4] which was an eternal kingdom and eternal liberty; and they understood this, after their own manner, in a secondary sense, of which God takes small account, namely that of temporal dominion and temporal liberty, which in God's eyes is neither kingdom nor liberty at all. Wherefore, being blinded by the insufficiency of the letter, and not understanding its spirit and truth, they took the life of their God and Lord, even as Saint Paul said in these words: *Qui enim habitabant Jerusalem, et principes ejus, hunc ignorantes et voces prophetarum, quæ per omne Sabbatum leguntur, judicantes impleverunt.*[5] Which signifies: They that dwelt in Jerusalem, and her rulers, not knowing Who He was, nor understanding the sayings of the prophets, which are read every Sabbath day, have fulfilled them by judging Him.

9. And to such a point did they carry this inability to understand the sayings of God as it behoved them, that even His own disciples, who had gone about with Him, were deceived, as were those two who, after His death, were going to the village of Emmaus, sad and disconsolate, saying: *Nos autem sperabamus quod ipse esset redempturus Israel.*[6] That is: We hoped that it was He that should have redeemed Israel. They, too, understood that this dominion and redemption were to be temporal; but Christ our Redeemer, appearing to them, reproved them as foolish and heavy and gross[7] of heart as to their belief in the things that the prophets had spoken.[8] And, even when He was going to Heaven, some of them were still in that state of grossness of heart, and asked Him, saying: *Domine, si in tempore hoc restitues Regnum Israel.*[9] That is: Lord, tell us if Thou wilt restore at this time the kingdom of Israel. The Holy Spirit causes many things to be said which

---

[1] A, B, e.p.: 'Lord of all the earth.'
[2] E.p.: 'from the hands and the power of the devil.' A, B: 'from the hands of the devil.'
[3] E.p. omits: 'against . . . helper.' A, B have 'powerful' for 'mighty.'
[4] [*Lit.*, 'of Christ and of His followers.' The addition is necessary to the sense.]
[5] Acts xiii, 27.   [6] St. Luke xxiv, 21.
[7] So Alc. The other MSS., and e.p. have: 'foolish and hard.'
[8] St. Luke xxiv, 25.   [9] Acts i, 6.

bear another sense than that which men understand; as can be seen in that which He caused to be said by Caiphas concerning Christ: that it was meet that one man should die lest all the people should perish.[1] This he said not of his own accord; and he said it and understood it in one sense, and the Holy Spirit in another.[2]

10. From this it is clear that, although sayings and revelations may be of God, we cannot always be sure of their meaning; for we can very easily be greatly deceived by them because of our manner of understanding them. For they are all[3] an abyss and a depth of the spirit, and to try to limit them to what we can understand concerning them, and to what our sense can apprehend, is nothing but to attempt to grasp the air, and to grasp some particle in it that the hand touches: the air disappears and nothing remains.

11. The spiritual teacher must therefore strive that the spirituality of his disciple be not cramped by attempts to interpret all supernatural apprehensions, which are no more than spiritual particles, lest he come to retain naught but these, and have no spirituality at all. But let the teacher wean his disciple from all visions and locutions, and impress upon him the necessity of dwelling in the liberty and darkness of faith, wherein are received spiritual liberty and abundance,[4] and consequently the wisdom and understanding necessary to interpret the sayings of God. For it is impossible for a man, if he be not spiritual, to judge of the things of God or understand them in a reasonable way, and he is not spiritual when he judges them according to sense; and thus, although they come to him beneath the disguise of sense, he understands them not. This Saint Paul well expresses in these words: *Animalis autem homo non percipit ea quæ sunt spiritus Dei: stultitia enim est illi, et non potest intelligere: quia de spiritualibus examinatur. Spiritualis autem judicat omnia.*[5] Which signifies: The animal man perceives not the things which are of the Spirit of God, for unto him they are foolishness and he cannot understand them because they are spiritual; but he that is spiritual judgeth all things. By the animal man is here meant one that uses sense alone; by the spiritual man, one that is not bound or guided by sense. Wherefore it is temerity to presume to have intercourse with God by way of a supernatural apprehension effected by sense, or to allow anyone else to do so.

12. And that this may be the better understood let us here set down

---

[1] St. John xi, 50.
[3] E.p. omits 'all.'
[5] 1 Corinthians ii, 14.

[2] E.p. adds: 'and a very different one.'
[4] A, B, e.p.: 'abundance of spirit.'

a few examples. Let us suppose that a holy man is greatly afflicted because his enemies persecute him, and that God answers him, saying: I will deliver thee from all thine enemies. This prophecy may be very true, yet, notwithstanding, his enemies may succeed in prevailing, and he may die at their hands. And so if a man should understand this after a temporal manner he would be deceived; for God might be speaking of the true and principal liberty and victory, which is salvation, whereby the soul is delivered, freed and made victorious[1] over all its enemies, and much more truly so and in a higher sense than if it were delivered from them here below. And thus, this prophecy was much more true and comprehensive than the man could understand if he interpreted it only with respect to this life; for, when God speaks, His words are always to be taken in the sense which is most important and profitable, whereas man, according to his own way and purpose, may understand the less important sense, and thus may be deceived. This we see in that prophecy which David makes concerning Christ in the second Psalm, saying: *Reges eos in virga ferrea, et tamquam vas figuli confringes eos.*[2] That is: Thou shalt rule all the people with a rod of iron and thou shalt dash them in pieces like a vessel of clay. Herein God speaks of the principal and perfect dominion, which is eternal dominion; and it was in this sense that it was fulfilled, and not in the less important sense, which was temporal, and which was not fulfilled in Christ during any part of His temporal life.

13. Let us take another example. A soul has great desires to be a martyr. It may happen that God answers him, saying: Thou shalt be a martyr. This will give him inwardly great comfort and confidence that he is to be martyred; yet it may come to pass that he dies not the death of a martyr, and notwithstanding this the promise may be true. Why, then, is it not fulfilled literally? Because it will be fulfilled, and is capable of being fulfilled,[3] according to the most important and essential sense of that saying—namely, in that God will have given that soul the love and the reward which belong essentially to a martyr;[4] and thus in truth He gives to the soul that which it formally desired and that which He promised it. For the formal desire[5] of the soul was, not that particular manner of death, but to do God a martyr's service, and to

---

[1] [*Lit.*, 'free and victorious.'] So Alc., e.p. A, B have: 'whence the soul remains free and with victory.'

[2] Psalm ii, 9.   [3] E.p. omits: 'and is . . . fulfilled.'

[4] E.p. adds: 'and by His making him a martyr of love, and granting him a prolonged martyrdom in sufferings, the continuance whereof is more painful than death.'

[5] E.p.: 'For the chief part of the desire.'

show its love for Him as a martyr does. For that manner of death is of no worth in itself without this love, the which love and the showing forth thereof and the reward belonging to the martyr may be given to it more perfectly by other means. So that, though it may not die like a martyr, the soul is well satisfied that it has been given that which it desired. For, when they are born of living love, such desires, and others like them, although they be not fulfilled in the way wherein they are described and understood, are fulfilled in another and a better way, and in a way which honours God more greatly than that which they might have asked. Wherefore David says: *Desiderium pauperum exaudivit Dominus.*[1] That is: The Lord has granted the poor their desire. And in the Proverbs Divine Wisdom says: *Desiderium suum justis dabitur.*[2] 'The just shall be given their desire.' Hence, then, since we see that many holy men have desired many particular things for God's sake, and that in this life their desires have not been granted them, it is a matter of faith that,[3] as their desires were just and true, they have been fulfilled for them perfectly in the next life. Since this is truth, it would also be truth for God to promise it to them in this life, saying to them: Your desire shall be fulfilled; and for it not to be fulfilled in the way which they expected.

14. In this and other ways, the words and visions of God may be true and sure and yet we may be deceived by them, through being unable to interpret them in a high and important sense, which is the sense and purpose wherein God intends them. And thus the best and surest course is to train souls in prudence so that they flee from these supernatural things, by accustoming them, as we have said, to[4] purity of spirit in dark faith, which is the means of union.

CHAPTER XX

Wherein is proved by passages from Scripture how the sayings and words of God, though always true, do not always rest upon stable causes.

WE have now to prove the second reason why visions and words which come from God, although in themselves they are always true, are not always stable in their relation to ourselves. This is because of their causes, whereon[5] they are founded; for

---

[1] Psalm ix, 17 [A.V., x, 17].   [2] Proverbs x, 24.
[3] E.p.: 'it is certain that . . .'   [4] A, B: 'by bringing them, as we have said, into . . .'
[5] E.p.: 'of the causes and motives whereon . . .'

God often makes statements founded upon creatures and their effects, which are changeable and liable to fail, for which reason the statements which are founded upon them are liable also to be changeable and to fail; for, when one thing depends on another, if one fails, the other fails likewise. It is as though[1] God should say: In a year's time I shall send upon this kingdom such or such a plague; and the cause and foundation for this warning is a certain offence which has been committed against God in that kingdom. If the offence should cease or change, the punishment might cease;[2] yet the threat was true because it was founded upon the fault committed at the time, and, if this had continued, it would have been carried out.[3]

2. This, we see, happened in the city of Ninive, where God said: *Adhuc quadraginta dies, et Ninive subvertetur.*[4] Which signifies: Yet forty days and Ninive[5] shall be destroyed. This was not fulfilled, because the cause of the threat ceased—namely, the sins of the city, for which it did penance—but, if this had not been so, the prophecy would have been carried into effect. We read likewise in the Third Book of the Kings that, when King Achab had committed a very great sin, God sent to prophesy[6] a great punishment—our father Elias being the messenger[7]—which should come upon his person, upon his house and upon his kingdom.[8] And, because Achab rent his garments with grief and clothed himself in haircloth and fasted, and slept in sackcloth and went about in a humble and contrite manner, God sent again, by the same prophet, to declare to him these words: *Quia igitur humiliatus est mei causa, non inducam malum in diebus ejus, sed in diebus filii sui.*[9] Which signifies: Inasmuch as Achab has humbled himself for love of Me, I will not send the evil whereof I spake in his days, but in the days of his son. Here we see that, because Achab changed his spirit and his former affection, God likewise changed His sentence.[10]

3. From this we may deduce, as regards the matter under discussion, that, although God may have revealed or affirmed something to a soul,

---

[1] E.p. abbreviates: 'This is because of the causes and motives whereon they are founded; and it is to be understood that they will be so for as long as the cause endures which determines God (let us say) to chasten. It is as though . . .'

[2] E.p.: 'cease or change.'

[3] E.p. adds: 'And these warnings or revelations are minatory or conditional.'

[4] Jonas iii, 4.

[5] E.p.: '. . . where God sent the prophet Jonas to proclaim this threat from Him in Ninive: Yet forty days and the city of Ninive . . .'

[6] [*Lit.*, 'to promise.'] A, B: 'God sent to threaten him with.' E.p.: 'God sent him the threat of.'

[7] A, B omit: 'our father . . . messenger.'

[8] 3 Kings [A.V., 1 Kings] xxi, 21.   [9] 3 Kings xxi, 27–9.

[10] E.p.: '. . . . because Achab changed, the threat and sentence of God ceased likewise.'

whether good or evil, and whether relating to that soul itself or to others, this may, to a greater or a lesser extent, be changed or altered or entirely withdrawn, according to the change or variation in the affection of this soul, or the cause whereon God based His judgment,[1] and thus it would not be fulfilled in the way expected, and oftentimes none would have known why, save only God. For God is wont to declare and teach and promise many things, not that they may be understood or possessed at the time, but that they may be understood at a later time, when it is fitting that a soul may have light concerning them, or when their effect is attained. This, as we see, He did with His disciples, to whom He spake many parables, and pronounced many judgments, the wisdom whereof[2] they understood not until the time when they had to preach it, which was when the Holy Spirit came upon them, of Whom Christ had said to them that He would explain to them all the things that He had spoken to them in His life. And, when Saint John speaks of that entry of Christ into Jerusalem, he says: *Hæc non cognoverunt discipuli ejus primum: sed quando glorificatus est Jesus, tunc recordati sunt quia hæc erant scripta de eo.*[3] And thus there may pass through the soul many detailed messages from God which neither the soul nor its director will understand until the proper time.

4. Likewise, in the First Book of the Kings, we read that, when God was wroth against Heli, a priest of Israel, for his sins in not chastising his sons, he sent to him by Samuel to say, among other words, these which follow: *Loquens locutus sum, ut domus tua, et domus patris tui, ministraret in conspectu meo, usque in sempiternum. Verumtamen absit hoc a me.* And this is as though He had said:[4] In very truth I said aforetime that thy house and the house of thy father should serve Me continually in the priesthood in My presence for ever, but this purpose is far from Me; I will not do this thing. For this office of the priesthood was founded for giving honour and glory to God, and to this end God had promised to give it to the father of Heli for ever if he failed not.[5] But, when Heli failed in zeal for the honour of God (for, as God Himself complained when He sent him the message, he honoured his sons more than God, overlooking their sins so as not to offend them),[6] the

---

[1] E.p.: 'the cause to which God had regard.'
[2] Thus Alc., e.p. A, B have: 'the meaning whereof.'
[3] St. John xii, 16.
[4] 1 Kings [A.V., 1 Samuel] ii, 30.
[5] So Alc., e.p. Alc., however, probably by an oversight, omits: 'if he failed not.' A, B have: 'and to this end He had promised the priesthood to his father,' etc., B adding: '[his father] for ever, if for ever good service and zeal continued in them.'
[6] A, B omit the parenthesis.

promise also failed which would have held good for ever if the good service and zeal of Heli had lasted for ever. And thus there is no reason to think that, because sayings and revelations[1] come from God, they must invariably come to pass in their apparent sense, especially when[2] they are bound up with human causes which may vary, change or alter.

5. And when they are dependent upon these causes[3] God Himself knows, though He does not always declare it, but pronounces the saying, or makes the revelation, and sometimes says nothing of the condition, as when He definitely told the Ninivites that they would be destroyed after forty days.[4] At other times He lays down the condition, as He did to Roboam, saying to him: 'If thou wilt keep My commandments, as did My servant David, I will be with thee even as I was with him, and will set thee up a house as I did to My servant David.'[5] But, whether He declares it or no, the soul must not rely upon its own understanding; for it is impossible to understand the hidden truths of God which are in His sayings, and the multitude of their meanings. He is above the heavens, and speaks according to the way of eternity;[6] we blind souls are upon the earth and understand only the ways of flesh and time.[7] It was for that reason, I believe, that the Wise Man said: 'God is in Heaven, and thou art upon earth; wherefore be not thou lengthy or hasty in speaking.'[8]

6. You will perhaps ask me: Why, if we are not to understand these things, or to play any part in them, does God communicate them to us? I have already said that everything will be understood in its own time by the command of Him Who spake it, and he whom God wills shall understand it, and it will be seen that it was fitting; for God does naught save with due cause and in truth. Let it be realized, therefore, that there is no complete understanding of the meaning[9] of the sayings and things of God, and that this meaning cannot be decided by what it seems to be, without great error, and, in the end, grievous confusion. This was very well known to the prophets, into whose hands was given the word of God, and who found it a sore trial to prophesy concerning

---

[1] E.p. adds: 'true in themselves.'
[2] E.p. adds: 'by the command of God Himself.'
[3] E.p.: 'And when this is so.'
[4] Jonas iii, 4.
[5] 3 Kings [A.V., 1 Kings] xi, 38. [Actually it was to Jeroboam that this was said]
[6] [Lit., 'on the road of eternity.']
[7] E.p.: '. . . earth, so that we cannot attain to His secrets.'
[8] Ecclesiastes v, 1 [A.V., v, 2].
[9] E.p.: 'of the full meaning.'

the people; for, as we have said, many of the people saw that things came not to pass literally, as they were told them, for which cause they laughed at the prophets and mocked them greatly; so much so that Jeremias went as far as to say: 'They mock me all the day long, they scorn and despise me every one, for I have long been crying against evil and promising them destruction; and the word of the Lord has been made a reproach and a derision to me continually. And I said, I must not remember Him, neither speak any more in His name.'[1] Herein, although the holy prophet was speaking with resignation and in the form of a weak man who cannot endure the ways and workings[2] of God, he clearly indicates the difference between the way wherein the Divine sayings are fulfilled and the ordinary meaning which they appear to have; for the Divine prophets[3] were treated as mockers, and suffered so much from their prophecy that Jeremias himself said elsewhere: *Formido et laqueus facta est nobis vaticinatio et contritio.*[4] Which signifies: Prophecy has become to us fear and snares and contradiction of spirit.

7. And the reason why Jonas fled when God sent him to preach the destruction of Ninive was this, namely, that he knew the different meanings of the sayings of God with respect to the understanding of men and with respect to the causes of the sayings.[5] And thus, lest they should mock him when they saw that his prophecy was not fulfilled, he went away and fled in order not to prophesy; and thus he remained waiting all the forty days outside the city, to see if his prophecy was fulfilled; and, when it was not fulfilled, he was greatly afflicted, so much so that he said to God: *Obsecro, Domine, numquid non hoc est verbum meum, cum adhuc essem in terra mea? propter hoc præoccupavi, ut fugerem in Tharsis.*[6] That is: I pray Thee, O Lord, is not this what I said when I was yet in my own country? Therefore was I vexed, and fled away to Tharsis. And the saint was wroth and besought God to take away his life.

8. Why, then, must we marvel that God should speak and reveal certain things to souls which come not to pass in the sense wherein they understand them? For, if God should affirm or represent such or such a thing to the soul, whether good or evil, with respect to itself or to another, and if that thing be founded upon a certain affection or service or offence of that soul, or of another, at that time, with respect

---

[1] Jeremias xx, 7–9.   [2] E.p.: 'ways and secrets.'
[3] A, B: 'the sacred prophets.'   [4] Lamentations iii, 47.
[5] E.p.: '. . . namely, that he understood not the truth of the sayings of God and knew not wholly their meaning.'   [6] Jonas iv, 2.

to God, so that, if the soul persevere therein, it will be fulfilled; yet even then its fulfilment[1] is not certain, since it is not certain that the soul will persevere. Wherefore we must rely,[2] not upon understanding, but upon faith.

CHAPTER XXI

Wherein is explained how at times, although God answers the prayers that are addressed to Him, He is not pleased that we should use such methods. It is also shown how, although He condescend to us and answer us, He is oftentimes wroth.

CERTAIN spiritual men, as we have said, assure themselves that it is a good thing to display curiosity, as they sometimes do, in striving to know certain things by supernatural methods, thinking that,[3] because God occasionally answers their importunity, this is a good method and pleasing to Him. Yet the truth is that, although He may answer them, the method is not good, neither is it pleasing to God, but rather it is displeasing to Him; and not only so, but oftentimes He is greatly offended and wroth.[4] The reason for this is that it is lawful[5] for no creature to pass beyond the limits that God has ordained for its governance after the order of nature.[6] He has laid down rational and natural limits for man's governance;[7] wherefore to desire to pass beyond them is not lawful,[8] and to desire to seek out and attain to anything by supernatural means is to go beyond these natural limits.[9] It is therefore an unlawful thing,[10] and it is therefore not pleasing to God,[11] for He is offended by all that is unlawful. King Achaz was well aware of this, since, although Isaias told him from God to ask for a sign, he would not do so, saying: *Non petam, et non tentabo Dominum.*[12] That is: I will not ask such a thing, neither will I tempt

---

[1] E.p. adds: 'as it sounds' [i.e., in the sense which it seems to bear].
[2] A, B, e.p. add: 'and take our stand.'
[3] E.p.: 'Certain spiritual men, as we have said, assure themselves—not reflecting much upon the curiosity which they sometimes display in striving to know certain things by supernatural means—and think that . . .'
[4] E.p.: 'oftentimes He is very grieved and wroth at it.'
[5] E.p.: 'it is fitting.'
[6] E.p. omits: 'after the order of nature.'   [7] E.p. omits: 'and natural.'
[8] E.p.: 'is not fitting.'   [9] E.p. omits 'natural.'
[10] E.p.: 'It is not a holy or a fitting thing.'
[11] E.p. omits the remainder of this paragraph.
[12] Isaias vii, 12. [The Spanish has 'Achab' for 'Achaz.']

God. For it is tempting God to seek to commune with Him by extra-ordinary ways, such as those that are supernatural.

2. But why, you will say, if it be a fact that God is displeased, does He sometimes answer? I reply that it is sometimes the devil who answers. And, if it is God Who answers,[1] I reply that He does so because of the weakness of the soul that desires to travel along that road, lest it should be disconsolate and go backward, or lest it should think that God is wroth with it and should be overmuch afflicted;[2] or for other reasons known to God, founded upon the weakness of that soul, whereby God sees that it is well that He should answer it and deigns to do so in that way. In a like manner, too, does He treat many weak and tender souls, granting them favours and sweetness in sensible converse with Himself, as has been said above; this is not because He desires or is pleased that they should commune with Him after that manner or by these methods; it is that He gives to each one, as we have said, after the manner best suited to him. For God is like a spring, whence everyone draws water according to the vessel which he carries. Sometimes a soul is allowed to draw it by these extraordinary channels; but it follows not from this that it is lawful to draw water[3] by them, but only that God Himself can permit this, when, how and to whom He wills, and for what reason He wills, without the party concerned having any right in the matter. And thus, as we say, He sometimes deigns to satisfy the desire and the prayer of certain souls, whom, since they are good and sincere, He wills not to fail to succour, lest He should make them sad, but it is not because He is pleased with their methods that He wills it. This will be the better understood by the following comparison.

3. The father of a family has on his table many and different kinds of food, some of which are better than others. A child is asking him for a certain dish, not the best, but the first that meets its eye, and it asks for this dish because it would rather eat of it than any other; and as the father sees that, even if he gives it the better kind of food, it will not take it, but will have that which it asks for, since that alone pleases it, he gives it that, regretfully, lest it should take no food at all and be miserable. In just this way, we observe, did God treat the children of Israel when they asked Him for a king: He gave them one, but unwillingly, because it was not good for them. And thus He said to Samuel: *Audi*

---

[1] Alc. omits: 'I reply that . . . God Who answers,' probably by an oversight.
[2] E.p.: 'overmuch tempted.'
[3] E.p.: 'that it is fitting to seek to draw water.'

vocem populi in omnibus quæ loquuntur tibi: non enim te abjecerunt, sed me.[1] Which signifies: Hearken unto the voice of this people and grant them the king whom they ask of thee, for they have not rejected thee but Me, that I should not reign over them. In this same way God condescends to certain souls, and grants them that which is not best for them, because they will not or cannot walk by any other road. And thus certain souls attain to tenderness and sweetness of spirit or sense; and God grants them this[2] because they are unable to partake of the stronger and more solid food of the trials of the Cross of His Son, which He would prefer them to take, rather than aught else.

4. I consider, however, that the desire to know things by supernatural means is much worse than the desire for other spiritual favours pertaining to the senses; for I cannot see how the soul that desires them can fail to commit, at the least, venial sin, however good may be its aims, and however far advanced it may be on the road to perfection; and if anyone should bid the soul desire them, and consent to it, he sins likewise. For there is no necessity for any of these things, since the soul has its natural reason and the doctrine and law of the Gospel, which are quite sufficient for its guidance, and there is no difficulty or necessity that cannot be solved and remedied by these means, which are very pleasing to God and of great profit to souls; and such great use must we make of our reason and of Gospel doctrine that, if certain things be told us supernaturally, whether at our desire or no, we must receive only that which is in clear conformity with reason and Gospel law. And then we must receive it, not because it is revelation, but because it is reason, and not allow ourselves to be influenced by the fact that it has been revealed. Indeed, it is well in such a case to look at that reason and examine it very much more closely[3] than if there had been no revelation concerning it; inasmuch as the devil utters many things that are true, and that will come to pass, and that are in conformity with reason, in order that he may deceive.

5. Wherefore, in all our needs, trials and difficulties, there remains to us no better and surer means than prayer and hope that God will provide for us, by such means as He wills.[4] This is the advice given to us in the Scriptures, where we read that, when King Josaphat was

[1] 1 Kings [A.V., 1 Samuel] viii, 7.
[2] E.p.: 'And if certain souls . . . or sense, God grants them this,' etc.
[3] E.p. abbreviates: 'And then we must receive that which is in conformity with reason and Gospel law; and even then it is well to look at it and examine it very much more closely . . .'
[4] A: 'than hope through the means that He wills.'

greatly afflicted and surrounded by enemies, the saintly King gave himself to prayer, saying to God: *Cum ignoremus quid facere debeamus, hoc solum habemus residui, ut oculos nostros dirigamus ad te.*[1] Which is as though he had said: When means fail and reason is unable to succour us in our necessities, it remains for us only to lift up our eyes to Thee, that Thou mayest succour us as is most pleasing to Thee.

6. And further, although this has also been made clear, it will be well to prove, from certain passages of Scripture, that, though God may answer such requests, He is none the less sometimes wroth. In the First Book of the Kings it is said that, when King Saul begged[2] that the prophet Samuel, who was now dead, might speak to him, the said prophet appeared to him, and that God was wroth with all this, since Samuel at once reproved Saul for having done such a thing, saying: *Quare inquietasti me, ut suscitarer?*[3] That is: Why hast thou disquieted me, in causing me to arise? We also know that, in spite of having answered the children of Israel and given them the meat that they besought of Him, God was nevertheless greatly incensed against them; for He sent fire from Heaven upon them as a punishment, as we read in the Pentateuch,[4] and as David relates in these words: *Adhuc escæ eorum erant in ore ipsorum, et ira Dei descendit super eos.*[5] Which signifies: Even as they had the morsels in their mouths, the wrath of God came down upon them. And likewise we read in Numbers that God was greatly wroth[6] with Balaam the prophet, because he went to the Madianites when Balac their king sent for him, although God had bidden him go, because he desired to go and had begged it of God; and while he was yet in the way there appeared to him an angel with a sword, who desired to slay him, and said to him: *Perversa est via tua, mihique contraria.*[7] 'Thy way is perverse and contrary to Me.' For which cause he desired to slay him.

7. After this manner and many others God deigns to satisfy the desires of souls though He be wroth with them. Concerning this we have many testimonies in Scripture, and, in addition, many illustrations,[8] though in a matter that is so clear these are unnecessary.

---

[1] 2 Paralipomenon [A.V., 2 Chronicles] xx, 12.
[2] E.p. has 'desired' for 'begged.'
[3] 1 Kings [A.V., 1 Samuel] xxviii, 15.
[4] E.p. is more precise: 'in the Book of Numbers.'
[5] Psalm lxxvii, 30–1 [A.V., lxxviii, 30–1].
[6] E.p.: 'that God was none the less wroth.'
[7] Numbers xxii, 32.
[8] So A, B. E.p. has: 'Concerning this there are many more testimonies in Divine Scripture, and many illustrations.'

I will merely say that to desire to commune with God by such means is a most perilous thing, more so than I can express, and that one who is affectioned to such methods will not fail to err greatly and will often find himself in confusion. Anyone who in the past has prized them will understand me from his own experience. For over and above the difficulty that there is in being sure that one is not going astray[1] in respect of locutions and visions which are of God, there are ordinarily many of these locutions and visions which are of the devil; for in his converse with the soul the devil habitually wears the same guise as God assumes in His dealings with it, setting before it things that are very like to those which God communicates to it, insinuating himself, like the wolf in sheep's clothing, among the flock, with a success so nearly complete that he can hardly be recognized. For, since he says many things that are true, and in conformity with reason, and things that come to pass as he describes them,[2] it is very easy for the soul to be deceived, and to think that, since these things come to pass as he says, and the future is correctly foretold, this can be the work of none save God; for such souls know not that it is a very easy thing for one that has clear natural light to be acquainted, as to their causes, with things, or with many of them, which have been or shall be.[3] And since the devil has a very clear light of this kind, he can very easily[4] deduce effect from cause, although it may not always turn out as he says, because all causes[5] depend upon the will of God. Let us take an example.

8. The devil knows that the constitution of the earth and the atmosphere, and the laws ruling the sun, are disposed in such manner and in such degree that, when a certain moment has arrived, it will necessarily follow, according to the laws of nature laid down for these elements, that they will infect[6] people with pestilence, and he knows in what places this will be more severe and in what places less so. Here you have a knowledge of pestilence in respect of its causes. What a wonderful thing it seems[7] when the devil reveals this to a soul, saying: 'In a year or in six months from now there will be pestilence,' and it happens as he says! And yet this is a prophecy of the devil. In the same way he may have a knowledge of earthquakes, and, seeing that the

---

[1] So e.p. The Codices have: 'that there is in not going astray.'
[2] [*Lit.*, 'that come out true.'] E.p.: 'that come out exact.'
[3] E.p. adds: 'and thus [such a] one will predict many things of the future.'
[4] E.p. omits: 'very easily.'   [5] E.p.: 'all things.'
[6] E.p. abbreviates: 'according to their laws, that they will infect.'
[7] [Or: 'Is it such a wonderful thing . . . as he says? It is merely a prophecy of the devil.']

bowels of the earth are filling with air, will say: 'At such a time there will be an earthquake.' Yet this is only natural knowledge,[1] for the possession of which it suffices for the spirit to be free from the passions of the soul, even as Boetius says in these words: *Si vis claro lumine cernere verum, gaudia pelle, timorem, spemque fugato, nec dolor adsit.*[2] That is: If thou desire to know truths with the clearness of nature, cast from thee rejoicing and fear and hope and sorrow.

9. And likewise supernatural events and[3] happenings may be known, in their causes, in matters concerning Divine Providence, which deals most justly and surely as is required by their good or evil causes as regards the sons of men.[4] For one may know by natural means[5] that such or such a person, or such or such a city, or some other place, is in such or such necessity, or has reached such or such a point, so that God, according to His providence and justice, must deal with such a person or thing in the way required by its cause, and in the way that is fitting for it, whether by means of punishment or of reward, as the cause merits. And then one can say: 'At such a time God will give you this, or will do this, or that will come to pass, of a surety.'[6] It was this that holy Judith said to Holofernes,[7] when, in order to persuade him that the children of Israel would without fail be destroyed, she first related to him many of their sins and the evil deeds that they did. And then she said: *Et, quoniam hæc faciunt, certum est quod in perditionem dabuntur.* Which signifies: Since they do these things, it is certain that they will be destroyed. This is to know the punishment in the cause,[8] and it is as though she had said: It is certain that such sins must be the cause of such punishments, at the hand of God Who is most just. And as the Divine Wisdom says: *Per quæ quis peccat, per hæc et torquetur.*[9] With respect to that and for that wherein a man sins, therein is he punished.

10. The devil may have knowledge of this, not only naturally, but

---

[1] E.p. omits the remainder of the paragraph.
[2] The exact reading in Boetius is: 'Tu quoque si vis lumine claro cernere verum—Tramite recto carpere callem—Gaudia pelle—Pelle timorem—Spemque fugato—Nec dolor adsit' (Migne, Vol. LXXV, p. 122).
[3] A, B omit: 'events and.'
[4] E.p.: 'And likewise to some extent particular events and happenings may be deduced from Divine Providence, which is wont to deal most justly according to the good and evil [doings] of the sons of men.'
[5] So Alc.   E.p. omits: 'by natural means.' A, B: 'one may know clearly.'
[6] E.p. omits: 'of a surety.'   [7] Judith xi, 12.
[8] E.p.: 'It is this that Achior meant when he said to Holofernes (Judith v, 18): *Quotiescumque praeter Deum suum alterum coluerunt, dati sunt in praedam, et in gladium et in opprobrium.* This is to know the punishment in the cause.'
[9] Wisdom xi, 17 [A.V., xi, 16].

also by the experience which he has of having seen God do similar things, and he can foretell it and do so correctly.[1] Again, holy Tobias was aware of the punishment of the city of Ninive because of its cause, and he thus admonished his son, saying: 'Behold, son, in the hour when I and thy mother die, go thou forth from this land, for it will not remain.'[2] *Video enim quia iniquitas ejus finem dabit ei.*[3] I see clearly that its own iniquity will be the cause of its punishment, which will be that it shall be ended and destroyed altogether. This might have been known by the devil as well as by Tobias, not only because of the iniquity of the city, but by experience, since they had seen that for the sins of the world God destroyed it in the Flood,[4] and that the Sodomites, too, perished for their sins by fire; but Tobias knew it also through the Divine Spirit.

11. And the devil may know that one Peter[5] cannot, in the course of nature, live more than so many years, and he may foretell this; and so with regard to many other things and in many ways that it is impossible to recount fully—nor can one even begin to recount many of them, since they are most intricate and subtle—he insinuates falsehoods;[6] from which a soul cannot free itself save by fleeing from all revelations and visions and locutions that are supernatural.[7] Wherefore God is justly angered with those that receive them, for He sees that it is temerity on their part to expose themselves to such great peril and presumption and curiosity, and things that spring from pride, and are the root and foundation of vainglory, and of disdain for the things of God, and the beginning of many evils[8] to which many have come. Such persons have succeeded in angering God so greatly that He has of set purpose allowed them to go astray and be deceived and to blind their own spirits and to leave the ordered paths of life and give rein to their vanities and fancies, according to the word of Isaias, where he says: *Dominus miscuit in medio ejus spiritum vertiginis.*[9] Which is as much as to say: The Lord hath mingled in the midst thereof the spirit of dissension and confusion. Which in our ordinary vernacular signifies the spirit of misunderstanding. What Isaias is here

---

[1] E.p. adds: 'at times.'   [2] E.p. has 'city' for 'land.'

[3] Tobias xiv, 13.

[4] So Alc. E.p.: 'had destroyed men in the Flood.' A, B: 'since they had seen the sins for which God had destroyed the world with the Flood.'

[5] [i.e., any individual.]

[6] E.p. omits: 'he insinuates falsehoods.'

[7] E.p. omits: 'that are supernatural.'

[8] So Alc. A, B: 'and the cause of many evils.' E.p.: 'and many evils.'

[9] Isaias xix, 14.

very plainly saying is to our purpose, for he is speaking of those who were endeavouring by supernatural means to know things that were to come to pass. And therefore he says that God mingled in their midst the spirit of misunderstanding; not that God willed them, in fact, to have the spirit of error, or gave it to them, but that they desired to meddle with that to which by nature they could not attain. Angered by this, God allowed them to act foolishly, giving them no light as to that wherewith He desired not that they should concern themselves. And thus the Prophet says that God mingled that spirit in them, privatively.[1] And in this sense God is the cause of such an evil—that is to say, He is the privative cause, which consists in His withdrawal of His light and favour, to such a point that they must needs fall into error.[2]

12. And in this way God gives leave to the devil to blind and deceive many, when their sins and audacities merit it; and this the devil can do and does successfully, and they give him credence and believe him to be a good spirit; to such a point that, although they may be quite persuaded that he is not so, they cannot undeceive themselves, since, by the permission of God, there has already been insinuated into them the spirit of misunderstanding, even as we read was the case with the prophets of King Achab, whom God permitted to be deceived by a lying spirit, giving the devil leave to deceive them, and saying: *Decipies, et prævalebis; egredere, et fac ita.*[3] Which signifies: Thou shalt prevail with thy falsehood and shalt deceive them; go forth and do so. And so well was he able to work upon the prophets and the King, in order to deceive them, that they would not believe the prophet Micheas, who prophesied the truth to them, saying the exact contrary of that which the others had prophesied, and this came to pass because God permitted them to be blinded, since their affections were attached to that which they desired to happen to them, and God answered them according to their desires and wishes; and this was a most certain preparation and means for their being blinded and deceived, which God allowed of set purpose.

13. Thus, too, did Ezechiel prophesy in the name of God. Speaking against those who began to desire to have knowledge direct from God, from motives of curiosity, according to the vanity[4] of their spirit, he says: When such a man comes to the prophet to enquire of Me through

---

[1] E.p. has 'permissively' for 'privatively.'
[2] E.p.: '. . . and favour, wherefore it follows that they must infallibly fall into error.'
[3] 3 Kings [A.V., 1 Kings] xxii, 22.
[4] Alc. has: 'to the variety.'

him, I, the Lord, will answer him by Myself, and I will set My face in
anger against that man; and, as to the prophet, when he has gone
astray in that which was asked of him, *Ego Dominus decepi prophetam
illum.*[1] That is: I, the Lord, have deceived that prophet. This is to be
taken to mean, by not succouring him with His favour so that he
might not be deceived; and this is His meaning when He says: I the
Lord will answer him by Myself in anger[2]—that is, God will withdraw
His grace and favour from that man. Hence necessarily[3] follows deception by reason of his abandonment by God. And then comes the devil
and makes answer according to the pleasure and desire of that man,
who, being pleased thereat, since the answers and communications
are according to his will,[4] allows himself to be deceived greatly.

14. It may appear that we have to some extent strayed from the
purpose that we set down in the title of this chapter, which was to
prove that, although God answers, He sometimes complains. But, if it
be carefully considered,[5] all that has been said goes to prove our intention; for it all shows that God desires not that we should wish for
such visions, since He makes it possible for us to be deceived by them
in so many ways.

CHAPTER XXII

*Wherein is solved[6] a difficulty—namely, why it is not lawful, under the
law of grace,[7] to ask anything of God by supernatural means, as it was
under the old law. This solution is proved by a passage from Saint Paul.[8]*

DIFFICULTIES keep coming to our mind, and thus we cannot
progress with the speed that we should desire. For as they
occur to us, we are obliged of necessity[9] to clear them up, so
that the truth of this teaching may ever be plain and carry its full
force. But there is always[10] this advantage in these difficulties, that,
although they somewhat impede our progress, they serve nevertheless

---

[1] Ezechiel xiv, 7–9.   [2] [Ezechiel xiv, 7.]
[3] E.p.: 'Hence infallibly.'
[4] E.p.: 'are in conformity with his will.'
[5] The passage from the beginning of the paragraph to this point is found only in Alc.
and e.p. The latter reads 'is wroth' for 'complains.'
[6] E.p.: 'is treated.'   [7] E.p.: 'under the New Law.'
[8] E.p. adds: 'Is is somewhat delectable for an understanding of the mysteries of our
holy faith.'
[9] E.p. omits: 'of necessity.'   [10] Alc. alone has 'always.'

to make our intention the clearer and more explicit,[1] as will be the case with the present one.

2. In the previous chapter, we said that it is not the will of God that souls should desire to receive anything distinctly, by supernatural means, through visions, locutions, etc. Further, we saw in the same chapter, and deduced from the testimonies which were there brought forward from Scripture, that such[2] communion with God was employed in the Old Law and was lawful; and that not only was it lawful, but God commanded it. And when they used not this opportunity, God reproved them,[3] as is to be seen in Isaias, where God reproves the children of Israel because they desired to go down[4] to Egypt without first enquiring of Him, saying: *Et os meum non interrogastis.*[5] That is: Ye asked not first at My own mouth what was fitting. And likewise we read in Josue that, when the children of Israel themselves are deceived by the Gabaonites, the Holy Spirit reproves them for this fault, saying: *Susceperunt ergo de cibariis eorum, et os Domini non interrogaverunt.*[6] Which signifies: They took of their victuals and they enquired not at the mouth of God. Furthermore, we see in the Divine Scripture that Moses always enquired of God, as did King David and all the kings of Israel with regard to their wars and necessities, and the priests and prophets of old, and God answered and spake with them and was not wroth, and it was well done; and if they did it not it would be ill done; and this is the truth. Why, then, in the new law—the law of grace—may it not now be as it was aforetime?

3. To this it must be replied that the principal reason why in the law of Scripture[7] the enquiries that were made of God were lawful, and why it was fitting that prophets and priests should seek visions and revelations of God, was because at that time faith had no firm foundation, neither was the law of the Gospel established; and thus it was needful that men should enquire of God and that He should speak, whether by words or by visions and revelations or whether by figures and similitudes or by many other ways of expressing His meaning. For all that He answered and spake and revealed belonged to the mysteries of our faith and things touching it or leading to it. And, since the things of faith are not of man, but come from the mouth of God

---

1 [*Lit.*, 'they serve nevertheless for the greater doctrine and clearness of our intention.']
2 E.p. abbreviates: 'Further, we know that such . . .'
3 E.p. adds: 'for it.'
4 A, B, e.p.: 'they thought of going down.'
5 Isaias xxx, 2.   6 Josue ix, 14.
7 A, B, e.p.: 'why in the Old Law.'

Himself, God Himself reproved them because they enquired not at His mouth in their affairs, so that He might answer,[1] and might direct their affairs and happenings toward the faith, of which at that time they had no knowledge, because it was not yet founded.[2] But now that the faith is founded in Christ, and, in this era of grace, the law of the Gospel has been made manifest, there is no reason to enquire of Him in that manner, nor for Him to speak or to answer as He did then. For, in giving us, as He did, His Son, which is His Word—and He has no other—He spake to us all together, once and for all, in this single Word, and He has no occasion to speak further.

4. And this is the sense of that passage with which Saint Paul begins, when he tries to persuade the Hebrews that they should abandon those first manners and ways of converse with God which are in the law of Moses, and should set their eyes on Christ alone, saying: *Multifariam multisque modis olim Deus loquens patribus in Prophetis: novissime autem diebus istis locutus est nobis in Filio.*[3] And this is as though he had said: That which God spake of old in the prophets to our fathers, in sundry ways and divers manners, He has now, at last, in these days, spoken to us once and for all in the Son. Herein the Apostle declares that God has become, as it were, dumb, and has no more to say,[4] since that which He spake aforetime, in part, to the prophets, He has now spoken altogether in Him, giving us the All, which is His Son.

5. Wherefore he that would now enquire of God, or seek any vision or revelation, would not only be acting foolishly, but would be committing an offence against God,[5] by not setting his eyes altogether upon Christ, and seeking no new thing or aught beside. And God might answer him after this manner, saying: If I have spoken all things to thee in My Word, Which is My Son, and I have no other word, what answer can I now make to thee, or what can I reveal to thee which is greater than this?[6] Set thine eyes on Him alone, for in Him I have spoken and revealed to thee all things, and in Him thou shalt find yet more than that which thou askest and desirest. For thou

---

[1] E.p.: '. . . of God Himself, and by His very mouth were spoken; therefore it was needful that, as we have said, they should enquire at the mouth of God Himself; wherefore He answered them, when they did it not, so that He might answer them . . .'

[2] E.p. omits: 'because it was not yet founded.'

[3] Hebrews i, 1.

[4] E.p.: '. . . declares that God has spoken so much already, in this [way], that He has no more to desire.'

[5] E.p.: '. . . or revelation, would seem to be committing an offence against God.'

[6] E.p. omits: 'and I have . . . greater than this.'

askest locutions and revelations, which are the part; but if thou set thine eyes upon Him, thou shalt find the whole; for He is My complete locution and answer, and He is all My vision and all My revelation; so that I have spoken to thee, answered thee, declared to thee and revealed to thee, in giving Him to thee as thy brother,[1] companion and master, as ransom and prize. For since that day when I descended upon Him with My Spirit on Mount Tabor, saying: *Hic est filius meus dilectus, in quo mihi bene complacui, ipsum audite*[2] (which is to say: This is My beloved Son, in Whom I am well pleased; hear ye Him), I have left off all these manners of teaching and answering, and I have entrusted this to Him. Hear Him; for I have no more faith to reveal, neither have I any more things to declare. For, if I spake aforetime,[3] it was to promise Christ; and, if they enquired of Me, their enquiries[4] were directed to petitions for Christ and expectancy concerning Him, in Whom they should find every good thing (as is now set forth in all the teaching of the Evangelists and the Apostles); but now, any who would enquire of Me after that manner, and desire Me to speak to him or reveal aught to him, would in a sense be asking Me for Christ again, and asking Me for more faith, and be lacking in faith, which has already been given in Christ; and therefore he would be committing a great offence against My beloved Son, for not only would he be lacking in faith, but he would be obliging Him again first of all to become incarnate and pass through life and death. Thou shalt find[5] naught to ask of Me, or to desire of Me,[6] whether revelations or visions; consider this well, for thou shalt find that all has been done for thee and all has been given to thee—yea, and much more also—in Him.

6. If thou desirest Me to answer thee with any word of consolation, consider My Son, Who is subject to Me, and bound by love of Me, and afflicted,[7] and thou shalt see how fully He answers thee. If thou desirest Me to expound to thee secret things, or happenings, set thine eyes on Him alone, and thou shalt find the most secret mysteries, and the

[1] E.p.: 'for He is the Truth, the Guide and the Life, and I have given Him to thee as thy brother,' etc.

[2] St. Matthew xvii, 5.

[3] E.p. abbreviates: '. . . on Mount Tabor, saying: "This is My beloved Son in Whom I am well pleased; hear ye Him." Thou must seek no new manners of teaching and answering. For if I spake aforetime . . .'

[4] Alc.: 'their hopes.'

[5] E.p. abbreviates: '. . . would in some degree be not content with Christ, and thus he would be committing a great offence against My beloved Son. If thou hast Him, thou shalt find . . .'

[6] E.p. omits: 'of Me.'

[7] E.p.: '. . . consider My Son, obedient to Me and afflicted for love of Me . . .'

wisdom and wondrous things of God, which are hidden in Him, even as My Apostle says: *In quo sunt omnes thesauri sapientiae et scientiae Dei absconditi.*[1] That is: In this Son of God are hidden all the treasures of wisdom and knowledge of God. These treasures of wisdom shall be very much more sublime and delectable and profitable for thee than the things that thou desiredst to know. Herein the same Apostle gloried, saying: That he had not declared to them that he knew anything,[2] save Jesus Christ and Him crucified.[3] And if thou shouldst still desire other Divine or bodily revelations and visions, look also at Him made man, and thou shalt find therein more than thou thinkest, for the Apostle says likewise: *In ipso habitat omnis plenitudo Divinitatis corporaliter.*[4] Which signifies: In Christ dwelleth all the fullness of the Godhead bodily.

7. It is not fitting, then, to enquire of God by supernatural means, nor is it now necessary that He should answer; since all the faith has been given us in Christ, and there is therefore no more of it to be revealed, nor will there ever be.[5] And he that now desires to receive anything in a supernatural manner, as we have said,[6] is, as it were, finding fault with God for not having given us a complete sufficiency in His Son. For, although such a person may be assuming the faith, and believing it, nevertheless he is showing a curiosity which belongs to faithlessness. We must not expect, then,[7] to receive instruction, or aught else, in a supernatural manner. For, at the moment when Christ gave up the ghost upon the Cross, saying, *Consummatum est,*[8] which signifies, 'It is finished,' an end was made, not only of all these forms, but also of all those other ceremonies and rites of the Old Law. And so we must now be guided in all things by the law of Christ made man, and by that of His Church, and of His ministers, in a human and a visible manner, and by these means we must remedy our spiritual weaknesses and ignorances, since in these means we shall find abundant medicine for them all. If we leave this path, we are guilty not only of curiosity, but of great audacity: nothing is to be believed in a supernatural way, save only that which is the teaching of Christ made man, as I say, and of His ministers, who are men.[9] So much so that Saint

---

[1] Colossians ii, 3.   [2] E.p.: '. . . saying: That he knew no other thing . . .'
[3] 1 Corinthians ii, 2.   [4] Colossians ii, 9.
[5] E.p.: 'since, having spoken in Christ, He leaves no more to be desired.'
[6] E.p. has: 'in an extraordinary supernatural manner,' and omits: 'as we have said.'
[7] E.p. adds: 'with this curiosity.'   [8] St. John xix, 30.
[9] These two sentences are based on A and B. Alc. omits several lines, apparently by an oversight. E.p. has 'by the doctrine of Christ' for 'by the law of Christ made man'; omits 'in a human and a visible manner'; and adds 'and withdraw from' to 'If we leave.'

Paul says these words: *Quod si Angelus de coelo evangelizaverit, praeterquam quod evangelizavimus vobis, anathema sit.*[1] That is to say: If any angel from Heaven preach any other gospel unto you than that which we men[2] preach unto you, let him be accursed and excommunicate.

8. Wherefore, since it is true that we must ever be guided by that which Christ taught us, and that all things else are as nothing, and are not to be believed unless they are in conformity with it, he who still desires to commune with God after the manner of the Old Law acts vainly. Furthermore, it was not lawful at that time for everyone to enquire of God, neither did God answer all men, but only the priests and prophets, from whose mouths it was that the people had to learn law and doctrine; and thus, if a man desired to know anything of God, he enquired of Him through the prophet or the priest and not of God Himself. And, if David enquired of God at certain times upon his own account, he did this because he was a prophet, and yet, even so, he did it not without the priestly vestment, as it is clear was the case in the First Book of the Kings, where he said to Abimelech the priest: *Applica ad me Ephod*[3]—which ephod was one of the chief of the priestly vestments, having which he then spake with God. But at other times he spake with God through the prophet Nathan and other prophets. And by the mouths of these prophets and of the priests men were to believe that that which was said to them came from God; they were not to believe it because of their own opinions.

9. And thus, men were not authorized or empowered at that time to give entire credence to what was said by God, unless it were approved by the mouths of priests and prophets. For God is so desirous that the government and direction of every man should be undertaken by another man like himself,[4] and that every man should be ruled and governed by natural reason,[5] that He earnestly desires us not to give entire credence to the things that He communicates to us supernaturally, nor to consider them as being securely and completely confirmed until they pass through this human aqueduct of the mouth of man. And thus, whenever He says or reveals something to a soul, He gives this same soul to whom He says it a kind of inclination to tell it

---

[1] Galatians i, 8.
[2] E.p. omits 'men,' and also 'who are men' above.
[3] [It was to Abiathar that this was said.] 1 Kings [A.V., 1 Samuel] xxiii, 9.
[4] [P. Silverio reads: 'like Himself,' but the context seems to require the interpretation here adopted.]
[5] E.p. omits: 'and that . . . natural reason.'

to the person to whom it is fitting that it should be told. Until this has been done, it is not wont to give entire satisfaction, because the man has not taken it[1] from another man like himself.[2] We see in the Book of the Judges that the same thing happened to the captain Gedeon, to whom God had said many times that he should conquer the Madianites, yet he was fearful and full of doubts (for God had allowed him to retain that weakness) until he heard from the mouth of men what God had said to him. And it came to pass that, when God saw that he was weak, He said to him: 'Rise up and go down to the camp.' *Et cum audieris quid loquantur, tunc confortabuntur manus tuae, et securior ad hostium castra descendes.*[3] That is: When thou shalt hear what men are saying there, then shalt thou receive strength in that which I have said to thee, and thou shalt go down with greater security to the hosts of the enemy. And so it came to pass that, having heard a dream related by one of the Madianites to another, wherein the Madianite had dreamed that Gedeon should conquer them, he was greatly strengthened, and began to prepare for the battle with great joy. From this it can be seen that God desired not that he should feel secure, since He gave him not the assurance by supernatural means alone, but caused him first to be strengthened by natural means.[4]

10. And even more surprising is the thing that happened in this connection to Moses, when God had commanded him, and given him many instructions, which He confirmed with the signs of the wand changed into a serpent and of the leprous hand, enjoining him to go and set free the children of Israel. So weak was he and so uncertain[5] about this going forward that, although God was angered, he had not the courage to summon up the complete faith necessary for going,[6] until God encouraged him through his brother Aaron, saying: *Aaron frater tuus Levites, scio quod eloquens sit: ecce ipse egredietur in occursum tuum, vidensque te, laetabitur corde. Loquere ad eum, et pone verba mea in ore ejus: et ego ero in ore tuo, et in ore illius*, etc.[7] Which is as though He had said: I know that thy brother Aaron is an eloquent man: behold,[8] he will come forth to meet thee, and, when he seeth thee, he will be glad at heart; speak to him and tell him all My words, and I will be in thy

---

1 A, B, e.p.: 'in order that the man may take it.'
2 E.p. adds: 'whom God has set in His place.'
3 Judges vii, 11.
4 E.p.: 'should feel secure, until he had heard the same thing by the mouth of others.'
5 [*Lit.*, 'and so dark.'] E.p.: 'and so hesitating and dark.'
6 E.p. has 'strength' for 'faith.'
7 Exodus iv, 14–15.
8 Alc. alone has 'behold.'

mouth and in his mouth, so that each of you shall believe that which is in the mouth of the other.[1]

11. Having heard these words, Moses at once took courage, in the hope of finding consolation in the counsel which his brother was to give him; for this is a characteristic of the humble soul, which dares not converse alone with God, neither can be completely satisfied without human counsel and guidance. And that this should be given to it is the will of God, for He draws near to those who come together to converse of truth, in order to expound and confirm it in them, upon a foundation of natural reason,[2] even as He said that He would do when Moses and Aaron should come together—namely, that He would be in the mouth of the one and in the mouth of the other. Wherefore He said likewise in the Gospel that *Ubi fuerint duo vel tres congregati in nomine meo, ibi sum ego in medio eorum.*[3] That is: Where two or three have come together, in order to consider that which is for the greater honour and glory of My name, there am I in the midst of them. That is to say, I will make clear and confirm in their hearts the truths of God. And it is to be observed that He said not: Where there is one alone, there will I be; but: Where there are at least two. In this way He showed that God desires not that any man by himself alone should believe his experiences to be of God,[4] or should act in conformity with them,[5] or rely upon them, but rather should believe the Church and[6] her ministers, for God will not make clear and confirm the truth in the heart of one who is alone, and thus such a one will be weak and cold.

12. Hence comes that whereon the Preacher insists, where he says: *Vae soli, quia cum ceciderit, non habet sublevantem se. Si dormierint duo, fovebuntur mutuo; unus quomodo calefiet? et si quispiam praevaluerit contra unum, duo resistent ei.*[7] Which signifies: Woe to the man that is alone, for when he falleth he hath none to raise him up. If two sleep together, the one shall give warmth to the other (that is to say: with the warmth of God Who is between them[8]); but one alone, how shall he be warm? That is to say: How shall he be other than cold as to the things of God? And if any man can fight and prevail against one enemy (that is, the devil, who can fight and prevail against those that are alone and desire to be alone as regards the things of God), two men

---

[1] E.p. omits: 'so that . . . the other.'
[2] E.p. omits: 'upon . . . reason.'   [3] St. Matthew xviii, 20.
[4] [*Lit.*, 'the things which he has to be of God.']
[5] A, e.p.: 'neither should confirm them' [*confirme* for *conforme*].
[6] [*Lit.*, '. . . with them, without the Church or . . .'] E.p. has: '. . . with them, without the counsel and government of the Church or . . .'
[7] Ecclesiastes iv, 10–12.   [8] The parenthetical words are omitted in A and B.

together will resist him—that is, the disciple and the master[1] who come together to know and do[2] the truth. And until this happens such a man is habitually weak and feeble in the truth, however often he may have heard it from God; so much so that, despite the many occasions on which Saint Paul preached the Gospel, which he said that he had heard, not of men, but of God, he could not be satisfied until he had gone to consult with Saint Peter and the Apostles, saying: *Ne forte in vacuum currerem, aut cucurrissem.*[3] Which signifies: Perchance he should run, or had run, in vain,[4] having no assurance of himself, until man had given him assurance. This seems a noteworthy thing, O Paul, that He Who revealed to thee this Gospel could not likewise reveal to thee the assurance of the fault which thou mightest have committed in preaching the truth concerning Him.[5]

13. Herein it is clearly shown that a man must not rely upon the things that God reveals, save in the way that we are describing; for, even in cases where a person is in possession of certainty, as Saint Paul was certain of his Gospel (since he had already begun to preach it), yet, although the revelation be of God, man may still err with respect to it,[6] or in things relating to it. For, although God reveals one thing, He reveals not always the other; and oftentimes He reveals something without revealing the way in which it is to be done. For ordinarily He neither performs nor reveals anything that can be accomplished by human counsel and effort, although He may commune with the soul for a long time, very lovingly. Of this Saint Paul was very well aware, since, as we say, although he knew that the Gospel was revealed to him by God, he went to take counsel with Saint Peter. And we see this clearly in the Book of Exodus, where God had communed most familiarly with Moses, yet had never given him that salutary counsel which was given him by his father-in-law Jethro—that is to say, that he should choose other judges to assist him, so that the people should not be waiting from morning till night.[7] This counsel God approved, though it was not He Who had given it to him, for it was a thing that fell within the limits of human judgment and reason. With respect to Divine visions and revelations and locutions, God is not wont to reveal them,[8] for He is ever desirous that men should make such use of

---

[1] [i.e., the penitent and the confessor or director.]
[2] E.p.: 'and work.'
[3] Galatians ii, 2.
[4] E.p. omits the rest of this paragraph.
[5] A, B: 'the truth of the Lord.'
[6] E.p.: 'may still err in the execution of it.'
[7] Exodus xviii, 21-2.
[8] E.p.: 'for it was a thing that pertained to human counsel and judgment. And thus God is not wont to reveal all things concerning the visions and locutions of God that may pertain to human counsel and reason . . .'

their own reason as is possible, and all such things have to be governed by reason,[1] save those that are of faith, which transcend all judgment and reason, although these are not contrary to faith.[2]

14. Wherefore let none think that, because it may be true that God and the saints commune with him familiarly about many things, they will of necessity explain to him the faults that he commits with regard to anything, if it be possible for him to recognize these faults by other means. He can have no assurance about this; for, as we read came to pass in the Acts of the Apostles, Saint Peter, though a prince of the Church, who was taught directly by God, went astray nevertheless with respect to a certain ceremony that was in use among the Gentiles, and God was silent. So far did he stray that Saint Paul reproved him, as he affirms, saying: *Cum vidissem, quod non recte ad veritatem Evangelii ambularent, dixi coram omnibus: Si tu judaeus cum sis, gentiliter vivis, quomodo Gentes cogis judaizare?*[3] Which signifies: When I saw (says Saint Paul) that the disciples walked not uprightly according to the truth of the Gospel, I said to Peter before them all: If thou, being a Jew, as thou art, livest after the manner of the Gentiles, how feignest thou to force the Gentiles to live as do the Jews? And God reproved not Saint Peter Himself for this fault, for that simulation was a thing that had to do with reason, and it was possible for him to know it by rational means.[4]

15. Wherefore on the day of judgment God will punish for their many faults and sins many souls with whom He may quite habitually have held converse here below, and to whom He may have given much light and virtue; for, as to those things that they have known that they ought to do, they have been neglectful, and have relied upon that converse that they have had with God and upon the virtue that He has given them.[5] And thus, as Christ[6] says in the Gospel, they will marvel at that time, saying: *Domine, Domine, nonne in nomine tuo prophetavimus, et in nomine tuo daemonia ejecimus, et in nomine tuo virtutes multas fecimus?*[7] That is: Lord, Lord, were the prophecies that Thou spakest to us perchance not prophesied in Thy name? And in Thy name cast we not out devils?[8] And in Thy name performed we not

---

1 E.p. omits: 'and all such . . . by reason.'
2 A, B, e.p.: 'they are not contrary to reason and judgment.'
3 Galatians ii, 14.
4 E.p.: 'for it was a thing that he might know by ordinary means.'
5 A, B, e.p. add: 'and on that account being neglectful.'
6 So Alc.   A, B: 'as Christ our Lord.' E.p.: 'as our Lord Jesus.'
7 St. Matthew vii, 22.
8 Alc. omits this sentence. E.p. adds: 'Indeed we have cast out devils.'

many miracles and mighty works? And the Lord says that He will answer them in these words: *Et tunc confitebor illis, quia numquam novi vos: discedite a me omnes qui operamini iniquitatem.*[1] That is to say: Depart from Me, ye workers of iniquity, for I never knew you. Of the number of these was the prophet Balaam and others like to him, who, though God spake with them and gave them thanks,[2] were sinners. But the Lord will likewise give their proportion of reproof to His friends and chosen ones, with whom He communed familiarly here below, as to the faults and sins of neglect that they may have committed; whereof there was no need that God should Himself warn them, since He had already warned them through the natural reason and law that He had given to them.

16. In concluding this part of my subject, therefore, I say, and I infer from what has already been said, that anything, of whatsoever kind, received by the soul through supernatural means, must clearly and plainly, fully and simply,[3] be at once communicated to the spiritual director. For although there may seem no reason to speak of it, or to spend time upon doing so, since the soul is acting safely, as we have said, if it rejects it and neither pays heed to it nor desires it[4]— especially if it be a question of visions or revelations or other supernatural communications, which are either quite clear or very nearly so —nevertheless, it is very necessary to give an account of all these, although it may seem to the soul that there is no reason for so doing. And this for three causes.[5] First, because, as we have said, God communicates many things, the effect, power,[6] light and certainty whereof He confirms not wholly in the soul, until, as we have said, the soul consults him whom God has given to it as a spiritual judge, which is he that has the power to bind or to loose, and to approve or to blame, as we have shown by means of the passages quoted above;[7] and we can show it daily by experience, for we see humble souls to whom these things come to pass, and who, after discussing them with the proper persons, experience a new satisfaction, power, light and certainty; so much so that to some it seems that they have no effect upon them, nor do they even belong to them, until they have communicated them to the director, whereupon they are given to them anew.

---

[1] St. Matthew vii, 23.   [2] E.p. omits: 'and gave them thanks.'
[3] E.p. adds: 'with all truth.'   [4] E.p. omits: 'nor desires it.'
[5] So Alc.   B has: 'three reasons'; A, e.p.: 'three things.'
[6] A, B: 'the worth, effect . . .' [The word here rendered 'worth' is *esfuerzo*, which in the sixteenth century had that meaning among others, though its usual sense to-day is effort.']
[7] A, B omit: 'by means of the passages quoted above.'

17. The second cause is that the soul habitually needs instruction upon the things that come to pass within it, so that it may be led by that means to spiritual poverty and detachment, which is the dark night. For if it begins to relinquish this instruction—even when it desires not the things referred to—it will gradually, without realizing it, become callous[1] as it treads the spiritual road, and draw near again to the road of sense; and it is partly with respect to this that these distinct things happen.[2]

18. The third cause is that, for the sake of the humility and submission and mortification of the soul, it is well to relate everything to the director, even though he make[3] no account of it all and consider it of no importance. There are some souls who greatly dislike speaking of such things, because they think them to be unimportant, and know not how the person to whom they should relate them will receive them; but this is lack of humility, and for that very reason it is needful for them to submit themselves and relate these things. And there are others who are very timid in relating them, because they see no reason why they should have these experiences, which seem to belong to saints, as well as other things which they are sorry to have to describe; for which cause they think there is no reason to speak of them because they make no account of them; but for this very reason it is well for them to mortify themselves and relate them, until in time they come to speak of them humbly, unaffectedly, submissively and readily, and after this they will always find it easy to do so.

19. But, with respect to what has been said, it must be pointed out that, although we have insisted so much[4] that such things should be set aside, and that confessors should not encourage their penitents to discuss them, it is not well that spiritual fathers should show displeasure in regard to them, or should seek to avoid speaking of them or despise them, or make their penitents reserved and afraid to mention them, for it would be the means of causing them many inconveniences if the door were closed upon their relating them. For, since they are a means and manner[5] whereby God guides such souls, there is no reason for thinking ill of them or for being alarmed or scandalized by them; but rather there is a reason for proceeding[6] very quietly and kindly, for

---

[1] A, e.p. read 'rude' for 'callous.' [The change is a slight one: *enrudeciendo* for *endureciendo*.]

[2] E.p. omits: 'and it is partly . . . happen.'

[3] [The Spanish phrase equally admits the reading: 'even though the soul make.']

[4] B: 'so rigorously.'

[5] E.p.: 'For, as we have said, they are a means; and, since they are a means and manner . . .'   [6] None of the MSS. have 'proceeding,' which e.p. supplies.

encouraging these souls and giving them an opportunity to speak of these things; if necessary, they must be exhorted to speak; and, in view of the difficulty that some souls experience in describing such matters, this is sometimes quite essential. Let confessors direct their penitents into faith,[1] advising them frankly to turn away their eyes from all such things, teaching them how to void the desire and the spirit of them, so that they may make progress, and giving them to understand how much more precious in God's sight is one work or act of the will performed in charity than are all the visions and communications[2] that they may receive from Heaven, since these imply neither merit nor demerit.[3] Let them point out, too, that many souls who have known nothing of such things have made incomparably greater progress than others who have received many of them.

CHAPTER XXIII

Which begins to treat of the apprehensions of the understanding that come in a purely spiritual way, and describes their nature.

ALTHOUGH the instruction that we have given with respect to the apprehensions of the understanding which come by means of sense is somewhat brief, in comparison with what might be said about them, I have not desired to write of them at greater length; I believe, indeed, that I have already been too lengthy for the fulfilment of my present intention, which is to disencumber the understanding of them and direct the soul into the night of faith. Wherefore we shall now begin to treat of those other four apprehensions of the understanding, which, as we said in the tenth chapter,[4] are purely spiritual—namely, visions, revelations, locutions and spiritual feelings. These we call purely spiritual, for they do not (as do those that are corporeal and imaginary) communicate themselves to the understanding by way of the corporeal senses; but, without the intervention of any inward or outward corporeal sense, they present themselves to the understanding, clearly and distinctly, by supernatural means, passively—that is to say,

---

[1] [i.e., into the night of faith: cf. Chap. xxiii, § 4, below.]
[2] E.p.: 'than are all the visions and revelations.' A, B: 'than are all the visions and revelations and communications.'
[3] E.p. omits: 'since these . . . demerit.'
[4] It is in Chapter x (and not in viii, as is said in A, B and e.p.) that the author treats of these spiritual apprehensions.

without the performance of any act or operation on the part of the soul itself, at the least actively.[1]

2. It must be known, then, that, speaking broadly and in general terms, all these four apprehensions may be called visions of the soul; for we term the understanding of the soul also its sight. And since all these apprehensions are intelligible to the understanding, they are described, in a spiritual sense, as 'visible.' And thus the kinds of intelligence that are formed in the understanding may be called intellectual visions. Now, since all the objects of the other senses, which are all that can be seen, and all that can be heard, and all that can be smelt and tasted and touched, are objects of the understanding in so far as they fall within the limits of truth or falsehood, it follows that, just as to the eyes of the body all that is visible in a bodily way causes bodily vision, even so, to the spiritual eyes of the soul—namely, the understanding—all that is intelligible causes spiritual vision; for, as we have said, for the soul, to understand is for it to see. And thus, speaking generally, we may call these four apprehensions visions. This cannot be said, however, of the other senses, for no one of them is capable, as such, of receiving the object of another one.

3. But, since these apprehensions present themselves to the soul in the same way as they do to the various senses, it follows that, speaking properly and specifically, we shall describe that which the understanding receives by means of sight (because it can see things spiritually, even as the eyes can see bodily) as a vision; and that which it receives by apprehending and understanding new things (as it were through the hearing, when it hears things that are not heard[2]) we describe as revelation; and that which it receives by means of hearing we call locution; and that which it receives through the other senses, such as the perception of sweet spiritual fragrance, and of spiritual taste and of spiritual delight which the soul may enjoy supernaturally, we call spiritual feelings. From all these the soul derives spiritual vision or intelligence, without any kind of apprehension concerning form, image or figure of natural fancy or imagination[3]; these things are communicated to the soul directly by supernatural means and a supernatural process.

4. Of these, likewise (even as we said of the other imaginary corporeal apprehensions), it is well that we[4] should here disencumber the understanding, leading and directing it by means of them into the

---

[1] E.p.: 'actively and as on its own account.'   [2] E.p. omits the words in parenthesis.
[3] E.p. adds: 'whence it may derive them.'   [4] A reads: 'they.'

spiritual night of faith, to the Divine and substantial union of God;[1]
lest, by letting such things encumber and stultify it, it should be
hindered upon the road to solitude and detachment from all things,
which is necessary to that end. For, although these apprehensions are
nobler and more profitable and much more certain than those which
are corporeal and imaginary, inasmuch as they are interior and purely
spiritual, and are those which the devil is least able to counterfeit,
since they are communicated to the soul more purely and subtly without any effort of its own or of the imagination, at least actively,[2] yet
not only may the understanding be encumbered by them upon this
road, but it is possible for it, through its own imprudence, to be sorely
deceived.

5. And although, in one sense, we might conclude with these four
kinds of apprehension, by treating them all together and giving advice
which applies to them all, as we have given concerning all the others—
namely, that they should neither be desired nor aspired to—yet, since
we shall presently throw more light upon the way in which this is to be
done, and certain things will be said in connection with them, it will
be well to treat of each one of them in particular, and thus we shall
now speak of the first apprehensions, which are intellectual or spiritual
visions.

CHAPTER XXIV

Which treats of two kinds of spiritual vision that come supernaturally.

SPEAKING now strictly of those visions which are spiritual, and are
received without the intervention of any bodily sense, I say that
there are two kinds of vision that can be received by the understanding: the one kind is of corporeal substances; the other, of incorporeal or separated substances. The corporeal visions have respect
to all material things that are in Heaven and on earth, which the soul is
able to see, even while it is still in the body, by the aid of a certain
supernatural illumination, derived from God, wherein it is able to see
all things that are not present, both in Heaven and on earth,[3] even as
Saint John saw, as we read in the twenty-first chapter of the Apocalypse,
where he describes and relates the excellence of the celestial Jerusalem,

---

[1] The 1630 edition emends: 'of the love of God.'
[2] E.p. adds: 'and on its own account.'
[3] The remainder of this paragraph is omitted by e.p.

which he saw in Heaven. Even so, again, we read of Saint Benedict that in a spiritual vision he saw the whole world.[1] This vision, says Saint Thomas in the first of his Quodlibets, was in the light that is derived from above, as we have said.

2. The other visions, which are of incorporeal substances, cannot be seen by the aid of this derived illumination, whereof we are here speaking, but only by another and a higher illumination which is called the illumination of glory. And thus these visions of incorporeal substances, such as angels and souls,[2] are not of this life, neither can they be seen in the mortal body; for, if God were pleased to communicate them to the soul, in essence as they are, the soul would at once go forth from the flesh and would be loosed from this mortal life. For this reason God said to Moses, when he entreated Him to show him His Essence: *Non videbit me homo, et vivet.*[3] That is: Man shall not see Me and be able to remain alive. Wherefore, when the children of Israel thought that they were to see God, or had seen Him, or some angel, they feared death, as we read in the Book of Exodus, where, fearing these things, they said: *Non loquatur nobis Dominus, ne forte moriamur.*[4] As if they had said: Let not God communicate Himself to us openly, lest we die. And likewise in the Book of Judges, Manue, father of Samson, thought that he and his wife had seen in essence the angel who spake with them (and who had appeared to them in the form of a most beautiful man) and he said to his wife: *Morte moriemur, quia vidimus Dominum.*[5] Which signifies: We shall die, because we have seen the Lord.[6]

---

[1] St. Gregory: *Dial.,* Bk. II, Chap. xxxv. 'Omnis etiam mundus velut sub uno solis radio collectus, ante oculos eius adductus est.'
[2] The Toledo edition reads: 'such as the Divine Being, angels, souls.' This is based on an erroneous reading attributed incorrectly to Andrés de la Encarnación, who does not say, in fact, that any MS. so varies the text, but that it *might be* so varied in accordance with the context. No MS. has: 'the Divine Being.'
[3] Exodus xxxiii, 20.   [4] Exodus xx, 19.   [5] Judges xiii, 22.
[6] E.p. abbreviates this paragraph thus: 'The other visions, which are of incorporeal substances, demand another and a higher illumination; and thus these visions of incorporeal substances, such as angels and souls, do not occur habitually, nor are they proper to this life; still less is that of the Divine Essence, which is proper to the Blessed in Heaven, save that it may be communicated to a soul fleetingly and as in passing.' The next two paragraphs are omitted from e.p. P. Jerónimo de San José, in the edition of 1630, copies from e.p. the lines given in this note above, and then continues: '[save when] God so allows, in spite of the condition of our natural life, withdrawing the spirit from it occasionally, as happened to the apostle Saint Paul, when he says that he saw unspeakable secrets in the third heaven.' The adjustments made by P. Salablanca and amplified by P. Jerónimo in the rest of the paragraph [cf. notes below] follow the most usual scholastic doctrine. Among the Discalced Carmelite writers who deal most fully and competently with this doctrine of spiritual visions are the authors of the *Cursus Theologiæ Mysticæ,* Vol. IV, Disp. xx, xxi; Felipe de la Santísima Trinidad: *Summa Theologiæ Mysticæ,* Pt. II, Tract. III, Disc. iv; *Médula Mística,* Trat. VI. St. Thomas (I p., q. 88, a. 1) says that we cannot *quidditative* know separated substances.

3. And thus these visions occur not in this life, save occasionally and fleetingly, when, making an exception to the conditions which govern our natural life, God so allows it. At such times He totally withdraws the spirit from this life, and the natural functions of the body are supplied by His favour. This is why, at the time when it is thought that Saint Paul saw these (namely, the incorporeal substances in the third heaven), that Saint says :[1] *Sive in corpore, nescio, sive extra corpus, nescio, Deus scit.*[2] That is, he was enraptured, and of that which he saw he says that he knows not if it was in the body or out of the body, but that God knows. Herein it is clearly seen that the limits of natural means of communication[3] were passed, and that this was the work of God. Likewise, it is believed that God showed His Essence to Moses, for we read that God said to him that He would set him in the cleft of the rock, and would protect him, by covering him with His right hand, and protecting him so that he should not die when His glory passed; the which glory passed indeed, and was shown to him fleetingly, and the natural life of Moses was protected by the right hand of God.[4] But these visions that were so substantial—like that of Saint Paul and Moses, and that of our father[5] Elias, when he covered his face at the gentle whisper of God—although they are fleeting, occur only very rarely—indeed, hardly ever—and to very few; for God performs such a thing in those that are very strong[6] in the spirit of the Church and the law of God, as were the three men named above.

4. But, although these visions of spiritual substances cannot[7] be unveiled and be clearly seen in this life by the understanding, they can nevertheless be felt in the substance of the soul, with the sweetest touches and unions, all of which belongs to spiritual feelings, whereof, with the Divine favour, we shall treat presently; for our pen is being directed and guided to these—that is to say, to the Divine bond and union of the soul with Divine Substance. We shall speak of this when we treat of the dark and confused mystical understanding which remains to be described, wherein we shall show how, by means of this dark and loving knowledge, God is united with the soul in a lofty and Divine degree;[8] for, after some manner, this dark and loving

---

[1] Alc. omits: 'namely . . . Saint says.' [2] 2 Corinthians xii, 2.
[3] A, B: 'that the limits of life.' [4] Exodus xxxiii, 22.
[5] Only Alc. and the edition of 1630 have: 'our father.'
[6] The edition of 1630 omits 'very.' A, B [by changing one letter and writing *fuentes* for *fuertes*] read: 'that are spiritual fountains.'
[7] The edition of 1630 adds: 'according to the ordinary law.'
[8] This description the Saint probably accomplished, or intended to accomplish, in his commentaries on the last five stanzas of the *Dark Night*, which have not come down to us.

knowledge, which is faith, serves as a means to Divine union in this life, even as, in the next life, the light of glory serves as an intermediary to the clear vision of God.

5. Let us, then, now treat of the visions of corporeal substances, received spiritually in the soul, which come after the manner of bodily visions. For, just as the eyes see bodily visions by means of natural light, even so does the soul, through the understanding, by means of supernaturally derived light, as we have said, see those same natural things inwardly, together with others, as God wills; the difference between the two kinds of vision is only in the mode and manner of them. For spiritual and intellectual visions are much clearer and subtler than those which pertain to the body. For, when God is pleased to grant this favour to the soul, He communicates to it that supernatural light whereof we speak, wherein the soul sees the things that God wills it to see, easily and most clearly, whether they be of Heaven or of earth, and the absence or presence of them is no hindrance to the vision. And it is at times as though a door were opened before it into a great brightness, through which the soul sees a light, after the manner of a lightning flash, which, on a dark night, reveals things suddenly, and causes them to be clearly and distinctly seen, and then leaves them in darkness, although the forms and figures of them remain in the fancy. This comes to pass much more perfectly in the soul,[1] because those things that the spirit has seen in that light remain impressed upon it in such a way that whensoever it observes[2] them it sees them in itself as it saw them before;[3] even as in a mirror the forms that are in it[4] are seen whensoever a man looks in it, and in such a way that those forms of the things that he has seen are never wholly removed from his soul, although in course of time they become somewhat remote.[5]

6. The effect which these visions produce in the soul is that of quiet, illumination, joy like that of glory, sweetness, purity and love, humility and inclination or elevation of the spirit in God; sometimes more so, at other times less; with sometimes more of one thing, at other times more of another, according to the spirit wherein they are received and according as God wills.

7. The devil likewise can produce[6] these visions, by means of a

---

[1] E.p. omits the rest of the paragraph.
[2] 'Whensoever, enlightened by God, it observes . . .' reads the edition of 1630.
[3] A : 'it sees them even as it saw them before.'
[4] Edition of 1630: 'that are represented in it.'
[5] *Ibid.* : 'more remote.'
[6] *Ibid.* : 'can produce or imitate.'

certain natural light,[1] whereby he brings things clearly before the mind, through spiritual suggestion, whether they be present or absent. There is that passage in Saint Matthew, which says of the devil and Christ: *Ostendit omnia regna mundi, et gloriam eorum.*[2] That is to say: He showed Him all the kingdoms of the world and the glory of them. Concerning this certain doctors say that he did it by spiritual suggestion,[3] for it was not possible to make Him see so much with the bodily eyes as all the kingdoms of the world and the glory of them. But there is much difference between these visions that are caused by the devil and those that are of God. For the effects produced in the soul by the devil's visions are not like those produced by good visions; the former produce aridity of spirit as to communion with God and an inclination to esteem oneself highly, and to receive and set store by the visions aforesaid, and in no wise do they produce the gentleness of humility and love of God. Neither do the forms of such visions remain impressed upon the soul with the sweetness and brightness of the others; nor do they last, but are quickly effaced from the soul, save when the soul greatly esteems them, in which case this high esteem itself causes it to recall them naturally, but with great aridity of spirit, and without producing that effect of love and humility which is produced by good visions when the soul recalls them.

8. These visions, inasmuch as they are of creatures, wherewith God has no essential conformity or proportion,[4] cannot serve the understanding as a proximate means to union[5] with God. And thus the soul must conduct itself in a purely negative way concerning them, as in the other things that we have described, in order that it may progress by the proximate means—namely, by faith. Wherefore the soul must make no store or treasure of the forms of such visions as remain impressed upon it, neither must it lean upon them; for to do this would be to be encumbered with those forms, images and persons which remain inwardly within it, and thus the soul would not progress toward God by denying itself all things. For, even if these forms should be permanently set before the soul, they will not greatly hinder this progress, if the soul has no desire to set store by them. For, although it is true that the remembrance of them impels the soul to a certain love of God and contemplation, yet it is impelled and exalted much more by pure

---

[1] E.p. adds: 'making use of the fancy.'
[2] St. Matthew iv, 8. Thus the Codices. E.p. omits the Latin text.
[3] E.p.: '. . . by intelligible suggestion.' On this passage, cf. Cornelius a Lapide (*Commentaria in Matthæum*, Cap. IV) and St. Thomas (III p., q. 41, ad. 3).
[4] A, B: 'or communication.'   [5] A, B: 'to essential union.'

faith and detachment in darkness from them all, without its knowing how or whence it comes to it. And thus it will come to pass that the soul will go forward, enkindled with yearnings of purest love for God, without knowing whence they come to it, or on what they are founded. The fact is that, while faith has become ever more deeply rooted and infused in the soul by means of that emptiness and darkness and detachment from all things, or spiritual poverty, all of which may be spoken of as one and the same thing, at the same time the charity of God has become rooted and infused in the soul ever more deeply also. Wherefore, the more the soul desires obscurity and annihilation with respect to all the outward or inward things that it is capable of receiving, the more is it infused by faith, and, consequently, by love and hope, since all these three theological virtues go together.[1]

9. But at certain times the soul neither understands this love nor feels it; for this love resides, not in sense, with its tender feelings, but in the soul, with fortitude and with a courage and daring that are greater than they were before, though sometimes it overflows into sense and produces gentle and tender feelings. Wherefore, in order to attain to that love, joy and delight which such visions produce and cause in the soul, it is well that the soul should have fortitude and mortification and love,[2] so that it may desire to remain in emptiness and darkness as to all things, and to build its love and joy upon that which it neither sees nor feels, neither can see nor feel in this life, which is God, Who is incomprehensible and transcends all things. It is well, then, for us to journey to Him by denying ourselves everything. For otherwise, even if the soul be so wise, humble and strong that the devil cannot deceive it by visions or cause it to fall into some sin of presumption, as he is wont to do, he will not allow it to make progress; for he sets obstacles in the way of spiritual detachment and poverty of spirit and emptiness in faith, which is the essential condition for union of the soul with God.

10. And, as the same teaching that we gave in the nineteenth and twentieth chapters, concerning supernatural apprehensions and visions of sense, holds good for these visions, we shall not spend more time here in describing them.[3]

---

[1] E.p. omits: 'since . . . together.'
[2] E.p. omits: 'and love.'
[3] A, B, e.p.: 'in treating them more extensively.'

CHAPTER XXV

Which treats of revelations, describing their nature and making a distinction between them.

ACCORDING to the order which we are here following, we have next to treat of the second kind of spiritual apprehension, which we have described above as revelations, and which properly belongs[1] to the spirit of prophecy. With respect to this, it must first be known that revelation is naught else than the discovery of some hidden truth or the manifestation of some secret or mystery. Thus God may cause the soul to understand something by making clear to the understanding the truth concerning it, or He may reveal to the soul certain things which He is doing or proposes to do.

2. Accordingly, we may say that there are two kinds of revelation. The first is the disclosure to the understanding of truths which are properly called intellectual knowledge or intelligence; the second is the manifestation of secrets, which are called revelations with more propriety than the others. For the first kind cannot strictly be called revelations, since they consist in this, that God causes the soul to understand naked truths, not only with respect to temporal things, but likewise with respect to spiritual things, revealing them to the soul clearly and openly. These I have desired to treat under the heading of revelations: first, because they have close kinship and similarity with them: secondly, in order not to multiply distinctions.

3. According to this method, then, we shall now be well able to divide revelations into two kinds of apprehension. The one kind we shall call intellectual knowledge, and the other, the manifestation of secrets and hidden mysteries of God. With these we shall conclude in two chapters as briefly as we may, and in this chapter following we shall treat of the first.[2]

---

[1] E.p.: 'some of which properly belong.'
[2] So Alc. A, B omit: 'and in . . . the first.' E.p. has: 'treating, in this first chapter, intellectual knowledge.'

CHAPTER XXVI

Which treats of the intuition of naked truths in the understanding, explaining how they are of two kinds and how the soul is to conduct itself with respect to them.

IN order to speak properly of this intuition of naked truths which is conveyed to the understanding, the writer would need God to take his hand and to guide his pen; for know, dear reader, that[1] what they are to the soul cannot be expressed in words. But, since I speak not of them here of set purpose, but only that through them I may instruct the soul and lead it to Divine union, I shall suffer myself to speak of them here in a brief and modified form, as is sufficient for the fulfilment of that intention.

2. This kind of vision (or, to speak more properly, of knowledge of naked truths) is very different from that of which we have just spoken in the twenty-fourth chapter. For it is not like seeing bodily things with the understanding; it consists rather in comprehending and seeing with the understanding the truths of God, whether of things that are, that have been or that will be, which is in close conformity with the spirit of prophecy, as perchance we shall explain hereafter.

3. Here it is to be observed that this kind of knowledge is distinguishable according to two divisions: the one kind comes to the soul with respect to the Creator; the other with respect to creatures, as we have said. And, although both kinds are very delectable to the soul, yet the delight caused in it by the kind that relates to God is comparable to nothing whatsoever, and there are no words or terms wherein it can be described. This kind of knowledge is of God Himself, and the delight is in God Himself, whereof David says: 'There is naught soever like to Him.'[2] For this kind of knowledge comes to the soul in direct relation to God, when the soul, after a most lofty manner, has a perception of some attribute of God—of His omnipotence, of His might, of His goodness and sweetness, etc.; and, whensoever it has such a perception, that which is perceived cleaves to the soul. Inasmuch as this is pure contemplation, the soul clearly sees that there is no way wherein it can say aught concerning it, save to speak, in certain general terms, of the abundance of delight and blessing which it has felt, and this is expressed by souls that experience it; but not to the end that

---

[1] A, B: 'for you must know that.'   [2] [Psalm xxxix, 6: cf. A.V., xl, 5.]

what the soul has experienced and perceived may be wholly apprehended.

4. And thus David, speaking for himself when something of this kind had happened to him, used only common and general terms, saying: *Judicia Domini vera, justificata in semetipsa. Desiderabilia super aurum et lapidem pretiosum multum; et dulciora super mel et favum.*[1] Which signifies: The judgments of God[2]—that is, the virtues and attributes which we perceive in God—are in themselves true, justified, more to be desired than gold and very much more than precious stones, and sweeter than the honeycomb and honey. And concerning Moses we read that, when God gave him a most lofty manifestation of knowledge from Himself on an occasion when He passed before him, he said only that which can be expressed in the common terms above mentioned. And it was so that, when the Lord passed before him in that manifestation of knowledge, Moses quickly prostrated himself upon the ground,[3] saying: *Dominator Domine Deus, misericors et clemens, patiens, et multæ miserationis, ac verax. Qui custodis misericordiam in millia.*[4] Which signifies: Ruler,[5] Lord, God, merciful and clement, patient, and of great compassion, and true, that keepest mercy promised unto thousands. Here it is seen that Moses could not express that which he had learned from God in one single manifestation of knowledge, and therefore he expressed and gave utterance to it in all these words. And although at times, when such knowledge is given to a soul, words are used, the soul is well aware that it has expressed no part of what it has felt; for it knows that there is no fit name by which it can name it. And thus Saint Paul, when he was granted that lofty knowledge of God, made no attempt to describe it, saying only that it was not lawful for man to speak of it.

5. These Divine manifestations of knowledge which have respect to God never relate to particular matters, inasmuch as they concern the Chief Beginning, and therefore can have no particular reference, unless it be a question of some truth concerning a thing less than God, which is involved in the perception of the whole; but these Divine manifestations themselves—no, in no way whatsoever.[6] And these lofty manifestations of knowledge can come only to the soul that

---

[1] Psalm xviii, 10–11 [A.V., xix, 9–10].
[2] E.p.: 'That which we judge and perceive concerning God.'
[3] A, B omit 'quickly.'   [4] Exodus xxxiv, 6–7.
[5] [*Lit.*, 'Emperor.']
[6] E.p.: 'and therefore can have no particular reference, unless this knowledge should be extended to some other truth concerning something less than God which is capable of being described in some way; but these general manifestations—no.'

attains to union with God, for they are themselves that union; and to receive them is equivalent to a certain contact with the Divinity[1] which the soul experiences, and thus it is God Himself Who is perceived and tasted therein. And, although He cannot be experienced manifestly and clearly, as in glory, this touch of knowledge and delight is nevertheless so sublime and profound that it penetrates the substance[2] of the soul, and the devil cannot meddle with it or produce any manifestation like to it, for there is no such thing, neither is there aught that compares with it, neither can he infuse pleasure or delight that is like to it; for such kinds of knowledge savour of the Divine Essence and of eternal life, and the devil cannot counterfeit a thing so lofty.

6. Nevertheless he might make some pretence of imitating it, by representing to the soul certain great matters and things which enchant the senses and can readily be perceived by them, and endeavouring to persuade the soul that these are God; but he cannot do this in such wise that they enter into the substance[3] of the soul and of a sudden[4] renew it and enkindle it with love, as do the manifestations of God. For there are certain kinds of knowledge, and certain of these touches effected by God in the substance of the soul, which enrich it after such wise that not only does one of them suffice to take from the soul once and for all the whole of the imperfections that it had itself been unable to throw off during its whole life, but it leaves the soul full of virtues and blessings[5] from God.

7. And these touches are so delectable to the soul, and the delight they produce is so intimate, that if it received only one of them it would consider itself well rewarded for all the trials that it had suffered in this life, even had they been innumerable; and it is so greatly encouraged and given such energy to suffer many things for God's sake that it suffers especially in seeing that it is not suffering more.

8. The soul cannot attain to these lofty degrees of knowledge by means of any comparison or imagination of its own, because[6] they are loftier than all these; and so God works them in the soul without making use of its own capacities. Wherefore, at certain times, when the soul is least thinking of it and least desiring it, God is wont to give it these Divine touches, by causing it certain remembrances of Himself.

---

[1] E.p. has 'Divine Truth' for 'Divinity.'   [2] E.p.: 'the inmost part.'
[3] E.p.: 'into the very interior part.' A: 'into the wisdom.'
[4] So Alc., D. A, B, C, P, e.p. have: 'and sublimely.' [The difference is slight: *subidamente* for *subitamente*.]
[5] A, erroneously, has: 'and visions.'   [6] E.p. adds: 'as we have said.'

And these are sometimes suddenly caused in the soul by its mere recollection of certain things—sometimes of very small things. And they are so readily perceived[1] that at times they cause not only the soul, but also the body, to tremble. But at other times they come to pass in the spirit when it is very tranquil, without any kind of trembling, but with a sudden[2] sense of delight and spiritual refreshment.

9. At other times, again, they come when the soul repeats or hears some word, perhaps from Scripture or possibly from some other source; but they are not always equally efficacious and sensible, for oftentimes they are extremely faint; yet, however faint they may be, one of these recollections and touches of God is more profitable to the soul than many other kinds of knowledge or many meditations upon the creatures and the works of God. And, since these manifestations of knowledge come to the soul suddenly,[3] and independently of its own free will, it must neither desire to have them, nor desire not to have them[4]; but must merely be humble and resigned concerning them, and God will perform His work how and when He wills.

10. And I say not that the soul should behave in the same negative manner with regard to these apprehensions as with regard to the rest, for, as we have said, they are a part of the union towards which we are leading the soul, to which end we are teaching it to detach and strip itself of all other apprehensions. And the means by which God will do this must be humility and suffering for love of God with resignation[5] as regards all reward; for these favours are not granted to the soul which still cherishes attachments, inasmuch as they are granted through a very special love of God toward the soul which loves Him likewise with great detachment. It is to this that the Son of God referred, in Saint John, when He said: *Qui autem diligit me, diligetur a Patre meo, et ego diligam eum, et manifestabo ei me ipsum.*[6] Which signifies: He that loves Me shall be loved of My Father, and I will love him and will manifest Myself to him. Herein are included the kinds of knowledge and touches to which we are referring, which God manifests to the soul that truly loves Him.[7]

11. The second kind of knowledge or vision of interior truths[8] is very different from this that we have described, since it is of things

---

1 E.p.: 'And they are so efficacious.'
2 So Alc. The other authorities read: 'with a sublime' [*subido* for *súbito*, as above.]
3 E.p. adds: 'as we have said.'
4 E.p.: 'it must neither strive to have them nor strive not to have them.'
5 E.p. adds: 'and disinterestedness.'   6 St. John xiv, 21.
7 A, B: 'that draws near to Him and truly loves Him.'
8 A, B: 'or of interior truths.'

lower than God. And herein is included the perception of the truth of things in themselves, and that of the events and happenings which come to pass among men. And this knowledge is of such a kind that, when the soul learns these truths, they sink into it, independently of any suggestion from without, to such an extent that, although it may be given a different interpretation of them, it cannot make inward assent to this, even though it endeavour to do so by putting forth a great effort; for within the spirit it is learning otherwise through the spirit that is teaching it that thing,[1] which is equivalent to seeing it clearly. This pertains[2] to the spirit of prophecy and to the grace which Saint Paul calls the gift of the discernment of spirits.[3] Yet, although the soul holds something which it understands to be quite certain and true, as we have said, and although it may be unable to cease giving it that passive interior consent, it must not therefore cease to believe and to give the consent of reason to that which its spiritual director tells it and commands it,[4] even though this may be quite contrary to its own feelings, so that it may be directed in faith to Divine union, to which a soul must journey by believing rather than by understanding.

12. Concerning both these things we have clear testimonies in Scripture. For, with respect to the spiritual knowledge[5] of things that may be acquired, the Wise Man says these words: *Ipse dedit mihi horum, quæ sunt, scientiam veram, ut sciam dispositionem orbis terrarum, et virtutes elementorum, initium et consummationem temporum, vicissitudinum permutationes, et consummationes temporum, et morum mutationes, divisiones temporum, et anni cursus, et stellarum dispositiones, naturas animalium et iras bestiarum, vim ventorum, et cogitationes hominum, differentias virgultorum, et virtutes radicum, et quæcumque sunt abscondita, et improvisa didici: omnium enim artifex docuit me sapientia.*[6] Which signifies: God hath given me true knowledge of things that are: to know the disposition of the round world[7] and the virtues of the elements; the beginning, and ending, and midst of the times, the alterations in the changes[8] and the consummations of the seasons, and the changes of customs, the divisions of the seasons,[9] the courses of the

---

[1] E.p.: 'otherwise in that which has been spiritually represented to it.'
[2] E.p.: 'This may pertain.'   [3] 1 Corinthians xii, 10.
[4] E.p. abbreviates: 'as we have said, it cannot cease to follow that which its spiritual director commands.'
[5] E.p.: 'to the particular spiritual knowledge.'
[6] Wisdom vii, 17–21. The reading of the Latin text is that of Alc.
[7] [*Lit.*, 'of the roundness of the lands.']   [8] E.p.: 'the changes in events.'
[9] A omits this phrase, and B, this and the phrase preceding.

year and the dispositions of the stars; the natures of animals, and the furies of the beasts, the strength and virtue of the winds, and the thoughts of men; the diversities in plants and trees and the virtues of roots and all things that are hidden, and those that are not foreseen[1]: all these I learned, for Wisdom, which is the worker of all things, taught me. And although this knowledge which the Wise Man here says that God gave him concerning all things was infused[2] and general, the passage quoted furnishes sufficient evidence for all particular kinds of knowledge which God infuses into souls, by supernatural means, when He wills. And this not that He may give them a general habit of knowledge as He gave to Solomon in the matters aforementioned; but that He may reveal to them at times certain truths with respect to any of all these things that the Wise Man here enumerates. Although it is true that into many souls Our Lord infuses habits which relate to many things, yet these are never of so general a kind as they were in the case of Solomon. The differences between them are like to those between the gifts distributed by God which are enumerated by Saint Paul; among these he sets wisdom, knowledge, faith, prophecy, discernment or knowledge of spirits, understanding of tongues, interpretation of spoken words, etc.[3] All these kinds of knowledge are infused habits,[4] which God gives freely to whom He will, whether naturally or supernaturally; naturally,[5] as to Balaam, to other idolatrous prophets and to many sybils, to whom He gave the spirit of prophecy; and supernaturally, as to the holy prophets and apostles and other saints.[6]

13. But over and above these habits or graces[7] freely bestowed,[8] what we say is that persons who are perfect or are making progress in perfection are wont very commonly to receive enlightenment and knowledge of things present or absent; these they know through their spirit,[9] which is already enlightened and purged. We can interpret that passage from the Proverbs in this sense, namely: *Quomodo in aquis resplendent vultus prospicientium sic corda hominum manifesta sunt prudentibus.*[10] Even as there appear in the waters the faces of those that look therein, so the hearts of men are manifest to the prudent. This is

---

[1] E.p. omits: 'and . . . foreseen.'
[2] A abbreviates: 'which is the worker of all things, was infused.'
[3] [*Lit.*, 'exposition of words'; the reference is clearly to 1 Corinthians xii, 8–10.]
[4] E.p.: 'infused gifts.'   [5] Alc. alone has 'naturally.'
[6] E.p. abbreviates: 'to whom He will, as to the holy prophets and apostles and to other saints.'
[7] E.p.: 'But over and above these graces.'
[8] [The original has *gratis datas*.]
[9] E.p.: 'through the light which they receive in their spirit.'
[10] Proverbs xxvii, 19.

understood of those that have the wisdom of saints, which the sacred Scripture calls prudence. And in this way these spirits sometimes learn of other things also, although not whensoever they will; for this belongs only to those that have the habit, and even to these it belongs not always and with respect to all things, for it depends upon God's will to help them.

14. But it must be known that those whose spirits are purged can learn by natural means with great readiness,[1] and some more readily than others, that which is in the inward spirit or heart, and the inclinations and talents of men, and this by outward indications, albeit very slight ones, as words, movements and other signs. For, even as the devil can do this, since he is spirit, even so likewise can the spiritual man, according to the words of the Apostle, who says: *Spiritualis autem judicat omnia.*[2] 'He that is spiritual judgeth all things.' And again he says: *Spiritus enim omnia scrutatur, etiam profunda Dei.*[3] 'The spirit searcheth all things, yea, the deep things of God.' Wherefore, although spiritual persons cannot by nature know thoughts, or things that are in the minds of others,[4] they may well interpret them through supernatural enlightenment or by signs. And, although they may often be deceived in their interpretation of signs, they are more generally correct. Yet we must trust neither to the one means nor to the other, for the devil meddles herein greatly, and with much subtlety, as we shall afterwards say, and thus we must ever renounce such kinds of knowledge.

15. And that spiritual persons may have knowledge of the deeds and happenings of men, even though they be elsewhere, we have witness and example in the Fourth Book of the Kings, where Giezi, the servant of our father Eliseus,[5] desired to hide from him the money which he had received from Naaman the Syrian, and Eliseus said: *Nonne cor meum in præsenti erat, quando reversus est homo de curru suo in occursum tui?*[6] 'Was not my heart perchance present, when Naaman turned back from his chariot and went to meet thee?' This happens spiritually; the spirit sees it as though it were happening in its presence. And the same thing is proved in the same book, where we read likewise of the same Eliseus, that, knowing all that the King of Syria did with his princes in his privy chamber, he told it to the King of Israel, and thus the counsels of the King of Syria were of no effect; so much so that, when the King

---

[1] E.p.: 'can learn with greater readiness.'
[3] 1 Corinthians ii, 10.
[5] This phrase is found only in Alc. and e.p.

[2] 1 Corinthians ii, 15.
[4] [*Lit.*, 'in the interior.']
[6] 4 Kings [A.V., 2 Kings] v, 26.

of Syria saw that all was known, he said to his people[1]: Why do ye not tell me which of you is betraying me to the King of Israel? And then one of his servants said: *Nequaquam, Domine mi Rex, sed Eliseus Propheta, qui est in Israel, indicat Regi Israel omnia verba, quæcumque locutus fueris in conclavi tuo.*[2] 'It is not so, my lord, O king, but Eliseus, the prophet that is in Israel, telleth the king of Israel all the words that thou speakest in thy privy chamber.'

16. Both kinds of this knowledge of things, as well as other kinds of knowledge, come to pass[3] in the soul passively, so that for its own part it does naught. For it will come to pass that, when a person is inattentive to a matter and it is far from his mind, there will come to him a vivid understanding of what he is hearing or reading, and that much more clearly than could be conveyed by the sound of the words; and at times, though he understand not the words, as when they are in Latin and he knows not that tongue, the knowledge of their meaning comes to him, despite his not understanding them.

17. With regard to the deceptions which the devil can bring about, and does bring about, concerning this kind of knowledge and understanding, there is much that might be said, for the deceptions which he effects in this way are very great and very difficult to unmask. Inasmuch as, through suggestion,[4] he can represent to the soul many kinds of intellectual knowledge and implant them so firmly that it appears impossible that they should not be true, he will certainly cause the soul to believe innumerable falsehoods if it be not humble and cautious. For suggestion has sometimes great power over the soul, above all when it is to some extent aided by the weakness of sense, causing the knowledge which it conveys to sink into the soul with such great power, persuasiveness and determination that the soul needs to give itself earnestly to prayer and to exert great strength if it is to cast it off. For at times the devil is accustomed to represent to the soul the sins of others, and evil consciences and evil souls,[5] falsely but very vividly, and all this he does to harm the soul, trusting that it may spread abroad his revelations, and that thus more sins may be committed, for which reason he fills the soul with zeal by making it believe that these revelations are granted it so that it may commend the persons concerned to God. Now, though it is true that God sometimes sets before holy souls the necessities of their neighbours, so that they may commend them to

---

[1] A, B: 'to his counsellors.'   [2] 4 Kings [A.V., 2 Kings] vi, 12.
[3] E.p.: 'Both kinds of this knowledge of things also come to pass.'
[4] E.p. adds: 'making use of the bodily senses.'
[5] A, B: 'and the evil souls of others.'

God or relieve them, even as we read that He revealed to Jeremias the weakness of the prophet Baruch, that he might give him counsel concerning it,[1] yet it is more often the devil who does this, and speaks falsely about it, in order to cause infamy, sin and discouragement, whereof we have very great experience. And at other times he implants other kinds of knowledge with great assurance, and persuades the soul to believe them.

18. Such knowledge as this, whether it be of God or no, can be of very little assistance to the progress of the soul[2] on its journey to God if the soul desire it and be attached to it; on the contrary, if it were not scrupulous in rejecting it, not only would it be hindered on its road, but it would even be greatly harmed and led far astray. For all the perils and inconveniences which, as we have said, may be involved in the supernatural apprehensions whereof we have treated up to this point, may occur here, and more also. I will not, therefore, treat more fully of this matter here, since sufficient instruction about it has already been given in past chapters; I will[3] only say that the soul must always be very scrupulous in rejecting these things, and seek to journey to God by the way of unknowing; and must ever relate its experiences to its spiritual confessor, and be ever attentive to his counsel. Let the confessor guide the soul past this, laying no stress upon it, for it is of no kind of importance for[4] the road to union; for when these things are granted to the soul passively they always leave in it such effect as God wills shall remain, without necessity for the soul to exert any diligence in the matter.[5] And thus it seems to me that there is no reason to describe here either the effect which is produced by true knowledge, or that which comes from false knowledge, for this would be wearisome and never-ending. For the effects of this knowledge cannot all be described in a brief instruction, the knowledge being great and greatly varied, and its effects being so likewise, since good knowledge produces good effects, and evil knowledge, evil effects,[6] etc. In saying that all should be rejected,[7] we have said sufficient for the soul not to go astray.[8]

---

[1] Jeremias xlv, 3.　　　　　　　　　[2] E.p. : 'can bring very little profit to the soul.'
[3] A, B : 'therefore I will . . .'
[4] E.p. : '. . . laying no stress upon it, (and) treating it as of no account for . . .'
[5] E.p. omits: 'without . . . in the matter.'
[6] A, B, e.p. have: '. . . good effects [leading] to good, and evil knowledge evil effects [leading] to evil.' Alc. ends the chapter here.
[7] E.p. adds: 'and how this is to be done.'
[8] E.p. omits: 'for the soul not to go astray.' We follow A and B in our reading of this last sentence.

CHAPTER XXVII

Which treats of the second kind of revelation, namely, the disclosure of hidden secrets.[1] *Describes the way in which these may assist the soul toward union with God, and the way in which they may be a hindrance; and how the devil may deceive the soul greatly in this matter.*

W E were saying that the second kind of revelation was the manifestation of hidden mysteries and secrets. This may come to pass in two ways. The first with respect to that which God is in Himself, wherein is included the revelation of the mystery of the Most Holy Trinity and Unity of God. The second is with respect to that which God is in His works, and herein are included the other articles of our Catholic faith,[2] and the propositions deducible from them which may be laid down explicitly as truths. In these are included and comprised a great number of the revelations of the prophets, of promises and threatenings of God, and of other things which have happened and shall happen concerning this matter of faith.[3] Under this second head we may also include many other particular things which God habitually reveals, both concerning the universe in general as also in particular concerning kingdoms, provinces and states and families and particular persons. Of these we have examples in abundance in the Divine writings, both of the one kind and of the other, especially in all the Prophets, wherein are found revelations of all these kinds. As this is a clear and plain matter, I will not here spend time in quoting these examples, but will only say[4] that these revelations do not come to pass by word alone, but that God gives them in many ways and manners, sometimes by word alone, sometimes by signs and figures alone, and by images and similitudes alone, sometimes in more than one way at once, as is likewise to be seen in the Prophets, particularly throughout the Apocalypse, where we find not only all the kinds of revelation which we have described, but likewise the ways and manners to which we are here referring.

2. As to these revelations which are included under our second head, God grants them still in our time to whom He will. He is wont, for example, to reveal to some persons how many days they still have

---

[1] A, B, e.p. add : 'and mysteries.'
[2] E.p. : 'of our holy Catholic faith.'
[3] E.p. omits : 'concerning this matter of faith.'
[4] A, B : '. .. I do not speak of them; I only say . . .'

to live, or what trials they are to suffer, or what is to befall such and such a person, or such and such a kingdom, etc. And even as regards the mysteries of our faith, He will reveal and expound to the spirit the truths concerning them,[1] although, since this has already been revealed once, it is not properly to be termed revelation, but is more correctly a manifestation or explanation of what has been revealed already.

3. In this kind of revelation[2] the devil may meddle freely. For, as revelations of this nature come ordinarily through words, figures and similitudes, etc., the devil may very readily counterfeit others like them, much more so than when the revelations are in spirit alone.[3] Wherefore, if with regard to the first and the second kind of revelation which we are here describing, as touching our faith, there be revealed to us anything new, or different, we must in no wise give our consent to it, even though we had evidence that it was spoken by an angel from Heaven.[4] For even so says Saint Paul, in these words: *Licet nos, aut Angelus de cœlo evangeliʒet vobis præterquam quod evangeliʒavimus vobis, anathema sit.*[5] Which signifies: Even though an angel from Heaven declare or preach unto you aught else than that which we have preached unto you, let him be anathema.

4. Since, then, there are no more articles to be revealed concerning the substance of our faith than those which have already been revealed to the Church, not only must[6] anything new which may be revealed to the soul concerning this be rejected, but it behoves the soul[7] to be cautious and pay no heed to any novelties implied therein, and for the sake of the purity of the soul it behoves it to rely on faith alone. Even though the truths already revealed to it be revealed again, it will believe them, not because they are now revealed anew, but because they have already been sufficiently revealed to the Church: indeed, it must close its understanding to them, holding[8] simply to the doctrine of the Church and to its faith, which, as Saint Paul says, enters through hearing.[9] And let not its credence and intellectual assent be given to these matters of the faith which have been revealed anew, however

---

[1] E.p. adds: 'with particular light and impressiveness.'
[2] So the MSS.   E.p. reads: 'With regard, then, to what we call revelations (for I speak not now of what has already been revealed, such as the mysteries of the faith) . . .'
[3] E.p. omits: 'much more . . . spirit alone.'
[4] E.p. omits: 'even though . . . from Heaven.'   [5] Galatians i, 8.
[6] E.p. begins the sentence thus: 'And thus, not only must . . .'
[7] E.p. adds: 'apart from this.'
[8] E.p. abbreviates: 'it behoves it to rely on faith alone, closing its understanding and holding . . .'
[9] Romans x, 17.

fitting and true they may seem to it, if it desire not to be deceived.[1] For, in order to deceive the soul and to instil falsehoods into it, the devil first feeds it with truths and things that are probable in order to give it assurance and afterwards to deceive it.[2] He resembles one that sews leather with a bristle, first piercing the leather with the sharp bristle, after which enters the soft thread; the thread could not enter unless the bristle guided it.

5. And let this be considered carefully; for, even were it true that there was no peril in such deception, yet it greatly behoves the soul not to desire to understand clearly things that have respect to the faith,[3] so that it may preserve the merit of faith, in its purity and entirety, and likewise that it may come, in this night of the understanding, to the Divine light of Divine union. And it is equally necessary to consider any new revelation with one's eyes closed, and holding fast the prophecies of old, for the Apostle Saint Peter, though he had seen the glory of the Son of God after some manner[4] on Mount Tabor, wrote, in his canonical epistle, these words: *Et habemus firmiorem propheticum sermonem; cui benefacitis attendentes, etc.*[5] Which is as though he had said: Although the vision that we have seen of Christ on the Mount is true, the word of the prophecy that is revealed to us is firmer and surer, and, if ye rest your soul upon it, ye do well.

6. And if it is true that, for the reasons already described, it behoves the soul to close its eyes to the aforementioned revelations which come to it, and which concern the propositions of the faith,[6] how much more necessary will it be neither to receive nor to give credit to other revelations relating to different things, wherein the devil habitually meddles so freely that I believe it impossible[7] for a man not to be deceived in many of them unless he strive to reject them, such an appearance of truth and security does the devil give them? For he brings together so many appearances and probabilities, in order that they may be believed, and plants them so firmly in the sense and the imagination, that it seems to the person affected that what he says will certainly happen; and in such a way does he cause the soul to grasp and hold them, that, if it

---

[1] E.p. has 'be easily given,' and omits 'of the faith' and 'however fitting and true they may seem to it.'
[2] E.p. omits: 'and afterwards to deceive it.'
[3] E.p. omits: 'that have respect to the faith.'
[4] E.p. omits these three words.
[5] 2 St. Peter i, 19.
[6] So Alc. A, B: 'to close its eyes to the things that happen which concern the propositions or new revelations of the faith.' E.p.: 'not to open its eyes curiously to the new revelations which come to it and which concern the propositions of the faith.'
[7] E.p.: 'I believe it almost impossible.'

have not humility, it will hardly be persuaded to reject them and made to believe the contrary. Wherefore, the soul that is pure, cautious, simple and humble must resist revelations and other visions with as much effort and care as though they were very perilous temptations.[1] For there is no need to desire them; on the contrary, there is need not to desire them, if we are to reach the union of love. It is this that Solomon meant when he said: 'What need has a man to desire and seek things that are above his natural capacity?'[2] As though we were to say: He has[3] no necessity, in order to be perfect, to desire supernatural things[4] by supernatural means, which are above his capacity.[5]

7. And as the objections that can be made to this have already been answered, in the nineteenth and twentieth chapters of this book, I refer the reader to these, saying only that the soul must keep itself from all revelations[6] in order to journey, in purity and without error, in the night of faith, to union.

CHAPTER XXVIII

Which treats of interior locutions that may come to the spirit supernaturally. Says of what kinds they are.

THE discreet reader has ever need to bear in mind the intent and end which I have in this book, which is the direction of the soul, through all its apprehensions, natural and supernatural, without deception or hindrance, in purity of faith, to Divine union with God. If he does this, he will understand that, although with respect to apprehensions of the soul and the doctrine that I am expounding I give not such copious instruction neither do I particularize so much or make so many divisions as the understanding perchance requires, I am not being over-brief in this matter. For with respect to all this I believe that sufficient cautions, explanations and instructions are given for the soul to be enabled to behave prudently in every contingency, outward

---

[1] E.p. omits: 'with as . . . temptations.'
[2] Ecclesiastes vii, 1. E.p. omits 'natural.'
[3] A, B: 'Man has.'   [4] E.p.: 'supernatural and extraordinary things.'
[5] A, B add: 'for perfection.'
[6] So Alc. A, B read: 'I refer [the reader] to them in that which touches this matter of revelations; for it is sufficient to know that it behoves the soul to keep itself from them all. . . .' E.p.: '. . . referring [the reader] to them, I cease as touching this matter of revelations; for it is sufficient to know that it behoves the soul to keep itself prudently from them all. . . .'

or inward, so as to make progress. And this is the reason why I have so briefly dismissed the subject of prophetic apprehensions and the other subjects allied to it; for there is so much more to be said of each of them, according to the differences and the ways and manners[1] that are wont to be observed in each,[2] that I believe one could never know it all perfectly. I am content that, as I believe, the substance and the doctrine thereof have been given, and the soul has been warned of the caution which it behoves it to exercise in this respect, and also concerning all other things of the same kind that may come to pass within it.

2. I will now follow the same course with regard to the third kind of apprehension, which, we said, was that of supernatural locutions,[3] which are apt to come to the spirits of spiritual persons[4] without the intervention of any bodily sense. These, although they are of many kinds, may, I believe, all be reduced to three, namely: successive, formal and substantial. I describe as successive certain words and arguments which the spirit is wont to form and fashion when it is inwardly recollected. Formal words are certain clear and distinct words[5] which the spirit receives, not from itself, but from a third person, sometimes when it is recollected and sometimes when it is not. Substantial words are others which also come to the spirit formally, sometimes when it is recollected and sometimes when it is not; these cause in the substance of the soul[6] that substance and virtue which they signify. All these we shall here proceed to treat in their order.

CHAPTER XXIX

Which treats of the first kind of words that the recollected spirit sometimes forms within itself. Describes the cause of these and the profit and the harm which there may be in them.

THESE successive words always come when the spirit is recollected and absorbed very attentively in some meditation; and, in its reflections upon that same matter whereon it is thinking, it proceeds from one stage to another, forming[7] words and

---

[1] E.p. omits: 'and manners.'   [2] E.p. omits: 'in each.'
[3] E.p. has 'apprehensions' for 'locutions.'
[4] E.p. omits: 'the spirits of.' A, B have 'may' for 'are wont to.'
[5] [*Lit.*, 'certain distinct and formal words.']
[6] E.p.: 'in the inmost part of the soul.'
[7] A, B have 'founding' for 'forming.'

arguments which are very much to the point, with great facility and distinctness, and by means of its reasoning discovers[1] things which it knew not with respect to the subject of its reflections, so that it seems not to be doing this itself, but rather it seems that another person is supplying the reasoning within its mind or answering its questions or teaching it. And in truth it has good cause for thinking this, for the soul itself is reasoning with itself and answering itself as though it were two persons conversing together; and in some ways this is really so; for, although it is the spirit itself that works as an instrument,[2] the Holy Spirit oftentimes aids it to produce and form those true reasonings, words and conceptions. And thus it utters them to itself as though to a third person. For, as at that time the understanding is recollected and united with the truth of that whereon it is thinking, and the Divine Spirit is likewise united with it in that truth, as it is always united in all truth,[3] it follows that, when the understanding communicates in this way with the Divine Spirit by means of this truth, it begins to form within itself, successively, those other truths which are connected with that whereon it is thinking, the door being opened to it and illumination being given to it continually by the Holy Spirit Who teaches it. For this is one of the ways wherein the Holy Spirit teaches.

2. And when the understanding is illumined and taught in this way by this master, and comprehends these truths, it begins of its own accord[4] to form the words which relate to the truths that are communicated to it from elsewhere. So that we may say that the voice is the voice of Jacob and the hands are the hands of Esau.[5] And one that is in this condition will be unable to believe that this is so, but will think that the sayings and the words come from a third person. For such a one knows not the facility with which the understanding can form words inwardly, as though they came from a third person, and having reference to conceptions and truths which have in fact been communicated to it by a third person.

3. And although it is true that, in this communication and enlightenment of the understanding, no deception is produced in the soul itself, nevertheless, deception may, and does, frequently occur in the formal words and reasonings which the understanding bases upon it. For, inasmuch as this illumination which it receives is at times very subtle and spiritual, so that the understanding cannot attain to a clear apprehen-

---

[1] B has 'reflects upon' [*discurriendo*] for 'discovers' [*descubriendo*].
[2] E.p. omits: 'as an instrument.'   [3] E.p. omits: 'in that . . . all truth.'
[4] E.p. omits: 'of its own accord.'   [5] Genesis xxvii, 22.

sion of it, and it is the understanding that, as we say, forms the reasonings of its own accord, it follows that those which it forms are
frequently false, and on other occasions are only apparently true, or
are imperfect. For since at the outset the soul began to seize the truth,
and then brought into play the skilfulness or the clumsiness of its own
weak understanding, its perception of the truth may easily be modified
by the instability of its own faculties of comprehension, and act all the
time exactly as though a third person were speaking.

4. I knew a person who had these successive locutions: among
them were some very true and substantial ones concerning the most
holy Sacrament of the Eucharist, but others were sheer heresy.[1] And I
am appalled at what happens in these days—namely, when some soul
with the very smallest experience[2] of meditation, if it be conscious of
certain locutions of this kind in some state of recollection, at once
christens them all as coming from God, and assumes that this is the
case, saying: 'God said to me . . .'; 'God answered me . . .'; whereas
it is not so at all, but, as we have said, it is for the most part they who
are saying these things to themselves.

5. And, over and above this, the desire which people have for
locutions, and the pleasure which comes to their spirits from them, lead
them to make answer to themselves and then to think that it is God
Who is answering them and speaking to them. They therefore commit
great blunders unless they impose a strict restraint upon themselves,
and unless their director obliges them to abstain from these kinds of
reflection. For they are apt to gain from them mere nonsensical talk
and impurity of soul rather than humility and mortification of spirit,
if they think, 'This was indeed a great thing' and 'God was speaking'; whereas it will have been little more than nothing, or nothing at
all, or less than nothing. For, if humility and charity be not engendered
by such experiences, and mortification and holy simplicity and
silence, etc., what can be the value of them? I say, then, that these
things may hinder the soul greatly in its progress to Divine union
because, if it pay heed to them, it is led far astray from the abyss
of faith, where the understanding must remain in darkness, and
must journey in darkness, by love and in faith, and not by much
reasoning.

6. And if you ask me why the understanding must be deprived of

---

[1] E.p.: 'but others contained much error.'
[2] [*Lit.*, 'with four maravedís' worth of experience.' The *maravedí* was a small coin,
worth 1/375 of a gold ducat, the unit of coinage at this time in Castile.]

these truths, since through them it is illumined by the Spirit of God, and thus they[1] cannot be evil, I reply that the Holy Spirit illumines the understanding which is recollected, and illumines it according to the manner of its recollection,[2] and that the understanding cannot find any other and greater recollection than in faith; and thus the Holy Spirit will illumine it in naught more than in faith. For the purer and the more refined in faith[3] is the soul, the more it has of the infused charity of God; and the more charity it has, the more is it illumined and the more gifts of the Holy Spirit are communicated to it, for charity is the cause and the means whereby they are communicated to it.[4] And although it is true that, in this illumination of truths, the Holy Spirit communicates a certain light to the soul, this is nevertheless as different in quality from that which is in faith, wherein is no clear understanding, as is the most precious gold from the basest metal; and, with regard to its quantity,[5] the one is as much greater than the other as the sea is greater than a drop of water. For in the one manner there is communicated to the soul wisdom concerning one or two or three truths, etc., but in the other there is communicated to it all the wisdom of God in general, which is the Son of God, Who communicates Himself to the soul in faith.[6]

7. And if you tell me that this is all good, and that the one impedes not the other, I reply that it impedes it greatly if the soul sets store by it; for to do this is to occupy itself with things which are clear and of little importance, yet which are sufficient to hinder the communication of the abyss of faith, wherein God supernaturally and secretly instructs the soul, and exalts it in virtues and gifts in a way that it knows not. And the profit which these successive communications will bring us cannot come by our deliberately applying the understanding to them, for if we do this they will rather lead us astray, even as Wisdom says to the soul in the *Songs*: 'Turn away thine eyes from me, for they make

----

[1] [*Lit.*, 'and thus it.']

[2] This profound and important principle, which has often been developed in mystical theology, is well expounded by P. José de Jesús María in a treatise called *Reply to a question* [*Respuesta a una duda*]. Here, among other things, he says: 'As St. Thomas proves (*De Veritate*, q. 12, a. 6), Divine illumination, like every other spiritual form, is communicated to the soul after the manner of the receiver of it, whether according to sense or according to spirit, to the particular or to the universal. And thus, he that receives it must prepare himself for it to be communicated to him further, whether in small measure (as we say) or according to sense, or in large measure or intellectually.'

[3] E.p.: 'in perfection of living faith.'

[4] E.p. omits 'of the Holy Spirit' and 'for charity . . . communicated to it.'

[5] E.p.: 'and, as to the abundance of its light.'

[6] E.p.: 'in general, by a simple and universal knowledge which is given to the soul in faith.'

me to fly away.'[1] That is to say: They make me to fly far away from
thee and to set myself higher. We must therefore not apply the understanding[2] to that which is being supernaturally communicated to it, but
simply and sincerely apply the will to God with love,[3] for it is through
love that these good things are communicated and through love they
will be communicated in greater abundance than before. For if the
ability of the natural[4] understanding or of other faculties be brought
actively to bear upon these things which are communicated supernaturally and passively, its imperfect nature will not reach them, and
thus they will perforce be modified according to the capacity of the
understanding, and consequently will perforce be changed; and thus
the understanding will necessarily go astray[5] and begin to form reasonings within itself, and there will no longer be anything supernatural
or any semblance thereof, but all will be merely natural and most
erroneous and unworthy.

8. But there are certain types of understanding so quick and subtle
that, when they become recollected during some meditation, they
invent conceptions, and begin naturally, and with great facility, to form
these conceptions into the most lifelike words and arguments, which
they think, without any doubt, come from God. Yet all the time they
come only from the understanding, which, with its natural illumination, being to some extent freed from the operation of the senses, is
able to effect all this, and more, without any supernatural aid. This
happens very commonly, and many persons are greatly deceived by it,
thinking that they have attained to a high degree of prayer and are
receiving communications from God, wherefore they either write
this down or cause[6] it to be written. And it turns out[7] to be nothing,
and to have the substance of no virtue, and it serves only to encourage
them in vanity.

9. Let these persons learn to be intent upon naught, save only upon
grounding the will in humble love, working diligently, suffering and
thus imitating the Son of God in His life and mortifications,[8] for it is
by this road that a man will come to all spiritual good, rather than by
much inward reasoning.

10. In this type of locution—namely, in successive interior words—

---

[1] [Canticles vi, 4.]   [2] E.p.: 'the strength of the understanding.'
[3] A, B: 'apply the will to the love of God.'
[4] E.p. omits 'natural.'
[5] E.p.: 'will necessarily be in peril of straying.'
[6] E.p.: '. . . from God, and they write down what happens to them or cause . . .'
[7] E.p.: 'And it all turns out . . .'
[8] E.p.: 'in His life, and mortifying themselves in all things.'

the devil frequently intervenes, especially in the case of such as have some inclination or affection for them. At times when such persons begin to be recollected, the devil is accustomed to offer them ample material for distractions, forming conceptions or words by suggestion in their understanding, and then corrupting[1] and deceiving it most subtly with things that have every appearance of being true. And this is one of the manners wherein he communicates[2] with those who have made some implicit or expressed compact with him; as with certain heretics, especially with certain heresiarchs, whose understanding he fills with most subtle, false and erroneous conceptions and arguments.

11. From what has been said, it is evident that these successive locutions may proceed in the understanding from three causes, namely: from the Divine Spirit, Who moves and illumines the understanding; from the natural illumination of the same understanding; and from the devil, who may speak to the soul by suggestion. To describe[3] now the signs and indications by which a man may know when they proceed from one cause and when from another would be somewhat difficult, as also to give examples and indications.[4] It is quite possible, however, to give some general signs, which are these. When in its words and conceptions the soul finds itself loving God, and at the same time is conscious not only of love but also of humility and reverence, it is a sign that the Holy Spirit is working within it, for, whensoever He grants favours, He grants them with this accompaniment.[5] When the locutions proceed solely from the vivacity and brilliance of the understanding, it is the understanding that accomplishes everything, without the operation of the virtues (although the will, in the knowledge and illumination of those truths, may love naturally); and, when the meditation is over, the will remains dry, albeit inclined neither to vanity nor to evil, unless the devil should tempt it afresh about this matter. This, however, is not the case when the locutions have been prompted by a good spirit; for then, as a rule, the will is afterwards affectioned to God and inclined to well-doing. At certain times, nevertheless, it will happen that, although the communication has been the work of a good spirit, the will remains in aridity, since God ordains it so for certain causes which are of assistance to the soul. At other times the soul will not be very conscious of the operations or motions of those virtues, yet that

---

1 [*Lit.*, 'and then throwing it down.']
2 E.p.: ' It is in this way that he is wont to communicate . . .'
3 E.p.: 'But to describe.'
4 E.p.: 'examples and signs.'
5 [*Lit.*, 'He grants them wrapped up in this.']

which it has experienced will be good. Wherefore I say that the difference between these locutions is sometimes difficult to recognize, by
reason of the varied effects which they produce; but these which have
now been described are the most common, although sometimes they
occur in greater abundance and sometimes in less. But those that come
from the devil are sometimes difficult to understand and recognize,
for, although it is true that as a rule they leave the will in aridity with
respect to love of God, and the mind inclined to vanity, self-esteem or
complacency, nevertheless they sometimes inspire the soul with a false
humility and a fervent affection of the will rooted in self-love, so that at
times a person must be extremely spiritually-minded to recognize it.
And this the devil does in order the better to protect himself; for he
knows very well how sometimes[1] to produce tears by the feelings which
he inspires in a soul, in order that he may continue to implant in it the
affections that he desires. But he always strives to move its will so that
it may esteem those interior communications, attach great importance
to them, and, as a result, give itself up to them and be occupied in that
which is not virtue, but is rather the occasion of losing such virtue as
the soul may have.

12. Let us remember, then, this necessary caution, both as to the
one type of locution and as to the other, so that we may not be deceived
or hindered by them. Let us treasure none of them, but think only of
learning to direct our will determinedly to God, fulfilling His law and
His holy counsels perfectly, which is the wisdom of the Saints, and
contenting ourselves with knowing the mysteries and truths with the
simplicity and truth wherewith the Church sets them before us. For
this is sufficient to enkindle the will greatly, so that we need not pry
into other deep and curious[2] things wherein it is a wonder if there is no
peril. For with respect to this Saint Paul says: It is not fitting to know
more than it behoves us[3] to know.[4] And let this suffice with respect to
this matter of successive words.

[1] E.p. omits 'sometimes.'   [2] A, B omit: 'and curious.'
[3] [The verbs used in the Spanish for 'is fitting' and 'behoves' are the same.]
[4] Romans xii, 3.

CHAPTER XXX

Which treats of the interior words that come to the spirit formally by super-natural means. Warns the reader of the harm which they may do and of the caution that is necessary in order that the soul may not be deceived by them.

THE interior words belonging to the second type are formal words, which at certain times come to the spirit by super-natural means, without the intervention of any of the senses, sometimes when the spirit is recollected and at other times when it is not. I call them formal because they are communicated to the spirit formally by a third person,[1] the spirit itself playing no part in this. And they are therefore very different from those which we have just described; because not only is there this difference, that they come without any such intervention of the spirit itself as takes place in the other case; but also, as I say, they sometimes come when the spirit is not recollected and even when it is far from thinking of the subject of what is being said to it. This is not so in the first type of locution—namely, that of successive words—which always has some relation to the subject which the soul is considering.

2. These words are sometimes very clearly formed and sometimes less so; for they are frequently like conceptions in which something is said to the spirit, whether in the form of a reply to it or in that of another manner of address. Sometimes there is only one word; sometimes there are two or more; sometimes the words succeed one another like those already described, for they are apt to be continuous, either instructing the soul or discussing something with it; and all this comes to pass without any part being played therein by the spirit, for it is just as though one person were speaking with another. In this way, we read, it came to pass with Daniel, who says that the angel spoke within him.[2] This was a formal and successive discourse within his spirit, which instructed him, even as the angel declared at the time, saying that he had come to instruct him.

3. When these words are no more than formal, the effect which they produce upon the soul is not great. For ordinarily they serve only to instruct or illumine with respect to one thing; and, in order to produce this effect, it is not necessary that they should produce any

---

[1] A, B: 'because it seems to the spirit that a third person communicates them formally.'
[2] Daniel ix, 22.

other effect more efficacious than the purpose to which they are leading. And when they are of God they invariably work this in the soul;
for they make it ready and quick to do that which it is commanded or
instructed to do; yet at times they take not from it the repugnance or
the difficulty which it feels, but are rather wont to increase these,
according as God ordains for the better instruction, increased humility
and greater good of the soul. And this repugnance most commonly
occurs when the soul is commanded to do things of a high order, or
things of a kind that may exalt it; when things are commanded it that
conduce to its greater lowliness and humility, it responds with more
readiness and ease. And thus we read in Exodus that, when God commanded Moses to go to Pharao and deliver the people, he showed such
great repugnance that He had to command him three times to do it
and to perform signs for him; and all this was of no avail until God
gave him Aaron for a companion to take part of the honour.[1]

4. When, on the other hand, the words and communications are of
the devil, it comes to pass that the soul responds with more ease and
readiness to things that are of greater weight,[2] and for lowlier things
it conceives repugnance. The fact is that God so greatly abhors seeing
souls attracted by high position that, even when He commands and
obliges them to accept such positions, He desires them not to be ready
and anxious to command. It is this readiness which God commonly
inspires in the soul, through these formal words, that constitutes one
great difference between them and those other successive words: the
latter move not the spirit so much, neither do they inspire it with such
readiness, since they are less formal, and since the understanding has
more to do with them. Nevertheless successive words may sometimes
produce a greater effect by reason of the close communication that
there is at times between the Divine Spirit and the human. It is in the
manner of their coming that there is a great difference between the
two kinds of locution. With respect to formal words the soul can have
no doubt as to whether or no it is pronouncing them itself, for it sees
quite clearly that it is not, especially when it has not been thinking of
the subject of that which has been said to it; and even when it has been
so thinking it feels very clearly and distinctly that the words come from
elsewhere.

5. The soul must no more attach importance to all these formal
words than to the other, or successive, words; for, apart from the fact

---

[1] Exodus iii, iv.
[2] [*Lit.*, 'greater worth.'] A, B: 'greater truth and worth.'

that to do so would occupy the spirit with that which is not a legitimate and proximate means to union with God—namely, faith—it might also very easily cause it to be deceived by the devil. For sometimes it is hardly possible to know what words are spoken by a good spirit, and what by an evil spirit. By their effects they can hardly be distinguished at all, since neither kind produces effects of much importance: sometimes, indeed, with imperfect souls, words which come from the devil have more efficacy[1] than have these others, which come from a good spirit, with souls that are spiritual. The soul, then, must take no account of what these words may express, nor attach any importance to them, whether the spirit from which they come be good or evil. But the words must be repeated to an experienced confessor, or to a discreet and learned person, that he may give instruction and see what it is well to do, and impart his advice; and the soul must behave, with regard to them, in a resigned and negative way. And, if such an expert person cannot be found, it is better to attach no importance to these words[2] and to repeat them to nobody; for it is easy to find persons who will ruin the soul rather than edify it. Souls must not be given into the charge of any kind of director, since in so grave a matter it is of the greatest importance whether one goes astray or acts rightly.

6. And let it be carefully noted that a soul should never act according to its own opinion or accept anything of what these locutions express, without much reflection and without taking advice of another.[3] For strange and subtle deceptions may arise in this matter; so much so that I myself believe that the soul that does not set itself against accepting such things cannot fail to be deceived by many of them.[4]

7. And since we have treated of these deceptions and perils, and of the caution to be observed with regard to them, in Chapters seventeen, eighteen, nineteen and twenty of this book, I refer the reader to these and say no more on this matter here; I only repeat that my chief instruction is that the soul should attach no importance to these things in any way.[5]

---

[1] A, e.p.: 'more sensible efficacy.'

[2] E.p.: 'it is better to take the substantial and secure part of what these words bring, and otherwise to attach no importance to them.'

[3] E.p. omits: 'of another.'

[4] A, B, e.p. add: 'either to a small, or to a great extent.'

[5] So Alc. A, B: '... my chief instruction, and the surest, to this end, is that the soul should attach no importance whatever to these things, however highly it may think of them, but should be guided in all things by reason and by what the Church has already taught us and teaches us daily.'

CHAPTER XXXI

Which treats of the substantial words that come interiorly to the spirit.
Describes the difference between them and formal words, and the profit
which they bring and the resignation and respect which the soul must
observe with regard to them.[1]

THE third kind of interior words, we said, is called substantial.
These substantial words, although they are likewise formal,
since they are impressed upon the soul in a definitely formal way,
differ, nevertheless, in that substantial words produce vivid and substantial effects upon the soul, whereas words which are merely formal
do not. So that, although it is true that every substantial word is formal,
every formal word is not therefore substantial, but only, as we said
above, such a word as impresses substantially[2] on the soul that which it
signifies. It is as if Our Lord were to say formally to the soul: 'Be
thou good'; it would then substantially be good. Or as if He were to
say to it: 'Love thou Me'; it would then have and feel within itself the
substance of love for God.[3] Or as if it feared greatly and He said to it:
'Fear thou not'; it would at once feel within itself great fortitude and
tranquillity. For the saying of God, and His word, as the Wise Man
says, is full of power;[4] and thus that which He says to the soul He
produces substantially within it. For it is this that David meant when
he said: 'See, He will give to His voice a voice of virtue.'[5] And even so
with Abraham, when He said to him: 'Walk in My presence and be
perfect':[6] he was then perfect and walked ever in the fear of God. And
this is the power of His word in the Gospel, wherewith He healed the
sick, raised the dead, etc., by no more than a word. And after this

---

[1] This chapter is notable for the hardly surpassable clarity and precision with which
the Saint defines substantial locutions. Some critics, however, have found fault with him
for saying that the soul should not fear these locutions, but accept them humbly and
passively, since they depend wholly on God. The reply is that, when God favours the
soul with these locutions, its own restless effort can only impede His work in it, as has
already been said. The soul is truly co-operating with God by preparing itself with
resignation and humble affection to receive His favours: it should not, as some critics
have asserted, remain completely inactive. As to the fear of being deceived by these
locutions, both St. Thomas and all the principal commentators are in conformity with
the Saint's teaching. St. Teresa, too, took the same attitude as St. John of the Cross. Cf.
her *Life*, Chap. xxv, and *Interior Castle*, VI, iii.

[2] E.p.: 'impresses truly.'

[3] E.p. modifies thus: 'Or as if He were to say formally to the soul: "Love thou Me": it
would then have and feel within itself impulses of love for God.' The edition of 1630 has:
'... the substance of love—that is, true love of God,' reading otherwise as in the text.

[4] Ecclesiastes viii, 4.   [5] Psalm lxvii, 34 [A.V., lxviii, 33].   [6] Genesis xvii, 1.

manner He gives certain souls locutions which are substantial; and they are of such moment and price that they are life and virtue and incomparable good to the soul; for one of these words works[1] greater good within the soul than all that the soul itself has done throughout its life.

2. With respect to these words, the soul should do nothing. It should neither desire them nor refrain from desiring them; it should neither reject them nor fear them. It should do nothing[2] in the way of executing what these words express, for these substantial words are never pronounced by God in order that the soul may translate them into action, but that He may so translate them within the soul; herein they differ from formal and successive words. And I say that the soul must neither desire nor refrain from desiring, since its desire is not necessary for God to translate these words into effect, nor is it sufficient for the soul to refrain from desiring in order for the said effect not to be produced. Let the soul rather be resigned and humble with respect to them. It must not reject them,[3] since the effect of these words remains substantially within it and is full of the good which comes from God. As the soul receives this good passively, its action is at no time of any importance. Nor should it fear any deception; for neither the understanding nor the devil can intervene herein, nor can they succeed[4] in passively producing this substantial effect in the soul, in such a way that the effect and habit of the locution may be impressed upon it, unless the soul should have given itself to the devil by a voluntary compact, and he should have dwelt in it as its master, and impressed upon it these effects, not of good, but of evil.[5] Inasmuch as that soul would be already voluntarily united to him in perversity, the devil might easily impress upon it the effects of his sayings and words with evil intent.[6] For we see by experience that in many things and even upon good souls he works great violence, by means of suggestion, making his suggestions very efficacious; and if they were evil he might

---

[1] E.p. adds: 'perhaps.'

[2] Alc. omits: 'It should neither desire . . . should do nothing.'

[3] E.p. abbreviates this paragraph thus: 'With respect to these words, the soul should itself do nothing and desire nothing at the time, but conduct itself with resignation and humility, giving its free consent to God; neither should it reject anything, nor fear anything. It should not labour in executing what these words express, for by these substantial words God works in the soul; wherein they differ from formal and successive words. It must not reject them,' etc.

[4] E.p. : 'nor can this evil one succeed . . .'

[5] E.p. has (for 'unless the soul . . . of evil'): 'although in souls that were given to the devil by a voluntary compact, in whom he dwelt as their master, he could by suggestion impel them to [produce] results of great malignity.'

[6] So A, B. Alc. omits this sentence. E.p. has: 'For, as such souls would already be voluntarily united to him in perversity, the devil could easily impel them thereto.'

work in them the consummation of these suggestions.[1] But he cannot leave upon a soul effects similar to those of locutions which are good; for there is no comparison between the locutions of the devil and those of God. The former are all as though they were not, in comparison with the latter, neither do they produce any effect at all compared with the effect of these. For this cause God says through Jeremias: 'What has the chaff to do with the wheat? Are not My words perchance as fire, and as a hammer that breaketh the rock in pieces?'[2] And thus these substantial words are greatly conducive to the union of the soul with God; and the more interior they are, the more substantial are they, and the greater is the profit that they bring. Happy is the soul to whom God addresses these words. Speak, Lord, for Thy servant heareth.[3]

CHAPTER XXXII

Which treats of the apprehensions received by the understanding from interior feelings which come supernaturally to the soul. Describes their cause, and the manner wherein the soul must conduct itself so that they may not obstruct its road to union with God.

IT is now time to treat of the fourth and last kind of intellectual apprehension which we said might come to the understanding through the spiritual feelings which are frequently produced supernaturally in the souls of spiritual persons and which we count amongst the distinct apprehensions of the understanding.

2. These distinct spiritual feelings may be of two kinds. The first kind is in the affection of the will. The second, in the substance of the soul.[4] Each of these may be of many kinds. Those of the will, when they are of God, are most sublime; but those that are of the substance of the soul are very high and of great good and profit.[5] As to these, neither the soul nor he that treats with it can know or understand the cause whence they proceed, or what are the acts whereby God may grant it these favours; for they depend not upon any works performed by the soul, nor upon its meditations, although both these things are a good

---

[1] E.p.: 'he might impel them more violently still.'
[2] Jeremias xxiii, 28–9. A, B, e.p. read 'stones' for 'rocks.'
[3] 1 Kings [A.V., 1 Samuel] iii, 10.
[4] E.p.: 'The second, feelings that, though they are also in the will, are most intense, sublime, profound and secret, and therefore seem not to touch the will, but to be wrought in the substance of the soul.'
[5] E.p.: 'but the second are very high and of great good and profit.'

preparation for them: God grants these favours to whom He wills and for what reason He wills.[1] For it may come to pass that a person will have performed many good works, yet that He will not give him these touches of His favour; and another will have done far fewer good works, yet He will give him them to a most sublime degree and in great abundance. And thus it is not needful that the soul should be actually employed and occupied in spiritual things (although it is much better that it should be so employed if it is to have these favours) for God to give it these touches in which the soul experiences the said feelings; for in the majority of cases the soul is completely heedless of them. Of these touches, some are distinct and pass quickly away; others are less distinct and last longer.

3. These feelings, inasmuch as they are feelings only,[2] belong not to the understanding but to the will; and thus I refrain, of set purpose, from treating of them here, nor shall I do so until we treat of the night and purgation of the will in its affections: this will be in the third book, which follows this.[3] But since frequently, and even in the majority of cases, apprehensions and knowledge and intelligence overflow from them into the understanding, it would be well to make mention of them here, for that reason only. It must be known, then, that from these feelings, both from those of the will and from those which are in the substance of the soul, whether[4] they are caused suddenly by the touches of God, or are durable and successive, an apprehension of knowledge or intelligence frequently overflows, as I say, into the understanding; and this is normally a most sublime perception of God, most delectable to the understanding, to which no name can be given, any more than to the feeling whence it overflows. And these manifestations of knowledge are sometimes of one kind and sometimes of another; sometimes they are clearer and more sublime, according to the nature of the touches which come from God and which produce the feelings whence they proceed, and according also to their individual characteristics.[5]

4. It is unnecessary here to spend a great store of words[6] in caution-

---

[1] A, B: 'and how He wills.' Note that the Saint does not deprecate good works, as did the Illuminists [alumbrados], who bade the perfect soul set them aside for contemplation, even though they were works of obligation. On the contrary, he asserts that good works have a definite, though a preparatory, part to play in the life of a contemplative.

[2] E.p.: '. . . they are feelings only of the kind whereof we here speak . . .'

[3] Alc. alone has: 'which follows this.' The Saint does not, in fact, return to this matter, either in the third book or elsewhere.

[4] E.p.: 'that from all these feelings, whether . . .'

[5] E.p.: 'to their capacity.'   [6] E.p.: 'to spend many words.'

ing and directing the understanding, through these manifestations of knowledge, in faith, to union with God. For albeit the feelings which we have described are produced passively in the soul, without any effective assistance to that end on its own part, even so likewise is the knowledge of them received passively in the understanding, in a way called by the philosophers 'passible,' wherein the understanding plays no part. Wherefore, in order not to go astray on their account nor to impede the profit which comes from them, the understanding must do nothing in connection with these feelings, but must conduct itself passively,[1] and not interfere by applying to them its natural capacity. For, as we have said is the case with successive locutions, the understanding, with its activity, would very easily disturb and ruin the effect of these delicate manifestations of knowledge, which are a delectable supernatural intelligence that human nature cannot attain or apprehend by its own efforts, but only by remaining in a state of receptivity.[2] And thus the soul must not strive to attain them or desire to receive them,[3] lest the understanding should form other manifestations of its own, or the devil should make his entry with still more that are different from them and false. This he may very well do by means[4] of the feelings aforementioned, or of those which he can himself infuse into the soul that devotes itself to these kinds of knowledge.[5] Let the soul be resigned, humble and passive herein, for, since it receives this knowledge passively from God, He will communicate it whensoever He is pleased, if He sees the soul to be humble and detached. And in this way the soul will do nothing to counteract the help which these kinds of knowledge give it in its progress toward Divine union, which help is great; for these touches are all touches of union, which is wrought passively in the soul.[6]

[1] E.p. adds here: 'inclining the will to free consent and gratitude.'

[2] [Lit., 'or apprehend by doing, but by receiving.']

[3] E.p. omits: 'or desire to receive them.'

[4] The edition of 1630 has: '. . . do in the soul, when it gives itself to these kinds of knowledge, by means . . .'

[5] E.p. substitutes for 'or of those . . . kinds of knowledge' the words: 'making use of the bodily senses.'

[6] Some editions here add a long paragraph, which, however, is the work of P. Jerónimo de San José, who was responsible for the edition of 1630. It appears neither in the MSS. nor in e.p. It runs as follows:

All the instruction which has been given in this book on total abstraction and passive contemplation, wherein, oblivious to all created things and detached from images and figures, we allow ourselves to be guided by God, dwelling with simple regard upon supreme truth, is applicable not only to that act of most perfect contemplation, the lofty and wholly supernatural repose of which is still prevented by the daughters of Jerusalem (namely, good reflections and meditations), if at that time the soul desires them, but also to the whole of the time during which Our Lord

5. What has been said concerning this suffices, for no matter what may happen to the soul with respect to the understanding, cautions and instructions have been given it in the sections already mentioned. And although a case may appear to be different and to be in no way included herein, there is none that cannot be referred to one of these, and thus may be deduced the instruction necessary for it.[1]

communicates the simple, general and loving attentiveness aforementioned, or during which the soul, aided by grace, places itself in that state. For at that time the soul must always strive to keep its understanding in repose, without the interference of other forms, figures or particular kinds of knowledge, save very fleetingly and quite superficially; and it must have a loving sweetness which will enkindle it ever more. But, except at this time, in all its exercises, acts and works, the soul must make use of good meditations and remembrances, so as to experience the greater devotion and profit, most of all with respect to the life, passion and death of Our Lord Jesus Christ, so that its actions, practices and life may be made like to His.

[1] Thus Alc. A, B, e.p. read: 'This suffices to conclude (our treatment of) the supernatural apprehensions of the understanding, so far as concerns the guidance of the understanding, by their means, in faith, to Divine union. And I think that what has been said with regard to this suffices, for, no matter what happens to the soul with respect to the understanding, instructions and cautions concerning it will be found in the sections already mentioned. And, if something should happen, apparently so different that none of them deals with it (although I think there will be nothing relating to the understanding which cannot be referred to one of the four kinds of distinct knowledge), instructions and cautions concerning it can be deduced from what has been said of others similar to it. And with this we will pass to the third book, where, with the Divine favour, we shall treat of the interior spiritual purgation of the will with regard to its interior affections which we here call active night.'

C, D have: 'From what has been said may be deduced instructions and cautions for guidance in whatever may happen to the soul with regard to the understanding, even if it seem so different that it includes none of the four distinct kinds, although I think there will be nothing relating to the understanding which cannot be referred to one of them. And so we will pass to the third book.'

The edition of 1630 follows A, B and e.p., and adds further: 'I therefore beg the discreet reader to read these things in a benevolent and simple spirit; for, when this spirit is not present, however sublime and perfect be the instruction, it will not yield the profit that it contains, nor will it earn the esteem that it merits. How much truer is this in the present case, since my style is in so many ways deficient!'

BOOK THE THIRD

Which treats of the purgation of the active night of the memory and will.
Gives instruction how the soul is to behave with respect to the appre-
hensions of these two faculties, that it may come to union with God,
according to the two faculties aforementioned, in perfect hope and
charity.[1]

CHAPTER I

THE first faculty of the soul, which is the understanding, has
now been instructed, through all its apprehensions, in the first
theological virtue, which is faith, to the end that, according to
this faculty, the soul may be united with God by means of the purity
of faith. It now remains to do likewise with respect to the other two
faculties of the soul, which are memory and will, and to purify them
likewise with respect to their apprehensions, to the end that, according
to these two faculties also, the soul may come to union with God in
perfect hope and charity. This will briefly be effected in this third
book. We have now concluded our treatment of the understanding,
which is the receptacle of all other objects according to its mode of
operation;[2] and in treating of this we have gone a great part of the
whole way. It is therefore unnecessary for us to write at equal length
with respect to these faculties;[3] for it is not possible that, if the spiritual
man instructs his understanding in faith according to the doctrine
which has been given him, he should not, in so doing, instruct the
other two faculties in the other two virtues likewise; for the operations
of each faculty depend upon the others.

2. But since, in order to follow our manner of procedure, and in
order, too, that we may be the better understood, we must necessarily
speak of the proper and determinate matter, we shall here be obliged to

---

[1] So Alc., A, B. This first chapter, in e.p., is called the 'Argument' of the book, and
the numbering of the chapters differs correspondingly from that of the MSS. Cf. the
Exposition of Book II (p. 63, above).

[2] E.p.: '. . . of all the other objects that pass to these faculties.'

[3] E.p. omits the rest of this paragraph.

set down the apprehensions proper to each faculty,[1] and first, those of the memory, making here such distinction between them as suffices for our purpose. This we shall be able to deduce from the distinction between their objects, which are three: natural,[2] imaginary and spiritual; according to which there are likewise three kinds of knowledge which come from the memory, namely: natural and supernatural,[3] imaginary and spiritual.

3. All these, by the Divine favour, we shall treat here in due course, beginning with natural knowledge, which pertains to the most exterior objects. And we shall then treat of the affections of the will, wherewith we shall conclude this third book of the active spiritual night.

CHAPTER II

Which treats of the natural apprehensions of the memory and describes how the soul must be voided of them in order to be able to attain to union with God according to this faculty.

IT is necessary that, in each of these books, the reader should bear in mind the purpose of which we are speaking. For otherwise there may arise within him many such questions with respect to what he is reading as might by this time be occurring to him with respect to what we have said of the understanding, and shall say now of the memory, and afterwards shall say of the will. For, seeing how we annihilate the faculties with respect to their operations, it may perhaps seem to him that we are destroying the road of spiritual practice rather than constructing it.

2. This would be true if we were seeking here only to instruct beginners, who are best prepared through these apprehensible and discursive apprehensions. But, since we are here giving instruction to those who would progress farther in contemplation, even to union with God, to which end all these means and exercises of sense concerning the faculties must recede into the background, and be put to silence, to the end that God may of His own accord work Divine

---

[1] E.p.: 'we shall here have to treat of the acts of each faculty.'

[2] 'Natural and supernatural,' says the edition of 1630, basing its reading upon the similar one two lines below.

[3] It will be seen from what follows that in practice the Saint preserves the strictly tripartite division given in the text above, supernatural knowledge being found in each of the sections.

union in the soul, it is necessary to proceed by this method of disencumbering and emptying the soul, and causing it to reject the natural jurisdiction and operations of the faculties, so that they may become capable of infusion and illumination from supernatural sources; for their capacity cannot attain to so lofty an experience, but will rather hinder it, if it be not disregarded.

3. And thus, if it be true, as it is, that the soul must proceed in its growing knowledge of God by learning that which He is not rather than that which He is, in order to come to Him, it must proceed by renouncing and rejecting, to the very uttermost, everything in its apprehensions that it is possible to renounce, whether this be natural or supernatural. We shall proceed with this end in view with regard to the memory, drawing it out from its natural state and limitations, and causing it to rise above itself—that is, above all distinct knowledge and apprehensible possession—to the supreme hope of God, Who is incomprehensible.

4. Beginning, then, with natural knowledge, I say that natural knowledge in the memory consists of all the kinds of knowledge that the memory can form concerning the objects of the five bodily senses— namely: hearing, sight, smell, taste and touch—and all kinds of knowledge of this type which it is possible to form and fashion. Of all these forms and kinds of knowledge the soul must strip and void itself, and it must strive to lose the imaginary apprehension of them, so that there may be left in it no kind of impression of knowledge, nor trace of aught soever, but rather the soul must remain barren and bare,[1] as if these forms had never passed through it, and in total oblivion and suspension. And this cannot happen unless the memory be annihilated as to all its forms, if it is to be united with God. For it cannot happen save by total separation from all forms which are not God; for God comes beneath no definite form or kind of knowledge whatsoever, as we have said in treating of the night of the understanding. And since, as Christ says,[2] no man can serve two masters,[3] the memory cannot be united[4] both with God and with forms and distinct kinds of knowledge; and, as God has no form or image that can be comprehended by the memory, it follows that, when the memory is united with God (as is seen, too, every day by experience), it remains without form and

---

[1] E.p.: '. . . impression of knowledge, but [the soul] must remain as completely detached as it can.'
[2] E.p.: 'as our Redeemer teaches.'
[3] [St. Matthew vi, 24.]
[4] E.p.: 'united in perfection.'

without figure, its imagination being lost and itself being absorbed in a supreme good, and in a great oblivion, remembering nothing. For that Divine union voids its fancy and sweeps it[1] clean of all forms and kinds of knowledge and raises it to the supernatural.

5. Now there sometimes comes to pass here a notable thing; for occasionally, when God brings about these touches of union in the memory, the brain (where memory has its seat) is so perceptibly upset that it seems as if it becomes quite inert, and its judgment and sense are lost. This is sometimes more perceptible and sometimes less so, according to the strength of this touch, and then, by reason of this union, the memory is voided and purged, as I say, of all kinds of knowledge. It remains in oblivion—at times in complete oblivion[2]—so that it has to put forth a great effort and to labour greatly in order to remember anything.

6. And sometimes this oblivion of the memory and suspension of the imagination reach such a point, because of the union of the memory with God, that a long time passes without the soul's perceiving it, or knowing what has taken place during that period. And, as the imaginative faculty is then in suspension, it feels naught that is done to it, not even things that cause pain; for without imagination there is no feeling, not even coming through thought, since this exists not.[3] And, to the end that God may bring about these touches of union, the soul must needs withdraw its memory from all apprehensible kinds of knowledge. And it is to be noted that these suspensions come not to pass in those that are already perfect, since they have attained to perfect union, and these suspensions belong to the beginnings of union.

7. Someone will remark that all this seems very well, but that it leads to the destruction of the natural use and course of the faculties, and reduces man to the state of a beast—a state of oblivion and even worse—since he becomes incapable of reasoning or of remembering his natural functions and necessities. It will be argued that God destroys not nature, but rather perfects it; and that from this teaching there necessarily follows its destruction, when that which pertains to morality and reason is not practised and is forgotten, neither is that which is natural practised; for (it will be said) none of these things

---

[1] E.p.: 'and seems to sweep it.'
[2] So Alc., P. A: 'It remains in oblivion, and, at times, [is] oblivious to itself.' B: 'It remains transported, and, at times, [is] oblivious to itself.' E.p. omits the whole of the paragraph down to this point, continuing the preceding paragraph, thus: '. . . raises it to the supernatural, leaving it in such oblivion that it has to put forth . . .'
[3] Alc. ends the sentence at 'feeling.'

can be remembered, as the soul is deprived of[1] forms and kinds of knowledge which are the means of remembrance.

8. To this I reply that, the more nearly the memory attains to union with God, the more do distinct kinds of knowledge become perfected within it, until it loses them entirely—namely, when it attains to the state of union in perfection. And thus, at the beginning, when this is first taking place, the soul cannot but fall into great oblivion with respect to all things, since forms and kinds of knowledge are being erased from it; and therefore it is very negligent concerning its outward behaviour and usage—forgetting to eat or drink, and being uncertain if it has done this or no, if it has seen this or no, if it has said this or no—because of the absorption of the memory in God.[2] But when once it attains to the habit of union, which is a supreme blessing, it no longer has these periods of oblivion, after this manner, in that which pertains to natural and moral reason; actions which are seemly and necessary, indeed, it performs with a much greater degree of perfection,[3] although it performs them no longer by means of forms and manners of knowledge pertaining to the memory. For, when it has the habit of union, which is a supernatural state, memory and the other faculties fail it completely in their natural functions, and pass beyond their natural limitations, even to God, Who is supernatural. And thus, when the memory is transformed in God, it cannot receive impressions of forms or kinds of knowledge. Wherefore the functions of the memory and of the other faculties in this state are all Divine; for, when at last God possesses the faculties and has become the entire master of them, through their transformation into Himself, it is He Himself Who moves and commands them divinely, according to His Divine Spirit and will;[4] and the result of this is that the operations of the soul are not distinct, but all that it does is of God, and its operations are Divine, so that, even as Saint Paul says, he that is joined unto God becomes one spirit with Him.[5]

9. Hence it comes to pass that the operations of the soul in union are of the Divine Spirit and are Divine. And hence it comes that the actions of such souls are only those that are seemly and reasonable, and not those that are ill-beseeming. For the Spirit of God teaches them

---

[1] E.p.: 'as the soul pays no heed to.'
[2] E.p. abbreviates: '. . . union with God, the less it heeds distinct kinds of knowledge, and this increases in proportion as it draws nearer to the state of union through the absorption of the memory in God.'
[3] E.p. omits the rest of this sentence and the whole of the next.
[4] E.p. omits the rest of this paragraph and the first sentence of the next.
[5] 1 Corinthians vi, 17.

that which they ought to know, and causes them to be ignorant of that which it behoves them not to know, and to remember that which they have to remember, with or without forms, and to forget that which they should forget; and it makes them love that which they have to love, and not to love that which is not in God. And thus,[1] all the first motions of the faculties of such souls are Divine and it is not to be wondered at that the motions and operations of these faculties should be Divine, since they are transformed in the Divine Being.[2]

10.[3] Of these operations I will give a few examples. Let this be one. A person asks another who is in this state to commend him to God. This person will not remember to do so by means of any form or kind of knowledge that remains in his memory concerning that other person; if it be right that he should recommend him to God (which will be if God desires to receive a prayer for that person), He will move his will and give him a desire to pray for him; and if God desires not such prayer, that other person will not be able nor will desire to pray,'[4] though he make great efforts to do so; and at times God will cause him to pray for others of whom he has no knowledge nor has ever heard. And this is because, as I have said, God alone moves the faculties of these souls to do those works which are meet, according to the will and ordinance of God, and they cannot be moved to do others; and thus the works and prayers of these souls are always effectual. Such were those of the most glorious Virgin Our Lady, who, being raised to this high estate from the beginning, had never the form of any creature[5] imprinted in her soul, neither was moved by such, but was invariably guided by the Holy Spirit.

11. Another example. At a certain time a person in this state has to attend to some necessary business. He will remember it by no kind of form, but, without his knowing how, it will come to his soul,[6] at the time and in the manner that it ought to come, and that without fail.

12. And not only in these things does the Holy Spirit give such

[1] E.p. substitutes for this sentence: 'For He [i.e., the Spirit of God] specially governs and moves them so that they may perform those actions which are seemly, according to the will and ordinance of God.'

[2] P. José de Jesús María, in his *Vida y excelencias de la Santísima Virgen María* (I, xl), quotes this and part of the last paragraph from what he claims to be an original MS. of St. John of the Cross, but his text varies considerably from that of any MS. now known. [P. Silverio considers that this and other similar citations are quite untrustworthy.]

[3] E.p. omits paragraphs 10, 11, 12, all of which, however, are restored in the edition of 1630.

[4] Edition of 1630: 'will not pray nor will desire to pray.'

[5] *Ibid.*: 'of any creature that would turn her aside from God.'

[6] Edition of 1630 adds here: 'by the stirring up of his memory described above.'

persons light, but also in many others, relating both to the present and to the future, and even, in many cases, as regards those absent from them; and although at times this comes to pass through intellectual forms, it frequently happens without the intervention of any forms that can be apprehended, so that these persons know not how they know.[1] But this comes to them from the Divine Wisdom; for, since these souls exercise themselves in knowing and apprehending nothing with the faculties,[2] they come in general, as we have said in the Mount,[3] to know everything, according to that which the Wise Man says: 'The worker of all things, who is Wisdom, taught me all things.'[4]

13. You will say, perhaps, that the soul will be unable to void and deprive its memory of all forms and fancies to such an extent as to be able to attain to so lofty a state; for there are two things so difficult that their accomplishment surpasses human ability and strength, namely, to throw off with one's natural powers that which is natural, which is hard enough,[5] and to attain and be united to the supernatural, which is much more difficult—indeed, to speak the truth, is impossible with natural ability alone. The truth, I repeat, is that God must place the soul in this supernatural state; but the soul, as far as in it lies, must be continually preparing itself; and this it can do by natural means, especially[6] with the help that God is continually giving it. And thus, as the soul, for its own part, enters into this renunciation and self-emptying of forms, so God begins to give it the possession of union; and this God works passively in the soul, as we shall say, *Deo dante*, when we treat of the passive night of the soul. And thus, when it shall please God, and according to the manner of the soul's preparation, He will grant it the habit of perfect and Divine union.[7]

14. And the Divine effects which God produces in the soul when He has granted it this habit, both as to the understanding and as to the memory and will, we shall not describe in this account of the soul's active purgation and night, for this alone will not bring the soul to Divine union. We shall speak of these effects, however, in treating of the passive night, by means of which is brought about the union of the

---

1 Edition of 1630 abbreviates: '. . . as regards those absent from them, so that these persons know not how they know.'

2 Edition of 1630: 'and apprehending with the faculties nothing that can impede them.'

3 The reference is to the drawing of the Mount of Perfection. Cf. p. xxxii, above.

4 Wisdom vii, 21.

5 [*Lit.*, 'which cannot be' (*que no puede ser*), but this is a well-known Spanish hyperbole describing what is extremely difficult.]

6 E.p. omits 'especially.'   7 E.p. omits: 'and Divine.'

soul with God.[1] And so I shall speak here only of the necessary means whereby the memory may place itself actively in this night and purgation, as far as lies in its power. And these means are that the spiritual man must habitually exercise caution, after this manner. All the things that he hears, sees, smells, tastes or touches, he must be careful not to store up or collect in his memory, but he must allow himself to forget them immediately, and this he must accomplish, if need be, with the same efficacy as that with which others contrive to remember them, so that there remains in his memory no knowledge or image of them whatsoever. It must be with him as if they existed not in the world, and his memory must be left free and disencumbered of them, and be tied to no consideration, whether from above or from below, as if he had no faculty of memory; he must freely allow everything to fall into oblivion as though all things were a hindrance to him; and in fact everything that is natural, if one attempt to make use of it in supernatural matters, is a hindrance rather than a help.

15. And if those questions and objections which arose above with respect to the understanding should also arise here (the objections, that is to say, that the soul is doing nothing, is wasting its time and is depriving itself of spiritual blessings which it might well receive through the memory), the answer to this has already been given,[2] and will be given again farther on, in our treatment of the passive night;

---

[1] E.p. omits all the rest of this paragraph, substituting the following passage, which it introduces in order [says P. Silverio] to describe the scope of the Saint's teaching, and which is copied in the edition of 1630:

In [treating of] this purgation of the memory, I speak here only of the necessary means whereby the memory may place itself actively in this night and purgation, as far as lies in its power. And these means are that the spiritual man must habitually exercise caution, after this manner. Of all the things that he sees, hears, smells, tastes or touches he must make no particular store in the memory, or pay heed to them, or dwell upon them, but must allow them to pass and must remain in holy oblivion without reflecting upon them, save when necessary for some good reflection or meditation. And this care to forget and forsake knowledge and images is never applicable to Christ and His Humanity. For, although occasionally, at the height of contemplation and simple regard of the Divinity, the soul may not remember this most sacred Humanity, because God, with His own hand, has raised the soul to this, as it were, confused and most supernatural knowledge, yet it is in no wise seemly to study to forget it, since looking and meditating lovingly upon it will aid the soul to [attain] all that is good, and it is by its means that the soul will most readily rise to the most lofty state of union. And it is clear that, although other bodily and visible things are a hindrance and ought to be forgotten, we must not include among these Him Who became man for our salvation, and Who is the truth, the door, the way and the guide to all good things. This being assumed, let the soul strive after complete abstraction and oblivion, so that, in so far as is possible, there may remain in its memory no more knowledge or image of created things than though they existed not in the world; and let it leave the memory free and disencumbered for God, and, as it were, lost in holy oblivion.

[2] E.p.: '. . . through the memory) much has already been said here in reply to them, and there, too, they have been completely answered.'

wherefore there is no need for us to dwell upon it here. It is needful only to observe that, although at certain times the benefit of this suspension of forms and of all knowledge may not be realized, the spiritual man must not for that reason grow weary, for in His own time God will not fail to succour him. To attain so great a blessing it behoves the soul to endure much and to suffer with patience and hope.

16. And, although it is true that hardly any soul will be found that is moved by God in all things and at all times, and has such continual union with God that, without the mediation of any form, its faculties[1] are ever moved divinely, there are nevertheless souls who in their operations are very habitually moved by God, and these are not they that are moved of themselves, for, as Saint Paul says, the sons of God, who are transformed and united in God, are moved by the Spirit of God,[2] that is, are moved to perform Divine work in their faculties. And it is no marvel that their operations should be Divine, since the union of the soul is Divine.

CHAPTER III

Wherein are described three kinds of evil which come to the soul when it enters not into darkness with respect to knowledge and reflections in the memory. Herein is described the first.

To three kinds of evil and inconvenience the spiritual man is subject when he persists in desiring to make use of all natural knowledge and reflections of the memory in order to journey toward God, or for any other purpose: two of these are positive and one is privative. The first comes from things of the world; the second, from the devil; the third, which is privative, is the impediment and hindrance to Divine union caused and effected in the soul.

2. The first evil, which comes from the world,[3] consists in the subjection of the soul, through knowledge[4] and reflection, to many kinds of harm, such as falsehoods, imperfections, desires, opinions, loss of time, and many other things which breed many kinds of impurity in the soul. And it is clear that the soul must of necessity fall into many perils of falsehood, when it admits knowledge and reasoning; for oftentimes that which is true must appear false, and that which is

[1] E.p. omits: 'without the mediation of any form.'
[2] Romans viii, 14.   [3] E.p.: 'from the things of the world.'
[4] A, B: 'through much knowledge.'

certain, doubtful; and contrariwise; for there is scarcely a single truth of which we can have complete knowledge. From all these things the soul is free if the memory enters into darkness with respect to every kind of reflection and knowledge.

3. Imperfections meet the soul at every step if it sets its memory upon that which it has heard, seen, touched, smelt and tasted; for there must then perforce cling to it some affection, whether this be of pain, of fear, of hatred, of vain hope, vain enjoyment, vainglory, etc.; for all these are, at the least, imperfections, and at times are downright[1] venial sins; and they leave much impurity most subtly in the soul, even though the reflections and the knowledge have relation to God.[2] And it is also clear that they engender desires within the soul, for these arise naturally from the knowledge and reflections afore-mentioned, and if one wishes only to have this knowledge and these reflections, even that is a desire. And it is clearly seen that many occasions of judging others will come likewise; for, in using its memory, the soul cannot fail to come upon that which is good and bad in others, and, in such a case, that which is evil oftentimes seems good, and that which is good, evil. I believe there is none who can completely free himself from all these kinds of evil, save by blinding his memory and leading it into darkness with regard to all these things.

4. And if you tell me that a man is well able to conquer all these things when they come to him, I reply that, if he sets store by know-ledge, this is simply and utterly impossible; for countless imperfec-tions and follies insinuate themselves into such knowledge, some of which are so subtle and minute that, without the soul's realization thereof, they cling to it of their own accord, even as pitch clings to the man that touches it; so that it is better to conquer once for all by deny-ing the memory completely. You will say likewise that by so doing the soul deprives itself of many good thoughts and meditations upon God, which are of great profit to it and whereby God grants it favours. I reply that to this end purity of soul is of the greatest profit,[3] which means that there clings to the soul no creature affection, or temporal

---

[1] [*Lit.*, 'good.'] E.p. reads 'known' for 'downright.'
[2] So Alc., A, B.   E.p. reads: '. . . venial sins: all of these [being] things which disturb perfect purity and most simple union with God.'
[3] E.p. inserts, after 'grants it favours': 'I reply that it is not that which is purely God and which aids this simple, pure, universal and confused knowledge that is to be rejected, but that which detains [the memory] in images, forms, figures or similitudes of created things.' It continues: 'And, speaking of this purgation, in order that God may accom-plish it, purity of soul is of the greatest profit. . . .' The insertion is also found in the edition of 1630.

affection, or effective advertence; which I believe cannot but cling to
the soul because of the imperfection which the faculties have in their
own operations. Wherefore it is best to learn to silence the faculties
and to cause them to be still, so that God may speak. For, as we have
said, in order to attain to this state the natural operations must be
completely disregarded, and this happens, as the Prophet says, when
the soul comes into solitude, according to these its faculties, and God
speaks to its heart.[1]

5. And if you again reply, saying that the soul will have no blessing
unless it meditates upon God and allows its memory to reflect upon
Him, and that many distractions and negligences will continually enter
it, I say that it is impossible, if the memory be recollected with regard
both to things of the next life and to things here below, that evils or
distractions should enter it, nor any other follies or vices (the which
things always enter when the memory wanders), since there is no exit
or entrance for them. This would come to pass if, when we had shut
the door upon considerations and reflections concerning things above,
we opened it to things below; but in this state we shut the door to all
things whence distraction may come,[2] causing the memory to be still
and dumb, and the ear of the spirit to be attentive, in silence, to God
alone, saying with the Prophet: 'Speak, Lord, for Thy servant heareth.'[3]
It was thus that the Spouse in the Songs said that his Bride should be, in
these words: 'My sister is a garden enclosed and a fountain sealed up'[4]—
that is to say, enclosed and sealed up against all things that may enter.

6. Let the soul, then, remain 'enclosed,' without anxieties and
troubles, and He that entered in bodily form to His disciples when the
doors were shut, and gave them peace,[5] though they neither knew nor
thought that this was possible nor knew how it was possible,[6] will
enter spiritually into the soul, without its knowing how He does so,
when the doors of its faculties—memory, understanding and will—
are enclosed against all apprehensions. And He will fill them with
peace, coming down upon the soul, as the prophet says, like a river of
peace,[7] and taking from it all the misgivings and suspicions, disturbances and darknesses which caused it to fear that it was lost or
was on the way to being so. Let it not grow careless about prayer, and
let it wait in detachment and emptiness, for its blessing will not tarry.

---

[1] Osee ii, 14.
[2] [*Lit.*, 'whence that may come.'] E.p.: 'We shut the door to all things which are a
hindrance to union, and whence distraction may come.'
[3] 1 Kings [A.V., 1 Samuel] iii, 10.   [4] Canticles iv, 12.   [5] [St. John xx, 19].
[6] E.p. omits: 'nor knew how it was possible.'   [7] Isaiah xlviii, 18.

CHAPTER IV[1]

Which treats of the second kind of evil that may come to the soul from the devil by way of the natural apprehensions of the memory.

THE second positive evil that may come to the soul by means of the knowledge of the memory proceeds from the devil, who by this means obtains great influence over it. For he can continually bring it new forms, kinds of knowledge and reflections, by means whereof he can taint the soul with pride, avarice, wrath, envy, etc., and cause it unjust hatred, or vain love, and deceive it in many ways. And besides this, he is wont to leave impressions,[2] and to implant them in the fancy, in such wise that those that are false appear true, and those that are true, false. And finally all the worst deceptions which are caused by the devil, and the evils that he brings to the soul, enter by way of knowledge and reflections of the memory. Thus if the memory enter into darkness with respect to them all, and be annihilated in its oblivion to them, it shuts the door altogether upon this evil which proceeds from the devil, and frees itself from all these things, which is a great blessing. For the devil has no power over the soul unless it be through the operations of its faculties, principally by means of knowledge,[3] whereupon depend almost all the other operations of the other faculties. Wherefore, if the memory be annihilated with respect to them, the devil can do naught; for he finds no foothold, and without a foothold he is powerless.[4]

2. I would that spiritual persons might clearly see how many kinds of harm are wrought by evil spirits in their souls by means of the memory, when they devote themselves frequently to making use of it, and how many kinds of sadness and affliction and vain and evil[5] joys they have, both with respect to their thoughts about God, and also with respect to the things of the world; and how many impurities are left rooted in their spirits;[6] and likewise how greatly they are distracted from the highest recollection, which consists in the fixing of the whole soul, according to its faculties, upon the one incomprehensible Good, and in withdrawing it from all things that can be appre-

---

[1] P. omits this chapter.
[2] [*Lit.*, 'to leave things.'] A, B, e.p.: 'to fix things.'
[3] E.p.: 'by means of forms and species.'
[4] [*Lit.*, 'he finds nothing to seize upon, and with nothing he can do nothing.']
[5] E.p. omits: 'and evil.'
[6] Alc. omits: 'and how many . . . spirits.'

hended, since these are not incomprehensible Good.[1] This is a great
good (although less good results from this emptiness than from the
soul's fixing itself upon God), simply because it is the cause whereby
the soul frees itself from many griefs and afflictions and sorrows, over
and above the imperfections and sins from which it is freed.

CHAPTER V

*Of the third evil which comes to the soul by way of the distinct natural
knowledge of the memory.*

THE third evil which comes to the soul through the natural
apprehensions of the memory is privative; for these apprehensions can hinder moral good and deprive us of spiritual
good. And, in order that we may first of all explain how these apprehensions hinder moral good in the soul, it must be known that moral
good consists in the restraining of the passions and the curbing of disorderly desires, from which restraint there come to the soul tranquillity, peace and rest, and moral virtues, all of which things are moral
good. This restraining and curbing of the passions cannot be truly
accomplished by the soul that forgets not and withdraws not itself
from things pertaining to itself, whence arise the affections; and no
disturbances ever arise in the soul save through the apprehensions of
the memory. For, when all things are forgotten, there is naught that
can disturb peace or that moves the desires; since, as they say, that
which the eye sees not the heart desires not.

2. This we are constantly learning by experience; for we observe
that, whenever the soul begins to think of any matter, it is moved and
disturbed, either much or little, with respect to that thing, according to
the nature of its apprehension. If it be a troublesome and grievous
matter, the soul finds sadness[2] in it; if pleasant, desire and joy,[3] and so
forth. Wherefore the result of the changing of that apprehension is
necessarily disturbance; and thus the soul is now joyful, now sad; now
it hates, now loves; and it cannot continue in one and the same
attitude (which is an effect of moral tranquillity) save when it strives
to forget all things. It is clear, then, that knowledge greatly hinders
the good of the moral virtues in the soul.

[1] E.p. omits: 'since . . . Good.'
[2] E.p.: 'sadness or hate.'
[3] E.p.: 'if pleasant, joy and desire.'

3. Again, what has been said clearly proves that an encumbered memory also hinders spiritual good;[1] for the soul that is disturbed, and has no foundation of moral good, is to that extent incapable of spiritual good, which impresses itself only upon souls that are restrained and at peace. And besides this, if the soul pays attention and heed to the apprehensions of the memory—seeing that it can attend to but one thing at a time—and busies itself with things that can be apprehended, such as the knowledge of the memory, it is not possible for it to be free to attend to the incomprehensible, which is God. For, in order to approach God, the soul must proceed by not comprehending rather than by comprehending; it must exchange the mutable and comprehensible for the immutable and incomprehensible.

CHAPTER VI

Of the benefits which come to the soul from forgetfulness and emptiness of all thoughts and knowledge which it may have in a natural way with respect to the memory.

FROM the evils which, as we have said, come to the soul through the apprehensions of the memory, we can likewise infer the benefits which are contrary to them and come to the soul as a result of its forgetting them and emptying itself of them. For, as natural philosophy puts it, the same doctrine which serves for one thing serves likewise for its contrary. In the first place, the soul enjoys tranquillity and peace of mind, since it is freed from the disturbance and the changeableness which arise from thoughts and ideas of the memory, and consequently, which is more important, it enjoys purity of conscience and soul. And herein the soul has ample preparation for the acquiring of Divine and human wisdom, and of the virtues.

2. In the second place, it is freed from many suggestions, temptations and motions of the devil, which he infuses into the soul by means of thoughts and ideas, causing it to fall into many impurities and sins,[2] as David says in these words: 'They have thought and spoken wickedness.'[3] And thus, when these thoughts have been completely removed, the devil has naught wherewith to assault the soul by natural means.[4]

---

[1] The edition of 1630 reads: 'spiritual or mystical good.'
[2] A, B, e.p.: 'to fall, at the least, into many impurities, and, as we have said, into sins.'
[3] Psalm lxxii, 8 [A.V., lxxiii, 8]. E.p.: 'and found wickedness.'
[4] E.p. omits: 'by natural means.'

3. In the third place, the soul has within itself, through this recollection of itself and this forgetfulness as to all things, a preparedness to be moved by the Holy Spirit and taught by Him, for, as the Wise Man says, He removes Himself from thoughts that are without understanding.[1] Even if a man received no other benefit from this forgetfulness and emptiness of the memory than being freed thereby from troubles and disturbances, it would be great gain and good for him. For the troubles and storms which adverse things and happenings arouse in the soul are of no use or help[2] for bringing peace and calm;[3] indeed, as a rule, they make things worse and also harm the soul itself. Wherefore David said: 'Of a truth every man is disquieted in vain.'[4] For it is clear that to disquiet oneself is always vain since it brings profit to none. And thus, even if everything came to an end and were destroyed, and if all things went wrong and turned to adversity, it would be vain to disturb oneself; for such disturbance hurts a man rather than relieves him. Whereas to bear everything with equable and peaceful tranquillity not only brings the soul the profit of many blessings, but likewise causes it, even in the midst of its adversities, to form a truer judgment about them and to find them a fitting remedy.

4. For this reason Solomon, being well acquainted both with the evil and with the benefit of which we are speaking, said: 'I knew that there was naught better for man than to rejoice and to do good in his life.'[5] By this he meant that, in everything that happens to us, howsoever adverse it be, we should rejoice rather than be disturbed, so that we may not lose a blessing which is greater than any kind of prosperity —namely, tranquillity and peace of mind in all things, which, whether they bring adversity or prosperity, we must bear in the same manner. This a man would never lose if he were not only to forget all kinds of knowledge and put aside all thoughts, but would even withdraw himself from hearing, sight and commerce with others, in so far as was possible for him. Our nature is so frail and unstable that, however well it be disciplined, it will hardly fail to stumble upon the remembrance of things which will disturb and change a mind that was in peace and tranquillity when it remembered them not. For this cause said Jeremias: 'With memory I will remember, and my soul will fail me for pain.'[6]

---

[1] Wisdom i, 5.   [2] E.p. omits: 'or help.'
[3] [*Lit.*, 'for the peace and calm of the same things and happenings.'] E.p. omits: 'things and.'
[4] Psalm xxxviii, 7 [A.V., xxxix, 6].
[5] Ecclesiastes iii, 12.   [6] Lamentations iii, 20.

CHAPTER VII

Which treats of the second kind of apprehension of the memory—namely, imaginary apprehensions—and of supernatural knowledge.

ALTHOUGH in writing of natural apprehensions of the first kind we also gave instruction concerning the imaginary, which are likewise natural, it was well to make this division because of the love which the memory always has for other forms and kinds of knowledge, which are of supernatural things, such as visions, revelations, locutions and feelings which come in a supernatural way. When these things have passed through the soul, there is wont to remain impressed upon it some image, form, figure or idea, whether in the soul or in the memory or fancy, at times very vividly and effectively. Concerning these images it is also needful to give advice, lest the memory be encumbered with them and they be a hindrance to its union with God in perfect and pure hope.

2. I say that the soul, in order to attain that blessing, must never reflect upon the clear and distinct objects which may have passed through its mind by supernatural means, in such a way as to preserve within itself the forms and figures and knowledge of those things. For we must ever bear in mind this principle: the greater heed the soul gives to any clear and distinct apprehensions, whether natural or supernatural, the less capacity and preparation it has for entering into the abyss of faith, wherein are absorbed all things else. For, as has been said, no supernatural forms or kinds of knowledge which can be apprehended by the memory are God,[1] and, in order to reach God, the soul must void itself of all that is not God. The memory must also strip itself of all these forms and kinds of knowledge, that it may unite itself with God in hope.[2] For all possession is contrary to hope, which, as Saint Paul says, belongs to that which is not possessed.[3] Wherefore, the more the memory dispossesses itself, the greater is its hope; and the more it has of hope, the more it has of union with God; for, with respect to God, the more the soul hopes, the more it attains. And it hopes most when it is most completely dispossessed; and, when it shall be perfectly dispossessed, it will remain with the perfect possession of

---

[1] E.p. adds: 'nor do they bear any proportion to Him nor can serve as proximate means to union with Him.'

[2] E.p.: '. . . unite itself with God in a manner of mystical and perfect hope.'

[3] Hebrews xi, 1.

God,[1] in Divine union. But there are many who will not deprive themselves of the sweetness and delight which memory finds in those forms
and notions, wherefore they attain not to supreme possession and
perfect sweetness. For he that renounces not all that he possesses
cannot be the disciple of Christ.[2]

CHAPTER VIII

*Of the evils which may be caused in the soul by the knowledge of super-
natural things, if it reflect upon them. Says how many these evils are.*[3]

THE spiritual man incurs the risk of five kinds of evil if he pays
heed to, and reflects upon, these forms and ideas which are
impressed upon him by the things which pass through his mind
in a supernatural way.

2. The first is that he is frequently deceived, and mistakes one thing
for another. The second is that he is like to fall, and is exposed to the
danger of falling, into some form of presumption or vanity. The third
is that the devil has many occasions of deceiving him by means of the
apprehensions aforementioned. The fourth is that he is hindered as to
union in hope with God. The fifth is that, for the most part, he has a
low judgment of God.

3. As to the first evil, it is clear that, if the spiritual man pays heed
to these forms and notions, and reflects upon them, he must frequently
be deceived in his judgment of them; for, as no man can have a complete understanding of the things that pass through his imagination
naturally, nor a perfect and certain judgment about them, he will be
much less able still to have this with respect to supernatural things,
which are above our capacity to understand, and occur but rarely.
Wherefore he will often think that what comes but from his fancy
pertains to God; and often, too, that what is of God is of the devil, and
what is of the devil is of God. And very often there will remain with
him deep-seated impressions of forms and ideas concerning the good
and evil of others, or of himself, together with other figures which
have been presented to him: these he will consider to be most certain
and true, when in fact they will not be so, but very great falsehoods.

---

[1] E.p. adds: 'in so far as may be in this life.'
[2] St. Luke xiv, 33.
[3] A, B, e.p. add: 'and treats here of the first.'

And others will be true, and he will judge them to be false, although this error I consider safer, as it is apt to arise from humility.

4. And, even if he be not deceived as to their truth, he may well be deceived as to their quantity or quality,[1] thinking that little things are great, and great things, little. And with respect to their quality, he may consider what is in his imagination to be this or that, when it is something quite different; he may put, as Isaias says, darkness for light, and light for darkness, and bitter for sweet, and sweet for bitter.[2] And finally, even though he be correct as to one thing, it will be a marvel if he goes not astray with respect to the next; for, although he may not desire to apply his judgment to the judging of them, yet, if he apply it in paying heed to them, this will be sufficient to make some evil to cling to him as a result of it,[3] at least passively; if not evil of this kind, then of one of the four other kinds of which we shall shortly speak.

5. It behoves the spiritual man, therefore, lest he fall into this evil of being deceived in his judgment, not to desire to apply his judgment in order to know the nature of his own condition or feelings, or the nature of such and such a vision, idea or feeling; neither should he desire to know it or to pay heed[4] to it. This he should only desire in order to speak of it to his spiritual father, and to be taught by him how to void his memory of these apprehensions.[5] For, whatever may be their intrinsic nature, they cannot help him to love God as much as the smallest act of living faith and hope performed in the emptiness and renunciation of all things.[6]

CHAPTER IX

Of the second kind of evil, which is the peril of falling into self-esteem and vain presumption.

THE supernatural apprehensions of the memory already described are also a frequent occasion to spiritual persons of falling into some kind of presumption or vanity, if they give heed to them and set store by them. For, even as he who knows nothing of them is

---

[1] E.p.: 'quality and value.'   [2] Isaias v, 20.
[3] The 1630 edition adds: 'and for him to suffer from it.'
[4] E.p.: 'pay much heed.'
[5] E.p. adds: 'or [to do] what in his particular case may be most expedient, with this same detachment.'
[6] E.p.: 'in the emptiness of all this.'

quite free from falling into this vice, since he sees in himself no occasion of presumption, even so, in contrary wise, he that has experience of them has close at hand an occasion for thinking himself to be some-thing, since he possesses these supernatural communications. For, although it is true that he may attribute them to God, hold himself[1] to be unworthy of them, and give God the thanks, yet nevertheless there is wont to remain in his spirit a certain secret satisfaction, and a self-esteem and a sense of their value, from which, without his know-ledge, there will come to him great spiritual pride.

2. This may be observed very clearly by such as will consider the dislike and aversion caused them by any who do not praise their spirituality, or esteem the experiences which they enjoy, and the mortification which they suffer when they think or are told that others have just those same experiences, or even superior ones. All this arises from secret self-esteem and pride, and they can never quite realize that they are steeped in pride up to their very eyes. For they think that a certain degree of recognition of their own wretchedness suffices, and, although they have this, they are full of secret self-esteem and self-satisfaction, taking more delight in their own spirituality and spiritual gifts[2] than in those of others. They are like the Pharisee who gave thanks to God that he was not as other men, and that he practised such and such virtues, whereat he was satisfied with himself and pre-sumed thereon.[3] Such men, although they may not use the Pharisee's actual words, habitually resemble him in spirit. And some of them even become so proud that they are worse than the devil. For, observing in themselves, as they imagine, certain apprehensions and feelings con-cerning God which are devout and sweet, they become self-satisfied to such an extent that they believe themselves to be very near God; and those that are not like themselves they consider very low and despise them after the manner of the Pharisee.[4]

3. In order to flee from this pestilent evil, abhorrent in the eyes of God, they must consider two things. First, that virtue consists not in apprehensions and feelings concerning God, howsoever sublime they be, nor in anything of this kind that a man can feel within himself; but, on the contrary, in that which has nothing to do with feeling—namely, a great humility and contempt of oneself and of all that pertains to oneself, firmly rooted in the soul and keenly felt by it; and likewise in

---

[1] E.p.: 'feel himself.'
[2] E.p.: 'spirituality and gifts.'
[3] St. Luke xviii, 11–12.
[4] A, B: 'and despise them as the Pharisee despised the publican.'

being glad that others feel in this very way concerning oneself and in not wishing to be of any account in the esteem[1] of others.

4. Secondly, it must be noted that all visions, revelations and feelings coming from Heaven, and any thoughts that may proceed from these, are of less worth than the least act of humility. And humility is one of the effects of charity, which esteems not its own things nor strives to attain them; nor thinks evil, save of itself; nor thinks any good thing of itself, but only of others. It is well, therefore, that these supernatural apprehensions should not attract men's eyes, but that they should strive to forget them in order that they may be free.

CHAPTER X

Of the third evil that may come to the soul from the devil, through the imaginary apprehensions of the memory.

FROM all that has been said above it may be clearly understood and inferred how great is the evil that may come to the soul from the devil by way of these supernatural apprehensions. For not only can he represent to the memory and the fancy many false forms and ideas, which seem true and good, impressing them on spirit and sense with great effectiveness and certifying them to be true by means of suggestion (so that it appears to the soul that it cannot be otherwise, but that everything is even as he represents it; for, as he transfigures himself into an angel of light, he appears as light to the soul); but he may also tempt the soul in many ways with respect to true knowledge, which is of God, moving its desires[2] and affections, whether spiritual or sensual, in unruly fashion with respect to these; for, if the soul takes pleasure in such apprehensions, it is very easy for the devil to cause its desires and affections to grow[3] within it, and to make it fall into spiritual gluttony and other evils.

2. And, in order the better to do this, he is wont to suggest and give pleasure, sweetness and delight to the senses with respect to these same things of God, so that the soul is corrupted and bewildered[4] by that sweetness, and is thus blinded with that pleasure and sets its eyes on

---

1 [*Lit.*, 'in the heart.']   2 A, B: 'its will and desires.'

3 A, B and many of the editions (not, however, e.p.) have *creer* ('believe') for *crecer* ('grow'), so that we should have to read: 'to cause it to believe its desires and affections.'

4 [The two verbs, in the original, have very definite and concrete meanings, 'sweetened with honey' and 'dazzled by a lamp' respectively.]

pleasure rather than on love (or, at least, very much more than upon love), and gives more heed to the apprehensions than to the detachment and emptiness which are found in faith and hope and love of God. And from this he may go on gradually to deceive the soul and cause it to believe his falsehoods with great facility. For to the soul that is blind falsehood no longer appears to be falsehood, nor does evil appear to be evil, etc.; for darkness appears to be light, and light, darkness; and hence that soul comes to commit a thousand foolish errors,[1] whether with respect to natural things, or to moral things, or to spiritual things; so that that which was wine to it becomes vinegar. All this happens to the soul because it began not, first of all, by denying itself the pleasure of those supernatural things. At first this is a small matter, and not very harmful, and the soul has therefore no misgivings, and allows it to continue, and it grows,[2] like the grain of mustard seed, into a tall tree. For a small error at the beginning, as they say, becomes a great error in the end.

3. Wherefore, in order to flee from this great evil, which comes[3] from the devil, the soul must not desire to have any pleasure in such things, because such pleasure will most surely lead it to become blind and to fall. For of their own nature, and without the help of the devil,[4] pleasure and delight and sweetness blind[5] the soul. And this was the meaning of David when he said: 'Perhaps darkness shall blind me in my delights and I shall have the night for my light.'[6]

CHAPTER XI

Of the fourth evil that comes to the soul from the distinct supernatural apprehensions of the memory, which is the hindrance that it interposes to union.

CONCERNING this fourth evil there is not much to be said, since it has already been treated again and again in this third book, wherein we have proved how, in order that the soul may come to union with God in hope, it must renounce every possession of the memory; for, in order that its hope in God may be perfect, it must have

---

[1] E.p. adds here: 'so that that which was wine to it becomes vinegar,' omitting this same phrase where it occurs below.
[2] E.p.: 'to continue and grow.'   [3] E.p.: 'which may come.'
[4] E.p. omits: 'and without the help of the devil.'
[5] E.p.: 'dull and blind.'   [6] Psalm cxxxviii, 11 [A.V., cxxxix, 11].

naught in the memory that is not God. And, as we have likewise said, no form or figure or image or other kind of knowledge that may come to the memory can be God, neither can be like Him, whether it be of heaven or of earth,[1] natural or supernatural, even as David teaches, when he says: 'Lord, among the gods there is none like unto Thee.'[2]

2. Wherefore, if the memory desires to pay heed to any of these things, it hinders the soul from reaching God; first, because it encumbers it, and next because, the more the soul has of possession, the less it has of hope.[3] Wherefore it is needful for the soul to be stripped of the distinct forms and the knowledge of supernatural things, and to become oblivious to them, so that the memory may cause no hindrance to its union with God in perfect hope.

CHAPTER XII

Of the fifth evil that may come to the soul in supernatural imaginary forms and apprehensions, which is a low and unseemly judgment of God.

No less serious is the fifth evil that comes to the soul from its desire to retain in the memory and imagination the said forms and images of things that are supernaturally communicated to it, above all if it desires to use them as a means to Divine union. For it is a very easy thing to judge of the Being and greatness of God less worthily and nobly than befits His incomprehensible nature; for, although our reason and judgment may form no express conception that God is like any one of these things, yet the very esteeming of these apprehensions, if in fact the soul esteems them, makes and causes it not to esteem God,[4] or not to feel concerning Him, as highly as faith teaches, since faith tells us that He is incomparable, incomprehensible, and so forth. For, quite apart from the fact that the soul takes from God all that it gives to the creature, it is natural that its esteem of these apprehensible things should lead it to make a certain inward comparison between such things and God, which would prevent it from judging and esteeming God as highly as it ought. For the creatures, whether terrestrial or celestial, and all distinct images and kinds of knowledge,[5]

---

[1] E.p. omits: 'whether it be of heaven or of earth.'
[2] Psalm lxxxv, 8 [A.V., lxxxvi, 8].   [3] E.p.: 'of perfection of hope.'
[4] E.p. abbreviates: 'the very esteeming of these apprehensions makes the soul not to esteem God . . .'
[5] E.p.: 'and all the forms and images.'

both natural and supernatural, that can be encompassed by the faculties of the soul, however lofty they be in this life, have no comparison or proportion with the Being of God, since God falls within no genus and no species, whereas the creatures do, or so the theologians tell us.[1] And the soul in this life is not capable of receiving in a clear and distinct manner aught save that which falls within genus and species. For this cause Saint John says that no man hath seen God at any time.[2] And Isaias says it has not entered into the heart of man what God is like.[3] And God said to Moses that he could not see Him while he was in this mortal state.[4] Wherefore he that encumbers his memory and the other faculties of the soul with that which they can comprehend cannot esteem God, neither feel concerning Him, as he ought.

2. Let us make a comparison on a lower level. It is clear that the more a man fixes his eyes[5] upon the servants of a king, and the more notice he takes of them, the less notice does he take of the king himself, and the less does he esteem him; for, although this comparison may not be formally and distinctly present in the understanding, it is inherent in the act, since, the more attention the man gives to the servants, the more he takes from their lord; and he cannot have a very high opinion of the king if the servants appear to him to be of any importance while they are in the presence of the king, their lord. Even so does the soul treat its God when it pays heed to the creatures[6] aforementioned. This comparison, however, is on a very low level, for, as we have said, God is of another being than His creatures in that He is infinitely far from them all. For this reason they must all be banished from sight, and the soul must withdraw its gaze from them in all their forms, that it may set its gaze on God through faith and hope.[7]

3. Wherefore those who not only pay heed to the imaginary apprehensions aforementioned, but suppose God to be like to some of them, and think that by means of them they will be able to attain to union with God, have already gone far astray and will ever continue to lose the light[8] of faith in the understanding, through which this faculty is united with God; neither will they grow in the loftiness of hope, by means whereof the memory is united with God in hope,[9] which must be brought about through disunion from all that is of the imagination.

---

[1] E.p. ends this sentence at 'no species.'   [2] St. John i, 18.
[3] Isaias lxiv, 4.   [4] Exodus xxxiii, 20.
[5] E.p.: 'fixes the eyes of his esteem.'   [6] A, B, e.p.: 'to the things.'
[7] E.p.: 'and perfect hope.'   [8] E.p.: 'and profit not greatly by the light.'
[9] E.p. omits: 'in hope.'

CHAPTER XIII

Of the benefits which the soul receives through banishing from itself the apprehensions of the imagination. This chapter answers a certain objection and explains a difference which exists between apprehensions that are imaginary, natural and supernatural.[1]

THE benefits that come from voiding the imagination of imaginary forms can be clearly observed in the five evils aforementioned which they inflict upon the soul, if it desires to retain them, even as we also said of the natural forms. But, apart from these, there are other benefits for the spirit—namely, those of great rest and quiet. For, setting aside that natural rest which the soul obtains when it is free from images and forms, it likewise becomes free from anxiety as to whether they are good or evil, and as to how it must behave with respect to the one and to the other. Nor has it to waste the labour and time of its spiritual masters by requiring them to decide if these things are good or evil, and if they are of this kind or of another; for the soul has no need to desire to know all this if it pays no heed to them.[2] The time and energies which it would have wasted in dealing with these images and forms[3] can be better employed in another and a more profitable exercise, which is that of the will with respect to God, and in having a care to seek detachment and poverty of spirit and sense, which consists in desiring earnestly to be without any consoling support that can be apprehended, whether interior or exterior. This we practise well when we desire and strive to strip ourselves of these forms, since from this there will proceed no less a benefit than that of approach to God (Who has no image, neither form nor figure), and this will be the greater according as the soul withdraws itself the more completely from all forms, images and figures of the imagination.[4]

2. But perchance you will say: 'Why do many spiritual persons counsel the soul to strive to profit by the communications and feelings which come from God, and to desire to receive them from Him, that it may have something to give Him; since, if He gives us nothing, we shall give Him nothing likewise? And wherefore does Saint Paul say:

---

[1] So Alc., e.p. The other authorities have the first sentence of the title only.
[2] E.p. adds: 'but [needs] only to reject them in the sense already mentioned.'
[3] E.p. abbreviates: 'which would have been wasted upon this.'
[4] E.p. omits: 'of the imagination.'

" Quench not the spirit ?"[1] And the Spouse to the Bride: " Set Me as a seal[2] upon thy heart and as a seal upon thine arm ?"[3] This certainly denotes some kind of apprehension. And, according to the instruction given above, not only must all this not be striven after, but, even though God sends it, it must be rejected and cast aside. But surely it is clear that, since God gives it, He gives it to a good purpose, and it will have a good effect. We must not throw away pearls. And it is even a kind of pride to be unwilling to receive the things of God, as if we could do without them and were self-sufficient.'

3. In order to meet this objection it is necessary to recall what we said in the fifteenth and sixteenth chapters[4] of the second book, where to a great extent the difficulty is solved. For we said there that the good that overflows in the soul from supernatural apprehensions, when they come from a good source, is produced passively in the soul at that very instant[5] when they are represented to the senses, without the working of any operation of the faculties. Wherefore it is unnecessary for the will to perform the act of receiving them; for, as we have also said, if at that time the soul should try to labour with its faculties,[6] the effect of its own base and natural operation would be to hinder the super-natural graces[7] which God is even then working in it rather than that, through these apprehensions, God should cause it to derive any benefit from its active labour. Nay, rather, as the spirituality coming from those imaginary apprehensions is given passively to the soul, even so must the soul conduct itself passively with respect to them, setting no store by its inward or outward actions.[8] To do this is to preserve the feelings that have their source in God, for in this way they are not lost through the soul's base manner of working. And this is not quenching the spirit; for the spirit would be quenched by the soul if it desired to behave in any other manner than that whereby God is leading it. And this it would be doing if, when God had given it spiritual graces[9] passively, as He does in these apprehensions, it should then desire to exert itself actively with respect to them, by labouring[10] with its understanding[11] or by seeking to find something in

---

1 1 Thessalonians v, 19.   2 D, P: 'as a sign.'
3 Canticles viii, 6.   4 More correctly, in Chaps. xvi and xvii.
5 E.p. omits: 'at that very instant.'
6 A, B: 'labour with the favour of its faculties.' E.p.: 'labour according to the ability of its faculties.'
7 [Lit., 'the supernatural.']   8 E.p. adds: 'in the sense mentioned above.'
9 [Lit., 'had given it spirit' (or 'spirituality').]
10 E.p. inserts: 'of itself.'
11 E.p. ends the paragraph here, but the 1630 edition adds 'beyond what God gives it' and continues, with the variants noted below.]

them. And this is clear because, if the soul desires to labour at that time with its own exertions, its work cannot be more than natural, for of itself[1] it is capable of no more; for supernaturally[2] it neither moves itself nor can move itself—it is God that moves it and brings it to this state.[3] And thus, if the soul at that time desires to labour with its own exertions (as far as lies in its power), its active working will hinder the passive work[4] that God is communicating to it, which is spirit.[5] It will be setting itself to its own work, which is of another and an inferior kind than that which God communicates to it; for the work of God is passive and supernatural, and that of the soul is active and natural;[6] and in this way the soul would therefore be quenching the spirit.

4. That this activity of the soul is an inferior one is also clear from the fact that the faculties of the soul cannot, of their own power,[7] reflect and act, save upon some form, figure and image, and this is the rind and accident of the substance and spirit which lie beneath this rind and accident. This substance and spirit unite not with the faculties of the soul in true understanding and love, save when at last the operation of the faculties ceases. For the aim and end of this operation is only that the substance which can be understood and loved and which lies beneath these forms may come to be received in the soul. The difference, therefore, between active and passive operation, and the superiority of the latter, corresponds to the difference between that which is being done and that which is done already, or between that which a man tries to attain and effect and that which is already effected. Hence it may likewise be inferred that, if the soul should desire to employ its faculties actively on these supernatural apprehensions, wherein God, as we have said, bestows the spirit of them passively, it would be doing nothing less than abandoning what it had already done, in order to do it again, neither would it enjoy what it had done, nor could it produce any other result, by these actions of its own, save that of impeding what had been done already. For, as we say, the faculties cannot of their own power attain to the spirituality which God bestows upon the soul without any operation of their own. And thus the soul

---

[1] The 1630 edition adds: 'or, at most, if it be supernatural, it must be very much inferior to that which God would work in it, for of itself.'

[2] The 1630 edition has: 'for in this most sublime and supernatural way.'

[3] The 1630 edition adds: 'when it gives its consent.'

[4] The 1630 edition has: 'it will, with its working, hinder the work.'

[5] [Or 'spirituality.' Cf. p. 235, n. 9, above.]

[6] The 1630 edition omits: 'for the work . . . active and natural.'

[7] E.p.: 'cannot, according to their natural and ordinary method.'

would be directly quenching the spirituality[1] which God infuses through these imaginary apprehensions aforementioned if it were to set any store by them; wherefore it must set them aside, and take up a passive and negative attitude with regard to them.[2] For at that time God is moving the soul to things which are above its own power and knowledge. For this cause the Prophet said: 'I will stand upon my watch and set my step upon my tower, and I will watch to see that which will be said to me.'[3] This is as though he were to say: I will stand on guard over my faculties and I will take no step forward as to my actions, and thus I shall be able to contemplate that which will be said to me—that is, I shall understand and enjoy that which will be communicated to me supernaturally.

5. And the passage which has been quoted concerning the Spouse is to be understood as referring to the love that He entreats of[4] the Bride, the office of which love between two lovers is to make one like to the other[5] in the most vital part of them. Wherefore He tells her to set Him as a seal upon her heart,[6] where all the arrows strike that leave the quiver of love, which arrows are the actions and motives of love. So they will all strike Him Who is there as a mark[7] for them; and thus all will be for Him, so that the soul will become like Him through the actions and motions of love, until it be transformed in Him. Likewise he bids her set Him as a seal[8] upon her arm, because the arm performs[9] the exercise of love, for by the arm the Beloved is sustained and comforted.

6. Therefore all that the soul has to endeavour to do with respect to all the apprehensions which come to it from above, whether imaginary or of any other kind—it matters not if they be visions, locutions, feelings or revelations—is to make no account of the letter or the rind (that is, of what is signified or represented or given to be understood), but to pay heed only to the possession of the love of God which they cause interiorly within the soul. And in this case the soul will make account, not of feelings of sweetness or delight, nor of figures, but of the feelings of love which they cause it. And with this sole end in view it may at times recall that image and apprehension caused it by love, in order to set the spirit on its course of love. For, though the effect of that apprehension

---

1 [Or 'the spirit.' Cf. p. 235, n. 9, above.]
2 E.p. omits 'and negative' and adds 'as we say.'
3 Habacuc ii, 1. [The original has 'munition' for 'tower' and 'contemplate' for 'watch and see.']
4 A, B: 'that He has to.'
5 E.p. omits the rest of this sentence.
6 Canticles viii, 6. A, B: 'as a sign.'
7 A, e.p.: 'as a sign.'
8 E.p.: 'as a sign.'
9 [Lit., 'because in the arm is.']

be not so great afterwards, when it is recalled, as it was on the first occasion when it was communicated, yet, when it is recalled, love is renewed, and the mind is lifted up to God, especially when the recollection is of certain figures, images or feelings which are supernatural, and are wont to be sealed and imprinted upon the soul in such a way that they continue for a long time—some of them, indeed, never leave the soul. And those that are thus sealed upon the soul produce in it Divine effects of love, sweetness, light and so forth, on almost every occasion when the soul returns to them, sometimes more so and sometimes less; for it was to this end that they were impressed upon it. And thus this is a great favour for the soul on which God bestows it, for it is as though it had within itself a mine of blessings.

7. The figures which produce effects such as these are deeply implanted in the soul,[1] and are not like other images and forms that are retained in the fancy. And thus the soul has no need to have recourse to this faculty when it desires to recall them, for it sees that it has them within itself, and that they are as an image seen in the mirror. When it comes to pass that any soul has such figures formally within itself, it will then do well to recall them to the effect of love to which I have referred, for they will be no hindrance to the union of love in faith, since the soul will not desire to be absorbed in the figure, but only to profit by the love; it will immediately set aside the figure, which thus will rather be a help to it.

8. Only with great difficulty can it be known when these images are imprinted upon the soul, and when upon the fancy.[2] For those which touch the fancy are as apt to occur very frequently as are the others; for certain persons are accustomed habitually to have imaginary visions in their imagination and fancy, which are presented to them in one form with great frequency; sometimes because the apprehensive power of the organ concerned is very great, and, however little they reflect upon it, that habitual figure is at once presented to, and outlined upon, their fancy; sometimes because it is the work of the devil; sometimes, again, because it is the work of God; but the visions are not formally imprinted upon the soul. They may be known, however, by their effects. For those that are natural, or that come from the devil, produce no good effect upon the soul, however frequently they be recalled, nor work its spiritual renewal, but the contemplation of them simply

---

[1] E.p. adds: 'according to its intellectual memory.'
[2] E.p.: '. . . when these images touch the spiritual part of the soul directly and when they belong to the fancy.'

produces aridity. Those that are good, however, produce some good effect when they are recalled, like that[1] which was produced in the soul upon the first occasion. But the formal images which are imprinted upon the soul almost invariably produce some effect in it, whensoever they are remembered.

9. He that has experienced these will readily distinguish the one kind from the other, for the great difference[2] between them is very clear to anyone that has experience of them. I will merely say that those which are formally and durably imprinted upon the soul are of very rare occurrence. But, whether they be of this kind or of that, it is good for the soul to desire to understand nothing, save God alone, through faith, in hope. And if anyone makes the objection that to reject these things, if they are good, appears to be pride, I reply that it is not so, but that it is prudent humility to profit by them in the best way, as has been said, and to be guided by that which is safest.

CHAPTER XIV

Which treats of spiritual knowledge in so far as it may concern the memory.

WE classed spiritual forms of knowledge as the third division of the apprehensions of the memory, not because they belong to the bodily sense of the fancy, as do the others, for they have no bodily form and image,[3] but because they are likewise apprehensible by spiritual memory and reminiscence. Now, after the soul has had experience of one of these apprehensions, it can recall it whensoever it will; and this is not by the effigy[4] and image that the apprehension has left in the bodily sense, for, since this is of bodily form, as we say, it has no capacity for spiritual forms; but because it recalls it, intellectually and spiritually, by means of that form which it has left impressed upon the soul, which is likewise a formal or spiritual form or notion or image, whereby it is recalled, or by means of the effect that it has wrought. It is for this reason that I place these apprehensions among those of the memory, although they belong not to the apprehensions of the fancy.

[1] So e.p. The MSS. [and P. Silverio] read: 'in that.'
[2] E.p.: 'the aforementioned difference.'
[3] E.p. omits: 'for they have no bodily form and image.'
[4] E.p.: 'not by the figure.'

2. What these kinds of knowledge are, and how the soul is to conduct itself with respect to them in order to attain to union with God, are sufficiently described in the twenty-fourth chapter[1] of the second book, where we treated this knowledge as apprehensions of the understanding. Let this be referred to, for we there described how it was of two kinds: either uncreated[2] or of the creatures. I speak now only of things relating to my present purpose—namely, how the memory must behave with respect to them in order to attain to union. And I say, as I have just said of formal knowledge in the preceding chapter (for this, being of created things, is of the same kind), that these apprehensions may be recalled when they produce good effects, not that they may be dwelt upon, but that they may quicken the soul's love and knowledge of God. But, unless the recollection of them produces good effects, let the memory never give them even passing attention. With regard to uncreated knowledge,[3] I say that the soul should try to recall it as often as possible, for it will produce most beneficial effects. As we said above, it produces touches and impressions of union with God, which is the aim towards which we are directing the soul. And by no form, image or figure which can be impressed upon the soul does the memory recall these (for these touches and impressions of union with the Creator[4] have no form), but only by the effects which they have produced upon it of light, love, joy and spiritual renewal, and so forth, some of which are wrought anew in the soul whensoever they are remembered.

CHAPTER XV

Which sets down the general method whereby the spiritual person must govern himself with respect to this sense.

IN order to conclude this discussion on the memory, it will be well at this point to give the spiritual reader an account of[5] the method which he must observe, and which is of universal application, in order that he may be united with God according to this sense.[6] For, although what has been said makes the subject quite clear, it will nevertheless be more easily apprehended if we summarize it here. To this end

---

[1] Really the chapter is the twenty-sixth.   [2] E.p.: 'either of uncreated perfections.'
[3] E.p.: 'With regard to the knowledge of things uncreated.'
[4] A, B: 'with God.'   [5] Only Alc. and e.p. have: 'an account of.'
[6] E.p.: 'this faculty.'

it must be remembered that, since our aim is the union of the soul
with God in hope, according to the memory, and since that which is
hoped for is that which is not possessed, and since, the less we possess
of other things, the greater scope and the greater capacity have we for
hoping, and consequently the greater hope,[1] therefore, the more things
we possess, the less scope and capacity is there for hoping, and consequently the less hope[2] have we. Hence, the more the soul dispossesses
the memory of forms and things which may be recalled by it, which are
not God,[3] the more will it set its memory upon God, and the emptier
will its memory become, so that it may hope for Him Who shall fill it.
What must be done, then, that the soul may live in the perfect and pure
hope of God is that, whensoever these distinct images, forms and ideas
come to it, it must not rest in them, but must turn immediately to God,
voiding the memory of them entirely, with loving affection. It must
neither think of these things nor consider them beyond the degree
which is necessary for the understanding and performing of its obligations, if they have any concern with these. And this it must do without
setting any affection or inclination upon them, so that they may produce no effects[4] in the soul. And thus a man must not fail to think and
recall that which he ought to know and do, for, provided he preserves
no affection or attachments, this will do him no harm. For this matter
the lines of the Mount, which are in the thirteenth chapter[5] of the first
book, will be of profit.

2. But here it must be borne in mind that this doctrine of ours does
not agree, nor do we desire that it should agree, with the doctrine of
those pestilent men, who, inspired by Satanic pride and envy, have
desired to remove from the eyes of the faithful the holy and necessary
use, and the worthy[6] adoration, of images of God and of the saints.
This teaching of ours is very different from that; for we say not here,
as they do, that images should not exist, and should not be adored; we
simply explain the difference between images and God. We exhort men
to pass beyond that which is superficial[7] that they may not be hindered

---

[1] E p.: 'the greater perfection of hope.'

[2] E.p.: 'the less perfection of hope.'

[3] E.p.: 'which are not Divinity or God made human, the memory of Whom is
always a help to that end, since He is the true Way and Guide and Author of all good.'
With this addition, cf. that quoted on p. 218, n. 1, above.

[4] E.p.: 'no effects or perturbations.'

[5] So e.p. A, B have: 'in the first chapter,' referring apparently to the drawing
described above (p. xxxii). Alc., C, D [followed by P. Silverio] read: 'in the chapter.'

[6] [The Spanish word, ínclita, is stronger than this, meaning 'distinguished,'
'illustrious.']

[7] [Lit., 'which is painted.']

from attaining to the living truth beneath it, and to make no more account of the former than suffices for attainment to the spiritual. For means are good and necessary to an end; and images are means which serve to remind us of God and of the saints. But when we consider and attend to the means more than is necessary for treating them as such, they disturb and hinder us as much, in their own way, as any different thing;[1] the more so, when we treat of supernatural visions and images,[2] to which I am specially referring, and with respect to which arise many deceptions and perils. For, with respect to the remembrance and adoration and esteem of images, which the Catholic Church sets before us,[3] there can be no deception or peril, because naught is esteemed therein other than that which is represented;[4] nor does the remembrance of them fail to profit the soul, since they are not preserved in the memory save with love for that which they represent; and, provided the soul pays no more heed to them than is necessary for this purpose,[5] they will ever assist it to union with God, allowing the soul to soar upwards (when God grants it that favour) from the superficial image[6] to the living God, forgetting every creature and everything that belongs to creatures.[7]

CHAPTER XVI

Which begins to treat of the dark night of the will. Makes a division between the affections of the will.[8]

W E should have accomplished nothing by the purgation of the understanding in order to ground it in the virtue of faith, and by the purgation of the memory[9] in order to ground it in hope, if we purged not the will also according to the third virtue, which is charity,[10] whereby the works that are done in faith live and have great

1 E.p. adds: 'disturbs and hinders us.'
2 E.p.: 'of images and visions that are interior and are formed in the soul.'
3 B: 'sets corporeally before us' [P. Silverio, in a note, prefers this reading]. A, Alc.: 'sets naturally before us.' E.p.: 'which our mother the Church sets before us.'
4 E.p. omits: 'because naught . . . represented.'
5 E.p.: 'and, provided the soul uses them for this purpose.'
6 [*Lit.*, 'the painted image.']
7 A, B have here: 'End of the third book,' the chapters which follow being placed in the fourth book.
8 A, B omit this second sentence.
9 E.p. adds: 'in the sense referred to in the sixth chapter of the second book.'
10 E.p.: 'if we purged not the will also with respect to charity.'

merit, and without it are of no worth. For, as Saint James says: 'Without works of charity, faith is dead.'[1] And, now that we have to treat of the active detachment and night of this faculty, in order to form it and make it perfect in this virtue of the charity of God, I find no more fitting authority than that which is written in the sixth chapter of Deuteronomy, where Moses says: 'Thou shalt love the Lord thy God with thy whole heart and with thy whole soul and with thy whole strength.'[2] Herein is contained all that the spiritual man ought to do, and all that I have here to teach him, so that he may truly attain to God, through union of the will, by means of charity. For herein man is commanded to employ all the faculties and desires and operations and affections of his soul in God, so that all the ability and strength of his soul may serve for no more than this, according to that which David says, in these words: *Fortitudinem meam ad te custodiam.*[3]

2. The strength of the soul consists in its faculties, passions and desires, all of which are governed by the will. Now when these faculties, passions and desires are directed by the will toward God, and turned away from all that is not God, then the strength of the soul is kept for God, and thus the soul is able to love God with all its strength. And, to the end that the soul may do this, we shall here treat of the purgation from the will of all its unruly affections, whence arise unruly operations, affections and desires,[4] and whence also arises its failure to keep all its strength for God. These affections and passions are four, namely: joy, hope, grief and fear. These passions, when they are controlled by reason according to the way of God, so that the soul rejoices only in that which is purely the honour and glory of God, and hopes for naught else, neither grieves save for things that concern this, neither fears aught save God alone, it is clear that the strength and ability of the soul are being directed toward God and kept for Him. For, the more the soul rejoices in any other thing than God, the less completely will it centre its rejoicing in God;[5] and the more it hopes in aught else, the less will it hope in God; and so with the other passions.

3. And in order to give fuller instructions concerning this, we shall treat, in turn and in detail, as is our custom, of each of these four passions and of the desires of the will. For the whole business of attaining to union with God consists in purging the will from its affections

---

[1] St. James ii, 20.   [2] Deuteronomy vi, 5.
[3] Psalm lviii, 10 [A.V., lix, 9].
[4] E.p. omits: 'whence arise . . . and desires.'
[5] [*Lit.*, 'the less strongly will its rejoicing be employed in God.']

and desires; so that thus it may no longer be a base, human will, but may become a Divine will, being made one[1] with the will of God.

4. These four passions have the greater dominion in the soul, and assail it the more vehemently, when the will is less strongly attached to God and more dependent on the creatures. For then it rejoices very readily at things that merit not rejoicing, hopes in that which brings no profit, grieves over that in which perchance it ought to rejoice, and fears where there is no reason for fearing.

5. From these affections, when they are unbridled, arise in the soul all the vices and imperfections which it possesses, and likewise, when they are ordered and composed, all its virtues. And it must be known that, if one of them should become ordered and controlled by reason, the rest will become so likewise; for these four passions of the soul are so closely and intimately united to one another that the actual direction of one is the virtual direction of the others; and if one be actually recollected the other three will virtually and proportionately be recollected likewise. For, if the will rejoice in anything, it will as a result hope for the same thing to the extent of its rejoicing, and herein are virtually included grief and fear with regard to the same thing; and, in proportion as desire for these is taken away, fear and grief concerning them are likewise gradually lost, and hope for them is removed.[2] For the will, with these four passions, is denoted by that figure which was seen by Ezechiel, of four beasts with one body, which had four faces; and the wings of the one were joined to those of the other, and each one went straight before his face, and when they went forward they turned not back.[3] And thus in the same manner the wings of each one of these affections are joined to those of each of the others, so that, in whichever direction one of them turns—that is, in its operation— the others of necessity go with it virtually also; and, when one of them descends, as is there said, they must all descend, and, when one is lifted up, they will all be lifted up. Where thy hope is, thither will go thy joy and fear and grief; and, if thy hope returns, the others will return, and so of the rest.

. 6. Wherefore thou must take note[4] that, wheresoever one of these passions is, thither will go likewise the whole soul and the will and the other faculties, and they will all live as captives to this passion, and the

---

[1] [The original is stronger: 'one same thing.']
[2] E.p. adds: 'after the manner (though it is not this that is there meant) of those four beasts that were seen by Ezechiel.'
[3] Ezechiel i, 5-9.
[4] A, B, e.p. add: 'O spiritual man.'

other three passions[1] will be living in it also, to afflict the soul with their captivity,[2] and not to allow it to fly upward to the liberty and rest of sweet contemplation and union. For this cause Boetius told thee that, if thou shouldst desire to understand truth with clear light, thou must cast from thee joys, hope, fear and grief.[3] For, as long as these passions reign, they allow not the soul to remain in the tranquillity and peace which are necessary for the wisdom which, by natural or supernatural means, it is capable of receiving.

CHAPTER XVII

Which begins to treat of the first affections of the will. Describes the nature of joy and makes a distinction between the things in which the will can rejoice.

THE first of the passions of the soul and affections of the will is joy, which, in so far as concerns that[4] which we propose to say about it, is naught else than a satisfaction of the will together with esteem for something which it considers desirable; for the will never rejoices save when an object affords it appreciation and satisfaction. This has reference to active joy, which arises when the soul clearly and distinctly understands the reason for its rejoicing, and when it is in its own power to rejoice or not. There is another and a passive joy, a condition in which the will may find itself rejoicing without understanding clearly and distinctly the reason for its rejoicing, and which also occurs at times when it does understand this; but it is not in the soul's power[5] to rejoice or not. Of this condition we shall speak hereafter. For the present we shall speak of joy when it is active and voluntary and arises from things that are distinct and clear.

2. Joy may arise from six kinds of good things or blessings,[6] namely: temporal, natural, sensual, moral, supernatural and spiritual. Of these we shall speak in their order, controlling the will with regard to them so that it may not be encumbered by them and fail to place the strength of its joy in God. To this end it is well to presuppose one

---

1 A: 'and the other three faculties, or rather passions.'
2 E.p. omits: 'with their captivity.'
3 Cf. p. 158, above.   4 E.p.: 'which, with regard to that.'
5 E.p. adds: 'at that time.'
6 [*Lit.*, 'things or blessings.' The word here translated 'blessings' is *bienes*, often rendered 'goods.' I use 'blessings' or 'good things' in the following chapters, according as best suits the context.]

fundamental truth, which will be as a staff whereon we should ever lean as we progress; and it will be well to have understood it, because it is the light whereby we should be guided and whereby we may understand this doctrine, and direct our rejoicing in all these blessings to God. This truth is that the will must never rejoice save only in that which is to the honour and glory of God; and that the greatest honour we can show to Him is that of serving Him according to evangelical perfection; and anything that has naught to do with this is of no value and profit to man.

CHAPTER XVIII

Which treats of joy with respect to temporal blessings. Describes how joy in them must be directed to God.

THE first kind of blessing of which we have spoken is temporal. And by temporal blessings we here understand riches, rank, office and other things that men desire; and children, relatives, marriages, etc.: all of which are things wherein the will may rejoice. But it is clear how vain a thing it is for men to rejoice in riches, titles, rank, office and other such things which they are wont to desire; for, if a man were the better servant of God for being rich, he ought to rejoice in riches; but in fact they are rather a cause[1] for his giving offence to God, even as the Wise Man teaches, saying: 'Son, if thou be rich, thou shalt not be free from sin.'[2] Although it is true that temporal blessings do not necessarily of themselves cause sin, yet, through the frailty of its affections, the heart of man habitually clings to them and fails God (which is a sin, for to fail God is sin[3]); it is for this cause that the Wise Man says: 'Thou shalt not be free from sin.' For this reason the Lord[4] described riches, in the Gospel, as thorns,[5] in order to show that he who touches them[6] with the will shall be wounded by some sin. And that exclamation which He makes in the Gospel,[7] saying: 'How hardly shall they that have riches enter the Kingdom of the heavens'—that is to say, they that have joy in riches—clearly shows that man must not rejoice in riches, since he exposes himself thereby

---

[1] E.p.: 'but rather they may be a cause.' [2] Ecclesiasticus xi, 10.
[3] E.p. omits: 'for to fail God is sin.'
[4] E.p.: 'For this reason Jesus Christ our Lord.'
[5] St. Matthew xiii, 22; St. Luke viii, 14. [6] [*Lit.*, 'handles them.']
[7] So Alc. A, B: 'which He makes in Saint Luke, and which is so much to be feared.' E.p.: 'which He makes in Saint Matthew, and which is so much to be feared.'

to such great peril.[1] And David, in order to withdraw us from this peril, said likewise: 'If riches abound, set not your heart on them.'[2] And I will not here quote further testimony on so clear a matter.

2. For in that case I should never cease quoting Scripture, nor should I cease[3] describing the evils which Solomon imputes to riches in Ecclesiastes. Solomon was a man who had possessed great riches, and, knowing well what they were, said: 'All things that are under the sun are vanity of vanities, vexation of spirit and vain solicitude of the mind.'[4] And he that loves riches, he said, shall reap no fruit from them.[5] And he adds that riches are kept to the hurt of their owner,[6] as we see in the Gospel, where it was said from Heaven to the man that rejoiced because he had kept[7] many fruits for many years: 'Fool, this night shall thy soul be required of thee to give account thereof, and whose shall be that which thou hast provided?'[8] And finally, David teaches us the same, saying: 'Let us have no envy when our neighbour becomes rich, for it will profit him nothing in the life to come;'[9] meaning thereby that we might rather have pity on him.

3. It follows, then, that a man must neither rejoice in riches when he has them, nor when his brother has them,[10] unless they help them to serve God. For if ever it is allowable to rejoice in them,[11] it will be when they are spent and employed in the service of God, for otherwise no profit will be derived from them. And the same is to be understood of other blessings (titles, offices, etc.), in all of which it is vain to rejoice if a man feel not that God is the better served because of them and the way to eternal life is made more secure. And as it cannot be clearly known if this is so (if God is better served, etc.), it would be a vain thing to rejoice in these things deliberately, since such a joy[12] cannot be reasonable. For, as the Lord says: 'If a man gain all the world, he may yet lose his soul.'[13] There is naught, then, wherein to rejoice save in the fact that God is better served.

4. Neither is there cause for rejoicing in children because they are many, or rich, or endowed with natural graces and talents and the good things of fortune, but only if they serve God. For Absalom, the

---

[1] St. Matthew xix, 23; St. Luke xviii, 24.   [2] Psalm lxi, 11 [A.V., lxii, 10].
[3] E.p. omits: 'quoting Scripture, nor should I cease.'
[4] Ecclesiastes i, 14.   [5] Ecclesiastes v, 9.   [6] Ecclesiastes v, 12.
[7] [guardados.] Alc., erroneously, has: 'he had gained' [ganados].
[8] St. Luke xii, 20.   [9] Psalm xlviii, 17–18 [A.V., xlix, 16–17].
[10] E.p.: '. . . rejoice because he has riches, nor because his brother has them.'
[11] A, Alc. [and P. Silverio] add: 'as one will rejoice in riches.'
[12] E.p.: 'such a joy in them.'
[13] St. Matthew xvi, 26. E.p. has: 'If a man gain all the world, it profits him little, if he suffers detriment in his soul.'

son of David, found neither his beauty nor his riches nor his lineage of any service to him because he served not God.[1] Hence it was a vain thing to have rejoiced in such a son. For this reason it is also a vain thing for men to desire to have children, as do some who trouble and disturb everyone with their desire for them, since they know not if such children will be good and serve God. Nor do they know if their satisfaction in them will be turned into pain; nor if the comfort and consolation which they should have from them will change to disquiet and trial; and the honour which they should bring them, into dishonour; nor if they will cause them to give greater offence to God, as happens to many. Of these Christ says that they go round about the sea and the land to enrich them and to make them doubly the children of perdition which they are themselves.[2]

5. Wherefore, though all things smile upon a man and all that he does turns out prosperously,[3] he ought to have misgivings rather than to rejoice; for these things increase the occasion and peril of his forgetting God.[4] For this cause Solomon says, in Ecclesiastes, that he was cautious: 'Laughter I counted error and to rejoicing I said, "Why art thou vainly deceived?"'[5] Which is as though he had said: When things smiled upon me I counted it error and deception to rejoice in them; for without doubt it is great error and folly on the part of a man if he rejoice when things are bright and pleasant for him, knowing not of a certainty that there will come to him thence some eternal good. The heart of the fool, says the Wise Man, is where there is mirth, but that of the wise man is where there is sorrow.[6] For mirth[7] blinds the heart and allows it not to consider things and ponder them; but sadness makes a man open his eyes and look at the profit and the harm of them. And hence it is that, as he himself says, anger is better than laughter.[8] Wherefore it is better to go to the house of mourning than to the house of feasting; for in the former is figured the end of all men,[9] as the Wise Man says likewise.

6. It would therefore be vanity for a woman or her husband to rejoice in their marriage when they know not clearly that they are serving God better thereby. They ought rather to feel confounded, since matrimony is a cause, as Saint Paul says, whereby each one sets

---

[1] 2 Kings [A.V., 2 Samuel] xiv, 25.   [2] St. Matthew xxiii, 15.
[3] E.p. adds: 'and, as they say, [good things] fall into his mouth.'
[4] A, B, e.p. add: 'and of offending Him, as we have said.'
[5] Ecclesiastes ii, 2.   [6] Ecclesiastes vii, 5.
[7] E.p.: 'For vain mirth.'   [8] Ecclesiastes vii, 4.
[9] Ecclesiastes vii, 3.

his heart upon the other and keeps it not wholly with God. Wherefore he says: 'If thou shouldst find thyself free from a wife, desire not
to seek a wife; while he that has one already should walk with such
freedom of heart as though he had her not.'[1] This, together with what
we have said concerning temporal blessings, he teaches us himself, in
these words: 'This is certain; as I say to you, brethren, the time is
short; it remaineth that they also who have wives be as if they had
none; and they that weep, as them that weep not; and they that rejoice,
as them that rejoice not; and they that buy, as them that possess not;
and they that use this world, as them that use it not.'[2] All this he says to
show us that we must not set our rejoicing[3] upon any other thing than
that which tends to the service of God, since the rest is vanity and a
thing which profits not; for joy that is not according to God can bring
the soul no profit.[4]

CHAPTER XIX

Of the evils that may befall the soul when it sets its rejoicing upon temporal
blessings.

IF we had to describe the evils which encompass the soul when it
sets the affections of its will upon temporal blessings, neither ink
nor paper would suffice us and our time would be too short. For
from very small beginnings a man may attain to great evils and destroy
great blessings; even as from a spark of fire, if it be not quenched, may
be enkindled great fires which set the world ablaze. All these evils have
their root and origin in one important evil of a privative kind that is
contained in this joy—namely, withdrawal from God. For even as, in
the soul that is united with Him by the affection of its will, there are
born all blessings, even so, when it withdraws itself from Him because
of this creature affection, there beset it all evils and disasters proportionately to the joy and affection wherewith it is united with the
creature; for this is inherent in[5] withdrawal from God. Wherefore a

---

[1] 1 Corinthians vii, 27.   [2] 1 Corinthians vii, 29–30.
[3] [The original reads: 'to show us that to set,' etc., leaving the sentence grammatically
incomplete. P. Gerardo omits 'since the rest' and reads: 'to show us that to set . . .
service of God is vanity,' etc.] Alc. omits all the paragraph down to this point, reading:
'And thus we must not set our rejoicing . . .'
[4] [*Lit.*, 'bring it no profit.'] A, B: '. . . to God cannot please the soul.' E.p.: '. . . to
God cannot do the soul good.'
[5] [*Lit.*, 'for this is.']

soul may expect the evils which assail it to be greater or less according to the greater or lesser degree of its withdrawal from God. These evils may be extensive or intensive; for the most part they are both together.

2. This privative evil, whence, we say, arise other privative and positive evils, has four degrees, each one worse than the other. And, when the soul compasses the fourth degree, it will have compassed all the evils and depravities that arise in this connection.[1] These four degrees are well indicated by Moses in Deuteronomy in these words, where he says: 'The beloved grew fat and kicked. He grew fat and became swollen and gross.[2] He forsook God his Maker and departed from God his Salvation.'[3]

3. This growing fat of the soul, which was loved before it grew fat,[4] indicates absorption in this joy of creatures. And hence arises the first degree of this evil, namely the going backward; which is a certain blunting of the mind with regard to God, an obscuring of the blessings of God like the obscuring of the air by mist, so that it cannot be clearly illumined by the light of the sun. For, precisely when the spiritual person sets his rejoicing upon anything, and gives rein to his desire for foolish things, he becomes blind as to God, and the simple intelligence of his judgment becomes clouded, even as the Divine Spirit teaches in the Book of Wisdom, saying: 'The use and association of vanity[5] and scorn obscureth good things, and inconstancy of desire overturneth and perverteth the sense and judgment that are without malice.'[6] Here the Holy Spirit shows that, although there be no malice[7] conceived in the understanding of the soul, concupiscence and rejoicing in creatures suffice of themselves to create in the soul the first degree of this evil, which is the blunting of the mind and the darkening of the judgment, by which the truth is understood and each thing honestly judged as it is.

4. Holiness and good judgment suffice not to save a man from falling into this evil, if he gives way to concupiscence or rejoicing in temporal things. For this reason God warned us by uttering these words through Moses: 'Thou shalt take no gifts, which blind even the prudent.'[8] And this was addressed particularly to those who were to be

---

[1] [Lit., 'that can be told in this case.']
[2] E.p.: 'The beloved became fat and returned; he became swollen and gross.'
[3] Deuteronomy xxxii, 15.
[4] E.p.: 'This becoming fat of the soul, which previously was loved . . .'
[5] E.p.: 'The false appearance of vanity.'   [6] Wisdom iv, 12.
[7] E.p.: 'no precedent malice.'   [8] Exodus xxiii, 8.

judges; for these have need to keep their judgment clear and alert, which they will be unable to do if they covet and rejoice in gifts. And for this cause likewise God commanded Moses to appoint judges from those who abhorred avarice, so that their judgment should not be blunted with the lust of the passions.[1] And thus he says not only that they should not desire it, but that they should abhor it. For, if a man is to be perfectly defended from the affection of love, he must preserve an abhorrence of it, defending himself by means of the one thing against its contrary. The reason why the prophet Samuel, for example, was always so upright and enlightened a judge is that (as he said in the Book of the Kings) he had never received a gift from any man.[2]

5. The second degree of this privative evil arises from the first, which is indicated in the words following the passage already quoted, namely: 'He grew fat and became swollen and gross.'[3] And thus this second degree is dilation of the will through the acquisition of greater liberty in temporal things; which consists in no longer attaching so much importance to them, nor troubling oneself about them, nor esteeming so highly the joy and pleasure that come from created blessings. And this will have arisen in the soul from its having in the first place given rein to rejoicing; for, through giving way to it, the soul has become swollen with it, as is said in that passage, and that fatness of rejoicing and desire has caused it to dilate and extend its will more freely toward the creatures. And this brings with it great evils. For this second degree causes the soul to withdraw itself from the things of God, and from holy practices, and to take no pleasure in them, because it takes pleasure in other things and devotes itself continually to many imperfections and follies[4] and to joys and vain pleasures.

6. And when this second degree is consummated, it withdraws a man wholly from the practices which he followed continually and makes his whole mind and covetousness to be given to secular things. And those who are affected by this second degree not only have their judgment and understanding darkened so that they cannot recognize truth and justice, like those who are in the first degree, but they are also very weak and lukewarm and careless[5] in acquiring knowledge of, and in practising, truth and justice, even as Isaias says of them in these words: 'They all love gifts and allow themselves to be carried away by

---

[1] Exodus xviii, 21–2.   [2] 1 Kings [A.V., 1 Samuel] xii, 3.
[3] Deuteronomy xxxii, 15. E.p. omits: 'grew fat and.'
[4] E.p.: 'and many follies.'   [5] E.p. omits: 'and careless.'

rewards, and they judge not the orphan, neither doth the cause of the widow come unto them that they may give heed to it.'[1] This comes not to pass in them without sin, especially when to do these things is incumbent upon them because of their office. For those who are affected by this degree are not free from malice as are those of the first degree. And thus they withdraw themselves more and more from justice and virtues, since their will reaches out more and more[2] in affection for creatures. Wherefore, the characteristics of those who are in this second degree are great lukewarmness in spiritual things and failure to do their duty by them; they practise them from formality or from compulsion or from the habit which they have formed of practising them, rather than because they love them.

7. The third degree of this privative evil is a complete falling away from God, neglect to fulfil His law in order not to lose worldly things and blessings,[3] and relapse into mortal sin through covetousness. And this third degree is described in the words following the passage quoted above, which says: 'He forsook God his Maker.'[4] In this degree are included all who have the faculties of the soul absorbed in things of the world and in riches and commerce,[5] in such a way that they care nothing for fulfilling the obligations of the law of God. And they are very forgetful and dull with respect to that which touches their salvation, and have a correspondingly greater ardour and shrewdness with respect to things of the world. So much so that in the Gospel Christ calls them children of this world, and says of them that they are more prudent and acute in their affairs than are the children of light in their own.[6] And thus they are as nothing in God's business, whereas in the world's business they are everything. And these are the truly avaricious, who have extended and dispersed their desire and joy on things created, and this with such affection that they cannot be satisfied; on the contrary, their desire and their thirst grow all the more because they are farther withdrawn from the only source that could satisfy them, which is God. For it is of these that God Himself speaks through Jeremias, saying: 'They have forsaken Me, Who am the fountain of living water, and they have digged to themselves broken cisterns that can hold no water.'[7] And this is the reason why the covetous man finds

---

[1] Isaiah i, 23.
[2] A, e.p.: '. . . their will becomes more and more enkindled . . .' [The change is a slight one: *encendiendo* for *extendiendo*.]
[3] E.p.: 'not to lose the trifling things of the world.'
[4] Deuteronomy xxxii, 15.   [5] E.p.: 'commerce with it.'
[6] St. Luke xvi, 8.   [7] Jeremias ii, 13.

naught among the creatures wherewith he can quench his thirst, but only that which increases it. These persons are they that fall into countless kinds of sin through love of temporal blessings and the evils which afflict them are innumerable. And of these David says: *Transierunt in affectum cordis*.[1]

8. The fourth degree of this privative evil is indicated in the last words of our passage, which says: 'And he departed from God his Salvation.'[2] To this degree come those of the third degree whereof we have just spoken. For, through his not giving heed to setting his heart upon the law of God because of temporal blessings, the soul of the covetous man departs far from God according to his memory, understanding and will, forgetting Him as though He were not his God, which comes to pass because he has made for himself a god of money and of temporal blessings,[3] as Saint Paul says when he describes avarice as slavery to idols.[4] For this fourth degree leads a man as far as to forget God, and to set his heart, which he should have set formally upon God, formally upon money, as though he had no god beside.

9. To this fourth degree belong those who hesitate not to subject Divine and supernatural things to temporal things, as to their God, when they ought to do the contrary, and subject temporal things to God, if they considered Him as their God, as would be in accordance with reason.[5] To these belonged the iniquitous[6] Balaam, who sold the grace that God had given to him.[7] And also Simon Magus, who thought to value the grace of God in terms of money, and desired to buy it.[8] In doing this he showed a greater esteem for money; and he thought there were those who similarly esteemed it, and would give grace for money. There are many nowadays who in many other ways belong to this fourth degree; their reason is darkened to spiritual things by covetousness; they serve money and not God, and are influenced by money and not by God, putting first the cost of a thing and not its Divine worth and reward, and in many ways making money their principal god and end, and setting it before the final end, which is God.

10. To this last degree belong also those miserable souls who are so

---

1 ['They have passed into the affection of the heart.'] Psalm lxxii, 7 [A.V. lxxiii, 7]. Only e.p. has this quotation in its Spanish form. Alc. adds the word *exponat*.
2 Deuteronomy xxxii, 15.
3 A, e.p.: '. . . he has made money and temporal blessings a god for himself.'
4 Colossians iii, 5.
5 E.p. omits: 'if they considered Him as their God.'
6 E.p.: 'the impious.'   7 Numbers xxii, 7.   8 Acts viii, 18–19.

greatly in love with their own goods that they take them for their god, so much so that they scruple not to sacrifice their lives for them, when they see that this god of theirs is suffering some temporal harm. They abandon themselves to despair and take their own lives for their miserable ends, showing by their own acts how wretched is the reward which such a god as theirs bestows. For when they can no longer hope for aught from him he gives them despair[1] and death; and those whom he pursues not to this last evil of death he condemns to a dying life[2] in the griefs of anxiety and in many other miseries, allowing no mirth to enter their heart, and naught that is of earth to bring them satisfaction. They continually pay the tribute of their heart to money by their yearning for it and hoarding of it for the final calamity of their just perdition, as the Wise Man warns them, saying: 'Riches are kept to the hurt of their owner.'[3]

11. And to this fourth degree belong those of whom Saint Paul says: *Tradidit illos in reprobum sensum.*[4] For joy, when it strives after possessions as its final goal, drags man down to these evils. But those on whom it inflicts lesser evils are also to be sorely pitied, since, as we have said, their souls are driven far backward upon the way[5] of God. Wherefore, as David says: Be not thou afraid when a man shall be made rich: that is, envy him not, thinking that he outstrips thee, for, when he dieth, he shall carry nothing away, neither shall his glory nor his joy descend with him.[6]

CHAPTER XX

Of the benefits that come to the soul from its withdrawal of joy from temporal things.

THE spiritual man, then, must look carefully to it that his heart and his rejoicing begin not to lay hold upon temporal things; he must fear lest from being little it should grow to be great, and should increase from one degree to another. For little things, in time, become great; and from a small beginning there comes in the

---

1 The remainder of this chapter is omitted in Alc.
2 So e.p. [*lit.*, 'to live dying']. A: 'to live living'; B: 'to die living.'
3 Ecclesiastes v, 11–12.
4 ['He delivered them up to a reprobate sense.'] Romans i, 28.
5 E.p.: 'upon the road.'
6 Psalm xlviii, 17–18 [A.V., xlix, 16–17].

end a great matter,[1] even as a spark suffices to set a mountain on fire
and to burn up the whole world.[2] And let him never be self-confident
because his attachment is small, and fail to uproot it instantly because
he thinks that he will do so later. For if, when it is so small and in its
beginnings, he has not the courage to make an end of it, how does he
suppose, and presume, that he will be able to do so when it is great and
more deeply rooted. The more so since Our Lord said in the Gospel:
'He that is unfaithful in little will be unfaithful also in much.'[3] For he
that avoids the small sin will not fall into the great sin; but great evil
is inherent in the small sin,[4] since it has already penetrated within the
fence and wall of the heart; and as the proverb says: Once begun, half
done. Wherefore David warns us, saying: 'Though riches abound, let
us not apply our heart to them.'[5]

2. Although a man might not do this for the sake of God and of the
obligations of Christian perfection, he should nevertheless do it
because of the temporal advantages that result from it, to say nothing
of the spiritual advantages, and he should free his heart completely
from all rejoicing in the things mentioned above. And thus, not only
will he free himself from the pestilent evils which we have described in
the last chapter, but, in addition to this, he will withdraw his joy from
temporal blessings and acquire the virtue of liberality, which is one of
the principal attributes of God,[6] and can in no wise coexist with
covetousness. Apart from this, he will acquire liberty of soul, clarity
of reason, rest, tranquillity and peaceful confidence in God and a true
reverence and worship of God which comes from the will.[7] He will
find greater joy and recreation in the creatures through his detachment from them, for he cannot rejoice in them if he look upon them
with attachment to them as to his own. Attachment is an anxiety that,
like a bond, ties the spirit down to the earth and allows it no enlarge-
ment of heart. He will also acquire, in his detachment from things, a
clear conception of them, so that he can well understand the truths

---

[1] Thus the Codices. E.p. alters this to 'a great evil.' [P. Silverio supports the emendation.]

[2] E.p. omits: 'and to burn up the whole world.' [The word rendered 'mountain'
may also mean 'wood.' Cf. St. James iii, 5, Vulgate.]

[3] St. Luke xvi, 10.

[4] [The word 'sin' is not in the original of this sentence, which reads 'the small . . .
the great . . .' etc.]

[5] Psalm lxi, 11 [A.V., lxii, 10. Cf. p. 247, n. 2, above]. E.p.: 'let us not attach our heart
to them.'

[6] So Alc., e.p.   A, B: 'one of the principal virtues of God, or, rather, attributes.'

[7] A, B: 'which comes from liberty.' [The word translated 'reverence' normally
implies respectful acquiescence.]

relating to them, both naturally and supernaturally. He will therefore enjoy them very differently from one who is attached to them, and he will have a great advantage and superiority over such a one. For, while he enjoys them according to their truth, the other enjoys them according to their falseness;[1] the one appreciates the best side of them and the other the worst; the one rejoices in their substance; the other, whose sense is bound to them, in their accident. For sense cannot grasp or attain to more than the accident, but the spirit, purged of the clouds and species of accident, penetrates the truth and worth of things, for this is its object. Wherefore joy, like a cloud, darkens the judgment, since there can be no voluntary joy in creatures without voluntary attachment, even as there can be no joy which is passion when there is no habitual attachment in the heart;[2] and the renunciation and purgation of such joy leave the judgment clear, even as the mists leave the air clear when they are scattered.

3. This man, then, rejoices in all things—since his joy is dependent upon none of them—as if he had them all; and this other, through looking upon them with a particular sense of ownership, loses in a general sense all the pleasure of them all. This former man, having none of them in his heart, possesses them all, as Saint Paul says, in great freedom.[3] This latter man, inasmuch as he has something of them through the attachment of his will, neither has nor possesses anything; it is rather they that have possessed[4] his heart, and he is, as it were, a sorrowing captive. Wherefore, if he desire to have a certain degree of joy in creatures, he must of necessity have an equal degree of disquietude and grief in his heart, since it is seized and possessed by them. But he that is detached is untroubled by anxieties, either in prayer or apart from it; and thus, without losing time, he readily gains great spiritual treasure. But the other man loses everything, running to and fro upon the chain by which his heart is attached and bound; and with all his diligence he can still hardly free himself for a short time from this bond of thought and rejoicing by which his heart is bound. The spiritual man, then, must restrain the first motion of his heart towards creatures, remembering the premiss which we have here laid down, that there is naught wherein a man must rejoice, save in his service of God, and in his striving for His glory and honour in all things, directing all things solely to this end and turning aside from

---

[1] Alc. omits the rest of this sentence and the whole of the next.
[2] E.p. [for 'when . . . heart'] reads: 'without voluntary attachment.'
[3] 2 Corinthians vi, 10.   [4] A, B: 'they that have seized.'

vanity in them, looking in them neither for his own joy nor for his consolation.

4. There is another very great and important benefit in this detachment of the rejoicing from creatures—namely, that it leaves the heart free for God. This is the dispositive foundation of all the favours which God will grant to the soul, and without this disposition He grants them not. And they are such that, even from the temporal standpoint, for one joy which the soul renounces for love of Him and for the perfection of the Gospel, He will give him a hundred in this life, as His Majesty promises in the same Gospel.[1] But, even were there not so high a rate of interest, the spiritual man should quench these creature joys in his soul because of the displeasure which they give to God. For we see in the Gospel that, simply because that rich man rejoiced at having goods laid up for many years, God was so greatly angered that He told him that his soul would be brought to account on that same night.[2] Therefore, we must believe[3] that, whensoever we rejoice vainly, God is beholding us and preparing some punishment and bitter draught according to our deserts, so that the pain which results from the joy may sometimes be a hundred times greater[4] than the joy. For, although it is true, as Saint John says on this matter, in the Apocalpyse, concerning Babylon, that as much as she had rejoiced and lived in delights, so much torment and sorrow should be given her,[5] yet this is not to say that the pain will not be greater than the joy, which indeed it will be, since for brief pleasures are given eternal torments. The words mean that there shall be nothing without its particular punishment, for He Who will punish the idle word will not pardon vain rejoicing.

CHAPTER XXI

Which describes how it is vanity to set the rejoicing of the will upon the good things of nature, and how the soul must direct itself, by means of them, to God.

BY natural blessings we here understand beauty, grace, comeliness, bodily constitution and all other bodily endowments; and likewise, in the soul, good understanding, discretion and other things that pertain to reason. Many a man sets his rejoicing upon all

---

[1] St. Matthew xix, 29.   [2] St. Luke xii, 20.
[3] E.p.: 'Therefore, we may fear.'   [4] E.p.: '. . . may often be greater.'
[5] Apocalypse xviii, 7.

these gifts, to the end that he himself, or those that belong to him, may possess them, and for no other reason, and gives no thanks to God Who bestows them on him so that He may be the better known and loved by him because of them. But to rejoice for this cause alone is vanity and deception, as Solomon says in these words: 'Deceitful is grace and vain is beauty; the woman who fears God, she shall be praised.'[1] Here he teaches us that a man ought rather to be fearful because of these natural gifts, since he may easily be distracted[2] by them from the love of God, and, if he be attracted by them, he may fall into vanity and be deceived. For this reason bodily grace is said to be deceptive because it deceives a man in the way[3] and attracts him to that which beseems him not, through vain joy and complacency, either in himself or in others that have such grace. And it is said that beauty is vain because it causes a man to fall in many ways when he esteems it and rejoices in it, for he should rejoice only if he serves God or others through it. But he ought rather to fear and harbour misgivings lest perchance his natural graces and gifts should be a cause of his offending God, either by his vain presumption or by the extreme affection[4] with which he regards them. Wherefore he that has such gifts should be cautious and live carefully, lest, by his vain ostentation, he give cause to any man to withdraw his heart in the smallest degree from God. For these graces and gifts of nature are so full of provocation and occasion of evil, both to him that possesses them and to him that looks upon them, that there is hardly any who entirely escapes from binding and entangling his heart in them. We have heard that many spiritual persons, who had certain of these gifts, had such fear of this that they prayed God to disfigure them, lest they should be a cause and occasion of any vain joy or affection to themselves or to others, and God granted their prayer.

2. The spiritual man, then, must purge his will, and make it to be blind to this vain rejoicing, bearing in mind that beauty and all other natural gifts are but earth, and that they come from the earth and will return thither; and that grace and beauty are the smoke and vapour belonging to this same earth; and that they must be held and esteemed as such by any man who desires not to fall into vanity, but will direct his heart to God in these matters, with rejoicing and gladness, because God is in Himself all these beauties and graces in the most eminent degree, and is infinitely high above all created things. And, as David says, they are all like a garment and shall grow old and pass away, and

---

[1] Proverbs xxxi, 30.   [2] A, B: 'be kept back.'
[3] A, B: 'in the road.'   [4] A, B, e.p.: 'the strange affection.'

He alone remains immutable for ever.[1] Wherefore, if in all these matters a man direct not his rejoicing to God, it will ever be false and deceptive. For of such a man is that saying of Solomon to be understood, where he addresses joy in the creatures, saying: 'To joy I said: "Why art thou vainly deceived?"'[2] That is, when the heart allows itself to be attracted by the creatures.

CHAPTER XXII

Of the evils which come to the soul when it sets the rejoicing of its will upon the good things of nature.

ALTHOUGH many of these evils and benefits that I am describing in treating of these kinds of joy are common to all, yet, because they follow directly from joy and detachment from joy (although comprised under any one of these six divisions which I am treating), therefore I speak under each heading of some evils and benefits which are also found under another, since these, as I say, are connected with that joy which belongs to them all. But my principal intent is to speak of the particular evils and benefits which come to the soul, with respect to each thing, through its rejoicing or not rejoicing in it. These I call particular evils, because they are primarily and immediately caused by one particular kind of rejoicing, and are not, save in a secondary and mediate sense, caused by another. The evil of spiritual lukewarmness, for example, is caused directly by any and every kind of joy, and this evil is therefore common to all these six kinds; but fornication is a particular evil, which is the direct result only of joy in the good things of nature of which we are speaking.

2. The spiritual and bodily evils, then, which directly and effectively come to the soul when it sets its rejoicing on the good things of nature are reduced to six principal evils. The first is vainglory, presumption, pride and disesteem of our neighbour; for a man cannot cast[3] eyes of esteem on one thing without taking them from the rest. From this follows, at the least, a real disesteem[4] for everything else; for naturally, by setting our esteem on one thing, we withdraw our heart from all things else and set it upon the thing esteemed; and from this real contempt it is very easy to fall into an intentional and voluntary contempt

[1] Psalm ci, 27 [A.V., cii, 26–7].   [2] Ecclesiastes ii, 2.
[3] E.p.: 'cannot excessively cast.'
[4] E.p.: 'a real and, as it were, negative disesteem.'

for all these other things, in particular or in general, not only in the heart, but also in speech, when we say that such a thing or[1] such a person is not like such another. The second evil is the moving of the senses to complacency and sensual delight and lust.[2] The third evil comes from falling into adulation and vain praise, wherein is deception and vanity, as Isaias says in these words: 'My people, he that praises thee deceives thee.'[3] And the reason is that, although we sometimes speak the truth when we praise grace and beauty, yet it will be a marvel if there is not some evil enwrapped therein or if the person praised is not plunged into vain complacency and rejoicing, or his imperfect intentions and affections are not directed thereto. The fourth evil is of a general kind: it is a serious[4] blunting of the reason and the spiritual sense, such as is effected by rejoicing in temporal good things. In one way, indeed, it is much worse. For as the good things of nature are more closely connected with man than are temporal good things, the joy which they give leaves an impression and effect and trace upon the senses more readily and more effectively, and deadens them more completely. And thus reason and judgment are not free, but are clouded with that affection of joy which is very closely connected with them; and from this arises the fifth evil, which is distraction of the mind by created things. And hence arise and follow lukewarmness and weakness of spirit, which is the sixth evil, and is likewise of a general kind; this is apt to reach such a pitch that a man may find the things of God very tedious and troublesome, and at last even come to abhor them. In this rejoicing purity of spirit is invariably lost—at least, in its essence. For, if any spirituality is discerned, it will be of such a gross and sensual kind as to be hardly spiritual or interior or recollected at all, since it will consist rather in pleasure of sense than in strength of spirit. Since, then, the spirituality of the soul is of so low and weak a character at that time as not to quench the habit of this rejoicing (for this habit alone suffices to destroy pure spirituality, even when the soul is not consenting to the acts of rejoicing), the soul must be living, so to say, in the weakness of sense rather than in the strength of the spirit. Otherwise,[5] it will be seen in the perfection and fortitude which the soul will have when the occasion demands it. Although I do not deny that many virtues may exist together with serious imperfections, no pure or delectable inward spirituality can exist while these joys are

---

[1] E.p. omits: 'such a thing or.'
[3] Isaias iii, 12.
[5] E.p. omits: 'otherwise.'
[2] E.p. omits: 'and lust.'
[4] [*Lit.*, 'the great.']

not quenched; for the flesh reigns[1] within, warring against the spirit, and, although the spirit may be unconscious of the evil, yet at the least it causes it secret distraction.

3. Returning now to speak of that second evil, which contains within itself innumerable other evils, it is impossible to describe with the pen or to express in words the lengths to which it can go, but this is not unknown or secret,[2] nor is the extent of the misery that arises from the setting of our rejoicing on natural beauty and graces. For every day we hear of its causing numerous deaths, the loss by many of their honour, the commission of many insults, the dissipation of much wealth, numerous cases of emulation and strife, of adultery, rape and fornication,[3] and of the fall[4] of many holy men, comparable in number to that third part of the stars of Heaven which was swept down by the tail of the serpent on earth.[5] The fine gold has lost its brilliance and lustre and is become mire; and the notable and noble men of Sion, who were clothed in finest gold, are counted as earthen pitchers that are broken and have become potsherds.[6] How far does the poison of this evil not penetrate?

4. And who drinks not, either little or much, from this golden chalice of the Babylonian woman of the Apocalypse?[7] She seats herself on that great beast, that had seven heads and ten crowns, signifying that there is scarce any man, whether high or low, saint or sinner, who comes not to drink of her wine, to some extent enslaving his heart thereby, for, as is said of her in that place, all the kings of the earth have become drunken with the wine of her prostitution. And she seizes upon all estates of men, even upon the highest and noblest estate— the service of the sanctuary and the Divine priesthood—setting her abominable cup, as Daniel says, in the holy place,[8] and leaving scarcely a single strong man without making him to drink, either little or much, from the wine of this chalice, which is vain rejoicing. For this reason it is said that all the kings of the earth have become drunken with this wine, for very few will be found, however holy they may have been, that have not been to some extent stupefied and bewildered by this draught of the joy and pleasure of natural graces and beauty.

---

[1] E.p.: 'the flesh almost reigns here.'   [2] E.p. omits: 'but . . . secret.'
[3] E.p.: 'of adultery and rape.'
[4] The Codices [followed by P. Silverio] have 'of the fall to the ground' which e.p. abbreviates [as in the text].
[5] Apocalypse xii, 4.   [6] Lamentations iv, 1–2.
[7] Apocalypse xvii, 3–4. Here eleven pages are missing from Alc., which P. Andrés de la Encarnación supplies, taking them from the old MS. which in his time was preserved at Duruelo.   [8] Daniel ix, 27.

5. This phrase 'have become drunken' should be noted. For, how-ever little a man may drink of the wine of this rejoicing, it at once takes hold upon the heart, and stupefies it and works the evil of darkening the reason, as does wine to those who have been corrupted by it. So that, if some antidote be not at once taken against this poison, whereby it may be quickly expelled, the life of the soul is endangered. Its spiritual weakness will increase, bringing it to such a pass that it will be like Samson, when his eyes[1] were put out and the hair of his first strength was cut off, and like Samson it will see itself grinding in the mills, a captive among its enemies;[2] and afterwards, peradventure, it will die the second death among its enemies, even as did he,[3] since the drinking of this rejoicing will produce in them spiritually all those evils that were produced in him physically, and does in fact produce them in many persons to this day. Let his enemies come and say to him after-wards, to his great confusion: Art thou he that broke the knotted cords,[4] that tore asunder the lions, slew the thousand Philistines, broke down the gates and freed himself from all his enemies?

6. Let us conclude, then, by giving the instruction necessary to counteract this poison. And let it be this: As soon as thy heart feels moved by this vain joy in the good things of nature, let it remember how vain a thing it is to rejoice in aught save the service of God, how perilous and how pernicious. Let it consider how great an evil it was for the angels to rejoice and take pleasure in their natural endowments and beauty, since it was this that plunged them into the depths of shame.[5] Let them think, too, how many evils come to men daily through this same vanity, and let them therefore resolve in good time to employ the remedy which the poet commends to those who begin to grow affectioned to such things. 'Make haste now,' he says, 'and use the remedy at the beginning; for when evil things have had time to grow in the heart, remedy and medicine come late.'[6] Look not upon the wine, as the Wise Man says, when its colour is red and when it shines in the glass; it enters pleasantly and bites like a viper and sheds abroad poison like a basilisk.[7]

[1] The Codices have: 'when the eyes of his sight . . .' This reading [adopted by P. Silverio] is shortened by e.p., as being pleonastic, to 'when his eyes . . .'
[2] Judges xvi.
[3] The 1630 edition reads: 'even as he died the first [death].'
[4] E.p.: 'the three knotted cords.'
[5] [*Lit.*, 'since it was through this they fell into the vile abysses.']
[6] So Alc. The other authorities have only: 'medicine comes late.'
[7] Proverbs xxiii, 31-2. Only Alc. and e.p. have: 'and sheds abroad poison [really 'poisons'] like a basilisk.' A, B have 'its poison' and use the word *basilisco*, where Alc., e.p. have *régulo*, with the same meaning.

CHAPTER XXIII

Of the benefits which the soul receives from not setting its rejoicing upon the good things of nature.

MANY are the benefits which come to the soul through the withdrawal of its heart from this rejoicing; for, besides preparing itself for the love of God and the other virtues, it makes a direct way for its own humility, and for a general charity toward its neighbours. For, as it is not led by the apparent[1] good things of nature, which are deceitful, into affection for anyone, the soul remains free and able[2] to love them all rationally and spiritually, as God wills them to be loved. Here it must be understood that none deserves to be loved, save for the virtue that is in him. And, when we love in this way, it is very pleasing to the will of God, and also brings great freedom; and if there be attachment in it, there is greater attachment to God. For, in that case, the more this love grows, the more grows our love toward God; and, the more grows our love toward God, the greater becomes our love for our neighbour. For, when love is grounded in God, the reason for all love is one and the same and the cause of all love is one and the same also.

2. Another excellent benefit comes to the soul from its renunciation of this kind of rejoicing,[3] which is that it fulfils and keeps[4] the counsel of Our Saviour which He gives us through Saint Matthew. 'Let him that will follow Me', He says, 'deny himself.'[5] This the soul could in no wise do if it were to set its rejoicing upon the good things[6] of nature; for he that makes any account of himself neither denies himself nor follows Christ.

3. There is another great benefit in the renunciation of this kind of rejoicing, which is that it produces great tranquillity in the soul, empties it of distractions and brings recollection to the senses, especially to the eyes. For the soul that desires not to rejoice in these things desires neither to look at them nor to attach the other senses to them, lest it should be attracted or entangled by them.[7] Nor will it spend time or thought upon them, being like the prudent serpent, which stops its

---

[1] E.p. omits 'apparent.'   [2] [*Lit.*, 'free and clear.']
[3] 'From . . . rejoicing' are words found in Alc. only.
[4] E.p. adds: 'with perfection.'
[5] St. Matthew xvi, 24.   [6] A, B, e.p. read: 'the gifts.'
[7] E.p. omits: 'or entangled by them.'

ears that it may not hear the charmers[1] lest they make some impression upon it.[2] For, by guarding its doors, which are the senses, the soul guards itself safely and increases its tranquillity and purity.

4. There is another benefit of no less importance to those that have become proficient in the mortification of this kind of rejoicing, which is that evil things and the knowledge of them neither make an impression upon them nor stain them as they do those to whom they still give any delight. Wherefore the renunciation and mortification of this rejoicing result in spiritual cleanness of soul and body; that is, of spirit and sense; and the soul comes to have an angelical conformity with God, and becomes, both in spirit and in body, a worthy temple of the Holy Spirit. This cannot come to pass if the heart rejoices in natural graces and good things.[3] For this reason it is not necessary to have given consent to any evil thing, or to have remembrance of such;[4] for that rejoicing suffices to stain the soul and the senses with impurity by means of the knowledge of evil;[5] for, as the Wise Man says, the Holy Spirit will remove Himself from thoughts that are without understanding—that is, without the higher reason that has respect to God.[6]

5. Another benefit of a general kind follows, which is that, besides freeing ourselves from the evils and dangers aforementioned, we are delivered also from countless vanities, and from many other evils, both spiritual and temporal; and especially from falling into the small esteem in which are held all those that are seen to glory or rejoice in the said natural gifts, whether in their own or in those of others. And thus these souls are held and esteemed as wise and prudent, as indeed are all those who take no account of these things, but only of that which pleases God.

6. From these said benefits follows the last, which is a generosity of the soul, as necessary to the service of God as is liberty of spirit, whereby temptations are easily vanquished and trials faithfully endured, and whereby, too, the virtues[7] grow and become prosperous.

---

[1] So Alc. A, B: 'incantations.' E.p.: 'charms.'

[2] Psalm ivii, 5 [A.V., lviii, 4–5].

[3] E.p.: 'if the heart allows itself to be to any extent carried away by rejoicing in natural graces and good things.'

[4] E.p. omits: 'or to have remembrance of such.'

[5] E.p. concludes this paragraph here, but the 1630 edition continues, as do the Codices, which we here follow.

[6] Wisdom i, 5. [7] A, B: 'the virtues of the soul.'

CHAPTER XXIV

Which treats of the third kind of good thing whereon the will may set the
affection of rejoicing, which kind pertains to sense. Indicates what these
good things are and of how many kinds, and how the will has to be
directed to God and purged of this rejoicing.

WE have next to treat of rejoicing with respect to the good
things of sense, which is the third kind of good thing
wherein we said that the will may rejoice. And it is to be
noted that by the good things of sense we here understand everything
in this life that can be apprehended by the senses of sight, hearing,
smell, taste or touch, and by the interior fashioning of imaginary
reflections, all of which things belong to the bodily senses, interior and
exterior.

2. And, in order to darken the will and purge it of rejoicing with
respect to these sensible objects, and direct it to God by means of them,
it is necessary to assume one truth, which is that, as we have frequently
said, the sense of the lower part of man, which is that whereof we are
treating, is not, neither can be, capable of knowing or understanding
God as God is. So that the eye cannot see Him, or aught that is like
Him; neither can the ear hear His voice, or any sound that resembles
it; neither can the sense of smell perceive a perfume so sweet as He;
neither can the taste detect a savour so sublime and delectable; neither
can the touch feel a movement so delicate and full of delight, nor
aught like to it; neither can His form or any figure that represents Him
enter into the thought or imagination. Even as says Isaias: 'Eye hath
not seen Him, nor hath ear heard Him, neither hath it entered into the
heart of man.'[1]

3. And here it must be noted that the senses may receive pleasure
and delight, either from the spirit, by means of some communication
that it receives from God interiorly, or from outward things communicated to them. And, as has been said, neither by way of the spirit
nor by that of sense can the sensual part of the soul know God. For,
since it has no capacity for attaining to such a point, it receives in the
senses both that which is of the spirit and that which is of sense,[2] and
receives them in no other way. Wherefore it would be at the least but

---

[1] Isaias lxiv, 4; 1 Corinthians ii, 9.
[2] E.p. reads: 'and that which is of the intellect.'

vanity to set the rejoicing of the will upon pleasure caused by any of these apprehensions, and it would be hindering the power of the will from occupying itself with God and from setting its rejoicing upon Him alone. This the soul cannot perfectly accomplish, save by purging itself and remaining in darkness as to rejoicing of this kind, as also with respect to other things.

4. I said advisedly that if the rejoicing of the will were to rest in any of these things it would be vanity. But, when it does not rest upon them, but, as soon as the will finds pleasure in that which it hears, sees and does, soars upward to rejoice in God—so that its pleasure acts as a motive and strengthens it to that end—this is very good. In such a case not only need the said motions not be shunned when they cause this devotion and prayer, but the soul may profit by them, and indeed should so profit, to the end that it may accomplish this holy exercise. For there are souls who are greatly moved by objects of sense to seek God. But much circumspection must be observed herein and the resulting effects must be considered; for oftentimes many spiritual persons indulge in the recreations of sense aforementioned under the pretext of offering prayer and devotion to God; and they do this in a way which must be described as recreation rather than prayer, and which gives more pleasure to themselves than to God. And, although[1] the intention that they have is toward God, the effect which they produce[2] is that of recreation of sense, wherein they find weakness and imperfection, rather than revival of the will and surrender thereof to God.

5. I wish, therefore, to propose a test whereby it may be seen when these delights of the senses aforementioned are profitable and when they are not. And it is that, whensoever a person hears music and other things, and sees pleasant things,[3] and is conscious of sweet perfumes, or tastes things that are delicious, or feels soft touches, if his thought and the affection of his will are at once centred upon God and if that thought of God gives him more pleasure than the movement of sense which causes it, and save for that he finds no pleasure in the said movement, this is a sign that he is receiving benefit therefrom, and that this thing of sense is a help to his spirit. In this way such things may be used, for then such things of sense subserve the end for which God created and gave them, which is that He should be the better loved and known because of them. And it must be known, furthermore, that one upon whom these things of sense cause the pure spiritual effect which

---

[1] E.p.: 'although it seems that.'   [2] E.p.: 'which they cause.'
[3] A, e.p.: 'hears music or other pleasant things.'

I describe has no desire for them, and makes hardly any account of them, though they cause him great pleasure when they are offered to him, because of the pleasure which, as I have said, they cause him in God. He is not, however, solicitous for them, and when they are offered to him, as I say, his will passes from them at once and he abandons it to God and sets it upon Him.

6. The reason why he cares little for these motives, although they help him on his journey to God, is that the spirit which is ready to go by every means and in every way to God is so completely nourished and prepared and satisfied by the Spirit of God that it lacks nothing and desires nothing; or, if it desires anything to that end, the desire at once passes and is forgotten, and the soul makes no account of it. But one that feels not this liberty of spirit in these things and pleasures of sense, but whose will rests in these pleasures and feeds upon them, is greatly harmed by them and should withdraw himself from the use of them. For, although his reason may desire to employ them to journey to God, yet, inasmuch as his desire finds pleasure in them which is according to sense, and their effect is ever dependent upon the pleasure which they give, he is certain to find hindrance in them rather than help, and harm rather than profit. And, when he sees that the desire[1] for such recreation reigns in him, he must mortify it; for, the stronger it becomes, the more imperfection he will have and the greater will be his weakness.

7. So whatever pleasure coming from sense presents itself to the spiritual person, and whether it come to him by chance or by design, he must make use of it only for God, lifting up to Him the rejoicing of his soul so that his rejoicing may be useful and profitable[2] and perfect; realizing that all rejoicing which implies not renunciation[3] and annihilation of every other kind of rejoicing, although it be with respect to something apparently very lofty, is vain and profits not, but is a hindrance towards the union of the will in God.

---

[1] E.p.: 'that the spirit.'   [2] Alc. alone has: 'and profitable.'
[3] [*Lit.*, 'that is not in renunciation . . .']

CHAPTER XXV

Which treats of the evils that afflict the soul when it desires to set the rejoicing of its will upon the good things of sense.

IN the first place, if the soul does not darken and quench the joy which may arise within it from the things of sense, and direct its rejoicing to God, all the general kinds of evil which we have described as arising from every other kind of rejoicing follow from this joy in the things of sense: such evils are darkness in the reason, lukewarmness, spiritual weariness, etc. But, to come to details, many are the evils, spiritual, bodily and sensual, into which the soul may fall through this rejoicing.

2. First of all, from joy in visible things, when the soul denies not itself therein in order to reach God, there may come to it, directly, vanity of spirit and distraction of the mind, unruly covetousness, immodesty, outward and inward unseemliness, impurity of thought, and envy.

3. From joy in hearing useless things there may directly arise distraction of the imagination, gossiping, envy, rash judgments and vacillating thoughts; and from these arise many other and pernicious evils.

4. From joy in sweet perfumes, there arise loathing of the poor, which is contrary to the teaching of Christ, dislike of serving others, unruliness of heart in humble things, and spiritual insensibility, at least to a degree proportionate with its desire for this joy.

5. From joy in the savour of meat and drink, there arise directly such gluttony and drunkenness, wrath, discord and want of charity with one's neighbours and with the poor, as had that Epulon,[1] who fared sumptuously every day, with Lazarus.[2] Hence arise bodily disorders, infirmities and evil motions, because the incentives to luxury become greater. Directly, too, there arises great spiritual torpor, and the desire for spiritual things is corrupted, so that the soul can derive no enjoyment or satisfaction from them nor can even speak of them. From this joy is likewise born distraction of the other senses and of the heart, and discontent with respect to many things.

6. From joy in the touch of soft things arise many more evils and more pernicious ones, which more quickly cause sense to overflow

---

[1] E.p.: 'as had that rich eater.'　　　　[2] St. Luke xvi, 19.

into spirit,[1] and quench all spiritual strength and vigour. Hence arises the abominable vice of effeminacy, or the incentives thereto, according to the proportion of joy of this kind which is experienced. Hence luxury increases, the mind becomes effeminate and timid, and the senses grow soft and delicate and are predisposed to sin and evil. Vain gladness and joy are infused into the heart; the tongue takes to itself licence and the eyes roam unrestrainedly; and the remaining senses are blunted and deadened, according to the measure[2] of this desire. The judgment is put to confusion, being nourished by spiritual folly and insipidity; moral cowardice and inconstancy increase; and, by the darkness of the soul and the weakness of the heart, fear is begotten even where no fear is. At times, again, this joy begets a spirit of confusion, and insensibility with respect to conscience and spirit; wherefore the reason is greatly enfeebled, and is affected in such a way that it can neither take nor give good counsel, and remains incapable of moral and spiritual blessings and becomes as useless as a broken vessel.

7. All these evils are caused by this kind of rejoicing—in some more intensely,[3] according to the intensity of their rejoicing, and also according to the complacency or weakness or variableness of the person who yields to it. For there are natures that will receive more detriment from a slight occasion of sin than will others from a great one.

8. Finally, from joy of this kind in touch, a person may fall into as many evils and perils as those which we have described as concerning the good things of nature; and, since these have already been described, I do not detail them here; neither do I describe many other evils wrought thus, such as a falling-off in spiritual exercises and bodily penance and lukewarmness and lack of devotion in the use of the sacraments of penance and of the Eucharist.

[1] E.p.: 'which more quickly hurt the spirit.'
[2] [Lit., 'to the quantity.'] E.p.: 'to the degree.'
[3] E.p.: 'in some more, in others less, more or less intensely . . .'

CHAPTER XXVI

Of the benefits that come to the soul from self-denial in rejoicing as to things of sense, which benefits are spiritual and temporal.

MARVELLOUS are the benefits that the soul derives from self-denial in this rejoicing: some of these are spiritual and some temporal.

2. The first is that the soul, by restraining its rejoicing as to things of sense, is restored from the distraction into which it has fallen through excessive use of the senses, and is recollected in God. The spirituality and the virtues that it has acquired are preserved; nay, they are increased and increase continually.[1]

3. The second spiritual benefit which comes from self-denial in rejoicing as to things of sense is exceeding great. We may say with truth that that which was sensual becomes spiritual, and that which was animal becomes rational; and even that the soul is journeying from a human life to a portion which is angelical; and that, instead of being temporal and human, it becomes celestial and divine. For, even as a man who seeks the pleasure of things of sense and sets his rejoicing upon them neither merits nor deserves any other name than those which we have given him—that is, sensual, animal, temporal, etc.—even so, when he exalts his rejoicing above these things of sense, he merits all those other names—to wit, spiritual, celestial, etc.

4. And it is clear that this is true; for, although the use of the senses and the power of sensuality are contrary, as the Apostle says, to the power and the exercises of spirituality,[2] it follows that, when the one kind of power is diminished and brought to an end, the other contrary kinds, the growth of which was hindered by the first kinds, are increased. And thus, when the spirit is perfected (which is the higher part of the soul and the part that has relations with God and receives His communications), it merits all these attributes aforementioned, since it is perfected in the heavenly and spiritual gifts and blessings of God. Both these things are proved by Saint Paul, who calls the sensual man (namely, the man that directs the exercise of his will solely to sense) the animal man, who perceives not[3] the things of God. But this

---

[1] [*Lit.,* 'and gain continually.'] So Alc. A, B add 'anew.' E.p. omits: 'and increase continually.'

[2] Galatians v, 17.   [3] A, B: 'who is he that perceives not . . .'

other man, who lifts up his will to God, he calls the spiritual man,
saying that this man penetrates and judges all things, even the deep
things of God.[1] Therefore the soul gains herein the marvellous[2]
benefit of a disposition well able to receive the blessings and spiritual
gifts of God.

5. The third benefit is that the pleasures and the rejoicing of the
will in temporal matters are very greatly increased; for, as the Saviour
says, they shall receive an hundredfold in this life.[3] So that, if thou
deniest thyself one joy, the Lord will give thee an hundredfold in this
life, both spiritually and temporally; and likewise, for one joy that
thou hast in these things of sense, thou shalt have an hundredfold of
affliction and misery. For, through the eye that is purged from the joys
of sight, there comes to the soul a spiritual joy, directed to God in all
things that are seen, whether Divine or profane.[4] Through the ear that
is purged from the joy of hearing, there comes to the soul joy most
spiritual an hundredfold, directed to God in all that it hears, whether
Divine or profane.[5] Even so is it with the other senses when they are
purged. For, even as in the state of innocence all that our first parents
saw and said and ate in Paradise furnished them with greater sweetness
of contemplation, so that the sensual part of their nature might be duly
subjected to, and ordered by, reason; even so the man whose senses are
purged from all things of sense and made subject to the spirit receives,
in their very first motion, the delight of delectable knowledge and
contemplation of God.

6. Wherefore, to him that is pure, all things, whether high or low,
are an occasion of greater good and further purity; even as the man
that is impure is apt to derive evil from things both high and low,
because of his impurity. But he that conquers not the joy of desire will
not enjoy the serenity of habitual rejoicing in God through His
creatures and works. In the man that lives no more according to sense,
all the operations of the senses and faculties are directed to Divine
contemplation. For, as it is true in good philosophy that each thing
operates according to its being, and to the life that it lives, so it is
clear, beyond contradiction, that if the soul lives a spiritual life, the
animal life[6] being mortified, it must be journeying straight to God,

---

[1] 1 Corinthians ii, 9, 10, 14.
[2] Here P. Juan Evangelista's copy recommences (cf. p. 261, n. 7, above).
[3] St. Matthew xix, 29.   [4] E.p.: 'or human.'
[5] E.p.: 'or human.'
[6] E.p.: '. . . that according to the being which everything has is the life that it lives,
therefore, in a soul [*lit.*, 'in him'] that has a spiritual being, the animal life . . .'

since all its spiritual actions and motions pertain to the life of the spirit. Hence it follows that such a man, being pure in heart, finds in all things a knowledge of God which is joyful and pleasant, chaste, pure, spiritual, glad and loving.

7. From what has been said I deduce the following doctrine— namely that, until a man has succeeded in so habituating his senses to the purgation of the joys of sense that from their first motion[1] he is gaining the benefit aforementioned of directing all his powers to God, he must needs deny himself joy and pleasure with respect to these powers, so that he may withdraw his soul from the life of sense. He must fear that since he is not yet spiritual, he may perchance derive from the practice of these things a pleasure and an energy which is of sense rather than of spirit; that the energy which is of sense may predominate in all his actions; and that this may lead to an increase of sensuality and may sustain and nurture it. For, as Our Saviour says, that which is born of the flesh is flesh, and that which is born of the Spirit is spirit.[2] Let this be closely considered, for it is the truth. And let not him that has not yet mortified his pleasure in things of sense dare to make great use of the power and operation of sense with respect to them, thinking that they will help him to become more spiritual; for the powers of the soul will increase the more without the intervention of these things of sense—that is, if it quench the joy and desire for them rather than indulge its pleasure in them.

8. There is no need to speak of the blessings of glory that, in the life to come, result from the renunciation of these joys. For, apart from the fact that the bodily gifts of the life of glory, such as agility and clarity, will be much more excellent than in those souls who have not denied themselves, there will be an increase in the essential glory of the soul corresponding to its love of God, for Whose sake it has renounced the things of sense aforementioned. For every momentary, fleeting joy that has been renounced, as Saint Paul says, there shall be laid up an exceeding weight of glory eternally.[3] And I will not here recount the other benefits, whether moral, temporal or spiritual, which result from this night of rejoicing; for they all are those that have already been described, and to a more eminent degree; since these joys that are renounced are more closely linked to the natural man, and therefore he that renounces them acquires thereby a more intimate purity.

[1] E.p. omits: 'from their first motion.'
[2] St. John iii, 6.
[3] 2 Corinthians iv, 17.

CHAPTER XXVII

Which begins to treat of the fourth kind of good—namely, the moral.
Describes wherein this consists, and in what manner joy of the will therein
is lawful.

THE fourth kind of good wherein the will may rejoice is moral.
By this we here understand the virtues, and the habits of the
virtues, in so far as these are moral, and the practice of any
virtue, and the practice of works of mercy, the keeping of the law of
God, and of that of the commonweal,[1] and the putting into practice
of all good intentions and inclinations.

2. These kinds of moral good, when they are possessed and practised, deserve perhaps more than any of the other kinds aforementioned
that the will should rejoice in them. For a man may rejoice in his own
affairs for one of two reasons, or for both reasons together—namely,
for that which they are in themselves, or for the good which they
imply and bring with them as a means and instrument. We shall find
that the possession of the three kinds of good already mentioned merits
no rejoicing of the will. For of themselves, as has been said, they do
no good to man, nor in themselves have they any good, since they are
so fleeting and frail; rather, as we have likewise said, they cause and
bring him trouble and grief and affliction of spirit. Now, although they
might merit that man should rejoice in them for the second reason—
which is that he may profit by them for journeying to God—this is so
uncertain that, as we commonly see, they more often harm man than
bring him profit. But good things of a moral kind merit a certain
degree of rejoicing in him that possesses them, and this for the first
reason—namely, for their intrinsic nature and worth. For they bring
with them peace and tranquillity, and a right and ordered use of the
reason and actions that are consistent therewith, so that a man cannot,
humanly speaking, have anything better in this life.

3. Thus, since these virtues deserve to be loved and esteemed,
humanly speaking, for their own sakes, a man may well rejoice in the
possession of them, and may practise them for that which they are in
themselves, and for the blessing which they bring to man in human

---

[1] [*Lit.*, *política*, the 'political' virtue of Aristotle and St. Thomas—i.e., the 'social,'
as opposed to the 'moral,' 'intellectual' and 'theological' virtues. P. Silverio glosses the
word as meaning 'good government in the commonweal, courtesy and other social
virtues.'] A, B read *plática* ['conversation'], thereby entirely altering the sense.

and temporal form. In this way and for this reason[1] philosophers and wise men and princes of old esteemed and praised them, and endeavoured to possess and practise them; and, although they were heathen, and regarded them only in a temporal manner, merely considering the blessings which they knew would result from them—temporal, corporeal and natural—they not only obtained by means of them the temporal renown and benefits which they sought, but, apart from this, God, Who loves all that is good (even in barbarians and heathen) and, as the Wise Man says, hinders the doing of naught that is good,[2] gave them longer life, greater honour, dominion and peace (as He did for example to the Romans), because they made just laws; for He subjected nearly the whole world to them, and gave rewards of a temporal kind for their good customs to those who because of their unbelief were incapable of eternal reward. For God loves moral good so much that, merely because Solomon asked wisdom of Him that he might teach his people, govern them justly and bring them up in good customs, God Himself was greatly pleased with him, and told him that, because he had asked for wisdom to that end, this should be given him, and there should also be given him that which he had not asked, namely, riches and honour, so that no king, either in the past or in the future, should be like him.[3]

4. But, although the Christian should rejoice in this first way in the moral good that he possesses and in the good works of a temporal kind which he does, since they lead to the temporal blessings which we have described, he must not allow his joy to stop at this first stage (as we have said the heathen did, because their spiritual sight extended not beyond the things of this mortal life); but, since he has the light of faith, wherein he hopes for eternal life, without which nothing that belongs to this life and the next will be of any value to him, he must rejoice principally and solely in the possession and employment of this moral good after the second manner—namely, in that by doing these works for the love of God he will gain eternal life. And thus he should set his eyes and his rejoicing solely on serving and honouring God with his good customs and virtues. For without this intention the virtues are of no worth in the sight of God, as is seen in the ten virgins of the Gospel, who had all kept their virginity and done good works; and yet, because the joy of five of them was not of the second kind (that is, because they had not directed their joy to God), but was rather

---

[1] E.p. omits: 'and for this reason.'
[2] Wisdom vii, 22.   [3] 3 Kings [A.V., 1 Kings] iii, 11–13.

after the first and vain kind, for they rejoiced[1] in the possession of their
good works, they were cast out[2] from Heaven with no acknowledge-
ment or reward from the Bridegroom. And likewise many persons of
old had many virtues[3] and practised good works, and many Christians
have them[4] nowadays and accomplish great acts, which will profit
them nothing for eternal life, because they have not sought in them the
glory and honour which belong to God alone.[5] The Christian, then,
must rejoice, not in the performing of good works and the following
of good customs, but in doing them for the love of God alone, without respect to aught else soever. For, inasmuch as good works that
are done to serve God alone will have the greater reward in glory, the
greater will be the confusion in the presence of God of those who have
done them for other reasons.

5. The Christian, then, if he will direct his rejoicing to God with
regard to moral good, must realize that the value of his good works,
fasts, alms, penances, etc., is based, not upon the number or the quality
of them, but upon the love of God which inspires him to do them; and
that they are the more excellent when they are performed with a
purer and sincerer love of God, and when there is less in them of self-
interest, joy, pleasure, consolation and praise, whether with reference
to this world or to the next. Wherefore the heart must not be set upon
pleasure, consolation and delight, and the other interests which good
works and practices commonly bring with them, but it must concentrate its rejoicing upon God. It must desire to serve Him in its
good works, and purge itself from this other rejoicing, remaining in
darkness with respect to it and desiring that God alone shall have joy
in its good works and shall take secret pleasure therein, without any
other intention and delight than those relating to the honour and glory
of God. And thus, with respect to this moral good, the soul will concentrate all the strength of its will upon God.

[1] A, B, e.p. add: 'and boasted.'   [2] E.p.: 'were dismissed.'
[3] E.p.: 'certain virtues.'
[4] E.p.: 'have and practise them.'
[5] E.p. adds: 'and His love above all things.'

CHAPTER XXVIII

Of seven evils into which a man may fall if he set the rejoicing of his will upon moral good.

THE principal evils into which a man may fall through vain rejoicing in his good works and habits I find to be seven; and they are very hurtful because they are spiritual.[1]

2. The first evil is vanity, pride, vainglory and presumption; for a man cannot rejoice in his works without esteeming them. And hence arise boasting and like things, as is said of the Pharisee in the Gospel, who prayed and congratulated himself before God,[2] boasting that he fasted and did other good works.

3. The second evil is usually linked with this: it is our judging others, by comparison with ourselves, as wicked and imperfect, when it seems to us that their acts and good works are inferior to our own; we esteem them the less highly in our hearts, and at times also in our speech. This evil was likewise that of the Pharisee, for in his prayer he said: 'I thank Thee that[3] I am not as other men are: robbers, unjust and adulterers.'[4] So that by one single act he fell into these two evils, esteeming himself and despising others, as do many nowadays, saying: I am not like such a man, nor do I do this and that, as does such or such a man. And many of these are even worse than the Pharisee. He, it is true, not only despised others, but also pointed to an individual, saying: 'Nor am I like this publican.' But they, not satisfied with either of these things, go so far as to be angry and envious when they see that others are praised, or do more, or are of greater use, than themselves.

4. The third evil is that, as they look for pleasure in their good works, they usually perform them only when they see that some pleasure and praise will result from them. And thus, as Christ says, they do everything *ut videantur ab hominibus*,[5] and work not for the love of[6] God alone.

5. The fourth evil follows from this. It is that they will have no reward from God, since they have desired in this life to have joy or consolation or honour or some other kind of interest as a result of their good works: of such the Saviour says that herein they have

---

[1] A, B, e.p. add: 'These I shall here briefly describe.'
[2] St. Luke xviii, 11–12.   [3] E.p. omits: 'I thank Thee that.'
[4] St. Luke xviii, 11.   [5] St. Matthew xxiii, 5.
[6] A, B, e.p. omit: 'the love of.'

received their reward.[1] And thus they have had[2] naught but the labour of their work and are confounded, and receive no reward. There is so much misery among the sons of men which has to do with this evil that I myself believe that the greater number of good works which they perform in public are either vicious or will be of no value to them, or are imperfect[3] in the sight of God, because they are not detached from these human intentions and interests. For what other judgment can be formed of some of the actions which certain men perform, and of the memorials which they set up, when they will not perform these actions at all unless they are surrounded by human respect and honour, which are the vanity of life, or unless they can perpetuate in these memorials their name, lineage or authority, even setting up their emblems[4] and escutcheons in the very churches, as if they wished to set themselves, in the stead of images, in places where all bend the knee? In these good works which some men perform, may it not be said that they are worshipping[5] themselves more than God? This is certainly true if they perform them for the reason described and otherwise would not perform them at all.[6] But leaving aside these, which are the worst cases, how many are there who fall into these evils in their good works in many ways? Some wish to be praised, others to be thanked, others enumerate their good works and desire that this person and that shall know of them, and indeed the whole world; and sometimes they wish an intermediary to present their alms, or to perform other of their charitable deeds,[7] so that more may be known of them; and some desire all these things. This is the sounding of the trumpet, which, says the Saviour in the Gospel, vain men do, for which reason they shall have no reward for their works from God.[8]

6. In order to flee from this evil, such persons must hide their good works so that God alone may see them, and must not desire anyone to take notice of them. And they must hide them, not only from others, but even from themselves. That is to say, they must find no satisfaction in them, nor esteem them as if they were of some worth, nor derive pleasure from them at all. It is this that is spiritually indicated in those words of Our Lord: 'Let not thy left hand know what thy right hand doeth.'[9] Which is as much as to say: Esteem not with thy carnal and temporal eye the work that thou doest spiritually. And in this way the

---

[1] St. Matthew vi, 2.
[2] E.p.: 'And thus they will have.'
[3] A, e.p.: 'or are imperfect and defective.'
[4] A, B: 'their names.'
[5] [*Lit.*, 'are adoring.'] E.p.: 'are esteeming.'
[6] E.p. omits this entire sentence.
[7] [*Lit.*, 'to present their alms or that which they do.']
[8] St. Matthew vi, 2.
[9] St. Matthew vi, 3.

strength of the will is concentrated upon God, and a good deed bears fruit in His sight; so that not only will it not be lost, but it will be of great merit.[1] And in this sense must be understood that passage from Job: 'If I have kissed my hand with my mouth, which is a great sin and iniquity, and my heart hath rejoiced in secret.'[2] Here by the hand is understood good works, and by the mouth is understood the will which finds satisfaction in them. And since this is, as we say, finding satisfaction in oneself, he says: If my heart hath rejoiced in secret, which is a great iniquity against God and a denial of Him. And this is as though he were to say that he had no satisfaction, neither did his heart rejoice in secret.[3]

7. The fifth of these evils is that such persons make no progress on the road of perfection. For, since they are attached to the pleasure and consolation which they find in their good works, it follows that, when they find no such pleasure and consolation in their good works and exercises, which ordinarily happens when God desires to lead them on, by giving them the dry bread of the perfect and taking from them the milk of babes, in order to prove their strength and to purge their delicate appetites so that they may be able to enjoy the food of grown men, they commonly faint and cease to persevere, because their good works give them no pleasure. In this way may be spiritually understood these words of the Wise Man: 'Dying flies spoil the sweetness of ointment.'[4] For, when any mortification comes to these persons, they die to their good works and cease to practise them; and thus they lose their perseverance, wherein are found sweetness of spirit and interior consolation.

8. The sixth of these evils is that such persons commonly deceive themselves, thinking that the things and good works which give them pleasure must be better than those that give them none. They praise and esteem the one kind and depreciate the other;[5] yet as a rule those works whereby a man is most greatly mortified (especially when he is not proficient in perfection) are more acceptable and precious in the

[1] So Alc. A, B, e.p. read: 'where [sic. Read: 'where otherwise'] not only will it be lost, but oftentimes, through inward vanity and boasting, the soul will sin greatly before God.'
[2] Job xxxi, 27–8.
[3] So Alc. A, B and (with slight variations) e.p. add: 'For to assign and attribute good works to oneself is to deny them to God, to Whom belongs every good work; this Lucifer did, rejoicing in himself and denying to God that which was His, and exalting himself because of it, which was the cause of his perdition.'
[4] Ecclesiastes x, 1.
[5] So Alc. A, B: 'and reprehend and despise the other.' E.p.: 'and condemn and despise the other.'

sight of God, by reason of the self-denial which a man must observe
in performing them, than are those wherein he finds consolation and
which may very easily be an occasion of self-seeking. And in this
connection Micheas says of them: *Malum manuum suarum dicunt
bonum.*[1] That is: That which is bad in their works they call good. This
comes to them because of the pleasure which they take in their good
works, instead of thinking only of giving pleasure to God. The extent
to which this evil predominates, whether in spiritual men or in ordinary
persons, would take too long to describe, for hardly anyone can be
found who is moved to do such works simply for God's sake, without
the attraction of some advantage of consolation or pleasure, or some
other consideration.

9. The seventh evil is that, in so far as a man stifles not vain rejoicing
in moral works, he is to that extent incapable of receiving reasonable
counsel and instruction with regard to good works that he should
perform. For he is fettered by the habit of weakness that he has
acquired through performing good works with attachment to vain
rejoicing; so that he cannot consider the counsel of others as best, or,
even if he considers it to be so, he cannot follow it, through not having
the necessary strength of mind. Such persons as this are greatly
weakened in charity toward God and their neighbour; for the self-
love with respect to their good works in which they indulge causes
their charity to grow cold.

CHAPTER XXIX

*Of the benefits which come to the soul through the withdrawal of its
rejoicing from moral good.*

VERY great are the benefits which come to the soul when it
desires not to set the vain rejoicing of its will on this kind of
good. For, in the first place, it is freed from falling into many
temptations and deceits of the devil, which are involved in rejoicing
in these good works, as we may understand by that which is said in
Job, namely: 'He sleepeth under the shadow, in the covert of the reed[2]
and in moist places.'[3] This he applies to the devil, who deceives the
soul in the moisture of rejoicing and in the vanity of the reed—that is,

---

[1] Micheas vii, 3.
[2] This is the emendation of e.p. The Codices [followed by P. Silverio] have: 'of the
feather,' as also in the following sentence.   [3] Job xl, 16 [A.V., xl, 21].

in vain works. And it is no wonder if the soul is secretly deceived by the devil in this rejoicing; for, apart altogether from his suggestions, vain rejoicing is itself deception. This is especially true when there is any boasting of heart concerning these good works, as Jeremias well says in these words: *Arrogantia tua decepit te*.[1] For what greater deception is there than boasting? And from this the soul that purges itself from this rejoicing is freed.

2. The second benefit is that the soul performs its good works with greater deliberation and perfection than it can if there be in them the passion of joy and pleasure. For, because of this passion of joy, the passions of wrath and concupiscence are so strong that they will not submit to reason,[2] but ordinarily cause a man to be inconsistent in his actions and purposes, so that he abandons some and takes up others, and begins a thing only to abandon it without completing any part of it. For, since he acts under the influence of pleasure, and since pleasure is variable, being much stronger in some natures than in others, it follows that, when this pleasure ceases, both the action and its purpose cease, important though they may be. To such persons the joy which they have in their work is the soul and the strength thereof; and, when the joy is quenched,[3] the work ceases and perishes, and they persevere therein no longer. It is of such persons that Christ says: 'They receive the word with joy, and then the devil taketh it away from them, lest they should persevere.'[4] And this is because they have no strength and no roots save in the joy aforementioned. To take and to withdraw their will, therefore, from this rejoicing is the cause of their perseverance and success.[5] This benefit, then, is a great one, even as the contrary evil is great likewise. The wise man sets his eyes upon the substance and benefit of his work, not upon the pleasure and delight which it gives him; and so he is not beating the air, but derives from his work a stable joy, without any meed of bitterness.[6]

3. The third benefit is divine. It is that, when vain joy in these good works is quenched, the soul becomes poor in spirit, which is one of the blessings spoken of by the Son of God when He says: 'Blessed are the poor in spirit, for theirs is the Kingdom of Heaven.'[7]

---

[1] Jeremias xlix, 16. E.p. adds the translation: 'Thy arrogance hath deceived thee.'
[2] [*Lit.*, 'will not give place to the weight of reason.']
[3] A, B: 'when the joy ceases.'   [4] St. Luke viii, 12.
[5] E.p.: '. . . is an excellent preparation for perseverance and success.'
[6] E.p.: 'without demanding any meed of pleasure.' [The word translated 'bitterness' in the text is *sinsabor*, the contrary of *sabor*, which is translated above 'pleasure.' The chief idea beneath *sinsabor* is that of insipidity and boredom.]
[7] St. Matthew v, 3.

4. The fourth benefit is that he that denies himself this joy will be meek, humble and prudent in his actions. For he will not act impetuously and rapidly, through being impelled[1] by the wrath and concupiscence which belong to joy; neither presumptuously, through being affected by the esteem of his own work which he cherishes because of the joy that he has in it; neither incautiously, through being blinded by joy.[2]

5. The fifth benefit is that he becomes pleasing to God and man, and is freed from spiritual sloth, gluttony and avarice, and from spiritual envy and from a thousand other vices.

CHAPTER XXX

Which begins to treat of the fifth kind of good wherein the will may rejoice, which is the supernatural. Describes the nature of these supernatural good things, and how they are distinguished from the spiritual, and how joy in them is to be directed to God.

IT now behoves us to treat of the fifth kind of good thing wherein the soul may rejoice, which is the supernatural. By this term we here understand all the gifts and graces given by God which transcend natural virtue and capacity and are called *gratis datæ*. Such as these are the gifts of wisdom and knowledge which God gave to Solomon, and the graces whereof Saint Paul speaks[3]—namely, faith, gifts of healing, the working of miracles, prophecy, knowledge and discernment of spirits, interpretation of words and likewise the gift of tongues.

2. These good things, it is true, are also spiritual, like those of the same kind of which we have to speak presently; yet, since the two are so different, I have thought well to make a distinction between them. The practice of these has an intimate relation with the profit of man, and it is with a view to this profit and to this end that God gives them. As Saint Paul says: 'The spirit is given to none save for the profit of the rest;'[4] this is to be understood of these graces. But the use and practice of spiritual graces has to do with the soul and God alone, and with God and the soul, in the communion of understanding and will, etc., as we shall say hereafter. And thus there is a difference in their object, since

---

[1] E.p.: 'being carried away.'
[3] 1 Corinthians xii, 9–10.

[2] Alc. omits: 'neither . . . by joy.'
[4] 1 Corinthians xii, 7.

spiritual graces have to do only with the Creator and the soul;[1] whereas supernatural graces have to do with the creature, and furthermore differ[2] in substance, and therefore in their operation, and thus of necessity the instruction which we give concerning them differs also.

3. Speaking now of supernatural graces and gifts as we here understand them, I say that, in order to purge ourselves of vain joy in them, it is well here to notice two benefits which are comprised in this kind of gift—namely, temporal and spiritual. The temporal benefits are the healing of infirmities, the receiving of their sight by the blind, the raising of the dead, the casting out of devils, prophesying concerning the future so that men may take heed to themselves, and other things of the kind. The spiritual and eternal benefit is that God is known and served through these good works by him that performs them, or by those in whom and in whose presence they are performed.

4. With respect to the first kind of benefit—namely, the temporal—supernatural works and miracles merit little or no rejoicing on the part of the soul; for, without the second kind of benefit, they are of little or no importance to man, since they are not in themselves a means for uniting the soul with God, as charity is. And these supernatural works and graces may be performed by those who are not in a state of grace and charity, whether they truly give thanks and attribute their gifts to God,[3] as did the wicked prophet Balaam, and Solomon, or whether they perform them falsely, through the agency of the devil, as did Simon Magus, or by means of other secrets of nature. These works and marvels, if any of them were to be of any profit to him that worked them, would be true works given by God. And Saint Paul teaches us what these are worth[4] without the second kind of benefit, saying: 'Though I speak with the tongues of men and of angels, and have not charity, I am become as a sounding bell or metal. And though I have prophecy and know all mysteries and all knowledge; and though I have all faith, even as much as may remove[5] mountains, and have not charity, I am nothing, etc.'[6] Wherefore Christ will refuse the requests of many who have esteemed their good works in this way, when they beg Him for glory because of them, saying[7]: Lord, have

---

1 E.p.: 'spiritual graces are between God and the soul.'
2 E.p.: 'but the other supernatural graces of which we were speaking have relation to other creatures and are for their profit. And furthermore they differ.'
3 [*Lit.*, 'give thanks and gifts to God.']   4 A, B omit 'worth.'
5 [*traspasar*: *lit.*, 'go over,' 'go through.']
6 1 Corinthians xiii, 1–2.
7 A, B: 'and say to Him.' The other authorities omit 'saying.'

we not prophesied in Thy name and worked many miracles? Then
Christ will say to them: 'Depart from Me, workers of iniquity.'[1]

5. A man, then, should rejoice, not when he has such graces and
makes use of them, but when he reaps from them the second spiritual
fruit, namely that of serving God in them with true charity, for herein
is the fruit of eternal life. For this cause Our Saviour reproved the
disciples who were rejoicing because they cast out devils, saying:
'Desire not to rejoice in this, that devils are subject to you, but rather
because your names are written in the book of life.'[2] This, according to
good theology, is as much as to say: Rejoice if your names are written
in the book of life. By this it is understood that a man should not
rejoice save when he is walking in the way of life, which he may do by
performing good works in charity; for where is the profit and what is
the worth in the sight of God of aught that is not love of God? And
this love is not perfect if it be not strong and discreet in purging the
will of joy in all things, and if it be not set upon doing the will of God
alone. And in this manner the will is united with God through these
good things which are supernatural.

CHAPTER XXXI

*Of the evils which come to the soul when it sets the rejoicing of the will upon
this kind of good.*

THREE principal evils, it seems to me, may come to the soul when
it sets its rejoicing[3] upon supernatural good. These are: that it
may deceive and be deceived; that it may fall away from the
faith; and that it may indulge in vainglory or some other such vanity.

2. As to the first of these, it is a very easy thing to deceive others,
and to deceive oneself, by rejoicing in this kind of operation. And the
reason is that, in order to know which of these operations are false
and which are true, and how and at what time they should be practised, much counsel and much light from God are needful, both of
which are greatly impeded by joy in these operations and esteem for
them. And this for two reasons: first, because joy blunts and obscures
the judgment; second, because, when a man has joy in these things,
not only does he the more quickly become eager for them, but he is also

---

[1] St. Matthew vii, 22–3.   [2] St. Luke x, 20.
[3] E.p.: 'may come to man when he sets his rejoicing.'

the more impelled[1] to practise them out of the proper season. And even supposing the virtues and operations which are practised to be genuine, these two defects suffice for us to be frequently deceived in them, either through not understanding them as they should be understood, or through not profiting by them and not using them at the times and in the ways that are most meet. For, although it is true that, when God gives these gifts and graces, He gives light by which to see them, and the impulse whereby a man may know at what times and in what ways to use them; yet these souls, through the attachment and imperfection which they may have with regard to them, may greatly err, by not using them with the perfection that God desires of them therein, and in the way and at the time that He wills. We read that Balaam desired to do this, when, against the will of God, he determined to go[2] and curse the people of Israel, for which reason God was wroth and purposed to slay him.[3] And Saint James and Saint John[4] desired to call down fire from Heaven upon the Samaritans because they gave not lodging to Our Saviour, and for this He reproved them.[5]

3. Here it is evident that these persons[6] were led to determine to perform these works, when it was not meet for them to do so, by a certain imperfect passion, which was inherent in their joy in them and esteem for them. For, when no such imperfection exists, the soul is moved and determined to perform these virtues only in the manner wherein God so moves it, and at His time, and until then it is not right that they should be performed. It was for this reason that God complained of certain prophets, through Jeremias, saying: 'I sent not the prophets, and they ran; I spake not to them, and they prophesied.'[7] And later He says: 'They deceived My people by their lying and their miracles, when I had not commanded them, neither had I sent them.'[8] And in that place He says of them likewise: 'They see the visions of their heart, and speak of them'[9]; which would not happen if they had not this abominable attachment to these works.

4. From these passages it is to be understood that the evil of this rejoicing not only leads men to make wicked and perverse use of these graces given by God, as did Balaam and those of whom the prophet here says that they worked miracles whereby they deceived the

---

[1] E.p.: 'the more inclined.'
[3] Numbers xxii, 22-3.
[5] St. Luke ix, 54-5.
[6] E.p.: 'that these imperfect persons of whom we are speaking.'
[7] Jeremias xxiii, 21.
[9] Jeremias xxiii, 26.

[2] E.p.: 'he dared to go.'
[4] E.p. adds: 'carried away by zeal.'
[8] Jeremias xxiii, 32.

people, but it even leads them to use these graces without having been given them by God, like those who prophesied their own fancies and published the visions which they invented or which the devil represented to them. For, when the devil sees them affectioned to these things, he opens a wide field to them, gives them abundant material and interferes with them in many ways; whereupon they spread their sails and become shamelessly audacious in the freedom wherewith they work these marvels.

5. Nor does the evil stop here. To such a point does their joy in these works and their eagerness for them extend that, if before they had a secret compact with the devil (and many of them do in fact perform these works by such secret compacts), it now makes them bold enough to work with him by an explicit and manifest compact, submitting themselves to him, by agreement, as his disciples and allies. Hence we have wizards, enchanters, magicians, soothsayers and sorcerers. And so far does the joy of these persons in their works carry them that, not only do they seek to purchase gifts and graces with money, as did Simon Magus, in order to serve the devil, but they even strive to obtain sacred things, and (which cannot be said without trembling) Divine things,[1] for even the very Body[2] of our Lord Jesus Christ has been seen to be usurped for the use of their wicked deeds and abominations. May God here extend and show to them His great mercy!

6. Everyone will clearly understand how pernicious are such persons to themselves and how prejudicial to Christianity.[3] It may be noted here that all those magicians and soothsayers who lived among the children of Israel, whom Saul destroyed out of the land, because they desired to imitate the true prophets of God, had fallen into such abominations and deceits.

7. He, then, that has supernatural gifts and graces ought to refrain from desiring to practise them, and from rejoicing in so doing, nor ought he to care to exercise them;[4] for God, Who gives Himself to such persons, by supernatural means, for the profit of His Church and of its members, will move them likewise supernaturally[5] in such a manner and at such time as He desires. As He commanded His faithful ones[6] to take no thought as to what they were to say, or as to how they

---

[1] The remainder of this sentence is omitted from e.p.
[2] [*Lit.*, 'the awful Body.']   [3] A, B, e.p.: 'to the Christian commonweal.'
[4] Thus Alc. and B.   A: 'to name them.' E.p. omits: 'nor ought he to care to exercise them.'
[5] E.p. adds: 'to exercise them.'   [6] E.p.: 'His disciples.'

were to say it, since this is the supernatural business of faith, it will likewise be His will (as these operations are no less a supernatural matter) that a man should wait and allow God to work by moving his heart, since it is in the virtue of this working that there will be wrought all virtue. The disciples (so we read in the Acts of the Apostles), although these graces and gifts had been infused within them, prayed to God, beseeching Him to be pleased to stretch forth His hand in making signs and performing works of healing through them, that they might introduce the faith of our Lord Jesus Christ into men's hearts.[1]

8. From this first evil may proceed the second, which is a falling away from the faith; this can come to pass after two manners. The first has respect to others; for, when a man sets out, unseasonably and needlessly, to perform a marvel or a mighty work, apart from the fact that this is tempting God, which is a great sin, it may be that he will not succeed, and will engender in the hearts of men discredit and contempt for the faith. For, although at times such persons may succeed because for other reasons and purposes God so wills it, as in the case of Saul's witch[2] (if it be true that it was indeed Samuel who appeared on that occasion), they will not always so succeed; and, when they do so, they go astray none the less and are blameworthy for having used these graces when it was not fitting. The second manner in which we may fall away is in ourselves[3] and has respect to the merit of faith; for, if a man make much account of these miracles, he ceases to lean upon the substantial practice of faith, which is an obscure habit; and thus, where signs and witnesses abound, there is less merit in believing. In this way Saint Gregory says that faith has no merit when human reason provides experience.[4] And thus these marvels are never worked by God save when they are really necessary for belief.[5] Therefore, to the end that His disciples should not be without merit, though they had experience of His resurrection, He did many things before He showed Himself to them, so that they should believe Him without seeing Him. To Mary Magdalene, first of all, He showed the empty tomb, and afterwards bade the angels speak to her[6] (for, as Saint Paul says, faith comes by hearing);[7] so that, having heard, she should

---

[1] Acts iv, 29–30. [2] 1 Kings [A.V., 1 Samuel] xxviii, 7, ff.
[3] Alc. has 'in like manner' [asimismo] for 'in ourselves' [en sí mismo].
[4] 'Nec fides habet meritum cui humana ratio præbet experimentum.' St. Gregory, Hom. 26 in Evang. (Migne, Vol. LXXVI, p. 1,137). The translation in the text is that of Alc. A, B, e.p. have: '. . . when reason provides experience of a human and palpable kind'
[5] E.p. adds: 'and for other ends concerning His glory and His saints.'
[6] [St. Luke xxiv, 6; St. John xx, 2.] [7] [Romans x, 17.]

believe before she saw. And, although she saw Him, it was as an ordinary man,[1] that, by the warmth of His presence, He might completely instruct her in the belief which she lacked. And He first sent to
tell His disciples, with the women, and afterwards they went to see the
tomb. And, as to those who went to Emmaus, He first of all enkindled
their hearts in faith so that they might see Him, dissembling with them
as He walked.[2] And finally He reproved them all because they had not
believed those who had announced to them His resurrection.[3] And He
reproved Saint Thomas because he desired to have the witness of His
wounds, by telling him that they who saw Him not and yet believed
Him were blessed.[4]

9. And thus it is not the will of God that miracles should be
wrought: when He works them, He does so, as it were, because He
cannot do otherwise.[5] And for this cause He reproved the Pharisees
because they believed not save through signs, saying: 'Unless ye see
marvels and signs, ye believe not.'[6] Those, then, who love to rejoice
in these supernatural works lose much in the matter of faith.

10. The third evil is that, because of their joy in these works, men
commonly fall into vainglory or some other vanity. For even their
joy in these wonders, when it is not, as we have said, purely in God and
for God, is vanity; which is evident in the reproof given by Our Lord
to the disciples because they had rejoiced that devils were subject to
them;[7] for which joy, if it had not been vain, He would not have
reproved them.

CHAPTER XXXII

*Of two benefits which are derived from the renunciation of rejoicing in the
matter of the supernatural graces.*

BESIDES the benefits which the soul gains by being delivered from
the three evils aforementioned through its renunciation of this
joy, it acquires two excellent benefits. The first is that it magni-
fies and exalts God: the second is that it exalts itself. For God is exalted

---

[1] E.p.: 'as a gardener' [St. John xx, 15].   [2] St. Luke xxiv, 15.
[3] [St. Luke xxiv, 25–6.]   [4] St. John xx, 29.
[5] [The phrase translated 'as it were' is *como dicen*, 'as they say,' and is explained by
the fact that *a más no poder*, here rendered 'because He cannot do otherwise,' is an idio-
matic expression, probably less common then than it is now.] E.p. omits: 'when He . . .
do otherwise.'
[6] St. John iv, 48.   [7] St. Luke x, 20.

in the soul after two manners: first, by the withdrawal of the heart and the joy of the will from all that is not God, in order that they may be set upon Him alone. This David signified in the verse[1] which we quoted when we began to speak of the night of this faculty; namely: 'Man shall attain to a lofty heart, and God shall be exalted.'[2] For, when the heart is raised above all things, the soul is exalted above them all.

2. And, because in this way the soul centres itself in God alone, God is exalted and magnified, when He reveals to the soul His excellence and greatness; for, in this elevation of joy, God bears witness of Who He Himself is. This cannot be done save if the will be voided of joy and consolation with respect to all things, even as David said also, in these words: 'Be still and see that I am God.'[3] And again he says: 'In a desert land, dry and pathless, have I appeared before Thee, to see Thy power and Thy glory.'[4] And, since it is true that God is exalted by the fixing of the soul's rejoicing upon detachment from all things, He is much more highly exalted when the soul withdraws itself from the most wondrous of these things in order to fix its rejoicing on Him alone. For these, being supernatural, are of a nobler kind; and thus for the soul to cast them aside, in order to set its rejoicing upon God alone, is for it to attribute greater glory and excellence to God than to them. For, the more and the greater things a man despises for the sake of another, the more does he esteem and exalt that other.

3. Furthermore, God is exalted after the second manner when the will is withdrawn from this kind of operation; for, the more God is believed and served without testimonies and signs, the more He is exalted by the soul, for it believes more concerning God than signs and miracles can demonstrate.

4. The second benefit wherein the soul is exalted consists in this, that, withdrawing the will from all desire for apparent[5] signs and testimonies, it is exalted in purest faith, which God increases and infuses within it much more intensely. And, together with this, He increases in it the other two theological virtues, which are charity and hope, wherein the soul enjoys the highest Divine knowledge by means of the obscure and detached habit of faith; and it enjoys great delight of love by means of charity, whereby the will rejoices in naught else

---

[1] E.p.: 'in the place.'
[2] Psalm lxiii, 7 [A.V., lxiv, 6–7].
[3] Psalm xlv, 11 [A.V., xlvi, 10].
[4] Psalm lxii, 3 [A.V., lxiii, 1–2].
[5] [i.e., that are perceived by the faculties of the soul in other ways than by pure faith.]

than in the living God; and likewise it enjoys satisfaction in the memory[1] by means of hope. All this is a wondrous benefit, which leads essentially and directly to the perfect union of the soul with God.

CHAPTER XXXIII

Which begins to treat of the sixth kind of good wherein the soul may rejoice. Describes its nature and makes the first division under this head.[2]

SINCE the intention of this work of ours is to lead the spirit through these good things of the spirit even to the Divine union of the soul with God, it will now behove both myself and the reader to give our consideration to this matter with particular care. For, in speaking of this sixth kind of good, we have to treat of the good things of the spirit, which are those that are of the greatest service to this end. For it is quite certain, and quite an ordinary occurrence,[3] that some persons, because of their lack of knowledge, make use of spiritual things with respect only to sense, and leave the spirit empty. There will scarcely be anyone whose spirit is not to a considerable degree corrupted by sweetness of sense; since, if the water be drunk up before it reaches the spirit, the latter becomes dry and barren.

2. Coming to this matter, then, I say that by good things of the spirit I understand all those that influence and aid the soul in Divine things and in its intercourse with God, and the communications of God to the soul.

3. Beginning by making a division between these supreme kinds of good, I say that good things of the spirit are of two kinds: the one kind is delectable and the other painful. And each of these kinds is likewise of two manners; for the delectable kind consists of clear things that are distinctly understood, and also of things that are not understood clearly or distinctly. The painful kind, likewise, may be of clear and distinct things, or of things dark and confused.

4. Between all these we may likewise make distinctions with respect to the faculties of the soul. For some kinds of spiritual good, being of knowledge, pertain to the understanding; others, being of affection, pertain to the will; and others, inasmuch as they are imaginary, pertain to the memory.

---

[1] A, B, e.p.: 'in the will.'
[2] This last sentence is found in A, B and e.p. only.
[3] [*Lit.*, 'thing.'] E.p.: 'For it is quite a certain thing . . .'

5. We shall leave for later consideration those good things that are painful, since[1] they pertain to the passive night, in treating of which we shall have to speak of them; and likewise the delectable blessings which we described as being of things confused and not distinct, of which we shall treat hereafter, since they pertain to that general, confused and loving knowledge wherein is effected the union of the soul with God, and which we passed over in the second book, deferring it so that we might treat of it later[2] when we should make a division between the apprehensions of the understanding.[3] We shall speak here and now of those delectable blessings which are of things clear and distinct.

CHAPTER XXXIV

Of those good things of the spirit which can be distinctly apprehended by the understanding and the memory. Describes how the will is to behave in the matter of rejoicing in them.

WE might spend much time here upon the multitude of the apprehensions of the memory and the understanding, teaching how the will is to conduct itself with regard to the joy that it may have in them, had we not treated of this at length in the second and the third book. But, since we there spoke of the manner wherein it behoves these two faculties to act with respect to them, in order that they may take the road to Divine union, and since it behoves the will to conduct itself likewise as regards rejoicing in them, it is unnecessary to go over this here; for it suffices to say that wheresoever we there said that those faculties should void themselves of this or that apprehension, it is to be understood also that the will should likewise be voided of joy in them. And in the way wherein it is said that memory and understanding are to conduct themselves with regard to all these apprehensions, the will must conduct itself likewise; for, since the understanding and the other faculties cannot admit or reject anything unless the will intervene therein, it is clear that the same teaching that serves for the one will serve also for the other.

2. It may there be seen, then, what is requisite in this case, for

---

[1] E.p.: 'inasmuch as.'
[2] Cf. p. 119, n. 3, above.
[3] Alc. omits: 'when we should . . . understanding.' E.p. adds to this last phrase: 'and this we shall duly do in the book of the *Dark Night*.'

the soul will fall into all the evils and perils to which we there referred if it cannot direct the rejoicing of the will to God in all those
apprehensions.[1]

CHAPTER XXXV

*Of the delectable spiritual good things which can be distinctly apprehended
by the will. Describes the kinds of these.*

WE can reduce all the kinds of good which can distinctly cause
joy to the will to four: namely, motive, provocative, direc-
tive and perfective. Of these we shall speak in turn, each in
its order; and first, of the motive kind—namely, images and portraits
of saints, oratories and ceremonies.

2. As touching images and portraits, there may be much vanity and
vain rejoicing in these. For, though they are most important for Divine
worship and most necessary to move the will to devotion, as is shown
by the approval given to them and the use made of them by our Mother
Church (for which reason it is always well that we should employ them,
in order to awaken our lukewarmness), there are many persons who
rejoice rather in the painting and decoration of them than in what
they represent.

3. The use of images has been ordained by the Church for two
principal ends—namely, that we may reverence the saints in them, and
that the will may be moved and devotion to the saints awakened by
them. When they serve this purpose they are beneficial and the use of
them is necessary; and therefore we must choose those that are most
true and lifelike, and that most move the will to devotion, and our
eyes must ever be fixed upon this motive rather than upon the value
and cunning of their workmanship and decoration. For, as I say, there
are some who pay more attention to the cunning with which an image
is made, and to its value, than to what it represents; and that interior
devotion which they ought to direct spiritually to the saint whom
they see not, forgetting the image at once, since it serves only as a
motive,[2] they squander upon the cunning and the decoration of its
outward workmanship. In this way sense is pleased and delighted, and

---

[1] Alc. abbreviates: 'It may there be seen what is requisite herein, for the soul will fall
into all those evils if it cannot direct itself to God.'
[2] E.p. omits the phrase: 'forgetting . . . as a motive.'

the love and rejoicing of the will remain there. This is a complete hindrance to true spirituality, which demands annihilation of the affections as to all particular things.

4. This will become quite clear from the detestable custom which certain persons observe with regard to images in these our days. Holding not in abhorrence the vain trappings of the world, they adorn images with the garments which from time to time vain persons invent in order to satisfy their own pleasures and vanities.[1] So they clothe images with garments reprehensible even in themselves, a kind of vanity which was, and is still, abhorrent to the saints whom the images represent. Herein, with their help, the devil succeeds in canonizing his vanities, by clothing the saints with them, not without causing them great displeasure. And in this way the honest and grave devotion of the soul, which rejects and spurns all vanity and every trace of it, becomes with them little more than a dressing of dolls; some persons use images merely as idols upon which they have set their rejoicing.[2] And thus you will see certain persons who are never tired of adding one image to another, and wish them to be of this or that kind and workmanship, and to be placed in this or that manner, so as to be pleasing to sense; and they make little account of the devotion of the heart. They are as much attached to them as was Michas to his idols,[3] or as was Laban;[4] for the one ran out of his house crying aloud because they were being taken from him; and the other, having made a long journey and been very wroth because of them, disturbed all the household stuff of Jacob, in searching for them.

5. The person who is truly[5] devout sets his devotion principally upon that which is invisible; he needs few images and uses few, and chooses those that harmonize with the Divine rather than with the human, clothing them, and with them himself, in the garments of the world to come, and following its fashions rather than those of this world. For not only does an image belonging to this world in no way influence his desire; it does not even lead him to think of this world, in spite of his having before his eyes something worldly, akin to the world's interests. Nor is his heart attached to the images that he uses; if they are taken from him, he grieves very little, for he seeks within himself the living image, which is Christ crucified, for Whose sake he even desires that all should be taken from him and he should have

---

[1] A, B, e.p. have 'frivolities' for 'vanities.'
[2] E.p. abbreviates: '. . . little more than curiosity and vanity.'
[3] Judges xviii, 22–4.   [4] Genesis xxxi, 34–7.
[5] Alc. alone has 'truly.'

nothing. Even when the motives and means which lead him closest to God[1] are taken from him, he remains in tranquillity. For the soul is nearer perfection when it is tranquil and joyous, though it be deprived of these motives, than if it has possession of them together with desire and attachment. For, although it is good to be pleased to have such images as assist the soul to greater devotion (for which reason it is those which move it most that must always be chosen), yet it is something far removed from perfection to be so greatly attached to them as to possess them with attachment, so that, if they are taken away from the soul, it becomes sad.

6. Let the soul be sure that, the more closely it is attached to an image or a motive,[2] the less will its devotion and prayer mount to God. For, although it is true that, since some are more appropriate than others, and excite devotion more than others, it is well, for this reason alone, to be more affectioned to some than to others, as I have just now said,[3] yet there must be none of the attachment and affection which I have described. Otherwise, that which has to sustain the spirit in its flight to God, in total forgetfulness, will be wholly occupied by sense, and the soul will be completely immersed in a delight afforded it by what are but instruments. These instruments I have to use, but solely in order to assist me in devotion; and, on account of my imperfection, they may well serve me as a hindrance, no less so than may affection and attachment to anything else.[4]

7.[5] But, though perhaps in this matter of images you may think that there is something to be said on the other side, if you have not clearly understood how much detachment and poverty of spirit is required by perfection, at least you cannot excuse the imperfection which is commonly indulged with regard to rosaries; for you will hardly find anyone who has not some weakness with regard to these, desiring them to be of this workmanship rather than of that,[6] or of this colour or metal rather than of that, or decorated in some one style or in some other. Yet no one style is better than another for the hearing of a prayer by God, for this depends upon the simple and true heart,[7]

---

[1] E.p.: 'Even when the means that seemed to be leading him closest to God . . .'
[2] E.p.: 'or a motive of sense.'
[3] Alc. omits: 'as I have just now said.'
[4] E.p. omits: 'no less . . . anything else.'
[5] [In this and the next paragraph the Saint is more than usually personal in his approach to the reader. The word *tú* (you) is repeated many times, and placed in emphatic positions, in a way which cannot be exactly reproduced in English.]
[6] E.p.: 'than of the other.
[7] E.p.: 'and upright heart.'

which looks at no more than pleasing God, and, apart from the question of indulgences, cares no more for one rosary than for another.

8. Our vain concupiscence is of such a nature and quality that it tries to establish itself in everything; and it is like the worm which destroys healthy wood, and works upon things both good and evil. For what else is your desire to have a rosary of cunning workmanship, and your wish that it shall be of one kind rather than of another, but the fixing of your rejoicing upon the instrument? It is like desiring to choose one image rather than another, and considering, not if it will better awaken Divine love within you, but only if it is more precious and more cunningly made. If you employed your desire and rejoicing solely in the love of God, you would care nothing for any of these considerations. It is most vexatious to see certain spiritual persons so greatly attached to the manner and workmanship of these instruments and motives, and to the curiosity and vain pleasure which they find in them: you will never see them satisfied; they will be continually leaving one thing for another, and forgetting and forsaking spiritual devotion for these visible things, to which they have affection and attachment, sometimes of just the same kind as that which a man has to temporal things; and from this they receive no small harm.[1]

CHAPTER XXXVI

Which continues to treat of images, and describes the ignorance of certain persons with respect to them.

THERE is much that might be said of the stupidity which many persons display with regard to images; their foolishness reaches such a point that some of them place more confidence in one kind of image than in another, believing that God will hear them more readily because of these than because of those, even when both represent the same thing, as when there are two of Christ or two of Our Lady. And this happens because they have more affection for the one kind of workmanship than for the other; which implies the crudest ideas concerning intercourse with God and the worship and honour that are owed to Him, which has solely to do with the faith and the

---

[1] So A, B, e.p. Alc. abbreviates the last sentence thus: 'And it is a pity to see certain spiritual persons so greatly attached to the manner and workmanship of these instruments, and having the [same] affection and attachment to them as to other temporal things,' C, D also abbreviate, but resemble the other authorities rather than Alc.

purity of heart of him that prays.[1] For if God sometimes grants more favours by means of one image rather than by another of the same kind, it is not because there is more virtue to this effect in one than in another (however much difference there may be in their workmanship), but because some persons better awaken their own devotion by one than by another. If they had the same devotion for the one as for the other (or even without the use of either), they would receive the same favours from God.[2]

2. Hence the reason for which God works[3] miracles and grants favours by means of one kind of image rather than by another is not that these should be esteemed more than those, but to the end that, by means of the wonder that they cause, there may be awakened sleeping devotion and the affection of the faithful for prayer. And hence it comes that, as the contemplation of the image at that time enkindles devotion and makes us to continue in prayer (both these being means whereby God hears and grants that which is asked of Him), therefore, at that time and by means of that same image, God continues to work favours and miracles because of the prayer and affection which are then shown; for it is certain that God does it not because of the image, which in itself is no more than a painted thing, but because of the devotion and faith which the person has toward the saint whom it represents. And so, if you had the same devotion and faith in Our Lady before one image representing her as before another, since the person represented is the same (and even, as we have said, if you had no such image at all), you would receive the same favours. For it is clear from experience that, when God grants certain favours and works miracles, He does so as a rule by means of certain images which are not well carved or cunningly formed or painted, so that the faithful may attribute nothing to the figure or the painting.[4]

3. Furthermore, Our Lord is frequently wont to grant these favours by means of those images that are most remote and solitary. One reason for this is that the effort necessary to journey to them causes the

---

[1] E.p. reads: '. . . in one kind of image than in another, being influenced herein solely by the affection which they have for one figure rather than for another. This implies the crudest and meanest ideas concerning intercourse with God and the worship and honour that are owed to Him, which has principally to do with the faith and the purity of heart of him that prays.'

[2] E.p.: '. . . of the same kind, it is (although there may be much difference in their workmanship) to the end that people may awaken their own devotion better by means of one than by means of another.' This concludes the paragraph, the last sentence being omitted.

[3] [Lit. 'awakens.' Cf. the use of the same metaphor below.]

[4] A, B, e.p.: 'to the painting or the workmanship.'

affections to be increased and makes the act of prayer more earnest.
Another reason is that we may withdraw ourselves from noise and
from people when we pray, even as did the Lord. Wherefore he that
makes a pilgrimage does well if he makes it at a time when no others
are doing so, even though the time be unusual. I should never advise
him to make a pilgrimage when a great multitude is doing so; for, as a
rule, on these occasions, people return in a state of greater distraction
than when they went. And many set out on these pilgrimages and
make them for recreation rather than for devotion. Where there is
devotion and faith, then, any image will suffice; but, if there is none,
none will suffice.[1] Our Saviour was a very living image in the world;
and yet those that had no faith, even though they went about with
Him and saw His wondrous works, derived no benefit from them. And
this was the reason why, as the Evangelist says, He did few mighty
works in His own country.[2]

4. I desire also to speak here of certain supernatural effects which are
sometimes produced by certain images upon particular persons.
To certain images God gives a particular spiritual influence upon such
persons, so that the figure of the image and the devotion caused by it
remain fixed in the mind, and the person has them ever present before
him; and so, when he suddenly thinks of the image, the spiritual
influence which works upon him is of the same kind as when he saw
it—sometimes it is less, but sometimes it is even greater—yet, from
another image, although it be of more perfect workmanship, he will
not obtain the same spiritual effect.

5. Many persons, too, have devotion to one kind of workmanship
rather than to another, and to some they will have no more than a
natural inclination and affection, just as we prefer seeing one person's
face to another's. And they will naturally become more attracted to a
particular image, and will keep it more vividly in their imagination,[3]
even though it be not as beautiful as others, just because their nature is
attracted to that kind of form and figure which it represents. And some
persons will think that the affection which they have for such or such
an image is devotion, whereas it will perhaps be no more than natural
inclination and affection. Again, it may happen that, when they look
at an image, they will see it move, or make signs and gestures and indications, or speak. This, and the variety of supernatural effects caused

---

[1] E.p.: 'Where there is no devotion and faith, then, no image will suffice.'
[2] St. Luke iv, 24. [Rather St. Matthew xiii, 58 or St. Mark vi, 5.]
[3] A: '. . . and will keep it more vividly, because it is a natural thing and [sic] to have it
ever in the memory.'

by images of which we have here been speaking, are,[1] it is true, quite
frequently good and true effects, produced by God either to increase
devotion or so that the soul may have some support on which to lean,
because it is somewhat weak, and so that it may not be distracted. Yet
frequently, again, they are produced by the devil[2] in order to cause
deception and harm. We shall therefore give instruction concerning
this in the chapter following.

CHAPTER XXXVII

Of how the rejoicing of the will must be directed, by way of images, to God,
so that the soul may not go astray because of them or be hindered by them.

JUST as images are of great benefit for remembering God and the
saints, and for moving the will to devotion when they are used in
the ordinary way,[3] as is fitting, so they will lead to great error if,
when supernatural happenings come to pass in connection with them,
the soul should not be able to conduct itself as is fitting for its journey
to God. For one of the means by which the devil lays hold on incautious souls, with great ease, and obstructs the way of spiritual truth
for them, is the use of extraordinary and supernatural[4] happenings, of
which he gives examples by means of images, both the material and
corporeal images used by the Church, and also those which he is wont
to fix in the fancy in relation to such or such a saint, or an image of
him, transforming himself into an angel of light that he may deceive.
For in those very means which we possess for our relief and help the
astute devil contrives to hide himself in order to catch us when we are
least prepared. Wherefore it is concerning good things that the soul
that is good must ever have the greatest misgivings, for evil things
bear their own testimony with them.

2. Hence, in order to avoid all the evils which may happen to the
soul in this connection, which are its being hindered from soaring
upward to God, or its using images in an unworthy and ignorant

---

[1] A: '. . . or speak in this manner or in another. But concerning the supernatural
effects, etc., . . . they are.'
[2] E.p.: 'Yet at other times they are not true [effects] and are apt to be produced by
the devil.'
[3] Alc. omits: 'in the ordinary way.'
[4] E.p.: 'and rare.' Cf. p. 124, n. 5, above.

manner, or its being deceived by them through natural or supernatural means,[1] all of which are things that we have touched upon
above; and in order likewise to purify the rejoicing of the will in them
and by means of them to lead the soul to God, for which reason the
Church recommends their use, I desire here to set down only one
warning, which will suffice for everything; and this warning is that,
since images serve us as a motive for invisible things, we must strive
to set the motive and the affection and the rejoicing of our will only
upon that which in fact they represent. Let the faithful soul, then, be
careful that, when he sees the image, he desire not that his senses
should be absorbed by it, whether the image be corporeal or imaginary,
whether beautifully made, whether richly adorned, whether the
devotion that it causes be of sense or of spirit, whether it produce
supernatural manifestations or no. The soul must on no account set
store by these accidents, nor even regard them, but[2] must raise up its
mind from the image to that which it represents, centring the sweetness
and rejoicing of its will, together with the prayer and devotion of its
spirit, upon God or upon the saint who is being invoked; for that
which belongs to the living reality and to the spirit should not be
usurped by sense and by the painted object. If the soul do this, it will
not be deceived, for it will set no store by anything that the image
may say to it, nor will it occupy its sense or its spirit in such a way that
they cannot travel freely to God, nor will it place more confidence in
one image than in another. And an image which would cause the soul
devotion by supernatural means will now do so more abundantly,
since the soul will now go with its affections directly to God. For,
whensoever God grants these and other favours, He does so by
inclining the affection of the joy of the will to that which is invisible,
and this He wishes us also to do, by annihilating the power and
sweetness of the faculties with respect to these visible things of sense.

[1] E.p. omits: 'through natural or supernatural means.'
[2] E.p. here interpolates: 'having paid to the image the adoration which the Church
commands.'

CHAPTER XXXVIII

Continues to describe motive good. Speaks of oratories and places dedicated to prayer.

I THINK it has now been explained how the spiritual person may find as great imperfection in the accidents of images, by setting his pleasure and rejoicing[1] upon them, as in other corporeal and temporal things, and perchance imperfection more perilous still. And I say perchance more perilous, because, when a person says that the objects of his rejoicing are holy, he feels more secure, and fears not to cling to them and become attached to them in a natural way. And thus such a person is sometimes greatly deceived, thinking himself to be full of devotion because he perceives that he takes pleasure in these holy things, when, perchance, this is due only to his natural desire and temperament, which lead him to this just as they lead him to other things.

2. Hence it arises (we are now beginning to treat of oratories) that there are some persons who never tire of adding to their oratories images of one kind and then of another, and take pleasure in the order and array in which they set them out, so that these oratories may be well adorned and pleasing to behold. Yet they love God no more when their oratories are ornate than when they are simple—nay, rather do they love Him less, since, as we have said, the pleasure which they set upon their painted adornments is stolen from the living reality. It is true that all the adornment and embellishment and respect that can be lavished upon images amounts to very little, and that therefore those who have images and treat them with a lack of decency and reverence are worthy of severe reproof, as are those who have images so ill-carved that they take away devotion rather than produce it, for which reason some image-makers who are very defective and unskilled in this art should be forbidden to practise it. But what has that to do with the attachment and affection and desire which you have[2] for these outward adornments and decorations, when your senses are absorbed by them in such a way that your heart is hindered from journeying to God, and from loving Him and forgetting all things for love of Him?

---

[1] E.p. omits: 'and rejoicing.'
[2] [Again the Saint begins, repeatedly and emphatically, to employ the pronoun *tú*. Cf. p. 293, n. 5, above.]

If you fail in the latter aim for the sake of the former, not only will God not esteem you for it, but He will even chasten you for not having sought His pleasure in all things rather than your own. This you may clearly gather from the description of that feast which they made for His Majesty when He entered Jerusalem. They received Him with songs and with branches, and the Lord wept;[1] for their hearts were very far removed from Him and they paid Him reverence only with outward adornments and signs. We may say of them that they were making a festival for themselves rather than for God; and this is done nowadays by many, who, when there is some solemn festival in a place,[2] are apt to rejoice because of the pleasure which they themselves will find in it—whether in seeing or in being seen, or whether in eating or in some other selfish thing—rather than to rejoice at being acceptable to God. By these inclinations and intentions they are giving no pleasure to God. Especially is this so when those who celebrate festivals invent ridiculous and undevout things to intersperse in them, so that they may incite people to laughter, which causes them greater distraction. And other persons invent things which merely please people rather than move them to devotion.

3. And what shall I say of persons who celebrate festivals for reasons connected with their own interests? They alone, and God Who sees them, know if their regard and desire are set upon such interests rather than upon the service of God. Let them realize, when they act in any of these ways, that they are making festivals in their own honour rather than in that of God. For that which they do for their own pleasure, or for the pleasure of men, God will not account as done for Himself. Yea, many who take part in God's festivals will be enjoying themselves even while God is wroth with them, as He was with the children of Israel when they made a festival, and sang and danced before their idol, thinking that they were keeping a festival in honour of God; of whom He slew many thousands.[3] Or again, as He was with the priests Nadab and Abiu, the sons of Aaron, whom He slew with the censers in their hands, because they offered strange fire.[4] Or as with the man that entered the wedding feast ill-adorned[5] and ill-garbed, whom the king commanded to be thrown into outer darkness, bound hand and foot.[6] By this it may be known how ill God suffers these irreverences in assemblies that are held for His service. For how many

---

[1] St. Matthew xxi, 9. [Cf. St. Luke xix, 41.]   [2] E.p.: 'when there is a solemnity.'
[3] Exodus xxxii, 7–28.   [4] Leviticus x, 1–2.
[5] E.p.: 'ill-clad.'   [6] St. Matthew xxii, 12–13.

festivals, O my God, are made Thee by the sons of men to the devil's
advantage rather than to Thine! The devil takes a delight in them,
because such gatherings bring him business, as they might to a trader.
And how often wilt Thou say concerning them : 'This people honoureth
Me with their lips alone, but their heart is far from Me, for they serve
Me from a wrong cause!'[1] For the sole reason[2] for which God must be
served is that He is Who He is, and not for any other mediate ends.
And thus to serve Him for other reasons than solely that He is Who
He is, is to serve Him without regard for Him as the Ultimate Reason.[3]

4. Returning now to oratories, I say that some persons deck them
out for their own pleasure rather than for the pleasure of God; and
some persons set so little account by the devotion which they arouse
that they think no more of them than of their own secular ante-
chambers; some, indeed, think even less of them, for they take more
pleasure in the profane than in the Divine.

5. But let us cease speaking of this and speak only of those who are
more particular[4]—that is to say, of those who consider themselves
devout persons. Many of these centre their desire and pleasure upon
their oratory and its adornments, to such an extent that they squander
on them all the time that they should be employing in prayer to God
and interior recollection. They cannot see that, by not arranging their
oratory with a view to the interior recollection and peace of the soul,
they are as much distracted by it as by anything else, and will find the
pleasure which they take in it a continual occasion of unrest, and more
so still if anyone endeavours to deprive them of it.

CHAPTER XXXIX

*Of the way in which oratories and churches should be used, so that the
spirit may be directed to God.*

WITH regard to the direction of the spirit to God through this
kind of good, it is well to point out that it is certainly lawful,
and even expedient, for beginners to find some sensible
sweetness and pleasure in images, oratories and other visible objects

---

1 St. Matthew xv, 8. [*Lit.*, 'they serve Me without cause.']
2 E.p.: 'For the principal cause.'
3 This last sentence is omitted in e.p.
4 [*Lit.*, 'that spin more finely'—a common Spanish metaphor.]

of devotion, since they have not yet weaned or detached their desire[1] from things of the world, so that they can leave the one pleasure for the other. They are like a child holding something in one of its hands; to make it loosen its hold upon it we give it something else to hold in the other hand lest it should cry because both its hands are empty. But the spiritual person that would make progress must strip himself of all those pleasures and desires wherein the will can rejoice, for pure spirituality is bound very little to any of those objects, but only to interior recollection and mental converse with God. So, although he makes use of images and oratories, he does so only fleetingly; his spirit at once comes to rest in God and he forgets all things of sense.

2. Wherefore, although it is best to pray where there is most decency, yet notwithstanding one should choose the place where sense and spirit are least hindered from journeying to God. Here we should consider that answer made by Our Saviour to the Samaritan woman, when she asked Him which was the more fitting place wherein to pray, the temple or the mountain, and He answered her[2] that true prayer was not connected with the mountain or with the temple,[3] but that those who adored the Father and were pleasing to Him were those that adored Him in spirit and in truth.[4] Wherefore, although churches and pleasant places are[5] set apart and furnished for prayer (for a church must not be used for aught else), yet, for a matter as intimate[6] as converse held with God, one should choose that place which gives sense the least occupation and the least encouragement. And thus it must not be a place that is pleasant and delectable to sense (like the places that some habitually contrive to find), for otherwise, instead of the recollection of the spirit in God, naught will be achieved save recreation and pleasure and delight of sense. Wherefore it is good to choose a place that is solitary, and even wild, so that the spirit may resolutely and directly soar upward to God, and not be hindered or detained by visible things; for, although these sometimes help to raise up the spirit, it is better to forget them at once and to rest in God. For this reason Our Saviour was wont to choose solitary places for prayer, and such as occupied the senses but little, in order to give us an example. He chose places that lifted up the soul to God, such as mountains,[7] which are

1 [*Lit.*, 'their palate.']
2 E.p. omits: 'and He answered her.'
3 E.p. omits: 'or with the temple.'
4 St. John iv, 23–4.
5 E.p. has 'may be' for 'are.'
6 A, B: 'as important and intimate'.
7 Alc. ends the paragraph here.

lifted up above the earth, and are ordinarily bare, thus offering no occasion for recreation of the senses.

3. The truly spiritual man, then, is never tied to a place of prayer because of its suitability in this way or in that, nor does he even consider such a thing, for, if he did so, he would still be tied to sense. But, to the end that he may attain interior recollection, and forget everything, he chooses[1] the places most free from sensible objects and attractions, withdrawing his attention from all these, that he may be able to rejoice in his God and be far removed from all things created. But it is a remarkable thing to see some spiritual persons, who waste all their time in setting up oratories and furnishing places which please their temperaments or inclinations, yet make little account of interior recollection, which is the most important thing, but of which they have very little. If they had more of it, they would be incapable of taking pleasure in those methods and manners of devotion, which would simply weary them.

CHAPTER XL

Which continues to direct the spirit to interior recollection with reference to what has been said.

THE reason, then, why some spiritual persons never enter perfectly into the true joys of the spirit is that they never succeed in raising their desire for rejoicing above these things that are outward and visible. Let such take note that, although the visible oratory and temple is a decent place set apart for prayer, and an image is a motive to prayer, the sweetness and delight of the soul must not be set upon the motive or the visible temple, lest the soul should forget to pray in the living temple, which is the interior recollection of the soul. The Apostle, to remind us of this, said: 'See that your bodies are living temples of the Holy Spirit, Who dwelleth in you.'[2] And this thought is suggested by the words of Christ which we have quoted, namely that they who truly adore God must needs adore Him in spirit and in truth.[3] For God takes little heed of your oratories and your places set apart for prayer if your desire and pleasure are

---

[1] E.p. abbreviates, from the beginning of the paragraph: 'Wherefore the truly spiritual man, considering only interior recollection and forgetting everything, chooses.'

[2] 1 Corinthians iii, 16. E.p. adds: 'And Christ said through Luke: The kingdom of God is within you' (St. Luke xvii, 21).   [3] St. John iv, 24.

bound to them, and thus you have little interior detachment, which is spiritual poverty and renunciation of all things that you may possess.

2. In order, then, to purge the will from vain desire and rejoicing in this matter, and to lead it to God in your prayer, you must see only to this, that your conscience is pure, and your will perfect with God, and your spirit truly set upon Him. Then, as I have said, you should choose the place that is the farthest withdrawn and the most solitary that you can find, and devote all the rejoicing of the will to calling upon God and glorifying Him; and you should take no account of those whims about outward things, but rather strive to renounce them. For, if the soul be attached to the delight of sensible devotion, it will never succeed in passing onward to the power of spiritual delight, which is found in spiritual detachment coming through interior recollection.

CHAPTER XLI

Of certain evils into which those persons fall who give themselves to pleasure in sensible objects and who frequent places of devotion in the way that has been described.

MANY evils, both interior and exterior, come to the spiritual person when he desires to follow after sweetness of sense in these matters aforementioned. For, as regards the spirit, he will never attain to interior spiritual recollection, which consists in neglecting all such things, and in causing the soul to forget all this sensible sweetness, and to enter into true recollection, and acquire the virtues by dint of effort. As regards exterior things, he will become unable to dispose himself for prayer in all places, but will be confined to places that are to his taste; and thus he will often fail in prayer, because, as the saying goes, he can understand no other book than his own village.

2. Furthermore, this desire leads such persons into great inconstancy. Some of them never continue in one place or even always in one state: now they will be seen in one place, now in another; now they will go to one hermitage, now to another; now they will set up this oratory, now that.[1] Some of them, again, wear out their lives in changing from one state or manner of living to another. For, as they possess only the sensible fervour and joy to be found in spiritual

---

[1] Alc. omits: 'now they . . . now that.'

things, and have never had the strength to attain to spiritual recollection by the renunciation of their own will, and submitting to suffering
inconveniences, whenever they see a place which they think well
suited for devotion, or any kind of life or state well adapted to their
temperament and inclination, they at once go after it and leave the
condition or state in which they were before. And, as they have come
under the influence of that sensible pleasure, it follows that they soon
seek something new, for sensible pleasure is not constant, but very
quickly fails.[1]

CHAPTER XLII

*Of three different kinds of place for devotion and of how the will should
conduct itself with regard to them.*

I CAN think of three kinds of place by means of which God is wont
to move the will to devotion. The first consists in certain dispositions of the ground and situation, which, by means of a pleasing
effect of variety, whether obtained by the arrangement of the ground or
of trees, or by means of quiet solitude, naturally awaken devotion.
These places it is beneficial to use, if they at once lead the will to God
and cause it to forget the places themselves, even as, in order to reach
one's journey's end, it is advisable not to pause and consider the means
and motive of the journey more than is necessary. For those who
strive to refresh their desires and to gain sensible sweetness will rather
find spiritual aridity and distraction; for spiritual sweetness and satisfaction are not found save in interior recollection.

2. When they are in such a place, therefore, they should forget it
and strive to be inwardly with God, as though they were not in that
place at all. For, if they be attached to the pleasure and delight of the
place, as we have said, they are seeking refreshment of sense and instability of spirit rather than spiritual repose. The anchorites and other
holy hermits, who in the most vast and pleasing wildernesses selected
the smallest places that sufficed for them, built there the smallest cells
and caves, in which to imprison themselves. Saint Benedict was in such
a place for three years, and another—namely, Saint Simon[2]—bound
himself with a cord that he might have no more liberty nor go any

---

[1] E.p.: 'and very quickly fails.'
[2] E.p. omits: 'namely, Saint Simon.' The allusion is, of course, to St. Simon Stylites.

farther than to places within its reach; and even so did many who are too numerous ever to be counted. Those saints understood very clearly that, if they quenched not the desire and eagerness for spiritual sweetness and pleasure, they could not attain to spirituality.

3. The second kind is of a more special nature, for it relates to certain places (not necessarily deserts, but any places whatsoever) where God is accustomed to grant to a few special persons certain very delectable spiritual favours; ordinarily, such a place attracts the heart of the person who has received a favour there, and sometimes gives him great desires and yearnings to return to it; although, when he goes there, what happened to him before is not repeated, since this is not within his control. For God grants these favours[1] when and how and where He pleases, without being tied to any place or time, nor to the free-will of the person to whom He grants them. Yet it is good to go and pray in such places at times if the desire is free from attachment; and this for three reasons. First, because although, as we said, God is not bound to any place, it would seem that He has willed to be praised by a soul in the place where He has granted it a favour. Secondly, because in that place the soul is more mindful to give thanks to God for that which it has received there. Thirdly, because, by remembering that favour, the soul's devotion is the more keenly awakened.

4. It is for these reasons that a man should go to such places, and not because he thinks that God is bound to grant him favours there, in such a way as to be unable to grant them wheresoever He wills, for the soul is a fitter and more comely place for God than any physical place. Thus we read in Holy Scripture that Abraham built an altar in the very place where God appeared to him, and invoked His holy name there, and that afterwards, coming from Egypt, he returned by the same road where God had appeared to him, and called upon God there once more at the same altar which he had built.[2] Jacob, too, marked the place where God had appeared to him, leaning upon a ladder, by raising there a stone which he anointed with oil.[3] And Agar gave a name to the place where the angel had appeared to her, and prized it highly, saying: 'Of a truth I have here seen the back of Him that seeth me.'[4]

5. The third kind consists of certain special places which God chooses that He may be called upon and served there, such as Mount Sinai, where He gave the law to Moses.[5] And the place that He showed

---

[1] A, B: 'since it is not within his power to receive those favours; God grants them . . .
[2] Genesis xii, 8; xiii, 4.   [3] Genesis xxviii, 13–19.
[4] Genesis xvi, 13.   [5] Exodus xxiv, 12.

Abraham, that he might sacrifice his son there.[1] And likewise Mount Horeb, where He appeared to our father Elias.[2]

6. The reason for which God chooses these places rather than others, that He may be praised there, is known to Himself alone. What it behoves us to know is that all is for our advantage, and that He will hear our prayers there, and also in any place where we pray to Him with perfect faith; although there is much greater opportunity for us to be heard in places dedicated to His service, since the Church has appointed and dedicated those places to that end.

CHAPTER XLIII

Which treats of other motives for prayer that many persons use—namely, a great variety of ceremonies.

THE useless joys and the imperfect attachment which many persons have to the things which we have described are perhaps to some extent excusable, since these persons act more or less innocently with regard to them. But[3] the great reliance which some persons place in many kinds of ceremonies introduced by uninstructed persons who lack the simplicity of faith is intolerable. Let us here disregard those which bear various extraordinary names or use terms that signify nothing, and also other things that are not sacred which persons who are foolish and gross and mistrustful in spirit are wont to interpolate in their prayers. For these are clearly evil, and involve sin, and many of them imply a secret compact with the devil; by such means these persons provoke God to wrath and not to mercy, wherefore I treat them not here.

2. I wish to speak solely of those ceremonies into which enters nothing of a suspicious nature, and of which many people make use nowadays with indiscreet devotion, attributing such efficacy and faith to these ways and manners wherein they desire to perform their

---

[1] Genesis xxii, 2.

[2] 3 Kings [A.V., 1 Kings] xix, 8. A, B, e.p. amplify, thus: 'And likewise Mount Horeb, whither God sent for our father Elias to come, that He might show Himself to him there. And the place which Saint Michael set apart for his service, namely Mount Garganus, when he appeared to the bishop of Siponto, and said that he was the guardian of that place and that an oratory should be dedicated to God in memory of the angels. And the glorious Virgin chose (by the remarkable sign of snow) a place for the church, to be named after her, which she desired Patricius to build.'

[3] E.p. alone has 'but.'

devotions and prayers, that they believe that, if they fail to the very slightest extent in them, or go beyond their limits, God will not be served by them nor will He hear them. They place more reliance upon these methods and kinds of ceremony than upon the reality of their prayer, and herein they greatly offend and displease God. I refer, for example, to a Mass at which there must be so many candles, neither more nor fewer; which has to be said by the priest in such or such a way; and must be at such or such an hour, and neither sooner nor later; and must be after a certain day, and neither sooner nor later; and the prayers and stations must be made at such and such times, with such or such ceremonies, and neither sooner nor later nor in any other manner; and the person who makes them must have such or such qualities or qualifications. And there are those who think that, if any of these details which they have laid down be wanting, nothing is accomplished.[1]

3. And, what is worse, and indeed intolerable, is that certain persons desire to feel some effect in themselves, or to have their petitions fulfilled, or to know that the purpose of these ceremonious prayers of theirs will be accomplished. This is nothing less than to tempt God and to anger Him greatly, so much so that He sometimes gives leave to the devil to deceive them, making them feel and understand things that are far removed from the benefit of their soul, which they deserve because of the attachment that they show in their prayers, not desiring God's will, rather than their own desires, to be done therein; and thus, because they place not their whole confidence in God, nothing goes well with them.[2]

[1] A, B add: 'and [there are] a thousand other things that are offered and used.' So e.p., but omitting: 'offered and.'
[2] With the last word of this chapter, which is also the last word of the page in Alc., the copy of P. Juan Evangelista comes to an end. The remainder of Alc. comes from another very early copy which, in the time of P. Andrés, existed at Duruelo (cf. p. xxvi, above).

CHAPTER XLIV

Of the manner wherein the rejoicing and strength of the will must be directed to God through these devotions.

LET these persons, then, know that, the more reliance they place on these things and ceremonies,[1] the less confidence they have in God, and that they will not obtain of God that which they desire. There are certain persons who pray[2] for their own ends rather than for the honour of God. Although they suppose that a thing will be done if it be for the service of God, and not otherwise, yet, because of their attachment to it and the vain rejoicing which they have in it, they multiply a large number of petitions for a thing, when it would be better for them to substitute others of greater importance to them, such as for the true cleansing of their consciences, and for a real application to things concerning their own salvation, leaving to a much later season all those other petitions of theirs which are not of this kind. And in this way they would attain that which is of the greatest importance to them, and at the same time all the other things that are good for them (although they might not have prayed for them), much better and much earlier than if they had expended all their energy on those things. For this the Lord promised, through the Evangelist, saying: 'Seek ye first and principally the Kingdom of God and His righteousness, and all these other things shall be added unto you.'[3]

2. This is the seeking and the asking that is most pleasing to God, and, in order to obtain the fulfilment of the petitions which we have in our hearts, there is no better way than to direct the energy of our prayer to the thing that most pleases God. For then not only will He give that which we ask of Him, which is salvation, but also that which He sees to be fitting and good for us, although we pray not for it. This David makes clear in a psalm where he says: 'The Lord is nigh unto those that call upon Him in truth,'[4] that beg Him[5] for the things that are in the highest degree true, such as salvation; for of these he then says: 'He will fulfil the will of them that fear Him, and will hear their

---

[1] B: 'the more they rely on their ceremonies.' E.p.: 'the more they lean on these their ceremonies.'

[2] A, e.p.: 'who work' [*obran* for *oran*].

[3] St. Matthew vi, 33.   [4] Psalm cxliv, 18 [A.V., cxlv, 18].

[5] E.p., keeping near the Latin text of the psalm, has: '. . . that call upon Him, to those that call upon Him in truth. And those that call upon Him in truth are such as beg Him.'

cries, and will save them. For God is the guardian of those that truly love Him.'¹ And thus, this nearness to God of which David here speaks is naught else than His being ready to satisfy them and grant them even that which it has not passed through their minds to ask. Even so we read that, because Solomon did well in asking God for a thing that was pleasing to Him—namely, wisdom to lead and rule his people righteously—God answered him, saying: 'Because more than aught else thou didst desire wisdom, and askedst not victory over thine enemies, with their deaths, nor riches, nor long life, I will not only give thee the wisdom that thou askest to rule My people righteously, but I will likewise give thee that which thou hast not asked—namely, riches and substance and glory—so that neither before thee nor after thee shall there be any king like unto thee.'² And this He did, giving him peace also from his enemies, so that all around him should pay tribute to him and trouble him not. We read of a similar incident in Genesis, where God promised Abraham to increase the generation of his lawful son, like the stars of Heaven, even as he had asked of Him, and said to him: 'Likewise I will increase the son of the bondwoman, for he is thy son.'³

3. In this way, then, the strength of the will and its rejoicing must be directed to God in our petitions, and we must not be anxious to cling to ceremonial inventions which are not used or approved by the Catholic Church. We must leave the method and manner of saying Mass to the priest, whom the Church sets there in her place, giving him her orders as to how he is to do it. And let not such persons use new methods, as if they knew more than the Holy Spirit and His Church. If, when they pray in their simplicity, God hears them not, let them not think that He will hear them any the more however many may be their inventions. For God is such that, if they behave towards Him as they should, and conformably to His nature, they will do with Him whatsoever they will; but, if they act from selfish ends, they cannot speak with Him.⁴

4. With regard to further ceremonies connected with prayer and other devotions, let not the will be set upon other ceremonies and forms of prayer than those which Christ⁵ taught us.⁶ For it is clear that, when His disciples besought Him that He would teach them to pray, He would tell them all that is necessary in order that the Eternal

---

¹ Psalm cxliv, 19–20 [A.V., cxlv, 19–20].
² 2 Paralipomenon [A.V., 2 Chronicles] i, 11–12.   ³ Genesis xxi, 13.
⁴ So Alc. E.p. omits the sentence: 'For God . . . speak with Him.'
⁵ E.p.: 'Christ and His Church.'   ⁶ St. Luke xi, 1–4.

Father may hear us, since He knew the Father's nature so well. Yet all that He taught them was the Pater Noster, with its seven petitions, wherein are included all our needs, both spiritual and temporal;[1] and He taught them not many other kinds of prayer, either in words or in ceremonies. On the contrary, He told them that when they prayed they ought not to desire to speak much, since our heavenly Father knows well what is meet for us.[2] He charged them only, but with great insistence, that they should persevere in prayer (that is, in the prayer of the Pater Noster), saying elsewhere: 'It behoves us always to pray and never to fail.'[3] But He taught not a variety of petitions, but rather that our petitions should be repeated frequently and with fervour and care. For, as I say, in them is contained all that is the will of God and all that is meet for us. Wherefore, when His Majesty drew near three times to the Eternal Father, He prayed all these three times, using those very words of the Pater Noster, as the Evangelists tell us, saying: 'Father, if it cannot be but that I must drink this cup, Thy will be done.'[4] And the ceremonies which He taught us to use in our prayers are only two. Either we are to pray in the secret place of our chamber, where without noise and without paying heed to any we can pray with the most perfect and pure heart, as He said in these words: 'When thou shalt pray, enter into thy chamber and shut the door and pray.'[5] Or else He taught us to go to a solitary and desert place, as He Himself did, and at the best and quietest time of night. And thus there is no reason to fix any limit of time, or any appointed days, or to set apart one time more than another for our devotions, neither is there any reason to use[6] other forms, in our words and prayers, nor phrases with double meanings, but only those which the Church uses and in the manner wherein she uses them; for all are reduced to those which we have described—namely, the Pater Noster.

5. I do not for this reason condemn—nay, I rather approve—the fixing of days on which certain persons sometimes arrange to make their devotions, such as novenas,[7] or other such things. I condemn only their conduct as concerns the fixity of their methods and the ceremonies with which they practise them. Even so did Judith rebuke and reprove the people of Bethulia because they had limited God as to the

---

[1] A, B: 'both corporeal and spiritual.'   [2] St. Matthew vi, 7–8.
[3] St. Luke xviii, 1.   [4] St. Matthew xxvi, 39.
[5] St. Matthew vi, 6.
[6] E.p. abbreviates: 'And thus there is no reason to fix times or fixed [sic] days, nor is there any reason to use.'
[7] So A, B. The other authorities [and P. Silverio] read: 'such as to fast.'

time wherein they awaited His mercy,[1] saying: 'Do ye set God a time for His mercies?' To do this, she says, is not to move God to clemency, but to awaken His wrath.[2]

CHAPTER XLV

Which treats of the second kind of distinct good, wherein the will may rejoice vainly.

THE second kind of distinct and delectable good wherein the will may rejoice vainly is that which provokes or persuades us to serve God and which we have called provocative. This class comprises preachers, and we might speak of it in two ways, namely, as affecting the preachers themselves and as affecting their hearers. For, as regards both, we must not fail to observe that both must direct the rejoicing of their will to God, with respect to this exercise.

2. In the first place, it must be pointed out to the preacher, if he is to cause his people profit and not to embarrass himself[3] with vain joy and presumption, that preaching is a spiritual exercise rather than a vocal one. For, although it is practised by means of outward words, its power and efficacy reside not in these but in the inward spirit. Wherefore, however lofty be the doctrine that is preached, and however choice the rhetoric and sublime the style wherein it is clothed, it brings as a rule no more benefit than is present in the spirit of the preacher. For, although it is true that the word of God is of itself efficacious, according to those words of David, 'He will give to His voice a voice of virtue,'[4] yet fire, which has also a virtue—that of burning—will not burn when the material is not prepared.

3. To the end that the preacher's instruction may exercise its full force, there must be two kinds of preparation: that of the preacher and that of the hearer; for as a rule the benefit derived from a sermon depends upon the preparation of the teacher. For this reason it is said that, as is the master, so is wont to be the disciple. For, when in the Acts of the Apostles those seven sons of that chief priest of the Jews[5] were wont to cast out devils in the same form as Saint Paul, the devil rose up against them, saying: 'Jesus I confess and Paul I know, but you, who are ye?'[6] And then, attacking them, he stripped and wounded

---

[1] A, B: 'awaited mercy from His hand.'   [2] Judith viii, 11–12.
[3] E.p.: 'and not to become vain.'   [4] Psalm lxvii, 34 [A.V., lxviii, 33].
[5] E.p.: 'those seven sons of Sceva.'   [6] Acts xix, 15.

them. This was only because they had not the fitting preparation, and not because Christ willed not that they should do this in His name. For the Apostles once found a man, who was not a disciple, casting out a devil in the name of Christ, and they forbade him, and the Lord reproved them for it, saying: 'Forbid him not, for no man that has done any mighty works in My name shall be able to speak evil of Me after a brief space of time.'[1] But He is angry with those who, though teaching the law of God, keep it not, and, while preaching spirituality, possess it not. For this reason God says, through Saint Paul: 'Thou teachest others and teachest not thyself. Thou who preachest that men should not steal, stealest.'[2] And through David the Holy Spirit says: 'To the sinner, God said: "Why dost thou declare My justice and take My law in thy mouth, when thou hast hated discipline and cast My words behind thee?"'[3] Here it is made plain that He will give them no spirituality whereby they may bear fruit.

4. It is a common matter of observation that, so far as we can judge here below, the better is the life of the preacher, the greater is the fruit that he bears, however undistinguished his style may be, however small his rhetoric and however ordinary his instruction. For it is the warmth that comes from the living spirit that clings; whereas the other kind of preacher will produce very little profit, however sublime be his style and his instruction. For, although it is true that a good style and gestures and sublime instruction and well-chosen language influence men and produce much effect when accompanied by true spirituality, yet without this, although a sermon give[4] pleasure and delight to the sense and the understanding, very little or nothing of its sweetness remains in the will. As a rule, in this case, the will remains as weak and remiss with regard to good works as it was before. Although marvellous things may have been marvellously said by the preacher, they serve only to delight the ear, like a concert of music or a peal of bells; the spirit, as I say, goes no farther from its habits than before, since the voice has no virtue to raise one that is dead from his grave.

5. Little does it matter that one kind of music should sound better than another if the better kind move me not more than the other to do good works. For, although marvellous things may have been said, they are at once forgotten if they have not fired the will. For, not only do they of themselves bear little fruit, but the fastening of the sense

---

[1] St. Mark ix, 38–9.   [2] Romans ii, 21.
[3] Psalm xlix, 16–17 [A.V., l, 16–17].
[4] So Alc. The other authorities have: 'although it give . . .'

upon the pleasure that it finds in that sort of instruction hinders the instruction from passing to the spirit, so that only the method and the accidents of what has been said are appreciated, and the preacher is praised for this characteristic or for that, and followed from such motives as these rather than because of the purpose of amendment of life which he has inspired. This doctrine is well explained to the Corinthians by Saint Paul, where he says: 'I, brethren, when I came to you, came not preaching Christ with loftiness of instruction and of wisdom, and my words and my preaching consisted not in the rhetoric of human wisdom, but in the showing forth of the spirit and of the truth.'[1]

6. Although the intention of the Apostle here, like my own intention, is not to condemn good style and rhetoric and phraseology, for, on the contrary, these are of great importance to the preacher, as in everything else, since good phraseology and style raise up and restore things that are fallen and ruined, even as bad phraseology ruins and destroys good things. . . .[2]

---

[1] 1 Corinthians ii, 1–4. B, e.p.: 'and of virtue.'

[2] E.p. adds: 'End of the *Ascent of Mount Carmel*.' The treatise thus remains incomplete, the chapter on the preacher being unfinished and no part of any chapter upon the hearer having come down to us. Further, the last two divisions of the four mentioned in Chap. xxxv, § 1 are not treated in any of the MSS. or early editions.

The fragments which P. Gerardo [*Obras*, etc., I, 402–10] added to the *Ascent*, forming two chapters, cannot be considered as a continuation of this book. They are in reality a long and admirable letter [Letter XI in this edition: Vol. III, p. 255], written to a religious, who was one of the Saint's spiritual sons, and copied by P. Jerónimo de San José in his *History of St. John of the Cross* (Bk. VI, Chap. vii). There is not the slightest doubt that the letter, which was written at Segovia, and is fully dated, is a genuine letter, and not an editor's maltreatment of part of a treatise. Only the similarity of its subject with that of these last chapters is responsible for its having been added to the *Ascent*. It is hard to see how P. Gerardo could have been misled about a matter which is so clear.

[This question was re-opened, in 1950, by P. Sobrino (see Vol. III, p. 240), who adds TG and a codex belonging to the Discalced Carmelite Fathers of Madrid to the list of the MSS. which give the fragments as part of the *Ascent*, making six authorities in all, against which can be set only the proved and admitted reliability of P. Jerónimo de San José. P. Sobrino, who discusses the matter (*Estudios*, etc., pp. 166–93) in great detail, hazards a plausible and attractive solution, which he reinforces with substantial evidence—that of a 'double redaction.' According to this theory, the Saint, in writing to the religious of Letter XI, made use, for the substance of his instruction, of two fragments which were to have gone into the *Ascent*. Considering how often in his writings he doubled passages, to say nothing of whole works, it is quite understandable that he should have utilized two unincorporated, and indeed unfinished, passages for a private letter.]

DARK NIGHT OF THE SOUL

INTRODUCTION

SOMEWHAT reluctantly, out of respect for a venerable tradition, we publish the *Dark Night* as a separate treatise, though in reality it is a continuation of the *Ascent of Mount Carmel* and fulfils the undertakings given in it:

The first night or purgation is of the sensual part of the soul, which is treated in the present stanza, and will be treated in the first part of this book. And the second is of the spiritual part; of this speaks the second stanza, which follows; and of this we shall treat likewise, in the second and the third part, with respect to the activity of the soul; *and in the fourth part, with respect to its passivity.*[1]

This 'fourth part' is the *Dark Night.* Of it the Saint writes in a passage which follows that just quoted:

And the second night, or purification, pertains to those who are already proficient, occurring at the time when God desires to bring them to the state of union with God. And this latter night is a more obscure and dark and terrible purgation, as we shall say afterwards.[2]

In his three earlier books he has written of the Active Night, of Sense and of Spirit; he now proposes to deal with the Passive Night, in the same order. He has already taught us how we are to deny and purify ourselves with the ordinary help of grace, in order to prepare our senses and faculties for union with God through love. He now proceeds to explain, with an arresting freshness, how these same senses and faculties are purged and purified by God with a view to the same end—that of union. The combined description of the two nights completes the presentation of active and passive purgation, to which the Saint limits himself in these treatises, although the subject of the stanzas which he is glossing is a much wider one, comprising the whole of the mystical life and ending only with the Divine embraces of the soul transformed in God through love.

[1] *Ascent*, Bk. I, chap. i, § 2 (p. 18, above). Cf. p. 2, above.
[2] *Op. cit.*, § 3 (p. 18, above).

The stanzas expounded by the Saint are taken from the same poem in the two treatises. The commentary upon the second, however, is very different from that upon the first, for it assumes a much more advanced state of development. The Active Night has left the senses and faculties well prepared, though not completely prepared, for the reception of Divine influences and illuminations in greater abundance than before. The Saint here postulates a principle of dogmatic theology —that by himself, and with the ordinary aid of grace, man cannot attain to that degree of purgation which is essential to his transformation in God. He needs Divine aid more abundantly. 'However greatly the soul itself labours,' writes the Saint, 'it cannot actively purify itself so as to be in the least degree prepared for the Divine union of perfection of love, if God takes not its hand and purges it not in that dark fire.'[1]

The Passive Nights, in which it is God Who accomplishes the purgation, are based upon this incapacity. Souls 'begin to enter' this dark night

when God draws them forth from the state of beginners—which is the state of those that meditate on the spiritual road—and begins to set them in the state of progressives—which is that of those who are already contemplatives —to the end that, after passing through it, they may arrive at the state of the perfect, which is that of the Divine union of the soul with God.[2]

Before explaining the nature and effects of this Passive Night, the Saint touches, in passing, upon certain imperfections found in those who are about to enter it and which it removes by the process of purgation. Such travellers are still untried proficients, who have not yet acquired mature habits of spirituality and who therefore still conduct themselves as children. The imperfections are examined one by one, following the order of the seven deadly sins, in chapters (ii–viii) which once more reveal the author's skill as a director of souls. They are easy chapters to understand, and of great practical utility, comparable to those in the first book of the *Ascent* which deal with the active purgation of the desires of sense.

In Chapter viii, St. John of the Cross begins to describe the Passive Night of the senses, the principal aim of which is the purgation or stripping of the soul of its imperfections and the preparation of it for fruitive union. The Passive Night of Sense, we are told, is 'common' and 'comes to many,' whereas that of Spirit 'is the portion

Dark Night, Bk. I, chap. iii, § 3.   [2] *Op. cit.*, Bk. I, chap. i, § 1.

of very few.'[1] The one is 'bitter and terrible' but 'the second bears no comparison with it,' for it is 'horrible and awful to the spirit.'[2] A good deal of literature on the former Night existed in the time of St. John of the Cross and he therefore promises to be brief in his treatment of it. Of the latter, on the other hand, he will 'treat more fully . . . since very little has been said of this, either in speech or in writing, and very little is known of it, even by experience.'[3]

Having described this Passive Night of Sense in Chapter viii, he explains with great insight and discernment how it may be recognized whether any given aridity is a result of this Night or whether it comes from sins or imperfections, or from frailty or lukewarmness of spirit, or even from indisposition or 'humours' of the body. The Saint is particularly effective here, and we may once more compare this chapter with a similar one in the *Ascent* (II, xiii)—that in which he fixes the point where the soul may abandon discursive meditation and enter the contemplation which belongs to loving and simple faith.

Both these chapters have contributed to the reputation of St. John of the Cross as a consummate spiritual master. And this not only for the objective value of his observations, but because, even in spite of himself, he betrays the sublimity of his own mystical experiences. Once more, too, we may admire the crystalline transparency of his teaching and the precision of the phrases in which he clothes it. To judge by his language alone, one might suppose at times that he is speaking of mathematical, rather than of spiritual operations.

In Chapter x, the Saint describes the discipline which the soul in this Dark Night must impose upon itself; this, as might be logically deduced from the *Ascent*, consists in 'allowing the soul to remain in peace and quietness,' content 'with a peaceful and loving attentiveness toward God.'[4] Before long it will experience enkindlings of love (Chapter xi), which will serve to purify its sins and imperfections and draw it gradually nearer to God; we have here, as it were, so many stages of the ascent of the Mount on whose summit the soul attains to transforming union. Chapters xii and xiii detail with great exactness the benefits that the soul receives from this aridity, while Chapter xiv briefly expounds the last line of the first stanza and brings to an end what the Saint desires to say with respect to the first Passive Night.

At only slightly greater length St. John of the Cross describes the Passive Night of the Spirit, which is at once more afflictive and

---

[1] *Dark Night*, Bk. I, chap. viii, § 1.   [2] *Op. cit.*, Bk. I, chap. viii, § 2.
[3] *Ibid.*   [4] *Op. cit.*, Bk. I, chap. x, § 4.

more painful than those which have preceded it. This, nevertheless, is the Dark Night *par excellence*, of which the Saint speaks in these words: 'The night which we have called that of sense may and should be called a kind of correction and restraint of the desire rather than purgation. The reason is that all the imperfections and disorders of the sensual part have their strength and root in the spirit, where all habits, both good and bad, are brought into subjection, and thus, until these are purged, the rebellions and depravities of sense cannot be purged throughly.'[1]

Spiritual persons, we are told, do not enter the second night immediately after leaving the first; on the contrary, they generally pass a long time, even years, before doing so,[2] for they still have many imperfections, both habitual and actual (Chapter ii). After a brief introduction (Chapter iii), the Saint describes with some fullness the nature of this spiritual purgation or dark contemplation referred to in the first stanza of his poem and the varieties of pain and affliction caused by it, whether in the soul or in its faculties (Chapters iv–viii). These chapters are brilliant beyond all description; in them we seem to reach the culminating point of their author's mystical experience; any excerpt from them would do them an injustice. It must suffice to say that St. John of the Cross seldom again touches those same heights of sublimity.

Chapter ix describes how, although these purgations seem to blind the spirit, they do so only to enlighten it again with a brighter and intenser light, which it is preparing itself to receive with greater abundance. The following chapter makes the comparison between spiritual purgation and the log of wood which gradually becomes transformed through being immersed in fire and at last takes on the fire's own properties. The force with which the familiar similitude is driven home impresses indelibly upon the mind the fundamental concept of this most sublime of all purgations. Marvellous, indeed, are its effects, from the first enkindlings and burnings of Divine love, which are greater beyond comparison than those produced by the Night of Sense, the one being as different from the other as is the body from the soul. 'For this (latter) is an enkindling of spiritual love in the soul, which, in the midst of these dark confines, feels itself to be keenly and sharply wounded in strong Divine love, and to have a certain realization and foretaste of God.'[3] No less wonderful are the effects of the power-

---

[1] *Dark Night*, Bk. II, chap. iii, § 1.   [2] *Op. cit.*, Bk. II, chap. i, § 1.
[3] *Op. cit.*, Bk. II, chap. xi, § 1.

ful Divine illumination which from time to time enfolds the soul in the splendours of glory. When the effects of the light that wounds and yet illumines are combined with those of the enkindlement that melts the soul with its heat, the delights experienced are so great as to be ineffable.

The second line of the first stanza of the poem is expounded in three admirable chapters (xi–xiii), while one short chapter (xiv) suffices for the three lines remaining. We then embark upon the second stanza, which describes the soul's security in the Dark Night—due, among other reasons, to its being freed 'not only from itself. but likewise from its other enemies, which are the world and the devil.'[1]

This contemplation is not only dark, but also secret (Chapter xvii), and in Chapter xviii is compared to the 'staircase' of the poem. This comparison suggests to the Saint an exposition (Chapters xviii, xix) of the ten steps or degrees of love which comprise St. Bernard's mystical ladder. Chapter xxi describes the soul's 'disguise,' from which the book passes on (Chapters xxii, xxiii) to extol the 'happy chance' which led it to journey 'in darkness and concealment' from its enemies, both without and within.

Chapter xxiv glosses the last line of the second stanza—'my house being now at rest.' Both the higher and the lower 'portions of the soul' are now tranquillized and prepared for the desired union with the Spouse, a union which is the subject that the Saint proposed to treat in his commentary on the five remaining stanzas. As far as we know, this commentary was never written. We have only the briefest outline of what was to have been covered in the third, in which, following the same effective metaphor of night, the Saint describes the excellent properties of the spiritual night of infused contemplation, through which the soul journeys with no other guide or support, either outward or inward, than the Divine love 'which burned in my heart.'

It is difficult to express adequately the sense of loss that one feels at the premature truncation of this eloquent treatise.[2] We have already given our opinion[3] upon the commentaries thought to have been written on the final stanzas of the 'Dark Night.' Did we possess them, they would explain the birth of the light—'dawn's first breathings in the heav'ns above'—which breaks through the black darkness of the Active and the Passive Nights; they would tell us, too, of the soul's further progress towards the Sun's full brightness. It is true, of course, that some part of this great gap is filled by St. John of the Cross himself

---

[1] *Dark Night*, Bk. II, chap. xvi, § 2.   [2] [On this, see Sobrino, pp. 159–66.]
[3] Cf. pp. liv–lviii, above.

in his other treatises, but it is small compensation for the incomplete state in which he left this edifice of such gigantic proportions that he should have given us other and smaller buildings of a somewhat similar kind. Admirable as are the *Spiritual Canticle* and the *Living Flame of Love*, they are not so completely knit into one whole as is this great double treatise. They lose both in flexibility and in substance through the closeness with which they follow the stanzas of which they are the exposition. In the *Ascent* and the *Dark Night*, on the other hand, we catch only the echoes of the poem, which are all but lost in the resonance of the philosopher's voice and the eloquent tones of the preacher. Nor have the other treatises the learning and the authority of these. Nowhere else does the genius of St. John of the Cross for infusing philosophy into his mystical dissertations find such an outlet as here. Nowhere else, again, is he quite so appealingly human; for, though he is human even in his loftiest and sublimest passages, this intermingling of philosophy with mystical theology makes him seem particularly so. These treatises are a wonderful illustration of the theological truth that grace, far from destroying nature, ennobles and dignifies it, and of the agreement always found between the natural and the supernatural—between the principles of sound reason and the sublimest manifestations of Divine grace.

Manuscripts of the *DARK NIGHT*

The autograph of the *Dark Night*, like that of the *Ascent of Mount Carmel*, is unknown to us: the second seems to have disappeared in the same period as the first. There are extant, however, as many as twelve early copies of the *Dark Night*, some of which, though none of them is as palæographically accurate as the best copy of the *Ascent*, are very reliable; there is no trace in them of conscious adulteration of the original or of any kind of modification to fit the sense of any passage into a preconceived theory. We definitely prefer one of these copies to the others but we nowhere follow it so literally as to incorporate in our text its evident discrepancies from its original.

MS. 3,446. An early MS. in the clear masculine hand of an Andalusian: MS. 3,446 in the National Library, Madrid. Like many others, this MS. was transferred to the library from the Convento de San Hermenegildo at the time of the religious persecutions in the early nineteenth century; it had been presented to the Archives of the

Reform by the Fathers of Los Remedios, Seville—a Carmelite house founded by P. Gracián in 1574. It has no title and a fragment from the *Living Flame of Love* is bound up with it.

This MS. has only two omissions of any length; these form part respectively of Book II, Chapters xix and xxiii, dealing with the Passive Night of the Spirit. It has many copyist's errors. At the same time, its antiquity and origin, and the good faith of which it shows continual signs, give it, in our view, primacy over the other copies now to come under consideration. It must be made clear, nevertheless, that there is no extant copy of the *Dark Night* as trustworthy and as skilfully made as the Alcaudete MS. of the *Ascent*.

MS. of the Carmelite Nuns of Toledo. Written in three hands, all early. Save for a few slips of the copyist, it agrees with the foregoing; a few of its errors have been corrected. It bears no title, but has a long sub-title which is in effect a partial summary of the argument.

MS. of the Carmelite Nuns of Valladolid. This famous convent, which was one of St. Teresa's foundations, is very rich in Teresan autographs, and has also a number of important documents relating to St. John of the Cross, together with some copies of his works. That here described is written in a large, clear hand and probably dates from the end of the sixteenth century. It has a title similar to that of the last-named copy. With few exceptions it follows the other most important MSS.

MS. Alba de Tormes. What has been said of this in the introduction to the *Ascent* (pp. 5–6) applies also to the *Dark Night*. It is complete, save for small omissions on the part of the amanuensis, the 'Argument' at the beginning of the poem, the verses themselves and a few lines from Book II, Chapter vii.

MS. 6,624. As we have seen (p. 6), this copy is almost identical with the foregoing. It omits the 'Argument' and the poem itself but not the lines from Book II, Chapter vii.

MS. 8,795. This contains the *Dark Night, Spiritual Canticle, Living Flame of Love*, a number of poems by St. John of the Cross and the *Spiritual Colloquies between Christ and the soul His Bride*. It is written in various hands, all very early and some feminine. A note by P. Andrés de la Encarnación, on the reverse of the first folio, records that the copy was presented to the Archives of the Reform by the Discalced Carmelite nuns of Baeza. This convent was founded in 1589, two years before the Saint's death, and the copy may well date from about this period. On the second folio comes the poem 'I entered in—I knew not where.' On the reverse of the third folio begins a kind of preface to the *Dark Night*, opening with the words: 'Begin the stanzas by means of which a soul may occupy itself and become fervent in the love of God. It deals with the Dark Night and is divided into two books. The first treats of the purgation of sense, and the second of the spiritual purgation of man. It was written by P. Fr. Juan de la Cruz, Discalced Carmelite.' On the next folio, a so-called 'Preface: To the Reader' begins: 'As a beginning and an explanation of these two purgations of the Dark Night which are to be expounded hereafter, this chapter will show how narrow is the path that leads to eternal life and how completely detached and disencumbered must be those that are to enter thereby.' This fundamental idea is developed for the space of two folios. There follows a sonnet on the *Dark Night*,[1] and immediately afterwards comes the text of the treatise.

The copy contains many errors, but its only omission is that of the last chapter. There is no trace in it of any attempt to modify its original; indeed, the very nature and number of the copyist's errors are a testimony to his good faith.

MS 12,658. A note by P. Andrés states that he acquired it in Madrid but has no more detailed recollection of its *provenance*. 'The *Dark Night*,' it adds, 'begins on folio 43; our holy father is described simply as "the second friar of the new Reformation,"[2] which is clear evidence of its antiquity.'

The Codex contains a number of opuscules, transcribed no doubt with a devotional aim by the copyist. Its epoch is probably the end of the sixteenth century; it is certainly earlier than the editions. There is no serious omission except that of six lines of the 'Argument.' The authors of the other works copied include St. Augustine, B. Juan de Ávila, P. Baltasar Álvarez and P. Tomás de Jesús.

The copies which remain to be described are all mutilated or abbreviated and can be disposed of briefly:

MS. 13,498. Cf. p. 6, above. This copy omits less of the *Dark Night* than of the *Ascent* but few pages are without their omissions. In one place a meticulous pair of scissors has removed the lower half of a folio on which the Saint deals with spiritual luxury.

---

[1] [It contains a series of paradoxical statements, after the style of those in *Ascent*, Bk. I, chap. xiii, and is of no great literary merit. P. Silverio reproduces it in Spanish on p. 302 (note) of his first volume.]

[2] The 'first friar' would be P. Antonio de Jesús (p. xxvi, above), who was senior to St. John of the Cross in the Carmelite Order, though not in the Reform.

MS. of the Carmelite Friars of Toledo. Dates from early in the seventeenth century and has numerous omissions, especially in the chapters on the Passive Night of the Spirit. The date is given (in the same hand as that which copies the title) as 1618. This MS. also contains an opuscule by Suso and another entitled 'Brief compendium of the most eminent Christian perfection of P. Fr. Juan de la Cruz.'

MS. 18,160. Cf. p. 7, above. The copyist has treated the *Dark Night* little better than the *Ascent*; except from the first ten and the last three chapters, he omits freely.

MS. 12,411. Entitled by its copyist 'Spiritual Compendium,' this MS. contains several short works of devotion, including one by Ruysbroeck. Of St. John of the Cross's works it copies the *Spiritual Canticle* as well as the *Dark Night*; the latter is headed: 'Song of one soul alone.' It also contains a number of poems, some of them by the Saint, and many passages from St. Teresa. It is in several hands, all of the seventeenth century. The copy of the *Dark Night* is most unsatisfactory; there are omissions and abbreviations everywhere.

MS. of the Carmelite Nuns of Pamplona. Cf. p. 7, above. This MS. also omits and abbreviates continually, especially in the chapters on the Passive Night of Sense, which are reduced to a mere skeleton.

Editio princeps. This is much more faithful to its original in the *Dark Night* than in the *Ascent*. Both the passages suppressed[1] and the interpolations[2] are relatively few and unimportant. Modifications of phraseology are more frequent and alterations are also made with the aim of correcting hyperbaton. In the first book about thirty lines are suppressed; in the second, about ninety. All changes which are of any importance have been shown in the notes.

The present edition. We have given preference, as a general rule, to *MS.* 3,446, subjecting it, however, to a rigorous comparison with the other copies. Mention has already been made (pp. liii–lv, above) of certain apparent anomalies and a certain lack of uniformity in the Saint's method of dividing his commentaries. This is nowhere more noticeable than in the *Dark Night*. Instead of dividing his treatise into books, each with its proper title, the Saint abandons this method and uses titles only occasionally. As this makes comprehension of his

---

[1] The longest of these are one of ten lines in Bk. I, chap. iv, [in the original] and those of Bk. II, chaps. vii, viii, xii, xiii, which vary from eleven to twenty-three lines. Bk. II, chap. xxiii, has also considerable modifications.

[2] The chief interpolation is in Bk. I, chap. x.

argument the more difficult, we have adopted the divisions which were introduced by P. Salablanca and have been copied by successive editors.

M. Baruzi (*Bulletin Hispanique*, 1922, Vol. xxiv, pp. 18–40) complains that this division weighs down the spiritual rhythm of-the treatise and interrupts its movement. We do not agree. In any case, we greatly prefer the gain of clarity, even if the rhythm occasionally halts, to the other alternative—the constant halting of the understanding. We have, of course, indicated every place where the title is taken from the *editio princeps* and was not the work of the author.

The following abbreviations are adopted in the footnotes:

A = MS. of the Discalced Carmelite Friars of Alba.
B = MS. 6,624 (National Library, Madrid).
Bz. = MS. 8,795 (N.L.M.).
C = MS. 13,498 (N.L.M.).
G = MS. 18,160 (N.L.M.).
H = MS. 3,446 (N.L.M.).
M = MS. of the Discalced Carmelite Nuns of Toledo.
Mtr. = MS. 12,658.
P = MS. of the Discalced Carmelite Friars of Toledo.
V = MS. of the Discalced Carmelite Nuns of Valladolid.
E.p. = *Editio princeps* (1618).

MS. 12,411 and the MS. of the Discalced Carmelite nuns of Pamplona are cited without abbreviations.

DARK NIGHT[1]

Exposition of the stanzas describing the method followed by the soul in its journey upon the spiritual road to the attainment of the perfect union of love with God, to the extent that is possible in this life. Likewise are described the properties[2] belonging to the soul that has attained to the said perfection, according as they are contained in the same stanzas.[3]

PROLOGUE[4]

IN this book are first set down all the stanzas which are to be expounded; afterwards, each of the stanzas is expounded separately, being set down before its exposition; and then each line is expounded separately and in turn, the line itself also being set down before the exposition. In the first two stanzas are expounded the effects of the two spiritual purgations: of the sensual part of man and of the spiritual part. In the other six are expounded various and wondrous effects of the spiritual illumination and union of love with God.

STANZAS OF THE SOUL

1. On a dark night, Kindled in love with yearnings—oh, happy chance!—
I went forth without being observed, My house being now at rest.

2. In darkness and secure, By the secret ladder, disguised—oh, happy chance!—
In darkness and in concealment, My house being now at rest.

3. In the happy night, In secret, when none saw me,
Nor I beheld aught, Without light or guide, save that which burned in my heart.

---

[1] This title is lacking in all the MSS. except Mtr. and P.
[2] C [incorrectly]: 'prosperities.'
[3] This sub-title is found in C, G, M, Mtr., which add some such words as 'by Fray Juan de la Cruz, Discalced Carmelite.' The *editio princeps* has both title and sub-title.
[4] So G, M. Bz. has 'Proem' and e.p. 'Argument.'

4. This light guided me   More surely than the light of noonday
   To the place where he (well I knew who!) was awaiting me—
   A place where none appeared.

5. Oh, night that guided me,   Oh, night more lovely than the
   dawn,
   Oh, night that joined Beloved with lover,   Lover transformed in the Beloved!

6. Upon my flowery breast,   Kept wholly for himself alone,
   There he stayed sleeping, and I caressed him,   And the
   fanning of the cedars made a breeze.

7. The breeze blew from the turret   As I parted his locks ;
   With his gentle hand he wounded my neck   And caused all
   my senses to be suspended.

8. I remained, lost in oblivion ;   My face I reclined on the
   Beloved.
   All ceased and I abandoned myself,   Leaving my cares
   forgotten among the lilies.

Begins the exposition of the stanzas which treat of the way and manner which the soul follows upon the road of the union of love with God.[1]

Before we enter upon the exposition of these stanzas, it is well to understand here that the soul that utters them is now in the state of perfection, which is the union of love with God, having already passed through severe trials and straits, by means of spiritual exercise in the narrow way of eternal life whereof Our Saviour speaks in the Gospel, along which way the soul ordinarily passes in order to reach this high and happy union with God.[2] Since this road (as the Lord Himself says likewise) is so strait, and since there are so few that enter by it,[3] the soul considers it a great happiness and good chance to have

---

[1] Thus H, M and other authorities. Some (including H) add the author's name. Others omit the title. A, B have: 'Book the fifth of the Dark Night.' E.p. has: 'Exposition of the intent of the Stanzas.'
[2] Thus the Codices. E.p. and M read: 'along which the soul ordinarily passes in order to reach this high and Divine union with God.'
[3] St. Matthew vii, 14.

passed along it to the said perfection of love, as it sings in this first stanza,[1] calling this strait road with full propriety 'dark night,' as will be explained hereafter in the lines of the said stanza. The soul, then, rejoicing at having passed along this narrow road whence so many blessings have come to it, speaks after this manner.

[1] Bz.: 'as it relates in this stanza.'

BOOK THE FIRST

Which treats of the Night of Sense.[1]

STANZA THE FIRST

**On a dark night,   Kindled in love with yearnings—oh, happy
chance!—
I went forth without being observed,   My house being now at
rest.**

EXPOSITION

IN this first stanza the soul relates the way and manner which it
followed in going forth, as to its affection, from itself and from all
things, and in dying to them all and to itself, by means of true
mortification, in order to attain to living the sweet and delectable life
of love with God; and it says that this going forth from itself and from
all things was a 'dark night,' by which, as will be explained hereafter,
is here understood purgative contemplation, which causes passively[2] in
the soul the negation of itself and of all things referred to above.

2. And this going forth it says here that it was able to accomplish in
the strength and ardour which love for its Spouse gave to it for that
purpose in the dark contemplation aforementioned. Herein it extols[3]
the great happiness which it found in journeying to God through this
night with such signal success that none of the three enemies, which are
world, devil and flesh (who are they that ever impede[4] this road),
could hinder it; inasmuch as the aforementioned night of purgative[5]
contemplation lulled to sleep and mortified, in the house of its sensuality, all the passions and desires with respect to their mischievous
desires and motions.[6]

The line, then, says:

On a dark night

---

[1] The Codices all begin with the stanza. The title belongs to the e.p. only.
[2] E.p. omits 'passively.'   [3] V: 'desired to extol.'
[4] B, e.p.: 'disturb.'   [5] [More exactly: 'purificative.'] E.p.: 'purified.'
[6] Thus B, C, G, H, M, Mtr. The other authorities and e.p. have: 'with respect to their
mischievous motions.'

CHAPTER I

Sets down the first line and begins to treat of the imperfections of beginners.[1]

INTO this dark night souls begin to enter when God draws them forth from the state of beginners—which is the state of those that meditate on the spiritual road—and begins to set them in the state of progressives[2]—which is that of those who are already contemplatives—to the end that, after passing through it, they may arrive at the state of the perfect, which is that of the Divine union of the soul with God. Wherefore, to the end that we may the better understand and explain what night is this through which the soul passes, and for what cause God sets it therein, it will be well here to touch first of all upon certain characteristics of beginners (which, although we treat them with all possible brevity, will not fail to be of service likewise to the beginners themselves),[3] in order that, realizing the weakness of the state wherein they are, they may take courage, and may desire that God will bring them into this night, wherein the soul is strengthened and confirmed in the virtues, and made ready for the inestimable delights of the love of God. And, although we may tarry here for a time, it will not be for longer than is necessary, so that we may go on to speak at once of this dark night.

2. It must be known, then, that the soul, after it has been definitely converted to the service of God, is, as a rule, spiritually nurtured and caressed by God, even as is the tender child by its loving mother, who warms it with the heat of her bosom and nurtures it with sweet milk and soft and pleasant food, and carries it and caresses it in her arms; but, as the child grows bigger, the mother gradually ceases caressing it, and, hiding her tender love, puts bitter aloes upon her sweet breast, sets down the child[4] from her arms and makes it walk upon its feet, so that it may lose the habits of a child and betake itself to more important and substantial occupations. The loving mother is like the grace of God, for, as soon as the soul is regenerated by its new warmth and fervour for the service of God, He treats it in the same way; He makes

---

[1] From e.p.

[2] Thus [*aprovechantes*] A, B, C, E, G, H, Mtr. The other authorities, and e.p., read: *aprovechados* ['proficient.']

[3] E.p. omits this parenthesis, which, however, is found in all the Codices, except C and E.

[4] E.p. modifies these lines of the Codices, thus: 'and, hiding her tender breast, puts bitter aloes upon it, sets down the child.'

it to find spiritual milk, sweet and delectable, in all the things of God, without any labour of its own, and also great pleasure in spiritual exercises, for here God is giving to it the breast of His tender love, even as to a tender child.

3. Therefore, such a soul finds its delight in spending long periods —perchance whole nights—in prayer; penances are its pleasures; fasts its joys; and its consolations are to make use of the sacraments and to occupy itself in Divine things. In the which things spiritual persons (though taking part in them with great efficacy and persistence and using and treating them with great care) often find themselves, spiritually speaking, very weak and imperfect. For since they are moved to these things and to these spiritual exercises by the consolation and pleasure that they find in them, and since, too, they have not been prepared for them by the practice of earnest striving in the virtues, they have many faults and imperfections with respect to these spiritual actions of theirs; for, after all, any man's actions correspond to the habit of perfection attained by him. And, as these persons have not had the opportunity of acquiring the said habits of strength, they have necessarily to work like feeble[1] children, feebly. In order that this may be seen more clearly, and likewise how much these beginners in the virtues lack[2] with respect to the works in which they so readily engage with the pleasure aforementioned, we shall describe it by reference to the seven capital sins, each in its turn, indicating some of the many imperfections which they have under each heading; wherein it will be clearly seen how like to children are these persons in all they do. And it will also be seen how many blessings the dark night of which we shall afterwards treat brings with it, since it cleanses the soul and purifies it from all these imperfections.

[1] E.p. and M omit 'feeble.'
[2] Thus B, G, H, Mtr., P, V. The other Codices and e.p. have: 'how feeble are these beginners in the virtues.'

CHAPTER II

Of certain spiritual imperfections which beginners have with respect to the habit of pride.[1]

As these beginners feel themselves to be very fervent and diligent in spiritual things and devout exercises, from this prosperity[2] (although it is true that holy things of their own nature cause humility) there often comes to them, through their imperfections, a certain kind of secret pride, whence they come to have some degree of satisfaction with their works and with themselves. And hence there comes to them likewise a certain desire, which is somewhat vain, and at times very vain, to speak of spiritual things[3] in the presence of others, and sometimes even to teach such things rather than to learn them. They condemn others in their heart when they see that they have not the kind of devotion which they themselves desire; and sometimes they even say this in words, herein resembling the Pharisee, who boasted of himself, praising God for his own good works and despising the publican.[4]

2. In these persons the devil often increases the fervour that they have and the desire to perform these and other works more frequently, so that their pride and presumption may grow greater. For the devil knows quite well that all these works and virtues which they perform are not only valueless to them, but even become vices in them. And such a degree of evil are some of these persons wont to reach that they would have none appear good save themselves; and thus, in deed and word, whenever the opportunity occurs, they condemn them and slander them, beholding the mote in their brother's eye[5] and not considering the beam which is in their own;[6] they strain at another's gnat and themselves swallow a camel.[7]

3. Sometimes, too, when their spiritual masters, such as confessors and superiors, do not approve of their spirit and behaviour (for they are anxious that all they do shall be esteemed and praised), they consider that they do not understand them, or that, because they do not approve of this and comply with that, their confessors are themselves

---

[1] This title is found in e.p. and also in all the Codices.
[2] H, M: 'from this property.'
[3] E.p.: 'And hence there comes to them likewise a certain exceedingly vain desire to speak of spiritual things.'
[4] St. Luke xviii, 11–12.   [5] E.p.: 'in another's eye.'
[6] St. Matthew vii, 3.   [7] St. Matthew xxiii, 24.

not spiritual. And so they immediately desire and contrive to find some one else who will fit in with their tastes; for as a rule they desire to speak of spiritual matters with those who they think will praise and esteem what they do, and they flee, as they would from death, from those who disabuse them in order to lead them into a safe road— sometimes they even harbour ill-will against them. Presuming thus,[1] they are wont to resolve much[2] and accomplish very little. Sometimes they are anxious that others shall realize how spiritual and devout they are, to which end they occasionally give outward evidence thereof in movements, sighs and other ceremonies; and at times they are apt to fall into[3] certain ecstasies, in public rather than in secret, wherein the devil aids them, and they are pleased that this should be noticed, and are often eager that it should be noticed more.[4]

4. Many such persons desire to be the favourites of their confessors and to become intimate with them[5], as a result of which there beset them continual occasions of envy and disquiet.[6] They are too much embarrassed[7] to confess their sins nakedly, lest their confessors should think less of them, so they palliate them and make them appear less evil, and thus it is to excuse themselves rather than to accuse themselves that they go to confession. And sometimes they seek another confessor to tell the wrongs that they have done, so that their own confessor shall think they have done nothing wrong at all, but only good; and thus they always take pleasure in telling him what is good,[8] and sometimes in such terms as make it appear to be greater than it is rather than less, desiring that he may think them to be good, when it would be greater humility in them, as we shall say, to depreciate it, and to desire that[9] neither he nor anyone else should consider them of account.

5. Some of these beginners, too, make little of their faults, and at other times become over-sad when they see themselves fall into them, thinking themselves to have been saints already; and thus they become

[1] [Lit., 'Presuming.'] E.p. reads: 'Presuming upon themselves.'

[2] A, B abbreviate: '. . . who disabuse them in order to cause them fear. They are wont to resolve much.'

[3] The words 'they are apt to fall into' are found in e.p. alone.

[4] [The original merely has: 'and are often eager.'] E.p. modifies: 'that this about which they are so eager should be noticed.'

[5] E.p.: 'Many such desire to be intimate with their confessors.' H has: 'desire to preach [predicar for preceder] and to be intimate with their confessors,' which destroys the sense of the passage.

[6] [Lit., 'a thousand envies and disquietudes.']

[7] Bz.: 'They are ashamed.'

[8] A, B, M omit: 'and thus . . . is good.'

[9] E.p.: 'and to say naught, so that . . .'

angry and impatient with themselves, which is another imperfection. Often they beseech God, with great yearnings,[1] that He will take from them their imperfections and faults, but they do this that they may find themselves at peace, and may not be troubled by them, rather than for God's sake; not realizing that, if He should take their imperfections from them, they would probably become prouder and more presumptuous[2] still. They dislike praising others and love to be praised themselves; sometimes they seek out such praise. Herein they are like the foolish virgins, who, when their lamps could not be lit, sought oil from others.[3]

6. From these imperfections some souls go on to develop[4] many very grave ones, which do them great harm. But some have fewer and some more,[5] and some, only the first motions thereof or little beyond these; and there are hardly any such beginners who, at the time of these signs of fervour,[6] fall not into some of these errors.[7] But those who at this time are going on to perfection proceed very differently and with quite another temper of spirit; for they progress by means of humility and are greatly edified, not only thinking naught of their own affairs,[8] but having very little satisfaction with themselves; they consider all others as far better, and usually have a holy envy of them, and an eagerness to serve God as they do. For the greater is their fervour, and the more numerous are the works that they perform, and the greater is the pleasure that they take in them, as they progress in humility, the more do they realize how much God deserves of them, and how little is all that they do for His sake;[9] and thus, the more they do, the less are they satisfied. So much would they gladly do from charity and love for Him, that all they do seems to them naught; and so greatly are they importuned, occupied and absorbed[10] by this loving anxiety that they never notice what others do or do not; or if they do notice it, they always believe, as I say, that all others are far better than they themselves. Wherefore, holding themselves as of little worth, they are anxious that others too should thus hold them,[11] and should despise and depreciate that which they do. And further, if men should

---

1 M, e.p. omit 'great.'
2 M, e.p. omit: 'and more presumptuous.'
3 St. Matthew xxv, 8. [*Lit.*, 'who, having their lamps dead, sought oil from without.']
4 [*Lit.*, 'to have.'] A, M omit this verb and read: 'go on to many . . .'
5 E.p.: 'and others more.'   6 [*Lit.*, 'these fervours.']
7 [*Lit.*, 'into something of this.']   8 E.p.: 'their own works.'
9 H omits: 'and how . . . His sake.'
10 Bz. has 'fascinated' for 'absorbed.' E.p.: 'importuned and occupied.'
11 A, B omit this clause [interrupting the sense of the passage].

praise and esteem them, they can in no wise believe what they say; it seems to them strange that anyone should say these good things of them.

7. Together with great tranquillity and humbleness, these souls have a deep desire to be taught by anyone who can bring them profit; they are the complete opposite of those of whom we have spoken above, who would fain be always teaching, and who, when others seem to be teaching them, take the words from their mouths as if they knew them already. These souls, on the other hand, being far from desiring to be the masters of any, are very ready to travel and set out on another road than that which they are actually following, if they be so commanded, because they never think that they are right in anything whatsoever. They rejoice when others are praised; they grieve only because they serve not God like them. They have no desire to speak of the things that they do, because they think so little of them that they are ashamed to speak of them even to their spiritual masters, since they seem to them to be things that merit not being spoken of. They are more anxious to speak of their faults and sins, or that these should be recognized rather than their virtues;[1] and thus they incline to talk of their souls with those who account[2] their actions and their spirituality of little value. This is a characteristic of the spirit which is simple, pure, genuine and very pleasing to God. For as the wise Spirit of God dwells in these humble souls, He moves them and inclines them to keep His treasures secretly within and likewise to cast out from themselves all evil. God gives this grace to the humble, together with the other virtues, even as He denies it to the proud.

8. These souls will give their heart's blood to anyone that serves God, and will help others to serve Him as much as in them lies. The imperfections into which they see themselves fall they bear with humility, meekness of spirit[3] and a loving fear of God, hoping in Him. But souls who in the beginning journey with this kind of perfection are, as I understand, and as has been said, a minority, and very few are those who we can be glad do not fall into the opposite errors. For this reason, as we shall afterwards say, God leads into the dark night those whom He desires to purify from all these imperfections so that He may bring them farther onward.

---

[1] M, e.p.: 'or that it should be recognized that these [faults and sins] are not virtues.'
[2] E.p.: 'esteem.'
[3] H: 'with humility, humility of spirit.'

CHAPTER III

Of some imperfections which some of these souls[1] are apt to have, with respect to the second capital sin, which is avarice,[2] in the spiritual sense.

MANY of these beginners have also at times great spiritual avarice. They will be found to be discontented with the spirituality which God gives them; and they are very disconsolate and querulous because they find not in spiritual things the consolation that they would desire. Many can never have enough of listening to counsels and learning[3] spiritual precepts, and of possessing and reading many books which treat of this matter, and they spend their time on all these things rather than on works of mortification[4] and the perfecting[5] of the inward poverty of spirit which should be theirs. Furthermore, they burden themselves with images and rosaries which are very curious;[6] now they put down one, now take up another; now they change about, now change back again; now they want this kind of thing, now that, preferring one kind of cross to another, because it is more curious.[7] And others you will see adorned with agnusdeis[8] and relics and tokens,[9] like children with trinkets. Here I condemn the attachment of the heart, and the affection which they have for the nature, multitude and curiosity of these things, inasmuch as it is quite contrary to poverty of spirit, which considers only the substance of devotion, makes use only of what suffices for that end and grows weary of this other kind of multiplicity and curiosity. For true devotion must issue from the heart, and consists in the truth and

---

[1] E.p.: 'which some beginners.'

[2] Bz.: 'which is pride and boasting.'   [3] M, e.p. omit 'learning.'

[4] Bz., P insert here: 'and they have and read many spiritual books which treat of this vice and of gluttony, which generally lead them to attempt many kinds of exercise, either to make great use of their capital, from a craving for great profits or through mere pleasure and cupidity; whence comes inconstancy to them and lack of stability in their particular exercises, which are chiefly necessary in these beginnings; and this spoils their labour and makes it of none effect and vain, wasting their time in experiments and trials.'

[5] E.p. reads: 'rather than on works, without the mortification and the perfecting.'

[6] So H, P.   A, B, C, G, Mtr., V have: 'which are sometimes very curious and showy.' So Bz., but with 'costly' for 'showy.' M, e.p.: 'images and crosses which are very curious and costly.'

[7] Bz. adds: 'or costly.' Other authorities add: 'or valuable.'

[8] The *agnusdei* was a wax medal with a representation of the Lamb stamped upon it, often blessed by the Pope; at the time of the Saint such medals were greatly sought after, as we know from various references in St. Teresa's letters.

[9] [The word *nómina*, translated 'token,' and normally meaning 'list' or 'roll,' refers to a relic on which were written the names of saints. In modern Spanish it can denote a medal or amulet used superstitiously.]

substance[1] alone of what is represented by spiritual things; all the rest is affection and attachment proceeding from imperfection; and in order that one may pass to any kind of perfection[2] it is necessary for such desires to be killed.

2. I knew a person who for more than ten years made use of a cross roughly formed from a branch[3] that had been blessed, fastened with a pin twisted round it; he had never ceased using it, and he always carried it about with him until I took it from him; and this was a person of no small sense and understanding. And I saw another who said his prayers using beads that were made of bones from the spine of a fish; his devotion was certainly no less precious on that account in the sight of God, for it is clear that these things[4] carried no devotion in their workmanship or value. Those, then, who start from these beginnings and make good progress attach themselves to no visible instruments, nor do they burden themselves with such, nor desire to know more than is necessary in order that they may act well;[5] for they set their eyes only on being right with God and on pleasing Him, and therein consists their covetousness. And thus with great generosity they give away all that they have, and delight to know that they have it not, for God's sake and for charity to their neighbour,[6] no matter whether these be spiritual things or temporal. For, as I say, they set their eyes only upon the reality of interior[7] perfection, which is to give pleasure to God and in naught to give pleasure to themselves.

3. But neither from these imperfections nor from those others can the soul be perfectly purified until God brings it into the passive purgation of that dark night whereof we shall speak presently. It befits the soul, however, to contrive to labour, in so far as it can, on its own account, to the end that it may purge and perfect itself, and thus may merit being taken by God into that Divine care wherein it becomes healed of all things that it was unable of itself to cure. Because, however greatly the soul itself labours, it cannot[8] actively purify itself so as

---

[1] E.p. alone modifies thus: 'from the heart, in truth alone, and must consider only the truth and substance.'

[2] E.p. alone has: 'pass to the estate of perfection.'

[3] [No doubt a branch of palm, olive or rosemary, blessed in church on Palm Sunday, like the English palm crosses of to-day. 'Palm Sunday' is in Spanish *Domingo de ramos*: 'Branch Sunday.']

[4] Thus e.p. alone. The other authorities have 'these.'

[5] M: 'neither do they desire to know much in order to act [well].' [The word 'well' does not occur anywhere in the original.]

[6] E.p.: 'and for charity to their neighbour, ruling everything by the laws of this virtue.'

[7] M, e.p. omit 'interior.'   [8] E.p.: 'it cannot by its industry.'

to be in the least degree prepared for the Divine union of perfection of love, if God takes not[1] its hand and purges it not in that dark fire, in the way and manner that we have to describe.[2]

CHAPTER IV

Of other imperfections which these beginners are apt to have with respect to the third sin, which is luxury.[3]

MANY of these beginners have many other imperfections than those which I am describing with respect to each of the deadly sins, but these I set aside, in order to avoid prolixity, touching upon a few of the most important, which are, as it were, the origin and cause[4] of the rest. And thus, with respect to this sin of luxury (leaving apart the falling of spiritual persons[5] into this sin, since my intent is to treat of the imperfections which have to be purged by the dark night), they have many imperfections which[6] might be described as spiritual luxury, not because they are so, but because the imperfections proceed from spiritual things. For it often comes to pass that, in their very spiritual exercises, when they are powerless to prevent it, there arise and assert themselves in the sensual part of the soul impure acts and motions,[7] and sometimes this happens even when the spirit is deep in prayer, or engaged in the Sacrament of Penance or in the Eucharist. These things are not, as I say, in their power; they proceed from one of three causes.[8]

2. The first cause from which they often proceed is the pleasure which human nature takes in spiritual things.[9] For when the spirit and the sense are pleased, every part of a man is moved by that pleasure[10] to

---

[1] M, e.p.: 'of love with God, if He takes not.'
[2] E.p.: 'in the manner that we have to describe'; M: 'in the manner that we have described.'
[3] E.p. adds: 'spiritually understood.'   [4] Bz.: 'origin and head.'
[5] E.p. omits: 'of spiritual persons.' [This is a better reading: the omission throws into relief the author's contrast between the actual commission of the deadly sin and the imperfections connected with it.]
[6] So e.p. The Codices read [more emphatically]: 'many imperfections, many which.'
[7] E.p.: 'in the sensual part of the soul unclean motions.' The edition of 1630 reads: 'not because this is so, but because at times it is felt and experienced in the flesh, by reason of its weakness, when the soul receives spiritual things. For it often comes to pass that, in their very spiritual exercises, when they are powerless to prevent it, there arise and are experienced in the sensual part of the soul unclean motions.'
[8] Thus most of the Codices. Others, and e.p., read: 'three things.'
[9] E.p.: '. . . occasionally proceed, albeit rarely and in weak natures, is from,' etc.
[10] [*Lit.*, 'recreation.']

delight according to its proportion[1] and nature. For then the spirit, which is the higher part, is moved to pleasure[2] and delight in God; and the sensual nature, which is the lower part, is moved to pleasure and delight of the senses, because it cannot possess and lay hold upon aught else, and it therefore lays hold upon that which comes nearest to itself, which is the impure and sensual.[3] Thus it comes to pass that the soul is in deep prayer with God according to the spirit, and, on the other hand, according to sense it is passively conscious, not without great displeasure, of rebellions and motions and acts of the senses,[4] which often happens in Communion, for when the soul receives joy and comfort in this act of love, because this Lord bestows it (since it is to that end that He gives Himself), the sensual nature takes that which is its own likewise, as we have said, after its manner. Now as, after all, these two parts are combined in one individual, they ordinarily both participate in that which one of them receives, each after its manner; for, as the philosopher says, everything that is received is in the recipient[5] after the manner of the same recipient. And thus, in these beginnings, and even when the soul has made some progress, its sensual part, being imperfect, oftentimes receives the Spirit of God with the same imperfection.[6] Now when this sensual part is renewed by the purgation of the dark night which we shall describe, it no longer has these weaknesses; for it is no longer this part that receives aught, but rather it is itself received into the Spirit. And thus it then has everything after the manner of the Spirit.[7]

3. The second cause whence these rebellions sometimes proceed is the devil, who, in order to disquiet[8] and disturb the soul, at times when it is at prayer or is striving to pray, contrives to stir up these motions of impurity in its nature; and if the soul gives heed to any of these, they cause it great harm. For through fear of these not only do persons

---

[1] So H, P. The other authorities [followed by P. Silverio] have 'portion.'

[2] [Lit., 'recreation.']

[3] E.p. omits: 'and it . . . and sensual.'

[4] E.p. reads: 'Thus it comes to pass that the soul is in prayer with God according to the spirit, and, on the other hand, according to sense it is passively conscious, not without great displeasure, of rebellions and motions of the senses.' It then omits the following words: 'which often . . . after its manner.'

[5] E.p. omits: 'in the recipient.'

[6] E.p.: 'since its sensual part is imperfect, it occasionally partakes of spiritual pleasures with the same imperfection.'

[7] E.p. expands thus: '. . . has these weaknesses; for so abundantly does it receive the Divine Spirit that it seems rather to be received into that same Spirit—into One, in brief, that is very much greater. And thus it possesses everything after the manner of the Spirit, in a wondrous way, in Whom it is a partaker, being united with God.'

[8] M, V: 'to disgust'; Mtr.: 'to retaliate.'

become lax in prayer—which is the aim of the devil when he begins to strive with them—but some give up prayer altogether, because they think that these things attack them more during that exercise than apart from it, which is true, since the devil attacks them then more than at other times, so that they may give up spiritual exercises. And not only so, but he succeeds in portraying to them very vividly things that are most foul and impure, and at times are very closely related to certain spiritual things and persons that are of profit to their souls, in order to terrify them and make them fearful;[1] so that those who are affected by this dare not even look at anything or meditate upon anything, because they immediately encounter this temptation. And upon those who are inclined to melancholy this acts with such effect[2] that they become greatly to be pitied since they are suffering so sadly; for this trial reaches such a point in certain persons, when they have this evil humour, that they believe it to be clear that the devil is ever present with them and that they have no power to prevent this, although some of these persons can prevent his attack by dint of great effort and labour.[3] When these impurities[4] attack such souls through the medium of melancholy, they are not as a rule freed from them until they have been cured of that kind of humour, unless the dark night has entered the soul, and rids them of all impurities, one after another.[5]

4. The third source whence these impure motions are apt to proceed in order to make war upon the soul is often the fear which such persons have conceived for these impure representations and motions. Something that they see or say or think brings them to their mind, and this makes them afraid, so that they suffer from them through no fault of their own.

5.[6] There are also certain souls of so tender and frail a nature that, when there comes to them some spiritual consolation or some grace in prayer, the spirit of luxury is with them immediately, inebriating[7] and delighting their sensual nature in such manner that it is as if they were plunged into the enjoyment and pleasure of this sin; and the enjoyment remains, together with the consolation, passively, and

---

[1] E.p. has 'make an end of them' [acabarlas] for 'make them fearful' (acobardarlas].
[2] So H. A, B, Bz., G, Mtr., P, V have: 'with such effect and frequency.' M, e.p.: 'with such effect and vehemence.'
[3] E.p. omits: 'since they are suffering . . . effort and labour.' C also omits these lines and a number of other passages in this chapter.
[4] E.p.: 'these things.'
[5] [Lit., 'of everything.'] E.p.: 'and gradually purifies them altogether.'
[6] C omits most of this paragraph and e.p. omits it all.
[7] M has 'hindering' [embarga] for 'inebriating' [embriaga].

sometimes they are able to see that certain impure and unruly acts have taken place. The reason for this is that, since these natures are, as I say, frail and tender, their humours are stirred up and their blood is excited at the least disturbance.[1] And hence come these motions; and the same thing happens to such souls when they are enkindled with anger or suffer any disturbance or grief.[2]

6. Sometimes, again, there arises within these spiritual persons, whether they be speaking or performing spiritual actions, a certain vigour and bravado, through their having regard to persons who are present, and before these persons they display a certain kind of vain gratification. This also arises from luxury of spirit, after the manner wherein we here understand it, which is accompanied as a rule[3] by complacency in the will.

7.[4] Some of these persons make friendships of a spiritual kind with others, which oftentimes arise from luxury and not from spirituality; this may be known to be the case when the remembrance of that friendship causes not the remembrance and love of God to grow, but occasions remorse of conscience. For, when the friendship is purely spiritual, the love of God grows with it; and the more the soul remembers it, the more it remembers the love of God, and the greater the desire it has for God; so that, as the one grows, the other grows also. For the spirit of God has this property, that it increases good by adding to it more good, inasmuch as there is likeness and conformity between them. But, when this love arises from the vice of sensuality aforementioned, it produces the contrary effects; for the more the one grows, the more the other decreases, and the remembrance of it likewise. If that sensual love grows, it will at once be observed that the soul's love of God is becoming colder, and that it is forgetting Him as it remembers that love; there comes to it, too, a certain remorse of conscience. And, on the other hand, if the love of God grows in the soul, that other love becomes cold and is forgotten; for, as the two are

---

[1] V: 'the least operation.'

[2] All writers who comment upon this delicate matter go into lengthy and learned explanations of it, though in reality there is little that needs to be added to the Saint's clear and apt exposition. It will be remembered that St. Teresa once wrote to her brother Lorenzo, who suffered in this way: 'As to those stirrings of sense. . . . I am quite clear they are of no account, so the best thing is to make no account of them' (LL. 168). The most effective means of calming souls tormented by these favours is to commend them to a discreet and wise director whose counsel they may safely follow. The Illuminists committed the grossest errors in dealing with this matter.

[3] E.p. reads 'at times' for 'as a rule.'

[4] H, V insert here a sub-title: 'Rule for knowing the love which is with God and that which is not so.'

contrary to one another, not only does the one not aid the other, but the one which predominates quenches and confounds the other, and becomes strengthened in itself, as the philosophers say. Wherefore Our Saviour said in the Gospel: 'That which is born of the flesh is flesh, and that which is born of the Spirit is spirit.'[1] That is to say, the love which is born of sensuality ends in sensuality, and that which is of the spirit ends in the spirit of God and causes it to grow. This is the difference that exists between these two kinds of love, whereby we may know them.

8. When the soul enters the dark night, it brings these kinds of love under control. It strengthens and purifies the one, namely that which is according to God; and the other it removes and brings to an end;[2] and in the beginning it causes both to be lost sight of, as we shall say hereafter.

CHAPTER V

Of the imperfections into which beginners fall with respect to the sin of wrath.

BY reason of the concupiscence which many beginners have for spiritual consolations, their experience of these consolations is very commonly accompanied by many imperfections proceeding from the sin of wrath; for, when their delight and pleasure in spiritual things come to an end, they naturally become embittered,[3] and bear that lack of sweetness which they have to suffer with a bad grace, which affects all that they do; and they very easily become irritated over the smallest matter—sometimes, indeed, none can tolerate them. This frequently happens after they have been very pleasantly recollected in prayer according to sense; when their pleasure and delight therein come to an end, their nature is naturally vexed and disappointed, just as is the child when they take it from the breast of which it was enjoying the sweetness. There is no sin in this natural vexation,[4] when it is not permitted to indulge itself, but only imperfection, which must be purged by the aridity and severity of the dark night.

2. There are other of these spiritual persons, again, who fall into

---

[1] St. John iii, 6.
[2] E.p.: 'removes, brings to an end or mortifies.'
[3] [*desabridos*. Cf. note on *sinsabor*, p. 280, above.]
[4] M: 'natural disillusion.'

another kind of spiritual wrath: this happens when they become irritated at the sins of others, and keep watch on those others with a sort of uneasy zeal. At times the impulse comes to them to reprove them angrily, and occasionally they go so far as to indulge it[1] and set themselves up as masters of virtue. All this is contrary to spiritual meekness.

3. There are others who are vexed with themselves when they observe their own imperfectness,[2] and display an impatience that is not humility; so impatient are they about this that they would fain be saints in a day. Many of these persons purpose to accomplish a great deal and make grand[3] resolutions; yet, as they are not humble and have no misgivings about themselves,[4] the more resolutions they make, the greater is their fall and the greater their annoyance, since they have not the patience to wait for that which God will give them when it pleases Him; this likewise is contrary to the spiritual meekness[5] aforementioned, which cannot be wholly remedied save by the purgation of the dark night. Some souls, on the other hand, are so patient[6] as regards the progress which they desire that God would gladly see them less so.

CHAPTER VI

Of imperfections with respect to spiritual gluttony.

WITH respect to the fourth sin, which is spiritual gluttony, there is much to be said, for there is scarce one of these beginners who, however satisfactory his progress, falls not into some of the many imperfections which come to these beginners with respect to this sin, on account of the sweetness which they find at first in spiritual exercises. For many of these, lured by the sweetness and pleasure which they find in such exercises, strive more after spiritual sweetness than after spiritual purity and discretion,[7] which is

---

[1] [*Lit.*, 'they even do it.'] E.p.: 'they even carry it out.'
[2] M: 'impatience' for 'imperfectness.'
[3] Some Codices read: 'make many.'
[4] So A, G, H, M, Mtr. The other authorities read: 'nor trust in themselves' [*confían* for *desconfían*].
[5] All the MSS. have 'meekness.' H reads 'dishonour,' which a corrector has altered to 'misgivings' [*desconfían̨a*].
[6] E.p. adds: 'and travel so slowly.'
[7] E.p.: 'than after true devotion and purity.'

that which God regards and accepts throughout the spiritual journey.[1] Therefore, besides the imperfections into which the seeking for sweetness of this kind makes them fall, the gluttony which they now have makes them continually go to extremes, so that they pass beyond the limits of moderation within which the virtues are acquired and wherein they have their being. For some of these persons, attracted by the pleasure which they find therein, kill themselves with penances, and others weaken themselves with fasts, by performing more than their frailty can bear, without the order or advice of any,[2] but rather endeavouring to avoid those whom they should obey in these matters; some, indeed, dare to do these things even though the contrary has been commanded them.

2. These persons are most imperfect and unreasonable; for they set bodily penance before subjection and obedience, which is penance according to reason and discretion, and therefore a sacrifice more acceptable and pleasing to God than any other. But such one-sided penance is no more than the penance of beasts, to which they are attracted, exactly like beasts, by the desire and pleasure which they find therein.[3] Inasmuch as all extremes are vicious, and as in behaving thus such persons[4] are working their own will, they grow in vice rather than in virtue; for, to say the least, they are acquiring spiritual gluttony and pride in this way, through not walking in obedience. And many of these the devil assails,[5] stirring up this gluttony in them through the pleasures and desires which he increases within them, to such an extent that, since they can no longer help themselves, they either change or vary or add to that which is commanded them, as any obedience in this respect is so bitter[6] to them. To such an evil pass have some persons come that, simply because it is through obedience that they engage in these exercises, they lose the desire and devotion to perform them, their only desire and pleasure being to do what they themselves are inclined to do,[7] so that it would probably be more profitable for them not to engage in these exercises at all.

3. You will find that many of these persons are very insistent with their spiritual masters to be granted that which they desire, extracting it from them almost by force; if they be refused it they become as

---

[1] [*Lit.*, 'spiritual road.']

[2] A, P: 'without any order or advice.' H: 'without order and advice.'

[3] E.p. softens thus: 'Such one-sided penance is most imperfect, for they are attracted thereto only by the desire and pleasure which they find therein.'

[4] [*Lit.*, 'these persons.' M, e.p.: 'all persons.']

[5] E.p.: 'the devil deceives.'   [6] E.p.: 'so severe and bitter.'

[7] C, G, Mtr., V add: 'and not because it is commanded them.'

peevish as children and go about in great displeasure, thinking that they are not serving God when they are not allowed to do that which they would. For they go about clinging to their own will and pleasure, which they treat as though it came from God;[1] and immediately their directors[2] take it from them, and try to subject them to the will of God, they become peevish, grow faint-hearted and fall away. These persons think that their own satisfaction and pleasure are the satisfaction and service of God.

4. There are others, again, who, because of this gluttony, know so little of their own unworthiness and misery and have thrust so far from them the loving fear and reverence which they owe to the greatness of God, that they hesitate not to insist continually that their confessors shall allow them to communicate[3] often. And, what is worse, they frequently dare to communicate without the leave and consent[4] of the minister and steward of Christ, merely acting on their own opinion, and contriving to conceal the truth from him. And for this reason, because they desire to communicate continually, they make their confessions[5] carelessly,[6] being more eager to eat than to eat cleanly and perfectly, although it would be healthier and holier for them had they the contrary inclination and begged their confessors not to command them to approach the altar so frequently: between these two extremes, however, the better way is that of humble resignation. But the boldness referred to is[7] a thing that does great harm, and men may fear to be punished for such temerity.

5. These persons, in communicating, strive with every nerve to obtain some kind of sensible sweetness and pleasure, instead of humbly doing reverence and giving praise within themselves to God. And in such wise do they devote themselves to this that, when they have received no pleasure or sweetness in the senses, they think that they have accomplished nothing at all. This is to judge God very unworthily; they have not realized that the least of the benefits which come from this Most Holy Sacrament is that which concerns the senses; and that the invisible part of the grace that it bestows is much greater; for, in order that they may look at it with the eyes of faith, God oftentimes withholds from them these other consolations and sweetnesses of

---

1 [*Lit.*, 'and treat this as their God.'] This e.p. omits [softening the sense of the whole, as above (p. 344)].

2 [The Spanish is impersonal: 'immediately this is taken from them,' etc.]

3 G, M, e.p.: 'to confess and communicate.'

4 [*Lit.*, 'and opinion.']   5 H erroneously reads: 'their passions.'

6 [*Lit.*, 'anyhow.']

7 [*Lit.*, 'the other boldnesses are.'] A, e.p. read: 'the excessive boldnesses are.'

sense.[1] And thus they desire to feel and taste God as though He were comprehensible by them and accessible to them, not only in this, but likewise in other spiritual practices. All this is very great imperfection and completely opposed to the nature of God, since it is impurity in faith.[2]

6. These persons have the same defect as regards the practice of prayer, for they think that all the business of prayer consists in experiencing sensible pleasure and devotion and they strive to obtain this by great effort,[3] wearying and fatiguing their faculties and their heads; and when they have not found this pleasure they become greatly discouraged, thinking that they have accomplished nothing. Through these efforts they lose true devotion and spirituality, which consist in perseverance, together with patience and humility, and mistrust of themselves, that they may please God alone. For this reason, when they have once failed to find pleasure in this or some other exercise, they have great disinclination and repugnance to return to it, and at times they abandon it. They are, in fact, as we have said, like children, who are not influenced by reason, and who act, not from rational motives, but from inclination.[4] Such persons expend all their effort in seeking spiritual pleasure and consolation; they never tire, therefore, of reading books; and they begin, now one meditation, now another, in their pursuit of this pleasure which they desire to experience in the things of God. But God, very justly, wisely and lovingly, denies it to them, for otherwise this spiritual gluttony and inordinate appetite would breed innumerable evils. It is, therefore, very fitting that they should enter into the dark night, whereof we shall speak,[5] that they may be purged from this childishness.

7. These persons who are thus inclined to such pleasures have another very great imperfection, which is that they are very weak and remiss in journeying upon the hard[6] road of the Cross; for the soul that is given to sweetness naturally has its face set against all self-denial, which is devoid of sweetness.[7]

[1] M, e.p.: 'and favours of sense.' [The difference, in a Spanish MS., between *sabores* and *favores* would be of the slightest.]
[2] So the MSS. E.p. modifies the last clause and reads: 'Who demands the purest faith.'
[3] [*Lit.*, 'they strive to obtain this, as they say, by the strength of their arms.' The phrase is, of course, understood in the Spanish to be metaphorical, as the words 'as they say' clearly indicate.]
[4] [*Lit.*, 'who are not influenced, neither act by reason, but from pleasure.']
[5] [*Lit.*, 'which we shall give.'] E.p. omits: 'whereof we shall speak.' A, G, V: 'which we shall describe.'
[6] [*áspero*: harsh, rough, rugged.]
[7] [*Lit.*, 'against all the sweetlessness of self-denial.']

8. These persons have many other imperfections which arise hence, of which in time the Lord heals them by means of temptations, aridities and other trials, all of which are part of the dark night. All these I will not treat further here, lest I become too lengthy; I will only say that spiritual temperance and sobriety lead to another and a very different temper, which is that of mortification, fear and submission in all things. It thus becomes clear that the perfection and worth of things consist not in the multitude and the pleasantness of one's actions,[1] but in being able to deny oneself in them; this such persons must endeavour to compass, in so far as they may, until God is pleased to purify them indeed, by bringing them[2] into the dark night, to arrive at which I am hastening on with my account of these imperfections.

CHAPTER VII

Of imperfections with respect to spiritual envy and sloth.[3]

WITH respect likewise to the other two vices, which are spiritual envy and sloth, these beginners fail not to have many imperfections. For, with respect to envy, many of them are wont to experience movements[4] of displeasure at the spiritual good of others, which cause them a certain sensible grief at being outstripped upon this road, so that they would prefer not to hear others praised; for they become displeased at others' virtues and sometimes they cannot refrain from contradicting what is said in praise of them, depreciating it as far as they can; and their annoyance thereat grows[5] because the same[6] is not said of them, for they would fain be preferred in everything. All this is clean contrary to charity, which, as Saint Paul says, rejoices in goodness.[7] And, if charity has any envy, it is a holy envy, comprising grief at not having the virtues of others, yet also joy because others have them, and delight when others outstrip us in the service of God, wherein we ourselves are so remiss.

---

1 Bz., M: 'of one's things.' E.p. abbreviates: 'in the multitude of one's actions.'
2 [*Lit.*, 'causing them to enter.'] Bz.: 'putting them.'
3 Bz., H omit: 'and sloth.'   4 Bz. qualifies with 'many.'
5 [*Lit.*, 'and, as they say, their eye (*el ojo*) grows'—a colloquial phrase expressing annoyance.] E.p. omits this phrase altogether. Bz., G read *enojo* for *el ojo* [destroying the metaphor but not altering the sense of this translation.]
6 E.p.: 'and they greatly regret that the same.'
7 1 Corinthians xiii, 6. The Saint here cites the sense, not the letter, of the epistle. B, H give the quotation correctly, as 'rejoiceth in the truth.'

2. With respect also to spiritual sloth, beginners are apt to be irked by the things that are most spiritual, from which they flee because these things are incompatible with sensible pleasure. For, as they are so much accustomed to sweetness in spiritual things, they are wearied by things in which they find no sweetness. If once they failed to find in prayer the satisfaction which their taste required (and after all it is well that God should take it from them to prove them), they would prefer not to return to it: sometimes they leave it; at other times they continue it unwillingly. And thus because of this sloth they abandon the way of perfection (which is the way of the negation of their will and pleasure for God's sake) for the pleasure and sweetness of their own will, which they aim at satisfying in this way rather than the will of God.

3. And many of these would have God will that which they them-selves will, and are fretful at having to will that which He wills, and find it repugnant to accommodate their will to that of God.[1] Hence it happens to them that oftentimes they think that that wherein they find not their own will and pleasure is not the will of God; and that, on the other hand, when they themselves find satisfaction, God is satisfied. Thus they measure God by themselves and not themselves by God, acting quite contrarily to that which He Himself taught in the Gospel, saying: That he who should lose his will for His sake, the same should gain it; and he who should desire to gain it, the same should lose it.[2]

4. These persons likewise find it irksome when they are commanded to do that wherein they take no pleasure. Because they aim at spiritual sweetness and consolation, they are too weak to have the fortitude and bear the trials of perfection.[3] They resemble those who are softly nurtured and who run fretfully away from everything that is hard, and take offence at the Cross, wherein consist the delights of the spirit. The more spiritual a thing is, the more irksome they find it, for, as they seek to go about spiritual matters with complete freedom and accord-ing to the inclination of their will, it causes them great sorrow and repugnance to enter upon the narrow way, which, says Christ, is the way of life.[4]

5. Let it suffice here to have described these imperfections, among the many to be found in the lives of those that are in this first state of beginners, so that it may be seen how greatly they need God to set them in the state of proficients. This He does by bringing them into

---

[1] E.p.: 'to the Divine will.'
[2] St. Matthew xvi, 25.
[3] [*Lit.*, 'they are very weak for the fortitude and trial of perfection.']
[4] St. Matthew vii, 14.

the dark night whereof we now speak; wherein He weans them from the breasts of these sweetnesses and pleasures, gives them pure aridities and inward darkness, takes from them all these irrelevances[1] and puerilities, and by very different means causes them to win the virtues. For, however assiduously the beginner practises the mortification in himself of all these actions and passions of his, he can never completely succeed—very far from it—until God shall work it in him passively by means of the purgation of the said night. Of this I would fain speak in some way that may be profitable; may God, then, be pleased to give me His Divine light, because this is very needful in a night that is so dark and a matter that is so difficult[2] to describe and to expound.

The line, then, is:

In a dark night.

CHAPTER VIII

Wherein is expounded the first line of the first stanza, and a beginning is made of the explanation of this dark night.[3]

THIS night, which, as we say, is contemplation, produces in spiritual persons two kinds of darkness or purgation, corresponding to the two parts of man's nature—namely, the sensual and the spiritual. And thus the one night or purgation will be sensual, wherein the soul is purged according to sense, which is subdued to the spirit; and the other is a night or purgation which is spiritual, wherein the soul is purged and stripped[4] according to the spirit, and subdued and made ready for the union of love with God. The night of sense is common and comes to many: these are the beginners; and of this night[5] we shall speak first. The night of the spirit is the portion of very few, and these are they that are already practised and proficient, of whom we shall treat hereafter.

2. The first purgation or night is bitter and terrible to sense, as we shall now show.[6] The second bears no comparison with it, for it is

---

[1] M, P, e.p.: 'all these imperfections.'
[2] E.p. and a number of MSS. omit all that follows the word 'difficult.'
[3] The title is taken from e.p. The Codices have no title.
[4] E.p.: 'wherein a soul is purged or stripped.'
[5] E.p.: 'of whom.'   [6] [*Lit.*, 'say.']

horrible and awful[1] to the spirit, as we shall show[2] presently. Since the night of sense is first in order and comes first, we shall first of all[3] say something about it briefly, since more is written of it, as of a thing that is more common; and we shall pass on to treat more fully of the spiritual night, since very little has been said of this, either in speech[4] or in writing, and very little[5] is known of it, even by experience.

3. Since, then, the conduct of these beginners upon the way of God is ignoble,[6] and has much to do with their love of self and their own inclinations, as has been explained above, God desires to lead them farther. He seeks to bring them out of that ignoble kind of love to a higher degree of love for Him, to free them from the ignoble exercises of sense and meditation (wherewith, as we have said, they go seeking God so unworthily and in so many ways that are unbefitting), and to lead them to a kind of spiritual exercise wherein they can commune with Him more abundantly and are freed more completely from imperfections. For they have now had practice for some time in the way of virtue and have persevered in meditation and prayer, whereby, through the sweetness and pleasure that they have found therein, they have lost their love of the things of the world and have gained some degree of spiritual strength in God; this has enabled them to some extent to refrain from creature desires, so that for God's sake they are now able to suffer a light burden and a little aridity without turning back to a time[7] which they found more pleasant. When they are going about these spiritual exercises with the greatest delight and pleasure, and when they believe that the sun of Divine favour is shining most brightly upon them, God turns all this light of theirs into darkness, and shuts against them the door and the source of the sweet spiritual water which they were tasting in God whensoever and for as long as they desired. (For, as they were weak and tender, there was no door closed to them, as Saint John says in the Apocalypse, iii, 8). And thus He leaves them so completely in the dark that they know not whither to go with their sensible imagination and meditation; for they cannot[8] advance a step in meditation, as they were wont to do aforetime, their

---

[1] E.p.: 'for it is very awful.'   [2] [Lit., 'say.']
[3] E.p. omits: 'first of all.'
[4] [plática: the word is frequently used in Spanish to denote an informal sermon or address.]
[5] This 'very little' [which in the original comes in the emphatic final position] is omitted in e.p.
[6] [Lit., 'low'; the same word recurs below and is similarly translated.]
[7] [Lit., 'to the better time.']
[8] M, e.p.: 'for they know not how to.'

inward senses being submerged in this night, and left with such dry-ness that not only do they experience no pleasure and consolation in the spiritual things and good exercises wherein they were wont to find their delights and pleasures, but instead, on the contrary, they find insipidity and bitterness in the said things. For, as I have said, God now sees that they have grown a little, and are becoming strong enough to lay aside their swaddling clothes and be taken from the gentle breast; so He sets them down from His arms and teaches them to[1] walk on their own feet; which they feel to be very strange, for everything seems to be going wrong with them.

4. To recollected persons this commonly happens sooner after their beginnings than to others, inasmuch as they are freer from occasions of backsliding, and their desires turn more quickly from the things of the world, which is necessary if they are to begin to enter this blessed[2] night of sense. Ordinarily no great time passes after their beginnings before they begin to enter this night of sense; and the great majority of them do in fact enter it, for they will generally be seen to fall into these aridities.

5. With regard to this way of purgation of the senses, since it is so common, we might here adduce a great number of quotations from Divine Scripture, where many passages relating to it are continually found, particularly in the Psalms and the Prophets. However, I do not wish to spend time upon these, for he who knows not how to look for them there will find the common experience of this purgation to be sufficient.[3]

CHAPTER IX

Of the signs by which it will be known that the spiritual person is walking along the way of this night and purgation of sense.

BUT since these aridities might frequently proceed, not from the night and purgation of the sensual desires aforementioned, but from sins and imperfections, or from weakness and lukewarm-ness, or from some bad humour or indisposition of the body, I shall here set down certain signs by which it may be known if such aridity

---

[1] M, e.p.: 'and shows them how to.'
[2] E.p. has 'happy' for 'blessed.'
[3] C, e.p. omit this entire sentence, substituting: 'And, to avoid prolixity, we omit them, albeit we shall adduce certain of them later.'

proceeds from the aforementioned purgation, or if it arises from any of the aforementioned sins. For the making of this distinction I find that there are three principal signs.

2. The first is whether, when a soul finds no pleasure or consolation in the things of God, it also fails to find it in any thing created; for, as God sets the soul in this dark night to the end that He may quench and purge its sensual desire, He allows it not to find attraction or sweetness in anything whatsoever. In such a case it may be considered very probable[1] that this aridity and insipidity proceed not from recently committed sins or imperfections. For, if this were so, the soul would feel in its nature some inclination or desire to taste other things than those of God; since, whenever the desire is allowed indulgence in any imperfection, it immediately feels inclined thereto, whether little or much, in proportion to the pleasure and the love that it has put into it. Since, however, this lack of enjoyment in things above or below might proceed from some indisposition or melancholy humour, which often-times makes it impossible for the soul to take pleasure in anything, it becomes necessary to apply the second sign and condition.

3. The second sign whereby a man may believe himself to be experiencing the said purgation[2] is that the memory is ordinarily centred upon God, with painful care and solicitude, thinking that it is not serving God, but is backsliding, because it finds itself without sweetness in the things of God. And in such a case it is evident that this lack of sweetness and this aridity come not from weakness and lukewarmness; for it is the nature of lukewarmness not to care greatly or to have any inward solicitude for the things of God. There is thus a great difference between aridity and lukewarmness, for lukewarmness consists in great weakness and remissness in the will and in the spirit, without solicitude as to serving God; whereas purgative aridity is ordinarily accompanied by solicitude, with care and grief, as I say, because the soul is not serving God. And, although this may sometimes be increased by melancholy or some other humour (as it frequently is), it fails not for that reason to produce a purgative effect upon the desire, since the desire is deprived of all pleasure,[3] and has its care centred upon God alone. For, when mere humour is the cause, it spends itself in displeasure and ruin of the physical nature, and there are none of those desires to serve God which belong to purgative

---

[1] [*Lit.*, 'And in this it is known very probably.'] E.p. omits 'very.'
[2] E.p.: 'The second sign and condition of this purgation.'
[3] A, B: 'since it is completely purged as to [its] pleasure.'

aridity. When the cause is aridity, it is true that the sensual part of the soul has fallen low, and is weak and feeble in its actions, by reason of the little pleasure which it finds in them; but the spirit, on the other hand, is ready and strong.

4. For the cause of this aridity is that God transfers to the spirit the good things and the strength of the senses, which, since the soul's natural strength and senses are incapable of using them, remain barren, dry and empty. For the sensual part of a man has no capacity for that which is pure spirit, and thus, when it is the spirit that receives the pleasure, the flesh is left without savour and is too weak to perform any action. But the spirit, which all the time is being fed, goes forward in strength, and with more alertness and solicitude than before, in its anxiety not to fail God; and if it is not immediately conscious of spiritual sweetness and delight, but only of aridity and lack of sweetness, the reason for this is the strangeness of the exchange; for its palate has been accustomed to those other sensual pleasures upon which its eyes are still fixed, and, since the spiritual palate is not made ready or purged for such subtle pleasure, until it finds itself becoming prepared for it by means of this arid and dark night, it cannot experience spiritual pleasure and good, but only aridity and lack of sweetness, since it misses the pleasure which aforetime it enjoyed so readily.

5. These souls whom God is beginning to lead through these solitary places of the wilderness are like to the children of Israel, to whom in the wilderness God began to give food from Heaven, containing within itself all sweetness, and, as is there said,[1] it turned to the savour which each one of them desired. But withal the children of Israel felt the lack of the pleasures and delights of the flesh and the onions which they had eaten aforetime in Egypt, the more so because their palate was accustomed to these and took delight in them, rather than in the delicate sweetness of the angelic manna; and they wept and sighed for the fleshpots even in the midst of the food of Heaven.[2] To such depths does the vileness of our desires descend that it makes us to long for our own wretched food[3] and to be nauseated by the indescribable[4] blessings of Heaven.

6. But, as I say, when these aridities proceed from the way of the purgation of sensual desire, although at first the spirit feels no sweetness, for the reasons that we have just given, it feels that it is deriving

---

[1] E.p. abbreviates: 'God began to give such delicious food from Heaven that, as is there said.'
[2] Numbers xi, 5–6.   [3] [*Lit.*, 'makes us to desire our miseries.']
[4] [*Lit.*, 'incommunicable.'] E.p. has 'incommutable.'

strength and energy to act from the substance which this inward food
gives it, the which food is the beginning of a contemplation that is
dark and arid to the senses; which contemplation is secret and hidden
from the very person that experiences it; and ordinarily, together with
the aridity and emptiness which it causes in the senses, it gives the soul
an inclination and desire to be alone and in quietness, without being
able to think of any particular thing or having the desire to do so. If
those souls to whom this comes to pass knew how to be quiet at this
time, and troubled not about performing any kind of action, whether
inward or outward, neither had any anxiety about doing anything,[1]
then they would delicately experience this inward refreshment in that
ease and freedom from care. So delicate is this refreshment that ordinarily, if a man have desire or care[2] to experience it, he experiences it
not; for, as I say, it does its work when the soul is most at ease and
freest from care; it is like the air which, if one would close one's hand
upon it, escapes.

7. In this sense we may understand that which the Spouse said to
the Bride in the Songs, namely: 'Withdraw thine eyes from me, for
they make me to soar aloft.'[3] For in such a way does God bring the soul
into this state, and by so different a path does He lead it that, if it
desires to work with its faculties,[4] it hinders the work which God is
doing in it rather than aids it; whereas aforetime it was quite the contrary. The reason is that, in this state of contemplation, which the soul
enters when it forsakes meditation for the state of the proficient, it is
God Who is now working in the soul; He binds[5] its interior faculties,
and allows it not to cling to the understanding, nor to have delight in
the will, nor to reason with the memory. For anything that the soul
can do of its own accord at this time serves only, as we have said, to
hinder inward peace and the work which God is accomplishing in the
spirit by means of that aridity of sense. And this peace, being spiritual
and delicate, performs a work which is quiet and delicate, solitary,
productive of peace and satisfaction[6] and far removed from all those

---

[1] E.p. reads: '. . . [outward], which they strive with their labour and their reasoning
to perform, and had no anxiety to do anything save to allow themselves to be led by God,
to receive and to listen with loving interior attentiveness, then . . .' etc.

[2] E.p.: 'if a man have superadded and particular desire and care.'

[3] Canticles vi, 4 [A.V., vi, 5].

[4] E.p.: 'that, if it will work of itself and by its own ability.'

[5] Nearly all authorities read thus. M, e.p., however, have: 'He seems to bind,' and V:
'He veils.'

[6] [Lit., 'satisfactory and pacific.'] E.p. omits: 'solitary, productive of . . . satisfaction.'
H has 'solicitous' for 'solitary.' C omits 'solitary.' All other authorities read as in the
text.

earlier pleasures, which were very palpable and sensual. This is the peace which, says David, God speaks in the soul to the end that He may make it spiritual.[1] And this leads us to the third point.

8. The third sign whereby this purgation of sense may be recognized is that the soul can no longer meditate or reflect in the imaginative sphere of sense as it was wont,[2] however much it may of itself endeavour to do so. For God now begins to communicate Himself to it, no longer through sense, as He did aforetime, by means of reflections which joined and sundered its knowledge, but by pure spirit, into which consecutive reflections enter not; but He communicates Himself to it by an act of simple contemplation, to which neither the exterior nor the interior senses of the lower part of the soul can attain. From this time forward, therefore, imagination and fancy can find no support in any meditation,[3] and can gain no foothold by means thereof.

9. With regard to this third sign, it is to be understood that this embarrassment and dissatisfaction of the faculties proceed not from indisposition, for, when this is the case, and the indisposition, which never lasts for long,[4] comes to an end, the soul is able once again, by taking some trouble about the matter, to do what it did before, and the faculties find their wonted support. But in the purgation of the desire this is not so: when once the soul begins to enter therein, its inability to reflect with the faculties grows ever greater. For, although it is true that at first, and with some persons, the process is not as continuous[5] as this, so that occasionally they fail to abandon their pleasures and reflections[6] of sense (for perchance[7] by reason of their weakness it was not fitting to wean them from these immediately), yet this inability grows within them more and more and brings the workings of sense to an end, if indeed they are to make progress, for those who walk not in the way of contemplation act very differently. For this night of aridities is not usually continuous in their senses. At times they have these aridities; at others they have them not. At times they cannot meditate; at others they can. For God sets them in this night only to

---

[1] Psalm lxxxiv, 9 [A.V., lxxxv, 8].
[2] E.p. is slightly explicit: ' . . . or reflect, making use of the imaginative sphere of sense, that it may move it as it was wont.'
[3] E. p. : ' cannot find support or make a beginning with any meditation.'
[4] [The stress here is evidently on the transience of the distempers, whether they be moral or physical.]
[5] Bz. : 'as continent.'   [6] E.p. : 'and alleviations.'
[7] E.p. omits 'perchance.'

prove them and to humble them, and to reform their desires, so that they go not nurturing in themselves a sinful[1] gluttony in spiritual things. He sets them not there in order to lead them in the way of the spirit, which is this contemplation; for not all those who walk of set purpose in the way of the spirit are brought by God to contemplation, nor even the half of them[2]—why, He best knows. And this is why He never completely weans the senses of such persons from the breasts of meditations and reflections, but only for short periods and at certain seasons, as we have said.

CHAPTER X

Of the way in which these souls are to conduct themselves in this dark night.

DURING the time, then, of the aridities of this night of sense (wherein God effects the change of which we have spoken above, drawing forth the soul from the life of sense into that of the spirit—that is, from meditation to contemplation—wherein it no longer has any power to work or to reason with its faculties concerning the things of God, as has been said), spiritual persons suffer great trials, by reason not so much of the aridities which they suffer, as of the fear which they have of being lost on the road, thinking that all spiritual blessing is over for them and that God has abandoned them since they find no help or pleasure in good things.[3] Then they grow weary, and endeavour (as they have been accustomed to do) to concentrate their faculties with some degree of pleasure upon some object of meditation, thinking that, when they are not doing this and yet are conscious of making an effort, they are doing nothing. This effort they make not without great inward repugnance and unwillingness on the part of their soul, which was taking pleasure in being in that quietness and ease, instead of working with its faculties.[4] So they have abandoned the one pursuit,[5] yet draw no profit from the other; for, by seeking[6] what is prompted by their own spirit,[7] they lose the spirit of tranquillity and peace[8] which they had before. And thus they are like to

---

[1] E.p. omits: 'a sinful.'
[2] E.p. reads 'to perfect contemplation' and omits 'nor even the half of them.'
[3] H: 'no help whatever in good things.'
[4] E.p. omits: 'instead . . . faculties.'
[5] [*Lit.*, 'spoiling themselves in the one.'] E.p. has: 'turning aside in [i.e., from] the one.'
[6] A, B, M, e.p. have 'using.' Bz.: 'tasting.'
[7] [*Lit.*, 'because they seek their spirit.']   [8] G, H, P omit: 'and peace.'

one who abandons what he has done in order to do it over again, or to one who leaves a city only to re-enter it, or to one who is hunting and lets his prey go in order to hunt it once more. This is useless here, for the soul will gain nothing further by conducting itself in this way, as has been said.[1]

2. These souls turn back at such a time if there is none who understands them; they abandon the road or lose courage; or, at the least, they are hindered from going farther by the great trouble which they take in advancing along the road of meditation and reasoning. Thus they fatigue and overwork their nature, imagining that they are failing through negligence or sin. But this trouble that they are taking is quite useless, for God is now leading them by another road, which is that of contemplation, and is very different from the first; for the one is of meditation and reasoning, and the other belongs neither to imagination nor yet to reasoning.

3. It is well for those who find themselves in this condition to take comfort, to persevere in patience and to be in no wise afflicted. Let them trust in God, Who abandons not those that seek Him with a simple and right heart, and will not fail to give them what is needful for the road, until He bring them into the clear and pure light of love. This last He will give them by means of that other dark night, that of the spirit, if they merit His bringing them thereto.

4. The way in which they are to conduct themselves in this night of sense is to devote themselves not at all to reasoning and meditation, since this is not the time for it, but to allow the soul to remain in peace and quietness, although it may seem clear[2] to them that they are doing nothing and are wasting their time, and although it may appear to them[3] that it is because of their weakness that they have no desire in that state to think of anything. The truth is that they will be doing quite sufficient if they have patience and persevere in prayer without making any effort.[4] What they must do is merely to leave the soul free and disencumbered and at rest from all knowledge and thought, troubling not themselves, in that state, about what they shall think or meditate upon, but contenting themselves with merely a peaceful and loving attentiveness toward God, and in being without anxiety,

---

[1] G modifies and abbreviates the rest of the chapter considerably from this point onward.

[2] E.p. omits 'clear.'

[3] E.p. omits: 'although it may seem to them.'

[4] [*Lit.*, 'without doing anything themselves.'] E.p. abbreviates: 'persevere in prayer, only leaving the soul free,' etc.

without the ability and without desire[1] to have experience of Him or to perceive Him.[2] For all these yearnings disquiet and distract the soul from the peaceful quiet and sweet ease of contemplation which is here granted to it.

5. And although further scruples may come to them—that they are wasting their time, and that it would be well for them to do something else, because they can neither do nor think anything in prayer—let them suffer these scruples and remain in peace, as there is no question save of their being at ease and having freedom of spirit. For if such a soul should desire to make any effort of its own with its interior faculties, this means that it will hinder and lose the blessings which, by means of that peace and ease of the soul, God is instilling into it and impressing upon it. It is just as if some painter were painting or dyeing a face; if the sitter were to move because he desired to do something, he would prevent the painter from accomplishing anything and would disturb him in what he was doing. And thus, when the soul desires to remain in inward ease and peace, any operation and affection or attention[3] wherein it may then seek to indulge[4] will distract it and disquiet it and make it conscious of aridity and emptiness of sense. For the more a soul endeavours to find support in affection and knowledge, the more will it feel the lack of these, which cannot now be supplied to it upon that road.

6. Wherefore it behoves such a soul to pay no heed if the operations of its faculties become lost to it; it is rather to desire that this should happen quickly. For, by not hindering the operation of infused contemplation that God is bestowing upon it, it can receive this with more peaceful abundance, and cause[5] its spirit to be enkindled and to burn with the love which this dark and secret[6] contemplation brings with it and sets firmly in the soul.[7] For contemplation is naught else than a

---

[1] E.p. alters to: 'without excessive desire.' [As on p. 357, n. 4, this edition is endeavouring to soften expressions which might be taken as quietistic.]

[2] E.p.: 'to perceive Him or to have experience of Him.' Bz.: 'to have experience of Him or delight itself in perceiving Him.' [The word rendered 'have experience of' is *gustar*: *lit.*, 'taste.']

[3] E.p.: 'or anxious attention.'   [4] [*Lit.*, 'which it may then wish to have.']

[5] M, e.p.: 'and be refreshed and cause.'   [6] V: 'and secure.'

[7] E.p. here adds: 'I would not, however, have any general rule laid down here as to cessation from meditation or reflection; for such cessation should never come until meditation is no longer possible, and only when the Lord sets a hindrance to it either in the form of purgation and torment, or in that of most perfect contemplation. At other times, and on other occasions, this support and resource must always be used, and, further [the soul must meditate upon] the life and cross of Christ, which is the best means to purgation and patience, and to security on the road, and a wondrous help to lofty contemplation.'

secret, peaceful and loving infusion from God, which, if it be permitted, enkindles the soul with the spirit of love, according as the soul declares in the next lines, namely:

Kindled in love with yearnings.[1]

CHAPTER XI

Wherein are expounded the three lines of the stanza.[2]

THIS enkindling of love is not as a rule felt at the first, because it has not begun to take hold upon the soul, by reason of the impurity of human nature, or because the soul has not understood its own state, as we have said, and has therefore given it no peaceful abiding-place within itself. Yet sometimes, nevertheless, there soon begins to make itself felt a certain yearning toward God; and the more this increases, the more is the soul affectioned and enkindled in love toward God, without knowing or understanding how and whence this love and affection come to it, but from time to time seeing this flame and this enkindling grow so greatly within it that it desires God with yearning of love; even as David, when he was in this dark night, said of himself in these words,[3] namely: 'Because my heart was enkindled (that is to say, in love of contemplation), my reins also were changed': that is, my desires for sensual affections were changed,[4] namely from the way of sense to the way of the spirit, which is the aridity and cessation from all these things whereof we are speaking. And I, he says, was dissolved in nothing and annihilated, and I knew not; for, as we have said, without knowing the way whereby it goes, the soul finds itself annihilated with respect to all things above and below which were accustomed to please it; and it finds itself enamoured, without knowing how. And because at times the enkindling of love in the spirit grows greater, the yearnings for God become so great in the soul that the very bones seem to be dried up by this thirst, and the natural powers to be fading away, and their warmth and strength to be perishing through the intensity[5] of the thirst of love, for the soul feels

---

[1] G departs freely from the text throughout the exposition of this line.
[2] Thus e.p.   [3] Psalm lxxii, 21 [A.V., lxxiii, 21–2].
[4] Thus C, G, H, Mtr., V. The other authorities have only: 'my reins also were changed.' E.p. reads: 'my tastes and affections also were changed,' and continues: 'namely, from the way of sense,' etc.
[5] [*Lit.*, 'livingness': cf. the quotation below.]

that this thirst of love is a living thirst. This thirst David had and felt, when he said: 'My soul thirsted for the living God.'[1] Which is as much as to say: A living thirst was that of my soul. Of this thirst, since it is living, we may say that it kills. But it is to be noted that the vehemence of this thirst is not continuous, but occasional, although as a rule the soul is accustomed to feel it to a certain degree.[2]

2. But it must be noted that, as I began to say just now, this love is not as a rule felt at first, but only the dryness and emptiness are felt whereof we are speaking. Then in place of this love which afterwards becomes gradually enkindled, what the soul experiences in the midst of these aridities and emptinesses of the faculties is an habitual care and solicitude with respect to God, together with grief and fear that it is not serving Him. But it is a sacrifice which is not a little pleasing to God that the soul should go about afflicted and solicitous for His love. This solicitude and care leads the soul into that secret contemplation, until, the senses (that is, the sensual part) having in course of time been in some degree purged of the natural affections and powers by means of the aridities which it causes within them, this Divine love begins to be enkindled in the spirit. Meanwhile, however, like one who has began a cure, the soul knows only suffering in this dark and arid purgation of the desire; by this means it becomes healed of many imperfections, and exercises itself in many virtues, in order to make itself meet for the said love, as we shall now say with respect to the line following:

Oh, happy chance!

3. When God leads the soul into this night of sense in order to purge the sense of its lower part and to subdue it, unite it and bring it into conformity with the spirit, by setting it in darkness and causing it to cease from meditation (as He afterwards does in order to purify the spirit to unite it with God, as we shall afterwards say[3]), He brings it into the night of the spirit, and (although it appears not so to it) the soul gains so many benefits that it holds it to be a happy chance to have escaped from the bonds and restrictions of the senses of its lower self, by means of this night aforesaid;[4] and utters the present line, namely: Oh, happy chance! With respect to this, it behoves us here to note the benefits which the soul finds in this night, and because of which it

---

[1] Psalm xli, 3 [A.V., xlii, 2].
[2] E.p. substitutes for this last sentence: 'although the vehemence of this thirst is not continuous, but only occasional; howbeit this thirst is ordinarily felt to a certain degree.'
[3] E.p. omits: 'as we shall afterwards say.'   [4] E.p.: 'this happy night.'

considers it a happy chance to have passed through it; all of which benefits the soul includes in the next line, namely:

I went forth without being observed.

4. This going forth is understood of the subjection to its sensual part which the soul suffered when it sought God through operations so weak, so limited and so defective[1] as are those of this lower part; for at every step it stumbled into numerous imperfections and ignorances, as we have noted above in writing of the seven capital sins. From all these it is freed when this night quenches within it all pleasures, whether from above or from below, and makes all meditation darkness to it, and grants it other innumerable blessings in the acquirement of the virtues, as we shall now show. For it will be a matter of great pleasure and great consolation, to one that journeys on this road, to see how that which seems to the soul so severe and adverse, and so contrary to spiritual pleasure, works in it so many blessings. These, as we say, are gained when the soul goes forth, as regards its affection and operation, by means of this night, from all created things, and when it journeys to eternal things,[2] which is great happiness and good fortune:[3] first, because of the great blessing which is in the quenching of the desire and affection with respect to all things; secondly, because they are very few that endure and persevere in entering by this strait gate and by the narrow way which leads to life, as says Our Saviour.[4] The strait gate is this night of sense, and the soul detaches itself from sense and strips itself thereof that it may enter by this gate, and establishes itself in faith,[5] which is a stranger to all sense, so that afterwards it may journey by the narrow way, which is the other night—that of the spirit—and this the soul afterwards[6] enters in order to journey to God in pure faith,[7] which is the means whereby the soul is united to God. By this road, since it is so narrow, dark and terrible (though there is no comparison between this night of sense and that other,[8] in its darkness and trials, as we shall say later), they are far fewer that journey, but its benefits are far greater without comparison than those of this present night. Of these benefits we shall now begin to say something, with such brevity as is possible, in order that we may pass to the other night.

[1] E.p. omits: 'so . . . so . . . so . . .'   [2] V: 'to invisible things.'
[3] [Lit., 'and chance': the same word as in the verse-line above.]
[4] St. Matthew vii, 14.
[5] E.p.: 'ruling itself by faith.' Some Codices have: 'uniting itself in faith.'
[6] E.p.: 'later.'   [7] E.p.: 'in faith most pure.'   [8] E.p.: 'and that of the spirit.

CHAPTER XII

Of the benefits which this night[1] causes in the soul.

THIS night and purgation of the desire, a happy one for the soul, works in it so many blessings and benefits (although to the soul, as we have said, it rather seems that blessings are being taken away from it) that, even as Abraham made a great feast when he weaned his son Isaac,[2] even so is there joy in Heaven because God is now taking this soul from its swaddling clothes, setting it down from His arms, making it to walk upon its feet, and likewise taking from it the milk of the breast and the soft and sweet food proper to children, and making it to eat bread with crust, and to begin to enjoy the food of robust persons. This food, in these aridities and this darkness of sense, is now given to the spirit, which is dry and emptied of all the sweetness of sense. And this food is the infused contemplation whereof we have spoken.

2. This is the first and principal benefit caused by this arid and dark night of contemplation: the knowledge of oneself and of one's misery.[3] For, besides the fact that all the favours which God grants to the soul are habitually granted to them enwrapped in this knowledge, these aridities and this emptiness of the faculties, compared with the abundance which the soul experienced aforetime and the difficulty which it finds in good works, make it recognize its own lowliness and misery, which in the time of its prosperity it was unable to see. Of this there is a good illustration in the Book of Exodus, where God, wishing to humble the children of Israel and desiring that they should know themselves, commanded them to take away and strip off the festal garments and adornments wherewith they were accustomed to adorn themselves in the Wilderness, saying: 'Now from henceforth strip yourselves of festal ornaments and put on everyday working dress, that ye may know what treatment ye deserve.'[4] This is as though He had said: Inasmuch as the attire that ye wear, being proper to festival and rejoicing, causes you to feel less humble concerning yourselves than ye should, put off from you this attire, in order that henceforth, seeing yourselves clothed with vileness, ye may know that ye merit no more, and may

---

[1] E.p.: 'this night of sense.'   [2] Genesis xxi, 8.
[3] So H and the other Codices. E.p. has: 'And this is the first and principal benefit which the soul gains here, and from which almost all the others are derived. Of these, the first benefit is the knowledge of oneself and of one's misery.'
[4] Exodus xxxiii, 5.

know who ye are. Wherefore the soul knows the truth that it knew not at first, concerning its own misery; for, at the time when it was clad as for a festival and found in God much pleasure, consolation and support, it was somewhat more satisfied and contented, since it thought itself to some extent to be serving God. It is true that such souls may not have this idea explicitly in their minds; but some suggestion of it at least is implanted in them by the satisfaction which they find in their pleasant experiences. But, now that the soul has put on its other and working attire—that of aridity and abandonment—and now that its first lights have turned into darkness, it possesses these lights more truly in this virtue of self-knowledge, which is so excellent and so necessary,[1] considering itself now as nothing and experiencing no satisfaction in itself; for it sees that it does nothing of itself neither can do anything. And the smallness of this self-satisfaction, together with the soul's affliction at not serving God, is considered and esteemed by God as greater than all the consolations which the soul formerly experienced and the works which it wrought, however great they were, inasmuch as they were the occasion of many imperfections and ignorances. And from this attire[2] of aridity proceed, as from their fount and source of self-knowledge, not only the things which we have described already, but also the benefits which we shall now describe and many more which will have to be omitted.

3. In the first place, the soul learns to commune with God with more respect and more courtesy, such as a soul must ever observe in converse with the Most High. These it knew not in its prosperous times of comfort and consolation, for that comforting favour[3] which it experienced made its craving for God somewhat bolder than was fitting, and discourteous and ill-considered.[4] Even so did it happen to Moses, when he perceived that God was speaking to him; blinded[5] by that pleasure and desire, without further consideration, he would have made bold to go to Him if God had not commanded him to stay and put off his shoes. By this incident we are shown the respect and discretion in detachment of desire wherewith a man is to commune with God. When Moses had obeyed in this matter, he became so discreet and so attentive that the Scripture says that not only did he not

---

[1] E.p.: 'it more truly possesses and has this virtue of self-knowledge so excellent and so necessary.' Our reading is that of H.

[2] H: 'this labour,' probably in error [trabajo for traje].

[3] E.p. omits 'comforting [gustoso].' Bz. has: 'that fervour and comfort [gusto],' Mtr., V: 'that favour and comfort.'

[4] E.p. 'somewhat bolder and less courteous than was fitting.'

[5] E.p. has 'carried away' for 'blinded.'

make bold to draw near to God, but that he dared not even look at Him.[1] For, having taken off the shoes of his desires and pleasures, he became very conscious of his wretchedness in the sight of God, as befitted one about to hear the word of God. Even so likewise the preparation which God granted[2] to Job in order that he might speak with Him consisted not in those delights and glories which Job himself reports that he was wont to have in his God, but in leaving him naked upon a dung-hill,[3] abandoned and even persecuted by his friends, filled with anguish and bitterness, and the earth covered with worms. And then the Most High God, He that lifts up the poor man from the dung-hill, was pleased to come down and speak with him there face to face, revealing[4] to him the depths and heights[5] of His wisdom, in a way that He had never done in the time of his prosperity.

4. And here we must note another excellent benefit which there is in this night and aridity of the desire of sense, since we have had occasion to speak of it. It is that, in this dark night of the desire (to the end that the words of the Prophet may be fulfilled, namely: 'Thy light shall shine in the darkness'[6]), God will enlighten the soul, giving it knowledge, not only of its lowliness and wretchedness, as we have said, but likewise of the greatness and excellence of God. For, as well as quenching the desires and pleasures and attachments of sense, He cleanses and frees the understanding that it may understand the truth; for pleasure of sense and desire, even though it be for spiritual things, darkens and obstructs the spirit, and furthermore that straitness[7] and aridity of sense enlightens and quickens the understanding, as says Isaias.[8] Vexation makes us to understand how the soul that is empty and disencumbered, as is necessary for His Divine influence, is instructed supernaturally by God in His Divine wisdom, through this dark and arid night of contemplation,[9] as we have said; and this instruction God gave not in those first sweetnesses and joys.

5. This is very well explained by the same prophet Isaias, where he

---

[1] This is the reading of e.p. Cf. Exodus iii, 6. [P. Silverio reads, with] other authorities: 'dared not even reflect.'

[2] E.p.: 'to hear the Divine words. The preparation likewise which God granted . . .'

[3] [Job ii, 7–8.]

[4] E.p.: 'the Most High God, Who lifts up the poor man from the dung-hill, was pleased to communicate Himself to him with greater abundance and sweetness, revealing . . .'

[5] [Lit., 'the deep heights.']   [6] Isaias lviii, 10.

[7] A, B, Bz., C, H read 'appetite' [apetito] for 'straitness' [aprieto], presumably in error.

[8] Isaias xxviii, 19. [The author omits the actual text.]

[9] [To translate this passage at all, we must read the Dios cómo of P. Silverio (p. 403, l. 20), which is also found in P. Gerardo and elsewhere, as cómo Dios.]

says: 'Whom shall God teach His knowledge, and whom shall He make to understand the hearing?'[1] To those, He says, that are weaned from the milk and drawn away from the breasts.[2] Here it is shown that the first milk of spiritual sweetness is no preparation for this Divine influence, neither is there preparation in attachment to the breast of delectable meditations, belonging to the faculties of sense, which gave the soul pleasure; such preparation consists rather in the lack of the one and withdrawal from the other. Inasmuch as, in order to listen to God, the soul needs to stand upright and to be detached, with regard to affection and sense, even as the Prophet says concerning himself, in these words: I will stand upon my watch (this is that detachment of desire) and I will make firm my step (that is, I will not meditate with sense), in order to contemplate (that is, in order to understand that which may come to me from God).[3] So we have now arrived at this, that from this arid night there first of all comes self-knowledge, whence, as from a foundation, rises this other knowledge of God. For which cause Saint Augustine said to God: 'Let me know myself, Lord, and I shall know Thee.'[4] For, as the philosophers say, one extreme can be well known by another.

6. And in order to prove more completely how efficacious is this night of sense, with its aridity and its desolation, in bringing the soul that light which, as we say, it receives there from God, we shall quote that passage of David, wherein he clearly describes the great power which is in this night for bringing the soul this lofty knowledge of God. He says, then, thus: 'In the desert land, waterless, dry and pathless, I appeared before Thee, that I might see Thy virtue and Thy glory.'[5] It is a wondrous thing that David should say here that the means and the preparation for his knowledge of the glory of God were not the spiritual delights and the many pleasures which he had experienced, but the aridities and detachments of his sensual nature, which is here to be understood by the dry and desert land. No less wondrous is it that he should describe as the road to his perception and vision of the virtue of God, not the Divine meditations and conceptions of which he had often made use, but his being unable to form any conception of God or to walk by meditation produced by imaginary consideration, which is here to be understood by the pathless land. So that the means to a knowledge of God and of oneself is this dark night with its aridities

---

[1] E.p.: 'to hear His word.'
[2] Isaias xxviii, 9.
[3] Habacuc ii, 1.
[4] St. Augustine: Soliloq., Cap. ii.
[5] Psalm lxii, 3 [A.V., lxiii, 1–2].

and voids, although it leads not to a knowledge of Him of the same plenitude and abundance that comes from the other night of the spirit, since this is only, as it were, the beginning of that other.

7. Likewise, from the aridities and voids of this night of the desire, the soul draws spiritual humility, which is the contrary virtue to the first capital sin, which, as we said, is spiritual pride. Through this humility, which is acquired by the said knowledge of self, the soul is purged from all those imperfections whereinto it fell with respect to that sin of pride,[1] in the time of its prosperity. For it sees itself so dry and miserable that the idea never even occurs to it that it is making better progress than others, or outstripping them, as it believed itself to be doing before. On the contrary, it recognizes that others are making better progress than itself.

8. And hence arises the love of its neighbours, for it esteems them, and judges them not as it was wont to do aforetime, when it saw that itself had great fervour and others not so. It is aware only of its own wretchedness, which it keeps before its eyes to such an extent that it never forgets it, nor takes occasion to set its eyes on anyone else. This was described wonderfully by David, when he was in this night, in these words: 'I was dumb and was humbled and kept silence from good things and my sorrow was renewed.'[2] This he says because it seemed to him that the good that was in his soul had so completely departed that not only did he neither speak nor find any language concerning it, but with respect to the good of others he was likewise dumb because of his grief at the knowledge of his misery.

9. In this condition, again, souls become submissive and obedient upon the spiritual road, for, when they see their own misery, not only do they hear[3] what is taught them, but they even desire that anyone soever may set them on the way and tell them what they ought to do. The affective[4] presumption which they sometimes had in their prosperity is taken from them; and finally, there are swept away from them on this road all the other imperfections which we noted above with respect to this first sin, which is spiritual pride.[5]

---

1 E.p. omits: 'with respect to that sin of pride.'
2 Psalm xxxviii, 3 [A.V., xxxix, 2].   3 Bz.: 'do they obey.'
4 E.p. omits 'affective.'
5 E.p.: 'all the other imperfections are swept away from them which we touched on above when speaking of spiritual pride.' A, B add: 'as we have said.'

CHAPTER XIII

Of other benefits which this night of sense causes in the soul.[1]

WITH respect to the soul's imperfections of spiritual avarice, because of which it coveted this and that spiritual thing and found no satisfaction in this and that exercise by reason of its covetousness for the desire and pleasure which it found therein, this arid and dark night has now greatly reformed it. For, as it finds not the pleasure and sweetness which it was wont to find, but rather finds affliction and lack of sweetness, it has such moderate recourse to them that it might possibly now lose, through defective use, what aforetime it lost through excess; although as a rule God gives to those whom He leads into this night humility and readiness, albeit with lack of sweetness, so that what is commanded them they may do for God's sake alone; and thus they no longer seek profit in many things[2] because they find no pleasure in them.

2. With respect to spiritual luxury, it is likewise clearly seen that, through this aridity and lack of sensible sweetness which the soul finds in spiritual things, it is freed from those impurities which we there noted; for we said that, as a rule, they proceeded from the pleasure which overflowed from spirit into sense.

3. But with regard to the imperfections from which the soul frees itself in this dark night with respect to the fourth sin, which is spiritual gluttony,[3] they may be found above, though they have not all been described there, because they are innumerable; and thus I will not detail them here, for I would fain make an end of this night in order to pass to the next, concerning which we shall have to pronounce grave words and instructions.[4] Let it suffice for the understanding of the innumerable benefits which, over and above those mentioned, the soul gains in this night with respect to this sin[5] of spiritual gluttony, to say that it frees itself from all those imperfections which have there been described, and from many other and greater evils, and vile abominations[6] which are not written above, into which fell many of whom we have had experience, because they had not reformed their desire as concerning this inordinate love of spiritual sweetness. For in this arid

---

1 From e.p.
2 E.p.: 'and thus they detach themselves from many things.'
3 H erroneously reads: 'spiritual pleasure.'   4 E.p.: 'grave instructions.'
5 E.p.: 'against this sin.'   6 E.p. omits: 'and vile abominations.'

and dark night wherein He sets the soul, God has restrained its concupiscence and curbed its desire so that the soul cannot feed upon any
pleasure or sweetness of sense,[1] whether from above or from below;
and this He continues to do[2] after such manner that the soul is subjected, reformed and repressed with respect to concupiscence and
desire. It loses the strength of its passions and concupiscence and it
becomes sterile, because it no longer consults its likings. Just as, when
none is accustomed to take milk from the breast, the courses of the
milk[3] are dried up, so the desires of the soul are dried up. And besides[4]
these things there follow admirable benefits from this spiritual sobriety,
for, when desire and concupiscence are quenched, the soul lives in
spiritual tranquillity and peace; for, where desire and concupiscence
reign not, there is no disturbance, but peace and consolation of God.

4. From this there arises another and a second benefit, which is that
the soul habitually has remembrance of God, with fear and dread of
backsliding upon the spiritual road, as has been said. This is a great
benefit, and not one of the least that results from this aridity and purgation of the desire, for the soul is purified and cleansed of the imperfections that were clinging to it because of the desires and affections,
which of their own accord deaden and darken the soul.

5. There is another very great benefit for the soul in this night,
which is that it practises several virtues together, as, for example,
patience and longsuffering, which are often called upon in these times
of emptiness and aridity, when the soul endures and perseveres in its
spiritual exercises without consolation and without pleasure. It
practises the charity of God, since it is not now moved by the pleasure
of attraction and sweetness which it finds in its work, but only by God.
It likewise practises here the virtue of fortitude, because, in these
difficulties and insipidities which it finds in its work, it brings strength
out of weakness and thus becomes strong. All the virtues, in short—
the theological and also the cardinal and moral—both in body and in
spirit,[5] are practised by the soul in these times of aridity.

6. And that in this night the soul obtains these four benefits which
we have here described (namely, delight of peace, habitual remem-

---

[1] E.p.: 'so that it can hardly feed at all upon sweetnesses or pleasures of sense.'
[2] H omits: 'and this He continues to do.'
[3] A: 'of the breast of the milk'; Mtr.: 'of the veins of the milk.'
[4] E.p. omits freely, reading: 'and this He continues to do after such manner that the
soul is gradually correcting, mortifying and controlling itself, as regards concupiscence
and desire, so that it seems to be losing the strength of its passions; and besides . . .'
[5] E.p. reads: 'All the virtues, the cardinal, and also the theological and moral,' and
omits: 'both in body and in spirit.'

brance and thought of God, cleanness and purity of soul and the practice of the virtues which we have just described), David tells us, having experienced it himself when he was in this night, in these words: 'My soul refused consolations, I had remembrance of God, I found consolation and was exercised and my spirit failed.'[1] And he then says: 'And I meditated by night with my heart and was exercised, and I swept and purified my spirit'—that is to say, from all the affections.[2]

7. With respect to the imperfections of the other three spiritual sins which we have described above, which are wrath, envy and sloth, the soul is purged hereof likewise in this aridity of the desire and acquires the virtues opposed to them; for, softened and humbled by these aridities and hardships and other temptations and trials wherein God exercises it during this night, it becomes meek with respect to God, and to itself, and likewise with respect to its neighbour. So that it is no longer disturbed and angry with itself because of its own faults, nor with its neighbour because of his, neither is it displeased with God, nor does it utter unseemly complaints because He does not quickly make it holy.

8. Then, as to envy, the soul has charity toward others in this respect also; for, if it has any envy, this is no longer a vice as it was before, when it was grieved because others were preferred to it and given greater advantage. Its grief now comes from seeing how great is its own misery, and its envy (if it has any) is a virtuous envy, since it desires to imitate others, which is great virtue.

9. Neither are the sloth and the irksomeness which it now experiences concerning spiritual things vicious as they were before. For in the past these sins proceeded from the spiritual pleasures which the soul sometimes experienced and sought after when it found them not. But this new weariness proceeds not from this insufficiency of pleasure, because God has taken from the soul pleasure in all things in this purgation of the desire.

10. Besides these benefits which have been mentioned, the soul attains innumerable others by means of this arid contemplation. For often, in the midst of these times of aridity and hardship, God communicates to the soul, when it is least expecting it, the purest spiritual sweetness and love, together with a spiritual knowledge which is sometimes very delicate, each manifestation of which is of greater benefit and worth than those which the soul enjoyed aforetime; although in

---

[1] Psalm lxxvi, 4 [A.V., lxxvii, 3–4].
[2] Psalm lxxvi, 7 [A.V., lxxvii, 6].

its beginnings the soul thinks that this is not so, for the spiritual influence now granted to it is very delicate and cannot be perceived by sense.

11. Finally, inasmuch as the soul is now purged from the affections and desires of sense, it obtains liberty of spirit, whereby in ever greater degree it gains the twelve fruits of the Holy Spirit. Here, too, it is wondrously delivered from the hands of its three enemies—devil, world and flesh; for, its pleasure and delight of sense being quenched with respect to all things, neither the devil nor the world nor sensuality has any arms or any strength wherewith to make war upon the spirit.

12. These times of aridity, then, cause the soul to journey in all purity in the love of God, since it is no longer influenced in its actions by the pleasure and sweetness of the actions themselves, as perchance it was when it experienced sweetness, but only by a desire to please God. It becomes neither presumptuous nor self-satisfied, as perchance it was wont to become in the time of its prosperity, but fearful and timid with regard to itself, finding in itself no satisfaction whatsoever; and herein consists that holy fear which preserves and increases the virtues. This aridity, too, quenches natural energy and concupiscence, as has also been said. Save for the pleasure, indeed, which at certain times God Himself infuses into it, it is a wonder if it finds pleasure and consolation of sense, through its own diligence, in any spiritual exercise or action, as has already been said.

13. There grows within souls that experience this arid night concern for God and yearnings to serve Him, for in proportion as the breasts of sensuality, wherewith it sustained and nourished the desires that it pursued, are drying up, there remains nothing in that aridity and detachment save the yearning to serve God, which is a thing very pleasing to God. For, as David says, an afflicted spirit is a sacrifice to God.[1]

14. When the soul, then, knows that, in this arid purgation through which it has passed, it has derived and attained so many and such precious benefits[2] as those which have here been described, it tarries not in crying, as in the stanza of which we are expounding the lines, 'Oh, happy chance!—I went forth without being observed.' That is, 'I went forth' from the bonds and subjection of the desires of sense and the affections, 'without being observed'—that is to say, without the three enemies aforementioned being able to keep me from it. These

---

[1] Psalm l, 19 [A.V., li, 17].
[2] E.p.: 'attained such precious benefits, and so many.'

enemies, as we have said, bind the soul as with bonds,[1] in its desires and pleasures, and prevent it from going forth from itself to the liberty of the love[2] of God; and without these desires and pleasures they cannot give battle to the soul, as has been said.

15. When, therefore, the four passions of the soul—which are joy, grief, hope and fear—are calmed through continual mortification; when the natural desires have been lulled to sleep, in the sensual nature of the soul, by means of habitual times of aridity; and when the harmony of the senses and the interior faculties causes a suspension of labour and a cessation from the work of meditation, as we have said (which is the dwelling and the household of the lower part of the soul), these enemies cannot obstruct this spiritual liberty, and the house remains at rest and quiet, as says the following line:

My house being now at rest.[3]

CHAPTER XIV

Expounds this last line of the first stanza.[4]

WHEN this house of sensuality was now at rest—that is, was mortified—its passions being quenched and its desires put to rest and lulled to sleep by means of this blessed night of the purgation of sense, the soul went forth, to set out upon the road and way of the spirit, which is that of progressives and proficients,[5] and which, by another name, is called the way of illumination or of infused contemplation, wherein God Himself feeds and refreshes the soul, without meditation, or the soul's active help.[6] Such, as we have said, is the night and purgation of sense in the soul.[7] In those who have afterwards to enter the other and more formidable night of the spirit, in order to pass to the Divine union of love of God (for not all

---

[1] E.p. omits: 'as with bonds.'   [2] E.p.: 'of the perfect love.'
[3] [So e.p., which completes the sense of the paragraph. The other versions, which P. Silverio follows, leave it unfinished, reading: '. . . of the soul), which is that which the Lord (*sic*) here calls His house, she says: "My house being now at rest."']
[4] The title is from e.p. In the first four lines of the first paragraph the Codices show considerable variations in secondary matters. We here follow H.
[5] [*de los aprovechantes y aprovechados.*] E.p., Bz. omit: 'progressives and.'
[6] H: 'or the soul's active way.' The 1630 edition reads as in the text above, but adds: 'with labour.'
[7] E.p. omits: 'in the soul.'

pass habitually thereto, but only the smallest number), it is wont to be accompanied by formidable trials and temptations of sense, which last for a long time, albeit longer in some than in others. For to some the angel of Satan presents himself—namely, the spirit of fornication— that he may buffet their senses with abominable and violent temptations, and trouble their spirits with vile considerations and representations which are most[1] visible to the imagination, which things at times are a greater affliction to them than death.[2]

2. At other times in this night there is added to these things the spirit of blasphemy, which roams abroad, setting in the path of all the conceptions and thoughts of the soul intolerable blasphemies. These it sometimes suggests to the imagination with such violence that the soul almost utters them, which is a grave torment to it.

3. At other times another abominable spirit, which Isaias calls *Spiritus vertiginis*,[3] is allowed to molest them, not in order that they may fall, but that it may try them. This spirit darkens their senses in such a way that it fills them with numerous scruples and perplexities, so confusing that, as they judge, they can never, by any means, be satisfied concerning them, neither can they find any help for their judgment[4] in counsel or thought. This is one of the severest goads and horrors of this night, very closely akin to that which passes in the night of the spirit.

4. As a rule these storms and trials are sent by God in this night and purgation of sense to those whom afterwards He purposes to lead into the other night (though not all reach it), to the end that, when they have been chastened and buffeted, they may in this way continually exercise and prepare themselves, and continually accustom their senses and faculties to the union of wisdom which is to be bestowed upon them in that other night. For, if the soul be not tempted, exercised and proved with trials and temptations, it cannot quicken[5] its sense for Wisdom. For this reason it is said in Ecclesiasticus: 'He that has not been tempted, what does he know? And he that has not been proved, what are the things that he recognizes?'[6] To this truth Jeremias bears good witness, saying: 'Thou didst chastise me, Lord, and I was instructed.'[7] And the most proper form of this chastisement, for one

---

[1] Bz., e.p.: 'are very.'   [2] The next paragraph is lacking in V.
[3] [The 'spirit of giddiness' of D.V., and 'perverse spirit' of A.V., Isaias xix, 14.] E.p. adds: 'is allowed to try them,' and omits: 'not in order that they may fall, but.'
[4] So A. The other authorities [and P. Silverio] read: 'for the judgment.'
[5] So Bz., H, Mtr., P, V. A, B, C, M, e.p. read: 'arrive' [which involves a retranslation: 'its senses cannot arrive at wisdom'—this is not a natural reading in the Spanish].
[6] Ecclesiasticus xxxiv, 9–10.   [7] Jeremias xxxi, 18.

who will enter into Wisdom, is that of the interior trials which we are here describing, inasmuch as it is these which most effectively purge sense of all favours and consolations to which it was affected, with natural weakness, and by which the soul is truly humiliated in preparation for the exaltation which it is to experience.

5. For how long a time the soul will be held in this fasting and penance of sense, cannot be said with any certainty; for all do not experience it after one manner, neither do all encounter the same temptations. For this is meted out by the will of God, in conformity with the greater or the smaller degree of imperfection which each soul has to purge away. In conformity, likewise, with the degree of love of union[1] to which God is pleased to raise it, He will humble it with greater or less intensity or in greater or less time. Those who have the disposition and greater strength to suffer, He purges with greater intensity and more quickly. But those who are very weak are kept for a long time in this night, and these He purges very gently and with slight temptations. Habitually, too, He gives them refreshments of sense so that they may not fall away, and only after a long time do they attain to purity of perfection in this life, some of them never attaining to it at all. Such are neither properly in the night nor properly out of it; for, although they make no progress, yet, in order that they may continue in humility and self-knowledge, God exercises them for certain periods and at certain times[2] in those temptations and aridities; and at other times and seasons He assists them with consolations, lest they should grow faint and return to seek the consolations of the world. Other souls, which are weaker, God Himself accompanies, now appearing to them,[3] now moving farther away, that He may exercise them in His love; for without such turnings away they would not learn to reach God.

6. But the souls which are to pass on to that happy and high estate, the union of love, are wont as a rule to remain for a long time in these aridities and temptations,[4] however quickly God may lead them, as has been seen by experience. It is time, then, to begin to treat of the second night.[5]

---

[1] E.p.: 'of union of love.'   [2] [Lit., 'for certain days.']
[3] E.p.: 'now disappearing (from them).'   [4] E.p. omits: 'and temptations.'
[5] So end the MSS. A and B add: 'wherein God places the soul.' E.p. substitutes for the last sentence: 'Bringing here, then, this book to a close, let us begin to treat of the second night.' G ends: '. . . aridities and temptations, until God set it in the second night of the spirit, whereof we have next to treat.' Bz. has: 'End of the Night. End of the first night and purgation which is of sense. Laus Deus (sic). That which God wills.' P has: 'Finis. Laus Deo Optimo et Maximo. Es (sic) Deus in nobis agitante calescimus ipso.'

BOOK THE SECOND

Of the Dark Night of the Spirit.[1]

CHAPTER I

Which begins to treat of the dark night[2] *of the spirit and says at what time it begins.*

THE soul which God is about to lead onward is not led by His Majesty into this night of the spirit[3] as soon as it goes forth from the aridities and trials of the first purgation and night of sense; rather it is wont to pass a long time, even years, after leaving the state of beginners, in exercising itself in that of proficients. In this latter state it is like to one that has come forth from a rigorous imprisonment;[4] it goes about the things of God with much greater freedom and satisfaction of the soul, and with more abundant and inward delight than it did[5] at the beginning before it entered the said night. For its imagination and faculties are no longer bound, as they were before, by meditation and anxiety of spirit, since it now very readily finds in its spirit the most serene and loving contemplation and spiritual sweetness without the labour of meditation; although, as the purgation of the soul is not complete (for the principal part thereof, which is that of the spirit, is wanting, without which, owing to the communication that exists between the one part and the other,[6] since the subject is one only, the purgation of sense, however violent it may have been, is not yet complete and perfect), it is never without certain occasional necessities, aridities,[7] darknesses and perils which are sometimes much more intense than those of the past, for they are as tokens and heralds of the coming night of the spirit, and are not of as long duration as will

---

[1] The MSS. vary as to the title. Some have none. B begins: 'Book the Second of the Purgation of the Spirit called Dark Night.'
[2] Thus the Codices. E.p. has: 'the second night.'
[3] So H, P. Bz. has: 'into this night and purgation of the spirit.' E.p.: 'into the union of love.'
[4] [*Lit.*, 'from a narrow prison.']   [5] E.p.: 'than it had.'
[6] [i.e., between sense and spirit.]   [7] E.p. omits: 'occasional necessities.'

be the night which is to come. For, having passed through a period, or periods, or days of this night and tempest, the soul soon returns to its wonted serenity; and after this manner God purges certain souls which are not to rise to so high a degree of love as are others, bringing them at times, and for short periods, into this night of contemplation and purgation of the spirit, causing night to come upon them[1] and then dawn, and this frequently, so that the words of David may be fulfilled, that He sends His crystal—that is, His contemplation—like morsels;[2] although these morsels of dark contemplation are never as intense as is that terrible night of contemplation which we are to describe, into which, of set purpose, God brings the soul that He may lead it to Divine union.

2. This sweetness, then, and this interior pleasure which we are describing, and which these progressives find and experience in their spirits so easily and so abundantly, is communicated to them in much greater abundance than aforetime, overflowing into their senses more than was usual previously to this purgation of sense; for, inasmuch as the sense is now purer, it can more easily feel the pleasures of the spirit after its manner. As, however, this sensual part of the soul is weak and incapable of experiencing the strong things of the spirit, it follows that these proficients, by reason of this spiritual communication which is made to their sensual part, endure therein many frailties and sufferings and weaknesses of the stomach, and in consequence are fatigued in spirit. For, as the Wise Man says: 'The corruptible body presseth down the soul.'[3] Hence comes it that the communications that are granted to these souls cannot be very strong or very intense or very spiritual, as is required for Divine union with God, by reason of the weakness and corruption of the sensual nature which has a part in them. Hence arise the raptures and trances and dislocations of the bones which always happen when the communications are not purely spiritual—that is, are not given to the spirit alone, as are those of the perfect who are purified by the second night of the spirit, and in whom these raptures and torments of the body no longer exist, since they are enjoying liberty of spirit, and their senses are now neither clouded nor transported.

3. And in order that the necessity for such souls to enter this night of the spirit may be understood, we will here note certain imperfections and perils which belong to these proficients.

[1] A, B, M, e.p. omit: 'upon them.'
[2] Psalm cxlvii, 17 [D.V. and A.V.].   [3] Wisdom ix, 15.

CHAPTER II

Describes other imperfections[1] which belong to these proficients.

THESE proficients have two kinds of imperfection: the one kind is habitual; the other actual. The habitual imperfections are the imperfect habits and affections which have remained all the time in the spirit, and are like roots, to which the purgation of sense has been unable to penetrate. The difference between the purgation of these and that of this other kind is the difference between the root and the branch, or between the removing of a stain which is fresh and one which is old and of long standing. For, as we said, the purgation of sense is only the entrance and beginning of contemplation leading to the purgation of the spirit, which, as we have likewise said,[2] serves rather to accommodate sense to spirit than to unite spirit with God. But there still remain in the spirit the stains of the old man, although the spirit thinks not that this is so, neither can it perceive them; if these stains be not removed with the soap and strong lye of the purgation of this night, the spirit will be unable to come to the purity of Divine union.

2. These souls have likewise the *hebetudo mentis*[3] and the natural roughness which every man contracts through sin, and the distraction and outward clinging of the spirit, which must be enlightened, refined and recollected by the afflictions and perils of that night. These habitual imperfections belong to all those who have not passed beyond this state of the proficient; they cannot coexist, as we say,[4] with the perfect state of union through love.

3. To actual imperfections all are not liable in the same way. Some, whose spiritual good is[5] so superficial and so readily affected by sense, fall into greater[6] difficulties and dangers, which we described at the beginning of this treatise. For, as they find so many and such abundant spiritual[7] communications and apprehensions, both in sense and in spirit, wherein they oftentimes see imaginary and spiritual visions (for all these things, together with other delectable feelings, come to many

---

[1] [*Lit.*, 'Continues with other imperfections.'] The Codices read as in the text; but e.p. has: 'Of certain imperfections.'
[2] E.p. omits: 'as we have likewise said.'
[3] [i.e., 'deadening of the mind.']   [4] E.p. omits: 'as we say.'
[5] Bz.: 'spiritual pleasures are.'   [6] E.p.: 'into certain.'
[7] E.p. omits 'spiritual.'

souls in this state, wherein the devil and their own fancy very commonly practise deceptions on them), and, as the devil is apt to take such pleasure in impressing upon the soul and suggesting to it the said apprehensions and feelings, he fascinates and deludes it with great ease,[1] unless it takes the precaution of resigning itself to God, and of protecting itself strongly, by means of faith, from all these visions and feelings. For in this state the devil causes many to believe in vain visions[2] and false prophecies; and strives[3] to make them presume that God and the saints are speaking with them; and they often trust their own fancy. And the devil is also accustomed, in this state, to fill them with presumption and pride, so that they become attracted by vanity and arrogance, and allow themselves to be seen engaging in outward acts which appear holy, such as raptures and other manifestations. Thus they become bold with God, and lose holy fear, which is the key and the custodian of all the virtues; and in some of these souls so many are the falsehoods and deceits which tend to multiply, and so inveterate do they grow, that it is very doubtful if such souls will return[4] to the pure road of virtue and true spirituality. Into these miseries they fall because they are beginning to give themselves over to spiritual feelings and apprehensions with too great security, when they were beginning to make some progress upon the way.[5]

4. There is much more that I might say of these imperfections and of how they are the more incurable because such souls consider them to be more spiritual than the others, but I will leave this subject. I shall only add, in order to prove how necessary, for him that would go farther, is the night of the spirit, which is purgation, that none of these proficients, however strenuously he may have laboured, is free, at best, from many of those natural affections and imperfect habits, purification from which,[6] we said, is necessary if a soul is to pass to Divine union.

5. And over and above this (as we have said already), inasmuch as the lower part of the soul still has a share in these spiritual communications, they cannot be as intense, as pure and as strong as is needful for the aforesaid union; wherefore, in order to come to this union, the soul must needs enter into the second night of the spirit, wherein it

---

[1] A, M: 'with great difficulty': presumably a copyist's error.
[2] A, B, M, e.p.: 'causes to be believed many visions.'
[3] So e.p. The Codices [and also, rather meaninglessly, P. Silverio] read: 'here, in this place, he strives.'
[4] Bz.: 'it is very difficult for such to return.'
[5] E.p.: 'the spiritual way.'
[6] Bz.: 'mortification whereof.'

must strip sense and spirit perfectly from all these apprehensions and from all sweetness, and be made to walk in dark and pure faith, which is the proper and adequate means whereby the soul is united with God, according as Osee says, in these words: 'I will betroth thee—that is, I will unite thee—with Me through faith.'[1]

CHAPTER III

Annotation for that which follows.

THESE souls, then, have now become proficients, because of the time which they have spent in feeding the senses with sweet communications,[2] so that their sensual part, being thus attracted and delighted by spiritual pleasure, which came to it from the spirit, may be united with the spirit and made one with it; each part after its own manner eating of one and the same spiritual food and from one and the same dish, as one person and with one sole intent, so that thus they may in a certain way be united and brought into agreement, and, thus united, may be prepared for the endurance of the stern and severe purgation of the spirit which awaits them. In this purgation these two parts of the soul, the spiritual and the sensual, must be completely purged, since the one is never truly purged without the other, the purgation of sense becoming effective when that of the spirit has fairly begun. Wherefore the night which we have called that of sense may and should be called a kind of correction and restraint of the desire rather than purgation. The reason is that all the imperfections and disorders of the sensual part have their strength and root in the spirit, where all habits, both good and bad, are brought into subjection,[3] and thus, until these are purged, the rebellions and depravities of sense cannot be purged throughly.[4]

2. Wherefore, in this night following, both parts of the soul are purged together, and it is for this end that it is well to have passed through the corrections of the first night, and the period of tranquillity[5]

[1] Osee ii, 20. E.p. has: 'I will betroth thee with Me through faith.'
[2] E.p. begins: 'These [souls], then, have now become proficients because of the time which they have spent in experiencing these sweet communications.'
[3] E.p. omits: 'where . . . subjection.'
[4] E.p.: 'until the bad habits are purged, the rebellions and depravities of sense cannot be purged throughly.'
[5] E.p.: 'and to have attained to the period of tranquillity' [*lit.*, 'the fair weather'].

which proceeds from it, in order that, sense[1] being united with spirit, both may be purged after a certain manner and may then suffer with greater fortitude. For very great fortitude[2] is needful for so violent and severe a purgation, since, if the weakness of the lower part has not first been corrected and fortitude has not been gained from God through the sweet and delectable communion which the soul has afterwards enjoyed with Him, its nature will not have the strength or the disposition to bear it.

3. Therefore, since these proficients are still at a very low stage of progress, and follow their own nature closely[3] in the intercourse and dealings which they have with God, because the gold of their spirit is not yet purified and refined, they still think of God as little children, and speak of God as little children, and feel and experience God as little children, even as Saint Paul says,[4] because they have not reached perfection, which is the union of the soul[5] with God. In the state of union, however, they will work great things in[6] the spirit, even as grown men, and their works and faculties will then be Divine rather than human, as will afterwards be said. To this end God is pleased to strip them of this old man and clothe them with the new man, who is created according to God, as the Apostle says,[7] in the newness of sense. He strips their faculties, affections and feelings, both spiritual and sensual, both outward and inward, leaving the understanding dark, the will dry, the memory empty and the affections in the deepest affliction, bitterness and constraint, taking from the soul the pleasure and experience of spiritual blessings which it had aforetime, in order to make of this privation one of the principles which are requisite in the spirit so that there may be introduced into it and united with it the spiritual form of the spirit, which is the union of love. All this the Lord works in the soul by means of a pure and dark contemplation,[8] as the soul explains in the first stanza. This, although we originally[9] interpreted it with reference to the first night of sense, is principally understood by the soul of this second night of the spirit, since this is the principal part of the purification of the soul. And thus we shall set it down and expound it here again in this sense.

---

[1] Only Bz., H, Mtr., V have the word 'sense.'
[2] Most authorities omit 'fortitude' [which, however, the context supplies]. Bz. gives it explicitly; A has: 'great preparation.'
[3] E.p. omits: 'and . . . closely.'   [4] 1 Corinthians xiii, 11.
[5] E.p.: 'the union of love.'
[6] A, B, M, e.p. have 'with' for 'in.'   [7] [Ephesians iv, 24.]
[8] Bz.: 'of a dark and clean contemplation.'
[9] Only e.p. has: 'originally.'

CHAPTER IV

Sets down the first stanza and the exposition thereof.[1]

On a dark night, Kindled[2] **in love with yearnings—oh, happy chance!—**
I went forth without being observed,   **My house being now at rest.**

EXPOSITION[3]

INTERPRETING this stanza now with reference to purgation, contemplation or detachment or poverty of spirit, which here are almost one and the same thing, we can expound it after this manner and make the soul speak thus: In poverty, and without protection[4] or support in all the apprehensions of my soul—that is, in the darkness of my understanding and the constraint of my will, in affliction and anguish with respect to memory, remaining in the dark in pure faith, which is dark night for the said natural faculties, the will alone being touched by grief and afflictions and yearnings for the love of God—I went forth from myself—that is, from my low manner of understanding, from my weak mode of loving and from my poor and limited manner of experiencing God, without being hindered therein by sensuality or the devil.

2. This was a great happiness and a good chance for me; for, when the faculties had been perfectly annihilated and calmed, together with the passions, desires[5] and affections of my soul, wherewith I had experienced and tasted God after a lowly manner, I went forth from my own human dealings and operations to the operations and dealings of God.[6] That is to say, my understanding went forth from itself, turning from the human and natural to the Divine; for, when it is united with God by means of this purgation, its understanding no longer comes through its natural light and vigour,[7] but through the Divine Wisdom wherewith it has become united. And my will went forth from itself,

---

[1] So e.p. The Codices have only 'Stanza the First' or no title at all. V reads: 'Stanza for the third part.'

[2] B, G, H, M: 'aflame.'   [3] Omitted by A, B, e.p.

[4] E.p. omits: 'protection or.'   [5] E.p. omits 'desires.'

[6] E.p.: 'I went forth from the dealings and limited operations aforementioned to the operations and dealings of God.'

[7] E.p.: 'it no longer has understanding after the narrow and limited manner that it had aforetime.'

becoming Divine; for, being united with Divine love, it no longer loves with its natural strength after a lowly manner,[1] but with strength and purity from the Holy Spirit;[2] and thus the will, which is now near to God, acts not after a human manner, and similarly the memory has become transformed into eternal apprehensions of glory. And finally, by means of this night and purgation of the old man, all the energies and affections of the soul are wholly renewed into a Divine temper and Divine delight.

There follows the line:

On a dark night.

CHAPTER V

Sets down the first line and begins to explain how this dark contemplation is not only night for the soul but is also grief and torment.[3]

THIS dark night is an inflowing of God into the soul, which purges it from its ignorances and imperfections, habitual, natural and spiritual, and which is called by contemplatives infused contemplation, or mystical theology. Herein God secretly teaches the soul and instructs it in perfection of love, without its doing anything, or understanding of what manner is this infused contemplation.[4] Inasmuch as it is the loving wisdom of God, God produces striking effects[5] in the soul, for, by purging and illumining it, He prepares it for the union of love with God. Wherefore the same loving wisdom that purges[6] the blessed spirits and enlightens them is that which here purges the soul and illumines it.

2. But the question arises: Why is the Divine light (which, as we say, illumines and purges the soul from its ignorances) here called by the soul a dark night? To this the answer is that for two reasons[7] this Divine wisdom is not only night and darkness for the soul, but is likewise affliction and torment. The first is because of the height of

---

[1] E.p.: 'comes with the limited vigour and strength that it had aforetime.'
[2] E.p.: 'from the Divine Spirit.'
[3] So e.p. The Codices have no title.
[4] E.p.: 'without its doing any more than wait lovingly upon God, hear Him and receive His light, without understanding of what manner is this infused contemplation.'
[5] E.p.: '. . . of God, it produces special effects.'
[6] A, B, M: 'Wherefore the same wisdom, as a thing that purges.'
[7] So A, B, Bz. The other authorities have: 'for two things.'

Divine Wisdom, which transcends the talent of the soul, and in this way is darkness to it; the second, because of its vileness and impurity, in which respect it is painful and afflictive to it, and is also dark.

3. In order to prove the first point, we must here assume a certain doctrine of the philosopher, which says that, the clearer and more manifest are Divine things in themselves, the darker and more hidden are they to the soul naturally; just as, the clearer is the light, the more it blinds and darkens the pupil of the owl, and, the more directly we look at the sun, the greater is the darkness which it causes in our visual faculty, overcoming and overwhelming it through its own weakness. In the same way, when this Divine light of contemplation assails the soul which is not yet wholly enlightened, it causes spiritual darkness in it; for not only does it overcome it, but likewise it overwhelms it and darkens the act of its natural intelligence. For this reason Saint Dionysius and other mystical theologians call this infused contemplation a ray of darkness—that is to say, for the soul that is not enlightened and purged—for the natural strength of the intellect is transcended and overwhelmed by its great supernatural light. Wherefore David likewise said: That near to God and round about Him are darkness and cloud;[1] not that this is so in fact, but that it is so to our weak understanding, which is blinded and darkened by so vast a light, to which it cannot attain.[2] For this cause the same David then explained himself, saying: 'Through the great splendour of His presence passed clouds'[3]—that is, between God and our understanding. And it is for this cause that, when God sends it out from Himself to the soul that is not yet transformed, this illumining ray[4] of His secret wisdom causes[5] thick darkness in the understanding.

4. And it is clear that this dark contemplation is in these its beginnings painful likewise to the soul; for, as this Divine infused contemplation has many excellences that are extremely good, and the soul that receives them, not being purged, has many miseries that are likewise extremely bad,[6] hence it follows that, as two contraries cannot coexist in one subject—the soul—it must of necessity have pain and suffering, since it is the subject wherein these two contraries war against each other, working the one against the other, by reason of the purgation of

---

[1] Psalm xcvi, 2 [A.V., xcvii, 2].
[2] [Lit., 'not attaining.'] B, Bz.: 'not attaining to it.' E.p.: 'not attaining to so great a height.'
[3] Psalm xvii, 13 [A.V., xviii, 12].
[4] H has 'kingdom' for 'ray' [reino for rayo], an evident error.
[5] So e.p. The other authorities [and P. Silverio] read: 'produces.'
[6] E.p. omits: 'that . . . bad.'

the imperfections of the soul which comes to pass through this contemplation. This we shall prove inductively in the manner following.

5. In the first place, because the light and wisdom of this contemplation is most bright and pure, and the soul which it assails is dark and impure, it follows that the soul suffers great pain when it receives it in itself, just as, when[1] the eyes are dimmed by humours, and become impure and weak, the assault made upon them by a bright light causes them pain. And when the soul suffers the direct assault of this Divine light, its pain, which results from its impurity, is immense; because, when this pure light assails the soul, in order to expel its impurity, the soul feels itself to be so impure and miserable that it believes God to be against it, and thinks that it has set itself up against God. This causes it sore grief and pain, because it now believes that God has cast it away: this was one of the greatest trials which Job felt when God sent him this experience, and he said: 'Why hast Thou set me contrary to Thee, so that I am grievous and burdensome to myself?'[2] For, by means of this pure light,[3] the soul now sees its impurity clearly (although darkly), and knows clearly that it is unworthy of God or of any creature. And what gives it most pain is that it thinks that it will never be worthy[4] and that its good things are all over for it. This is caused by the profound immersion of its spirit in the knowledge and realization of its evils and miseries; for this Divine and dark light now reveals them all to the eye, that it may see clearly how in its own strength it can never have aught else. In this sense we may understand that passage from David, which says: 'For iniquity Thou hast corrected man and hast made his soul to be undone and consumed: he wastes away as the spider.'[5]

6. The second way in which the soul suffers pain is by reason of its weakness, natural, moral and spiritual; for, when this Divine contemplation assails the soul with a certain force, in order to strengthen it and subdue it, it suffers such pain in its weakness that it nearly swoons away. This is especially so at certain times when it is assailed with somewhat greater force; for sense and spirit, as if beneath some immense and dark load, are in such great pain and agony that the soul would find advantage and relief in death. This had been experienced

---

[1] E.p.: 'it follows that to receive it afflicts the soul greatly, even as when,' etc.
[2] Job vii, 20.
[3] Thus the Codices, except A, B, P, which read: 'this clear light.' E.p. has: 'this clear and pure light.'
[4] E.p.: 'is the fear that it will never be worthy.'
[5] Psalm xxxviii, 12 [A.V., xxxix, 11].

by the prophet Job, when he said: 'I desire not that He should have intercourse with me in great strength, lest He oppress me with the weight of His greatness.'[1]

7. Beneath the power of this oppression and weight the soul feels itself so far from being favoured that it thinks, and correctly so, that even that wherein it was wont to find some help has vanished with everything else, and that there is none who has pity upon it. To this effect Job says likewise: 'Have pity upon me, have pity upon me,[2] at least ye my friends, because the hand of the Lord has touched me.'[3] A thing of great wonder and pity is it that the soul's weakness and impurity should now be so great that, though the hand of God is of itself so light and gentle, the soul should now feel it to be so heavy and so contrary,[4] though it neither weighs it down nor rests upon it, but only touches it, and that mercifully, since He does this in order to grant the soul favours and not to chastise it.

CHAPTER VI

Of other kinds of pain that the soul suffers in this night.[5]

THE third kind of suffering and pain that the soul endures in this state results from the fact that two other extremes meet here in one, namely, the Divine and the human. The Divine is this purgative contemplation, and the human is the subject—that is, the soul. The Divine assails the soul in order to renew it[6] and thus to make it Divine; and, stripping it of the habitual affections and attachments of the old man, to which it is very closely united, knit together and conformed, destroys and consumes its spiritual substance,[7] and absorbs it in deep and profound darkness. As a result of this, the soul feels itself to be perishing and melting away, in the presence and sight of its miseries, in a cruel spiritual death, even as if it had been swallowed by

---

[1] Job xxiii, 6.   [2] Some Codices do not repeat this phrase.
[3] Job xix, 21.
[4] [There is a reference here to Job vii, 20: cf. § 5, above.]
[5] So e.p. The other authorities have no title.
[6] So H, V. A, B: 'purge it and renew it.' M: 'make it and renew it.' C, P: 'take it and renew it.' Bz.: 'cut it and renew it.' E.p.: 'season it and renew it.' As will be seen, there is a reading for every preference. We cannot be sure which is the true one.
[7] E.p. omits: 'its spiritual substance' and reads: 'breaks it up and bruises it.' The two verbs are greatly varied by the different authorities but their general sense remains much as in the text above, which gives the reading of H, Mtr., V.

a beast and felt itself being devoured in the darkness of its belly, suffering such anguish as was endured by Jonas in the belly of that beast of the sea.[1] For in this sepulchre of dark death it must needs abide until the spiritual resurrection which it hopes for.

2. A description of this suffering and pain, although in truth it transcends all description, is given by David, when he says: 'The lamentations of death compassed me about; the pains of hell surrounded me; I cried in my tribulation.'[2] But what the sorrowful soul feels most in this condition is its clear perception, as it thinks, that God has abandoned it, and, in His abhorrence of it, has flung it into darkness; it is a grave and piteous grief for it to believe that God has forsaken it. It is this that David also felt so much in a like case, saying: 'After the manner wherein the wounded are dead in the sepulchres,[3] being now cast off by Thy hand, so that Thou rememberest them no more, even so have they set me in the deepest and lowest lake, in the dark places and in the shadow of death, and Thy fury is confirmed upon me and all Thy waves Thou hast brought in upon me.'[4] For indeed, when this purgative contemplation is most severe, the soul feels very keenly the shadow of death and the lamentations of death[5] and the pains of hell, which consist in its feeling itself to be without God, and chastised and cast out, and unworthy of Him;[6] and it feels that He is wroth with it. All this is felt by the soul in this condition—yea, and more, for it believes[7] that it is so with it for ever.

3. It feels, too, that all creatures have forsaken it, and that it is contemned by them, particularly by its friends. Wherefore David presently continues, saying: 'Thou hast put far from me my friends and acquaintances; they have counted me an abomination.'[8] To all this will Jonas testify, as one who likewise experienced it in the belly of the beast, both bodily and spiritually. 'Thou hast cast me forth (he says) into the deep, into the heart of the sea, and the flood hath compassed me; all its billows and waves have passed over me. And I said, "I am cast away out of the sight of Thine eyes, but I shall once again see Thy holy temple" (which he says, because God purifies the soul in this state that it may see His temple); the waters[9] compassed me, even to the soul, the deep hath closed me round about, the ocean hath covered my head; I went down to the lowest parts of the mountains; the bars of

---

[1] Jonas ii, 1.
[2] Psalm xvii, 5–7 [A.V., xviii, 4–5].
[3] H omits: 'in the sepulchres.'
[4] Psalm lxxxvii, 6–8 [A.V., lxxxviii, 5–7].
[5] E.p. omits: 'of death.'
[6] E.p.: 'and He is angered with it.'
[7] E.p. adds: 'with a fearful apprehension,' but no MS. has this addition.
[8] Psalm lxxxvii, 9 [A.V., lxxxviii, 8].
[9] Bz.: 'the afflictions.'

the earth have shut me up[1] for ever.'[2] By these bars are here under-stood, in this sense, imperfections of the soul, which have impeded it from enjoying this delectable contemplation.

4. The fourth kind of pain is caused in the soul by another excellence of this dark contemplation, which is its majesty and greatness,[3] from which arises in the soul a consciousness of the other extreme which is in itself—namely, that of the deepest poverty and wretchedness: this is one of the chiefest pains that it suffers in this purgation. For it feels within itself a profound emptiness and impoverishment of three kinds of good, which are ordained for the pleasure of the soul, which are the temporal, the natural and the spiritual; and finds itself set in the midst of the evils contrary to these, namely, miseries of imperfection, aridity and emptiness of the apprehensions of the faculties and abandonment of the spirit in darkness. Inasmuch as God here purges the soul according to the substance of its sense and spirit, and according to the interior and exterior faculties, the soul must needs be in all its parts reduced to a state of emptiness, poverty and abandonment and must be left dry and empty and in darkness.[4] For the sensual part is purified in aridity, the faculties are purified in the emptiness of their perceptions and the spirit is purified in thick darkness.

5. All this God brings to pass by means of this dark contemplation; wherein the soul not only suffers this emptiness and the suspension of these natural supports and perceptions, which is a most afflictive suffer-ing (as if a man were suspended or held in the air so that he could not breathe), but likewise He is purging the soul, annihilating it, emptying it or consuming in it (even as fire consumes the mouldiness and the rust of metal) all the affections and imperfect habits which it has con-tracted in its whole life. Since these are deeply rooted in the substance of the soul, it is wont to suffer great undoing[5] and inward torment, besides the said poverty and emptiness, natural and spiritual, so that there may here be fulfilled that passage from Ezechiel which says: 'Heap together the bones and I will burn them in the fire; the flesh shall be consumed and the whole composition shall be burned and the bones shall be destroyed.'[6] Herein is understood the pain which is

---

[1] V: 'surrounded me.'   [2] Jonas ii, 4–7 [A.V., ii, 3–6].
[3] So Bz., C, G, H, Mtr., V. A, B, M omit this phrase. E.p. has: 'which is the majesty and greatness of God.' The Saint may mean that the soul acquires in this contemplation a greater knowledge of its own excellence, and in consequence has the greater obligation to God, in Whose image and likeness it is made.
[4] Bz.: 'and in black darkness.'
[5] A, B, M: 'great burdens and undoing'; Bz.: 'great sorrow.' The text follows e.p., H, Mtr., P, V.   [6] Ezechiel xxiv, 10.

suffered in the emptiness and poverty of the substance of the soul[1] both in sense and in spirit. And concerning this he then says: 'Set it also empty upon the coals, that its metal may become hot and molten, and its uncleanness may be destroyed within it, and its rust may be consumed.'[2] Herein is described the grave suffering which the soul here endures in the purgation of the fire of this contemplation, for the Prophet says here that, in order for the rust of the affections which are within the soul to be purified and destroyed, it is needful that, in a certain manner, the soul itself should be annihilated and destroyed, since these passions and imperfections have become natural to it.[3]

6. Wherefore, because the soul is purified in this furnace like gold in a crucible, as says the Wise Man,[4] it is conscious of this complete undoing of itself in its very substance, together with the direst poverty, wherein it is, as it were, nearing its end, as may be seen by that which David says of himself in this respect, in these words: 'Save me, Lord (he cries to God), for the waters have come in even unto my soul; I am made fast in the mire of the deep and there is no place where I can stand; I am come into the depth of the sea and a tempest hath overwhelmed me; I have laboured crying, my throat[5] has become hoarse, mine eyes have failed whilst I hope in my God.'[6] Here God greatly humbles the soul in order that He may afterwards greatly exalt it; and if He ordained not that, when these feelings arise within the soul, they should speedily be stilled, it would die[7] in a very short space; but there are only occasional periods when it is conscious of their greatest intensity. At times, however, they are so keen that the soul seems to be seeing hell and perdition opened. Of such are they that in truth go down alive into hell, being purged here on earth in the same manner as there,[8] since this purgation is that which would have to be accomplished there.[9] And thus the soul that passes through this[10] either enters not that place[11] at all, or tarries there but for a very[12] short time; for one hour of purgation here is more profitable than are many there.

---

[1] E.p.: 'and poverty of the soul.'   [2] Ezechiel xxiv, 11.
[3] Bz.: 'eradicated from it.'   [4] Wisdom iii, 6.
[5] So e.p. The other authorities use the plural form of 'throat' (*gargantas*).
[6] Psalm lxviii, 2–4 [A.V., lxix, 1–3].
[7] E.p.: 'it would forsake the body.'
[8] E.p.: 'being purged here in a kind of purgatory.' [This reading makes explicit what is evidently meant, the word 'hell,' as the preceding sentence shows, being used metaphorically—a 'concealed' quotation from Psalm liv, 16 (A.V., lv, 15).]
[9] E.p. adds: 'when it is for sins, even though they be venial.'
[10] E.p. adds: 'and is throughly purged.'   [11] [i.e., purgatory.]
[12] E.p. omits 'very.'

CHAPTER VII

Continues the same matter and considers other afflictions and constraints of the will.[1]

THE afflictions and constraints of the will are now very great likewise, and of such a kind that they sometimes transpierce the soul with a sudden remembrance of the evils in the midst of which it finds itself, and with the uncertainty of finding a remedy for them. And to this is added the remembrance of times of prosperity now past; for as a rule souls that enter this night have had many consolations[2] from God, and have rendered Him many services, and it causes them the greater grief to see that they are far removed from that happiness, and unable to enter into it. This was also described by Job, who had had experience of it, in these words: 'I, who was wont to be wealthy and rich, am suddenly undone and broken to pieces; He hath taken me by my neck; He hath broken me and set me up for His mark[3] to wound me; He hath compassed me round about with His lances; He hath wounded all my loins; He hath not spared; He hath poured out my bowels on the earth; He hath broken me with wound upon wound;[4] He hath assailed me as a strong giant; I have sewed sackcloth upon my skin and have covered my flesh with ashes; my face is become swollen with weeping and mine eyes are blinded.'[5]

2. So many and so grievous[6] are the afflictions of this night, and so many passages of Scripture are there which could be cited to this purpose, that time and strength would fail us to write of them, for all that can be said thereof is certainly less than the truth. From the passages already quoted some idea may be gained of them. And, that we may bring the exposition of this line to a close and explain more fully what is worked in the soul by this night, I shall tell what Jeremias felt about it, which, since there is so much of it, he describes and bewails in many words after this manner: 'I am the man that see my poverty in the rod of His indignation; He hath threatened me and brought me into darkness and not into light. So far hath He turned against me and hath converted His hand upon me all the day! My skin and my flesh hath He made old; He hath broken my bones; He hath

---

[1] So e.p. The Codices have no title.   [2] The noun occurs only in e.p.
[3] E.p.: 'for His target.'
[4] E.p.: 'He hath broken me and added wounds upon wounds.'
[5] Job xvi, 13–17 [A.V., xvi, 12–16].   [6] A, B, e.p.: 'and so great.'

made a fence around me and compassed me with gall and trial; He hath set me in dark places, as those that are dead for ever. He hath made a fence around me and against me, that I may not go out; He hath made my captivity heavy. Yea, and when I have cried[1] and have entreated, He hath shut out my prayer. He hath enclosed my paths and ways out with square stones; He hath thwarted my steps. He hath set ambushes[2] for me; He hath become to me a lion in a secret place. He hath turned aside my steps and broken me in pieces, He hath made[3] me desolate; He hath bent His bow and set me as a mark for His arrow. He hath shot into my reins the daughters of His quiver. I have become a derision to all the people, and laughter and scorn for them all the day. He hath filled me with bitterness and hath made me drunken with wormwood. He hath broken my teeth by number;[4] He hath fed me with ashes. My soul is cast out from peace; I have forgotten good things. And I said: "Mine end is frustrated and cut short, together with my desire and my hope from the Lord. Remember my poverty and my excess, the wormwood and the gall. I shall be mindful with remembrance and my soul shall be undone within me in pains."[5]

3. All these complaints Jeremias makes about these pains and trials, and by means of them he most vividly depicts the sufferings of the soul in this spiritual night and purgation.[6] Wherefore the soul that God sets in this tempestuous[7] and horrible night is deserving of great compassion. For, although it experiences much happiness by reason of the great blessings that must arise on this account within it, when, as Job says, God raises up profound blessings in the soul out of darkness, and brings up to light the shadow of death,[8] so that, as David says, His light comes to be as was His darkness;[9] yet notwithstanding, by reason of the dreadful pain which the soul is suffering, and of the great uncertainty which it has concerning the remedy for it, since it believes,[10] as this prophet says here, that its evil will never end, and it thinks, as David says likewise, that God set it in dark places like those that are dead,[11] and for this reason brought its spirit within it into anguish and troubled its heart,[12] it suffers great pain and grief, since there is added

---

[1] E.p.: 'when I am calling.'
[2] H, M read: 'bear [sic] ambushes' [cf. Lamentations iii, 10].
[3] E.p.: 'hath left.'   [4] E.p. [more exactly]: 'one by one.'
[5] Lamentations iii, 1–20.
[6] E.p.: 'wherein this spiritual night and purgation sets it.'
[7] E.p.: 'fearful.'   [8] Job xii, 22.
[9] Psalm cxxxviii, 12 [A.V., cxxxix, 12].
[10] E.p.: 'it thinks.'
[11] [Lit., 'like to the dead of the world (or of the age).']
[12] Psalm cxlii, 3 [A.V., cxliii, 3–4].

to all this (because of the solitude and abandonment caused in it by this dark night) the fact that it finds no consolation or support in any instruction nor in a spiritual master. For, although in many ways its director may show it good reason for being comforted because of the blessings which are contained in these afflictions, it cannot believe him. For it is so greatly absorbed and immersed in the realization of those evils wherein it sees its own miseries so clearly, that it thinks that, as its director observes not that which it sees and feels, he is speaking in this manner because he understands it not; and so, instead of comfort, it rather receives fresh affliction, since it believes that its director's advice contains no remedy for its troubles. And, in truth, this is so; for, until the Lord shall have completely purged it after the manner that He wills, no means or remedy is of any service or profit for the relief of its affliction; the more so because the soul is as powerless in this case as one who has been imprisoned in a dark dungeon, and is bound hand and foot, and can neither move nor see, nor feel any favour whether from above or from below, until the spirit is humbled, softened and purified, and grows so keen and delicate and pure that it can become one with the Spirit of God, according to the degree of union of love which His mercy is pleased to grant it; in proportion to this the purgation[1] is of greater or less severity and of greater or less duration.

4. But, if it is to be really effectual, it will last for some years, however severe it be; since the purgative process allows intervals of relief,[2] wherein, by the dispensation of God, this dark contemplation ceases to assail the soul in the form and manner of purgation, and assails it after an illuminative and a loving manner, wherein the soul, like one that has gone forth from this dungeon and imprisonment, and is brought into the recreation of spaciousness and liberty, feels and experiences great sweetness of peace and loving friendship with God, together with a ready abundance of spiritual communication. This is to the soul a sign of the health which is being wrought within it by the said purgation and a foretaste of the abundance for which it hopes. Occasionally this is so great that the soul believes its trials to be at last over. For spiritual things in the soul, when they are most purely spiritual, have this characteristic that, if trials come to it, the soul believes that it will never escape from them, and that all its blessings are now over, as has been seen in the passages quoted; and, if spiritual blessings come, the soul believes in the same way that its troubles are

---

[1] A, B, H, M, P, V have: 'the union.'
[2] A, V, e.p.: 'intervals and reliefs.'

now over, and that blessings will never fail it. This was so with David, when he found himself in the midst of them, as he confesses in these words: 'I said in my abundance: "I shall never be moved." '[1]

5. This happens because the actual possession by the spirit of one of two contrary things itself makes impossible the actual possession and realization of the other contrary thing; this is not so,[2] however, in the sensual part of the soul, because its apprehension is weak. But, as the spirit is not yet completely purged and cleansed from the affections that it has contracted from its lower part, while changing not in so far as it is spirit, it can be moved to further afflictions in so far as these affections sway it.[3] In this way, as we see, David was afterwards moved, and experienced many ills and afflictions, although in the time of his abundance he had thought and said that he would never be moved. Just so is it with the soul in this condition, when it sees itself moved by that abundance of spiritual blessings, and, being unable to see the root of the imperfection and impurity which still remain within it, thinks that its trials are over.

6. This thought, however, comes to the soul but seldom, for, until spiritual purification is complete and perfected, the sweet communication is very rarely so abundant as to conceal from the soul the root which remains hidden, in such a way that the soul can cease to feel that there is something that it lacks within itself or that it has still to do. Thus it cannot completely enjoy that relief, but feels as if one of its enemies were within it, and although this enemy is, as it were, hushed and asleep, it fears that he will come to life again and attack it.[4] And this is what indeed happens, for, when the soul is most secure and least alert,[5] it is dragged down and immersed again in another and a worse[6] degree of affliction which is severer and darker and more grievous than that which is past; and this new affliction will continue for a further period of time, perhaps longer than the first. And the soul once more comes to believe[7] that all its blessings are over for ever. Although it had thought during its first trial that there were no more afflictions which it could suffer, and yet, after the trial was over, it enjoyed great blessings, this experience is not sufficient to take away its belief, during

---

[1] Psalm xxix, 7 [A.V., xxx, 6].   [2] E.p.: 'which is not so much so.'
[3] E.p.: 'the affections that its lower part has contracted, although it has greater consistency and firmness, yet, in so far as it is affected by them, it is liable to further afflictions.'
[4] [*Lit.*, 'and play his tricks upon it.']
[5] E.p. omits: 'and least alert.'   [6] E.p. omits: 'and a worse.'
[7] E.p.: 'to persuade itself.' H omits: 'than the first. And then the soul once more comes to [believe that].'

this second degree of trial, that all is now over for it and that it will never again be happy as in the past. For, as I say, this belief, of which the soul is so sure, is caused in it by the actual apprehension of the spirit, which annihilates within it all that is contrary to it.[1]

7. This is the reason why those who lie in purgatory suffer great misgivings as to whether they will ever go forth from it and whether their pains will ever be over.[2] For, although they have the habit of the three theological virtues—faith, hope and charity—the present realization which they have of their afflictions and of their deprivation of God allows them not to enjoy the present blessing and consolation of these virtues. For, although they are able to realize that they have a great love for God, this is no consolation to them, since they cannot think that God loves them or that they are worthy that He should do so; rather, as they see that they are deprived of Him, and left in their own miseries, they think that there is that in themselves which provides a very good reason why they should with perfect justice be abhorred and cast out by God for ever.[3] And thus, although the soul in this purgation is conscious that it has a great love for God and would give a thousand lives for Him (which is the truth, for in these trials such

[1] E.p. has: 'which annihilates in it [the soul, not the spirit, as the gender of the Spanish noun shows] all that can cause it joy.' It then omits the next paragraph as far as the words 'cast out by God for ever.' A, V also make this omission, but not B, as P. Gerardo mistakenly asserts. G omits almost the whole of this chapter.

[2] M, probably in error [desean for de que se han]: 'and desire their pains to be over.' B reads very similarly [certainly with intention]. P omits: 'and . . . over.'

[3] B, Bz., C, H, Mtr. all have this long passage on the suffering of the soul in Purgatory. It would be rash, therefore, to deny that St. John of the Cross is its author, [or to suppose, as P. Gerardo did, that he deleted it during a revision of his works]. An admirably constructed synthesis of these questions will be found in B. Belarmino, De Purgatorio, Bk. II, chaps. iv, v. He asks if souls in Purgatory are sure of their salvation. This was denied by Luther, and by a number of Catholic writers, who held that, among the afflictions of these souls, the greatest is this very uncertainty; some maintain that, though they have in fact such certainty, they are unaware of it. Belarmino quotes among other authorities Denis the Carthusian, De quattuor novissimis, Gerson (Lect. I De Vita Spirituali) and John of Rochester (against Luther's 32nd article); these writers claim that, as sin which is venial is only so through the Divine mercy, it may with perfect justice be rewarded by eternal punishment, and thus souls that have committed venial sin cannot be confident of their salvation. He also shows, however, that the common opinion of theologians is that the souls in Purgatory are sure of their salvation, and considers various degrees of certainty, adding very truly that, while these souls experience no fear, they experience hope, since they have not yet the Beatific vision.
Uncertainty as to their salvation, it is said, might arise from ignorance of the sentence passed upon them by the Judge or from the deadening of their faculties by the torments which they are suffering. Belarmino refutes these and other suppositions with great force and effect. St. John of the Cross seems to be referring to the last named when he writes of the realization of their afflictions and their deprivation of God not allowing them to enjoy the blessings of the theological virtues. It is not surprising if the Saint, not having examined very closely this question, of which he would have read treatments in various authors, thought of it principally as an apt illustration of the purifying and refining effects of passive purgation; and an apt illustration it certainly is.

souls love their God very earnestly), yet this is no relief to it, but rather brings it greater affliction. For it loves Him so much that it cares about naught beside; when, therefore, it sees itself to be so wretched that it cannot believe that God loves it, nor that there is or will ever be reason why He should do so, but rather[1] that there is reason why it should be abhorred, not only by Him, but by all creatures for ever, it is grieved to see in itself reasons for deserving to be cast out by Him for Whom it has such great love and desire.

CHAPTER VIII

Of other pains which afflict the soul in this state.[2]

BUT there is another thing here[3] that afflicts and distresses the soul greatly, which is that, as this dark night has hindered its faculties and affections in this way, it is unable to raise[4] its affection or its mind to God, neither can it pray to Him, thinking, as Jeremias thought concerning himself, that God has set a cloud before it through which its prayer cannot pass.[5] For it is this that is meant by that which is said in the passage referred to, namely: 'He hath shut and enclosed my paths with square stones.'[6] And if it sometimes prays it does so with such lack of strength and of sweetness[7] that it thinks that God neither hears it nor pays heed to it, as this Prophet likewise declares in the same passage, saying: 'When I cry and entreat, He hath shut out my prayer.'[8] In truth this is no time for the soul to speak with God; it should rather put its mouth in the dust, as Jeremias says, so that perchance there may come to it some present hope,[9] and it may endure its purgation with patience.[10] It is God Who is passively[11] working here in the soul; wherefore the soul can do nothing. Hence it can neither pray nor pay attention when it is present at the Divine offices,[12] much less can it

---

[1] E.p.: 'when it sees itself to be so miserable, suspecting that God loves it not, and having then no certainty that there is anything in it worthy of love but rather . . .'

[2] So e.p. The Codices have no title.

[3] E.p.: 'There is in this state another thing.'

[4] E.p. adds here: 'as before.'   [5] Lamentations iii, 44.

[6] [Lamentations iii, 9.] E.p. omits 'shut and' and reads 'roads' for 'paths.'

[7] E.p.: 'with such aridity and lack of sweetness.'

[8] Lamentations iii, 8.   [9] Lamentations iii, 29.

[10] E.p.: 'In truth, this is the time to put, as Jeremias says, its mouth in the dust, enduring its purgation with patience.'

[11] E.p. omits 'passively.'

[12] [Lit., 'at the Divine things.'] Thus A, B, C, G, Mtr., P. M, e.p.: 'pay great attention.' H: 'present at the Divine things.' Bz.: 'present with devotion at the Divine things.'

attend to other things and affairs which are temporal. Not only so, but it has likewise such distractions and times of such profound forgetfulness of the memory that frequent periods pass by without its knowing what it has been doing or thinking, or what it is that it is doing or is going to do, neither can it pay attention, although it desire to do so, to anything that occupies it.[1]

2. Inasmuch as not only is the understanding here purged of its light,[2] and the will of its affections, but the memory is also purged of meditation and knowledge, it is well that it be likewise annihilated with respect to all these things, so that that which David says of himself in this purgation may be fulfilled, namely: 'I was annihilated and I knew not.'[3] This unknowing refers[4] to these follies and forgetfulnesses of the memory, which distractions and forgetfulnesses are caused by the interior recollection wherein this contemplation absorbs the soul. For, in order that the soul may be divinely prepared and tempered with its faculties for the Divine union of love, it would be well for it to be first of all absorbed, with all its faculties, in this Divine and dark spiritual light of contemplation, and thus to be withdrawn from all the affections and apprehensions of the creatures, which condition ordinarily[5] continues in proportion to its intensity. And thus, the simpler and the purer is this Divine light in its assault upon the soul, the more does it darken it, void it and annihilate it according to its particular apprehensions and affections, with regard both to things above and to things below; and similarly, the less simple and pure is it in this assault, the less deprivation it causes it and the less dark is it. Now this is a thing that seems incredible, to say that, the brighter and purer is supernatural and Divine light, the more it darkens the soul, and that, the less bright and pure is it, the less dark it is to the soul. Yet this may readily be understood[6] if we consider what has been proved above by the dictum of the philosopher—namely, that the brighter and the more manifest in themselves are supernatural things the darker are they to our understanding.[7]

3. And, to the end that this may be understood the more clearly, we shall here set down a similitude referring to common and natural

---

[1] E.p.: 'nor can it be very attentive, although it desire to be so, to anything that it is doing.'

[2] E.p.: 'of its imperfect knowledge.'   [3] Psalm lxxii, 22 [A.V., lxxiii, 22].

[4] E.p.: 'extends.'   [5] So M, e.p. The Codices have 'singularly.'

[6] The words 'this may readily be understood,' which are necessary to complete the sense of the passage, are only found in e.p. and Mtr.

[7] E.p. omits the next paragraph, doubtless because the same comparison has already been used in the *Ascent of Mount Carmel*, Bk. II, chap. xiv, § 9 (p. 115, above).

light. We observe that a ray of sunlight which enters through the window is the less clearly visible according as it is the purer and freer from specks, and the more of such specks and motes there are in the air, the brighter is the light to the eye. The reason is that it is not the light itself that is seen; the light is but the means whereby the other things that it strikes are seen, and then it is also seen itself, through its reflection in them; were it not for this, neither it nor they would have been seen. Thus if the ray of sunlight entered through the window of one room and passed out through another on the other side, traversing the room, and if it met nothing on the way, or if there were no specks in the air for it to strike, the room would have no more light than before, neither would the ray of light be visible. In fact, if we consider it carefully, there is more darkness where the ray is, since it absorbs and obscures any other light, and yet it is itself invisible, because, as we have said, there are no visible objects which it can strike.

4. Now this is precisely what this Divine ray of contemplation does in the soul. Assailing it with its Divine light, it transcends the natural power of the soul, and herein it darkens it and deprives it of all natural affections and apprehensions which it apprehended aforetime by means of natural light; and thus it leaves it[1] not only dark, but likewise empty, according to its faculties and desires, both spiritual and natural. And, by thus leaving it empty and in darkness, it purges and illumines it with Divine spiritual light, although the soul thinks not that it has this light, but believes itself to be in darkness, even as we have said of the ray of light, which, although it be in the midst of the room, yet, if it be pure and meet nothing on its path, is not visible. With regard, however, to this spiritual light by which the soul is assailed, when it has something to strike—that is, when something spiritual presents itself to be understood, however small a speck it be and whether of perfection or imperfection, or whether it be a judgment of the falsehood or the truth of a thing[2]—it then sees and understands much more clearly than before it was in these dark places. And exactly in the same

---

[1] E.p. greatly modifies the first part of this paragraph, thus:

'And thus, the ray of this lofty contemplation assails the soul with its Divine light, and, since it transcends the natural power of the soul itself, darkens it and deprives it of all the natural apprehensions and affections which it apprehended aforetime by means of natural light. Whereby it leaves it,' etc.

[2] E.p. has: '. . . even as we have said. But even as the ray of light, if it be pure and have nothing to strike or to meet, is hardly perceived, and when it strikes or reflects is the better seen, even so this spiritual light whereby the soul is assailed, since it is so pure, is not in itself observed or perceived; but when it has something to strike—that is, when some particular thing presents itself to be understood, of perfection, or judgment of the falsehood or truth of a thing,' etc.

way it discerns the spiritual light which it has in order that it may readily discern the imperfection which is presented to it; even as, when the ray of which we have spoken, within the room, is dark and not itself visible, if one introduce[1] a hand or any other thing into its path, the hand is then seen and it is realized that that sunlight is present.

5. Wherefore, since this spiritual light is so simple,[2] pure and general, not appropriated or restricted to any particular thing that can be understood, whether natural or Divine (since with respect to all these apprehensions the faculties of the soul are empty and annihilated), it follows that[3] with great comprehensiveness and readiness the soul discerns and penetrates whatsoever thing presents itself to it, whether it come from above or from below; for which cause the Apostle said: That the spiritual man searches all things, even the deep things of God.[4] For by this general and simple wisdom is understood that which the Holy Spirit says through the Wise Man, namely: That it reaches wheresoever it wills by reason of its purity;[5] that is to say, because it is not restricted to any particular object of the intellect or affection. And this is the characteristic of the spirit that is purged and annihilated with respect to all particular affections and objects of the understanding, that in this state wherein it has pleasure in 'nothing and understands nothing[6] in particular, but dwells in its emptiness, darkness and obscurity, it is fully prepared to embrace everything to the end that those words of Saint Paul may be fulfilled[7] in it: *Nihil habentes, et omnia possidentes*.[8] For such poverty of spirit as this would deserve such happiness.

CHAPTER IX

How, although this night brings darkness to the spirit, it does so in order to illumine it and give it light.[9]

IT now remains to be said that, although this happy night brings darkness to the spirit, it does so only to give it light in everything; and that, although it humbles it and makes it miserable, it does so only to exalt it and to raise it up; and, although it impoverishes it and

---

[1] E.p.: 'even as when the ray is in itself not perceived, yet, if one introduce,' etc.
[2] H: 'so sensible.'   [3] E.p. omits: 'it follows that.'
[4] 1 Corinthians ii, 10. [*Lit.*, 'penetrates all things.']
[5] Wisdom vii, 24.   [6] H omits: 'and understands nothing.'
[7] A, M, e.p. add 'mystically.'   [8] 2 Corinthians vi, 10.
[9] So e.p. The Codices have no title.

empties it of all natural affection and attachment, it does so only that it may enable it to stretch forward, divinely, and thus to have fruition and experience of all things, both above and below, yet to preserve its unrestricted liberty of spirit in them all. For just as the elements, in order that they may have a part in all natural entities and compounds, must have no particular colour, odour or taste, so as to be able to combine with all tastes, odours and colours, just so must the spirit be simple, pure and detached from all kinds of natural affection, whether actual or habitual, to the end that it may be able freely to share in the breadth of spirit of the Divine Wisdom, wherein, through its purity, it has experience of all the sweetness of all things in a certain pre-eminently excellent way.[1] And without this purgation it will be wholly unable to feel or experience the satisfaction of all this abundance of spiritual sweetness. For one single affection remaining in the spirit, or one particular thing to which, actually or habitually, it clings, suffices to hinder it from feeling or experiencing or communicating the delicacy and intimate sweetness of the spirit of love, which contains within itself all sweetness to a most eminent degree.[2]

2. For, even as the children of Israel, solely because they retained one single affection and remembrance—namely, with respect to the fleshpots and the meals which they had tasted in Egypt[3]—could not relish the delicate bread of angels, in the desert, which was the manna, which, as the Divine Scripture says, held sweetness for every taste and turned to the taste that each one desired;[4] even so the spirit cannot succeed in enjoying the delights of the spirit of liberty, according to the desire of the will, if it be still affectioned to any desire, whether actual or habitual, or to particular objects of understanding, or to any other apprehension.[5] The reason for this is that the affections, feelings and apprehensions of the perfect spirit, being Divine,[6] are of another kind and of a very different order from those that are natural. They are pre-eminent,[7] so that, in order both actually and habitually to possess the one, it is needful to expel and annihilate the other, as with two contrary things, which cannot exist together in one person.[8] Therefore it is most fitting and necessary, if the soul is to pass to these great

---

[1] [Lit., 'with a certain eminence of excellence.'] So C, H, M, Mtr., P, V. A, B, e.p.: 'certain kind of excellence.' Bz. omits a line or so here.
[2] [Lit., '. . . sweetness, with great eminence.']
[3] Exodus xvi, 3.   [4] Wisdom xvi, 21.
[5] Thus the Codices. E.p. has: 'any other limited apprehension.'
[6] E.p.: 'being so high and very specially Divine.'
[7] E.p. omits the last three words.
[8] E.p. omits: 'as with . . . person.'

things, that this dark night of contemplation should first of all annihilate and undo it in its meannesses, bringing it into darkness, aridity,
affliction and emptiness; for the light which is to be given to it is a
Divine light of the highest kind, which transcends all natural light,
and which by nature can find no place in the understanding.

3. And thus it is fitting that, if the understanding is to be united
with that light and become Divine in the state of perfection, it should
first of all be purged and annihilated as to its natural light, and, by
means of this dark contemplation, be brought actually into darkness.
This darkness should continue for as long as is needful in order to
expel and annihilate the habit which the soul has long since formed in
its manner of understanding, and the Divine light and illumination
will then take its place. And thus, inasmuch as that power of understanding which it had aforetime is natural, it follows that the darkness
which it here suffers is profound and horrible and most painful, for
this darkness, being felt in the deepest substance of the spirit, seems to
be substantial darkness.[1] Similarly, since the affection of love which is
to be given to it in the Divine union of love is Divine, and therefore
very spiritual, subtle and delicate, and very intimate, transcending
every affection and feeling[2] of the will, and every desire thereof, it is
fitting that, in order that the will may be able to attain to this Divine
affection and most lofty delight, and to feel it and experience it[3] through
the union of love, since it is not, in the way of nature, perceptible to the
will,[4] it be first of all purged and annihilated in all its affections and
feelings, and left in a condition of aridity and constraint, proportionate
to the habit of natural affections which it had before, with respect both
to Divine things and to human. Thus, being exhausted, withered and
throughly tried[5] in the fire of this dark contemplation, and having
driven away every kind[6] of evil spirit (as with the heart of the fish
which Tobias set on the coals[7]), it may have a simple and pure disposition, and its palate may be purged and healthy, so that it may feel

---

[1] E.p. reads: '. . . painful, for it touches, and is felt in, the depths of the spirit.'
[2] E.p.: 'every natural and imperfect affection and feeling.'
[3] E.p. omits: 'feel it and.'
[4] E.p. omits: 'since . . . will.'
[5] So H. There are many variants. A: 'that it may be dry and withered and well
proved.' B: 'that it may be dry, withered and well entangled (sic).' [Probably a copyist's
error: entrincada for extricada, 'wrung.'] Bz.: 'that it may be withered and well bruised.'
C, M, P: 'Thus, exhausted and withered and well wrung.' Mtr.: 'that it may be withered
and well wrung.' V: 'that it may be clean and withered and well wrung.' E.p.: 'Thus,
exhausted, withered and deprived (of every kind, etc.).'
[6] [Lit., 'from every kind.' But see Tobias viii, 2. The 'deprived' of e.p. gives the best
reading of this phrase, but the general sense is clear from the Scriptural reference.]
[7] Tobias viii, 2.

the rare and sublime touches of Divine love, wherein it will see itself divinely transformed, and all the contrarieties, whether actual or habitual, which it had aforetime, will be expelled, as we are saying.

4. Moreover, in order to attain the said union to which this dark night is disposing and leading it, the soul must be filled and endowed with a certain glorious magnificence in its communion with God, which includes within itself innumerable blessings springing from delights which exceed all the abundance that the soul can naturally possess. For by nature the soul is so weak and impure that it cannot receive all this. As Isaias says: 'Eye hath not seen, nor ear heard, neither hath it entered into the heart of man, that which God hath prepared, etc.'[1] It is meet, then, that the soul be first of all brought into emptiness and poverty of spirit and purged from all help, consolation and natural apprehension with respect to all things, both above and below. In this way, being empty, it is able indeed to be poor in spirit and freed from the old man, in order to live that new and blessed life which is attained by means of this night, and which is the state of union with God.

5. And because the soul is to attain to the possession of a sense, and of a Divine knowledge, which is very generous and full of sweetness, with respect to things Divine and human, which fall not within the common experience and natural knowledge of the soul (because it looks on them with eyes as different from those of the past as spirit is different from sense[2] and the Divine from the human), the spirit must be straitened[3] and inured to hardships as regards its common and natural experience, and be brought by means of this purgative contemplation into great anguish and affliction, and the memory must be borne far from all agreeable and peaceful knowledge, and have an intimate[4] sense and feeling that it is making a pilgrimage and being a stranger to all things, so that it seems to it that all things are strange and of a different kind from that which they were wont to be. For this night is gradually drawing the spirit away from its ordinary and common experience of things and bringing it nearer the Divine sense, which is a stranger and an alien to all human ways. It seems now to the soul that it is going forth from its very self, with much affliction.[5] At other times it wonders if it is under a charm or a spell, and it goes about marvelling at the things that it sees and hears, which seem to it

---

[1] Isaias lxiv, 4 [1 Corinthians ii, 9]. E.p. adds: 'for those that love Him.'
[2] E.p.: 'as the light and grace of the Holy Spirit differ from sense.'
[3] [*Lit.*, 'be made thin.']   [4] E.p.: 'a very intimate.'
[5] A, e.p.: '. . . human ways; so much so that it seems to the soul that it is going out from its very self.' So M, omitting the words 'much so.' B, Bz., C, H, V read as in the text.

very strange and rare, though they are the same that it was accustomed
to experience aforetime. The reason of this is that the soul is now becoming alien and remote from common sense and knowledge of things,
in order that, being annihilated in this respect, it may be informed with
the Divine—which belongs rather to the next life than to this.

6. The soul suffers all these afflictive purgations[1] of the spirit to the
end that it may be begotten anew in spiritual life by means of this
Divine inflowing, and in these pangs may bring forth the spirit of
salvation, that the saying of Isaias may be fulfilled: 'In Thy sight, O
Lord, we have conceived, and we have been as in the pangs of labour,
and we have brought forth the spirit of salvation.'[2] Moreover, since by
means of this contemplative night the soul is prepared for the attainment of inward peace and tranquillity, which is of such a kind and so
delectable that, as the Scripture[3] says, it passes all understanding,[4] it
behoves the soul to abandon all its former peace. This was in reality no
peace at all, since it was involved in imperfections; but to the soul
aforementioned it appeared to be so, because it was following its own
inclinations, which were for peace. It seemed, indeed, to be a twofold
peace—that is, the soul believed that it had already acquired the peace
of sense and that of spirit, for it found itself to be full of the spiritual
abundance of this peace of sense and of spirit—as I say, it is still
imperfect. First of all, then, it must be purged of that former peace and
disquieted concerning it and withdrawn from it.[5] Even so was Jeremias
when, in the passage which we quoted from him, he felt and lamented[6]
thus, in order to express the calamities of this night that is past, saying:
'My soul is withdrawn and removed from peace.'[7]

7. This is a painful disturbance, involving many misgivings,
imaginings and strivings which the soul has within itself, wherein, with
the apprehension and realization of the miseries in which it sees itself,
it fancies that it is lost and that its blessings have gone for ever.
Wherefore the spirit experiences[8] pain and sighing so deep that they

---

[1] A, B, M, Mtr., P: 'all these afflictions and purgations.' Bz., C: 'affective purgations.'
[2] Isaias xxvi, 17–18.
[3] [P. Silverio reads, with] A, B, M: 'the gloss.' [This was probably what the Saint
actually wrote.] Bz., C, H, Mtr., P [not understanding it] have: 'the Church' [la Iglesia
for la Glosa]. V, e.p. [give the correct sense by reading]: 'the Scripture.'
[4] [Philippians iv, 7.]
[5] [We have here split up a parenthesis of about seventy words.] E.p. abbreviates:
'[It seemed to be] a twofold peace, that is, of sense and spirit. First of all it must be purged
that it may be disquieted concerning that imperfect peace, and withdrawn from it.'
[6] [Lit., 'and wept.']   [7] Lamentations iii, 17.
[8] So C, H, Mtr., P, V. The other Codices and e.p. read: 'Wherefore there has entered
into the spirit.'

cause it vehement spiritual groans and cries, to which at times it gives vocal expression; when it has the necessary strength and power it dissolves into tears, although this relief comes but seldom. David[1] describes this very aptly, in a Psalm, as one who has had experience of it, where he says: 'I was exceedingly afflicted and humbled; I roared with the groaning of my heart.'[2] This roaring implies great pain; for at times, with the sudden and acute remembrance of these miseries wherein the soul sees itself, pain and affliction rise up and surround it, and I know not how the affections of the soul could be described[3] save in the similitude of holy Job, when he was in the same trials, and uttered these words: 'Even as the overflowing of the waters, even so is my roaring.'[4] For just as at times the waters make such inundations that they overwhelm and fill everything, so at times this roaring and this affliction of the soul grow to such an extent that they overwhelm it and penetrate it completely, filling it with spiritual pain and anguish in all its deep affections and energies, to an extent surpassing all possibility of exaggeration.

8. Such is the work wrought in the soul by this night that hides the hopes of the light of day. With regard to this the prophet Job says likewise: 'In the night my mouth is pierced with sorrows and they that feed upon me sleep not.'[5] Now here by the mouth is understood the will, which is transpierced with these pains that tear the soul to pieces, neither ceasing nor sleeping, for the doubts and misgivings which transpierce the soul in this way never cease.[6]

9. Deep is this warfare and this striving, for the peace which the soul hopes for will be very deep; and the spiritual pain is intimate and delicate,[7] for the love which it will possess will likewise be very intimate and refined. The more intimate and the more perfect the finished work is to be and to remain, the more intimate, perfect and pure must be the labour; the firmer the edifice, the harder the labour.[8] Wherefore, as Job says, the soul is fading within itself, and its vitals are being consumed without any hope.[9] Similarly, because in the state of perfection toward which it journeys by means of this purgative night the soul

---

[1] E.p.: 'The royal prophet David.'   [2] Psalm xxxvii, 9 [A.V., xxxviii, 8].
[3] [*Lit.*, '. . . sees itself, it arises and is surrounded with pain and affliction, the affections of the soul, that I know not how it could be described.' A confused, ungrammatical sentence, of which, however, the general meaning is not doubtful.] E.p. has: '. . . sees itself, the affections of the soul feels [*sic*] such pain and affliction.'
[4] Job iii, 24.   [5] Job xxx, 17.   [6] H: 'never sleep.'
[7] E.p. adds: 'and refined.'
[8] Some MSS. omit the words 'the labour,' but the meaning is evidently the same.
[9] Job. xxx, 16.

will attain to the possession and fruition of innumerable blessings, of gifts and virtues, both according to the substance of the soul and like-wise¹ according to its faculties, it must needs see and feel itself with-drawn from them all and deprived of them all and be empty and poor without them;² and it must needs believe itself to be so far from them that it cannot persuade itself that it will ever reach them, but rather it must be convinced that all its good things are over. The words of Jeremias have a similar meaning in that passage already quoted, where he says: 'I have forgotten good things.'³

10. But let us now see the reason why this light of contemplation, which is so sweet and blessed to the soul that there is naught more desirable (for, as has been said above, it is the same wherewith the soul must be united and wherein it must find all the good things in the state of perfection that it desires), produces, when it assails the soul, these beginnings which are so painful and these effects which are so disagreeable, as we have here said.

11. This question is easy for us to answer, by explaining, as we have already done in part, that the cause of this is that, in contemplation and the Divine inflowing, there is naught that of itself can cause affliction, but that they rather cause great sweetness and delight, as we shall say hereafter.⁴ The cause is rather the weakness and imperfection from which the soul then suffers, and the dispositions which it has in itself and which make it unfit for the reception of them. Wherefore, when⁵ the said Divine light assails the soul, it must needs cause it to suffer after the manner aforesaid.

CHAPTER X

*Explains this purgation fully by a comparison.*⁶

FOR the greater clearness of what has been said, and of what has still to be said, it is well to observe at this point that this purga-tive and loving knowledge or Divine light whereof we here speak acts upon the soul which it is purging and preparing for perfect

¹ E.p. omits 'likewise.'   ² E.p. omits: 'and be empty . . . them.'
³ Lamentations iii, 17.
⁴ So Bz., C, H, Mtr. A, B, M: 'as was [*sic*] afterwards given it.' E.p.: 'as will after-wards be given it.' V: 'as was said before.'
⁵ E.p. 'unfit [*lit.*, 'contrary': this also applies to our text] for the reception of that sweetness. And thus, when,' etc.
⁶ So e.p. The Codices have no title.

union with it in the same way as fire acts upon a log of wood in order
to transform it into itself; for material fire, acting upon wood, first of
all begins to dry it,[1] by driving out its moisture and causing it to shed
the water which it contains within itself. Then it begins to make it
black, dark and unsightly, and even to give forth a bad odour,[2] and,
as it dries it little by little, it brings out and drives away all the dark
and unsightly accidents which are contrary to the nature of fire. And,
finally, it begins to kindle it externally and give it heat, and at last
transforms it into itself and makes it as beautiful as fire. In this respect,
the wood has neither passivity nor activity of its own,[3] save for its
weight, which is greater, and its substance, which is denser, than that
of fire, for it has in itself[4] the properties and activities of fire. Thus it is
dry and it dries; it is hot and heats; it is bright and gives brightness;
and it is much less heavy than before. All these properties and effects
are caused in it by the fire.

2. In this same way we have to philosophize with respect to this
Divine fire of contemplative love, which, before it unites and transforms the soul in itself, first purges it of all its contrary accidents. It
drives out its unsightliness, and makes it black and dark, so that it seems
worse than before and more unsightly and abominable than it was wont
to be.[5] For this Divine purgation is removing[6] all the evil and vicious
humours which the soul has never perceived because they have been
so deeply rooted and grounded in it; it has never realized, in fact, that
it has had so much evil within itself. But now that they are to be driven
forth and annihilated, these humours reveal themselves, and become
visible to the soul because it is so brightly illumined by this dark light
of Divine contemplation (although it is no worse than before, either
in itself or in relation to God); and, as it sees in itself that which it saw
not before, it is clear to it that not only is it unfit to be seen by God,
but deserves His abhorrence, and that He does indeed abhor it. By
this comparison[7] we can now understand many things concerning
what we are saying and purpose to say.

3. First, we can understand how the very light and the loving
wisdom which are to be united with the soul and to transform it are
the same that at the beginning purge and prepare it: even as the very

---

[1] E.p.: 'to dry it up.'
[2] E.p. omits: 'and ... odour.'
[3] E.p. has 'proper to wood' for 'of its own.'
[4] E.p.: 'which is less subtle than that of fire; it has in itself.'
[5] E.p. omits: 'and more ... to be.'
[6] V: 'is consuming and removing.'
[7] Bz., H, V erroneously read: 'By this contemplation.'

fire which transforms the log of wood into itself, and makes it part of itself, is that which at the first was preparing it for that same purpose.

4. Secondly, we shall be able to see how these afflictions are not felt by the soul as coming from the said Wisdom, since, as the Wise Man says, all good things together come to the soul with her.[1] They are felt as coming from the weakness and imperfection which belong to the soul; without such purgation, the soul cannot receive its Divine light, sweetness and delight, even as the log of wood, when the fire acts upon it, cannot immediately be transformed until it be made ready; wherefore the soul is greatly afflicted.[2] This statement is fully supported by the Preacher, where he describes all that he suffered in order that he might attain to union with wisdom and to the fruition of it, saying thus: 'My soul hath wrestled with her and my bowels were moved in acquiring her; therefore it shall possess[3] a good possession.'[4]

5. Thirdly, we can learn here incidentally in what manner souls are afflicted in purgatory. For the fire would have no power over them, even though they came into contact with it, if they had no imperfections for which to suffer.[5] These are the material upon which the fire of purgatory seizes; when that material is consumed there is naught else that can burn. So here, when the imperfections are consumed, the affliction of the soul ceases and its fruition remains.[6]

6. The fourth thing that we shall learn here is the manner wherein the soul, as it becomes purged and purified by means of this fire of love, becomes ever more enkindled in love,[7] just as the wood grows hotter in proportion as it becomes the better prepared by the fire. This enkindling of love, however, is not always felt by the soul, but only at times when contemplation assails it less vehemently, for then it has occasion to see, and even to enjoy, the work which is being wrought in it, and which is then revealed to it. For it seems that the worker takes his hand from the work, and draws the iron out of the furnace, in order that something of the work which is being done may be seen; and then there is occasion for the soul to observe in itself the good which it saw not while the work was going on. In the same way, when the flame ceases to attack the wood, it is possible to see how much of it has been enkindled.

---

[1] Wisdom vii, 11.   [2] E.p.: 'wherefore the soul suffers greatly.'
[3] A, B: 'therefore shall I acquire.'
[4] Ecclesiasticus li, 28–9 [A.V., li, 19–21].
[5] E.p.: 'would have no power over them, if they were completely made ready to reign and be united with God in glory and had no faults for which to suffer.'
[6] E.p. adds: 'of the kind that in this life is possible.'
[7] E.p.: 'enkindled therein.'

7. Fifthly, we shall also learn from this comparison what has been said above—namely, how true it is that after each of these periods of relief the soul suffers once again, more intensely and keenly than before. For, after that revelation just referred to has been made, and after[1] the more outward imperfections of the soul have been purified, the fire of love once again attacks that which has yet to be consumed and purified more inwardly. The suffering of the soul now becomes more intimate, subtle and spiritual, in proportion as the fire refines away the finer,[2] more intimate and more spiritual imperfections, and those which are most deeply rooted in its inmost parts. And it is here just as with the wood, upon which the fire, when it begins to penetrate it more deeply, acts with more force and vehemence[3] in preparing its most inward part to possess it.

8.[4] Sixthly, we shall likewise learn here the reason why it seems to the soul that all its good is over, and that it is full of evil, since naught comes to it at this time but bitterness; it is like the burning[5] wood, which is touched by no air nor by aught else than by consuming fire. But, when there occur other periods of relief like the first, the rejoicing of the soul will be more interior because the purification has been more interior also.

9. Seventhly,[6] we shall learn that, although the soul has the most ample[7] joy at these periods (so much so that, as we said, it sometimes thinks that its trials[8] can never return again, although it is certain that[9] they will return quickly), it cannot fail to realize, if it is aware (and at times it is made aware) of a root of imperfection which remains, that its joy is incomplete, because a new assault seems to be threatening it;[10] when this is so, the trial returns quickly. Finally, that which still remains to be purged and enlightened most inwardly cannot well be concealed from the soul in view of its experience of its former purification;[11] even as also in the wood it is the most inward part that remains longest unkindled,[12] and the difference between it and that which has

---

[1] E.p.: 'and when at last.'
[2] [*Lit.*, 'more delicate.']   [3] [*Lit.*, 'fury.']
[4] This paragraph is only found in the Codices.
[5] Several codices omit 'burning.'
[6] E.p.: 'Sixthly.'   [7] E.p.: 'intense.'
[8] E.p. clarifies the sense of this passage by substituting for 'they' of the MSS., 'the trials.'
[9] Thus e.p. The other authorities have: 'yet when' [probably in the sense, however, of 'nevertheless,' as in our text].
[10] [The sudden change of metaphor is the author's. The 'assault' is, of course, the renewed growth of the 'root.']
[11] [*Lit.*, '. . . from the soul, with regard to that which has already been purified.']
[12] [*Lit.*, 'not enlightened': the word is the same as that used just above.]

already been purged is clearly perceptible; and, when this purification once more assails it most inwardly, it is no wonder if it seems to the soul once more that all its good is gone, and that it never expects to experience it again, for, now that it has been plunged into these most inward sufferings, all good coming from without is over.[1]

10. Keeping this comparison, then, before our eyes, together with what has already been said upon the first line of the first stanza concerning this dark night and its terrible properties, it will be well to leave these sad experiences of the soul and to begin to speak of the fruit of its tears and their blessed properties, whereof the soul begins to sing from this second line:

Kindled in love[2] with yearnings.

CHAPTER XI

Begins to explain the second line of the first stanza. Describes how, as the fruit of these rigorous constraints, the soul finds itself with the vehement passion of Divine love.[3]

IN this line the soul describes the fire of love which, as we have said, like the material fire acting upon the wood, begins to take hold upon the soul in this night of painful contemplation. This enkindling now described, although in a certain way it resembles that which we described above as coming to pass in the sensual part of the soul, is in some ways as different from that other as is the soul from the body, or the spiritual part from the sensual. For this present kind is an enkindling of spiritual love in the soul, which, in the midst of these dark confines, feels itself to be keenly and sharply wounded in strong Divine love, and to have a certain realization and foretaste of God, although it understands nothing definitely, for, as we say, the understanding is in darkness.

2. The spirit feels itself here to be deeply and passionately in love, for this spiritual enkindling produces the passion of love. And, inasmuch as this love is infused, it is passive rather than active,[4] and thus

---

[1] [The word translated 'over' is rendered 'gone' just above.] So A, B, M. [P. Silverio reads, with] Bz., C, H, Mtr., V: 'blinded' [i.e., 'is shut out from it']. E.p.: 'is hidden from it.'

[2] [*Lit.*, 'in loves'; and so throughout the exposition of this line.]

[3] So e.p. The Codices make no division here.

[4] E.p.: '. . . is infused, the soul here concurs rather with its passive aspect.'

it begets in the soul a strong passion of love. This love has in it something of union with God, and thus to some degree partakes of its properties, which are actions of God rather than of the soul, these being subdued within it passively. What the soul does here is to give its consent; the warmth and strength[1] and temper and passion of love—or enkindling, as the soul here calls it—belong[2] only to the love of God, which enters increasingly into union with it. This love finds in the soul more occasion and preparation to unite itself with it and to wound it, according as all the soul's desires are the more recollected,[3] and are the more withdrawn from and disabled for the enjoyment of aught either in Heaven or in earth.

3. This takes place to a great extent, as has already been said, in this dark purgation, for God has so weaned all the inclinations[4] and caused them to be so recollected[5] that they cannot find pleasure in anything they may wish. All this is done by God to the end that, when He withdraws them and recollects them in Himself, the soul may have more strength and fitness to receive this strong union of love of God, which He is now beginning to give it through this purgative way, wherein the soul must love with great strength and with all its desires and powers both of spirit and of sense; which could not be if they were dispersed in the enjoyment of aught else. For this reason David said to God, to the end that he might receive the strength of the love of this union with God: 'I will keep my strength for Thee;'[6] that is, I will keep the entire capacity and all the desires and energies of my faculties, nor will I employ their operation or pleasure in aught else than Thyself.

4. In this way it can be realized in some measure how great and how strong may be this enkindling of love in the spirit, wherein God keeps in recollection all the energies, faculties and desires of the soul, both of spirit and of sense, so that all this harmony may employ its energies and virtues in this love, and may thus attain to a true fulfilment of the first commandment, which sets aside nothing pertaining to man nor excludes from this love anything that is his, but says: 'Thou shalt love

---

[1] E.p.: 'which are more especially actions of God received in the soul than of the soul itself, the soul giving them its simple and loving consent. Yet the warmth and strength,' etc.

[2] [*Lit.*, 'cling,' 'adhere.']　　　　　　　　　[3] [*Lit.*, 'shut up.']

[4] A, B, M have 'unbound' for 'weaned.' E.p. reads: 'for God has so weaned all the faculties.'

[5] [Here, and below, the original has *recogidos*, the word normally translated 'recollected.']

[6] Psalm lviii, 10 [A.V., lix, 9].

thy God with all thy heart and with all thy mind, with all thy soul and with all thy strength.'[1]

5. When all the desires and energies of the soul, then, have been recollected in this enkindling of love, and when the soul itself has been touched and wounded in them all, and has been inspired with passion, what shall we understand the movements and digressions[2] of all these energies and desires to be, if they find themselves enkindled and wounded with strong love and without the possession and satisfaction thereof, in darkness and doubt? They will doubtless be suffering hunger, like the dogs of which David speaks as running about the city[3]; finding no satisfaction in this love, they keep howling and groaning. For the touch[4] of this love and Divine fire dries up the spirit and enkindles its desires,[5] in order to satisfy its thirst for this Divine love, so much so that it turns upon itself a thousand times and desires God in a thousand ways and manners, with the eagerness and desire of the appetite. This is very well explained by David in a psalm, where he says: 'My soul thirsted for Thee: in how many manners does my soul long for Thee!'[6]—that is, in desires. And another version reads: 'My soul thirsted for Thee, my soul is lost (or perishes) for Thee.'

6. It is for this reason that the soul says in this line that it was 'kindled in love with yearnings.'[7] For in all the things and thoughts that it revolves within itself, and in all the affairs and matters that present themselves to it, it loves in many ways, and also desires and suffers in the desire in many ways, at all times and in all places, finding rest in naught, and feeling this yearning in its enkindled wound,[8] even as the prophet Job declares, saying: 'As the hart[9] desireth the shadow, and as the hireling desireth the end of his work, so I also had vain months and numbered to myself wearisome and laborious nights. If I lie down to sleep, I shall say: "When shall I arise?" And then I shall await the evening and shall be full of sorrows even until the darkness of night.'[10] Everything becomes cramping to this soul: it cannot live[11]

---

[1] Deuteronomy vi, 5.   [2] E.p.: 'and affections.'

[3] Psalm lviii, 15–16 [A.V., lix, 14–15].

[4] E.p.: '. . . and without satisfaction thereof, in darkness thereof and doubt? Suffering greater hunger, doubtless, as they have greater experience of God. For the touch.'

[5] E.p.: 'its affections.'   [6] Psalm lxii, 2 [A.V., lxiii, 1].

[7] [Lit., as in the verses, 'in loves.'] Bz. adds: 'and says not "kindled in love with yearning."' H has: 'and says not "kindled in love and with yearning."'

[8] Thus the Codices. E.p. has: 'feeling this yearning enkindled and wounded.'

[9] [For ciervo, hart, read siervo, servant, and we have the correct quotation from Scripture. The change, however, was evidently made by the Saint knowingly. In P. Gerardo's edition, the Latin text, with cervus, precedes the Spanish translation, with ciervo.]

[10] Job vii, 2–4.   [11] [No cabe: lit., 'it cannot be contained,' 'there is no room for it.']

within itself; it cannot live either in Heaven or on earth; and it is filled with griefs until the darkness comes to which Job here refers, speaking spiritually and in the sense of our interpretation. What the soul here endures is affliction[1] and suffering without the consolation of a certain hope of any light and spiritual good. Wherefore the yearning and the grief of this soul in this enkindling of love are greater because it is multiplied in two ways: first, by the spiritual darkness wherein it finds itself, which afflicts it with its doubts and misgivings; and then by the love of God, which enkindles and stimulates it, and, with its loving wound, causes it a wondrous fear.[2] These two kinds of suffering at such a season are well described by Isaias, where he says: 'My soul desired Thee in the night'[3]—that is, in misery.

7. This is one kind of suffering which proceeds from this dark night; but, he goes on to say, with my spirit, in my bowels, until the morning, I will watch for Thee. And this is the second way of grieving in desire and yearning which comes from love in the bowels of the spirit, which are the spiritual affections. But in the midst of these dark and loving afflictions the soul feels within itself a certain companionship and strength, which bears it company and so greatly strengthens it that, if this burden of grievous darkness be taken away, it often feels itself to be alone, empty and weak. The cause of this is that, as the strength and efficacy of the soul were derived and communicated passively from the dark fire of love which assailed it, it follows that, when that fire ceases to assail it, the darkness and power and heat of love cease in the soul.[4]

[1] B, H, M: 'is expectation.'

[2] *Atemoriza* [evidently having puzzled the editor] is changed in e.p. into *atiza* ['stirs up'—the word used for poking the fire. I cannot think that the emendation, which repeats the idea of *estimula* above and finds no support in any MS., is worth adopting].

[3] Isaias xxvi, 9.   [4] H reads only: 'the darkness ceases.'

CHAPTER XII

Shows how this horrible night is purgatory, and how in it the Divine wisdom illumines men on earth with the same illumination that purges and illumines the angels in Heaven.[1]

FROM what has been said we shall be able to see how this dark night of loving fire, as it purges in the darkness, so also in the darkness enkindles the soul. We shall likewise be able to see that, even as spirits[2] are purged in the next life with dark material fire, so in this life they are purged and cleansed with the dark spiritual fire of love. The difference is that in the next life they are cleansed with fire, while here below they are cleansed and illumined with love only. It was this love that David entreated, when he said: *Cor mundum crea in me, Deus,* etc.[3] For cleanness of heart is nothing less than the love and grace of God. For the clean of heart are called by our Saviour 'blessed'; which is as if He had called them 'enkindled with love',[4] since blessedness is given by nothing less than love.

2. And Jeremias well shows how the soul is purged when it is illumined with this fire of loving wisdom (for God never grants mystical wisdom without love, since love itself infuses it), where he says: 'He hath sent fire into my bones, and hath taught me.'[5] And David says that the wisdom of God is silver tried in fire[6]—that is, in purgative fire of love. For this dark contemplation infuses into the soul love and wisdom jointly, to each one according to his capacity and need, enlightening the soul and purging it, in the words of the Wise Man, from its ignorances, as he said was done to himself.

3. From this we shall also infer that the very wisdom of God which purges these souls and illumines them[7] purges the angels from their ignorances, giving them knowledge, enlightening them as to that which they knew not,[8] and flowing down from God through the first hierarchies even to the last, and thence to men.[9] All the works, therefore, which are done by the angels, and all their inspirations, are said

---

[1] Chapter-heading and title are from e.p. The Codices make no division here.
[2] A, B: 'even as sins.' E.p.: 'even as the predestinate.'
[3] Psalm l, 12 [A.V., li, 10].　　　　　　　　[4] [*Lit.* 'enamoured.']
[5] Lamentations i, 13.　　　　　　　　[6] Psalm xi, 7 [A.V., xii, 6].
[7] The Codices omit the words 'purges . . . them', which are supplied by e.p.
[8] E.p. omits: 'giving . . . knew not.'
[9] The Schoolmen frequently assert that the lower angels are purged and illumined by the higher. Cf. St. Thomas, *Summa,* I, q. 106, a. 1, ad. 1.

in the Scriptures, with truth and propriety, to be the work of God and of themselves; for ordinarily these inspirations come through the angels, and they receive them likewise one from another without any delay—as quickly as a ray of sunshine is communicated through many windows arranged in order. For although it is true that the sun's ray itself passes through them all, still each one passes it on and infuses it into the next, in a modified form, according to the nature of the glass, and with rather more or rather less power and brightness, according as it is nearer to the sun or farther from it.

4. Hence it follows that, the nearer to God are the higher spirits and the lower,[1] the more completely are they purged and enlightened with more general purification; and that the lowest of them will receive this illumination[2] very much less powerfully and more remotely. Hence it follows that man, who is the lowest of all those to whom this loving contemplation flows down continually from God, will, when God desires to give it him, receive it perforce after his own manner in a very limited way and with great pain.[3] For, when the light of God illumines an angel, it enlightens him and enkindles[4] him in love, since, being pure spirit, he is prepared for that infusion. But, when it illumines man, who is impure and weak, it illumines him, as has been said above, according to his nature. It plunges him into darkness and causes him affliction and distress, as does the sun to the eye that is weak;[5] it enkindles him[6] with passionate yet afflictive love, until he be spiritualized and refined by this same fire of love; and it purifies him until he can receive with sweetness the union[7] of this loving infusion after the manner of the angels, being now purged, as by the help of the Lord we shall explain later.[8] But meanwhile he receives this contemplation and loving knowledge in the constraint and yearning of love of which we are here speaking.

5. This enkindling and yearning of love are not always perceived by the soul. For in the beginning, when this spiritual purgation commences, all this Divine fire is used in drying up and making ready the

---

[1] So e.p. The MSS. have: 'and those below.'

[2] E.p.: 'this enlightenment.'

[3] E.p. modifies thus: 'Hence it follows that, since man is lower than the angels, when God will give him this contemplation, he will perforce receive it after his manner, in a more limited way and with greater pain.'

[4] [*Lit.*, 'and softens.']

[5] [More literally, 'is sick.'] So most MSS. and e.p. Bz.: 'impure and sick.' H: 'bleared and sick.'

[6] A, e.p.: 'it enlightens him.'   [7] A, B, M: 'the infusion.'

[8] E.p. adds: 'For there are souls who in this life have received more perfect illumination than the angels.'

wood (which is the soul) rather than in giving it heat. But, as time goes on,[1] the fire begins to give heat to the soul, and the soul then very commonly feels this enkindling and heat of love. Further, as the understanding is being more and more purged by means of this darkness, it sometimes comes to pass that this mystical and loving theology, as well as enkindling the will, strikes and illumines the other faculty also—that of the understanding—with a certain Divine light and knowledge, so delectably and delicately[2] that it aids the will to conceive a marvellous fervour, and, without any action of its own,[3] there burns in it this Divine fire of love, in living flames, so that it now appears to the soul a living fire by reason of the living understanding which is given to it. It is of this that David speaks in a Psalm, saying: 'My heart grew hot within me, and, as I meditated, a certain fire was enkindled.'[4]

6. This enkindling of love, which accompanies the union of these two faculties, the understanding and the will, which are here united,[5] is for the soul a thing of great richness and delight; for it is a certain touch of the Divinity and is already the beginning[6] of the perfection of the union of love for which it hopes. Now the soul attains not to this touch of so sublime a sense and love of God, save when it has passed through many trials and a great part of its purgation. But for other touches which are much lower than these, and which are of ordinary occurrence, so much purgation is not needful.

7.[7] From what we have said it may here be inferred how in these spiritual blessings, which are passively infused by God into the soul, the will may very well love even though the understanding understand not; and similarly the understanding may understand and the will love not. For, since this dark night of contemplation consists of Divine light and love, just as fire contains light and heat, it is not unbefitting that, when this loving light is communicated, it should strike the will at times more effectively by enkindling it with love and leaving the understanding in darkness instead of striking it with light; and, at other times, by enlightening it with light, and giving it understanding, but leaving the will in aridity (as it is also true that the heat of the fire

---

[1] E.p. omits: 'as time goes on.'
[2] E.p.: 'and divinely.'
[3] E.p. omits: 'without . . . its own.'
[4] Psalm xxxviii, 4 [A.V., xxxix, 3].
[5] E.p. omits: 'which are here united.'
[6] [*Lit.*, 'the beginnings.'] E.p.: 'for it is certain that in this darkness it already has the beginnings.'
[7] The whole of this paragraph is omitted in e.p.

can be received without the light being seen, and also the light of it can be seen without the reception of heat); and this is wrought by the Lord, Who infuses as He wills.[1]

CHAPTER XIII

Of other delectable effects which are wrought in the soul by this dark night of contemplation.[2]

THIS type of enkindling will explain to us certain of the delectable effects which this dark night of contemplation works in the soul. For at certain times, as we have just said, the soul becomes enlightened in the midst of all this darkness, and the light shines in the darkness;[3] this mystical intelligence flows down into the understanding and the will remains in dryness—I mean, without actual union of love, with a serenity[4] and simplicity which are so delicate and delectable to the sense of the soul that no name can be given to them. Thus the presence of God is felt, now after one manner, now after another.

2. Sometimes, too, as has been said, it wounds the will at the same time, and enkindles love sublimely, tenderly and strongly; for we have already said that at certain times these two faculties, the understanding and the will, are united, when, the more they see,[5] the more perfect and delicate is the purgation of the understanding. But, before this state is reached, it is more usual for the touch of the enkindling of love to be felt in the will than for the touch of intelligence[6] to be felt in the understanding.

3.[7] But one question arises here, which is this: Why, since these two faculties are being purged together, are the enkindling and the love of purgative contemplation at first more commonly felt in the

---

[1] The Saint here treats a question often debated by philosophers and mystics—that of love and knowledge. Cf. also *Spiritual Canticle*, Stanza XVII (Vol. II, below), and *Living Flame*, Stanza III (Vol. III, below). Philosophers generally maintain that it is impossible to love without knowledge, and equally so to love more of an object than what is known of it. Mystics have, however, their own solutions of the philosophers' difficulty and the speculative Spanish mystics have much to say on the matter. (Cf., for example, the *Médula Mística*, Trat. V, Chap. iv, and the *Escuela de Oración*, Trat. XII, Duda v.)

[2] So e.p. The Codices make no division.   [3] St. John i, 5.

[4] E.p.: 'this mystical intelligence flows directly into the understanding and the will to some extent partakes of it, with a serenity,' etc.

[5] E.p. omits these four words, which are found in A, M. B, Bz., C, H, Mtr., V have: 'the more they go.' P: 'the more this is so.' [P. Gerardo follows P, which certainly best agrees with the general sense of the passage.]

[6] E.p.: 'of perfect intelligence.'   [7] E.p. omits this paragraph.

will than the intelligence thereof is felt in the understanding? To this it may be answered that this passive love does not now directly strike the will, for the will is free, and this enkindling of love is a passion of love rather than the free act of the will; for this heat of love strikes the substance of the soul and thus moves the affections passively. And so this is called passion of love rather than a free act of the will, an act of the will being so called only in so far as it is free. But these passions and affections subdue the will, and therefore it is said that, if the soul conceives passion with a certain affection, the will conceives passion; and this is indeed so, for in this manner the will is taken captive and loses its liberty, according as the impetus and power of its passion carry it away. And therefore we can say that this enkindling of love is in the will—that is, it enkindles the desire of the will; and thus, as we say, this is called passion of love rather than the free work of the will. And, because the receptive passion of the understanding can receive intelligence only in a detached and passive way (and this is impossible without its having been purged), therefore until this happens the soul feels the touch of intelligence less frequently than that of the passion of love. For it is not necessary to this end that the will should be so completely purged with respect to the passions, since these very passions help it to feel impassioned love.

4. This enkindling and thirst of love, which in this case belongs to the spirit, is very different from that other which we described in writing of the night of sense. For, though the sense has also its part here, since it fails not to participate in the labour of the spirit, yet the source and the keenness of the thirst of love is felt in the superior part of the soul—that is, in the spirit. It feels, and understands what it feels and its lack of what it desires, in such a way that all its affliction of sense, although greater without comparison than in the first night of sense, is as naught to it, because it recognizes within itself the lack of a great good which can in no way be measured.[1]

5. But here we must note that although, at the beginning, when this spiritual night commences, this enkindling of love is not felt, because this fire of love has not begun to take a hold,[2] God gives the soul, in place of it, an estimative love of Himself so great that, as we have said, the greatest sufferings and trials of which it is conscious in this night are the anguished thoughts that it[3] has lost God and the fears that He has abandoned it. And thus we may always say that from the very

---

[1] Bz., e.p.: 'be remedied.'   [2] E.p.: 'has not acted.'
[3] [Lit., 'the yearning to think if it.']

beginning of this night the soul is touched with yearnings of love, which is now that of estimation,[1] and now again, that of enkindling. And it is evident that the greatest suffering which it feels in these trials is this misgiving; for, if it could be certified at that time that all is not lost and over, but that what is happening to it is for the best—as it is—and that God is not wroth, it would care naught for all these afflictions, but would rejoice to know that God is making use of them for His good pleasure. For the love of estimation which it has for God is so great, even though it may not realize this and may be in darkness, that it would be glad,[2] not only to suffer in this way, but even to die many times over in order to give Him satisfaction. But when once the flame has enkindled the soul, it is wont to conceive, together with the estimation that it already has for God, such power and energy, and such yearning for Him, when He communicates to it the heat of love, that, with great boldness, it disregards everything and ceases to pay respect to anything, such are the power and the inebriation of love and desire. It regards not what it does, for[3] it would do strange and unusual things in whatever way and manner may present themselves, if thereby its soul might find Him Whom it loves.

6. It was for this reason that Mary Magdalene, though as greatly concerned for her own appearance as she was aforetime, took no heed[4] of the multitude of men who were at the feast,[5] whether they were of little or of great importance; neither did she consider that it was not seemly, and that it looked ill, to go and weep and shed tears among the guests, provided that, without delaying an hour or waiting for another time and season, she could reach Him for love of Whom her soul was already wounded and enkindled. And such is the inebriating power and the boldness[6] of love, that, though she knew her Beloved to be enclosed in the sepulchre by the great sealed stone, and surrounded by soldiers who were guarding Him lest His disciples should steal Him away,[7] she allowed none of these things to impede her, but went before daybreak with the ointments to anoint Him.

7. And finally, this inebriating power and yearning of love caused

---

1 [The word translated 'estimation' might also be rendered 'reverent love.' The 'love of estimation,' which has its seat in the understanding, is contrasted with the 'enkindling' or the 'love of desire,' which has its seat in the will. So elsewhere in this paragraph.]
2 E.p.: 'it would be very glad,' etc.
3 E.p. omits: 'such are the power . . . what it does, for.'
4 E.p.: 'Mary Magdalene, noble as she was, took no heed.'
5 E.p.: 'at the feast which was given at the house of the Pharisee, as Saint Luke says.'
6 H: 'and the superfluity.'
7 St. John xx, 1 [St. Matthew xxvii, 62–6].

her to ask one whom she believed to be a gardener and to have stolen Him away from the sepulchre, to tell her, if he had taken Him, where he had laid Him, that she might take Him away;[1] considering not that such a question, according to independent judgment and reason, was foolish;[2] for it was evident that, if the other had stolen Him, he would not say so, still less would he allow Him to be taken away. It is a characteristic of the power and vehemence of love that all things seem possible to it, and it believes all men to be of the same mind as itself. For it thinks that there is naught wherein one may be employed, or which[3] one may seek, save that which it seeks itself and that which it loves; and it believes that there is naught else to be desired, and naught wherein it may be employed, save that one thing, which is pursued by all.[4] For this reason, when the Bride went out to seek her Beloved, through streets and squares,[5] thinking that all others were doing the same, she begged them that, if they found Him, they would speak to Him and say[6] that she was pining for love of Him.[7] Such was the power of the love of this Mary that she thought that, if the gardener would tell her where he had hidden Him, she would go and take Him away, however difficult it might be made for her.

8. Of this manner, then, are the yearnings of love whereof this soul becomes conscious when it has made some progress in this spiritual purgation. For it rises up by night (that is, in this purgative darkness) according to the affections of the will. And with the yearnings and vehemence of the lioness or the she-bear going to seek her cubs when they have been taken away from her and she finds them not, does this wounded soul go forth to seek its God. For, being in darkness, it feels itself to be without Him and to be dying of love for Him. And this is that impatient love wherein the soul cannot long subsist without gaining its desire or dying. Such was Rachel's desire for children when she said to Jacob: 'Give me children, else shall I die.'[8]

9. But we have now to see how it is that the soul which feels itself so miserable and so unworthy of God, here[9] in this purgative darkness, has nevertheless strength, and is sufficiently bold and daring, to journey towards union with God. The reason is that, as love continually gives it strength wherewith it may love indeed, and as the property of love is to desire to be united, joined and made equal and like to the object

---

[1] St. John xx, 15.
[3] E.p.: 'or no other thing which.'
[5] [Lit., 'outskirts,' 'suburbs.']
[7] Canticles v, 8.
[9] E.p. has 'as it feels itself' for 'here.'

[2] E.p.: 'was not prudent.'
[4] E.p.: omits 'which . . . all.'
[6] E.p.: 'they would say of her.'
[8] Genesis xxx, 1.

of its love, that it may perfect itself in love's good things, hence it comes to pass that, when this soul is not perfected in love, through not having as yet attained to union, the hunger and thirst that it has for that which it lacks (which is union) and the strength set by love in the will which has caused it to become impassioned, make it bold and daring by reason of the enkindling of its will, although in its understanding, which is still dark and unenlightened,[1] it feels itself to be unworthy and knows itself to be miserable.

10. I will not here omit to mention the reason why this Divine light, which is always light to the soul, illumines it not as soon as it strikes it, as it does afterwards, but causes it the darkness and the trials of which we have spoken. Something has already been said concerning this, but the question must now be answered directly. The darkness and the other evils of which the soul is conscious when this Divine light strikes it are not darkness or evils caused by this light, but pertain to the soul itself, and the light illumines it so that it may see them. Wherefore it does indeed receive light from this Divine light; but the soul cannot see at first, by its aid, anything beyond what is nearest to it, or rather, beyond what is within it—namely, its darknesses or its miseries, which it now sees through the mercy of God, and saw not aforetime, because this supernatural light illumined it not. And this is the reason why at first it is conscious of nothing beyond darkness and evil; after it has been purged, however, by means of the knowledge and realization of these, it will have eyes to see, by the guidance of this light, the blessings of the Divine light; and, once all these darknesses and imperfections[2] have been driven out from the soul, it seems[3] that the benefits and the great blessings which the soul is gaining in this blessed night of contemplation become clearer.[4]

11. From what has been said, it is clear that God grants the soul in this state the favour of purging it and healing it with this strong lye of bitter purgation, according to its spiritual and its sensual part, of all the imperfect habits and affections which it had within itself with respect to temporal things and to natural, sensual[5] and spiritual things, its inward faculties being darkened, and voided of all these, its spiritual and sensual affections being constrained and dried up, and its natural

---

[1] E.p. omits: 'and unenlightened.'
[2] Bz., H, Mtr., P have 'impressions.' The other authorities read 'imperfections.'
[3] E.p.: 'it will have eyes to be shown the blessings of this Divine light, and once all these darknesses and these imperfections of the soul are driven out and taken away, it seems,' etc.
[4] E.p.: 'become known.'
[5] H adds 'speculative.'

energies being attenuated and weakened with respect to all this (a condition which it could never attain of itself, as we shall shortly say). In this way God makes it to die to all that is not naturally[1] God, so that, once it is stripped and denuded of its former skin, He may begin to clothe it anew. And thus its youth is renewed like the eagle's and it is clothed with the new man, which, as the Apostle says, is created according to God.[2] This is naught else but His illumination of the understanding with supernatural light, so that it is no more a human understanding but becomes Divine through union with the Divine. In the same way the will is informed[3] with Divine love, so that it is a will that is now no less than Divine, nor does it love otherwise than divinely, for it is made and united in one with the Divine will and love. So, too, is it with the memory; and likewise the affections and desires are all changed and converted[4] divinely, according to God. And thus this soul will now be a soul of heaven, heavenly, and more Divine than human. All this, as we have been saying, and because of what[5] we have said, God continues to do and to work in the soul by means of this night, illumining and enkindling it divinely with yearnings for God alone and for naught else whatsoever. For which cause the soul then very justly and reasonably adds the third line to the song, which says:[6]

. . . oh, happy chance!—
I went forth without being observed.

CHAPTER XIV

Wherein are set down and explained the last three lines of the first stanza.[7]

THIS happy chance was the reason for which the soul speaks, in the next lines, as follows:

I went forth without being observed,   My house being now at rest.

It takes the metaphor[8] from one who, in order the better to accomplish

---

[1] E.p. omits 'naturally.'   [2] Ephesians iv, 24.
[3] Mtr., V, e.p.: 'enkindled.'   [4] E.p. omits: 'and converted.'
[5] E.p.: 'as will have been clearly seen from what.'
[6] E.p.: '. . . to the song, which, with the other lines, we shall set down and explain in the chapter following.'   [7] Thus e.p.
[8] E.p. modifies thus: 'The happy chance whereof the soul sings in the first of these three lines was the reason for which it says in the two following . . . taking the metaphor,' etc.

something, leaves his house by night and in the dark, when those that are in the house are now at rest, so that none may hinder him. For this soul had to go forth to perform a deed so heroic and so rare—namely to become united with its Divine Beloved—and it had to leave its house, because the Beloved is not found save alone and without, in solitude. It was for this reason that the Bride desired to find Him alone, saying: 'Who would give Thee to me, my brother,[1] that I might find Thee alone, without, and that my love might be communicated to Thee.'[2] It is needful for the enamoured soul, in order to attain to its desired end, to do likewise, going forth at night, when all the domestics in its house are sleeping and at rest—that is, when the low operations, passions and desires of the soul (who are the people of the household) are, because it is night, sleeping and at rest. When these are awake, they invariably hinder the soul from seeking its good, since they are opposed to its going forth in freedom. These are they of whom Our Saviour speaks in the Gospel, saying that they are the enemies of man.[3] And thus it would be meet that their operations and motions should be put to sleep in this night, to the end that they may not hinder the soul from attaining the supernatural blessings of the union of love of God, for, while these are alive and active, this cannot be.[4] For all their work and their natural[5] motions hinder, rather than aid, the soul's reception of the spiritual blessings of the union of love, inasmuch as all natural ability is impotent with respect to the supernatural blessings that God, by means of His own infusion, bestows upon the soul passively, secretly and in silence. And thus it is needful that all the faculties should receive this infusion, and that, in order to receive it, they should remain passive,[6] and not interpose their own base acts and vile inclinations.

2. It was a happy chance for this soul that on this night God should put to sleep all the domestics in[7] its house—that is, all the faculties, passions, affections and desires which live in the soul, both sensually and spiritually. For thus it went forth 'without being observed'—that is, without being hindered by these affections, etc., for they were put to sleep and mortified in this night, in the darkness of which they were left, that they might not notice or feel anything after their own low and natural manner, and might thus be unable to hinder the soul from going forth from itself and from the house of its sensuality. And

---

[1] A, B, M have: 'my spouse, my brother.'
[2] Canticles viii, 1.   [3] St. Matthew x, 36.
[4] E.p.: 'this cannot be attained.'   [5] E.p. omits 'natural.'
[6] E.p. omits: 'and . . . passive.'   [7] E.p. has 'all the people of.'

thus only could the soul attain[1] to the spiritual union of perfect love of
God.[2]

3. Oh, how happy a chance is this for the soul which can free itself
from the house of its sensuality! None can understand it, unless, as it
seems to me, it be the soul that has experienced it. For such a soul will
see clearly how wretched was the servitude in which it lay and to how
many miseries it was subject when it was at the mercy of its faculties
and desires, and will know how the life of the spirit is true liberty and
wealth, bringing with it inestimable blessings. Some of these we shall
point out, as we proceed, in the following stanzas, wherein it will be
seen more clearly what good reason the soul has to sing of[3] the happy
chance of its passage from this dreadful night which has been described
above.

CHAPTER XV

Sets down the second stanza and its exposition.[4]

**In darkness and secure,   By the secret ladder, disguised—oh,
     happy chance!
In darkness and concealment,   My house being now at rest.**

IN this stanza the soul still continues to sing of certain properties of
the darkness of this night, reiterating how great is the happiness
which came to it through them. It speaks of them in replying to a
certain tacit objection, saying that[5] it is not to be supposed that, because
in this night and darkness it has passed through so many tempests of
afflictions, doubts, fears and horrors, as has been said, it has for that
reason run any risk of being lost. On the contrary, it says, in the darkness of this night it has gained itself. For in the night it has freed itself
and escaped subtly from its enemies, who were continually hindering
its progress. For in the darkness of the night it changed its garments
and disguised itself with three liveries and colours which we shall
describe hereafter; and went forth by a very secret ladder, which none

---

1 The verb 'could attain' is found in e.p. but, though necessary to the sense, is missing
from all the MSS.
2 So the MSS. E.p. modifies and shortens: 'which live in the sensual and spiritual soul,
that it might attain to the spiritual union of perfect love of God "without being observed"
—that is, without being hindered by them, because they were put to sleep and mortified
in that night, as has been said.'
3 A, P, e.p.: 'to relate.'
4 So e.p. The Codices have only: 'Stanza the Second.' A, B have no heading.
5 E.p.: 'pointing out that.'

in the house knew, the which ladder, as we shall observe likewise in the proper place, is living faith. By this ladder the soul went forth in such complete hiding and concealment, in order the better to execute its purpose, that it could not fail to be in great security; above all since in this purgative night the desires, affections and passions of the soul are put to sleep, mortified and quenched, which are they that, when they were awake and alive, consented not to this.[1]

The first line, then, runs thus:[2]

In darkness and secure.

CHAPTER XVI

Explains how, though in darkness, the soul walks securely.[3]

THE darkness which the soul here describes relates, as we have said, to the desires and faculties, sensual, interior and spiritual, for all these are darkened in this night as to their natural light, so that, being purged in this respect, they may be illumined with respect to the supernatural. For the spiritual and the sensual desires are put to sleep and mortified, so that they can experience[4] nothing, either Divine or human; the affections of the soul are oppressed and constrained, so that they can neither move nor find support in anything; the imagination is bound and can make no useful reflection; the memory is gone; the understanding is in darkness, unable to understand anything;[5] and hence the will likewise is arid and constrained and all the faculties are void and useless;[6] and in addition to all this a thick and heavy cloud is upon the soul, keeping it in affliction, and, as it were, far away from God.[7] It is in this kind of 'darkness' that the soul says here[8] it travelled 'securely.'

---

[1] Thus Bz., H, P. The other MSS. and e.p. have: 'they that, were they awake and alive, would not consent to this.'

[2] [*Lit.*, 'The line, then, continues, and says thus.' In fact, however, the author is returning to the first line of the stanza.]

[3] So e.p.   [4] [*Lit.*, 'taste.' E.p. adds 'delectably.']

[5] E.p. omits: 'unable to understand anything.'   [6] E.p. omits: 'and useless.'

[7] Some have considered this description exaggerated, but it must be borne in mind that all souls are not tested alike and the Saint is writing of those whom God has willed to raise to such sanctity that they drain the cup of bitterness to the dregs. We have already seen (Bk. I, chap. xiv, § 5) that 'all do not experience (this) after one manner . . . for (it) is meted out by the will of God, in conformity with the greater or the smaller degree of imperfection which each soul has to purge away, (and) in conformity, likewise, with the degree of love of union to which God is pleased to raise it' (p. 373, above).

[8] E.p.: 'It is in this kind of darkness that it says.'

2. The reason for this has been clearly expounded; for ordinarily the soul never strays save through its desires or its tastes or its reflections or its understanding or its affections; for as a rule it has too much or too little of these, or they vary or go astray, and hence the soul becomes inclined to that which behoves it not. Wherefore, when all these operations and motions are hindered, it is clear that the soul is secure against being led astray by them; for it is free, not only from itself, but likewise from its other enemies, which are the world and the devil. For when the affections and operations of the soul are quenched, these enemies cannot make war upon it by any other means or in any other manner.

3. It follows from this that, the greater is the darkness wherein the soul journeys and the more completely is it voided of its natural operations, the greater is its security. For, as the Prophet says,[1] perdition comes to the soul from itself alone—that is, from its sensual and interior desires and operations;[2] and good, says God, comes from Me alone. Wherefore, when it is thus hindered from following the things that lead it into evil, there will then come to it forthwith the blessings of union with God in its desires and faculties, which in that union He will make Divine and celestial. Hence, at the time of this darkness, if the soul considers the matter, it will see very clearly how little its desire and its faculties are being diverted to things that are useless and harmful; and how secure it is[3] from vainglory and pride and presumption, vain and false rejoicing and many other things. It follows clearly, then, that, by walking in darkness, not only is the soul not lost, but it has even greatly gained, since it is here gaining the virtues.

4. But there is a question which at once arises here—namely, since the things of God are of themselves profitable to the soul and bring it gain and security, why does God, in this night, darken the desires and faculties with respect to these good things likewise, in such a way that the soul can no more taste of them[4] or busy itself with them than with these other things, and indeed in some ways can do so less? The answer is that it is well for the soul to perform no operation touching spiritual things at that time and to have no pleasure in such things, because its faculties and desires are base, impure and wholly natural; and thus, although these faculties be given the desire and interest in things supernatural and Divine, they could not receive them save after

---

[1] Osee xiii, 9. [2] E.p. adds: 'not harmonized.'
[3] E.p.: 'to things that are useless and vain; and that it is secure,' etc.
[4] B, e.p.: 'can no more enjoy them.'

a base and a natural manner, exactly in their own fashion.[1] For, as the philosopher says, whatsoever is received comes to him that receives it after the manner of the recipient. Wherefore, since these natural faculties have neither purity nor strength nor capacity to receive and taste things that are supernatural after the manner of those things, which manner is Divine, but can do so only after their own manner, which is human and base, as we have said, it is meet that its faculties be in darkness concerning these Divine things likewise.[2] Thus, being weaned and purged and annihilated in this respect first of all, they may lose that base and human[3] way of receiving and acting, and thus all these faculties and desires of the soul may come to be prepared and tempered in such a way as to be able to receive, feel and taste that which is Divine and supernatural[4] after a sublime and lofty manner, which is impossible if the old man die not first of all.

5. Hence it follows that all spiritual things, if they come not from above and be not communicated by the Father of lights to human desire and free will (howsoever much a man may exercise his taste and faculties for God, and howsoever much it may seem to the faculties that they are experiencing these things), will not be experienced after a Divine and spiritual manner, but after a human and natural manner, just as other things are experienced, for spiritual blessings go not from man to God, but come from God to man.[5] With respect to this (if this were the proper place for it) we might here explain how there are many persons whose many tastes and affections and the operations of whose faculties are fixed upon God or upon spiritual things, and who may perhaps think that this is supernatural and spiritual, when it is perhaps no more than the most human[6] and natural desires[7] and actions. They regard these good things with the same disposition as they have for other things, by means of a certain natural facility which they possess for directing their desires and faculties to anything whatever.

6. If perchance we find[8] occasion elsewhere in this book, we shall

---

[1] E.p. modifies: 'that it is meet at that time for its operation and pleasure to be void as touching spiritual things; for its faculties and desires are base and impure; and thus, even though these faculties should be given desire and interest in things supernatural and Divine, they could not receive them save after a base manner.'

[2] E.p.: '. . . which manner is Divine, but after their own manner; it is meet that [its faculties] be in darkness concerning these Divine things likewise, for perfect purgation.'

[3] E.p. omits: 'and human.'   [4] E.p. omits: 'and supernatural.'

[5] E.p. modifies: 'howsoever much the taste and desire of man and his faculties with respect to God be exercised, and howsoever much it may seem to them that they experience Him, they experience Him not in this way divinely and perfectly.'

[6] E.p.: 'than very human.'

[7] A, B, M read 'trials' [aprietos] for 'desires' [apetitos].

[8] A, B, P, e.p.: 'we have.'

treat of this, describing certain signs which indicate when the interior actions and motions of the soul, with respect to communion with God, are only natural, when they are spiritual, and when they are both natural and spiritual. It suffices for us here to know that, in order that the interior motions and acts of the soul may come to be moved by God divinely, they must first be darkened and put to sleep and hushed to rest naturally[1] as touching all their capacity and operation, until they have no more strength.

7. Therefore, O spiritual soul, when thou seest thy desire obscured, thy affections arid and constrained, and thy faculties bereft of their capacity for any interior exercise, be not afflicted by this, but rather consider it a great happiness, since God is freeing thee from thyself and taking the matter from thy hands. For with those hands, howsoever well they may serve thee, thou wouldst never labour so effectively, so perfectly and so securely (because of their clumsiness and uncleanness) as now, when God takes thy hand and guides thee in the darkness, as though thou wert blind, to an end and by a way which thou knowest not. Nor couldst thou ever hope to travel with the aid of thine own eyes and feet, howsoever good thou be as a walker.

8. The reason, again, why the soul not only travels securely, when it travels thus in the darkness, but also achieves even greater gain and progress, is that usually, when the soul is receiving fresh advantage and profit, this comes by a way that it least understands—indeed, it quite commonly believes that it is losing ground. For, as it has never experienced that new feeling which drives it forth and[2] dazzles it and makes it depart recklessly from its former way of life, it thinks itself to be losing ground rather than gaining and progressing, since it sees that it is losing with respect to that which it knew and enjoyed, and is going by a way which it knows not and wherein it finds no enjoyment. It is like the traveller, who, in order to go to new and unknown lands,[3] takes new roads, unknown and untried, and journeys unguided by his past experience, but doubtingly and according to what others say. It is clear that such a man could not reach new countries, or add to his past experience, if he went not along new and unknown roads and abandoned those which were known to him.[4] Exactly so, one who is

---

1 A, e.p. [clarify the somewhat vague adverb by reading]: 'in that which is natural.'
2 E.p. omits: 'drives it forth and.'
3 M adds: 'and untried' and omits: 'takes . . . untried, and.'
4 E.p. modifies: 'unknown and untried by the report of any other person, and would clearly never reach new countries save by new and unknown roads, abandoning those which were known to him.'

learning fresh details concerning any office or art always proceeds in
darkness, and receives no guidance from his original knowledge, for if
he left not that behind he would get no farther nor make any progress;
and in the same way, when the soul is making most progress, it is
travelling in darkness, knowing naught. Wherefore, since God, as we
have said, is the Master and Guide of this blind soul, it may well and
truly rejoice, once it has learned to understand this, and say: 'In
darkness and secure.'

9. There is another reason why the soul has walked securely in this
darkness, and this is because it has been suffering; for the road of
suffering is more secure and even more profitable than that of fruition
and action: first, because in suffering the strength of God is added to
that of man, while in action and fruition the soul is practising its own
weaknesses and imperfections; and second, because in suffering the
soul continues to practise and acquire the virtues and become purer,
wiser and more cautious.

10. But there is another and a more important reason why the soul
now walks in darkness and securely;[1] this emanates from the dark light
or wisdom aforementioned. For in such a way does this dark night of
contemplation absorb and immerse the soul in itself, and so near does it
bring the soul to God, that it protects and delivers it from all that is
not God. For this soul is now, as it were, undergoing a cure, in order
that it may regain its health—its health being God Himself. His
Majesty restricts it to a diet and abstinence from all things, and takes
away its appetite for them all. It is like a sick man, who, if he is respected
by those in his house, is carefully tended so that he may be cured; the
air is not allowed to touch him, nor may he even enjoy the light, nor
must he hear footsteps, nor yet the noise of those in the house; and he
is given food that is very delicate, and even that only in great moderation—food that is nourishing rather than delectable.

11. All these particularities (which are for the security and safe-
keeping of the soul) are caused by this dark contemplation, because it
brings the soul nearer to God. For[2] the nearer the soul approaches
Him, the blacker is the darkness which it feels and the deeper is the
obscurity which comes through its weakness; just as, the nearer a man
approaches the sun, the greater are the darkness and the affliction
caused him through the great splendour of the sun and through the
weakness and impurity[3] of his eyes. In the same way, so immense is

---

[1] A, e.p.: 'now, walking in darkness, walks securely.'
[2] A, e.p.: 'For, in truth.'   [3] A, e.p. add: 'and defectiveness.'

the spiritual light of God, and so greatly does it transcend our natural understanding, that the nearer we approach it, the more it blinds and darkens us. And this is the reason why, in Psalm xvii, David says that God made darkness His hiding-place and covering, and His tabernacle around Him dark water in the clouds of the air.[1] This dark water in the clouds of the air is dark contemplation and Divine wisdom in souls, as we are saying. They continue to feel it as a thing which is near Him, as the tabernacle wherein He dwells, when God brings them ever nearer to Himself. And thus, that which in God is supreme light and refulgence is to man blackest darkness, as Saint Paul says, according as David explains in the same Psalm, saying: 'Because of the brightness which is in His presence, passed clouds and cataracts'[2]—that is to say, over the natural understanding, the light whereof, as Isaias says in Chapter V: *Obtenebrata est in caligine ejus.*[3]

12. Oh, miserable is the fortune of our life, which is lived in such great peril and wherein it is so difficult to find the truth! For that which is most clear and true is to us most dark and doubtful; wherefore, though it is the thing that is most needful for us, we flee from it. And that which gives the greatest light and satisfaction to our eyes we embrace and pursue, though it be the worst thing for us, and make us fall at every step. In what peril and fear does man live, since the very natural light of his eyes by which he has to guide himself[4] is the first light that dazzles him and leads him astray on his road to God! And if he is to know with certainty by what road he travels, he must perforce keep his eyes closed and walk in darkness, that he may be secure from the enemies who inhabit his own house—that is, his senses and faculties.

13. Well hidden, then, and well protected is the soul in these dark waters, when it is close to God. For, as these waters serve as a tabernacle and dwelling-place for God Himself, they will serve the soul in the same way and for a perfect protection and security, though it remain in darkness, wherein, as we have said, it is hidden[5] and protected from itself, and from all evils[6] that come from creatures; for to such the words of David refer in another Psalm, where he says: ' Thou shalt hide them in the hiding-place of Thy face from the disturbance of

---

[1] Psalm xvii, 12 [A.V., xviii, 11]. A alone gives the passage both in Latin and in Spanish.
[2] Psalm xvii, 13 [A.V., xviii, 12].
[3] Isaias v, 30.   [4] E.p.: 'wherewith he guides himself.'
[5] E.p.: 'though in darkness, where it is hidden.'
[6] A, V, e.p.: 'and from all the other evils.'

men; Thou shalt protect them in Thy tabernacle from the contradiction of tongues.'[1] Herein we understand all kinds of protection; for
to be hidden in the face of God from the disturbance of men is to be
fortified with this dark contemplation against all the chances which
may come upon the soul from men. And to be protected in His tabernacle from the contradiction of tongues is for the soul to be engulfed
in these dark waters, which are the tabernacle of David whereof we
have spoken. Wherefore, since the soul has all its desires and affections
weaned and its faculties set in darkness, it is free from all imperfections
which contradict the spirit, whether they come from its own flesh or
from other creatures. Wherefore this soul may well say that it journeys
'in darkness and secure.'

14. There is likewise another reason, which is no less effectual than
the last, by which we may understand how the soul journeys securely
in darkness;[2] it is derived from the fortitude by which the soul is at
once inspired in these obscure and afflictive dark waters of God. For
after all, though the waters be dark, they are none the less waters, and
therefore they cannot but refresh and fortify the soul in that which is
most needful for it, although in darkness and with affliction. For the
soul immediately perceives in itself a genuine determination and an
effectual desire to do naught which it understands to be an offence to
God, and to omit to do naught that seems to be for His service. For
that dark love cleaves to the soul, causing it a most watchful care and
an inward solicitude concerning that which it must do, or must not do,
for His sake, in order to please Him. It will consider and ask itself a
thousand times if it has given Him cause to be offended; and all this it
will do with much greater care and solicitude than before, as has
already been said with respect to the yearnings of love. For here all the
desires and energies and faculties of the soul are recollected from all
things else, and its effort and strength are employed in pleasing its God
alone.[3] After this manner the soul goes forth from itself and from all
created things to the sweet and delectable union of love of God, 'In
darkness and secure.'

By the secret ladder, disguised.

[1] Psalm xxx, 21 [A.V., xxxi, 20].
[2] E.p.: 'journeys well, though in darkness.'
[3] E.p.: '. . . of the soul, since they are recollected from all things else, employ their
effort and strength in pleasing their God alone.'

CHAPTER XVII

Explains how this dark contemplation is secret.[1]

THREE things have to be expounded with reference to three words contained in this present line. Two (namely, 'secret' and 'ladder') belong to the dark night of contemplation of which we are treating; the third (namely, 'disguised') belongs to the soul by reason of the manner wherein it conducts itself in this night.[2] As to the first, it must be known that in this line the soul describes this dark contemplation, by which it goes forth to the union of love, as a secret ladder, because of the two properties which belong to it—namely, its being secret and its being a ladder. We shall treat of each separately.[3]

2. First, it describes this dark contemplation as 'secret,' since, as we have indicated above, it is mystical theology, which theologians call secret wisdom,[4] and which, as Saint Thomas says, is communicated and infused into the soul through love.[5] This happens[6] secretly and in darkness, so as to be hidden from the work[7] of the understanding and of other faculties. Wherefore, inasmuch as the faculties aforementioned attain not to it, but the Holy Spirit infuses and orders it in the soul,[8] as says the Bride in the Songs, without either its knowledge or its understanding, it is called secret. And, in truth, not only does the soul not understand it, but there is none that does so, not even the devil; inasmuch as the Master Who teaches the soul is within it in its substance, to which the devil may not attain, neither may natural sense nor understanding.[9]

3. And it is not for this reason alone that it may be called secret, but likewise because of the effects which it produces in the soul. For it is secret not only in the darknesses and afflictions of purgation, when this wisdom of love[10] purges the soul, and the soul is unable to speak of

---

[1] So e.p. The Codices make no division.
[2] E.p.: 'but the third, which is "disguised," touches the manner wherein the soul conducts itself in this night.'
[3] E.p. abbreviates: 'which belong to it, and which we shall proceed to expound.'
[4] H: 'mystical wisdom.'
[5] 'Propter hoc Gregorius (Hom. 14 in Ezech.) constituit vitam contemplativam in charitate Dei.' Cf. *Summa Theologica*, 2a, 2æ, q. 45, a. 2.
[6] E.p.: 'through love more especially. And this happens.'
[7] A, e.p.: 'from the natural work.'
[8] E.p. omits: 'and orders.' A, B, M read: 'infuses and adorns it.'
[9] E.p. omits: 'to which . . . understanding.'
[10] A, B, e.p.: 'this secret wisdom.'

it, but equally so afterwards in illumination, when this wisdom is communicated to it most clearly. Even then it is still so secret that the soul cannot speak of it[1] and give it a name whereby it may be called; for, apart from the fact that the soul has no desire to speak of it, it can find no suitable way or manner or similitude by which it may be able to describe such lofty understanding and such delicate[2] spiritual feeling. And thus, even though the soul might have a great desire to express it and might find many ways in which to describe it, it would still be secret and remain undescribed.[3] For, as that inward wisdom is so simple, so general and so spiritual that it has not entered into the understanding enwrapped or cloaked in any form or image subject to sense,[4] it follows that sense and imagination (as it has not entered through them nor has taken their form and colour) cannot account for it or imagine it, so as to say anything concerning it,[5] although the soul be clearly aware that it is experiencing and partaking of that rare and delectable wisdom. It is like one who sees something never seen before, whereof he has not even seen the like; although he might understand its nature and have experience of it, he would be unable to give it a name, or say what it is, however much he tried to do so, and this in spite of its being a thing which he had perceived with the senses. How much less, then, could he describe a thing that has not entered through the senses! For the language of God has this characteristic that, since it is very intimate and spiritual[6] in its relations with the soul, it transcends every sense and at once makes all harmony and capacity of the outward and inward senses to cease and be dumb.

4. For this we have both authorities and examples in the Divine Scripture. For the incapacity of man to speak of it and describe it in words was shown by Jeremias,[7] when, after God had spoken with him, he knew not what to say, save 'Ah, ah, ah!' This interior incapacity—that is, of the interior sense of the imagination—and also that of the exterior sense corresponding to it was also demonstrated in the case of Moses, when he stood before God in the bush;[8] not only did he say to God that after speaking with Him he knew not neither was able to speak, but also that not even (as is said in the Acts of the Apostles)[9] with the interior imagination did he dare to meditate, for it

---

[1] E.p.: 'cannot discern it.' [2] E.p.: 'delicate and infused.'
[3] E.p.: 'it would ever remain secret.' [4] E.p. adds: 'as sometimes happens.'
[5] E.p.: 'or imagine it, in such a manner as to be able to say anything well concerning it.'
[6] E.p.: 'that, when it is very intimate, infused and spiritual.'
[7] Jeremias i, 6. [8] Exodus iv, 10 [cf. iii, 2].
[9] Acts vii. 32.

seemed to him that his imagination was very far away and was too dumb, not only to express any part of that which he understood concerning God, but even to have the capacity to receive aught therefrom. Wherefore, inasmuch as the wisdom of this contemplation is the language of God to the soul, addressed by pure spirit to pure spirit, naught that is less than spirit, such as the senses, can perceive it, and thus to them it is secret, and they know it not, neither can they say it,[1] nor do they desire to do so, because they see it not.[2]

5. We may deduce from this the reason why certain persons—good and fearful souls—who walk along this road and would like to give an account of their spiritual state to their director,[3] are neither able to do so nor know how. For the reason we have described,[4] they have a great repugnance in speaking of it,[5] especially when their contemplation is of the purer sort, so that the soul itself is hardly conscious of it. Such a person is only able to say that he is satisfied, tranquil and contented and that he is conscious of the presence of God, and that, as it seems to him, all is going well with him; but he cannot describe the state of his soul, nor can he say anything about it save in general terms like these. It is a different matter when the experiences of the soul are of a particular kind, such as visions, feelings, etc., which, being ordinarily received under some species wherein sense participates, can be described under that species, or by some other similitude. But this capacity for being described is not in the nature of pure contemplation, which is indescribable, as we have said,[6] for the which reason it is called secret.

6. And not only for that reason is it called secret, and is so, but likewise because this mystical knowledge has the property of hiding the soul within itself. For, besides performing its ordinary function, it sometimes absorbs the soul and engulfs it in its secret abyss, in such a way that the soul clearly sees that it has been carried far away from every creature and has become most remote therefrom;[7] so that it considers itself as having been placed in a most profound and vast retreat, to which no human creature can attain, such as an immense

---

[1] [Or: 'and they know not how to say it nor are able to do so.']
[2] E.p. abbreviates: 'was very far away and dumb. And as the wisdom of this contemplation is the language of God to the soul, of [or 'from'] pure spirit, the senses, which are not this [i.e., 'pure spirit'], perceive it not, and thus it is secret to them, and they know it not, neither can they say it.'
[3] [Lit., 'to him that rules them.']
[4] E.p.: 'And thus.'
[5] A, B: 'Hence arises the great repugnance that they have in speaking of it.'
[6] E.p.: 'which can hardly be described.'
[7] [Lit., 'that it is set most far away and most remote from every creature.'] E.p. has 'most completely abandoned' for 'most far away.'

desert, which nowhere has any boundary, a desert the more delectable, pleasant and lovely for its secrecy, vastness and solitude, wherein, the more the soul is raised up above all temporal creatures, the more deeply does it find itself hidden. And so greatly does this abyss of wisdom raise up and exalt the soul at this time, making it to penetrate the veins of the science of love, that it not only shows it how base are all properties of the creatures by comparison with this supreme knowledge and Divine feeling, but likewise it learns how base and defective, and, in some measure, how inapt, are all the terms and words which are used in this life to treat of Divine things, and how impossible it is,[1] in any natural way or manner, however learnedly and sublimely they may be spoken of, to be able to know and perceive them as they are, save by the illumination of this mystical theology. And thus, when by means of this illumination the soul discerns this truth, namely, that it cannot reach it, still less explain it, by common or human language, it rightly calls it secret.

7. This property of secrecy and superiority over natural capacity, which belongs to this Divine contemplation, belongs to it, not only because it is supernatural, but also inasmuch as it is a road that guides and leads the soul[2] to the perfections of union with God; which, as they are things unknown after a human manner, must be approached, after a human manner,[3] by unknowing and by Divine ignorance. For, speaking mystically, as we are speaking here, Divine things and perfections[4] are known and understood as they are, not when they are being sought after and practised,[5] but when they have been found and practised. To this purpose speaks the prophet Baruch concerning this Divine wisdom: 'There is none that can know her ways nor that can imagine her paths.'[6] Likewise the royal Prophet speaks in this manner concerning this road of the soul, when he says to God: 'Thy lightnings lighted and illumined the round earth; the earth was moved and trembled.[7] Thy way[8] is in the sea and Thy paths are in many waters; and Thy footsteps shall not be known.'[9]

---

[1] E.p.: 'and how it is not possible.'
[2] E.p.: 'inasmuch as it is a guide that guides the soul.'
[3] E.p. omits: 'after a human manner.'
[4] E.p. has 'these things' and omits 'and perfections.'
[5] E.p. omits: 'and practised.'
[6] Baruch iii, 31.
[7] P omits this passage and G omits an entire page here. Other MSS. have various words for that which is here rendered 'trembled' [but English has only the one word which fairly expresses them all].
[8] E.p.: 'Thy road.'
[9] Psalm lxxvi, 19–20 [A.V., lxxvii, 18–19].

8. All this, speaking spiritually, is to be understood in the sense wherein we are speaking. For the illumination of the round earth[1] by the lightnings[2] of God is the enlightenment which is produced by this Divine contemplation in the faculties of the soul; the moving and trembling of the earth is the painful purgation which is caused therein; and to say that the way and the road of God whereby the soul journeys to Him is in the sea, and His footprints are in many waters and for this reason shall not be known, is as much as to say that this road whereby the soul journeys to God is as secret and as hidden from the sense of the soul as the way of one that walks on the sea, whose paths and footprints are not known, is hidden from the sense of the body. The steps and footprints which God is imprinting upon the souls that He desires to bring near to Himself, and to make great in union with His Wisdom, have also this property, that they are not known. Wherefore in the Book of Job mention is made of this matter, in these words: 'Hast thou perchance known the paths of the great clouds or the perfect knowledges?'[3] By this are understood the ways and roads whereby God continually exalts souls and perfects them in His Wisdom, which souls are here understood by the clouds. It follows, then, that this contemplation which is guiding the soul to God is secret wisdom.

CHAPTER XVIII

Explains how this secret wisdom is likewise a ladder.[4]

IT now remains[5] to consider the second point—namely, how this secret wisdom is likewise a ladder. With respect to this it must be known that we can call this secret contemplation a ladder for many reasons. In the first place, because, just as men mount by means of ladders and climb up to possessions and treasures and things that are in strong places, even so also, by means of this secret contemplation, without knowing how, the soul ascends and climbs up to a knowledge and possession of[6] the good things and treasures of Heaven. This is well expressed by the royal prophet David, when he says: 'Blessed is he that hath Thy favour and help, for such a man hath placed in his

---

[1] [*Lit.*, 'of the roundness of the earth.']
[2] [*coruscaciones.*] A, P, e.p.: *ilustraciones* [the word translated 'lightnings' at the end of § 7; the singular is rendered 'enlightenment' in this present clause].
[3] Job xxxvii, 16.   [4] So e.p. There is no division in the Codices.
[5] E.p.: 'It remains.'   [6] [*Lit.*, 'rises to scale, know and possess.']

heart ascensions into the vale of tears in the place which he hath appointed;[1] for after this manner the Lord of the law shall give blessing, and they shall go from virtue to virtue as from step to step, and the God of gods shall be seen in Sion.'[2] This God is the treasure of the strong place of Sion, which is happiness.

2. We may also call it a ladder because, even as the ladder has those same steps in order that men may mount, it has them also that they may descend; even so is it likewise with this secret contemplation, for those same communications which it causes in the soul raise it up to God, yet humble it with respect to itself. For communications which are indeed of God have this property, that they humble the soul and at the same time exalt it. For, upon this road, to go down is to go up, and to go up, to go down, for he that humbles himself is exalted and he that exalts himself is humbled.[3] And besides the fact that the virtue of humility is greatness, for the exercise of the soul therein, God is wont to make it mount by this ladder so that it may descend, and to make it descend so that it may mount, that the words of the Wise Man may thus be fulfilled, namely: 'Before the soul is exalted, it is humbled; and before it is humbled, it is exalted.'[4]

3. Speaking now in a natural way,[5] the soul that desires to consider it will be able to see how on this road (we leave apart the spiritual aspect, of which the soul is not conscious) it has to suffer many ups and downs, and how the prosperity which it enjoys is followed immediately by certain storms and trials; so much so, that it appears to have been given that period of calm in order that it might be forewarned and strengthened against the poverty which has followed;[6] just as after misery and torment there come abundance and calm. It seems to the soul as if, before celebrating that festival, it has first been made to keep that vigil. This is the ordinary course and proceeding of the state of contemplation until the soul arrives at the state of quietness; it never remains in the same state for long together, but is ascending and descending continually.

4. The reason for this is that, as the state of perfection, which consists in the perfect love of God and contempt for self, cannot exist

---

[1] A: 'for such a man hath placed in his heart of sighs'; B: 'for such a man hath placed in his heart his sighs.'

[2] Psalm lxxxiii, 6 [A.V., lxxxiv, 7].

[3] St. Luke xiv, 11.   [4] Proverbs xviii, 12.

[5] So H. A, B, M read [hablando ahora manualmente, which in its context I take to mean]: 'Speaking now in a homely way'; Bz., Mtr., V: 'in a somewhat homely way.' E.p. has: 'Likewise, according to this quality of a ladder, the soul,' etc.

[6] E.p.: 'against its present hardships.'

unless it have these two parts, which are the knowledge of God and of oneself, the soul has of necessity to be practised first in the one and then in the other, now being given to taste of the one—that is, exaltation—and now being made to experience the other—that is, humiliation—until it has acquired perfect habits; and then this ascending and descending will cease, since the soul will have attained to God and become united with Him, which comes to pass at the summit of this ladder, for the ladder rests and leans upon Him. For this ladder of contemplation, which, as we have said, comes down from God, is prefigured by that ladder which Jacob saw as he slept, whereon angels were ascending and descending, from God to man, and from man to God, Who Himself was leaning upon the end of the ladder.[1] All this, says Divine Scripture, took place by night, when Jacob slept, in order to express how secret is this road and ascent to God, and how different from that of man's knowledge. This is very evident, since ordinarily that which is of the greatest profit in it—namely, to be ever losing oneself and becoming as nothing[2]—is considered the worst thing possible; and that which is of least worth, which is for a soul to find consolation and sweetness (wherein it ordinarily loses rather than gains), is considered best.

5. But, speaking now somewhat more substantially and properly of this ladder of secret contemplation, we shall observe that the principal characteristic of contemplation, on account of which it is here called a ladder, is that it is the science of love. This, as we have said,[3] is an infused and loving knowledge of God, which enlightens the soul and at the same time enkindles it with love, until it is raised up step by step, even unto God its Creator. For it is love alone that unites and joins the soul with God. To the end that this may be seen more clearly, we shall here indicate the steps of this Divine ladder one by one, pointing out briefly the marks and effects of each, so that the soul may conjecture hereby on which of them it is standing. We shall therefore distinguish them by their effects, as do Saint Bernard and Saint Thomas,[4] for to know them in themselves is not possible after a natural manner, inasmuch as this ladder of love is, as we have said, so secret that God alone is He that measures and weighs it.

---

[1] Genesis xxviii, 12.   [2] [*Lit.*, 'and annihilating oneself.']
[3] E.p. omits: 'as we have said.'
[4] 'Ut dicit Bernardus, Magna res est amor, sed sunt in eo gradus. Loquendo ergo aliquantulum magis moraliter quam realiter, decem amoris gradus distinguere possumus' (D. Thom., *De dilectione Dei et proximi*, cap. xxvii. Cf. Opusc. LXI of the edition of Venice, 1595).

CHAPTER XIX

Begins to explain the ten steps[1] of the mystic ladder of Divine love, according to Saint Bernard and Saint Thomas. The first five are here treated.[2]

WE observe, then, that the steps of this ladder of love by which the soul mounts, one by one, to God, are ten. The first step of love causes the soul to languish, and this to its advantage. The Bride is speaking from this step of love when she says: 'I adjure you, daughters of Jerusalem, that, if ye find my Beloved, ye tell Him that I am sick with love.'[3] This sickness, however, is not unto death, but for the glory of God, for in this sickness the soul[4] swoons as to sin and as to all things that are not God, for the sake of God Himself, even as David testifies, saying: 'My soul hath swooned away'[5]—that is, with respect to all things, for Thy salvation. For just as a sick man first of all loses his appetite and taste for all food, and his colour changes, so likewise in this degree of love the soul loses its taste and desire for all things and changes its colour and the other accidentals of its past life,[6] like one in love. The soul falls not into this sickness if excess of heat be not communicated to it from above,[7] even as is expressed in that verse of David which says: *Pluviam voluntariam segregabis, Deus, hæreditati tuæ, et infirmata est,*[8] etc. This sickness and swooning to all things, which is the beginning and the first step on the road to God, we clearly described above, when we were speaking of the annihilation wherein the soul finds itself when it begins to climb[9] this ladder of contemplative purgation,[10] when it can find no pleasure, support, consolation or abiding-place in anything soever. Wherefore from this step it begins at once to climb to the second.[11]

2. The second step causes the soul to seek God without ceasing.[12]

---

[1] [The word translated 'step' may also (and often more elegantly) be rendered 'degree.' The same word is kept, however, throughout the translation of this chapter except where noted below.]

[2] So e.p. The Codices make no division.   [3] Canticles v, 8.

[4] E.p.: 'for herein the soul.'   [5] Psalm cxlii, 7 [A.V., cxliii, 7].

[6] E.p. omits: 'and the . . . life.'

[7] E.p. adds: 'which is here the mystic fever.'

[8] Psalm lxvii, 10 [A.V., lxviii, 9]. The Latin text is found in all the Codices except C, G, P.

[9] [*Lit.*, 'to enter (upon).']   [10] V: 'of purgative contemplation.'

[11] E.p.: 'to climb to the rest.'

[12] The word 'God' is found only in A, B, e.p.

Wherefore, when the Bride says that she sought Him by night upon her bed (when she had swooned away according to the first step of love) and found Him not, she said: 'I will arise and will seek Him Whom my soul loveth.'¹ This, as we say, the soul does without ceasing, as David counsels it, saying: 'Seek ye ever the face of God, and seek ye Him in all things, tarrying not until ye find Him;'² like the Bride, who, having enquired for Him of the watchmen, passed on at once and left them. Mary Magdalene did not even notice the angels at the sepulchre.³ On this step the soul now walks so anxiously that it seeks the Beloved in all things. In whatsoever it thinks, it thinks at once of the Beloved. Of whatsoever it speaks, in whatsoever matters present themselves, it is speaking and communing at once with the Beloved. When it eats, when it sleeps, when it watches, when it does aught soever, all its care is about the Beloved, as is said above with respect to the yearnings of love. And now, as love begins to recover its health and find new strength in the love of this second step,⁴ it begins at once to mount to the third, by means of a certain degree⁵ of new purgation in the night, as we shall afterwards describe, which produces in the soul the following effects.

3. The third step of the ladder of love is that which causes the soul to work and gives it fervour so that it fails not. Concerning this the royal Prophet says: 'Blessed is the man that feareth the Lord, for in His commandments he is eager to labour greatly.'⁶ Wherefore if fear, being the son of love, causes within him this eagerness to labour,⁷ what will be done by love itself? On this step the soul considers great works undertaken for the Beloved as small; many things as few; and the long time for which it serves Him as short, by reason of the fire of love wherein it is now burning. Even so to Jacob, though after seven years he had been made to serve seven more, they seemed few because of the greatness of his love.⁸ Now if the love of a mere creature could accomplish so much in Jacob, what will love of the Creator be able to do when on this third step it takes possession of the soul? Here, for the great love which the soul bears to God, it suffers great pains and afflictions because of the little that it does for God; and if it were

---

¹ Canticles iii, 2.   ² Psalm civ, 4 [A.V., cv, 4].
³ St. John xx. [This is the reading of all MSS. and editions. The reference is presumably to *v*. 14. But cf. *vv*. 11–13.]
⁴ E.p.: '. . . its health, gathering strength on this second step.'
⁵ [The word in the Spanish is that elsewhere translated 'step.']
⁶ Psalm cxi, 1 [A.V., cxii, 1].
⁷ [*Lit.*, 'makes in him this labour of eagerness.'] E.p.: 'causes this effect of eagerness.'
⁸ Genesis xxix, 20.

lawful for it to be destroyed a thousand times for Him it would be comforted. Wherefore it considers itself useless in all that it does and thinks itself to be living in vain. Another wondrous effect produced here in the soul is that it considers itself as being, most certainly, worse than all other souls: first, because love is continually teaching it how much is due to God;[1] and second, because, as the works which it here does for God are many and it knows them all to be faulty and imperfect, they all bring it confusion and affliction, for it realizes in how lowly a manner it is working for God, Who is so high. On this third step, the soul is very far from vainglory or presumption, and from condemning others. These anxious effects, with many others like them, are produced in the soul by this third step;[2] wherefore it[3] gains courage and strength from them in order to mount to the fourth step, which is that that follows.

4. The fourth step of this ladder of love is that whereby there is caused in the soul an habitual suffering because of the Beloved, yet without weariness. For, as Saint Augustine says, love makes all things that are great, grievous and burdensome to be almost naught.[4] From this step the Bride was speaking when, desiring to attain to the last step, she said to the Spouse: 'Set me as a seal upon thy heart, as a seal upon thine arm; for love—that is, the act and work of love—is strong as death, and emulation and importunity last as long as hell.'[5] The spirit here has so much strength that it has subjected the flesh and takes as little account of it as does the tree of one of its leaves. In no way does the soul here seek its own consolation or pleasure, either in God, or in aught else, nor does it desire or seek to pray to God for favours, for it sees clearly that it has already received enough of these, and all its anxiety is set upon the manner[6] wherein it will be able to do something that is pleasing to God and to render Him some service such as He merits and in return for what it has received from Him, although it be greatly to its cost. The soul says in its heart and spirit: Ah, my God and Lord! How many are there that go to seek in Thee their own consolation and pleasure, and desire Thee to grant them favours and gifts; but those who long to do Thee pleasure and to give Thee something

---

[1] [*Lit.*, 'how much God merits.']
[2] E.p. adds: 'of love.'   [3] E.p.: 'wherefore the soul.'
[4] E.p. adds: 'and very light.' Cf. St. Augustine: *Serm. IX de Verbis Domini in Evang. secundum Math., in fine*: 'Omnia enim sæva et immania prorsus facilia et prope nulla efficit amor.'
[5] Canticles viii, 5.
[6] E.p.: 'or in aught else, nor from that motive of consolation or self-interest does it beg favours of God. For all its anxiety is now about the manner.'

at their cost, setting their own interests last, are very few. The failure, my God, is not in Thy unwillingness to grant us new favours, but in our neglect to use those that we have received in Thy service alone,[1] in order to constrain Thee to grant them to us continually. Exceeding lofty is this step of love; for, as the soul goes ever after God with love so true, imbued with the spirit of suffering for His sake, His Majesty oftentimes and quite habitually grants it joy, and visits it sweetly and delectably in the spirit; for the boundless love of Christ, the Word, cannot suffer the afflictions of His lover without succouring him. This He affirmed through Jeremias, saying: 'I have remembered thee, pitying thy youth and tenderness, when thou wentest after Me in the wilderness.'[2] Speaking spiritually, this denotes the detachment which the soul now has interiorly from every creature, so that it rests not and nowhere finds quietness. This fourth step enkindles the soul and makes it to burn in such desire for God that it causes it to mount to the fifth, which is that which follows.

5. The fifth step of this ladder of love makes the soul to desire and long for God impatiently. On this step the vehemence of the lover to comprehend the Beloved and be united with Him is such that every delay, however brief, becomes very long, wearisome and oppressive to it, and it continually believes itself to be finding the Beloved. And when it sees its desire frustrated (which is at almost every moment), it swoons away with its yearning, as says the Psalmist, speaking from this step, in these words: 'My soul longs and faints for the dwellings of the Lord.'[3] On this step the lover must needs see that which he loves, or die; at this step was Rachel,[4] when, for the great longing that she had for children, she said to Jacob, her spouse: 'Give me children, else shall I die.'[5] Here men suffer hunger like dogs and go about and surround the city of God. On this step, which is one of hunger,[6] the soul is nourished upon love; for, even as is its hunger, so is its abundance; so that it rises hence to the sixth step, producing the effects which follow.

[1] E.p.: 'For Thou, my God, failest not in willingness to grant us favours; it is we who fail to use those that we have received in Thy service alone.'
[2] Jeremias ii, 2.
[3] Psalm lxxxiii, 2 [A.V., lxxxiv, 2].
[4] E.p.: 'must needs attain that which he loves, or die, even as Rachel,' etc.
[5] Genesis xxx, 1.
[6] [Lit., 'On this hungering step.'] E.p. omits the whole of the preceding sentence and then abbreviates: 'Here the soul is nourished,' etc.

CHAPTER XX

Wherein are treated the other five steps of love.[1]

ON the sixth step the soul runs swiftly to God and touches Him again and again; and it runs without fainting[2] by reason of its hope. For here the love that has made it strong makes it to fly swiftly. Of this step the prophet Isaias speaks thus: 'The saints that hope in God shall renew their strength; they shall take wings as the eagle; they shall fly and shall not faint,[3]' as they did at the fifth step. To this step likewise alludes that verse of the Psalm: 'As the hart desires the waters, my soul desires Thee, O God.'[4] For the hart, in its thirst, runs to the waters with great swiftness. The cause of this swiftness in love which the soul has on this step is that its charity is greatly enlarged[5] within it, since the soul is here almost wholly purified, as is said likewise in the Psalm, namely: *Sine iniquitate cucurri.*[6] And in another Psalm: 'I ran the way of Thy commandments when Thou didst enlarge my heart';[7] and thus from this sixth step the soul at once mounts to the seventh, which is that which follows.

2. The seventh step of this ladder makes the soul to become vehement in its boldness. Here love employs not its judgment in order to hope,[8] nor does it take counsel so that it may draw back, neither can any shame restrain it; for the favour which God here grants to the soul causes it to become vehement in its boldness. Hence follows that which the Apostle says, namely: That charity believeth all things, hopeth all things and is capable of all things.[9] Of this step spake Moses, when he entreated God to pardon the people, and if not, to blot out his name from the book of life wherein He had written it.[10] Men like these obtain from God that which they beg of Him with desire. Wherefore David says: 'Delight thou in God and He will give thee the petitions of thy heart.'[11] On this step the Bride grew bold, and said:

---

[1] So e.p. The Codices make no division.
[2] E.p.: '... runs swiftly to God. And thus it runs without fainting.'
[3] Isaias xl, 31. So e.p. The Codices mistakenly attribute this passage to David.
[4] Psalm xli, 2 [A.V., xlii, 1].
[5] V: 'is very delicate' [probably an error: *delicada* for *dilatada*].
[6] Psalm lviii, 5 [A.V., lix, 4].   [7] Psalm cxviii, 32 [A.V., cxix, 32].
[8] E.p.: '... in its boldness, and it is carried away thereby with love and intensity, so that it allows not itself to be led away by its judgment in order to hope.'
[9] 1 Corinthians xiii, 7. The sentence 'Hence . . . of all things' is omitted from e.p.
[10] Exodus xxxii, 31–2.
[11] Psalm xxxvi, 4 [A.V., xxxvii, 4].

Osculetur me osculo oris sui.[1] To this step it is not lawful[2] for the soul to aspire boldly, unless it feel the interior favour of the King's sceptre extended to it, lest perchance it fall from the other steps which it has mounted up to this point, and wherein it must ever possess itself in humility. From this daring and power which God grants to the soul on this seventh step, so that it may be bold with God in the vehemence of love, follows the eighth, which is that wherein it takes the Beloved captive and is united with Him, as follows.[3]

3. The eighth step of love causes the soul to seize Him and hold Him fast without letting Him go, even as the Bride says, after this manner: 'I found Him Whom my heart and soul love; I held Him and I will not let Him go.'[4] On this step of union the soul satisfies her desire, but not continuously. Certain souls climb some way,[5] and then lose their hold; for, if this state were to continue, it would be glory itself in this life; and thus the soul remains therein[6] for very short periods of time.[7] To the prophet Daniel, because he was a man of desires, was sent a command from God[8] to remain on this step, when it was said to him: 'Daniel, stay upon thy step, because thou art a man of desires.'[9] After this step follows the ninth, which is that of souls now perfect, as we shall afterwards say, which is that that follows.[10]

4. The ninth step of love makes the soul to burn with sweetness. This step is that of the perfect, who now burn sweetly in God. For this sweet and delectable ardour is caused in them by the Holy Spirit by reason of the union which they have with God. For this cause Saint Gregory says, concerning the Apostles, that when the Holy Spirit came upon them visibly they burned inwardly and sweetly through love.[11] Of the good things and riches of God which the soul enjoys on this step, we cannot speak; for if many books were to be written concerning it the greater part would still remain untold. For this cause, and because we shall say something of it hereafter, I say no more here

---

1 Canticles i, 1.
2 E.p.: 'But it is to be emphasized here that it is not lawful,' etc.
3 E.p. omits: 'as follows.'   4 Canticles iii, 4.
5 [*Lit.*, 'attain to setting their foot.']
6 P: 'walks therein.'
7 So Bz., H, M, V. P reads as in the preceding note. The other Codices have: 'the soul spends very brief periods of time herein.' E.p. modifies the whole passage thus: 'for, if it were not so, and they remained on this step, they would have a certain kind of glory in this life, and thus the soul spends very short periods of time on this step.'
8 E.p.: 'The prophet Daniel . . . was told, on behalf of God,' etc.
9 Daniel x, 11. E.p. gives the passage in Latin also.
10 E.p. has only: 'as we shall say.'
11 'Dum Deum in ignis visione suscipiunt, per amorem suaviter arserunt' (*Hom. XXX in Evang.*).

than that after this follows the tenth and last step of this ladder of love, which belongs not to this life.

5. The tenth and last step of this secret ladder of love causes the soul to become wholly assimilated to God, by reason of the clear and immediate[1] vision of God which it then possesses; when, having ascended in this life to the ninth step, it goes forth from the flesh. These souls, who are few, enter not into purgatory, since they have already been wholly purged by love.[2] Of these Saint Matthew says: *Beati mundo corde: quoniam ipsi Deum videbunt.*[3] And, as we say, this vision is the cause of the perfect likeness of the soul to God, for, as Saint John says, we know that we shall be like Him.[4] Not because the soul will come to have the capacity of God, for that is impossible; but because all that it is will become like to God,[5] for which cause it will be called, and will be, God by participation.

6. This is the secret ladder whereof the soul here speaks, although upon these higher steps it is no longer very secret to the soul, since much is revealed to it by love, through the great effects which love produces in it. But, on this last step of clear vision, which is the last step of the ladder whereon God leans, as we have said already, there is naught that is hidden from the soul, by reason of its complete assimilation. Wherefore Our Saviour says: 'In that day ye shall ask Me nothing,' etc.[6] But, until that day, however high a point the soul may reach, there remains something hidden from it—namely, all that it lacks for total assimilation in the Divine Essence. After this manner, by this mystical theology and secret love, the soul continues to rise above all things and above itself, and to mount upward to God. For love is like fire,[7] which ever rises upward with the desire to be absorbed in the centre of its sphere.

---

[1] [i.e., direct, not mediate.] This adjective is omitted n e.p.

[2] E.p.: 'And these souls, who are few, love is wont to leave completely purged in this life, working that which in the next life is wrought in others by purgatory.'

[3] St. Matthew v, 8.

[4] 1 St. John iii, 2.

[5] E.p. modifies: 'We know that we shall be like Him, for we shall see Him as He is. Wherefore all that [the soul] is will be like to God.'

[6] St. John xvi, 23.

[7] So e.p. The other authorities [and P. Silverio] read: 'is assimilated to fire.'

CHAPTER XXI

Which explains the word 'disguised,' and describes the colours of the disguise of the soul in this night.[1]

Now that we have explained the reasons why the soul called this contemplation a 'secret ladder,' it remains for us to explain likewise the word 'disguised,' and the reason why the soul says also that it went forth by this 'secret ladder' in 'disguise.'

2. For the understanding of this it must be known[2] that to disguise oneself is naught else but to hide and cover oneself beneath another garb and figure than one's own—sometimes in order to show forth,[3] under that garb or figure, the will and purpose which is in the heart to gain the grace and will of one who is greatly loved; sometimes, again, to hide[4] oneself from one's rivals and thus to accomplish one's object better. At such times a man assumes the garments and livery which best represent and indicate the affection of his heart and which best conceal him from his rivals.

3. The soul, then, touched with the love of Christ the Spouse, and longing to attain to His grace and gain His goodwill, goes forth[5] here disguised with that disguise which most vividly represents the affections of its spirit and which will protect it most securely on its journey from its adversaries and enemies, which are the devil, the world and the flesh. Thus the livery which it wears is of three chief colours—white, green and purple—denoting the three theological virtues, faith, hope and charity. By these the soul will not only gain the grace and goodwill of its Beloved, but it will travel in security and complete protection from its three enemies: for faith is an inward tunic of a whiteness so pure that it completely dazzles the eyes of the understanding.[6] And thus, when the soul journeys in its vestment of faith, the devil can neither see it nor succeed in harming it, since it is well protected by faith—more so than by all the other virtues[7]—against the devil, who is at once the strongest and the most cunning of enemies.

---

1 So e.p. H lacks the first paragraph of this chapter.
2 E.p.: 'it is necessary to know.'
3 E.p. omits 'forth.' [The Spanish phrase has rather the meaning of 'abroad,' 'to those outside.']
4 E.p.: 'or to hide.'
5 E.p.: 'of Christ its Spouse, because it longs . . . goes forth.'
6 [*Lit.*, 'that it dislocates the sight of all understanding.']
7 E.p. omits: 'more . . . virtues.'

4. It is clear that Saint Peter could find no better protection than faith to save him from the devil, when he said: *Cui resistite fortes in fide*.[1] And in order to gain the grace of the Beloved, and union with Him, the soul cannot put on a better vest and tunic,[2] to serve as a foundation and beginning of the other vestments of the virtues, than this white garment[3] of faith, for without it, as the Apostle says, it is impossible to please God, and with it, it is impossible to fail to please Him.[4] For He Himself says through a prophet: *Sponsabo te mihi in fide*.[5] Which is as much as to say: If thou desirest, O soul, to be united and betrothed to Me, thou must come inwardly clad in faith.

5. This white garment of faith was worn by the soul on its going forth from this dark night, when, walking in interior constraint and darkness, as we have said before, it received no aid, in the form of light, from its understanding, neither from above, since Heaven seemed to be closed to it and God hidden from it, nor from below, since those that taught it satisfied it not. It suffered with constancy and persevered, passing through those trials without fainting or failing the Beloved, Who in trials and tribulations proves the faith of His Bride, so that afterwards she may truly repeat this saying of David, namely: 'By the words of Thy lips I kept hard ways.'[6]

6. Next, over this white tunic of faith the soul now puts on the second colour, which is a green vestment.[7] By this, as we said, is signified[8] the virtue of hope, wherewith, as in the first case, the soul is delivered and protected from the second enemy, which is the world. For this green colour of living hope in God gives the soul such ardour and courage and aspiration to the things of eternal life that, by comparison with what it hopes for therein, all things of the world seem to it to be, as in truth they are, dry and faded and dead and nothing worth. The soul now divests and strips itself of all these worldly vestments and garments, setting its heart upon naught that is in the world and hoping for naught, whether of that which is or of that which is to be, but living clad only in the hope of eternal life. Wherefore, when the heart is thus lifted up above the world, not only can the world neither touch

---

[1] I St. Peter v, 9.
[2] [*Lit*., 'a better undershirt and tunic.']
[3] [*Lit*., 'this whiteness.']
[4] A adds: 'if it be [a] living [faith].' E.p.: 'and with it, if it be [a] living [faith], it pleases Him and seems well to Him.'
[5] Osee ii, 20.
[6] Psalm xvi, 4 [A.V., xvii, 4].
[7] So e.p., substituting this more general word for the *almilla* [a kind of under-waist-coat] of the Codices.
[8] E.p.: 'By the which colour is signified.'

the heart[1] nor lay hold on it, but it cannot even come within sight of it.

7. And thus, in this green livery and disguise, the soul journeys in complete security from this second enemy, which is the world. For Saint Paul speaks of hope as the helmet of salvation[2]—that is, a piece of armour that protects the whole head, and covers it so that there remains uncovered only a visor through which it may look. And hope has this property, that it covers all the senses of the head of the soul, so that there is naught soever pertaining to the world in which they can be immersed, nor is there an opening through which any arrow of the world[3] can wound them. It has a visor, however, which the soul is permitted to use so that its eyes may look upward, but nowhere else; for this is the function which hope habitually performs in the soul, namely, the directing of its eyes upwards to look at God alone, even as David declared that his eyes were directed, when he said:[4] *Oculi mei semper ad Dominum.*[5] He hoped for no good thing elsewhere, save as he himself says in another Psalm: 'Even as the eyes of the handmaid are set upon the hands of her mistress, even so are our eyes set upon our Lord God, until He have mercy upon us as we hope in Him.'[6]

8. For this reason,[7] because of this green livery (since the soul is ever looking to God and sets its eyes on naught else, neither is pleased with aught save with Him alone), the Beloved has such great pleasure with the soul that it is true to say that the soul obtains from Him as much as it hopes for from Him. Wherefore the Spouse[8] in the Songs tells the Bride that, by looking upon Him with one eye alone, she has wounded His heart.[9] Without this green livery of hope in God alone it would be impossible for the soul to go forth to encompass this loving achievement, for it would have no success, since that which moves and conquers is the importunity of hope.

9. With this livery of hope the soul journeys in disguise through this secret and dark night whereof we have spoken;[10] for it is so completely voided of every possession and support that it fixes its eyes and its care upon naught but God, putting its mouth in the dust,[11] if so be there may be hope—to repeat the quotation made above from Jeremias.[12]

[1] E.p.: 'touch it.'
[2] 1 Thessalonians v, 8.
[3] E.p.: 'any arrow thereof.'
[4] E.p. abbreviates: 'even as David says.'
[5] Psalm xxiv, 15 [A.V., xxv, 15].
[6] Psalm cxxii, 2 [A.V., cxxiii, 2].
[7] E.p. omits: 'For this reason.'
[8] E.p.: 'Wherefore He.'
[9] Canticles iv, 9.
[10] E.p. omits: 'whereof we have spoken.'
[11] Lamentations iii, 29.
[12] *Ibid.* [For the quotation, see Bk. II, chap. viii, § 1, p. 393, above.]

10. Over the white and the green vestments, as the crown and perfection of this disguise and livery, the soul now puts on the third colour, which is a splendid garment of purple. By this is denoted the third virtue, which is charity. This not only adds grace to the other two colours, but causes the soul to rise to so lofty a point that it is brought near to God, and becomes very beautiful and pleasing to Him, so that it makes bold to say: 'Albeit I am black, O daughters of Jerusalem, I am comely; wherefore the King hath loved me and hath brought me into His chambers.'[1] This livery of charity, which is that of love, and causes greater love in the Beloved,[2] not only protects the soul and hides it from the third enemy, which is the flesh (for where there is true love of God there enters neither love of self nor that of the things of self), but even gives worth to the other virtues, bestowing on them vigour and strength to protect the soul, and grace and beauty to please the Beloved with them, for without charity no virtue has grace before God. This is the purple which is spoken of in the Songs,[3] upon which God reclines.[4] Clad in this purple livery the soul journeys when (as has been explained above in the first stanza) it goes forth from itself in the dark night, and from all things created, 'kindled in love with yearnings,' by this secret ladder of contemplation, to the perfect union of love of God, its beloved salvation.[5]

11. This, then, is the disguise which the soul says that it wears in the night of faith, upon this secret ladder, and these are its three colours. They constitute a most fit preparation for the union of the soul with God, according to its three faculties, which are understanding, memory and will. For faith voids and darkens the understanding as to all its natural intelligence, and herein prepares it for union with Divine Wisdom. Hope voids and withdraws the memory from all creature possessions; for, as Saint Paul says, hope is for that which is not possessed;[6] and thus it withdraws the memory from that which it is capable of possessing,[7] and sets it on that for which it hopes.[8] And for this cause hope in God alone prepares the memory purely for union with God.[9] Charity, in the same way, voids and annihilates the affections and desires of the will for whatever is not God, and sets

---

[1] Canticles i, 3. [A.V., i, 4.] [For 'chambers' the Spanish has 'bed.']
[2] E.p. omits: ' and . . . Beloved.'   [3] Canticles iii, 10.
[4] Some authorities add : 'whereby He goes up to the reclining-place.'
[5] [Or 'health.']   [6] Romans viii, 24.
[7] E.p. adds: 'in this life.'
[8] E.p.: 'on that which it hopes to possess.'
[9] E.p. substitutes for 'for union with God' 'according to the void caused in it that it may be united with Him.'

them upon Him alone; and thus this virtue prepares this faculty and unites it with God through love. And thus,[1] since the function of these virtues is the withdrawal of the soul from all that is less than God, their function is consequently that of joining it with God.

12. And thus, unless it journeys earnestly, clad in the garments of these three virtues, it is impossible for the soul to attain to the perfection of union with God through love.[2] Wherefore, in order that the soul might attain that which it desired, which was this loving and delectable union with its Beloved, this disguise and clothing which it assumed was most necessary and convenient. And likewise to have succeeded in thus clothing itself and persevering until it should obtain the end and aspiration which it had so much desired, which was the union of love, was a great and happy chance, wherefore in this line the soul also says:

Oh, happy chance!

CHAPTER XXII

Explains the third[3] line of the second stanza.[4]

IT is very clear that it was a happy chance for this soul to go forth with such an enterprise as this, for it was its going forth that delivered it[5] from the devil and from the world and from its own sensuality, as we have said.[6] Having attained liberty of spirit, so precious[7] and so greatly desired by all, it went forth from low things to high; from terrestrial, it became celestial; from human, Divine. Thus it came to have its conversation in the heavens, as has the soul in this state of perfection, even as we shall go on to say in what follows,[8] although with rather more brevity.

2. For the most important part of my task, and the part which chiefly led me to undertake it, was the explanation of this night to many souls who pass through it and yet know nothing about it, as was said in the prologue. Now this explanation and exposition has already been

---

1 E.p.: 'Wherefore.'
2 E.p.: 'to the perfection of love with God.'
3 [i.e., in the original Spanish and in our verse rendering of the poem in Vol. II.]
4 So e.p. The Codices make no division.
5 E.p. has [for 'for it . . . it'] 'wherein it was delivered.'
6 E.p. omits: 'as we have said.'
7 H has 'happy' for 'precious.'
8 E.p. omits: 'in what follows.'

half completed. Although much less has been said of it than might be said, we have shown how many are the blessings which the soul bears with it through the night and how happy is the chance whereby it passes through it, so that, when a soul is terrified by the horror of so many trials, it is also encouraged by the certain hope of so many and such precious blessings of God as it gains therein. And furthermore, for yet another reason, this was a happy chance for the soul; and this reason is given in the following line:

In darkness and in concealment.

CHAPTER XXIII

Expounds the fourth line[1] and describes the wondrous hiding-place wherein the soul is set during this night. Shows how, although the devil has an entrance into other places that are very high, he has none into this.[2]

'I n concealment' is as much as to say 'in a hiding-place,' or 'in hiding'; and thus, what the soul here says (namely,[3] that it went forth 'in darkness and in concealment') is a more complete explanation of the great security which it describes itself in the first line of the stanza as possessing, by means of this dark contemplation upon the road of the union of the love of God.

2. When the soul, then, says 'in darkness and in concealment,' it means that, inasmuch as it journeyed in darkness after the manner aforementioned, it went in hiding and in concealment from the devil and from his wiles and stratagems. The reason why, as it journeys in the darkness of this contemplation, the soul is free, and is hidden from the stratagems of the devil, is that the infused contemplation which it here possesses is infused into it passively and secretly, without the knowledge of[4] the senses and faculties, whether interior or exterior, of the sensual part. And hence it follows that, not only does it journey in hiding, and is free from the impediment which these faculties can set in its way because of its natural weakness, but likewise from the devil; who, except through these faculties of the sensual part, cannot reach or know that which is in the soul, nor that which is taking place

---

1 [i.e., in the original Spanish and in our verse rendering of the poem in Vol. II.]
2 So e.p. The Codices make no division.
3 E.p. omits 'namely.'
4 A, B, C, V: 'concealed by the darkness from.'

within it. Wherefore, the more spiritual, the more interior and the more remote from the senses is the communication, the farther does the devil fall short of understanding it.

3. And thus it is of great importance for the security of the soul that its inward communication with God should be of such a kind that its very senses of the lower part will remain in darkness[1] and be without knowledge of it, and attain not to it: first, so that it may be possible for the spiritual communication to be more abundant, and that the weakness of its sensual part may not hinder the liberty of its spirit; secondly because, as we say, the soul journeys more securely since the devil cannot penetrate so far. In this way we may understand that passage where Our Saviour, speaking in a spiritual sense, says: 'Let not thy left hand know what thy right hand doeth.'[2] Which is as though He had said: Let not thy left hand know that which takes place upon thy right hand, which is the higher and spiritual part of the soul; that is, let it be of such a kind that the lower portion of thy soul, which is the sensual part, may not attain to it; let it be a secret between the spirit and God alone.

4. It is quite true that oftentimes, when these very intimate and secret spiritual communications are present and take place in the soul, although the devil cannot get to know of what kind and manner they are, yet the great repose and silence which some of them cause in the senses and the faculties of the sensual part make it clear to him that they are taking place and that the soul is receiving a certain blessing[3] from them. And then, as he sees that he cannot succeed in thwarting them in the depth of the soul, he does what he can to disturb and disquiet the sensual part—that part to which he is able to attain—now by means of afflictions, now by terrors and fears, with intent to disquiet and disturb the higher and spiritual part of the soul by this means, with respect to that blessing which it then receives and enjoys. But often, when the communication of such contemplation makes its naked assault upon the soul and exerts its strength upon it, the devil, with all his diligence, is unable to disturb it; rather the soul receives a new and a greater advantage[4] and a securer peace. For, when it feels the disturbing presence of the enemy, then—wondrous thing!—without knowing how it comes to pass, and without any efforts of its own,[5] it enters farther into its own interior depths, feeling that it is indeed

---

[1] [The Spanish also admits of the rendering: 'remain shut off from it by darkness.']
[2] St. Matthew vi, 3.   [3] E.p.: 'a certain great blessing.'
[4] E.p.: 'a new advantage and love.'
[5] E.p. omits: 'and without any efforts of its own.'

being set in a sure refuge, where it perceives itself to be most completely withdrawn and hidden from the enemy. And thus its peace and
joy, which the devil is attempting to take from it, are increased; and all
the fear that assails it remains without; and it becomes clearly and
exultingly conscious of its secure enjoyment of that quiet peace and
sweetness of the hidden Spouse,[1] which neither the world nor the
devil can give it or take from it. In that state, therefore, it realizes the
truth of the words of the Bride about this, in the Songs, namely: 'See
how threescore strong men surround the bed of Solomon, etc.,
because of the fears of the night.'[2] It is conscious of this strength and
peace, although it is often equally conscious that its flesh and bones
are being tormented from without.

5. At other times, when the spiritual communication is not made in
any great measure to the spirit, but the senses have a part therein,[3]
the devil more easily succeeds in disturbing the spirit and raising a
tumult within it, by means of the senses, with these terrors. Great are
the torment and the affliction which are then caused in the spirit; at
times they exceed all that can be expressed. For, when there is a naked
contact of spirit with spirit, the horror is intolerable which the evil
spirit causes in the good spirit (I mean, in the soul), when its tumult
reaches it. This is expressed likewise by the Bride in the Songs, when
she says that it has happened thus to her at a time when she wished to
descend to interior recollection in order to have fruition of these
blessings. She says: 'I went down into the garden of nuts to see the
apples of the valleys, and if the vine had flourished. I knew not; my
soul troubled me because of the chariots'—that is, because of the
chariots and the noise of Aminadab, which is the devil.[4]

6. At other times it comes to pass that the devil is occasionally able
to see certain favours which God is pleased to grant the soul when they
are bestowed upon it by the mediation of a good angel; for of those
favours which come through a good angel God habitually allows the
enemy to have knowledge[5]: partly so that he may do that which he can
against them according to the measure of justice, and that thus he may
not be able to allege with truth that no opportunity is given him for
conquering the soul, as he said concerning Job.[6] This would be the

---

[1] E.p.: 'of the Spouse in hiding.'   [2] Canticles iii, 7-8.
[3] E.p.: 'is accompanied by [communications to] sense.'
[4] Canticles vi, 10 [A.V., vi, 11-12].
[5] E.p.: 'At other times this opposition of the devil takes place when God grants
favours to the soul by the mediation of a good angel; for these [favours] the devil is
occasionally able to see because God habitually allows the enemy to have knowledge
of them.'   [6] Job i, 1-11.

17*

case if God allowed not a certain equality between the two warriors—namely, the good angel and the bad—when they strive for the soul, so that the victory of either may be of the greater worth[1] and the soul that is victorious and faithful in temptation may be the more abundantly rewarded.

7. We must observe, therefore, that it is for this reason that, in proportion as God is guiding the soul and communing with it, He gives the devil leave to act with it after this manner. When the soul has genuine visions by the instrumentality of the good angel (for it is by this instrumentality that they habitually come, even though Christ reveal Himself, for He scarcely ever appears[2] in His actual person), God also gives[3] the wicked angel leave to present to the soul false visions of this very type in such a way that the soul which is not cautious may easily be deceived by their outward appearance, as many souls have been. Of this there is a figure in Exodus,[4] where it is said that all the genuine signs that Moses wrought were wrought likewise in appearance by the magicians of Pharao. If he brought forth frogs, they brought them forth likewise; if he turned water into blood, they did the same.

8. And not only does the evil one imitate God in this type of bodily vision, but he also imitates and interferes in spiritual communications which come through the instrumentality of an angel, when he succeeds in seeing them, as we say (for, as Job said[5]: *Omne sublime videt*). These, however, as they are without form and figure (for it is the nature of spirit to have no such thing), he cannot imitate and counterfeit like those others which are presented under some species or figure. And thus, in order to attack the soul, in the same way as that wherein it is being visited, his fearful spirit presents a similar vision in order to attack and destroy spiritual things by spiritual. When this comes to pass just as the good angel is about to communicate spiritual contemplation to the soul, it is impossible for the soul to shelter itself in the secrecy

[1] E.p. substitutes for this sentence: 'And thus it is meet that God should allow a certain equality between the two warriors—namely, the good angel and the bad—when they strive for the soul, that the victory may be of the greater worth.'

[2] Such is the unanimous opinion of theologians. Some, with St. Thomas (Pt. III, q. 57, a. 6), suppose that the appearance which converted St. Paul near Damascus was that of Our Lord Jesus Christ in person.

[3] E.p. modifies: '. . . for this reason that, at certain times, in that order whereby God is leading the soul, He gives leave to the devil to disquiet and tempt it, as happens when i t has genuine visions by the instrumentality of a good angel, and God also gives,' etc.

[4] Exodus vii, 11–22; viii, 7.

[5] Job xli, 25. E.p. modifies: '. . . of an angel, when he succeeds in seeing them; since, as Job said,' etc.

and hiding-place of contemplation with sufficient rapidity not to be observed by the devil; and thus he appears to it and produces a certain horror and perturbation of spirit[1] which at times is most distressing to the soul. Sometimes the soul can speedily free itself from him, so that there is no opportunity for the aforementioned horror of the evil spirit to make an impression on it; and it becomes recollected within itself, being favoured, to this end, by the effectual spiritual grace that the good angel then communicates to it.

9. At other times the devil prevails and encompasses the soul with a perturbation and horror which is a greater affliction to it than any torment in this life could be. For, as this horrible communication passes direct from spirit to spirit, in something like nakedness and clearly distinguished from all that is corporeal, it is grievous beyond what every sense can feel; and this lasts in the spirit for some time, yet not for long, for otherwise the spirit would be driven forth from the flesh by the vehement communication of the other spirit. Afterwards there remains to it the memory thereof, which is sufficient to cause it great affliction.[2]

10. All that we have here described comes to pass in the soul passively, without its doing or undoing anything of itself with respect to it.[3] But in this connection it must be known that, when the good angel permits the devil to gain this advantage of assailing the soul[4] with this spiritual horror, he does it to purify the soul and to prepare it by means of this spiritual vigil for some great spiritual favour and festival which he desires to grant it, for he never mortifies save to give life, nor humbles save to exalt, which comes to pass shortly afterwards. Then, according as was the dark and horrible[5] purgation which the soul suffered, so is the fruition now granted it of a wondrous and delectable spiritual contemplation,[6] sometimes so lofty that there is no language to describe it.[7] But the spirit has been greatly refined by the preceding horror of the evil spirit, in order that it may be able to

---

[1] E.p. abbreviates: 'his fearful spirit presents it [i.e., the vision] as it can, when the good angel is about to communicate to the soul spiritual contemplation, and produces a certain horror and perturbation of spirit.'

[2] E.p. abbreviates: 'At other times God allows this perturbation and horror to last longer, which is a greater affliction to the soul than any torment in this life could be. And afterwards there remains to it the memory thereof, which is sufficient to cause it great affliction.'

[3] E.p.: 'All that we have said comes to pass in the soul without its doing or undoing anything of itself with respect to this representation or feeling.'

[4] E.p.: 'when God permits the devil thus to afflict the soul.'

[5] E.p. omits: 'and horrible.'

[6] E.p. omits: 'wondrous and.'

[7] The remainder of this paragraph is omitted in e.p.

receive this blessing; for these spiritual visions belong to the next life rather than to this, and when one of them is seen this is a preparation for the next.

11. This is to be understood with respect to occasions when God visits the soul by the instrumentality of a good angel, wherein, as has been said, the soul is not so totally[1] in darkness and in concealment that the enemy cannot come within reach of it. But, when God Himself visits it, then the words of this line are indeed fulfilled, and it is in total darkness and in concealment from the enemy that the soul receives these spiritual favours of God. The reason for this is that, as His Majesty dwells[2] substantially in the soul, where neither angel nor devil can attain to an understanding of that which comes to pass, they cannot know the intimate and secret communications which take place there between the soul and God. These communications, since the Lord Himself works them, are wholly Divine and sovereign, for they are all substantial touches[3] of Divine union between the soul and God; in one of which the soul receives a greater blessing than in all the rest, since this is the loftiest degree[4] of prayer in existence.

12. For these are the touches that the Bride entreated of Him in the Songs, saying: *Osculetur me osculo oris sui.*[5] Since this is a thing which takes place in such close intimacy with God, whereto the soul desires with such yearnings to attain, it esteems and longs for a touch of this Divinity more than all the other favours that God grants it. Wherefore, after many such favours have been granted to the Bride in the said Songs, of which she has sung therein, she is not satisfied, but entreats Him for these Divine touches, saying: 'Who shall give Thee to me, my brother, that I might find Thee alone without, sucking the breasts of my mother, so that I might kiss Thee with the mouth of my soul, and that thus no man should despise me or make bold to attack me.'[6] By this she denotes the communication which God Himself alone makes to her, as we are saying,[7] far from all the creatures and without their knowledge,[8] for this is meant by 'alone and without, sucking, etc.'[9]—that is, drying up and draining the breasts of the desires and affections of the sensual part of the soul. This takes place when the soul,

---

1 E.p.: 'the soul is [*lit.*, goes] not secure, nor is so totally.'
2 E.p.: 'as His Majesty is the supreme Lord and dwells.'
3 E.p.: 'and, as it were, touches.'
4 [*Lit.*, 'step.' Cf. p. 435, n. 1, above.]
5 Canticles i, 1.   6 Canticles viii, 1.
7 E.p. omits: 'as we are saying.'
8 B, C, M, Mtr., V have: 'and concealed from them by darkness.'
9 The remainder of this sentence is omitted in e.p.

in intimate peace and delight, has fruition of these blessings, with liberty of spirit, and without the sensual part being able to hinder it, or the devil to thwart it by means thereof. And then the devil would not make bold to attack it, for he would not reach it, neither could he attain to an understanding of these Divine touches in the substance of the soul in[1] the loving substance of God.

13. To this blessing none attains save through intimate purgation and detachment and spiritual concealment from all that is creature; it comes to pass in the darkness, as we have already explained at length and as we say with respect to this line. The soul is in concealment and in hiding, in the which hiding-place, as we have now said, it continues to be strengthened[2] in union with God through love, wherefore it sings this in the same phrase, saying: 'In darkness and in concealment.'

14. When it comes to pass that those favours are granted to the soul in concealment (that is, as we have said, in spirit only), the soul is wont, during some of them, and without knowing how this comes to pass, to see itself so far withdrawn and separated[3] according to the higher and spiritual part, from the sensual and lower portion,[4] that it recognizes in itself two parts so distinct from each other that it believes that the one has naught to do with the other, but that the one is very remote and far withdrawn from the other. And in reality, in a certain way, this is so; for the operation is now wholly spiritual,[5] and the soul receives no communication in its sensual part. In this way the soul gradually becomes wholly spiritual; and in this hiding-place of unitive contemplation its spiritual desires and passions are to a great degree removed and purged away. And thus, speaking of its higher part, the soul then says in this last line:

My house being now at rest.[6]

---

[1] E.p.: 'with.'
[2] E.p. shortens this sentence thus: 'This is in darkness, in the which hiding-place the soul continues to be strengthened,' etc.
[3] E.p.: 'so far separated.'
[4] E.p.: 'according to the higher part, from the lower portion.'
[5] A, B, e.p.: 'the operation which now works is wholly spiritual.'
[6] See p. 10, n. 4, above.

CHAPTER XXIV

Completes the explanation of the second stanza.[1]

THIS is as much as to say: The higher portion of my soul being like the lower part also, at rest with respect to its desires and faculties, I went forth to the Divine union of the love of God. 2. Inasmuch as, by means of that war of the dark night, as has been said, the soul is combated[2] and purged after two manners—namely, according to its sensual and its spiritual part—with its senses, faculties and passions, so likewise after two manners—namely,[3] according to these two parts, the sensual and the spiritual—with all its faculties and desires, the soul attains to an enjoyment of peace and rest. For this reason, as has likewise been said, the soul twice pronounces this line— namely,[4] in this stanza and in the last—because of these two portions of the soul, the spiritual and the sensual, which, in order that they may go forth to the Divine union of love, must needs first be reformed, ordered and tranquillized[5] with respect to the sensual and to the spiritual, according to the nature of the state of innocence which was Adam's.[6] And thus this line which, in the first stanza, was understood of the repose of the lower and sensual portion,[7] is, in this second stanza, understood more particularly of the higher and spiritual part; for which reason it is repeated.[8]

3. This repose and quiet of this spiritual house the soul comes to attain, habitually and perfectly (in so far as the condition of this life allows), by means of the acts of the substantial touches[9] of Divine

---

[1] From e.p.　　　　　　[2] Bz. has: 'is converted'; [perhaps] in error.
[3] E.p. omits 'namely.'
[4] [*Lit.*, 'twice repeats'—a loosely used phrase.] E.p. omits 'namely.
[5] Bz. reads: 'and taken away' [*quitadas* for *quietas*], an error.
[6] H omits this last phrase, which is found in all the other Codices, and in e.p. The latter adds: 'notwithstanding that the soul is not wholly free from the temptations of the lower part.' The addition is made so that the teaching of the Saint may not be confused with that of the Illuminists, who supposed the contemplative in union to be impeccable, do what he might. The Saint's meaning is that for the mystical union of the soul with God such purity and tranquillity of senses and faculties are needful that his condition resembles that state of innocence in which Adam was created, but without the attribute of impeccability, which does not necessarily accompany union, nor can be attained by any, save by a most special privilege of God. Cf. St. Teresa's *Interior Castle*, VII, ii. St. Teresa will be found occasionally to explain points of mystical doctrine which St. John of the Cross takes as being understood.
[7] E.p.: 'part' for 'portion.'
[8] [*Lit.*, 'twice repeated.']
[9] E.p.: 'of these (as it were) substantial touches.'

union whereof we have just spoken; which, in concealment, and hidden from the perturbation of the devil, and of its own senses and passions, the soul has been receiving from the Divinity, wherein it has been purifying itself, as I say, resting, strengthening and confirming itself in order to be able to receive the said union once and for all, which is the Divine betrothal between the soul and the Son of God. As soon as these two houses of the soul have together become tranquillized and strengthened, with all their domestics—namely, the faculties and desires—and have put these domestics to sleep and made them to be silent with respect to all things, both above and below, this Divine Wisdom immediately unites itself with the soul by making a new bond of loving possession, and there is fulfilled that which is written in the Book of Wisdom, in these words:[1] *Dum quietum silentium contineret omnia, et nox in suo cursu medium iter haberet, omnipotens sermo tuus Domine a regalibus sedibus.*[2] The same thing is described by the Bride in the Songs,[3] where she says that, after she had passed by those who stripped her of her mantle by night and wounded her, she found Him Whom her soul loved.

4. The soul cannot come to this union without great purity, and this purity is not gained without great detachment from every created thing and sharp mortification. This is signified by the stripping of the Bride of her mantle and by her being wounded by night as she sought and went after the Spouse; for the new mantle which belonged to the betrothal could not be put on until the old mantle was stripped off. Wherefore, he that refuses to go forth in the night aforementioned to seek the Beloved, and to be stripped of his own will and to be mortified, but seeks Him upon his bed and at his own convenience, as did the Bride,[4] will not succeed in finding Him. For this soul says of itself that it found Him by going forth in the dark and with yearnings of love.

[1] E.p.: 'that which it [i.e., Wisdom] says.'
[2] Wisdom xviii, 14.
[3] Canticles v, 7.
[4] Canticles iii, 1.

CHAPTER XXV

Wherein is expounded the third stanza.[1]

**In the happy night,   In secret, when none saw me,
Nor I beheld aught, Without light or guide, save that which
burned in my heart.**

EXPOSITION

THE soul still continues the metaphor and similitude of temporal
night in describing this its spiritual night, and continues to
sing and extol the good properties which belong to it, and which
in passing through this night it found and used, to the end that it
might attain its desired goal with speed and security. Of these properties it here sets down three.

2. The first, it says, is that in this happy night of contemplation
God leads the soul by a manner of contemplation so solitary and secret,
so remote and far distant from sense, that naught pertaining to it,
nor any touch of created things, succeeds in approaching the soul in
such a way as to disturb it and detain it on the road of the union of
love.

3. The second property whereof it speaks pertains to the spiritual
darkness of this night, wherein all the faculties of the higher part of
the soul are in darkness. The soul sees naught, neither looks at aught
neither stays in aught that is not God, to the end that it may reach
Him, inasmuch as it journeys unimpeded by obstacles of forms and
figures, and of natural apprehensions, which are those that are wont to
hinder the soul from uniting with the eternal Being of God.[2]

4. The third is that, although as it journeys it is supported by no
particular interior light of understanding, nor by any exterior guide,
that it may receive satisfaction therefrom on this lofty road—it is
completely deprived of all this by this thick darkness—yet its love
alone, which burns[3] at this time, and makes its heart to long for the
Beloved, is that which now moves and guides it, and makes it to soar

---

[1] From e.p. Some of the Codices have 'Stanza the Third' and some simply 'Stanza.'
Bz., P omit the whole chapter.
[2] So G, H, Mtr. [*Lit.*, 'that it may not unite itself in the ever being of God.' *Siempre,*
'ever,' 'always,' is normally an adverb.] A, B have: 'that it may not unite itself always
and be with God.' C, M, e.p.: 'that it may not unite itself always with God.'
[3] E.p.: 'but it is love and faith which burn.'

upward to its God along the road of solitude, without its knowing how or in what manner.

There follows the line:

In the happy night.[1]

[1] Thus end the majority of the MSS. Cf. pp. xlix–liii, 319–20, above, on the incomplete state of this treatise. The MSS. say nothing of this, except that in the Alba de Tormes MS. we read: 'Thus far wrote the holy Fray John of the Cross concerning the purgative way, wherein he treats of the active and the passive [aspect] of it as is seen in the treatise of the *Ascent of the Mount* and in this of the *Dark Night*, and, as he died, he wrote no more. And hereafter follows the illuminative way, and then the unitive.' Elsewhere we have said that the lack of any commentary on the last five stanzas is not due to the Saint's death, since he lived for many years after writing the commentary on the earlier stanzas.